SOVEREIGN DEBT

The *Robert W. Kolb Series in Finance* provides a comprehensive view of the field of finance in all of its variety and complexity. The series is projected to include approximately 65 volumes covering all major topics and specializations in finance, ranging from investments, to corporate finance, to financial institutions. Each volume in the *Kolb Series in Finance* consists of new articles especially written for the volume.

Each volume is edited by a specialist in a particular area of finance, who develops the volume outline and commissions articles by the world's experts in that particular field of finance. Each volume includes an editor's introduction and approximately thirty articles to fully describe the current state of financial research and practice in a particular area of finance.

The essays in each volume are intended for practicing finance professionals, graduate students, and advanced undergraduate students. The goal of each volume is to encapsulate the current state of knowledge in a particular area of finance so that the reader can quickly achieve a mastery of that special area of finance.

Please visit www.wiley.com/go/kolbseries to learn about recent and forthcoming titles in the Kolb Series.

SOVEREIGN DEBT

From Safety to Default

Robert W. Kolb

The Robert W. Kolb Series in Finance

WILEY

John Wiley & Sons, Inc.

Library of Congress Cataloging-in-Publication Data:

Sovereign debt : from safety to default / Robert W. Kolb, editor.
        p. cm. – (Robert W. Kolb series in finance)
    Includes bibliographical references and index.
    ISBN 978-0-470-92239-2 (cloth); ISBN 978-1-118-01753-1 (ebk);
    ISBN 978-1-118-01754-8 (ebk); ISBN 978-1-118-01755-5 (ebk)
    1. Debts, Public.   I. Kolb, Robert W., 1949-
    HJ8015.S68 2011
    336.3′4–dc22   2010043306

To Lori, my sovereign

Contents

Introduction   xiii

Acknowledgments   xxiii

PART I   The Political Economy of Sovereign Debt   1

1   Sovereign Debt: Theory, Defaults, and Sanctions   3
Robert W. Kolb

2   The Institutional Determinants of Debt Intolerance   15
Raffaela Giordano and Pietro Tommasino

3   Output Costs of Sovereign Default   23
Bianca De Paoli, Glenn Hoggarth, and Victoria Saporta

4   Spillovers of Sovereign Default Risk: How Much Is the Private Sector Affected?   33
Udaibir S. Das, Michael G. Papaioannou, and Christoph Trebesch

5   Sovereign Debt Problems and Policy Gambles   43
Samuel W. Malone

6   Sovereign Debt and the Resource Curse   51
Mare Sarr, Erwin Bulte, Chris Meissner, and Swanson Tim

7   Sovereign Debt and Military Conflict   63
Zane M. Kelly

PART II   Making Sovereign Debt Work   71

8   Fiscal Policy, Government Institutions, and Sovereign Creditworthiness   73
Bernardin Akitoby and Thomas Stratmann

9   Corruption and Creditworthiness: Evidence from
    Sovereign Credit Ratings   79
    Craig A. Depken II, Courtney L. LaFountain, and Roger B. Butters

10 Institutions, Financial Integration,
    and Complementarity   89
    Nicola Gennaioli, Alberto Martin, and Stefano Rossi

11 Loans versus Bonds: The Importance of Potential
    Liquidity Problems for Sovereign Borrowers   101
    Issam Hallak and Paul Schure

12 First-Time Sovereign Bond Issuers: Considerations
    in Accessing International Capital Markets   111
    Udaibir S. Das, Michael G. Papaioannou, and Magdalena Polan

13 A Note on Sovereign Debt Auctions: Uniform
    or Discriminatory?   119
    Menachem Brenner, Dan Galai, and Orly Sade

14 Pension Reform and Sovereign Credit Standing   127
    Alfredo Cuevas, María González, Davide Lombardo, and Arnoldo López-Marmolejo

PART III   Sovereign Defaults, Restructurings,
and the Resumption of Borrowing   135

15 Understanding Sovereign Default   137
    Juan Carlos Hatchondo, Leonardo Martinez, and Horacio Sapriza

16 Are Sovereign Defaulters Punished?: Evidence
    from Foreign Direct Investment Flows   149
    Michael Fuentes and Diego Saravia

17 Supersanctions and Sovereign Debt Repayment   155
    Kris James Mitchener and Marc D. Weidenmier

18 Debt Restructuring Delays: Measurement and
    Stylized Facts   169
    Christoph Trebesch

19 IMF Interventions in Sovereign Debt Restructurings   179
    Javier Díaz-Cassou and Aitor Erce

**20 Resuming Lending to Countries Following a
Sovereign Debt Crisis**   189

Luisa Zanforlin

**PART IV   Legal and Contractual Dimensions of
Restructurings and Defaults**   195

**21 A Code of Conduct for Sovereign Debt Restructuring:
An Important Component of the International
Financial Architecture?**   197

Kathrin Berensmann

**22 Governing Law of Sovereign Bonds and
Legal Enforcement**   105

Issam Hallak

**23 Sovereign Debt Restructuring: The Judge,
the Vultures, and Creditor Rights**   211

Marcus H. Miller and Dania Thomas

**24 Sovereign Debt Documentation and the
Pari Passu Clause**   227

Umakanth Varottil

25 Collective Action Clauses in Sovereign Bonds   235

Sönke Häseler

26 Sovereignty, Legitimacy, and Creditworthiness   245

Odette Lienau

27 Odious Debts or Odious Regimes?   253

Patrick Bolton and David A. Skeel Jr.

**28 Insolvency Principles: The Missing Link
in the Odious Debt Debate**   261

A. Mechele Dickerson

PART V   Historical Perspectives   267

**29 The Baring Crisis and the Great Latin American
Meltdown of the 1890s**   269

Kris James Mitchener and Marc D. Weidenmier

**30 How Government Bond Yields Reflect Wartime
    Events: The Case of the Nordic Market**   279
Daniel Waldenström and Bruno S. Frey

**31 How Important Are the Political Costs of Domestic
    Default?: Evidence from World War II Bond Markets**   287
Daniel Waldenström

**32 Emerging Market Spreads at the Turn of the
    Twenty-First Century: A Roller Coaster**   295
Sergio Godoy

PART VI   Sovereign Debt in Emerging Markets   301

**33 Sovereign Default Risk and Implications for
    Fiscal Policy**   303
Gabriel Cuadra and Horacio Sapriza

34 Default Traps   309
Luis A.V. Catão, Ana Fostel, and Sandeep Kapur

35 Self-Fulfilling and Self-Enforcing Debt Crises   319
Daniel Cohen and Sebastien Villemot

**36 The Impact of Economic and Political Factors on
    Sovereign Credit Ratings**   325
Constantin Mellios and Eric Paget-Blanc

**37 Sovereign Bond Spreads in the New European
    Union Countries**   335
Ioana Alexopoulou, Irina Bunda, and Annalisa Ferrando

**38 Can Sovereign Credit Ratings Promote Financial
    Sector Development and Capital Inflows to
    Emerging Markets?**   345
Suk-Joong Kim and Eliza Wu

**39 Country Debt Default Probabilities in Emerging
    Markets: Were Credit Rating Agencies Wrong?**   353
*Angelina Georgievska, Ljubica Georgievska, Dr. Aleksandar Stojanovic,
and Dr. Natasa Todorovic*

40 The International Stock Market Impact of Sovereign Debt Ratings News 361

Miguel A. Ferreira and Paulo M. Gama

PART VII Sovereign Debt and Financial Crises 369

41 Equity Market Contagion and Co-Movement: Industry Level Evidence 371

Kate Phylaktis and Lichuan Xia

42 An Insolvency Procedure for Sovereign States: A Viable Instrument for Preventing and Resolving Debt Crises? 379

Kathrin Berensmann and Angélique Herzberg

43 From Banking to Sovereign Debt Crisis in Europe 387

Bertrand Candelon and Franz C. Palm

44 From Financial Crisis to Sovereign Risk 393

Carlos Caceres, Vincenzo Guzzo, and Miguel Segoviano

45 Sovereign Spreads and Perceived Risk of Default Revisited 401

Abolhassan Jalilvand and Jeannette Switzer

46 What Explains the Surge in Euro Area Sovereign Spreads During the Financial Crisis of 2007–2009? 407

Maria-Grazia Attinasi, Cristina Checherita, and Christiane Nickel

47 Euro Area Sovereign Risk During the Crisis 415

Silvia Sgherri and Edda Zoli

48 Facing the Debt Challenge of Countries That Are "Too Big To Fail" 425

Steven L. Schwarcz

Index 431

Introduction

Sovereign debt—borrowing by governments—has been a feature of world finance since antiquity. By its very nature, governmental borrowing is somewhat arcane and usually takes place beyond the purview of the typical citizen's personal interest. However, at all times, sovereign borrowing affects everyone in society—after all, when a government borrows it hands a piece of the obligation to every taxpayer. Normally obscure, sovereign debt sometimes suddenly seizes headlines and becomes spectacularly important for everyone in a society under stress. This volume offers the reader a comprehensive understanding of how sovereign debt works and how it affects the world today. Problems with sovereign debt shape the course of wars and help to determine national boundaries. In times of crisis, the management of sovereign debt even has an impact on the type and amount of food that people consume.

Today, issues of sovereign debt are more important than ever, and these concerns promise to reach into the lives of all of us to an unprecedented degree in the future. The last 15 years have witnessed rather spectacular events related to sovereign debt, debt crises, and default. In 1997, the Asian financial crisis swept across East Asia with devastating effects on economic growth and consumption in Thailand, South Korea, and Indonesia, and also afflicted Hong Kong, Malaysia, Laos, and the Philippines. Consumption plummeted in Thailand, and economic growth in the Philippines fell to nearly zero. At the same time, events forced Indonesia to devalue the rupiah. Widespread rioting followed, and Indonesia's government fell after decades of rule.

The Asian financial crisis led swiftly to a default by Russia, leading the International Monetary Fund and the World Bank to respond with a $23 billion bailout. Russia's nearby trading partners, many former Soviet republics, suffered considerably as well. Belarus and Ukraine sharply devalued their currencies, and in Uzbekistan the government placed restrictions on the sale of food to avoid panic. For their part, the Baltic states of Estonia, Latvia, and Lithuania fell into recession.

Having swept from Asia to Russia in a short period, financial distress came quickly to the United States with a dramatic effect on the hedge fund Long-Term Capital Management (LTCM), which was heavily invested in the Russian ruble. Events quickly proved that LTCM was pivotal in the global financial system, revealing a degree of interconnectedness that had previously been unthinkable. Policy makers soon realized that the collapse of LTCM threatened the entire financial system, and the Federal Reserve Bank of New York organized a bailout financed by $3.5 billion from the largest financial firms on Wall Street. The proud LTCM, which featured principals who had won the Nobel prize in economics,

completely collapsed.[1] The aftermath of these crises revealed to all attentive observers a new world financial structure that now possessed an astounding degree
of interconnectedness—a world in which financial distress could fly as quickly as
rumor.[2]

Against the background of the late 1990s, it was easier during the time from
2007 to 2009 to comprehend the speed with which financial distress could travel
from market to market and from firm to firm, even if the magnitude of that distress
shocked virtually everyone, from Wall Street titan to the small-holding pensioner.
These events have set a new stage for sovereign debt in a globalized financial
world—a world in which a financial hiccup in one region, market, country, or
company can cause convulsions in an economy previously thought to have been
quite remote from the original point of distress.

SOVEREIGN DEBT: A PIVOTAL FACTOR IN WORLD AFFAIRS

With the breakup of the Soviet Union in the early 1990s, some observers saw an
ultimate and permanent triumph of liberal democracies with an "end of history"
that initiated a stable future. This view was short-lived, and now others see an
enduring "clash of civilizations," or at least a "return of history and the end of
dreams."[3] The attacks of September 11, 2001, certainly provide a general awakening
to conflict at the level of civilizations, while the collapse of the dot-com bubble and
the financial crisis of 2007–2009 has made us all aware that we now live in a new
world of finance.

But we also live in a world being radically transformed by the rise of new
economic, political, and military powers. At least one leading economist foresees
China as quickly becoming the country with the world's largest GDP and succeeding in establishing an economic hegemony over the rest of the world.[4] With a
military that is still little threat to that of the United States, China has just passed
the United States in total number of warships. While some concede that the United
States and the Western democracies generally face a slowly developing eclipse,
others speculate that complex societies may be faced with sudden collapse and
specifically suggest that such rapid dissolution of world standing might be a near-
term fate for the United States.[5]

While any reasoned reading of geopolitical tea leaves suggests that the West
faces huge challenges ranging from an aging population to a loss of economic and
military primacy, it should be clear to all that much of the West's ability to navigate
the next decades will depend to a considerable degree on its financial strength. In
the United States, the collapse of home prices, the dislocations of the ensuing Great
Recession, the fiscal plight of many state governments, and the growing furor over
economic management at the federal level all make the financial challenges we
face evident to almost everyone.

These challenges face the Western democracies generally. Exhibit I.1 shows the
level of total societal debt—the sum of the debt of governments, households, financial institutions, and nonfinancial businesses—for the leading economic nations of
the world. By this measure, the United Kingdom and Japan are far and away the
most heavily indebted societies, with total debt exceeding more than four years

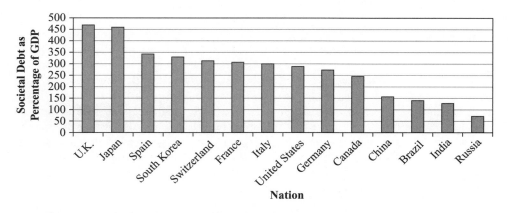

Exhibit I.1   Total Societal Debt as a Percentage of GDP
Source: McKinsey & Company, "Debt and Deleveraging: The Global Credit Bubble and Its Economic Consequences," January 2010, 20.

of the entire gross domestic product of these nations. The United States is only in the middle rank of these nations with slightly less than 300 percent of GDP as the burden of its societal debt. Notably, the large developing nations—the BRIC countries of Brazil, Russia, India, and China—carry the lowest debt burdens.[6]

For this same collection of nations, the rank ordering of sovereign debt as a percentage of GDP differs substantially from the ranking for total societal debt, as Exhibit I.2 shows. Japan's sovereign debt burden is almost twice as large relative to GDP as Italy's, which is second. Again, the United States falls in the middle rank of these countries. The BRIC nations, with uniformly lower levels of total societal debt, are diverse with respect to their sovereign debt levels. Most notably, Russia has very little sovereign debt, no doubt due to its sovereign default in 1998 and its subsequent exclusion from sovereign borrowing.

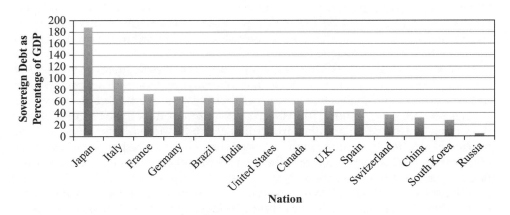

Exhibit I.2   Sovereign Debt as a Percentage of GDP
Source: McKinsey & Company, "Debt and Deleveraging: The Global Credit Bubble and Its Economic Consequences," January 2010, 20.

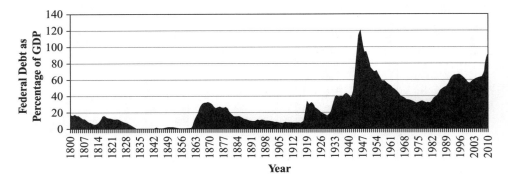

Exhibit I.3   U.S. Federal Debt as a Percentage of GDP
Source: www.usgovernmentspending.com/federal_debt_chart.html. Accessed September 1, 2010.

In the United States, the level of sovereign debt has varied dramatically over the years, showing a marked tendency to rise during times of war and to fall during times of peace. Exhibit I.3 shows the fluctuating level of sovereign debt for the United States from 1800 to 2010. The graph shows a clear pattern of debt that rose during periods of war: the Civil War, World War I, and during and immediately following World War II. The current debt level is second only to the level that resulted from World War II. In the United States, this unprecedentedly high level of sovereign debt in a period of relative peace, coupled with high levels of personal debt are two principal sources of the economic concern that resulted in the political realignments of the mid-term elections of 2010 and continue to threaten (or promise) continuing substantial political repercussions.

Concerns about sovereign debt are now widespread and intense. As a survey of sovereign debt conditions shows, the United States remains in a strong position as a borrower, despite having suffered a large worsening of fiscal conditions in a time of relative peace. Compare, for instance, the list of the world's riskiest sovereign borrowers, topped by Venezuela, as Exhibit I.4 shows. There is little doubt that Venezuela is capable of repaying its debts, given its substantial oil wealth. However, political posturing by an unreliable and perhaps unstable dictator there makes the honoring of Venezuela's debts a less-than-safe proposition. For Greece, the second riskiest sovereign borrower, the problem is quite otherwise. Greece worked itself into a bad situation through years of unsustainably generous social payments, a succession of governments that permitted themselves to be hostage to powerful unions, and a society committed to tax avoidance under the aegis of a government with poor tax-collection abilities. In late 2010, Credit Market Analysts, Ltd., the source of these rankings, gave both Venezuela and Greece a higher than 50 percent chance of default sometime during the next five years. Exhibit I.5 shows the most reliable borrowers, with Norway being the most likely to repay in full, due in no small part to its vast oil revenues, combined with its very substantial sovereign wealth fund. Despite the excited headlines, the United States remains a very reliable credit risk, ranked third for reliability by Credit Market Analysts, Ltd.

In late 2010, we appear to have reached the aftermath of the financial crisis of 2007–2009 as the Great Recession seems to recede or at least to moderate in its

Exhibit I.4   The World's Riskiest Sovereign
Borrowers (Ranked from Riskiest to Less Risky)

1	Venezuela
2	Greece
3	Argentina
4	Pakistan
5	Ukraine
6	Dubai
7	Iraq
8	Romania
9	Latvia
10	Bulgaria

Source: Credit Market Analysts, Ltd., "Global Sovereign
Credit Risk Report," Second Quarter, 2010, 4.

intensity. Nonetheless, the financial crisis and recession have left a very serious situation. This has been exposed by the crisis that rocked the European Union nations in 2010 as concern mounted over the economic viability of entire nations, the so-called PIIGS—Portugal, Ireland, Italy, Greece, and Spain—with Greece being the focal point of most intense concern. At one point in 2010, insuring Greek sovereign bonds against default for a single year exceeded 11 percent of the promised payment amount. The parlous state of world finance led the Bank for International Settlements to judge: "Fears of sovereign risk threaten to derail financial recovery."[7] However, comparison of sovereign debt levels with previous periods show them only as being high, not necessarily as being disastrous.

The elevated, but not necessarily dramatic, level of sovereign debt fails to disclose the whole picture, however. Some countries with the largest economies that have occupied positions of world leadership for decades are saddled not only with large levels of sovereign debt, but large levels of total societal debt, plus

Exhibit I.5   The World's Most Reliable Sovereign
Borrowers (Ranked from Most Reliable to Least
Reliable)

1	Norway
2	Finland
3	USA
4	Denmark
5	Sweden
6	Germany
7	Switzerland
8	Netherlands
9	Hong Kong
10	Australia

Source: Credit Market Analysts, Ltd., "Global Sovereign
Credit Risk Report," Second Quarter, 2010, 5.

structural budget deficits they seem unwilling to correct. Exhibit I.1 has already shown the high levels of societal debt for Japan, the United Kingdom, some other leading EU countries and the United States. However, these countries also have chronic national budget deficits. These countries have been characterized as having fallen into a "ring of fire"—a situation of high sovereign debt coupled with high governmental deficits. Unenviable membership in the ring of fire means that a country has ". . . the potential for public debt to exceed 90 percent of GDP within a few years' time, which would slow GDP [growth] by one percent or more."[8] As Exhibit I.6 indicates, these unfortunate countries in the ring of fire include the United States, the United Kingdom, Japan, France, and most of the PIIGS—Spain, Ireland, Italy, and Greece. By contrast, Norway, Sweden, Germany, Canada, and the Netherlands are in fairly good condition, with Finland, Denmark, and Australia holding the strongest positions on this measure.

Thus, the issue of sovereign debt must be considered against this two-fold background. First, sovereign debt is a key part of the picture of financial irresponsibility on the part of many of the presumably richest and most powerful nations of the West. Resolving the consequences of this longstanding irresponsibility will take a major societal effort over a long period in each of these countries. Second, this malaise affects the countries that have led the world toward the West's cherished values of individual freedom and democracy, and their economic weakness has come to a crisis point just as the rise of countries such as the BRICs

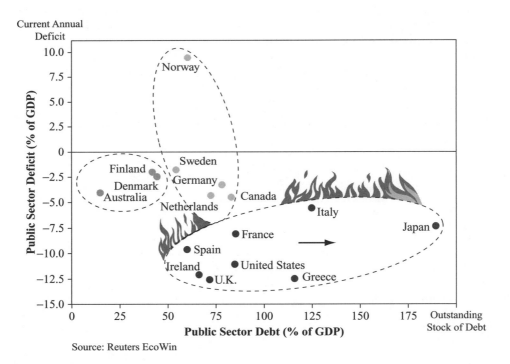

Source: Reuters EcoWin

Exhibit I.6 The Ring of Fire
Source: Bill Gross, "The Ring of Fire," *PIMCO Investment Outlook,* February 2010, 4.

presents a serious challenge to the economic primacy of liberal democracies. Also, a resurgence of Islam may presage a serious global confrontation with the West's values of personal freedom and representative government.

These factors combine to make sovereign debt a critical piece of the economic and social challenge that the Western nations must face. Not too long ago, sovereign debt was a concern primarily, or even only, for developing and impoverished countries. A mere decade ago, one of the largest issues in sovereign debt was debt relief for the poorest countries. Today, it is the rich (or formerly rich) countries that face their own problems with sovereign debt, and there is no one to forgive these debtors. These themes are the issue that stimulated the development of this book.

ABOUT THE TEXT

All of the chapters in this volume represent the cutting edge of thinking about sovereign debt. The contributions stem from the authors' deep expertise in the subject matter. Almost all of the contributions are based on formal academic research conducted in the last two years. Accordingly, this book spreads before the reader the best thinking on sovereign debt by specialists drawn from top universities and key international financial institutions, including central banks, the International Monetary Fund, and the World Bank. All of the contributions in this volume have been especially written for the intended reader—a nonfinance specialist interested in understanding the vital importance of sovereign debt for the world's economic future. The book is divided into seven sections, and each is preceded by a brief essay describing the chapters in that section:

    I. The Political Economy of Sovereign Debt
    II. Making Sovereign Debt Work
    III. Sovereign Defaults, Restructurings, and the Resumption of Borrowing
    IV. Legal and Contractual Dimensions of Restructurings and Defaults
    V. Historical Perspectives
    VI. Sovereign Debt in Emerging Markets
    VII. Sovereign Debt and Financial Crises

NOTES

1. For a riveting account of the rise and fall of Long-Term Capital Management, see Roger Lowenstein, *When Genius Failed: The Rise and Fall of Long-Term Capital Management*, New York: Random House, 2000.

2. This financial interconnectedness offers considerable benefits in normal times, but it also means that financial markets under stress can be subject to financial contagion—the propagation of financial distress in one firm, market, or economy to others. See Robert W. Kolb (ed.), *Financial Contagion: The Viral Threat to the Wealth of Nations* (Hoboken, NJ: John Wiley & Sons, 2011).

3. See Francis Fukuyama, "The End of History?" *The National Interest*, Summer 1989, and *The End of History and the Last Man* (New York: Free Press, 1992). Samuel P. Huntington advanced the clash of civilizations point of view: "The Clash of Civilizations," *Foreign*

Affairs (Summer 1993, 22–49), and *The Clash of Civilizations and the Remaking of the World Order* (New York: Simon & Schuster, 1996). See also Robert Kagan, *The Return of History and the End of Dreams* (New York: Knopf, 2008).

4. Robert Fogel, "$123,000,000,000,000," *Foreign Policy,* January/February 2010. By contrast, other well-placed observers see a more modest rise in Chinese economic power: Robert D. Kaplan, "The Geography of Chinese Power," *Foreign Affairs* (May/June 2010), 22–41.

5. For a gradualist perspective, see Fareed Zakaria, *The Post-American World* (New York: W.W. Norton, 2008). Zakaria sees the fall of the United States as resulting more from the "rise of the rest," rather than from an actual fall. Niall Ferguson represents the view that sees sudden collapse as possible: "Complexity and Collapse," *Foreign Affairs,* March/April 2010.

6. For the idea that the BRIC countries hold the key to world economic development, see Dominic Wilson and Roop Purushothaman, "Dreaming with BRICs: The Path to 2050," Goldman Sachs Global Economics Paper No. 99, October 1, 2003.

7. Bank for International Settlements, *80th Annual Report,* June 28, 2010, 23.

8. Bill Gross, "The Ring of Fire," *PIMCO Investment Outlook,* February 2010.

REFERENCES

Bank for International Settlements. 2010. *80th Annual Report.* June 28.

Credit Market Analysts, Ltd. 2010. "Global Sovereign Credit Risk Report." Second Quarter.

Ferguson, Niall. 2010. "Complexity and Collapse." *Foreign Affairs.* March/April.

Fogel, Robert. 2010. "$123,000,000,000,000." *Foreign Policy.* January/February.

Fukuyama, Francis. 1989. "The End of History?" *The National Interest.* Summer.

———. 1992. *The End of History and the Last Man.* New York: Free Press.

Gross, Bill. 2010. "The Ring of Fire." *PIMCO Investment Outlook.* February.

Huntington, Samuel P. 1993. "The Clash of Civilizations." *Foreign Affairs.* Summer, 22–49.

———. 1996. *The Clash of Civilizations and the Remaking of the World Order.* New York: Simon and Schuster.

Kagan, Robert. 2008. *The Return of History and the End of Dreams.* New York: Knopf.

Kaplan, Robert D. 2010. "The Geography of Chinese Power." *Foreign Affairs.* May/June, 22–41.

Lowenstein, Roger. 2000. *When Genius Failed: The Rise and Fall of Long-Term Capital Management.* New York: Random House.

Wilson, Dominic, and Roop Purushothaman. 2003. "Dreaming with BRICs: The Path to 2050." *Goldman Sachs Global Economics Paper* 99. October 1.

Zakaria, Fareed. 2008. *The Post-American World.* New York: W.W. Norton.

ABOUT THE EDITOR

Robert W. Kolb received two PhDs from the University of North Carolina at Chapel Hill (philosophy, 1974; finance, 1978), and has been a finance professor at the University of Florida, Emory University, the University of Miami, and the University of Colorado at Boulder. He was assistant dean of Business and Society, and director of the Center for Business and Society at the University of Colorado at Boulder. Kolb was also department chair at the University of Miami. He is currently at

Loyola University Chicago, where he holds the Frank W. Considine Chair in Applied Ethics.

Kolb has published more than 50 academic research articles and more than 20 books, most focusing on financial derivatives and their applications to risk management. In 1990, he founded Kolb Publishing Company to publish finance and economics university texts, built the company's list over the ensuing years, and sold the firm to Blackwell Publishers of Oxford, England in 1995. His recent writings include *Financial Derivatives 3e*; *Understanding Futures Markets 6e*; *Futures, Options, and Swaps 5e*; and *Financial Derivatives*, all co-authored with James A. Overdahl. Kolb also edited the monographs *The Ethics of Executive Compensation*, *The Ethics of Genetic Commerce, Corporate Retirement Security: Social and Ethical Issues*, and (with Don Schwartz) *Corporate Boards: Managers of Risk, Sources of Risk*. In addition, he was lead editor of the *Encyclopedia of Business Society and Ethics*, a five-volume work.

Two of Kolb's most recent books are *Lessons From the Financial Crisis: Causes, Consequences, and Our Economic Future*, an edited volume published by John Wiley & Sons, and *The Financial Crisis of Our Time*, published in 2011. In addition to the current volume, he also recently completed *Financial Contagion: The Viral Threat to the Wealth of Nations*.

Acknowledgments

N o one creates a book alone. In the first instance, this book was created by the many contributors who extended their wisdom and knowledge to the project. Also, Ronald MacDonald at Loyola University in Chicago served as an extremely capable editorial assistant, while Pooja Shah, also at Loyola, provided immediate and expert research assistance. At John Wiley & Sons, I have benefited from working closely with my editor Evan Burton, who encouraged me to undertake this project. Also at Wiley, Emilie Herman and Melissa Lopez have both managed the production of this volume with their typically high level of expertise.

To these approximately 100 people I extend my sincere gratitude for making this book possible.

ROBERT W. KOLB
Chicago
January 2011

SOVEREIGN DEBT

PART I

The Political Economy of Sovereign Debt

The chapters that comprise this section focus on the most sweeping issues of sovereign debt—the role that this debt plays in the essential economy of a nation and how sovereign debt interacts with societal dimensions beyond the merely financial. As the introduction has tried to make clear, sovereign debt has a worldwide economic importance that it has never had before, and this is due to the economic difficulties and societal challenges faced by so many of the heretofore most successful nations of the world. Accordingly, this section focuses on the overarching theory of sovereign debt, the levels of debt that nations can sustain, the problem of default, and the sanctions that lenders use to enforce their claims against governments that are reluctant to pay as promised.

In addition, these articles examine the effect of sovereign debt and defaults on the overall economic productivity of a nation. Further, some of the most egregious episodes in the history of sovereign debt arise from countries with a "resource curse"—a valuable resource that promises a horn of plenty but that has historically been associated with slow economic growth and a reluctance or inability to pay on sovereign debt.

A sovereign's ability to conduct war depends on money. As Cicero noted more than 2,000 years ago, "Endless money forms the sinews of war." Had Cicero lived in our time, he might have added: "And many nations attempt to fashion these sinews from debt," as many nations have attempted to construct these sinews by issuing sovereign debt, and success or failure in sovereign debt management has meant victory or defeat in many wars. Thus, sovereign debt connects with matters of great societal import—in some instances, sovereign debt determines the very survival of the state and society.

CHAPTER 1

Sovereign Debt

Theory, Defaults, and Sanctions

ROBERT W. KOLB
Professor of Finance and Considine Chair of Applied Ethics,
Loyola University Chicago

For more than 2,000 years, sovereign governments have borrowed and frequently defaulted. In many instances, the sovereign borrower possessed overweening power compared to the unlucky lender, leaving the hapless creditor little or no means of collecting the debt. In more recent historical times, sovereign borrowers have been smaller, weaker, and poorer nations, and their lenders have been financial institutions lodged in the world's most powerful states. On some occasions, those lenders were able to enlist the military power of their own countries to enforce their private claims against the sovereign borrowers to make them pay. (These governments were presumably willing to use their military power on behalf of their financial institutions because doing so met the perceived interests of the governments themselves, or at least the interests of those individuals who held office.)

These episodes of gunboat diplomacy or supersanctions were quite effective and far from rare in the period of 1870–1914, a time of widespread adherence to the gold standard in exchange rates. A clear instance of gunboat diplomacy occurred at the turn of the twentieth century. A revolution in Venezuela that began in 1898 destroyed considerable property, and the government stopped paying its foreign creditors. In response, Great Britain, Germany, and Italy blockaded Venezuelan ports and shelled coastal fortifications, compelling Venezuelan compliance. The experience of Egypt provides an example of a nongunboat supersanction. Under the leadership of Isma'il Pasha from 1863 to 1879, Egypt borrowed and spent, notably to finance a war with Ethiopia. Unable or unwilling to pay these debts as promised, Pasha sold the Suez Canal to Great Britain in 1875. With Egypt's debts still not satisfied, Great Britain pressured the Ottoman sultan to depose Isma'il and replace him with his son Tewfik Pasha in 1879. In response to a period of missing debt payments and internal unrest, Great Britain took effective control of Egypt's finances in 1882 and directed Egypt's financial resources to the repayment of its foreign debts.[1]

Today, attempts to secure repayment by gunboat diplomacy or seizing another sovereign state's finances are considered a bit outré, a circumstance that leads to the two central questions of the theory of sovereign debt: If the creditor cannot force the sovereign borrower to repay, why would the sovereign ever do so? Correlatively, without an ability to force repayment, why would any potential creditor ever lend to a sovereign borrower? The theory of sovereign debt addresses these two puzzles.

Before turning to a direct consideration of these issues, three preliminary points deserve mention. First, sovereign borrowers typically really do hold a different position from mere individuals or firms that borrow. While ordinary borrowers can be forced to repay through legal sanctions, sovereign borrowers today completely escape supersanctions and largely evade effective legal sanctions that might force repayment. Second, even in the post-supersanction period, and even with the inability to enforce collection with legal sanctions, sovereign lending remains quite robust. Despite a large number of defaults, sovereign debt is mostly repaid as promised. Third, the theory of sovereign debt attempts to explain the occurrence of lending and repayment in strictly economic terms. That is, the explanations that economists offer turn merely on the self-interest of the lender in extending credit and the borrower in making repayments. Economists never attempt to explain lending or borrowing behavior by reference to any moral obligation of fulfilling the promise to repay that borrowers make when they secure loans.

REPUTATIONAL EXPLANATIONS

One of the key rationales offered to account for the existence of sovereign lending turns on reputation. The argument asserts that sovereign governments want to maintain a reputation as a good credit risk to assure future access to international funds, so they repay the debts they owe now. As a result, lenders feel sufficient confidence to extend funds. There is no doubt considerable, yet somewhat limited, truth in this view. But the desire for continuing access to funds works hand in hand with the sanctions that do still prevail in the arena of sovereign debt. While these sanctions fall considerably short of the supersanction of invasion, they can have considerable force. For example, if lending institutions can punish a small developing nation that defaults by interfering with its international trade or by seizing that nation's assets held abroad, these sanctions can provide additional reasons for debtor countries to repay. Thus, the threat of sanctions also stimulates countries to repay. So reputational concerns interact with responses to limited sanctions to encourage sovereign debtors to pay.

From the point of view of theory, however, there is a question of whether reputational considerations alone are sufficient to make sovereigns pay. In the parlance of the theory of sovereign debt, if the value of a good reputation is sufficient to make lenders pay as promised and sufficient to encourage lenders to extend funds, then reputation is said to support sovereign lending.

To simplify matters, assume that there is a single lender (or that all lenders act monolithically), and if a country defaults, it is excluded from borrowing forever. Several studies advance reputation as grounds for sovereign lending (Eaton and Gersovitz 1981; Eaton, Gersovitz, and Stiglitz 1986). The first thing to notice about such theories is that they pertain to an environment in which borrowing continues infinitely, or at least indefinitely from year to year. If the borrower knows that the current year is a terminal year, after which there will be no lending, the borrower would refuse to repay for the simple reason that there is no fear of exclusion from future borrowing. But lenders, also knowing that the current year is the terminal year, would also recognize that they will not be repaid, so they will not lend for that final period. In the second-to-last year, the borrower would not repay because it would know it could not borrow in the terminal year for the reasons just given. But the lender is assumed to have the same information, so it would not lend in that penultimate year, because it would realize it would not be repaid. This argument of backward induction can be repeated for all years from the horizon back to the present, thereby showing that explanations of sovereign debt based on reputation alone can work only in an environment of perpetual lending and borrowing. Or at the very least, there must be some continuing probability of borrowing and repaying into the indefinite future.

If withholding future lending is the only sanction that lenders can impose, other potential breakdowns in lending arise. For simplicity, consider an environment of a single borrower and a single lender. Assume that the maximum debt capacity of the borrower is 100 units and the lender advances one unit in each loan up to this limit. When the debt capacity of the borrower reaches the limit of 100 units, the lender refuses to make new loans. However, at this point, the reputation for repayment has no prospect of securing future loans, because the borrower has borrowed so much it knows it can never borrow any more. In this situation, the threat of exclusion from future loans has no force, and a reputation for repayment has no value in securing future loans. Having reached this limit of borrowing with no future prospects for loans, the borrower would refuse to repay the loan. However, the lender will also recognize this prospect and will not allow that situation to arise.

But now consider the situation in which the lender has advanced 99 units of credit. The borrower knows that it cannot secure the additional loan of one unit of borrowing for the reasons just given. So the borrower will not repay the loan at the 99 units of borrowing. The lender, too, recognizes this rationale on the part of the borrower, so it will not be willing to fall into this position of extending credit up to 99 units either. The same process of backward induction that applied for each period from the terminal period back to the present also applies from some hypothetical upper loan limit back to an initial loan, with the result that the lender can never extend even the first loan.

These two thought experiments—when borrowers and lenders both know they have reached the last period for a loan or when they know that they have reached the upper bound of lending—show the limits to reputation alone as a rationale for explaining sovereign borrowing. In both cases, the certainty on the part of both lender and borrower makes the venture fail. Thus, it is uncertainty about the future that makes reputation valuable in sustaining lending. A borrower's reputation for paying as promised possesses value because of the prospect of securing a loan or expanding borrowing in the future.

BEYOND REPUTATIONAL EXPLANATIONS FOR SOVEREIGN DEBT

There are further limits to the reputational understanding of sovereign lending. Consider a country that has fluctuating production due to variable weather or other factors that affect harvests. Such a country might need to borrow in lean years to finance consumption, while repaying outstanding loans when harvests are bountiful or at least normal. Given these circumstances, this country might engage in sovereign borrowing followed by repayment with many repetitions in this cycle. For convenience, assume that the borrower country has reached its credit limit. At first glance, it may seem that the debtor nation has a choice of repaying with the prospect of future borrowings or defaulting and bearing the risk of future macroeconomic fluctuations on its own account.

However, a famous paper (Bulow and Rogoff 1989) shows that this is a false choice. Consider a country that has been borrowing in hard times and repaying when times get better but that has now borrowed up to the maximum any lender is willing to advance. In this situation, the country can also choose to refuse repayment and use the funds it owes to save against future macroeconomic shocks, earning interest until the shock occurs and the funds are needed. Thus, the country will be better off to default once it secures its maximum level of borrowing.[2]

Bulow and Rogoff (1989) consider an alternative to default and saving. The defaulting country might purchase insurance that pays when the country experiences future adverse macroeconomic events. Such an insurance contract would pay in those years in which production fell short. Therefore, Bulow and Rogoff contend, the country will also be better off if it defaults and purchases the macroeconomic insurance (or defaults and saves). As Bulow and Rogoff put the point, "Small countries will not meet loan obligations to maintain a reputation for repaying because, under fairly general conditions, it is impossible for them to have such a reputation" (p. 49). The purpose of Bulow and Rogoff's argument is not to assert that reputation plays no role in understanding international lending to sovereigns, but to prove that reputation by itself is not adequate to explain the world of sovereign debt that we actually observe, especially if both the prospective borrower and the prospective lender have perfect information about the incentives of the other party. As a consequence, lending "must be supported by the direct sanctions available to creditors, and cannot be supported by a country's 'reputation for repayment'" (p. 43).

Other limitations with simple reputational explanations are also evident under real-world considerations. For example, early reputational explanations assumed that lenders acted monolithically, that if a sovereign defaulted against one lender, no other lender would advance funds, and that one default meant permanent exclusion from international borrowing. Both assumptions are empirically incorrect. Sovereign debtors are often successful in gaining additional funds from not only the same lender against whom they defaulted but also new loans from other lenders. Further, sovereign borrowers are often successful in playing one lender off against others. As we will see, history offers considerable evidence of notorious defaulters quickly gaining renewed access to international credit markets.

Given that reputation alone cannot support or rationalize the occurrence of sovereign debt, other adverse consequences or lender-imposed sanctions must play some role. Many models of sovereign default consider the effect that a default on one lender may have on the willingness of other potential lenders to advance funds. However, the consequences of default may be quite a bit broader. If a nation defaults on one obligation, this can adversely affect a variety of other trust relationships that the sovereign may also value. As the leading exponents of this theory have maintained, default in one arena can lead to adverse "reputational spillovers" that affect trust relationships much more broadly. Thus, the fear of collateral damage from these spillovers can make it rational for the sovereign to honor its promises to pay when it might choose to default based on very narrow considerations of that borrowing relationship alone (Cole and Kehoe 1997). For example, if a sovereign defaults to a foreign bank, other suppliers for that government may require payment in advance before shipping goods or providing services. Similarly, a default by a government on an international loan may signal to domestic constituencies that the government is not to be trusted. So the default on a bank loan may provide a signal to labor groups, voters, and citizens generally that their government is not to be trusted. If a sovereign default impairs other important trust relationships that the sovereign values, this raises the total cost of the default. Thus, even though it might appear rational on narrow economic terms for the sovereign to default, the total cost of default might be high enough to encourage the sovereign to avoid default and to pay as promised.

Default by a sovereign borrower is almost always a choice, and because the default is by a government, such a choice necessarily has a political element. Recent research finds that states with certain political circumstances are more likely to default than others. There is a long-standing view that states with a weaker central government afford better protection for property rights and experience higher rates of economic growth (De Long and Shleifer 1993). More recent research suggests that similar factors may influence the probability of sovereign defaults. In brief, weaker central governmental authority coincides with a lower probability of sovereign default (Kohlscheen 2010; Saiegh 2009; Stasavage 2007). Thus, countries with coalition governments tend to default less than those dominated by a single strong party (Saiegh 2009). From a historical perspective, city-states with a strong merchant class default less often than do large territorial states; similarly, states with stronger constitutional restraints on the executive power have a lower probability of default that do those with a very powerful executive (Stasavage 2007). Further, faced with imminent default, states increase the riskiness of their economic policies in an effort to "gamble for redemption"—that is, to secure sufficient funds to avoid default (Malone 2011, forthcoming).

While the interaction of political factors and the propensity to default on sovereign debt remains incompletely understood, the general landscape of this interaction appears to be related to familiar issues in the realm of public choice economics. In particular, the interests of various political factions play a large role in determining the ultimate choice that states make with respect to default (Hatchondo, Martinez, and Sapriza 2007; Hatchondo, Martinez, and Sapriza 2011).

CREDITOR SANCTIONS AND SOVEREIGN DEFAULTS

We have already briefly considered an era in which rather extreme sanctions were enforced to collect sovereign debts. Assuming that invasion and gunboat diplomacy are no longer viable, what sanctions are available to creditors to encourage sovereign borrowers to pay as promised? This section briefly considers three famous episodes of sovereign default interacting with creditor sanctions across a span of more than 400 years. Together, they illustrate much of the broad range of the effectiveness and failure of creditor sanctions.

Defaults of the Spanish Empire in the Sixteenth Century

Historically, sanctions have sometimes been quite effective in securing repayment, even when the debtor appears to have all of the power in the relationship. In the late sixteenth century, the Spanish Empire under King Philip II from the house of Habsburg (reigned 1556–1598) held sway over much of Europe. Fueled by its silver revenues from the New World, Spain led European forces to victory at Lepanto in 1571 to turn back the Ottoman ascendancy in the Mediterranean, Spain's armada embarked on a failed invasion of England in 1588, and its armies pursued a brutal war in the Netherlands over much of Philip's reign. But the flood of silver from the mines of Latin America was not enough to sustain Spain's expenditures. Sovereign debt would play a determining role in Spain's attempt to solidify its control over the Netherlands.

During his 42-year reign, Philip borrowed from the banking magnates of Europe, and Spain defaulted four times: 1557, 1560, 1575, 1596. The most serious default and the one most illustrative of the import of sanctions was Philip's default on Spain's obligations to a coalition of bankers led by the Genoese in 1575. This default occurred at a critical moment in the war with the Netherlands: "The Habsburg default of 1575 led to a serious dislocation of international money markets at a delicate moment: prior to 1 September 1575 the Spanish position in the Netherlands had shown promise; after this date it proved impossible to satisfy the demand of the royal troops stationed in the Low Countries for pay and arrears. The Sack of Antwerp ('the Spanish Fury') which took place in the early days of November 1576 was a direct result" (Lovett 1980, p. 899).

While scholars generally agree that the default of 1575 resulted in a shortage of funds to meet Spain's military payroll and thus hampered the conduct of war in the Low Countries, they disagree on just how the bankers' sanctions brought Philip to heel. Philip paid his troops in coins, so it was absolutely necessary to obtain specie in the Netherlands. According to one leading explanation, this transfer of funds was under the management of the banking houses of Europe through letters of credit, as well as via physical shipments of bullion. When Spain defaulted, the bankers strangled the transfer of funds from Spain to the Netherlands, leaving the troops without pay: "The Genoese imposed an embargo on specie transfer on Philip. The Crown was unable to get appreciable funds to its troops in Flanders, with the result that in November 1576 troops mutinied over arrears and sacked Antwerp, a strategic entrepôt in Spanish possession" (Conklin 1998, p. 510).

Emphasizing the importance of the bankruptcy of 1575 and the bankers' consequent sanctions for the conduct of war in the Netherlands, Drelichman and Voth (2008) offer an alternative account of the sanctions that brought Philip to heel. In their view, the refusal of all bankers to lend following the default was the effective sanction. Drelichman and Voth maintained that transfers of specie actually continued at a healthy pace after the default: "There is no evidence that the Genoese 'transfer embargo' had any effect on the availability of funds in the Flanders theatre of war" (p. 22). Instead, Drelichman and Voth assert that the bankers of Europe successfully maintained their antilending cartel until Philip knuckled under to their financial demands, and it was this cessation of lending that kept the Spanish troops in Flanders unpaid.

Whether the interruption in pay to the Spanish troops stemmed from an embargo on transferring funds or from a refusal to lend, the sanctions imposed by Spain's creditors were the leading factors in forcing Philip to settle and resume payments on Spain's debt, which he did in 1577. As a result, lending resumed, paving the way for Philip's last default in 1596. While it might appear on first inspection that a coalition of bankers might have little power relative to the greatest empire in an age of empires, the fact turns out to be quite otherwise. Clearly, the bankers managed to make Spain comply with their demands, whether by blocking the transfer of coin to the Low Countries or by refusing to sustain Spain's need for additional financing.

Peru and Its Guano

In more recent times, the typical sovereign borrower has been a developing country with an economy based on the export of raw materials that acquires bank loans from international banks. As an exporter, the borrower country clearly gains from international trade and participates in the international financial system. Against this background, the role of sanctions in sovereign lending is to raise the cost of default sufficiently high to make repaying the foreign obligations in the self-interest of the sovereign debtor.

One of the most instructive instances of the value of sanctions comes from a situation in which sanctions were never actually enforced—a tale of a dog that did not bark—and it involves nineteenth-century Peru.[3] In the early 1820s, Peru fought for its independence against Spain and floated bond issues in London to finance its revolution. But Peru defaulted in 1826 and remained in default until 1849, with its bonds trading as low as 20 percent of par. As the low price of Peru's bonds during this period indicates, Peru's creditors had few effective sanctions to make Peru pay, and the bond market saw little prospect of Peru's actually paying on the bonds. However, Peru reached a settlement with its debtors in 1849 and then enjoyed more than 20 years of easy access to world capital markets at attractive borrowing rates. During this period, it floated many bond issues for purposes ranging from debt management to financing railway construction and other wars.

What rescued Peru from the mire of default? As with most sovereign defaults, Peru's problem from 1826 to 1849 was not its ability to pay, but its willingness. Peru's change from unwilling defaulter to active participant in world capital markets began with the travels of Alexander von Humboldt, a famous German scientist who traveled to Peru in 1802 and wrote of the rich deposits of guano on Peru's Chincha Islands, which lie 20 kilometers off Peru's coast. Production had already started in the early 1840s, but in 1849, the government of Peru attempted to rationalize the production and sale of this potentially valuable resource.

Europe, with its high demand for fertilizer, was the main market for the Peruvian guano, but Peru's principal unsatisfied creditors on its defaulted sovereign debt were also based in Europe, most notably in Great Britain. As a consequence, the Peruvian government feared that its guano exports would be seized in repayment of the outstanding debts. These fears were of real weight. The holders of the defaulted bonds had already noted in 1847 that the guano was by itself sufficient "to provide for the liquidation of its [Peru's] foreign debt, and that consequently the [British] government is bound by every principle of public faith and national honour to proceed to that stipulation without further delay." For its part, the Peruvian finance minister noted that "until the foreign debt is settled, the remission of guano abroad . . . could bring major complications that we must avoid" (Quoted in Vizcarra 2009, p. 371).

While these fears of seizure may have been exaggerated, Peru certainly faced the problem of restricted access to capital markets. With its bonds sitting in default, further financing from abroad was unlikely. Further, Peru very much needed new financing to make the extraction and sale of its guano possible. Loading a ship with guano could take a month, and the voyage to Europe was lengthy so the transportation cost was high. Further, "procurement of vessels and coordination of sales, foreign warehousing, and marketing were also costly and demanded a certain degree of expertise that the Peruvian government lacked" (Vizcarra 2009, p. 367). Peru solved this dilemma by contracting with a highly reputable British merchant bank, Anthony Gibbs and Sons, to manage this process and to collect its sales receipts in Europe. Peru authorized the Gibbs bank not only to collect all the guano revenues but also to withhold 50 percent of them to service Peru's foreign debt. The Gibbs company had considerable reputational capital of great value, so it was unlikely to cooperate with Peru to defraud new lenders.

With these new arrangements in place, Peru now had the means to capitalize on its guano deposits. Key to this was an arrangement that gave Peru's creditors confidence that Peru would pay. Because the proceeds from selling guano were realized outside the boundaries of Peru and passed through the hands of Gibbs and Sons, who had the confidence of Peru's foreign creditors, Peru had solved the problem of being able to make a "credible commitment" to pay its debts.

As an alternative to allowing Gibbs and Sons to control its guano-based cash flows, Peru might have tried to secure new financing to allow it to exploit its guano and to receive payment in Peru when the guano was loaded. However, given its record of defaults, new borrowing was unlikely. What lender would want to lend merely on Peru's promise of future payments? But having the revenues from guano realized outside the country by a reputable third party gave lenders the confidence they needed to advance new funds.

The Russian Federation in 1993

Shortly after the breakup of the Soviet Union, the Swiss firm known as Noga, led by Nessim Gaon, signed a deal with the first post-Soviet government in 1991. Noga exported goods including medicine and pesticides to Russia in exchange for oil, and the Russian Federation explicitly waived sovereign immunity. The deal quickly fell apart, after $1.5 billion in trade had already occurred, and Russia refused to send any more oil. Noga, claiming a loss of approximately $100 million, sued in 1993 and secured a court ruling that froze Russian government bank accounts in Luxembourg and Switzerland. Noga secured more legal victories, including an order by a French court to seize the bank accounts of many Russian state enterprises holding funds abroad.

Beyond freezing bank accounts, Noga also pursued other avenues of harassing the Russian government: "In 2000, the Royal Museum of Art and History in

Belgium was forced to abandon a show of Russian Art Treasures when it could not gain legal guarantees against the seizure of the art. . . . In 2000, a French presidential decree was made to prevent the seizure of president Putin's personal aircraft at Orly Airport in Paris. . . . [In 2000] the Russian tall ship Sedov . . . was impounded in the port of Brest in France. . . . Threats of seizure in 2000, led Russia to halt shipments of nuclear warheads to the USA for reprocessing until President Clinton signed an executive order guaranteeing immunity of the uranium from seizure" (Wright 2002, pp. 36–37).

Noga pursued its claims with remarkable persistence over the years. In 2001, Noga attempted to seize two Russian fighter jets at the Bourget air show, but the jets escaped with the warning and collusion of the show's organizers (Wright 2002, p. 37). In subsequent years, Russian planes were unaccustomedly missing from other European air shows, apparently due to fear of Noga's attempted seizures (Nadmitov, n.d., p. 56). Over the years, Noga continued its pursuit of restitution, winning a victory in a French court as recently as 2008 (Aris 2008). But Noga's quest apparently ended in 2009, when Noga lost a decision in the U.S. Court of Appeals for the Second Circuit.[4]

Although writing seven years before the final legal resolution of the matter, Sinyagina-Woodruff summarizes the ultimate outcome quite well: "Seizure of external assets, even with the blessings of international arbitration, can be more problematic still. The ongoing saga of the firm Noga which has struggled for almost 10 years to enforce court decisions against the Russian government, illustrates that. . . . This story demonstrates that the threat of seizing property outside the country's borders, a key 'stick' in some sanctioning theories of sovereign borrowing, is not credible and therefore cannot motivate repayment" (Sinyagina-Woodruff 2003, pp. 521, 538).

Why didn't Russia pay and avoid the embarrassment and interference with its image abroad? After all, the $100 million is a trivial amount in the broad scheme of Russian foreign debt. Some have speculated that Russia did not want to embolden other small creditors and wanted to show its ultimate mastery of the situation by settling with creditors equally and in its own way.

CONCLUSION

This chapter has attempted to survey some of the most important dimensions of sovereign debt. Today, sovereign borrowers are generally immune to physical force as a means of compelling repayment. So this fact raises the question of why sovereigns should ever repay, and the questionable incentives for sovereign repayment give rise to the question of why anyone should ever lend to a sovereign.

We have seen that, while a reputation as a reliable and responsible borrower may play an important role in understanding the behavior of borrowers and lenders, reputational considerations alone cannot account for sovereign repayment. However, when considerations of reputation are broadened to include the effect of default on constituencies beyond direct participants in borrowing and lending, reputational spillovers can have considerable effect. Further, the behavior of sovereign borrowers is largely influenced by political considerations and is related to the relationship between the executives and other political constituencies.

In addition, creditor sanctions do have an important role in securing repayment and in explaining the continuing existence of the sovereign debt market. Sanctions have mixed results in forcing payment. In some instances, the denial of further loans can be effective, especially if there is concerted action by a number of lenders. In a more swashbuckling era, governments could more successfully interfere with the international trade of smaller nations, thereby denying them the benefits of trade and making repayment more attractive than remaining in default. As the case of Peru and guano on the one hand, and Noga and Russia on the other hand illustrate, a creative and cooperative effort between creditor and defaulter, with sanctions held in the background, may prove to be a more effective means of securing repayment.

NOTES

1. For details on both of these episodes and many other supersanctions of both types, see three papers by Kris James Mitchener and Marc D. Weidenmier, "How Are Sovereign Debtors Punished? Evidence from the Gold Standard Era," Working Paper, September 2004; "Supersanctions and Sovereign Debt Repayment," in Robert W. Kolb, ed., *Sovereign Debt: From Safety to Default* (Hoboken, NJ: John Wiley & Sons); and 2010, "Supersanctions and Sovereign Debt Repayment," *Journal of International Money and Finance* 29, 19–36.

2. Bulow and Rogoff (1989) consider an alternative to default and saving. The defaulting country might purchase insurance that pays when the country experiences future adverse macroeconomic events. Such an insurance contract would pay in those years in which production fell short. Therefore, Bulow and Rogoff contend, the country will also be better off if it defaults and purchases the macroeconomic insurance (or defaults and saves).

3. This account of Peru's debt draws on W. M. Mathew. "A Primitive Export Sector: Guano Production in Mid-Nineteenth-Century Peru." *Journal of Latin American Studies* 9:1 (1977), 35–57; and Catalina Vizcarra, "Guano, Credible Commitments, and Sovereign Debt Repayment in Nineteenth-Century Peru," *Journal of Economic History* 69:2 (2009), 358–387.

4. See cgsh.com/zh-CHS/russian_federation_wins_appeal/. Accessed August 21, 2010.

REFERENCES

Aris, Ben. 2008. "A French Kiss Goodbye to Russia's Investment-Grade Credit Rating?" businessneweurope.eu/story1242. Accessed August 21, 2010.

Bulow, Jeremy, and Kenneth Rogoff. 1989. "Sovereign Debt: Is to Forgive to Forget?" *American Economic Review* 79:1, 43–50.

Cole, Harold L., and Patrick J. Kehoe. 1997. "Reviving Reputation Models of International Debt." *Federal Reserve Bank of Minneapolis Quarterly Review* 21:1, 21–30.

Conklin, James. 1998. "The Theory of Sovereign Debt and Spain under Philip II." *Journal of Political Economy* 106:3, 483–513.

De Long, J. Bradford, and Andrei Shleifer. 1993. "Princes and Merchants: European City Growth before the Industrial Revolutions." *Journal of Law and Economics* 36:2, 671–702.

Drelichman, Mauricio, and Hans-Joachim Voth. 2008. "Lending to the Borrower from Hell: Debt and Default in the Age of Philip II, 1556–1598." Working Paper.

Eaton, Jonathan, and Mark Gersovitz. 1981. "Debt with Potential Repudiation: Theoretical and Empirical Analysis." *Review of Economic Studies* 48: 289–309.

Eaton, Jonathan, Mark Gersovitz, and Joseph E. Stiglitz. 1986. "The Pure Theory of Country Risk." *NBER Working Paper*, No. 1894.

Hatchondo, Juan Carlos, Leonardo Martinez, and Horacio Sapriza. 2007. "The Economics of Sovereign Default." *Economic Quarterly* 163–187.

Hatchondo, Juan Carlos, Leonardo Martinez, and Horacio Sapriza. 2011. "Understanding sovereign default." In Robert W. Kolb, ed. *Sovereign Debt: From Safety to Default*, 137–147. Hoboken, NJ: John Wiley & Sons.

Kohlscheen, Emanuel. 2010. "Sovereign Risk: Constitutions Rule." *Oxford Economic Papers* 62: 62–86.

Lovett, A. W. 1980. "The Castilian Bankruptcy of 1575." *Historical Journal* 23:4, 899–911.

Malone, Samuel W. 2011. "Sovereign debt problems and policy gambles." In Robert W. Kolb, ed. *Sovereign Debt: From Safety to Default*, 43–49. Hoboken, NJ: John Wiley & Sons.

Malone, Samuel W. forthcoming. "Sovereign Indebtedness, Default, and Gambling for Redemption." *Oxford Economic Papers*.

Mathew, W. M. 1977. "A Primitive Export Sector: Guano Production in Mid-Nineteenth-Century Peru." *Journal of Latin American Studies* 9:1, 35–57.

Mitchener, Kris James, and Marc D. Weidenmier. 2004. "How Are Sovereign Debtors Punished? Evidence from the Gold Standard Era." Working Paper.

Mitchener, Kris James, and Marc D. Weidenmier. 2010. "Supersanctions and Sovereign Debt Repayment." *Journal of International Money and Finance* 29: 19–36.

Mitchener, Kris James, and Marc D. Weidenmier. 2011. "Supersanctions and sovereign debt repayment." In Robert W. Kolb, ed. *Sovereign Debt: From Safety to Default*, 155–166. Hoboken, NJ: John Wiley & Sons.

Nadmitov, Alexander, n.d. "Russian Debt Restructuring: Overview, Structure of Debt, Lessons of Default, Seizure Problems and the IMF SDRM Proposal." Working Paper.

Saiegh, Sebastian M. 2009. "Coalition Governments and Sovereign Debt Crises." *Economics and Politics* 21:2, 232–254.

Sinyagina-Woodruff, Yulia. 2003. "Russia, Sovereign Default, Reputation and Access to Capital Markets." *Europe-Asia Studies* 55:4, 521–551.

Stasavage, David. 2007. "Cities, Constitutions, and Sovereign Borrowing in Europe, 1274–1785," *International Organization* (Summer): 61, 489–525.

Vizcarra, Catalina. 2009. "Guano, Credible Commitments, and Sovereign Debt Repayment in Nineteenth-Century Peru." *Journal of Economic History* 69:2, 358–387.

Wright, Mark L. J. 2002. "Reputations and Sovereign Debt." Working Paper.

CHAPTER 2

The Institutional Determinants of Debt Intolerance

RAFFAELA GIORDANO
Bank of Italy—Research Department*

PIETRO TOMMASINO
Bank of Italy—Research Department

I t appears to be a historical regularity, first documented by Reinhart et al. (2003), that some countries are more likely to default than others.[1] Argentina, to give just an example, went bankrupt three times since 1980. Moreover, most debt repudiation episodes in these default-prone countries happened at relatively low levels of debt (in the most recent of its debt crises, Argentina had a debt-to-GDP ratio slightly above 50 percent). On the contrary, there are countries and governments that are able to sustain much higher borrowing levels. A striking case is Japan, whose public debt recently reached 170 percent of GDP without inducing significant market tensions.

It is of course very important to understand what determines the degree of debt (in)tolerance of a sovereign borrower, especially as the recent economic and financial crisis induced a dramatic increase in public debts all over the world, and both policy makers and investors appear increasingly worried by the risk of sovereign insolvency.

Several authors have argued that the debt intolerance ultimately depends on the institutional set-up of a country.[2] Indeed, governments, differently from firms—which are *forced* to go bankrupt when they do not have enough resources to repay their creditors—typically *choose* to default on their promises even if they could in principle find ways to honor the debt by cutting expenditures or increasing revenues or both.[3]

The choices made by governments facing high public debts should be explained from a political economy perspective, that is, starting from the assumption that policy makers are not benevolent welfare-maximizing planners but self-interested players advancing their own political objectives—*given the prevailing institutional constraints*. In this chapter, we would like to stress the role of political[4]

---

*The views expressed are those of the authors and do not necessarily reflect those of the Bank of Italy.

and monetary[5] institutions in shaping the decision to default and ultimately the reliability of a sovereign borrower.

THE ROLE OF POLITICAL INSTITUTIONS

Different strategies to cope with a high debt situation entail different redistributive consequences; social groups therefore often have conflicting economic interests with respect to the policy to pursue in the middle of a debt crisis.

A rational self-interested government will choose to default if and only if the implied costs for its constituency are lower than the benefits.

One dimension of conflict is related to differences in portfolio holdings (Giordano and Tommasino 2009). It is a well-documented fact that the composition of an individual's portfolio depends on that person's wealth.[6] The poorest part of the population is characterized by low saving rates and holds its wealth mostly in the form of cash, while the richest part has access to more sophisticated high-risk–high-return assets. Public debt is therefore mostly held by middle class households, which are consequently the most exposed to a government bankruptcy.

Moreover, the rich and the poor are likely to be those who pay the bill if the government decides to honor its debts and to follow a fiscal consolidation path. The poor would be worse off if consolidation were pursued through cuts in the welfare state, and the rich would be the most affected by increases in taxation, for example, through one-off wealth taxes.

Therefore, the presence of a politically influential middle class is likely to improve debt sustainability.[7] This effect will be enhanced if democratic institutions are in place, as they are more likely to protect the interests of the average citizen while limiting the influence of people at the extremes of the income spectrum.

Possible illustrations of our argument are the cases of Italy and Japan. In both countries, the presence of a large middle class for which treasury bonds represented a relatively safe and accessible means of saving probably made the accumulation of huge amounts of public debt easier (as lenders understood that defaulting on debt would have been politically self-defeating). In both countries, cultural biases against the stock market and high saving propensities may also have contributed to a strong domestic demand of government bonds by middle-income families.[8]

THE ROLE OF MONETARY INSTITUTIONS

In several episodes of sovereign default, the behavior of monetary authorities has been crucial in determining the outcome of the debt endgame (Alesina 1988). Even if in the middle of a debt crisis, the pressures of the government on the central bank to influence its policy increase, there are in most countries constitutional or legal rules that protect the bank's independence from that political pressure. The existence of checks and balances in the political process also limits the power of the government to override the monetary authority (Moser 1999).[9] Also, there are groups in society that might stand ready to defend central bank independence (for example, the financial community, as in Posen 1995).[10] Therefore, the monetary authority has always some degree of freedom in setting and pursuing its own objectives.

Moreover, such objectives are typically less partisan than those of the government. Indeed, the appointment of central bank officials typically involves other actors besides the executive, such as the parliament, or local governments (Lohmann 1998). Also, competing parties with extreme political preferences might reach an agreement and jointly appoint a moderate central bank if they are uncertain about election outcomes (Alesina and Gatti 1995).

In a debt crisis, the central bank fills the double role of guardian of price stability and exerciser of responsibility for the smooth functioning of the financial system. As a sovereign default often puts the financial system in jeopardy, for example, triggering bankruptcies of important financial institutions or inducing waves of panic selling (Kaminsky and Reinhart 1999; De Paoli et al. 2006), it will harm not only the debt holders, but also rich citizens who invested in the stock market. In such circumstances, they will pressure the central bank to inject liquidity to sustain the financial system, even if this policy will result in excessive inflation. Symmetrically, the poor will stand to lose from the bailout of the financial system because—due to the composition of their portfolio—they are the most exposed to its inflationary consequences. But, while each social group cares only about its own interests, a central bank is likely to protect the interests of the average citizen, opposing both the demand for an excessively loose monetary policy coming from a pro-rich government and that for an excessively tight policy coming from a pro-poor government, as both policies would benefit a minority at the expense of overall social welfare.[11]

Provided the central bank is sufficiently independent, even in the middle of a debt crisis it will effectively resist political pressures. This will in turn increase debt sustainability ex ante, as it implies that in the event of a sovereign debt crisis, both the rich and the poor—those who are more likely to prefer a default to a fiscal consolidation—would bear at least part of the costs of a sovereign default.[12]

To sum up, even in the presence of a small or politically weak middle class, the government has an incentive to honor its debt if there is a sufficiently independent central bank.

Some Evidence

In the previous section we argued that countries that lack proper political and monetary institutions are not able to sustain debt levels that are instead sustainable for others. According to the definition introduced by Reinhart et al. (2003), they suffer from debt intolerance. There is a country-specific debt threshold above which default occurs, and this threshold rises as the middle class increases its political power and the central bank gains greater independence.

In the present section, we bring some preliminary empirical evidence to support these conclusions.[13]

We report some measure of income distribution in Exhibit 2.1, central bank independence, and features of political institutions for 192 countries, some of which experienced one or more episodes of default. As in several countries, political or monetary institutions have changed in the last few decades, so we split our sample of default episodes into two subperiods: 1975 to 1990 and 1991 to 2006. This gives us 384 observations. We obtained data on sovereign default by merging the Standard & Poor's sovereign default database with the one built by Reinhart

Exhibit 2.1 Means and Standard Deviations and Ordinary Least Squares Estimation

	Whole Sample		No Default		At Least One Default	
	Mean	St. Dev.	Mean	St. Dev.	Mean	St. Dev.
Inequality (1)	39.24	9.85	38.04	9.52	44.58	9.67
CB indep. (2)	0.52	0.22	0.54	0.21	0.47	0.23
CB indep. (3)	0.50	0.22	0.51	0.22	0.43	0.20
Democracy (4)	0.73	7.33	1.09	7.56	−0.81	6.06
Democracy (5)	3.86	1.97	3.81	2.05	4.11	1.54
Observations	384		326		58	

Sources: (1) Gini coefficient from Deininger and Squire (1996); (2) from Crowe and Meade (2008); (3) from Arnone et al. (2008); (4) from Polity IV; (5) from Freedom House.

and Rogoff (2009). The former includes all sovereign defaults on loans or bonds with private agents between 1975 and 2002. The latter records defaults on domestic debt in the time from 1976 to 2006.[14]

Data on income inequality are from Deininger and Squire (1996): We consider the average Gini coefficient computed over periods that range, depending on the country, between 1975 and 1995. As proxies for the quality of political institutions, we consider both the Polity IV and the Freedom House indexes of democracy, available since 1972 and 1950, respectively.[15]

Finally, we use the measures of central bank independence computed by Grilli et al. (1991) and Cukierman et al. (1992) as recently updated by Arnone et al. (2008) and Crowe and Meade (2008).[16]

In 53 of the 192 countries included in our sample, one or more episodes of default occurred over the last 30 to 35 years; in five countries, such episodes occurred in both subperiods. On average, income inequality is significantly higher in countries that experienced at least one default episode, as already found by Berg and Sachs (1988) in a cross-section of middle income countries. Furthermore, consistent with our theoretical claims, the quality of monetary and political institutions is better (that is, the central bank is more independent and the government is more democratic) in countries that never experienced default. The same results hold if we perform a more formal analysis, regressing the number of default episodes against our measure of the size of the middle class (alone, and interacted to take the effects of political institutions into account) and central bank independence (alone, and interacted to capture the importance of the degree of conflict of interest between the central bank and the government). In line with our predictions, the size of the middle class and the degree of central bank independence turn out to be negatively related to the probability of default (Exhibit 2.2). Moreover, the estimated coefficients for the interaction terms suggest that there is a complementarity between better political institutions and a more equal income distribution, whereas central bank independence seems to be somewhat less important if the government is already disciplined by a larger middle class.

Exhibit 2.2 Ordinary Least Squares Estimation (Standard Errors in Parentheses)

	(1)		(2)		(3)	
Middle Class	−0.037	***	−0.048	***	−0.271	**
	(0.012)		(0.014)		(0.016)	
Middle Class * Demo	−0.003	**	−0.0003	*	−0.001	**
	(0.000)		(0.000)		(0.000)	
CB indep	−3.342	**	−4.309	***	−2.935	**
	(1.362)		(1.650)		(1.346)	
CB indep * middle class	0.048	**	0.063	**	0.042	**
	(0.021)		(0.026)		(0.021)	
Constant	2.803	***	3.529	***	2.403	***
	(0.741)		(0.876)		(0.715)	
R^2	0.150		0.180		0.120	
Observations	155		130		161	

Notes: ***: significant at 1 percent; **: significant at 5 percent; 8: significant at 10 percent.
(1) Dependent variable: number of default episodes. Importance of the middle class proxied by (1 − Gini coefficient); quality of political institutions proxied by the Polity IV index; Central bank independence proxied by the Crow and Meade (2008) index.
(2) As in (1) except for central bank independence, proxied by the Arnone et al. (2008) indexes.
(3) As in (1) except for the quality of political institutions measure, proxied by the Freedom House indicator.

Some Lessons for the Current Crisis

Looking at debt sustainability through the lens of political economy might also be useful in the current juncture, while the market perception of sovereign risk has increased for several EU countries. Those countries are characterized by large middle classes, which hold significant portions of the overall amount of outstanding public debt, and are well-established democracies. Furthermore, the European Central Bank can be credited with a very high degree of independence and a strong commitment to price stability. All these circumstances imply that the political costs of a default would be prohibitive for any government in the Eurozone, even if the alternative solution—a painful fiscal consolidation path involving measures both on the revenue and on the expenditure side—also involves high political costs.

All in all, the analysis conducted in this chapter allows a certain degree of optimism for the future of European sovereign debts.

NOTES

1. See also Reinhart and Rogoff (2009).
2. See, for example, the seminal paper by North and Weingast (1988), who argue that the increase in the power of the parliament in England significantly enhanced the borrowing capacity of the king.
3. Another possible way out, which we do not consider here, is inflating the debt away. Actually, this is not a viable option for many countries, either because debt is short-term or because it is denominated in a foreign currency.

4. See Kohlsheen (2007 and 2010), Van Rijckegem and Weder (2009), and Giordano and Tommasino (2009).

5. See Giordano and Tommasino (2009).

6. For example, stock market participation is in most countries limited to the richest part of the population (Guiso et al. 2003). Both the propensity and the possibility to buy risky assets increase with wealth: The poor exhibit a higher risk aversion (Guiso and Paiella 2008), a reduced awareness of the diversification possibilities offered by financial markets (Guiso and Jappelli 2005), and are more-than-proportionally harmed by the existence of fixed transaction costs. A thorough review of the related empirical literature is provided by Allen and Gale (2007).

7. This argument is consistent with the strand of the economic literature that highlights the economic costs of excessive inequality and political polarization (see, for example, Glaeser et al. 2003).

8. The importance of cultural factors in investment choices is documented by Guiso, Sapienza, and Zingales (2008).

9. North and Weingast (1989) argue that the introduction in the constitution of such checks and balances is optimal from an ex-ante point of view.

10. Beetsma (1996) argues that in this framework the policy maker will be more tempted to default if its constituency holds relatively few government bonds. The intuition that debt will be repaid if debt holders are politically more influential than the rest of the citizenry is also present in Dixit and Londregan (2000).

11. It has to be emphasized that even a seemingly implausible contrast between a dovish central bank and a hawkish government can sometimes take place. A recent example can be found in the critiques of the German chancellor, who blamed the European Central Bank for being excessively concerned with financial stability at the expense of price stability when it implemented measures to provide liquidity to distressed financial institutions. ("Germany Blasts 'Powers of the Fed,'" *Wall Street Journal,* June 3, 2009).

12. The idea that the risk of domestic financial market disruption deters government from defaulting has been formalized in Giordano and Tommasino (2009). In previous papers, default costs have been traced back to the exclusion of the defaulting sovereign from the debt market (Eaton and Gersovits 1981) and to broader reputational concerns (Cole and Kehoe 1998). Surveys of this literature can be found in Eaton and Fernandez (1995) and in Sturzenegger and Zettelmeyer (2006).

13. This section draws on Giordano and Tommasino (2009). Other related and supportive evidence already exists (Van Rijckegem and Weder 2009; Kohlscheen 2007), showing that default is less likely if the government is responsive to the needs of a wider set of citizens and political actors. For example, default seems less frequent if institutional checks and balances to the power of the executive are in place.

14. Reinhart and Rogoff (2009) include among default episodes forcible conversions of foreign currency bank deposits, arguing that they "constitute defaults on domestic debt because typically, the government simultaneously writes down the value of treasury debt held by banks."

15. The Polity IV index ranges from a minimum of −10 to a maximum of +10, for strongly autocratic and strongly democratic countries, respectively. Freedom House assigns scores between 1 and 7, which increase in the presence of lower guarantees for political rights and civil liberties.

16. Arnone et al. (2008) calculate indexes for 163 central banks, representing 181 countries, as of the end of 2003 and construct comparable indexes for a subgroup of 68 central banks as of the end of the 1980s. Their assessment is based on the methodologies developed

by Grilli et al. (1991) and Cukierman (1992). Crowe and Meade (2008) focus on the Cukierman, Webb, and Neyapti (1992) measure. They compute and update indexes for all but 3 of the 72 countries in the original Cukierman et al. (1992) sample and add 27 new countries.

REFERENCES

Alesina, A. 1988. "The End of Large Public Debts." In F. Giavazzi and L. Spaventa, eds. *High Public Debt: The Italian Experience.* Cambridge, UK: Cambridge University Press.

Alesina, A., and R. Gatti. 1995. "Independent Central Banks: Low Inflation at No Costs?" *American Economic Review* 85: 196–200.

Allen, F., and D. Gale. 2007. *Understanding Financial Crises.* Oxford, UK: Oxford University Press.

Arnone, M. B., J. Laurens, J. F. Segalotto, and M. Sommer. 2008. "Central Bank Autonomy: Lessons from Global Trends." *IMF Staff Papers.*

Beetsma, R. M. W. J. 1996. "Servicing Public Debt: The Role of Expectations. A Comment." *American Economic Review* 86:3, 675–679.

Berg, A., and J. Sachs. 1988. "The Debt Crisis: Structural Explanations of Country Performance." *Journal of Development Economics* 29: 271–306.

Cole, H. L., and P. J. Kehoe. 1998. "Models of Sovereign Debt: Partial versus General Reputations." *International Economic Review* 39: 55–70.

Crowe, C., and E. E. Meade. 2008. "Central Bank Independence and Transparency: Evolution and Effectiveness." *European Journal of Political Economy* 24: 763–777.

Cukierman A. 1992. *Central Bank Strategy, Credibility and Autonomy.* Cambridge, MA: MIT Press.

Cukierman A., S. B. Webb, and B. Neyapti. 1992. "Measuring the Independence of Central Banks and its Effects on Policy Outcomes." *World Bank Economic Review* 6: 353–398.

Deininger, K., and L. Squire. 1996. "A New Data Set Measuring Income Inequality." *World Bank Economic Review* 10:3, 565–591.

De Paoli, B., G. Hoggarth, and V. Saporta. 2006. "Costs of Sovereign Default." *Bank of England Quarterly Bulletin* 46:3, 297–307.

Dixit, A., and J. Londregan. 2000. "Political Power and the Credibility of Government Debt." *Journal of Economic Theory* 94: 80–105.

Eaton, J., and M. Gersovits. 1981. "Debt with Potential Repudiation: Theoretical and Empirical Analysis." *Review of Economic Studies* 48: 289–309.

Eaton, J., and M. Fernandez. 1995. "Sovereign Debt." In G. M. Grossman and K. Rogoff, eds. *Handbook of International Economics III.* Amsterdam, Holland: Elsevier.

Giordano, R., and Tommasino, P. 2009. "What Determines Debt Intolerance? The Role of Political and Monetary Institutions." *Bank of Italy, Economic Research Department, Working Papers.*

Glaeser, E., J. Scheinkman, and A. Shleifer. 2003. "The Injustice of Inequality." *Journal of Monetary Economics* 50:1, 199–222.

Grilli, V., D. Masciandaro, and G. Tabellini. 1991. "Political and Monetary Institutions and Public Financial Policies in the Industrial Countries." *Economic Policy* 13: 341–392.

Guiso, L., and T. Jappelli. 2005. "Awareness and Stock Market Participation." *Review of Finance* 9: 537–567.

Guiso, L., and M. Paiella. 2008. "Risk Aversion, Wealth, and Background Risk." *Journal of the European Economic Association* 6: 1109–1150.

Guiso, L., M. Haliassos, and T. Jappelli. 2003. "Equity Culture: Theory and Cross-Country Evidence." *Economic Policy* 18: 123–170.

Guiso, L., P. Sapienza, and L. Zingales. 2008. "Trusting the Stock Market." *Journal of Finance* 63: 2557–2600.

Kaminsky, G., and C. M. Reinhart. 1999. "The Twin Crises: The Causes of Banking and Balance-of-Payments Problems." *American Economic Review* 89:3, 473–500.

Kohlscheen, E. 2007. "Why Are There Serial Defaulters? Evidence from Constitutions." *Journal of Law and Economics* 50: 713–730.

Kohlscheen, E. 2010. "Sovereign Risk: Constitutions Rule." *Oxford Economic Paper* 62: 62–85.

Lohmann, S. 1998. "Institutional Checks and Balances and the Political Control of the Money Supply." *Oxford Economic Papers* 50: 360–377.

Moser, P. 1999. "Checks and Balances, and the Supply of Central Bank Independence." *European Economic Review* 43: 1569–1593.

North, D. C., and B. Weingast. 1989. "Constitutions and Commitment: The Evolution of Institutions Governing Public Choice in 17th-Century England." *Journal of Economic History* 49: 803–32.

Posen, A. S. 1995. "Declarations Are Not Enough: Financial Sector Sources of Central Bank Independence." In Bernanke, B. S. and J. J. Rotemberg, eds. *NBER Macroeconomics Annual.* Boston: MIT Press.

Reinhart, C. M., and K. Rogoff. 2009. *This Time Is Different:* Eight Centuries of Financial Folly. Princeton, NJ: Princeton University Press.

Reinhart, C. M., K. Rogoff, and M. S. Savastano. 2003. "Debt Intolerance." *Brookings Papers on Economic Activity* 1: 1–74.

Sturzenegger, F., and J. Zettelmeyer. 2006. *Debt Defaults and Lessons from a Decade of Crises.* Cambridge, MA: MIT Press.

Van Rijckegem, C., and B. Weder. 2004. "Political Institutions and Debt Crises." *Public Choice* 138: 387–408.

ABOUT THE AUTHORS

Raffaela Giordano is a senior economist in the research department of the Bank of Italy. She received an MA and a PhD from New York University. She has been an assistant professor at the Universitat Pompeu Fabra and at the Universidad Carlos III de Madrid. Dr. Giordano has done extensive work in the areas of fiscal policy and public spending, and public debt management. Giordano's writings include *Behind Public Sector Efficiency: The Role of Political Culture and Institutions; The Effects of Fiscal Policy in Italy: Evidence from a VAR Model; Funding a PAYG System: The Case of Italy; Budget Deficits and Coalition Governments; Wage Indexation, Employment and Inflation;* and *Default Risk and Optimal Debt Management.*

Pietro Tommasino is an economist in the research department of the Bank of Italy. He received an MSc and a PhD from Bocconi University, Milan. Dr. Tommasino has done work in the areas of fiscal policy, political economy, and public economics. Tommasino's recent writings include *Optimal Fiscal Policy in a Post-Crisis World; Behind Public Sector Efficiency: The Role of Political Culture and Institutions;* and *The Effect of Age on Portfolio Choices: Evidence from an Italian Pension Fund.*

CHAPTER 3

Output Costs of Sovereign Default

BIANCA DE PAOLI
Bank of England*

GLENN HOGGARTH
Bank of England

VICTORIA SAPORTA
Bank of England

S overeign defaults have been a feature of the international financial landscape for centuries. For example, Reinhart and Rogoff (2009), in their thorough historical survey of past financial crises, report that France defaulted on its sovereign debt eight times between 1500 and 1800, while Spain defaulted 14 times between 1500 and 1900. More recently, over the past quarter of a century, emerging market economies (EMEs) have defaulted on their sovereign debts frequently. And over the past year there has been increasing concerns about the actual and prospective sovereign debt levels in a number of developed countries, too.

But to the extent that default is voluntary there is an issue of why sovereigns did not default more frequently in the past. Sovereign nations—unlike companies—cannot be liquidated and there are also no national, or international, courts that can enforce payments on contract through, for example, transferring assets from the debtor to the creditor.[1] Defaulting, or restructuring, enables debtor countries to reduce the size or lengthen the maturity of their repayments, and thereby seek to provide a temporary boost to current consumption.

COSTS OF DEBT CRISES

There are, though, a number of potential costs of default that incentivize debtors to repay. Some are penalties imposed by external creditors on the cost or ability of defaulters to access *future* finance. So increasing consumption today may be at the expense of reducing consumption in the future. Moreover, given that defaulting

---

*The views expressed in this paper are those of the authors, and not necessarily those of the Bank of England.

may cause a broader financial crisis in which domestic activity and output are reduced even in the short run, any attempt to boost current spending temporarily through a default may not be successful.

Penalty Costs

In principle, defaulters may lose access to borrowing from financial markets. However, the empirical evidence suggests overall that sovereign default is not necessarily associated with a loss of market access, so fears about any such loss may not in themselves be a major deterrent to default. Lindert and Morton (1989) argue that in the 1930s, and again in the early 1980s, during periods when a number of countries defaulted, external credit was no more inaccessible to sovereign defaulters than to nondefaulters.[2] Jorgensen and Sachs (1989) find that in the two decades following the 1930s sovereign debt crisis, access to international capital markets for Latin American countries was severely restricted for previous nondefaulters as well as for defaulters. And once capital markets opened up in the 1960s, defaulters found it as easy to access capital as nondefaulters. More recently, assessing defaults since 1980, Medeiros et al. (2005) find that the probability of regaining market access after default depends partly on a country's external situation at the time of default and partly on its domestic macroeconomic performance.[3] More generally, Gelos et al. (2004) find that it only took past defaulters three and a half months, on average, to regain market access after defaulting during the 1990s compared with more than four and a half years during the 1980s.

Although the empirical evidence does not suggest that default necessarily closes off market access, it does point to an adverse effect on the government's *cost* of future borrowing. Ozler (1993) finds that during the tranquil period of the 1970s, lenders charged up to 50 basis points more for loans to previous (post-1930) defaulters. And more recently, Reinhart et al. (2003) find that EMEs with a history of defaulting on their external debts—especially serial defaulters—received a lower credit rating over the 1979 to 2000 period than nondefaulters that displayed similar financial strength.[4] Similarly, De Paoli et al. (2006) find that for a given debt to GDP ratio, past defaulters generally had a higher bond spread or lower credit rating than nondefaulters over the 2003 to 2005 period.

Broader Financial Costs

The costs discussed here represent penalties that sovereigns may face should they default. But governments may also want to maintain debt repayments so as to avoid broader losses to the domestic economy associated with default, beyond those caused by a tightening in the terms and conditions on borrowing imposed by foreign creditors. A number of studies suggest that default is often associated with a decline in output growth (for example, Cohen 1992, Dooley 2000, and Sturzenegger and Zettelmeyer 2006). But what are these broader output costs to the domestic economy resulting from sovereign default?

One mechanism by which a sovereign default may reduce GDP is through its impact on the domestic financial system. In many EMEs, domestic banks are major creditors of the government and so may be severely weakened, if not made insolvent, when the government defaults on, or restructures, its debt (including that owed to the domestic sector). In this case, banks may stop playing their inter-mediation role of providing liquidity and credit to the economy. This happened, for example, in Russia after the government suddenly defaulted on its domestic debt in the autumn of 1998. It has also been raised recently as a concern in the pe-ripheral Eurozone that sovereign problems may translate into banking ones (and vice versa). The impact of a sovereign default on the banking system is often accen-tuated through government debt having been taken up increasingly by domestic banks in the run-up to debt crises, when governments find it harder, or at least more expensive, to obtain external finance. Once banking problems emerge, any fiscal weakness, in turn, reduces the ability of the government to take measures to contain a crisis. For example, it is probably not credible for a highly indebted government to introduce a blanket guarantee to deposit holders so it can stem bank runs because depositors will not believe such a guarantee will be honored and their investments insured (see Hoelscher and Quintyn 2003).[5]

Foreign and domestic investors might also react to a sovereign defaulting on its external debt by questioning whether the government has sufficient foreign currency to defend the exchange rate. For net foreign currency borrowers, a sharp currency depreciation would, in turn, increase—when valued in domestic currency terms—the net foreign currency debts and debt service costs of the government, banks, and the nonbank private sector.[6] A tightening of monetary policy might limit the extent of exchange rate depreciation but at the expense, in the short run at least, of reducing domestic demand and liquidity in the financial system. Therefore, a triple—sovereign, banking, and currency—crisis may ensue, involving a run on both the domestic currency and the banking system (see Exhibit 3.1). But since depreciation tends to increase trade competitiveness, there would, after a time lag, be a potentially offsetting gain in net exports and output depending, inter alia, on the size of the traded goods sector (see Frankel 2005) and whether exporters have access to trade finance.

Measures of the Broader Financial Costs of Debt Crises

Despite research pointing to the importance of output losses as a reason why sovereigns would want to avoid defaulting, there have been few studies that have sought to quantify directly the losses following sovereign defaults. This gap in the literature is even more surprising given that similar studies have now been carried out extensively for banking and currency crises and their combination—so-called twin crises (see, for example, Kaminsky and Reinhart 1999, Bordo et al. 2001, Hoggarth et al. 2002, Cerra and Saxena 2005, Laeven and Valencia 2008, and IMF 2009). A recent study by us on the output losses of sovereign defaults is one exception (De Paoli et al. 2009).

De Paoli et al. define a sovereign default episode as occurring when either (1) the sovereign's arrears on principal are 15 percent or more of the total outstanding debt owed to the external private sector; (2) arrears on interest payments are 5 per-cent or more; or (3) a rescheduling agreement is reached with foreign private sector creditors.[7] Output losses are then estimated as the cumulative difference during the debt crisis period between actual GDP and estimates of what it would have been in the absence of a default. Having defined the episodes of default, there are two crucial measurement questions here—defining the beginning and end year of

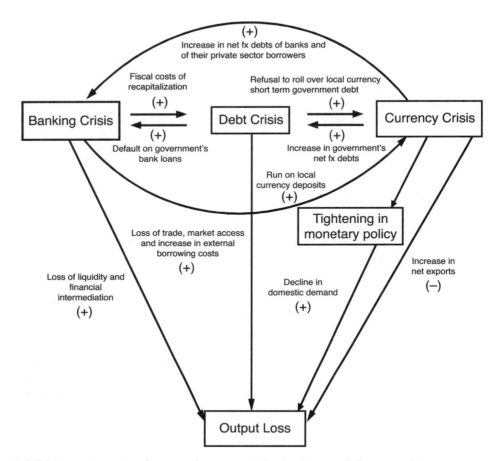

Exhibit 3.1 Interaction between Sovereign Debt, Banking, and Currency Crises
Note: Arrows show the direction of causation and +/− whether the impact is likely to accentuate or
alleviate the particular crisis or output loss.

the default period and estimating the output counterfactual. For governments that
fall into default, arrears usually build up gradually (and fall gradually after reaching a peak). So, having identified the default episodes, we define the beginning
of the crisis as the first year in which arrears on principal or on interest payments
rise above 5 percent and 1.5 percent, respectively, of outstanding debt (or when
an actual restructuring begins).[8] The end of a high arrears crisis period is more
difficult to pinpoint precisely so alternative specifications were considered.[9] But
for all variations of the assumed end point, crises were found, on average, to be
long-lasting. For the main output counterfactual (in the absence of a crisis), it was
assumed that output would have followed its pre-crisis trend (whereby the trend
is measured using a Hodrick Prescott (HP) filter on the available past GDP data). As
a check on the robustness of the results, an alternative output counterfactual was
also derived based on a conventional equation estimated to explain (per capita)
output growth.[10] This method produced qualitatively similar results.

Exhibit 3.2 Output Losses per Year During Different Types of EME Sovereign Crisis, 1970–2000

Type of Sovereign Default	Number of Crises	Average Mean Length of Crisis (years)	Median Loss, per Year[a]	Mean Cost per Year[a]
Sovereign only	5	3.2	−3.0[d]	0.5[d]
Sovereign and currency crisis[b]	14	8.1	2.3	6.2
Sovereign and banking crisis[b]	7	8.7	0.7	14.8
Triple crisis[b]	17	10.5	18.7	19.4
ALL CRISES	43	8.6	4.4	12.2
Restructured debt[c]	15	6.9	0.7	4.8
Unrestructured debt	28	9.5	11.5	16.1

[a]Cumulative difference per year between potential and actual output. Potential output is based on the country's pre-crisis (HP filter) trend.

[b]Defined as when a currency or banking crisis occurs at some point during the duration of the sovereign crisis. The definition of *banking crisis*, based on Caprio and Klingebiel (2003), is when "much or all" of the banking system's capital is exhausted, while that of *currency crisis*, based on Frankel and Rose (1986), is when the domestic nominal exchange rate against the dollar depreciates by at least 25 percent in any one year combined with a 10 percent increase in the rate of depreciation.

[c]Includes both pre- and post-arrears restructurings.

[d]A negative cost implies that actual output was higher during the crisis than suggested by its pre-crisis trend. Note, however, the small sample of default-only crises.

Source: De Paoli et al. (2009).

Exhibit 3.2 shows typical estimates of output losses from De Paoli et al. (2009). The estimated average *cumulative* output loss of the sample increases with the length of the crisis given that actual output remains below its counterfactual during most, if not all, of the crisis period.[11] Output losses are therefore shown on a per annum basis.

A number of features are suggested by Exhibit 3.2. First, output losses in the wake of sovereign default appear to be very large—almost 5 percent a year on the median measure—as well as long-lasting—on average for more than eight years. However, the counterfactuals likely overstate the path of output in the absence of the debt crisis because it is difficult to separate completely the loss due to default per se from the loss caused by the economic shock that triggered the default. Therefore, more weight should be attached to the relative costs from different types of crises than to the absolute estimates.

Second, sovereign defaults rarely occur in isolation—in only about 10 percent of the sample. More often, a debt crisis coincides with a banking and/or a currency crisis. In fact, almost one-half of the sample consists of triple (sovereign, banking, and currency) crises. In these cases, output losses appear to be particularly high—here the interactions between different sectors of the economy accentuate the decline in GDP. Banking crises often result in a sharp and prolonged reduction in the intermediation of credit to the private sector, with significant costs to economic efficiency. Although currency crises have the silver lining of stimulating exports—in two-thirds of the sample the share of domestic demand in total final expenditure falls during the crisis period (that is, the share of exports increases)—they also result in a marked deterioration in the balance sheet of the government or the private sector when measured in domestic currency terms since most EME external debt is denominated in foreign currency.

Third, the output losses *per year* tend to increase with the length of the crisis. This suggests that the longer that it takes to reduce arrears or complete a restructuring, the more output falls (relative to its trend or potential). Also, as shown in Exhibit 3.2, crisis countries that reschedule their debts appear to face smaller output losses than those that do not (despite having higher external debt-to-GDP ratios, on average, at the outset of the crisis). This suggests that countries that reschedule their debts—and thus start afresh with creditors—face a lower subsequent cost of finance or quicker renewed access to external finance. It might also indicate that an active policy of rescheduling has a less debilitating impact on the domestic financial system than a passive policy of remaining in arrears and not restructuring.

CONCLUSION

This chapter has assessed the output costs associated with sovereign default. The literature highlights a number of potential channels through which sovereign debtors incur costs through defaulting. Some of these costs are imposed by creditors, involving in particular a reduction in access to, or an increase in the cost of, future finance. In practice, in the aftermath of EME debt crises a decade ago, EMEs were often able to reaccess international capital markets quite quickly, although there is some evidence that they have had to pay a higher risk premium and been less able to issue in domestic currency, thereby increasing their vulnerability to currency risk.

There has been less focus in the literature on the broader output costs to the domestic economy associated with sovereign default and on the interaction with currency and banking crises. In practice, most EME sovereign crises over the past 25 years have been associated with a banking or a currency crisis. Sovereign defaults appear to have the biggest impact on domestic output when there is a triple (sovereign, banking, and currency) crisis. In some cases, such as following the Latin American crisis in the early 1980s and the Russian crisis in the late 1990s, sovereign defaults have precipitated broader instability in the global financial system.

Given that the costs of sovereign default appear to be high, one obvious but nonetheless important policy conclusion is that countries should take measures to reduce the risk of defaulting in the first place. At a broad level, authorities need to adopt sound macroeconomic policies and structural reform that should reduce the likelihood of crises as well as raise sustainable output growth. More specifically, the high cost of default points to the need for further development of early warning systems of crisis. The International Monetary Fund has a role to play here in carrying out stress tests of the fragility of the government's balance sheet and those of other sectors in its regular Article IV surveillance. This type of analysis should allow authorities time to change domestic policies and thereby reduce the likelihood of crisis. It also emphasizes the need for countries themselves to self-insure against the possibility of crises. Many EMEs have done this in recent years through building up foreign exchange reserves and reducing their reliance on foreign currency and short-term debt. This has reduced the likelihood of currency crises in particular and helped shelter EMEs from the recent banking crisis in developed countries. But government debts (relative to GDP) remain high in a number of EMEs and are often still significantly financed by the domestic banking system. This makes the latter vulnerable to sovereign weakness (and potentially vice versa if governments bail out weak banking systems). Actual and prospective government debt levels have also increased sharply recently in a number of developed countries.

Once in crisis, annual output losses seem to increase the longer countries stay in arrears or take to restructure their debts. There is also evidence that output losses are smaller for countries that restructure their debt than for those that do not. This emphasizes the importance of policy initiatives aimed at improving the speed and efficiency of debtor-creditor restructuring.

NOTES

1. Following the Foreign Sovereign Immunity Act (1976) in the United States and the State Immunity Act (1978) in the United Kingdom, it became common practice for most governments to waive sovereign immunity on foreign loans and bond contracts. In practice, however, this only allows creditors to have access to the debtor's assets held for commercial activity in the country in which the debt contract was issued. Moreover, a country considering default could remove its assets held in the foreign jurisdiction before any default.

2. Tomz (1998), however, finds that, during the interwar period, defaulting countries that were expected to default, given their poor fundamentals, could regain access to capital markets twice as quickly as countries that defaulted unexpectedly, given their better fundamentals.

3. As measured by GDP growth, inflation, the current account balance, and foreign currency reserves.

4. Measured by the ratios of external debt to both GDP and exports.

5. The large fiscal costs that are often incurred in resolving a banking crisis can also cause, or make worse, a sovereign crisis, for example, as happened in Indonesia in 1997–1998.

6. For the balance sheet channel of currency depreciation see, inter alia, Cespedes et al. (2004).

7. The higher threshold for arrears on principal than on interest payments is because, according to World Bank estimates, sovereign arrears on principal have been, on average, two to three times larger than on interest payments since 1970. The authors show that the probabilities of breaching these thresholds are low.

8. This was checked for consistency with other studies that include definitions of the start of debt crises.

9. For example, as soon as arrears on principal fall below 15 percent or arrears on interest payments below 5 percent, or when arrears fall below 5 percent on principal or below 1.5 percent on interest payments. Other things being equal, the first definition will clearly imply a shorter crisis period than the second one.

10. This is based on a panel regression of the crisis countries over the 1970–2000 period. GDP growth per capita was found to be a negative function of the initial level of GDP,

price inflation, the share of government consumption in GDP, and political instability and a positive function of the investment share in GDP and trade openness (see De Paoli et al. 2009).

11. In fact, output did not return to its pre-crisis trend at all during the crisis period in 60 percent of the sample.

REFERENCES

Bordo, M., B. Eichengreen, D. Klingebiel, and M. S. Martinez-Peria. 2001. "Is the Crisis Problem Growing More Severe?" *Economic Policy* 32: 51–82.

Caprio, G., and D. Klingebiel. 2003. "Episodes of Systemic and Borderline Banking Crises." World Bank.

Cerra, V., and S. C. Saxena. 2005. "Growth Dynamics: The Myth of Economic Recovery." *IMF Working Paper*, No. 147.

Cespedes, L., R. Chang, and A. Velasco. 2004. "Balance Sheets and Exchange Rate Policy." *American Economic Review* 94: 4.

Cohen, D. 1992. "The Debt Crisis, a Post Mortem." *NBER Macroeconomic Annual.*

De Paoli, B. S., G. Hoggarth, and V. Saporta. 2006. "Costs of Sovereign Default." *Bank of England Financial Stability Paper,* No. 1.

———. 2009. "Output Costs of Sovereign Crises: Some Empirical Estimates." *Bank of England Working Paper*, No. 362.

Dooley, M. 2000. "Can Output Losses Following International Financial Crises Be Avoided?" *NBER Working Paper*, No. 7531.

Frankel, J. A. 2005. *Contractionary Currency Crashes in Developing Countries.* Cambridge, MA: NBER.

Frankel, J. A., and A. K. Rose. 1996. "Currency Crashes in Emerging Markets: Empirical Indicators." *NBER Working Paper*, No. 5437.

Gelos, R. G., R. Sahay, and G. Sandleris. 2004. "Sovereign Borrowing by Developing Countries: What Determines Market Access?" *IMF Working Paper,* No. 221.

Hoelscher, D., and M. Quintyn. 2003. "Managing Systemic Banking Crises." *IMF Occasional Paper,* No. 22.

Hoggarth, G., R. Reis, and V. Saporta. 2002. "Costs of Banking System Instability: Some Empirical Estimates." *Journal of Banking and Finance* 26: 825–855.

International Monetary Fund. 2006. "Cross-Country Experience with Restructuring of Sovereign Debt and Restoring Debt Sustainability." *Policy Development and Review Department.*

Jorgensen, E., and J. Sachs. 1989. "Default and Renegotiation of Latin American Foreign Bonds in the Interwar Period." In B. Eichengreen and P. Lindert, eds. *The International Debt Crisis in Historical Perspective.* Cambridge, MA: MIT Press.

Kaminsky, G., and C. M. Reinhart. 1999. "The Twin Crises: The Cause of Banking and Balance of Payment Problems." *American Economic Review* 89: 473–500.

Laeven, L., and F. Valencia. 2008. "Systemic Banking Crises: A New Database." *IMF Working Paper,* No. 224.

Lindert, P. H., and P. J. Morton. 1989. "How Sovereign Debt Has Worked." In J. Sachs, ed. *Developing Country Debt and the World Economy.* Cambridge, MA: NBER.

Medeiros, C., M. Gapen, and L. Zanforlin. 2005. *Assessing the Determinants and Prospects for the Pace of Market Access by Countries Emerging from Crisis—Further Considerations.* Washington, DC: IMF, International Capital Markets Department.

Ozler, S. 1993. "Have Commercial Banks Ignored History?" *American Economic Review* 83: 608–620.

Reinhart, C., and K. Rogoff. 2009. *This Time Is Different: Eight Centuries of Financial Folly.* Princeton, NJ: Princeton University Press.

Reinhart, C., K. Rogoff, and M. Savastano. 2003. "Debt Intolerance." *NBER Working Paper*, No. 9908.

Sturzenegger, F., and J. Zettelmeyer. 2007. *Debt Defaults and Lessons from a Decade of Crises.* Cambridge, MA: MIT Press.

Tomz, M. 1998. "Do Creditors Ignore History? Reputation in International Capital Markets." Paper presented at the Latin American Studies Association, September 24–26, Chicago, Illinois.

ABOUT THE AUTHORS

Bianca De Paoli is a senior economist at the Bank of England, where she has been working in the field of monetary analysis since 2005. Before then, she received a PhD from the London School of Economics. Dr. De Paoli has done extensive work in the fields of international and monetary economics, and has published a series of articles on optimal monetary policy in open economies.

Glenn Hoggarth is currently senior economist in the Bank of England's International Finance Division. He previously worked in a number of divisions in the bank's financial and monetary stability areas as well as in its Centre for Central Banking Studies. He has been on a number of technical missions to other central banks advising on financial and monetary policy issues. He worked for a number of years as a private sector economist before joining the Bank of England.

Glenn was educated in economics at the University of Warwick (BA) and Churchill College, Cambridge (MPhil). He has numerous articles published on monetary and financial economics. His current research interests are international finance, EMEs, banking crises, and financial stability policies.

Victoria Saporta is head of the prudential policy division at the Bank of England. Her division is responsible for developing policy proposals on national and international prudential policy reform. Over the past 14 years, Victoria has held a number of policy and research positions in the financial stability and monetary analysis departments of the Bank. Victoria holds a PhD in economics and an MPhil in finance from the University of Cambridge and a BSc in mathematical economics and econometrics from the London School of Economics. She has published numerous articles on financial stability issues in books, professional journals, and Bank of England publications.

CHAPTER 4

Spillovers of Sovereign Default Risk

How Much Is the Private Sector Affected?

UDAIBIR S. DAS
IMF*

MICHAEL G. PAPAIOANNOU
IMF

CHRISTOPH TREBESCH
Free University of Berlin and Hertie School of Governance

The recent rise in sovereign risk perceptions has important consequences for debtor countries and the global economy. One crucial aspect is that sovereign default risk can adversely affect private corporations. In recent months, top-down risk spillovers from the sovereign to private entities have become increasingly relevant, but they have not been studied sufficiently (see ECB 2010). This chapter focuses on one type of such spillovers, namely the link between sovereign risk and corporate access to foreign capital. Our analysis is motivated by an awareness that private firms worldwide have gained unprecedented access to external finance in the last decades. Especially in emerging market countries, corporations have become more and more reliant on foreign sources of funding, meaning that they have been raising equity or debt on international capital markets in record amounts. However, in the wake of the ongoing financial crisis, some fiscally troubled governments have been partly or fully cut off from foreign capital. In these countries, corporations have also been struggling to raise capital in international markets, with grave consequences for domestic investment, production, and growth. These developments show that it is important to gain a better understanding on the collateral damage of sovereign risk.

---

*The views expressed herein are those of the authors and should not be attributed to the IMF, its executive board, or its management.

Our research on private sector access to external capital can be structured along two contributions. In Das, Papaioannou, and Trebesch (2009) we document a strong relationship between sovereign risk measures, such as sovereign bond spreads, ratings, or default, and the volume of foreign bonds and loans issued by domestic firms in emerging market economies. Trebesch (2009), in contrast, analyzes debt crisis episodes and debt renegotiations in more depth. His main finding is that debt renegotiation patterns and crisis resolution policies of governments vis-à-vis their creditors play a crucial role. Unilateral debtor policies, such as debt moratoria or forced debt exchanges, are associated with a sharp drop in the volume of debt issued by private firms—over and above the default effect, per se. Both papers, thereby, provide strong indication of top-down risk spillovers from the sovereign to the private sector in emerging market countries.

In the following, we provide a brief overview of our research. We discuss the existing empirical literature, our data and estimation approach, and the main results. We then conclude with a series of policy implications.

LITERATURE REVIEW: SOVEREIGN DEFAULT RISK AND CORPORATE ACCESS TO FINANCE

There is surprisingly little empirical work analyzing the scope of risk spillovers from the sovereign to the private sector.[1] A small set of recent papers provides evidence that sovereign risk and defaults can indeed affect emerging market firms—both in normal times and during crisis episodes. Borenzstein et al. (2007) show that sovereign ratings strongly determine corporate ratings. Levy-Yeyati et al. (2004) find that sovereign distress affects the behavior of depositors and can contribute to bank runs. In a similar vein, Borenzstein and Panizza (2008) provide evidence that debt crises may trigger systemic banking crises, but find no effect of defaults on industries that are more dependent on external finance. With regard to stock markets, Cruces (2007) finds sizable sovereign risk–related equity premia. According to his results, corporations in countries with credit ratings in the default range are forced to pay much higher expected rates of return compared to companies based in nondefault countries. Kaminsky and Schmukler (2002) also find that sovereign ratings have a strong effect on both bond and stock markets in emerging markets.

We are aware of only one study, by Arteta and Hale (2008), analyzing the specific effects of sovereign defaults on domestic corporations and their access to finance (for related theoretical papers, see Sandleris 2008, 2010 and Mendoza and Yue 2008). Their analysis was among the first to provide microevidence on the domestic costs of sovereign default. Specifically, the authors use aggregate firm-level data on external loan and bond issuances by domestic corporations in 30 emerging market economies as dependent variables. In a comprehensive analysis, they find that sovereign debt crises and restructurings have a strong negative impact on corporate external borrowing. They find the decline in credit to be much more pronounced in defaults with official (bilateral or multilateral) creditors, while the effect of defaults to private creditors is relatively small.

DATA AND EMPIRICAL STRATEGY

Our research assesses corporate access to international capital markets by focusing on the volume of primary market issuance. The dependent variable in both studies is aggregated from firm-level data on debt and equity issuances as reported in the Dealogic database. The advantage of using microdata is that it avoids some potential biases of capital flow data on the aggregate country level and allows identification of capital flows to private corporations only (the comprehensive Dealogic data allow the analyst to distinguish between private and publicly owned firms). In a first step, we retrieve all foreign corporate bond issues and foreign corporate syndicated loan contracts for 31 emerging economies in the period from January 1980 until December 2007. We then aggregate this data on a monthly (or quarterly) level to construct aggregate measures of external debt issuance. In Das et al. (2009) we also construct an additional dependent variable that captures the volume of equity securities issued by domestic corporations by country and quarter.

The country sample we employ is the same as in Arteta and Hale (2008), who exclude countries that had only limited access to foreign capital in the period of observation. We also exclude public corporations and domestic firms that are foreign owned, for example, by multinational corporations. The resulting aggregate figures on debt and equity issuances on the quarterly level are depicted in Exhibit 4.1. The caption also lists all 31 countries included in the analysis. The graph

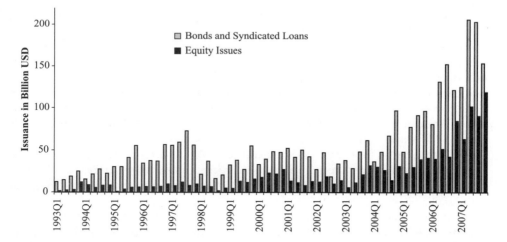

Exhibit 4.1 Bond, Syndicated Loan, and Equity Issuance by Private Domestic Firms in Emerging Markets, 1993–2007

Note: The authors' compilation is based on data from Dealogic. The figure shows aggregate equity and external debt (bonds and syndicated loans) issuance by domestic firms in 31 emerging market countries. Firms owned by the government or other public entities and firms owned by foreign companies are excluded. Q1 = first quarter. The countries included are Argentina, Brazil, Chile, China, Colombia, Croatia, Czech Republic, Egypt (Arab Rep. of), Hong Kong (China), Hungary, India, Indonesia, Korea (Rep. of), Malaysia, Mexico, Pakistan, Peru, Philippines, Poland, Qatar, Romania, Russian Federation, Saudi Arabia, Singapore, Slovak Republic, South Africa, Taiwan (China), Turkey, Venezuela (R. B. de), Thailand, and the United Arab Emirates.

clearly shows an increase in nominal primary market issuances of private firms in emerging markets since the early 1990s.

In our empirical analyses, we regress the dependent variables on debt and equity issuances on different measures of sovereign risk, as well as a large set of control variables and country and year fixed effects. To account for country fundamentals and global economic conditions, we choose a set of control variables by Arteta and Hale (2008). The authors construct various indexes through principal component analysis, thus summarizing a large set of mutually correlated variables, with the additional benefit of bridging data gaps in some of the series. The resulting composite indexes can be grouped into five broad categories: an international competitiveness index, an investment climate and monetary stability index, a financial development index, a long-run macroeconomic prospects index, and an index on the global supply of capital. To assess the robustness of our results, we also construct our own quarterly data set containing relevant financial and economic control variables that have been widely used in previous research on cross-border capital flows and corporate access to finance. Beyond this, we explicitly control for currency and banking crises and instances of sudden stops in capital flows as well as natural disasters. Finally, we include the real exchange rate, to account for possible currency mismatch effects on firms' balance sheets (a detailed overview of the variables and data sources is presented in Das et al. 2009).

MEASURING SOVEREIGN RISK AND DEFAULT

Sovereign default risk can be measured in various ways. Many researchers have used sovereign ratings or sovereign bond spreads as proxies for the level and variation in sovereign default risk, partly because these measures are readily available and accessible at high frequencies, that is, on a monthly or even daily level. While we also rely on these standard risk measures, a main novelty of our research is the use of newly collected data on sovereign risk and default. We take advantage of a new, comprehensive data set on sovereign debt crises and associated debt-renegotiation processes of the past three decades. This database was built by systematically evaluating more than 20,000 pages of case study material on crisis cases, as well as all standard reference books and other data sources (see Enderlein, Trebesch, and von Daniels 2009 and Trebesch 2008, 2009).

In Das et al. (2009), for example, we rely on novel, monthly data on the timing of debt crisis and debt restructurings, which allows for a more precise analysis of risk spillovers during crisis episodes. In contrast to Arteta and Hale, we focus mainly on defaults and debt renegotiations toward private external creditors, that is, banks and bondholders. In the dataset, the start of debt distress is coded as either the month of first missed payments beyond the grace period (the start of de facto default) or the beginning of debt talks and restructuring negotiations. The debt crisis ends with the successful closing of a restructuring agreement. We also use new measures on debt-crisis characteristics as explanatory variables, in particular a measure of negotiation delays stemming from political events and variable capturing cases of pre-restructuring litigation by creditors against debtor countries, as well as episodes of creditor holdouts.

Trebesch (2009) uses a further sovereign risk measure as a key explanatory variable. He draws on a data set by Enderlein, Trebesch, and von Daniels (2009), who code cooperative versus conflictual crisis resolution following sovereign default and debt distress. The index of government coerciveness proposed by the authors captures coercive actions that governments impose on their foreign banks and bondholders during debt renegotiation.[2] In principle, the index of coerciveness may be regarded as a complement to existing sovereign risk measures such as credit ratings, bond spreads, or political risk. In more general terms, however, the index may also be seen as a proxy of good versus bad government types or excusable versus inexcusable defaults, with high degrees of coerciveness signaling expropriative practices and unwillingness to pay (see Cole and Kehoe 1998; Grossman and Van Huyck 1988; Sandleris 2008).

The final index of debtor coerciveness consists of nine subindicators. These can be grouped into two broad categories of government behavior: (1) "Indicators of Payment Behavior," capturing government actions that have a direct impact on financial flows toward international banks or bondholders, and (2) "Indicators of Negotiation Behavior," measuring negotiation patterns and aggressive rhetoric of governments. Each subindicator is a dummy, which is coded as one if the respective action by the government can be observed in a given year—and zero otherwise. For details on the exact definitions, coding, and theoretical justification of the index and its subindicators, see Enderlein et al. (2010). The paper also presents coding results and new stylized facts from the data.

SUMMARY OF RESULTS

The main findings of our analyses can be summarized as follows: Both Das et al. (2009) and Trebesch (2009) find that sovereign defaults are associated with a significant drop in the volume of corporate external borrowing of up to 40 percent after controlling for fundamentals and shocks. In contrast to Arteta and Hale (2008), we find that defaults to private creditors have a significantly stronger impact than defaults to official creditors. Surprisingly, Das et al. (2009) find that creditor holdouts, intercreditor disputes, and creditor litigation against the sovereign have no impact on the volume of corporate borrowing. This indicates that government behavior in distress situations has more important consequences for the domestic economy than does creditor behavior.

A further main finding of Das et al. (2009) is that standard sovereign risk measures matter as well. Deteriorating risk perceptions, as measured by higher sovereign bond spreads and lower sovereign rating, are negatively associated with corporate access to capital, in particular, the volume of corporate external borrowing. We also find that the volume of equity issuances is closely linked to the level of country bond spreads, but little affected by sovereign ratings.

The key result of Trebesch (2009) is that crisis resolution policies, measured by the index of coerciveness, may play a crucial role for corporations and their external borrowing behavior. More coercive debt policies toward private external creditors are associated with a sizable drop in issuance volumes of corporate bonds and syndicated loans, an effect that holds during default episodes and for up to two years after the crisis has been resolved. The index of coercive government behavior has a high explanatory power beyond political risk and sovereign ratings and after controlling for a large set of variables capturing fundamentals and shocks. The decrease in corporate external borrowing during periods of confrontational debt policies is sizable, reaching 40 percent—over and above the default effect, per se. When disaggregating the index into its nine subcomponents, he finds that full payment moratoria and enforced, non-negotiated restructurings have a particularly large negative coefficient.

CONCLUSION

The results of our research indicate that governments need to be aware of the potentially adverse effects of sovereign risk for the domestic economy. Government policies affecting sovereign risk perceptions may have unintended consequences for the country's corporate sector and its access to capital. In light of the current financial crisis, excessive public deficits and rising debt-to-GDP ratios may pose upside risks for corporate debt yields and constrain firms and their external financing options for years to come. This, in turn, could reinforce negative feedback loops between the financial and real sectors. Policy makers should keep these risks in mind and possibly prepare mitigation strategies, so as to avoid adverse consequences for economic growth and financial stability.

With regard to default episodes, we provide a strong indication that crisis resolution strategies matter. In particular, we find that confrontational debtor policies may have negative consequences for economic agents in a defaulting country. This indicates that good faith debt renegotiations could help to reduce the domestic costs of sovereign defaults.

NOTES

1. There is a larger literature on private sector contingent claims and bottom-up risk transfers (see, for example, Gapen et al. 2008).

2. The index design and the subindicators chosen build on previous research like Cline (2004) and Roubini (2004) and prominent policy documents, in particular the good faith criteria outlined in the IMF's lending into arrears policy (IMF 1999, 2002), as well as the catalogue of best practices in the Institute of International Finance's "Principles for Stable Capital Flows and Fair Debt Restructuring in Emerging Markets" (Institute of International Finance, 2006).

REFERENCES

Arteta, Carlos, and Galina Hale. 2008. "Sovereign Debt Crises and Credit to the Private Sector." *Journal of International Economics* 74:1, 53–69.

Borensztein, Eduardo, Kevin Cowan, and Patricio Valenzuela. 2007. "Sovereign Ceilings 'Lite'? The Impact of Sovereign Ratings on Corporate Ratings in Emerging Market Economies." *IMF Working Paper*, No. 07/75. Washington, DC: International Monetary Fund.

Borensztein, Eduardo, and Ugo Panizza. 2008. "The Costs of Sovereign Default." *IMF Working Paper*, No. 08/238, Washington, DC: International Monetary Fund.

Cline, William R. 2004. "Private sector involvement in financial crisis resolution: Definition, measurement, and implementation." In A. Haldane, ed. *Fixing Financial Crises in the Twenty-First Century*, 61–94. London: Routledge.

Cole, Harold L., and Patrick Kehoe. 1998. "Models of Sovereign Debt: Partial versus General Reputations." *International Economic Review* 39: 55–70.

Cruces, Juan. 2007. *The Value of Pleasing International Creditors*. Buenos Aires, Argentina: Universidad Torcuato di Tella, Department of Economics.

Das, Udaibir, Michael Papaioannou, and Christoph Trebesch. 2009. "Sovereign default risk and private sector access to capital in emerging markets." In Carlos A. Primo Braga and Döerte Döemeland, eds. *Debt Relief and Beyond: Lessons Learned and Challenges Ahead*. Washington, DC: World Bank Publications.

Enderlein, Henrik, Christoph Trebesch, and Laura von Daniels. 2010. *Sovereign Debt Disputes*. Berlin, Germany: Hertie School of Governance.

European Central Bank. 2010. "Financial Stability Review." Frankfurt, Germany: European Central Bank.

Gapen, Michael, Dale Gray, Cheng Hoon Lim, and Yingbin Xiao. 2008. "Measuring and Analyzing Sovereign Risk with Contingent Claims." *IMF Staff Papers* 55:1, 109–148.

Grossman, Herschel I., and John B. Van Huyck. 1988. "Sovereign Debt as a Contingent Claim: Excusable Default, Repudiation, and Reputation." *American Economic Review* 78:5, 1088–1097.

International Monetary Fund. 1999. *IMF Policy on Lending into Arrears to Private Creditors*. Washington, DC: International Monetary Fund, Policy Development and Review and Legal Departments.

———. 2002. *Fund Policy on Lending into Arrears to Private Creditors—Further Consideration of the Good Faith Criterion*. Washington, DC: International Monetary Fund, Policy Development and Review and Legal Departments.

Institute of International Finance. 2006. *Principles for Stable Capital Flows and Fair Debt Restructuring in Emerging Markets. Report on Implementation by the Principles Consultative Group*. Washington, DC: Institute of International Finance.

Kaminsky, Graciela L., and Sergio L. Schmukler. 2002. "Emerging Market Instability: Do Sovereign Ratings Affect Country Risk and Stock Returns?" *World Bank Economic Review* 16:2, 171–195.

Levy-Yeyati, Eduardo, Maria S. Martinez Peria, and Sergio L. Schmukler. 2004. "Market Discipline under Systemic Risk: Evidence from Bank Runs in Emerging Economies." *Policy Research Working Paper*, No. 3440, Washington, DC: World Bank.

Mendoza, Enrique G., and Vivian Z. Yue. 2008. "A Solution to the Default Risk–Business Cycle Disconnect." *NBER Working Papers*, No. 13861. Cambridge, MA: National Bureau of Economic Research.

Roubini, Nouriel. 2004. "Private sector involvement in crisis resolution and mechanisms for dealing with sovereign debt problems." In Andrew Haldane, ed. *Fixing Financial Crises in the Twenty-First Century*, 101–142. London: Routledge.

Sandleris, Guido. 2008. "Sovereign Defaults: Information, Investment and Credit." *Journal of International Economics* 76:2, 267–275.

———. 2010. "Sovereign Defaults, Domestic Credit Market Institutions and Credit to the Private Sector," *Business School Working Papers*, No. 2010–01. Buenos Aires, Argentina: Universidad Torcuato Di Tella.

Trebesch, Christoph. 2008. *Delays in Sovereign Debt Restructurings: Should We Really Blame the Creditors?* Berlin, Germany: Free University of Berlin.
———. 2009. "The Cost of Aggressive Sovereign Debt Policies: How Much Is the Private Sector Affected?" *IMF Working Paper*, No. 09/29, Washington, DC: International Monetary Fund.

ABOUT THE AUTHORS

Udaibir S. Das is an assistant director in the Monetary and Capital Markets Department of the IMF where he heads the Sovereign Asset and Liability Management Division. Mr. Das leads a team that covers policy and operational issues relating to sovereign balance sheet risk management, debt, reserves and sovereign asset management, and local and regional sovereign bond markets. He is also associated with country-specific vulnerability assessments and financial stability surveillance.

Mr. Das joined the IMF in 1996. Before joining the IMF, Mr. Das was with the Reserve Bank of India for 18 years. He has participated in various financial sector assessment programs and technical assistance missions, and has been closely associated with several international and regional initiatives in financial sector and capital market areas. He was the resident adviser in Guyana (South America) from 1996 to 1998. In his career with the Fund, he has represented Fund staff on various OECD Working Parties, the Basel-based Joint Forum and the International Association of Insurance Supervisors, and the International Working Group of Sovereign Wealth Funds.

Mr. Das is a Fulbright-Humphrey scholar with graduate degrees in economics (U.S.) and management (U.S.). He was a lecturer in economics and finance at Boston University (U.S.) from 1989 to 1991. He has published in several international and professional journals and holds a research interest in central banking, sovereign asset liability management, nonbank financial institutions, and different aspects of debt and fixed income markets.

Michael G. Papaioannou is a deputy division chief at the Sovereign Asset and Liability Management Division, Monetary and Capital Markets Department of the International Monetary Fund. While at the IMF, he served as a special adviser to the governing board of the Bank of Greece. Before joining the IMF, he was a senior vice president for international financial services and director of the foreign exchange service at the WEFA Group (Wharton Econometrics Forecasting Associates) and served as chief economist of the Council of Economic Advisors of Greece. He has also taught at Temple University, School of Business and Management, Department of Finance, as an adjunct associate professor of finance and was a principal research fellow at the University of Pennsylvania, Department of Economics, LINK Central. He holds a PhD in economics from the University of Pennsylvania and an MA in economics from Georgetown University.

Christoph Trebesch is a PhD candidate in economics at Free University of Berlin. He has spent the 2009–2010 academic year at Yale University as Fox Fellow and also holds a postgraduate degree from the Kiel Institute for the World

Economy. He worked for the International Monetary Fund and the World Bank and is a research associate at Hertie School of Governance in Berlin. As part of his doctoral thesis, he is currently finalizing a comprehensive new database on sovereign default cases and debt restructurings between 1970 and 2010, including detailed information on debt renegotiation processes and the scope of debt relief ("haircuts").

CHAPTER 5

Sovereign Debt Problems and Policy Gambles

SAMUEL W. MALONE
Assistant Professor of Finance, University of the Andes School of Management

P oliticians, faced with the specter of losing office following a costly default, may be tempted to gamble for redemption by instituting policies that increase the volatility of output growth, possibly at the expense of reducing average growth. This intuition is especially relevant for the case of developing countries, in which weaker institutional environments tend to enhance the ability of leaders to siphon public funds for private gain, thereby sharpening the incentive for remaining in power, potentially by means that run counter to the greater public interest. In particular, the threat of some crisis event, such as imminent default on a debt payment to external creditors, can give politicians in weak institutional environments a strong incentive to double down when making policy choices so they can better increase the probability of repayment and of retaining power, even as they worsen the potential fallout in the case of failure.

This chapter draws upon a 2010 article in *Oxford Economic Papers* on "Sovereign Indebtedness, Default, and Gambling for Redemption." The basic chapter plan is as follows. First, we review some of the precedents for the intuition outlined earlier. We then sharpen the intuition by describing the basic set of conditions under which political gambling for redemption in the face of debt problems can occur. Finally, we devote the last third of the article to reviewing some of the main empirical evidence on policy gambling in the face of sovereign debt problems, gathered from the analysis of a database of 86 countries over the past 40 years.

Before proceeding, a couple of empirical findings in particular stand out from an examination of recent history. Sovereign defaults are clearly bad for the political careers of heads of state: for the average country in our sample, before controlling for other factors that affect job loss, a sovereign default nearly doubles the probability that the president or prime minister will lose that job within the following year. After controlling for other determinants of job loss, a default event raises the probability of job loss of the president or prime minister by 24 percent, and is comparable to a 3.5 standard deviation fall in economic growth. A priori, in other words, any policy gamble that would have the side effect of lowering economic growth while raising the volatility of revenue available for debt repayment would still probably be quite attractive from the career perspective of the leader, if the adverse growth consequences are anything but cataclysmic. When we turn to the evidence on indebtedness, cross-country regressions reveal that higher indebtedness is indeed associated with higher monetary, fiscal, and public investment policy volatility and with policies that increase output volatility at the expense of growth. With these basic results in mind, let us step back for a moment to consider the wider context surrounding sovereign gambling for redemption behavior, as well as its precedents in the world of finance.

BACKGROUND

While there is an ample literature on the determinants of sovereign default, as well as the effect of greater levels of foreign indebtedness on economic growth, much less is known about how indebtedness and the risk of sovereign default may affect the incentives of politicians with respect to influencing monetary, fiscal, and public investment policy in the developing world. In a recent article in the *Journal of Economic Literature* on the economics and law of sovereign debt and default, Panizza, Sturzenegger, and Zettelmeyer (2009) note that

> ... *a potential reason for why countries repay their debts is that defaults inflict costs on the politicians or government officials that make the decision to default, who may lose their jobs, or damage their political careers.... Richard N. Cooper (1971) and Jeffrey A. Frankel (2005) show that currency devaluations are often followed by electoral losses of the ruling party and reduce the tenure of the chief of the executive and the minister of finance; Borensztein and Panizza (2009) show that default episodes may have a similar effect.... To our knowledge, a systematic analysis of the relationship between sovereign debt, defaults, and political career concerns has not been undertaken and is an interesting area for future research. (682)*

A focus on political gambling for redemption in the face of sovereign debt problems is a natural and important direction for inquiry for several reasons. Most importantly, there is an ample theoretical literature in the area of finance related to the agency costs of financial distress and the risk-taking incentives induced by the existence of deposit guarantees (see, for example, Kareken and Wallace 1978 and Diamond and Dybvig 1986). That literature shows that situations that induce convexity into agent payoff functions can induce risk taking that harms other parties with a stake in the value of the assets (or income streams) under the agents' control.

The mathematical underpinning for the preceding findings rests on a couple of straightforward results about convex functions. A convex nondecreasing function $f(X)$ of a random variable X has the property that the expected value of the function is greater than the function evaluated at the expected value of X. This is known as Jensen's inequality. Thus, agents whose payoff is given by a convex function would rather accept the risk implicit in the underlying variable X that affects their payoff, rather than take the certain payoff given by the function $f(.)$ evaluated at the expected (or average) value of X. By a related result, it also follows that any risk-neutral decision maker who wishes to maximize his expected payoff will, if given scope to do so, increase the riskiness of X if his payoff function $f(X)$ is convex—even, in some cases, at the cost of lowering the expected value of X.

As a practical example of the preceding effect in the corporate finance context, managers in firms who face debt problems, who are likely to be fired in the event of a corporate default and may earn part of their compensation in the form of equity, possess convex payoff functions in the firm's future asset value. Such managers thus have an incentive to substitute safe assets, with secure payoff streams, for risky assets, with highly volatile payoff streams. This is known as the *asset substitution* problem, and is discussed in popular corporate finance textbooks such as Berk and DeMarzo (2007). One interesting aspect of the asset substitution problem, or the overinvestment problem, as it is sometimes referred to, is that if managers with perverse incentives have significant scope to channel more capital into risky investment strategies, total investment may increase rather than decrease. The losers, in this story, are the firm's creditors and bondholders, as such strategies unambiguously lower the fair value of the debt claims backed by the firm's assets and future income.

This story, with the appropriate modifications, can be translated into a theory of gambling for redemption in the sovereign context, with managers replaced by politicians, equity claims replaced by the government surplus after debt repayment, and corporate governance mechanisms for firing badly behaving managers replaced by the ballot box, or occasionally by a coup d'état or other nondemocratic transfer of power. More specifically, the possibility of sovereign default will induce convexity into politicians' payoff functions if two conditions hold: (1) default increases the probability of job loss, other things being equal; and (2) the ability to enjoy the rents associated with being in power is increasing in output, while the cost of losing access to these rents upon job loss is independent of the magnitude of the default event. Condition (1) can be verified, or rejected, directly by appealing to the data, and as indicated earlier, the data lend fairly strong support for this claim. On the other hand, while a direct empirical verification of condition (2) is more difficult, it stands to reason in light of the political economy literature that emphasizes rent seeking in the public sphere (see, for example, Tornell 1999 and Tornell and Lane 1999) that the returns to being in power are at least linear, if not increasing, in the value of windfalls that boost growth, while a loss of power is associated with a significant loss of direct access to rents, independently of how output growth subsequently evolves. Conditions (1) and (2) together create convexity in the politician's objective function, and an environment of weak political institutions, of the kind found in many developing countries, can provide them with the opportunity to act on the resulting motive to gamble by increasing the volatility of policies and output growth. The Malone (2010) article in *Oxford Economic Papers*, on which this chapter is based, provides a formal model based on these conditions that illustrates how policy gambling behavior, conceived primarily as an asset substitution effect, serves as a strategic complement to the incentive to exert low fiscal effort in the face of debt overhang problems, as was emphasized earlier in the work of Krugman (1988) and Sachs (1989).

Other authors have speculated recently that gambling behavior on the part of leading politicians may be quite important in practice, although the evidence has been mostly anecdotal.

Sturzenegger and Zettelmeyer (2007), for example, make this argument with regard to Argentina's 2001 default. A recent study by the Inter-American Development Bank (2007) notes, alternatively, that "the evidence on the political impact of recent events of default reveals that in 18 out of the 19 cases studied, the ruling coalitions lost votes after the default," and that politicians in this situation "may have an incentive for gambling for resurrection, namely, taking extreme measures that have a low chance of success but, if they do succeed, will bring clear political gains to the ruling administration."

TESTING THE THEORY OF POLITICAL GAMBLING FOR REDEMPTION

To take the sovereign gambling for redemption theory more definitively to the data, Malone (2010) assembles a database using macro data on growth, indebtedness, and other variables from the World Bank and IMF, job loss data from Frankel (2005) and Frankel and Wei (2005), and data on default events from Manasse, Roubini, and Schimmelpfennig (2003). The consequences of external indebtedness on policy gambling are assessed by studying macro variables drawn from the World Bank, the IMF, Euromonitor, and the Inter-American Development Bank, data from Everhart and Sumlinski (2001) on public investment, and additional control variables on systemic crises by Caprio and Klingebiel (1999), and on real exchange rate misalignment (one of several control variables) by Kubota (2008).

As stated at the beginning of the chapter, sovereign defaults spell bad news for the subsequent career prospects of the presidents and prime ministers who preside over them. Whether the existence of a political incentive to gamble under the duress of a possible default translates into actual policy choices consistent with gambling behavior, however, remains to be seen. To test the latter claim, Malone (2010) examines three slightly more specific hypotheses implied by the general gambling theory:

1. Policy volatility will increase with indebtedness, after controlling for other determinants.
2. Indebtedness will be associated with policies that are associated with higher output growth volatility and possibly lower output growth.
3. Indebtedness may also be associated directly with higher output growth volatility and possibly lower growth, after controlling for the channels in predictions (1) and (2), since it may, for example, induce a fall in the quality of investment that is difficult to observe directly (the asset substitution effect).

It turns out that there is significant evidence in favor of all three of the preceding hypotheses implied by the sovereign gambling for redemption theory. After controlling for a variety of other determinants of monetary, fiscal, and public investment policy, the external debt-to-GDP ratio of the country is significantly associated with monetary expansions and higher fiscal deficits, but not significantly associated with the level of public investment. The volatility of each of money supply growth, the fiscal surplus, and public investment is significantly and positively associated with higher indebtedness levels, after controlling for other determinants of policy volatility, as predicted by Hypothesis 1. The p-values of the debt-to-GDP coefficient in the cases of monetary and fiscal policy volatility exceed 1 percent, while for public investment the p-value exceeds the 10 percent level. With respect to Hypothesis 2, it was found that after controlling for other factors, fiscal deficits were significantly associated with lower economic growth and higher growth volatility, while the public investment-to-GDP ratio had no significance associated with either growth or its volatility. Both of these results are consistent with the sovereign gambling theory. With respect to monetary policy, it was found that monetary expansions are significantly associated with higher short-term economic growth, as we would naturally expect given that this is one of their primary purposes.

The latter result might appear, from the perspective of Hypothesis 2, to give us pause, as in general we expect higher indebtedness to be associated with policies that decrease, rather than increase, growth, and higher indebtedness is associated with expansionary monetary policy, which is associated with higher growth. We may settle any doubts on this score, however, by appealing to the evidence supporting Hypothesis 3. After controlling for the levels and volatilities of the monetary, fiscal, and public investment policy variables, in addition to a set of other control variables that include dummies for crisis events and measurements of the degree of real exchange rate misalignment, we find that higher indebtedness is indeed strongly associated (at the 1 percent level) with lower economic growth, as well as (at the 10 percent level) with higher growth volatility. One natural interpretation of the latter result, consistent with the fact that the quantity of public investment to GDP is not associated with growth or growth volatility, is that the quality of public investment deteriorates as the result of gambling for redemption behavior, perhaps by asset substitution, by political leaders in the face of sovereign debt problems. While confirming such behavior directly is notoriously difficult, the evidence overall provides solid support for the main implications of the gambling theory, and is consistent with the notion that high levels of indebtedness and greater default risk will lead to policy decisions that can increase income growth volatility at the expense of lower growth.

CONCLUSION

While the economics literature is only beginning to achieve an understanding of the political motivations that shape economic policy, especially in times of financial crisis, some important and useful results are beginning to emerge. In regard to the research discussed in this chapter, three main insights can be taken away. The careers of political leaders, in regard to their ability to maintain a hold on power, suffer significantly following a sovereign default event. The incentives facing leaders in weak institutional environments, in particular, strongly encourage policy gambling for political redemption, potentially at the cost of inducing more economic pain than necessary in the event that such risky policies fail. Finally, the relationships between indebtedness, economic policies, and growth and its volatility for a large sample of countries in recent history indicate that the consequences of such incentives predicted by the gambling theory are, by and large, borne out in the data. The messages for economic development initiatives are clear. In the first place, the gambling theory provides another strong rationale for strengthening institutions so as to counteract the ability of politicians to siphon unauthorized benefits from the public coffer while in power. In the second place, enacting impartial mechanisms to monitor the risk profile of public investments more carefully should be a high priority, with the results of such exercises disseminated widely and in a timely fashion to the voting public—not to mention foreign and domestic creditors.

REFERENCES

Berk, Jonathan, and Peter DeMarzo. 2007. *Corporate Finance*. Boston: Pearson.

Borensztein, Eduardo, and Ugo Panizza. 2009. "The Costs of Sovereign Default," *IMF Staff Papers* 56: 683–741.

Caprio, Gerard, and Daniela Klingebiel. 1999. *Episodes of Systemic and Borderline Financial Crises*. Washington, DC: World Bank.

Diamond, Douglas, and Philip Dybvig. 1986. "Banking Theory, Deposit Insurance, and Bank Regulation." *The Journal of Business* 59:1, 55–68.

Everhart, Stephen S., and Mariusz A. Sumlinski. 2001. *Trends in Private Investment in Developing Countries Statistics for 1970–2000 and the Impact on Private Investment of Corruption and the Quality of Public Investment*. Washington, DC: World Bank, International Finance Corporation, Discussion Paper No. 44.

Frankel, Jeffrey. 2005. "Contractionary Currency Crashes in Developing Countries." *IMF Staff Papers* 52:2, 149–192.

Frankel, Jeffrey A., and Shang-Jin Wei. 2005. "Managing macroeconomic crises: Policy lessons." In Joshua Aizenman and Brian Pinto, eds. *Economic Volatility and Crises: A Policy-Oriented Guide*. Washington, DC: World Bank.

Inter-American Development Bank. 2007. *Economic and Social Progress Report in Latin America: Living with Debt*. Cambridge, MA: Harvard University Press.

Kareken, John, and Neil Wallace. 1978. "Deposit Insurance and Bank Regulation: A Partial-Equilibrium Exposition." *The Journal of Business* 51:3, 413–438.

Krugman, Paul. 1988. "Financing versus Forgiving a Debt Overhang." *Journal of Development Economics* 29: 253–268.

Kubota, Megumi. 2009. *Real Exchange Rate Misalignments*. York, UK: University of York, Department of Economics, unpublished manuscript.

Malone, Samuel. 2010. "Sovereign Indebtedness, Default, and Gambling for Redemption." *Oxford Economic Papers*.

Manasse, Paolo, Nouriel Roubini, and Axel Schimmelpfennig. 2003. "Predicting Sovereign Debt Crises," *IMF Working Paper*, No. 03/221. Washington, DC: International Monetary Fund.

Panizza, Ugo, Federico Sturzenegger, and Jeromin Zettelmeyer. 2009. "The Economics and Law of Sovereign Debt and Default." *Journal of Economic Literature* 47:3, 651–698.

Sachs, Jeffrey. 1989. "The debt overhang of developing countries." In Guillermo Calvo, Ronald Findlay, Pentti Kouri, and Jorge Braga de Macedo, eds. *Debt, Stabilization and Development: Essays in Memory of Carlos Díaz-Alejandro*. Oxford, UK: Basil Blackwell.

Sturzenegger, Federico, and Jeromin Zettelmeyer. 2007. *Debt Defaults and Lessons from a Decade of Crises*. Cambridge, MA: MIT Press.

Tornell, Aaron. 1999. "Voracity and Growth in Discrete Time." *Economics Letters* 62:1, 139–145.

Tornell, Aaron, and Philip R. Lane. 1999. "The Voracity Effect." *American Economic Review* 89:1, 22–46.

ABOUT THE AUTHOR

Samuel W. Malone is an assistant professor of finance at the University of the Andes School of Management in Bogotá, Colombia. He holds a doctorate in economics from the University of Oxford, where he studied as a Rhodes Scholar, as well as undergraduate degrees in mathematics and economics from Duke

University, where he graduated summa cum laude and Phi Beta Kappa. Author of the book *Macrofinancial Risk Analysis* in the Wiley Finance series, with co-author Dale Gray and foreword by Robert Merton, Dr. Malone has published several refereed journal articles in finance, economics, and applied mathematics, and has delivered international courses in finance and economics in numerous countries in Europe and South America, in both central banks and academic institutions.

CHAPTER 6

Sovereign Debt and the Resource Curse

MARE SARR
Lecturer, Economics at the University of Cape Town*

ERWIN BULTE
Professor, Development Economics at Wageningen University

CHRIS MEISSNER
Associate Professor, Economics at the University of California

TIM SWANSON
Andre Hoffman Chair in Economics at the Graduate Institute, Geneva

Countries don't go out of business. . . . The infrastructure doesn't go away, the productivity of the people doesn't go away, the natural resources don't go away. And so their assets always exceed their liabilities, which is the technical reason for bankruptcy. And that's very different from a company.
　　　　　　　　　　　　　　　—Walter Wriston (Citicorp chairman, 1970–1984)

A n extensive literature documents that resource wealth can be a curse rather than a blessing for many countries. Until the 1980s, the general view among economists and political scientists was that a large endowment of natural

*This chapter is an abridged version of Sarr et al. (forthcoming). We would like to thank Toke Aidt, John Hartwick, Chris Knittel, Chen Le-Yu, Simon Lee, Lars Nesheim, Nicola Pavoni, Imran Rasul, Ragnar Torvik, and seminar participants at the University of Birmingham, University College London, University of Oxford, University of Cape Town, University of Warwick, Cornell University, Venice University, UCLA, Stanford GSB, and the Indian Statistical Institute Delhi for their valuable comments. We also thank Kirk Hamilton and Giovanni Ruta for sharing their data on natural resources with us. *Public Choice* Editor in Chief William Shughart and anonymous reviewers also provided helpful comments. Finally, Mare Sarr gratefully acknowledges financial support from Economic Research Southern Africa (ERSA) and Erwin Bulte would like to thank the Dutch Organization for Scientific Research (N.W.O.) for financial support (grant nr. 452-04-333). The usual disclaimer applies.

resources has a positive impact on a country's development prospects. Yet, over the past 40 years, casual observation and statistical studies indicate that natural resources often fail to deliver the expected economic benefits. On the contrary, resource wealth seems to impede the economic performance of many countries. In a series of highly influential papers, Sachs and Warner (1995, 1997) present empirical evidence suggesting that natural resource wealth (measured by the GDP share of primary exports in 1971) may be negatively associated with per capita GDP growth (see Exhibit 6.1). Various explanations have been offered ranging from the Dutch Disease to rent seeking, increased indebtedness (Manzano and Rigobon 2001), domestic conflict and political instability (Collier and Hoeffler 2004), and autocratic regimes and poor institutions (Ross 2001; Isham et al. 2005).

Our research contributes to a better understanding of the curse of natural resources by focusing on international credit market imperfections and institutional failures within resource-rich economies. In particular, we wish to examine how excessive resource-based lending by external financial institutions can induce debt, default, and regime change in autocratic developing countries. Moral hazard in the financial markets on the part of borrowers and lenders leading to excessive lending to sovereigns has been noted previously (Bulow 2002). The connection between inefficient lending, natural resources, and political instability is less clear.

The starting point for our work is a casual look at the data, which confirm there is a strong connection between international lending and commodity prices. Exhibit 6.2 shows the evolution of average lending and resource rents between 1970 and 2000. The lending curve mirrors the resource rents curve. This supports

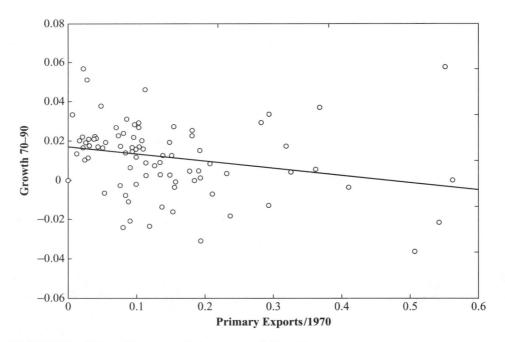

Exhibit 6.1 Natural Resource Abundance and Growth

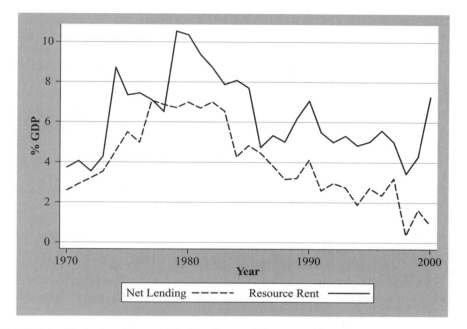

Exhibit 6.2 Evolution Average Net Lending and Resource Abundance

earlier claims that international financial markets lend money during commodity booms and restrict liquidity during busts. The evolution of these two indicators is indicative of the "boom-based borrowing capacity" highlighted by Usui (1997) and Manzano and Rigobon (2001). The latter argue that large credits offered on resource-based collateral in periods of commodity boom resulted in substantial debt overhang when commodity prices fell in the 1980s, which may have led to the resource curse.

The chapter is organized as follows. There is first a review of the resource curse literature focusing on the relationship between natural resource wealth and unsound lending. Then, we present a mechanism through which foreign lending to unchecked rulers in resource-rich nations may result in political instability and impede economic growth as well as the empirical evidence that supports our prediction. You find our conclusions at the end.

SOME PIECES OF THE PUZZLE FROM THE PREVIOUS LITERATURE

Sachs and Warner's statistical analysis confirms the findings made in earlier case studies documenting the apparent paradox that the resource boom in the 1970s and early 1980s did little to improve the growth prospects of primary commodity exporters (Gelb and Associates 1988; Auty 1994). A number of cross-country studies following Sachs and Warner have found evidence of the resource curse—Leite and Weidmann (2002), Isham et al. (2005), Bulte et al. (2005). These seemingly robust findings constitute a puzzle to analysts. More resources provide more options to a country and therefore should make it better off or at least as well off. If it was not the case, the possibility of leaving the resources in the ground is always an option. It is also a puzzle in light of economic history. Countries such as the United States, Canada, or Australia heavily relied on their large resource endowments and primary commodity exports at earlier stages of their development. For these countries, resources proved to be a blessing or at least did not prove to be a curse.

The crucial question is, what accounts for the apparent poor economic performance of resource-rich countries since the 1970s? There are at least four different explanations for the so-called resource curse:

1. Autocratic regimes and poor institutions (Ross 2001; Isham et al. 2005).
2. Increased indebtedness (Manzano and Rigobon 2001).
3. Domestic conflict and political instability (Collier and Hoeffler 2004).
4. Dutch Disease (Sachs and Warner 1995). We discuss only the first two explanations because they are what is relevant to our analysis.

The first explanation comes from Ross (2001), who addresses the question of the curse by exploring the link between resource abundance and political regimes. He finds evidence that oil and mineral wealth lead to less democratic regimes. There are two important channels. The first channel is the so-called rentier state effect, which holds that oil revenue can be used to sustain authoritarian regimes through low taxation and spending on patronage. The second channel is the repression effect, whereby authoritarian regimes in oil-rich countries seek to remain in power by relying heavily on defense and security expenditures. Thus, natural resource intensity not only may lead to lower growth, but it may also impede democracy.

The second explanation points to the relationship between resource wealth and debts (Usui 1997; Manzano and Rigobon 2001). Usui (1997) provided a case study on two oil-rich countries, Indonesia and Mexico, that sheds light on this link. He found that both Indonesia (in 1975) and Mexico (in 1978–1982) became attractive customers in the international credit market, and took advantage of the drastic improvement of the borrowing capacity during the periods of the boom of their resource sector. This unsound boom-based borrowing and lending resulted in the Pertamina crisis in 1975 in Indonesia and to Mexico's debt crisis in 1982.

Manzano and Rigobon's argument is based on debt overhang triggered by imperfect capital markets whereby credit is based on collateral, and resource stocks might serve as collateral. In the 1970s and early 1980s, international banks, such as Citicorp and Chase Manhattan, lent vast amounts of money to developing nations based on their natural resource endowment, virtually irrespective of their ability to repay such debts (Sampson 1982). The boom in resource prices in the 1970s increased the value of in situ resources, stretching the ability of resource-rich economies to attract foreign loans and run up debts. When resource prices subsequently came down, international credit became scarce and debt servicing turned out to be problematic with adverse consequences for growth.

The third explanation was popularized by Collier and Hoeffler (1998 and 2004). They argue that the presence of easily appropriable natural resources has a destabilizing effect in that it exacerbates power contests and violent conflicts. Their results suggest that resource abundance increases the likelihood of a civil war, albeit nonmonotonically. These results, however, have been recently challenged by both political scientists (Fearon 2005) and economists (Brunnschweiler and Bulte 2009).

The fourth explanation points to the Dutch Disease (Neary and van Wijnbergen 1986). The theory postulates that the rapid growth of primary exports will cause the exchange rate to appreciate, which in turn induces a contraction in manufacturing exports, or draws capital and labor away from manufacturing. This eventually results in poor economic performance. This theory, however, rests on the crucial assumption that the contraction in the manufacturing sector, the engine of growth, outweighs the boom in the resource sector.

While all four of these leading explanations have been informative, there is still a missing link. No research we are aware of has studied how governments make the joint choice regarding debt, investment, resource reliance, and oppression. The normative solution turns out to depend on a number of interesting inter-temporal trade-offs. Interestingly, we find strong support for such a stylized model in a data set covering a panel of 44 countries between 1972 and 1999.

MECHANISM AND EMPIRICAL RESULTS

This section elaborates upon the mechanisms by which resource-based lending contributes to low growth and political instability. A fundamental driver in our paper is moral hazard: International financial institutions perceive no downside risk to lending on the basis of resource-based collateral. Lenders have little reason to be concerned about the incentives their loans generate since the collateral (that is, the resources) remains behind even when the regime changes. (See the quote at the beginning of this chapter.)

Our view is that the resource curse can manifest itself as a form of looting. Akerlof and Romer (1994) proposed the idea of looting—bankruptcy at public expense and personal emolument—to describe the S&L crisis of the 1980s in the United States. In our model, states hold their natural resource stocks directly as sovereign assets so that no private entities (corporations, individuals) hold rights to these resources. The potential for poor governance is present in the form of an unchecked ruler with implicit property rights in the resources of the state. We are interested in how such an autocrat will elect to achieve a payout on these property rights and, in particular, the impact of lending market imperfections upon the dictator's choice between staying and looting. Staying involves the dictator's commitment to acquiring a return by holding on to power and investing in the country. Looting involves opting for a short-term hit-and-run strategy of maximum indebtedness, minimal investment, and immediate departure.

To gain the ability to loot, dictators must have the opportunity to leverage, or liquefy, their real assets. International financial institutions (banks, multilateral institutions, bond markets) consider natural resource stocks implicit collateral for their loans, and provide liquidity to resource-rich states in recognition of the expected future flows of value from the resource base. The discussion in the literature of odious debt highlights that contracts entered into by a ruler continue as obligations of that state beyond the individual tenure of that ruler (Jayachandran and Kremer 2006).

The ruler of the state concerned has unchecked power over the resource wealth and other assets of the state for the duration of his tenure. His problem is to determine how best to appropriate maximum personal benefit from his period of tenure over these resources. The basic decision comes down to whether to abscond with maximum liquidity today or to stay and invest in tenure and productivity of the non-resource-based economy so as to acquire a return from holding control over the productive capacities of the enterprise in the future. The ruler can affect the length of his tenure by means of investments in societal betterment or repression but faces the possibility of being ousted, and losing everything along with his loss of control. Thus, international lending gives the ruler the option of liquefying some additional proportion of the state's resource wealth, at the cost of an increase in the state's debt.

The dictator's fundamental trade-off concerns the refusal of amounts currently appropriable from the economy (through liquidity and looting) in pursuit of the amounts potentially producible in future periods (through investment and retention of tenure). The incentives to loot or to invest are determined by the rate of return on investment, the security of the autocrat, and the level of liquidity on offer. The optimal tenure of a dictator is more than one period, only if there is sufficient security and expectation of returns to render investment the preferred option. Our paper demonstrates how an inefficient sovereign debt contract (Bulow and Rogoff 1989; Kletzer and Wright 2000) is capable of inducing political instability and default, and demonstrates what is excessive liquidity in the context of a resource-rich but autocratic state.

We provide simulations to illustrate how liquidity is able to induce instability and hence underinvestment and lack of growth. These simulations demonstrate that an incoming autocrat may act as an owner or as a thief in regard to the economy, depending upon the level of liquidity on offer. Low levels of liquidity maintain the incentives to stay and to invest as the owner of the economy. The returns from control are secured by staying on the scene, maintaining control, and securing the flow of returns from earlier investments (see Exhibit 6.3). On the other hand, high levels of liquidity act as a prize to the winner of the contest for control, and create incentives for an ongoing system of hits and runs (see Exhibit 6.4). The returns from control in this case are secured simply by virtue of having control of the economy—then the banks pay the prize and the contest winner exits the stage.

Our key prediction is that unstructured lending into a country with resources heightens the incentive to loot and underinvest in the economy. This leads to slow economic growth because of lower investment. This result translates into empirically observable outcomes regarding lending, political instability, and economic growth.

To test our hypothesis, we use a sample of 44 autocracies between 1972 and 1999. Following Londregan and Poole (1990) and Alesina et al. (1996), we estimate two equations: the probability of political instability (or looting), and annual economic growth. The key determinants of looting are resource stocks, foreign lending, and their interaction. Our looting prediction would be substantiated if the marginal effect of lending in the presence of high resources were to be positive. Our growth equation includes determinants standard to the empirical growth literature (including a control for the Dutch Disease hypothesis) augmented with our looting indicator. We are interested in the indirect effect of lending and resources on growth due to political instability, which we identify as partially associated with looting behavior.

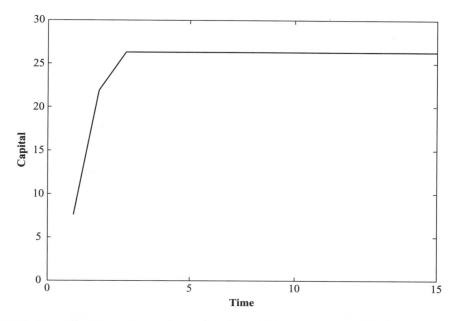

Exhibit 6.3 Simulation of capital accumulation without unstructured lending.
Note: The dictator chooses to accumulate capital and growth is high. The steady state level of capital is reached quickly and growth is stable.

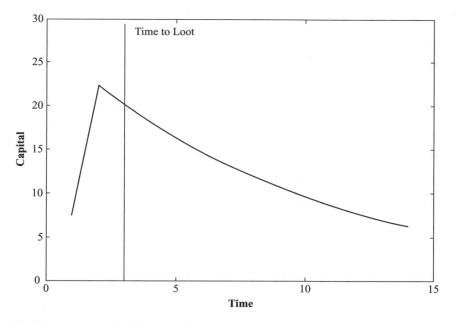

Exhibit 6.4 Simulation of capital accumulation when lending is unstructured.
Note: The dictator invests less than needed to achieve steady state, borrows heavily to consume privately, and departs or loots in order to avoid rebellion and zero utility. He can then continue consuming from the proceeds of prior lending. The country's growth subsequently slows because of this noninvestment from future rulers.

Our estimation results are consistent with our theoretical model. We find that the marginal impact of lending is positive and hence associated with a greater likelihood of turnover. This effect becomes more significant the greater the resource wealth. We also find a substantial rise in the predicted probability of looting (from 0.07 to 0.15) in resource-rich countries with poor governance. Both results indicate that greater lending in resource-rich countries is associated with greater political instability.

Furthermore, the effect of our looting indicator, proxied by a nondemocratic political turnover, is interesting. Here the impact of turnover on growth is negative and statistically significant. We find that output per capita drops by nearly 9 percent in the year of a political turnover. Since lending and natural resources are partially associated with this turnover, these factors have an impact on incomes and growth. We show that the effect of one standard deviation increase in lending results in an expected decrease in economic growth ranging from 0.47 to 0.72 percentage points. Together these findings provide strong evidence to support our predictions. Lending to resource-rich dictators raises the chance of political instability, leading to low growth.

CONCLUSION AND POLICY IMPLICATIONS

This paper attempts to unravel a mechanism through which the much-discussed resource curse operates. We view the problem as one of sovereign looting. Our main contribution is to model the impact of credit market imperfections on the intertemporal choices of dictators in resource-rich countries. Under certain conditions, instability and slow growth are optimal choices for a dictator. Our model suggests that a dictator will be fundamentally influenced in the choice between staying and looting by the level of lending afforded by external banking institutions. The opportunity cost to staying and investing in the economy increases directly with any increase in the liquidity being afforded.

Our story is closely related to the literature on odious debt (Jayachandran and Kremer 2006) and on efficient contracts for sovereign lending (Bulow 2002 and Kletzer and Wright 2000). Odious debt may result when lending to autocrats results in little for the country concerned other than debt. We have demonstrated here that unstructured resource-based lending is the antithesis of efficient sovereign loan contracting, and odious debts are the result. Our point here is that the indebtedness and poor performance of these resource-rich economies is as much a result of the poor contracting by the financial sector as it is of the unchecked power and poor institutions within the debtor regimes. It takes negligence or malfeasance by both the parties to make a bad contract. These bad contracts, together with the weak institutions in the resource-rich nations, create the environment within which non-investment, instability, and debt are generated—hence the resource curse.

The importance of restricting short-term liquidity to aid the enforceability of loan agreements has been long noted (Bulow and Rogoff 1989) as has been the tendency of banks to ignore such advice (Bulow 2002). The problem is argued to be one of moral hazard in the financial markets, where banks fail to internalize the risks of default because of the belief that sovereign debts will ultimately be worked out and particularly those with large amounts of natural resources underlying them.[1] The failure of the financial sector to internalize these risks places these costs upon the peoples of the countries concerned.

There are many approaches advocated to deal with this sort of moral hazard. Bulow (2002) believes that the problem is traceable, fundamentally, to the intervention of central banks and fiscal authorities in rescuing commercial banks and other creditors from defaults. Lenders engage in moral hazard in these lending practices on account of a fundamental failure of belief in the possibility of default. He recommends that banks should be made to execute loan agreements under domestic laws, enforceable only in domestic courts, in order to ensure that the debtor state's interests are taken into consideration. It is also argued by some that advance due diligence in lending should be a requirement for the enforceability of the resulting debt (Jayachandran, Kremer, and Schafter 2006). The result of requiring such a process would presumably be lower lending and lower incentives to loot the resources of the nation.

One other possibility is to require that loans come more in the form of structured obligations relying on specific investments rather than general assets. This would ensure that banks required hard investments as a result of loans, and that these investments were of a sort that could generate returns to the bank. It may also be more appropriate to encourage foreign direct investment rather than sovereign funding for local enterprises, again rendering recourse to domestic institutions necessary. All of these approaches may reduce the availability of debt in general, but our analysis indicates that this may be a good thing.

NOTE

1. Empirical work documents that private holdings of sovereign debt are not harmed by the fact of default. As Klingen et al. (2004) have demonstrated, "the strategy of rolling over and waiting for a debt restructuring with official backing seems to have worked well in containing losses and even making profits in some cases. From the banks' perspective, the write downs (. . .) were offset by the high prices of the restructured instruments, i.e., an expectation that the new claims would probably be honored."

REFERENCES

Akerlof, G., and P. Romer. 1994. "Looting: The Economic Underworld of Bankruptcy for Profit." *NBER Working Paper*, No. R1869. Cambridge MA: National Bureau of Economic Research.

Alesina A., S. Özler, N. Roubini, and P. Swagel. 1996. "Political Instability and Economic Growth." *Journal of Economic Growth* 1: 189–211.

Auty, R. M. 1994. "Industrial Policy Reform in Six Newly Industrializing Countries: The Resource Curse Thesis." *World Development* 22:1, 11–26.

Brunnschweiler, C., and E. H. Bulte. 2009. "Natural Resources and Violent Conflict: Resource Abundance, Dependence and the Onset of Civil Wars." *Oxford Economic Papers* 61: 651–674.

Bulow, J. 2002. "First World Governments and Third World Debt." *Brookings Papers on Economic Activity* 2002:1, 229–255.

Bulow, J., and K. Rogoff. 1989. "A Constant Recontracting Model of Sovereign Debt." *Journal of Political Economy* 97:1, 155–178.

Bulte, E., R. Damania, and R. Deacon. 2005. "Resource Intensity, Institutions and Development." *World Development* 33: 1029–1044.

Collier, P., and A. Hoeffler. 2004. "Greed and Grievance in Civil War." *Oxford Economic Papers* 56:4, 563–595.

Fearon, J. D. 2005. "Primary Commodity Exports and Civil War." *Journal of Conflict Resolution* 49:4, 483–507.

Gelb, A. H., and Associates. 1988. *Windfall Gains: Blessing or Curse?* New York: Oxford University Press.

Isham, J., M. Woolcock, L. Pritchett, and G. Busby. 2005. "The Varieties of Resource Experience: Natural Resource Export Structures Affect the Political Economy of Economic Growth." *World Bank Economic Review* 19: 141–174.

Jayachandran, S., and M. Kremer. 2006. "Odious Debt." *American Economic Review* 96:1, 82–92.

Jayachandran, S., M. Kremer, and S. Shafter. 2006. "Applying the Odious Debt Doctrine While Preserving Legitimate Lending." Paper presented at the Blue Sky conference organized by the Center for International Development, September 9, at Harvard University, Cambridge, MA.

Kletzer, K., and B. Wright. 2000. "Sovereign Debt as Intertemporal Barter." *American Economic Review* 90:3, 621–639.

Klingen, C. A., B. Weder, and J. Zettelmeyer. 2004. "How Private Creditors Fared in Emerging Debt Markets, 1970–2000." *IMF Working Paper*, WP/04/13. Washington, DC: International Monetary Fund.

Leite, C., and J. Weidmann. 2002. "Does Mother Nature Corrupt? Natural resources, Corruption and Economic Growth." In G. Abed and S. Gupta, eds., *Governance, Corruption, and Economic Performance*, 159–196. Washington, DC: International Monetary Fund.

Londregan, J. B., and K. T. Poole. 1990. "Poverty, the Coup Trap and the Seizure of Executive Power." *World Politics* 42: 151–183.

Manzano, O., and R. Rigobon. 2001. "Resource Curse or Debt Overhang?" *NBER Working Paper*, No. 8390. Cambridge, MA: National Bureau of Economic Research.

Neary, J. P., and S. van Wijnbergen. 1986. *Natural Resources and the Macroeconomy.* Cambridge, MA: MIT Press.

Ross, M. 2001. "Does Oil Hinder Democracy?" *World Politics* 53: 325–361.

Sachs, J., and A. Warner. 1995. "Natural Resource Abundance and Economic Growth." *NBER Working Paper*, No. 5398. Cambridge, MA: National Bureau of Economic Research.

———. 1997. "Sources of Slow Growth in African Economies." *Journal of African Economies* 6: 335–376.

Sampson, A. 1982. *The Money Lenders: Bankers and a World in Turmoil.* New York: Viking Press.

Sarr, M., E. Bulte, C. Meissner, and T. Swanson. 2010. "On the Looting of Nations." *Public Choice*, Forthcoming.

Usui, N. 1997. "Dutch Disease and Policy Adjustments to the Oil Boom: A Comparative Study of Indonesia and Mexico." *Resource Policy* 23: 151–162.

ABOUT THE AUTHORS

Mare Sarr is a lecturer in economics at the University of Cape Town. He is also a research fellow at the Environmental Economics Policy Research Unit (EPRU) and a research associate at the Southern Africa Labor and Development Research Unit (SALDRU). His research focuses on resource economics and intellectual property rights in the life sciences industries. He received his PhD in economics at University College London. He can be reached by e-mail at mare.sarr@uct.ac.za.

Erwin Bulte is a professor of development economics at Wageningen University, and a professor of environmental and natural resource economics at Tilburg University. He is also an external research fellow at Oxford University (OxCarre: the Oxford Center for the Analysis of Resource-Rich Economies) and Cambridge University (Department of Land Economy). He is associate editor of *Environment and Development Economics, Natural Resource Modeling,* and *Environmental & Resource Economics*. His main research interests are sustainable and efficient management of natural resources, institutional economics, the resource curse, and paleoeconomics. He can be reached by e-mail at erwin.bulte@wur.nl.

Chris Meissner is an associate professor of economics at the University of California, Davis. His research focuses on the economic history of the international economy, particularly between 1870 and 1913. He is also a research associate at the National Bureau of Economic Research (NBER) in the Development of the American Economy (DAE) program. Before joining the faculty at Davis, Meissner was on the economics faculty at Cambridge University. In Cambridge he was the director of studies in economics and a fellow of King's College. He has held visiting scholar positions at the International Monetary Fund and at Harvard. He was also a Houblon Norman fellow at the Bank of England. He can be reached by e-mail at cmmeissner@ucdavis.edu.

Tim Swanson holds the Andre Hoffman Chair in Economics at the Graduate Institute, Geneva. He was formerly the chair of law and economics at University College London. He teaches law and regulation and international environmental law in the law school, and teaches law and economics and institution building in the economics department. His research covers issues dealing with legal reform and institution building in the areas of the environment, intellectual property, and technology. He has advised the governments of China, India, and many international and development agencies. He can be reached by e-mail at tim.swanson@ucl.ac.uk.

CHAPTER 7

Sovereign Debt and Military Conflict

ZANE M. KELLY
University of Colorado

P ublic finance is a key factor for understanding state behavior. Without the ability to raise revenue, states are all but crippled. When it comes to war, every government must consider not only its military capabilities but also the anticipated costs of its actions. It is surprising, then, that political science has, until recently, focused very little attention on sovereign debt granted the great importance placed on it by such luminaries as Ricardo, Kant, Hume, Mill, and others. Extant research on the state agrees that taxes and war-making are intrinsically related but no such parallel body of work exists with respect to debt. This article presents two different approaches to the war-and-debt relationship. The first is rooted in observations from European history. It argues the sovereign debt allows states, especially large, powerful, and creditworthy states, to finance larger, longer, and bloodier wars. The second perspective tells us that there are several reasons to suspect that sovereign debt can reduce the overall incidence of conflict between nations.

SOVEREIGN DEBT AS A PERMISSIVE CAUSE OF WAR

The belief that public debt is a permissive cause of conflict is time-honored. David Ricardo posited that reliance on taxes to fund wars would ultimately deter belligerent governments. Not only do taxes suppress consumption, they should make wars shorter and less intense by reducing governments' available resources. By suddenly raising very high taxes to finance wars, governments would engender antiwar sentiment among the populace. In other words, citizens should prefer consumption today to wartime shortages and taxes. Immanuel Kant opposed debt to the degree that it figures into the preliminary articles of his well-known perpetual peace argument. David Hume warned in 1752 that unchecked credit would destroy Britain. Governments, however, seem inured to this advice, perhaps precisely because their interests lie in winning the wars they fight once they have begun.

Since the era of the Medicis, indeed even earlier, states have routinely borrowed money from private actors to supplement their wartime income. Generally speaking, there have been few exceptions to a wartime fiscal strategy of combining increased taxes with raising public debt. Seignorage or debasement is often an important part of the picture as well. Raising debt is an attractive funding mechanism for policy makers during wartime. Unlike seignorage, debt-induced inflation is easily managed. Inflation-indexed bonds accomplish this task quite efficiently. Compared to taxes, debt is voluntary and encourages domestic consumption; thus it is politically expedient.

Payments made by the U.S. government to the Europeans during World War I are a common example of direct financial intervention during conflict. Secretary of State William Jennings Bryan warned President Wilson that lending money to France would violate the principle of neutrality and lead the United States down a slippery slope to support for opposing sides in the war. Nevertheless, Americans eventually lent over $2 billion to the Triple Entente and over $27 million to the Triple Alliance.

At one extreme, the United States has benefited enormously as both a creditor and borrower over the twentieth century. The dollar's status as the world's reserve currency and high demand for dollars and U.S. Treasuries have allowed the U.S. government to finance huge deficits at very generous interest rates, although the Korean War stands out as an exception to this strategy. By some estimates, the Korean War was financed entirely through tax increases, following President Truman's commitment to suppressing the national debt.[1] The same was true of Great Britain during the late nineteenth century. A few privileged nations do seem to enjoy an advantage that allows them to fight war on the cheap while creditors bear the burden of wartime inflation. One such study links this phenomenon with democracy, arguing that democratic states are able to credibly reassure investors by virtue of providing transparent institutions. Historically, such democratic institutions as checks and balances on authority have played a role in influencing the direction of credit by making some borrowers more credible than those without such limits on authority.[2] Others have connected this borrowing advantage to Modelski's long-cycle theory, arguing that the best borrowers are ultimately the most successful in great power competitions for hegemony.[3]

Regular access to international credit has been a powerful tool in the portfolio of powerful states for centuries. As another illustration, one might consider French financiers who were heavily invested in Russian military infrastructure before World War I. Investments in Russian bonds dramatically outweighed foreign direct investment, particularly during the Russo-Japanese War, when the Tsarist government floated a number of new loans. These loans were quite agreeable to lenders in terms of interest rates and discounts and were specifically intended to help the Russians defeat the Japanese.

Although the arguments of many classical scholars point to a connection between sovereign debt and longer, more costly, and bloodier wars, there are reasons to believe that additional dynamics may be at work. These different processes should have a positive impact on international peace. Some more recent research into this topic argues that, particularly with respect to the United States, large stocks of sovereign debt can pose a significant impediment to achieving foreign policy goals.

SOVEREIGN DEBT AS A CONSTRAINT ON BELLIGERENCE

Contrary to the expectations of debt as a permissive cause of war, some empirical evidence demonstrates that larger stocks of public debt reduce incidence of interstate conflict. A useful observation from the late twentieth century is that large debt stocks in most of the world are not actually a consequence of sustained war efforts. Nor do they appear to be in preparation for such conflicts in most countries. Rather, sovereign borrowing abroad is now institutionalized and quite commonplace as diverse governments seek means to shore up domestic budgets. Although public debt can facilitate ongoing wars, there is an overall peace dividend associated with the broader phenomenon of expanding markets for government debt. Debtors are less likely to engage in conflict in the first place.[4]

There are several plausible mechanisms through which sovereign debt can reduce interstate conflict. First, public debt can grant creditors coercive leverage over debtors. Second, as government debts mount, leaders will find their range of choices increasingly constrained. Third, debt is a commitment mechanism. It is one arena in which debtors can signal their credibility and resolve. Fourth, with respect to interactions between nations, public debt aligns the interests of creditors and debtors. These last two mechanisms have spillover effects in other realms of international relations in terms of creating channels through which states can more clearly communicate their interests, intentions, and resolve over issues that might otherwise lead to conflict.

External, public sovereign debt, money owed to citizens and governments of other countries, represents shared interests between states, even though preferences between borrowers and lenders may vary significantly. Lenders prefer to maximize their returns and minimize their risks. Borrowers might prefer to forgo repayment entirely, but on the average they seek to obtain the lowest possible interest rates and to maximize the value of future borrowing. This last point is crucial for understanding how sovereign debt contributes to peace. Stability is important for lenders. Creditors should avoid the uncertainty associated with violent conflict and the chance that capital will be lost or destroyed during a costly war. Most creditors are expected to avoid or retreat from areas of conflict, although some may reasonably expect to profit from wars. This second point is especially true if a war involves a potential debtor such as the United States that is both very creditworthy and likely to win. On the demand side, borrowers should be deterred from conflict behavior that unnerves international markets so they can more easily attract continued, uninterrupted investment.

Debtors and creditors have a further mutual interest in peace that relates to wartime economies. When debts are denominated in a common currency, rather than local currency, then wartime inflation has two effects. First, it decreases the value of debts owed by war participants because inflation reduces the value of their currencies, in turn reducing the returns to capital. When a country owes debts denominated, for example, in dollars, domestic inflation as a result of wartime demands on the economy makes it more expensive to repay those dollars. Conversely, this makes debts denominated in dollars easier to pay for observers or nonparticipants to the conflict. Assuming positive gains in the exchange rate, it becomes relatively cheaper to repay dollar-denominated debts from the sidelines.

Large debtors thus have an incentive to avoid participating in other states' wars in which they owe money denominated in the belligerent states' currency.

To extend the preceding example, countries and individuals that hold dollar-denominated U.S. debt have an interest in American foreign policy. Creditors should prefer that the United States avoid costly wars because, insofar as those wars lead to dollar depreciation, they erode the value of other states' holdings. Of course, this preference is conditional on uncertainty about a great many factors such as the likelihood of wartime inflation, tax policy, the length of the conflict, and the relative value of other currencies that could serve as alternative holdings.

This argument suggests another concern. Governments that anticipate military conflict in the future may borrow ahead of time or take steps to reassure investors that they will be repaid. Pronouncements that wars will be short and inexpensive, such as those issued before the 2003 Iraq War, target multiple audiences, including political constituents and potential investors at home and abroad. There is historical precedent for government borrowing in anticipation of wars. The French government borrowed from the IMF in anticipation of the Suez Crisis in 1956, ostensibly justified by the losses incurred from nationalization of the Canal. The British did not, and consequently yielded to American financial pressure.[5]

Debt plays an important role in maintaining international peace by enhancing what political scientists call the shadow of the future. Simply put, borrowing and lending today increases the future value of such behavior. When two countries enhance their ties with one another and participate in actions that make long-term payoffs more valuable than short-term gains, militarized conflict between them is less likely. In the case of sovereign debt, even if both parties have an incentive to defect on their arrangement, for example, by defaulting on the use of force to collect on debts, they must consider the likely impact of such actions on future transactions. Debtors who frequently default earn a negative reputation that makes it more difficult and expensive to borrow in the future. Historically, there is scanty evidence suggesting that creditors should be expected to use military force to protect their investments, mainly stemming from nineteenth-century colonial imperialism, but not robust through the twentieth century. Anecdotally, there is evidence that governments that managed to service their external debts during the Great Depression were successful at continuing to raise capital, during a period when investors were extremely risk averse. The incentive for debtor nations to maintain positive relationships with investors rings true in the 2003 Brazilian elections. During the election, when it seemed clear that a left-leaning candidate would win, markets panicked, sending the real into a steep slide. When Lula da Silva won, he surprised both his constituents and international investors by committing to budget surpluses and debt repayment, successfully repaying Brazil's IMF obligations two years ahead of schedule.

Governments with large external debts should find themselves constrained by the burden of their financial obligations. Such a constraint derives from two sources. The first is what scholars call the guns-versus-butter trade-off. In this scenario, as government budget deficits and public debts grow, policy makers find themselves increasingly compelled to spend money repaying debt rather than investing in domestic programs. Public debt can thus limit the opportunities for interstate conflict, although it may not eliminate the reasons. Because wars create intense demand for discretionary spending, if sovereign debt burdens reduce the availability of such funding, they reduce the likelihood of conflict. As a brief illustration, approximately 35 percent of the U.S. budget is discretionary. Of that, a further 35 percent is security-related. As deficits grow, future revenues will increasingly need to be reallocated from discretionary spending to debt service.

The second source of policy constraint is outright coercion by creditors, as described earlier in the example of the Suez Crisis. Currently, there is no agreement as to the efficacy of this second mechanism. China, for example, has met with very limited success in translating its holdings of U.S. debt into coercive leverage over U.S. foreign policy. Creditors that hold sufficient debt often find themselves too intrinsically tied to the debtor nation to effectively assert leverage over other areas of foreign policy without threatening their own interests.[6]

Empirical tests linking conflict behavior and sovereign debt support the hypothesis that large stocks of public debt decrease the incidence of conflict. It is not clear, however, whether debt may also function in a way consistent with the expectations of Ricardo and Hume described earlier. Clearly, there have been distinct periods when sovereign debt served explicitly to finance ongoing conflicts. The two World Wars of the twentieth century and the American conflicts in Iraq and Afghanistan are only three such examples.

To the extent that governments' capacity depends on funding from a mix of other states and private actors, finance can act as a behavioral constraint and reduce the risk of violent conflict. A great deal of concern has been expressed over the consequences of extremely high public debts and government deficits in the developed world, most recently in economically weaker areas of the Eurozone. It is apparent that some countries have been beneficiaries of debt while others have indeed found themselves virtually handcuffed. Many governments are debtors, but few are grossly unsustainable borrowers. Indeed, robust public debt institutions are one of the hallmarks of the modern financial system. There is a great deal of room for further exploration of the relationship between debt finance and interstate conflict. Such projects are unfortunately limited by available data. Only approximately half of all countries provide robust statistics on external sovereign debt. Of those, only a handful publishes information on their specific creditors.

CONCLUSION

This article offers two primary perspectives on the relationship between sovereign debt and violent conflict, one arguing that external debt is a permissive cause of war, and the other positing that the institution of debt reduces the overall instance of war. There are a number of prominent examples of debt finance used specifically to fund wars. Early empirical evidence suggests, however, that these are not necessarily representative of a larger trend. As more states integrate into the global financial network as both creditors and debtors, the overall incidence of militarized conflict may decrease. Historical evidence also supports the first perspective, namely that large, powerful states that tend to attract credit find it easier to sustain costly wars when external creditors line up to provide fiscal support. Empirical research has currently relatively little to say about these interpretations.

As sovereign debt stocks grow, not only in the developed industrial world, but also in developing countries, these issues bear further exploration.

NOTES

1. Lee Ohanian, "The Macroeconomic Effects of War Finance in the United States: World War II and the Korean War," *The American Economic Review* 87 (1997): 23–40.

2. Kenneth A. Schultz and Barry R. Weingast, "The Democratic Advantage: Institutional Foundations of Financial Power in International Competition," *International Organization* 57 (2003): 3–42; David Staasavage, "Cities, Constitutions, and Sovereign Borrowing in Europe, 1274–1785," *International Organization* 61 (2007): 489–525; Richard M. Sweeney, "Sovereign Debt, Default and War in the 18th and 19th Centuries," unpublished manuscript.

3. Karen Rasler and William R. Thompson, "Global Wars, Public Debts, and the Long Cycle," *World Politics* 35 (1983): 489–516; Karen Rasler and William R. Thompson, "War Making and State Making: Governmental Expenditures, Tax Revenues, and Global Wars," *The American Political Science Review* 79 (1986): 491–507.

4. Zane M. Kelly, "The Cost of Conflict: Sovereign Debt and Interstate Disputes, 1970–2001," unpublished paper presented at the 2010 annual meeting of the Midwest Political Science Association, Chicago, IL, April 22–25, 2010.

5. Diane Kunz, *The Economic Diplomacy of the Suez Crisis* (Chapel Hill, NC: University of North Carolina Press, 1991).

6. Daniel Drezner, "Bad Debts: Assessing China's Financial Influence in Great Power Politics." *International Security* 34 (2009): 7–45.

REFERENCES

Drezner, Daniel. 2009. "Bad Debts: Assessing China's Financial Influence in Great Power Politics." *International Security* 34:2, 7–45.

Kelly, Zane M. 2010. "The Cost of Conflict: Sovereign Debt and Interstate Disputes, 1970–2001." Unpublished paper presented at the 2010 annual meeting of the Midwest Political Science Association, April 22–25, in Chicago, IL.

Kunz, Diane. 1991. *The Economic Diplomacy of the Suez Crisis*. Chapel Hill, NC: University of North Carolina Press.

Ohanian, Lee. 1997. "The Macroeconomic Effects of War Finance in the United States: World War II and the Korean War." *The American Economic Review* 87:1, 23–40.

Rasler, Karen, and William R. Thompson. 1983. "Global Wars, Public Debts, and the Long Cycle." *World Politics* 35:4, 489–516.

———. 1986. "War Making and State Making: Governmental Expenditures, Tax Revenues, and Global Wars." *The American Political Science Review* 79:2, 491–507.

Schultz, Kenneth A., and Barry R. Weingast. 2003. "The Democratic Advantage: Institutional Foundations of Financial Power in International Competition." *International Organization* 57:1, 3–42.

Staasavage, David. 2007. "Cities, Constitutions, and Sovereign Borrowing in Europe, 1274–1785." *International Organization* 61: 489–525.

Sweeney, Richard M. "Sovereign Debt, Default and War in the 18th and 19th Centuries." Unpublished manuscript.

ABOUT THE AUTHOR

Zane M. Kelly holds a PhD in political science from the University of Colorado at Boulder. From 2009 to 2010, he served as a Governing America in a Global Era (GAGE) fellow at the Miller Center of Public Affairs in Charlottesville, VA. His research is on the relationship between public finance and conflict behavior.

PART II

Making Sovereign Debt Work

G iven the importance of sovereign debt, successful national governance depends on the proper management of this source of finance. The ability to repay a sovereign's obligation depends on the fiscal management of the state, and part of that successful management is the deployment of sovereign borrowings to productive use. When borrowed funds are invested poorly or siphoned away through corruption, the state's ability to repay its obligations comes into jeopardy.

For the most part, smaller and developing nations secure sovereign financing by borrowing from international banks. For their part, the major industrial countries issue bills, notes, and bonds on their own account. While the very smallest nations are effectively restricted to bank borrowing, somewhat larger and more developed nations have a choice between borrowing from a bank and issuing their own debt. Chapters in this section consider the costs and benefits of the two approaches. This section also considers other matters in the management of sovereign debt and the interaction between sovereign debt and other obligations of the state such as pension obligations.

CHAPTER 8

Fiscal Policy, Government Institutions, and Sovereign Creditworthiness

BERNARDIN AKITOBY
Division Chief in the African Department of the International Monetary Fund[*]

THOMAS STRATMANN
Professor of Economics, George Mason University

T he international financial crisis has brought to the forefront the role of fiscal policy and institutions in restoring confidence in financial markets. This raises a number of critical questions. First, how do financial markets react to fiscal policy shocks, such as changes in government spending or taxes? Second, do financial markets differentiate between current expenditure–based and revenue-based adjustments? Third, do financial markets discriminate between tax-financed and debt-financed spending? Fourth, to the extent that institutions shape fiscal outcomes, a critical question is whether fiscal variables interact with the political institutions to affect financial markets. Finally, do political institutions have some independent influence on financial markets beyond the fiscal and economic outcomes they shape?

ANALYTICAL FRAMEWORK

To investigate these questions, we use a conceptual framework that builds on the theory of sovereign risk pricing (Edwards 1984) and the theoretical debate on whether the private sector's response to fiscal adjustment depends on the composition of fiscal adjustment (Alesina and Perotti 1997) and institutions that shape the fiscal outcome (Persson and Tabellini 2000). More specifically, we introduce fiscal policy and institutions variables into the empirical model of sovereign risk pricing. We then derive a testable equation for spreads, which we estimate using panel data techniques (see Akitoby and Stratmann 2008 and 2011).

---

[*]This chapter is based on Akitoby and Stratmann (2008 and 2011).

The data set for the dependent variable is the stripped spread obtained from the Emerging Markets Bond Index Global (EMBI Global). The EMBI Global tracks total returns for traded external debt instruments in emerging markets issued by sovereign and quasi-sovereign entities, and covers 32 countries.

For the choice of political institution variables, we consider the political system (presidential versus parliamentary), political constraints (Henisz 2000), the Freedom House indexes of political rights and civil liberties, the Kaufmann voice and accountability index, the democracy index (Polity) produced by the University of Maryland, the democratic accountability index of the International Country Risk Guide (ICRG), the ICRG political risk index, and whether there is an election in a particular year. Since many of these institutions are highly correlated, we estimate separate regressions for each. For the fiscal variables, we include government revenues, current expenditures, and government investment.

As for additional control variables, previous studies point to a large number of variables as possible determinants of sovereign risk. We aim for a parsimonious empirical model, capturing the key indicators of liquidity, solvency, and macroeconomic fundamentals. We therefore include the ratio of total debt outstanding to gross national income (GNI). This measure is a key indicator of a country's long-run solvency. Higher debt to GNI increases the default probability, and hence the sovereign risk. This variable is predicted to be positively associated with the spread.

Other control variables include the ratio of foreign exchange reserves to GDP, the inflation rate, the output gap, default history, and the regional spread index. The ratio of foreign exchange reserves to GDP is expected to reduce spreads, because it is a measure of a country's capacity to service external debt. The inflation rate is a key indicator of economic stability. Monetization of fiscal deficits can lead to high inflation, which reduces growth by raising the cost of acquiring capital. For this reason, higher inflation will tend to increase sovereign risk. We include the output gap to control for the economic cycle and monetary conditions because recent work has shown that the timing and type of fiscal adjustment also depend on the economic cycle. We include a country's default history as one of the control variables and hypothesize that it has a positive coefficient because defaults increase risk. Another control variable is a regional spread index that controls for contagion effects; the regions are Africa, Asia, Europe, and Latin America. All regressions include country and year fixed effects.

KEY FINDINGS

How do financial markets react to fiscal policy shocks such as changes in government spending or taxes? We find that revenue increases and current spending cuts reduce spreads. The impact of government investment is not statistically significant. Thus the size of public investment may not matter to investors. Quality of public investments may matter, but our data do not speak to this issue. Overall, these findings support the hypothesis that government revenues and current spending decisions affect financial markets.

Do financial markets differentiate between current expenditure–based and revenue-based adjustments? Contrary to the established view, financial markets favor revenue-driven adjustments more than current spending–driven adjustments.

Deficit-reducing tax increases of 1 percentage point lower interest rates on sovereign bonds by 20 percent, while a similar reduction in current spending lowers interest rates by only about 10 percent. Financial markets also react to the composition of spending, with cuts in current spending lowering spreads more than cuts in investment.

The result on the merits of spending-based versus revenue-based fiscal adjustments is consistent with the hypothesis that the three channels on which the success of spending-based fiscal adjustments rests—labor markets, expectation, and credibility—may not work well in emerging economies. First, in emerging economies, the transmission through labor markets may be hampered by labor market segmentation, the dominant role of government employment and regulation, and the low degree of labor mobility across sectors. Moreover, wage earners in emerging economies represent a smaller proportion of total employment than in industrialized countries. Second, the expectation channel may be ineffective, as liquidity constraints inhibit consumption smoothing. Finally, the credibility channel may not be effective if the social returns on government spending in developing countries are perceived to be higher than in developed countries.

Do financial markets discriminate between tax-financed and debt-financed spending? Financial markets do prefer the former to the latter. A one percentage point increase in current spending lowers spreads by 9.5 percent if financed by taxes, but will raise spreads by about 8.5 percent if financed by debt. If a country finances current spending by raising revenue, the increase in revenue will reduce the spread, thereby offsetting the impact of increasing current spending on spreads, whereas, in the case of the debt-financed current spending, the increase in the country's indebtedness will further heighten the country risk. Put differently, tax-financed current spending is not equivalent to debt-financed current spending, as far as the impact on spreads is concerned. We find that a one percentage point increase in debt to GNI leads to about a 1 percent increase in spreads, which implies that countries with higher debt are penalized in international markets. Similarly, like Edwards (1986), we also find that financial markets are sensitive to changes in reserves, evidence that liquidity concerns are important in the international investor's decision. A one percentage point increase in reserves to GDP causes the spreads to fall by about 4.5 percent. The magnitudes of the estimated coefficients on the debt and reserves indicate that each percentage increase in reserves is four times as effective in reducing spreads as each percentage reduction in debt.

Do fiscal variables interact with political institutions to affect financial markets? For example, for the same fiscal outcome, do market participants differentiate between right and left wing governments, or between majoritarian and proportional electoral systems? We find strong evidence that financial markets penalize left wing regimes that undertake spending-driven expansion. The penalty is estimated at about 3 percent higher interest rates. This may be because right wing governments are often associated with fiscal conservatism and a smaller government size while left wing governments are often associated with a larger government and broader social transfer programs. The findings also show that financial markets reward left wing governments more than they do right wing governments when government revenues increase. Put differently, right wing governments get lower benefits from a revenue-based consolidation. One reason for this could be that government spending is already low when the government is conservative, so that the marginal benefit from consolidation is less than if government spending is high.

With regard to the differentiation between majoritarian and proportional electoral systems, the results show that financial markets penalize majoritarian regimes—as opposed to proportional regimes—that undertake spending-driven expansion, presumably because these regimes are often associated with a larger government and broader transfer programs. This finding is also consistent with the view that the majority-rule countries tend to have what is called pork barrel spending in the United States, which is spending targeted to electoral districts. Financial markets may believe that pork barrel spending increases when current expenditures and government investment rise. Much of what may be contained in the category of government investment (building roads and bridges) may have low returns under a majoritarian system when it is spending targeted to districts or swing states.

Finally, do political institutions have some independent influence on financial markets beyond the fiscal and economic outcomes they shape? We find that political institutions matter for financial markets. The findings are robust to a wide range of indicators of institutional quality. First, democracy, regardless of how it is measured—the Kaufmann voice and accountability index, the Freedom House index of political rights, the Polity index, or the ICRG democratic accountability index—lowers spreads. The effects of democratic institutions are substantial. For example, a one standard deviation in the ICRG democratic accountability index decreases spreads by about 25 percent. More civil liberties also lower spreads, because civil liberties foster democracy. A one-point reduction in political rights, as measured by the Freedom House index on a one-to-six scale, reduces spreads by 8.5 percent, and the same reduction in civil rights reduces spreads by 19 percent. These results forcefully suggest that financial markets are giving a premium to democratic regimes. Put differently, the markets tend to penalize undemocratic regimes by charging them relatively higher interest rates. Because financial markets affect economic development through better resource allocation and risk diversification, our findings seem to suggest that democracy also matters for growth. Since we find that more government accountability, as measured by the ICRG index and the Kaufmann index, lowers spreads, our results lend support to the view that checks and balances increase creditworthiness.

We find a negative and statistically significant sign on the ICRG political risk variable. This shows that lower political risk reduces spreads, which confirms the widely held view that financial markets dislike political risk. We also find some evidence that sovereign borrowing costs tend to be higher in election years than in off-election years. This corroborates Block and Vaaler's (2004) finding that rating agencies and bondholders view elections negatively, presumably because elections are associated with uncertainty about the future.

POLICY IMPLICATIONS

This study suggests a number of policy implications for countries seeking to lower their borrowing cost on international capital markets. First, a country can pursue either revenue-based or expenditure-based fiscal adjustments, when fiscal adjustment is required to reassure financial markets. A country would be better off pursuing revenue-driven fiscal adjustments, however, whenever the labor market, the expectation, and the credibility channels are not present. Second, a country would be better off cutting current spending instead of public investment, because financial markets pay attention to the composition of fiscal consolidation. Third, since financial markets view high debt ratios negatively, reductions of debt through appropriate fiscal policy and debt management can lower spreads. Fourth, given the importance that the capital market attaches to the reserves-to-GDP ratio, governments can aim at increasing their foreign reserves position through appropriate macroeconomic and structural policies. Finally, a country would be better off if it strengthened checks and balances and democratic accountability.

REFERENCES

Akitoby, B., and T. Stratmann. 2008. "Fiscal Policy and Financial Markets." *The Economic Journal* 118: 1971–1985.

———. 2011. "The Value of Institutions for Financial Markets: Evidence from Emerging Markets." *Review of World Economics*. Forthcoming.

Alesina, A., and R. Perotti. 1997. "Fiscal Adjustments in OECD Countries: Composition and Macroeconomic Effects." *IMF Staff Papers* 44: 210–248.

Block, S., and P. Vaaler. 2004. "The Price of Democracy: Sovereign Risk Ratings, Bond Spreads and Political Business Cycles in Developing Countries." *Journal of International Money and Finance* 23: 917–946.

Edwards, S. 1984. "LDC's Foreign Borrowing and Default Risk: An Empirical Investigation." *The American Economic Review* 74: 726–734.

———. 1986. "The Pricing of Bonds and Bank Loans in International Markets: An Empirical Analysis of Developing Countries' Foreign Borrowing." *European Economic Review* 30: 565–589.

Henisz, Witold J. 2000. "The Institutional Environment for Economic Growth," *Economics and Politics* XII: 1–31.

Persson, T., and G. Tabellini. 2000. *Political Economics: Explaining Economic Policy*. Cambridge, MA: MIT Press.

ABOUT THE AUTHORS

Bernardin Akitoby holds a PhD in economics from the University of Montreal and degrees in business administration, finance, and accounting. He is currently division chief in the African department of the International Monetary Fund. Before joining the IMF, he worked in the World Bank's research department. Akitoby's research has been published in academic journals, including *The Economic Journal, European Journal of Political Economy, Review of World Economics, Economie Appliquée,* and *Revue Economique.* His research interests include real business cycles, growth, exchange rate, hyperinflation, fiscal policy, fiscal procyclicality, public investment and public-private partnerships, financial markets, economic institutions, and sovereign risk.

Thomas Stratmann is the university professor of economics and law at George Mason University. He holds a PhD in economics from the University of Maryland. He held previous appointments at the Montana State University and is a research professor at the Ifo Institute for Economic Research at the University of

Munich, Germany. Stratmann's research has been published in many economics and political science journals, including the *American Economic Review, American Journal of Political Science, American Political Science Review, Journal of Political Economy, Journal of Law and Economics,* and *Public Choice.* His research interests include political economy, law and economics, public finance, financial markets, and fiscal policy.

CHAPTER 9

Corruption and Creditworthiness

Evidence from Sovereign Credit Ratings

CRAIG A. DEPKEN II
Department of Economics, University of North Carolina–Charlotte*

COURTNEY L. LaFOUNTAIN
Government Accountability Office, Washington, DC

ROGER B. BUTTERS
Department of Economics, University of Nebraska–Lincoln

W e investigate the impact of public corruption on a country's creditworthiness, or willingness and ability to repay its sovereign debt. Corruption
and creditworthiness are linked by empirical evidence, suggesting that
public corruption drives economic activity such as production and investment, and
from the formal to the informal or unofficial sector of an economy. The informal
sector of an economy is, by design, beyond the reach of official tax collectors. Thus,
corruption reduces the tax revenue available to service sovereign debt, which in
turn may affect the sovereign's creditworthiness.[1]

Examples of how public corruption might be detrimental to an economy essentially involve some form of resource misallocation: Entrepreneurs pursue projects
that are best suited for the informal sector rather than the most valuable; talented
people spend time trying to capture rents rather than engaging in productive activities; public officials direct resources toward public goods that offer the best
opportunities to collect rents rather than those that generate the highest social
return; or bureaucrats design the regulatory structure to maximize rent-collecting
opportunities rather than to maximize social welfare. On the other hand, it may
be that the costs of corruption are inconsequential or that corruption introduces
market forces into bureaucracy, which improve efficiency.

---

*The opinions expressed herein are those of the authors and do not necessarily reflect the
position of the GAO or the U.S. federal government.

Thus, whether or not corruption is detrimental to an economy is an empirical question.

Each of the preceding examples illustrates how corruption may reduce overall tax collection from the formal sector. If the sovereign can raise revenue to repay debts only from the formal sector of an economy, then there is a strong positive correlation between economic activity that can be measured and economic activity that can be taxed. It follows that creditworthiness depends on measurable, rather than total, economic activity. Thus, corruption can have the same effect on creditworthiness whether it changes the overall level of economic activity or merely shifts economic activity from the formal to the informal sector.

In this study, we find that public corruption reduces creditworthiness as measured by sovereign credit ratings. Our estimates indicate that a one standard deviation increase in corruption causes credit ratings to fall by almost a full rating category on average. A rough calculation suggests that a one standard deviation decrease in corruption can save a country about $10,000 per $1 million of debt annually.[2]

To estimate the net impact of corruption on creditworthiness, we use *issuer* credit ratings from Standard & Poor's, which reflect the borrower's overall creditworthiness rather than the characteristics of a specific loan. Standard & Poor's publishes separate ratings of four different classes of debt: short-term local currency denominated debt, long-term local currency denominated debt, short-term foreign currency denominated debt, and long-term foreign currency denominated debt.

Short-term applies to a borrower's willingness and ability to repay obligations that are considered short-term by the market in which they are traded, typically debt with a maturity of one year or less. Standard & Poor's assigns one of nine possible short-term issuer credit ratings: A-1+, A-1, A-2, A-3, B, C, R, SD, and D, where A-1+ is the highest rating and D is the lowest. A borrower who is under regulatory supervision because of poor financial conditions receives a rating of R. A borrower who has defaulted on a specific loan or class of loans, but not on all obligations, receives a rating of SD. A borrower who has defaulted on most or all of its obligations receives a rating of D.

Long-term applies to a borrower's willingness and ability to repay obligations that are not short-term, and so typically have a maturity of more than one year. Standard & Poor's assigns sovereign borrowers one of 12 possible long-term credit ratings. The major ratings categories are AAA, AA, A, BBB, BB, B, CCC, CC, C, R, SD, and D, where AAA is the highest rating and D is the lowest. Credit ratings of AA through CCC may also be assigned a + or − sign to indicate relative creditworthiness within the major credit rating category. Ratings of R, SD, and D are assigned to borrowers in the same conditions as they are assigned for short-term debt.

For both short- and long-term debt, Standard & Poor's further differentiates debt according to currency of issue: local or foreign currency. Since the risk factors that influence a country's local currency denominated debt rating are a strict subset of those that influence a country's foreign currency denominated debt rating, different ratings are warranted for each type of issue.

We use the Corruption Perceptions Index (CPI), published by Transparency International, to measure public corruption in a country. The CPI is a composite index compiled from a variety of sources, including surveys of a country's residents, surveys of people doing business in a country, and assessments of experts. The values of the index range from 0 (highly corrupt) to 10 (highly clean). Transparency International requires information from a minimum of three independent sources before rating a country. The CPI is a noisy measure of the quantity of corruption in a country because it is based on subjective opinions and because the sources used to construct the index vary from year to year. However, the CPI is highly correlated with other measures of corruption, such as *The Economist's* Business International ratings, and it has been used in other research to measure corruption (Ciocchini et al. 2003). Each country's corruption score on the CPI is between 1 and 10, where larger numbers indicate less corruption. To make the empirical results more intuitive, we assign each country a corruption score equal to 10 minus the CPI, so larger values indicate more corruption.

A stylized fact in the data is that credit ratings and the CPI are negatively correlated, as Exhibit 9.1 and Exhibit 9.2 illustrate. In Exhibit 9.1, greater levels of public corruption correspond to lower short-term domestic currency bond ratings, which reflect a greater perceived risk of default. Exhibit 9.2 shows a similar relationship between long-term foreign currency bond ratings and public corruption. The relationships between public corruption and the two remaining bond ratings are similar. This stylized empirical finding is the motivation for our analysis.

As public corruption is not the only determinant of a country's creditworthiness, we control for several macroeconomic characteristics that the existing literature (Cantor and Packer 1996) suggests influence a country's credit rating: *GDP per capita* measures the tax base the government can tap to repay debt; *growth* is the annual percent change in real GDP per capita; *inflation* measures the quality of the government's finances and monetary policies, as well as the overall stability of the economy; *fiscal balance* is the government's budget surplus as a fraction of GDP; *external balance* is the current account as a fraction of GDP; *lagged default* is equal to one if a country defaulted on any of its debt in the previous year and zero otherwise; *EU membership* is equal to one if a country is a member of the European

Exhibit 9.1 Estimated Impact of One Standard Deviation Increase in Explanatory Variables on Creditworthiness

Independent Variable	Short-Term Local Currency	Long-Term Local Currency	Short-Term Foreign Currency	Long-Term Foreign Currency
Corruption score	−1.00	−1.18	−1.71	−1.00
Growth	0.04	0.07	0.12	0.04
Inflation	−0.20	−0.26	−0.38	−0.50
GDP per capita	2.34	1.62	1.78	1.50
Fiscal balance	−0.39	−0.72	−0.90	−0.56
External balance	−0.03	−0.19	−0.26	−0.15
Lagged default	−0.01	−0.07	−0.09	−0.05
EU membership	0.60	0.34	2.77	1.80
Trade openness	0.36	0.34	0.50	0.30

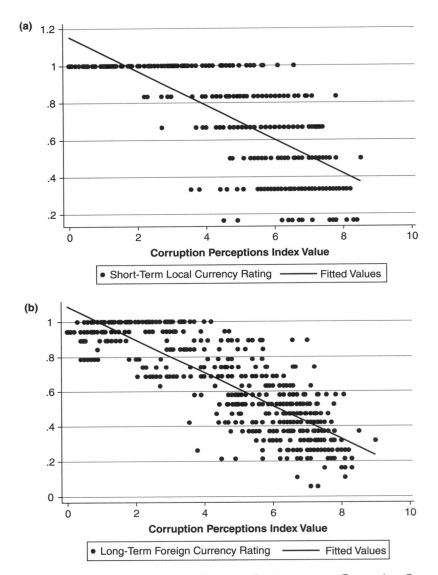

Exhibit 9.2 (a) Short-Term Domestic Currency Ratings versus Corruption Score and (b) Long-Term Foreign Currency Ratings versus Corruption Score

Union (EU) and zero otherwise; and *trade openness* is equal to a country's combined imports and exports as a fraction of GDP.

Our sample consists of data for 57 countries for at least one year between 1995 and 2003, inclusive. The sample includes both developed and developing countries, as well as countries from every region of the world. Data for every country are not available for every year, so our panel is unbalanced. Since credit ratings data are ordinal in nature, we employ an ordered probit estimator to estimate the impact of corruption on creditworthiness. The overall relationship between credit ratings and the explanatory variables is statistically significant at the 1 percent level.[3]

For all four types of debt, creditworthiness increases with GDP per capita and openness to trade, but decreases with the rate of inflation and a default in the previous year. Membership in the European Union has a positive impact on debt ratings in the case of foreign currency denominated debt but does not affect debt issued in the local currency. Growth in GDP per capita has a positive but statistically insignificant impact on creditworthiness. We find that creditworthiness decreases with fiscal balance and, for all but short-term local currency denominated debt, external balance. Previous research suggests that both fiscal balance and external balance should be positively related to creditworthiness. We conjecture that these results are driven by developed countries that tend to run deficits and have negative current account balances, but also good credit ratings.

Exhibit 9.1 reports the estimated impact of a one standard deviation increase in the particular variable on creditworthiness, holding all other variables at their sample means. We find that a one standard deviation increase in a country's corruption score causes that country's sovereign credit rating to deteriorate by almost one full rating category for all four types of debt. Furthermore, the effect is larger than a similar shock to any explanatory variable other than GDP per capita. However, these average effects mask considerable differences across countries.

For example, for the United States, a one standard deviation increase in its corruption score reduces its probability of getting the top rating in each class, and increases its probability of getting every other rating. For India, a one standard deviation increase in its corruption score reduces its probability of getting the top four short-term local currency credit ratings, the top four long-term local currency credit ratings, the top five short-term foreign currency credit ratings, and the top five long-term foreign currency debt ratings, and increases its probability of getting every other rating.

Combining the estimation results presented here with those of other authors facilitates a back-of-the-envelope calculation of the benefits from reducing corruption. Sy (2001) estimates that a one-unit increase in long-term foreign currency creditworthiness causes bond spreads to decrease by about 14.6 percent. In this case, the bond spread for a country is a weighted average of the difference between the interest rates on individual bonds issued by that country and the comparable U.S. Treasury bond. Controlling for the characteristics of the bond and creditworthiness is measured on a scale from 0 to 20. In our analysis, long-term foreign currency creditworthiness is measured on a scale from 1 to 11. It follows that a one-unit change in creditworthiness measured by Sy is equivalent to a 0.5 unit change in creditworthiness on our scale. Thus, a one-unit increase in creditworthiness, measured on our scale, corresponds to a 29 percent ($=100(0.146)(1=0.5)$) decrease in bond spread.

The average long-term foreign currency sovereign bond spread in a sample of emerging market countries was 347 basis points (Ciocchini et al. 2003). Thus, a one standard deviation decrease in corruption score causes the bond spread to fall by about $101(=0.29 \pounds 347)$ basis points. If the annual interest rate on a U.S. 10-year Treasury bond is about 6 percent, then this implies that the average interest rate on long-term foreign currency denominated debt is about 9.47 percent annually and falls to 8.46 percent.

These calculations suggest that a one standard deviation decrease in corruption leads to a savings of about $10,000 per $1 million of debt. For example, Argentina had about $127,687 million in debt outstanding at the end of 2003 (World Bank 2005). Reducing corruption in Argentina by one standard deviation in 2003, to the level of Tunisia, would save approximately $1,289 million in interest annually. In 2003, Argentina had a gross domestic product of approximately $129,596 million. Therefore, without accounting for the costs of reducing corruption, reducing corruption in Argentina by one standard deviation before the debt was issued could have saved as much as 1 percent of the nation's gross domestic product.

Another example is that of Chile. In 2003, Chile had approximately $35,727 million in outstanding debt (World Bank 2005). A one standard deviation improvement in Chile's corruption index would put that country on par with Finland, the least corrupt country in 2003. Chile would have been able to save approximately $361 million in annual interest payments had its corruption been reduced to this level when the debt was issued. In 2003, Chile's GDP was approximately $72,415 million. The reduced interest payments would represent about 0.5 percent of Chile's GDP.

We are not the first to investigate the relationship between public corruption and economic variables of interest. An alternative approach to measure corruption's impact on the cost of sovereign debt is to measure corruption's effect on bond spreads directly. Ciocchini et al. (2003) find that a one-point increase in the CPI increases the spread on foreign currency denominated bonds issued by an emerging market country by approximately 26 percent. The standard deviation of CPI values for the countries in their sample is about 1.5, whereas the standard deviation in our sample is 2.5, and the average sovereign bond spread for their sample is 347 basis points. Thus, a one standard deviation increase in the CPI will increase the spread on the average bond by about 135 basis points. Our estimate is slightly smaller—101 basis points.

Estimates of corruption's effect on U.S. state and municipal debt are qualitatively similar. Depken and LaFountain (2006) find that corruption imposes economically significant borrowing costs on U.S. states and municipalities. Butler et al. (2009) further point out that the magnitude of the cost varies dramatically with the institutional arrangement employed to issue a particular bond. For example, corrupt states are more likely to have credit insurance, to have a letter-of-credit backing, or to have their bonds underwritten by investment banks with good reputations. Whether sovereign countries can substitute similar third-party institutions for a lack of corruption to better signal creditworthiness to the market is an important matter for future research. This is important because sovereign debt carries no collateral or other enforceable guarantees of repayment.

Estimates of corruption's effect on creditworthiness contribute to the larger literature on the economic impact of corruption. Is corruption detrimental to an economy? If so, what is the magnitude of the problem? Micro-level studies find that corruption imposes economically significant costs on businesses and households. For example, the growth rate of sales of Ugandan firms in the mid-1990s fell by at least 3 percentage points, on average, when the fraction of sales allocated to bribes increased by 1 percent (Fisman and Svensson 2000); the prices public hospitals in Argentina paid for inputs produced in competitive markets fell by 10 to 15 percent following a crackdown on corruption during 1996 and 1997

(Di Tella and Schargrodsky 2003); primary schools in Uganda received only 13 percent, on average, of grants intended to finance their nonwage expenses (Reinikka and Svensson 2004); and approximately 18 percent of the rice intended for distribution to poor households in Indonesia in the late 1990s went missing (Olken 2005).

These studies provide relatively precise estimates of the costs of corruption in specific situations, but they are only partial equilibrium measures. If the corruption identified by these studies involves merely transfers of resources, then corruption might not have a significant aggregate economic effect.

Macro-level studies suggest that the aggregate effects of corruption are negative and economically significant. For example, corruption has been shown to be negatively correlated with education expenditures, infrastructure quality, birth weights, trade openness, political stability, investment, productivity, foreign direct investment, and net capital flows, and positively correlated with infant and childhood mortality rates and primary school dropout rates. Strikingly, there is no robust evidence that corruption has a significant impact on economic growth.

However, macro-level data can have two problems: First, when the unit of observation is the country, it is difficult to identify any truly exogenous variables. It is likely that the level of corruption and the dependent variables listed earlier are all outcomes of some underlying, unobserved process.

For example, high levels of corruption, low productivity, and political instability may all be equilibrium values of endogenous variables. Thus, it is not clear that corruption causes low productivity and political instability.

Second, the quality of the data used in these studies may itself be correlated with the level of corruption. If corruption in the formal sector drives economic activity into the informal sector, but data reflect only what takes place in the formal sector, then variables like investment and productivity will have measurement error. Furthermore, the measurement error will be positively related to the level of corruption. Thus, the results of many macro-level studies need to be interpreted with these issues in mind.

Our study is less likely to suffer from these problems as the dependent variables used here, sovereign credit ratings, reflect third-party opinions of the willingness and ability of sovereigns to repay their debt. Even if the quality of the data used by the ratings agencies is affected by corruption, the ratings agencies should incorporate this information in their final assessment. Bond spreads, the dependent variable used by Ciocchini et al. (2003), are determined by international capital markets, which are relatively competitive and in which any single emerging-market country is unlikely to have any market power. Thus, the processes determining sovereign credit ratings and bond spreads are likely to be independent of those determining corruption levels in different countries. As a result, we may place slightly more confidence in our results that corruption has a negative and economically significant impact on a country's creditworthiness.

NOTES

1. A thorough discussion of sovereign debt is beyond the scope of this paper. Hermalin and Rose (1999) provide a good start for looking into the issues.

2. Our results are robust across different estimators, including country-specific random effects, and controlling for selection bias. These additional empirical results are available upon request.

3. Empirical results are available upon request.

REFERENCES

Butler, Alexander W., Larry Fauver, and Sandra Mortal. 2009. "Corruption, Political Connections, and Municipal Finance." *Review of Financial Studies* 22:7, 2873–2905.

Cantor, Richard, and Frank Packer. 1996. "Determinants and Impact of Sovereign Credit Ratings." *Federal Reserve Bank of New York Economic Policy Review*. October, 37–53.

Ciocchini, Francisco, Erik Durbin, and David T. C. Ng. 2003. "Does Corruption Increase Emerging Market Bond Spreads?" *Journal of Economics and Business* 55: 503–528.

Depken, Craig, and Courtney LaFountain. 2006. "Fiscal Consequences of Public Corruption: Empirical Evidence from State Bond Ratings." *Public Choice* 126:1–2, 75–85.

Di Tella, Rafael, and Ernesto Schargrodsky. 2003. "The Role of Wages and Auditing during a Crackdown on Corruption in the City of Buenos Aires." *Journal of Law and Economics* 46:1, 269–292.

Fisman, Raymond, and Jakob Svensson. 2000. "Are Corruption and Taxation Really Harmful to Growth? Firm-Level Evidence." *World Bank Policy Research Working Paper*, No. 2485. http://ssrn.com/abstract=632555.

Hermalin, Benjamin E., and Andrew K. Rose. 1999. "Risks to Lenders and Borrowers in International Capital Markets." *NBER Working Paper*, No. 6886.

Olken, Benjamin. 2005. "Corruption and the Costs of Redistribution: Micro Evidence from Indonesia." *NBER Working Paper*, No. 11753.

Reinikka, Ritva, and Jakob Svensson. 2004. "Local Capture: Evidence from a Central Government Transfer Program in Uganda." *Quarterly Journal of Economics* 119:2, 679–705.

Sy, Amadou N. R. 2001. "Emerging Market Bond Spreads and Sovereign Credit Ratings: Reconciling Market Views with Economic Fundamentals." *IMF Working Paper*, No. 01/165. Available at SSRN: http://ssrn.com/abstract=292954 or DOI: 10.2139/ssrn.292954.

The World Bank. 2005. *World Development Indicators*. Washington, DC: The World Bank.

ABOUT THE AUTHORS

Craig A. Depken II holds a PhD in economics from the University of Georgia (1996). He has been an economics professor at the University of Texas at Arlington and is currently at the Belk College of Business at the University of North Carolina at Charlotte. He has published extensively in the areas of applied microeconomics, industrial organization, sports economics, and public choice. He is the author of more than 40 peer-reviewed articles and of the book *Microeconomics Demystified*, published by McGraw-Hill (2005).

Courtney L. LaFountain is an economist at the U.S. Government Accountability Office. She received her PhD from Washington University in Saint Louis. Dr. LaFountain has done research in urban and regional economics and public finance, and has published in the *Journal of Urban Economics, Public Choice*, the *Journal of Public Economic Theory*, and the *International Journal of Economic Theory*.

Roger B. Butters, PhD, is an assistant professor of economics at the University of Nebraska–Lincoln and the president of the Nebraska Council on Economic Education. His primary research interests are economic education, international finance, and growth. Dr. Butters has taught seminars on economics and international finance at universities in the United States, Europe, and China and has lectured on capitalism and poverty as part of the Goldman Sachs Leadership Institute in Brazil and Australia. His published works include assessments of economic learning and standardized testing instruments. He is a recipient of the *Lincoln Business Journal*'s 40 under 40 award, a Paul Harris Fellow and was recognized by the National Association of Economic Educators as the inaugural recipient of its Rising Star award. Dr. Butters can be reached at rbutters3@unl.edu.

CHAPTER 10

Institutions, Financial Integration, and Complementarity

NICOLA GENNAIOLI
Researcher, Centre de Recerca en Economia Internacional

ALBERTO MARTIN
Researcher, Centre de Recerca en Economia Internacional

STEFANO ROSSI
Assistant Professor of Finance, Imperial College Business School

We discuss the role of financial institutions in sustaining foreign borrowing by a country's private and public sectors, thus allowing it to benefit from financial integration. We exploit Gennaioli, Martin, and Rossi's (2010) notion of complementarity, which arises naturally whenever public defaults are disruptive of private financial markets. By boosting private borrowing, strong financial institutions reduce the risk of public defaults and boost public borrowing as well. We build on this notion to interpret some broad patterns of financial globalization of the last 30 years and we briefly explore its policy implications.

INTRODUCTION

Financial reform, defined as the strengthening of legal enforcement, investor rights, and corporate governance, scores high on the list of second-generation reforms that promise to enable emerging economies to reap the benefits of financial integration (IMF 1999; IADB 2006). Economic theory and empirical evidence confirm that better financial institutions enhance the ability of domestic financial systems to attract foreign funds and employ them efficiently (for example, Caballero and Krishnamurthy 2001; Alfaro, Kalemli-Ozcan, and Volosovych 2008). Despite its intuitive appeal, this view overlooks the fact that foreign investors in emerging economies are wary not only of the risks associated with the domestic legal and financial infrastructures, but also of those generated by the local government. That is, over and above direct expropriation by capital users, investors in emerging economies are subject to the risk that the government may indirectly hinder their returns through such policies as currency devaluation, inflation, and default (Tirole 2002). This possibility raises one key question: Does the presence of this type of government agency obliterate the role of financial reforms in support-ing effective globalization, or does it still leave significant room for them?

The importance of this question is evident in the case of public defaults, which represent a major form of government agency in the real world. During sovereign debt crises in Russia, Ecuador, Pakistan, Ukraine, and Argentina (see IMF 2002), public defaults have been followed by private financial turmoil, resulting in severe contractions in credit and output. In these episodes, default often spread to the private sector through banks' holdings of government bonds. For example, the Russian default in 1998 triggered large balance sheet losses on Russian banks, which had heavily invested in their government's bonds. The ensuing financial sector meltdown meant that foreign investors were doubly hurt: Besides the direct loss suffered through their holdings of public bonds, they also suffered an indirect loss through the default of private banks that were exposed to these bonds.

At first glance, these events seem to suggest that sound market institutions such as strong creditor rights and good corporate governance can play only a limited role because they do not directly constrain the government's ability to default. In reality, however, public default risk appears to be lower in countries characterized by stronger legal and financial systems (Reinhart, Rogoff, and Savastano 2003; Kraay and Nehru 2006), suggesting that—contrary to common intuition—financial institutions may indeed help to dampen public default risk even if they do not directly constrain the government.

Gennaioli et al. (2010) study this link between financial institutions and public default risk both theoretically and empirically. In their model, public defaults exert an adverse shock to the balance sheets of banks, leading to a contraction in credit, investment, and output. Crucially, better institutions render this contraction more severe by allowing banks to take on more leverage, for leverage amplifies the impact of an adverse shock to the balance sheet of banks. Consequently, the disruption in credit and output generated by government defaults, and thus their social cost, is predicted to be greater in countries having better financial institutions. These countries will thus be characterized by a lower risk of public default: Their governments will repay their debts to avoid inflicting large losses on the domestic banking sector. Gennaioli et al. (2010) provide thorough and systematic evidence showing that the post-default financial turmoil is indeed stronger in countries with better institutions, corroborating the key prediction of their model.

One crucial implication of this analysis is that better institutions promote a key complementarity between private and public sector borrowing. For a given amount of public debt, better financial institutions allow the country's private sector to attract more foreign financing, thereby boosting banks' leverage (and the cost of public default) above the level attainable in the absence of foreign lending. By so doing, strong institutions reduce the government's incentive to default and facilitate public borrowing as well. By contrast, the inability of institutionally weak countries to attract or retain private capital also boosts public default risk, reducing public as well as private foreign borrowing.

This notion of complementarity is absent from existing models of sovereign risk, which do not generally distinguish between public and private capital flows. In this chapter, we discuss how such complementarity can help shed important new light on the determinants of capital flows, on the costs and benefits of financial integration and—going back to our original question—on the role of financial reform in a world plagued by public default risk.

The chapter is organized as follows. The next section briefly summarizes the theoretical and empirical results of Gennaioli et al. (2010) on the link between public default risk and financial institutions. This section illustrates the working of complementarity and provides empirical evidence that supports it, providing the bedrock for the rest of our analysis. The section after that puts the notion of complementarity to work, discussing how it may help to rationalize some broad patterns of capital flows and financial crises in the last 30 years, and how it may shed light on the costs and benefits of financial openness. The last section discusses the normative implications of complementarity with respect to the form and timing of institutional reform in emerging economies.

INSTITUTIONS AND PUBLIC DEFAULT RISK

The model in Gennaioli et al. (2010) features a government that, although benevolent, is opportunistic and can choose to default on its debts. In the spirit of Broner and Ventura (2010), it is assumed that the government cannot discriminate between local and foreign bondholders. In this model, domestic banks choose to hold public bonds as a store of liquidity (Holmström and Tirole 1993), implying that the government's decision to default involves a trade-off. On the one hand, default beneficially increases total domestic resources for consumption, as some public bonds are held abroad. On the other hand, and in line with the aforementioned debt crises, a default also hurts domestic banks holding public bonds, thereby hampering credit, investment, and output.[1]

In this setup, better financial institutions increase the government's cost of default through two main effects. First, as previously described, better institutions boost the leverage of banks, which amplifies the adverse impact of defaults on bank intermediation. Second, for a given amount of public debt, better financial institutions allow the country's private sector to attract more foreign financing. Larger capital inflows to the country's private sector in turn increase the cost (and reduce the benefit) of defaulting for the government by allowing domestic banks to boost leverage further, enhancing credit and investment, and domestic agents to hold more public debt, reducing the share of such debt that is externally held.

If institutions are sufficiently good, these two effects are so strong that they discipline the government into repaying its debt. This is the notion of complementarity: By attracting private inflows, strong institutions reduce public default risk, facilitating public borrowing as well. By contrast, the inability of institutionally weak countries to attract or retain private capital boosts public default risk, reducing public as well as private borrowing.

Gennaioli et al. (2010) provide ample empirical evidence on the link between government default and domestic financial markets. They construct a large panel of emerging and developed countries spanning the period between 1980 and 2005. They measure the quality of financial institutions by using the creditor rights score of La Porta et al. (1998), which is the leading institutional predictor of credit market development around the world (Djankov, McLiesh, and Shleifer 2007). Consistently with anecdotal evidence, their econometric analysis shows that public defaults are followed by large and systematic contractions of aggregate financial activity in the defaulting country. In defaulting countries, the flow in private credit drops on average by 8.6 percent, which amounts to a decrease of 2.4 percent in terms of GDP. Crucially, and consistently with the subtler predictions of the model, the post-default credit crunch is stronger in countries in which banks hold more public debt, and where financial institutions are stronger. A one-standard-deviation increase in banks' holdings of public debt in a defaulting country is associated with a more severe contraction in the flow of private credit, which falls by an additional 69% of a standard deviation. An increase by one in the creditor rights score in a defaulting country (for example, moving from a score of 1, as in Argentina, to a score of 2, as in Chile) is associated with a more severe reduction in the flow of private credit of 5.7 percent, which amounts to 1.7 percent in terms of GDP.

These results are extremely robust. Gennaioli et al. (2010) control for country and time fixed effects,[2] as well as for a large set of (internal and external) country-specific economic shocks that may jointly affect private credit and a government's decision to default. They also control in various ways for ex ante default risk, which—in line with the predictions of the theoretical model—allows them to identify the effect of default on financial markets out of unanticipated default events. The data also show that, consistently with the model, government debt is more easily sustained in countries in which financial institutions are stronger and intermediaries hold more public debt.

CAPITAL FLOWS, PUBLIC DEFAULTS, AND COMPLEMENTARITY

The previous section has discussed how, during recent default episodes, the interaction between public default and private credit has been consistent with the notion of complementarity. We now argue that this same notion can be used to interpret some broad patterns that have characterized capital flows in the last 30 years.

Basic Facts

It is well known that, starting in the mid-1990s, there has been a steady increase in private capital flows to emerging economies (Kose et al. 2006). This boost in private flows has mainly financed the operations of private-sector actors such as industrial firms and financial institutions through private bonds, portfolio equity, and FDI (for example, Lane and Milesi-Ferretti 2007). If complementarity is present in the data, we would expect such boost in private capital inflows to have reduced public default risk.

Exhibit 10.1 displays raw data, for the 1980–2004 period, both for the number of sovereign defaults from Standard & Poor's[3] (solid line) and for a measure of privately held external debt over GDP (dashed line).[4] The data correspond to a representative sample from the World Bank of 56 emerging countries.

The pattern in Exhibit 10.1 is striking. The significant increase in (median) private flows to emerging markets during the 1990s, from about 3.5 percent to about 15 percent of GDP (left-hand side of the scale), was associated with a stark

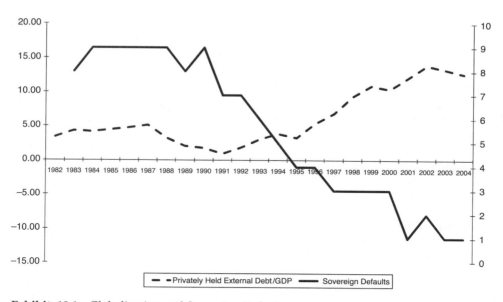

Exhibit 10.1   Globalization and Sovereign Defaults

decline in the total number of public defaults, from eight or nine per year in the 1980s to one or two at the beginning of the 2000s (right-hand side of the scale).

Naturally, this pattern could be due to many other reasons besides complementarity. It could, for example, result from a substitution of public with private debt that rendered the former more sustainable. During the period covered in Exhibit 10.1, public debt in Latin America (Cowan et al. 2006), as well as in Asia (Jeanne and Guscina 2006), was stable or moderately rising, however, which seems contrary to the possibility of substitution.

A second possible explanation for the pattern in Exhibit 10.1 lies in the period itself, since the 1990s were a tranquil period characterized by low interest rates and a wave of deregulation, privatizations, and liberalization programs in emerging countries. It is not surprising that the low cost of capital and the surge in private-sector investment opportunities jointly catalyzed private financing and reduced public default risk. Somewhat contrary to this period-based explanation, however, is that this co-movement between private financing and public default risk seems to be something of a historical regularity.

In this regard, Reinhart and Rogoff (2008) have recently adopted a broader historical perspective and shown that in the last 200 years boosts in private and public sector borrowing have gone hand in hand. During these booms, public and private debt crises were episodic and isolated. The end of these periods of bonanza, though, which was often due to turmoil in international financial markets, was associated with clusters of public defaults and banking crises.

Our model can help rationalize these patterns by stressing that since public and private borrowing complement one another, booms and busts in sovereign debt and private credit should be synchronized. Exhibit 10.1 is thus consistent with the possibility that the run-up of private capital flows during the last 30 years[5] has reduced public default risk by reducing the incentive of governments to default on public debt.

To further inquire about this possibility, our model invites the following subtler test. If it is the case that higher inflows progressively reduced public default risk by increasing the costs of public default, we should expect the disruptions in private credit experienced after public defaults to increase over time as private capital flows increase. To see whether this is the case, Exhibit 10.2 adds to Exhibit 10.1 the change in private credit to GDP experienced by defaulting countries.

Consistently with complementarity, Exhibit 10.2 shows that recent defaults are followed by progressively more severe reductions in private credit (as much as 10 percent of GDP, dotted line and right-hand side of the scale). This prediction, which follows naturally from complementarity, is harder to reconcile with the period-based explanation that views Exhibit 10.1 as the result of a tranquil international financial system. Not only does such a view fail to establish a causal link from public defaults to credit crunches, but it also seems to suggest that—even if they are purely coincidental and do not reflect any causal link—these credit crunches should, if anything, have become smaller in recent times, given booming liquidity and stable financial markets.

By contrast, Exhibit 10.2 seems consistent with the narrative of public defaults in the late 1990s such as those in Russia, Ecuador, and Indonesia. In each of these default episodes, there were particular idiosyncratic shocks that played an important role: In all of them, however, domestic banks suffered severe losses, not least because capital inflows had allowed these banks to become highly leveraged. Because of the ensuing fragility, public defaults greatly hurt private credit by hindering the ability of banks and firms to absorb new capital from domestic as

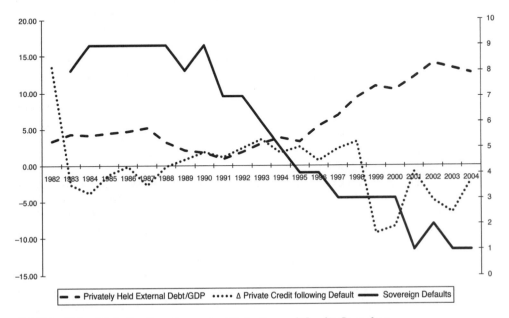

Exhibit 10.2 Globalization, Sovereign Defaults, and Credit Crunches

well as foreign investors (Arteta and Hale 2008). This narrative seems also consistent with complementarity: Just as capital inflows allow banks to expand their balance sheets ex ante, they also make these banks more vulnerable to unexpected shocks that induce the government to default ex post.

Threshold Effects and the Benefits of Financial Integration

The previous discussion suggests that complementarity can help interpret some of the evidence on the effects of financial liberalization. Indeed, one formal implication of Gennaioli et al. (2010) is that financial liberalization may have adverse effects in countries with weak financial institutions. In these countries, capital inflows in tranquil times allow the banking sector to become more leveraged despite the lack of strong institutions. This lack of institutions, though, means that these countries face a higher risk of experiencing capital-flow reversals leading to public defaults and thus to default-induced crises, which will be particularly severe precisely because of the high leverage of the banking sector. This effect may cause financial liberalization to be welfare decreasing. Even though a shutdown of capital inflows would reduce investment in these economies, it would also reduce their vulnerability to public default risk. This is not the case for countries having strong institutions, however. In these countries, private capital inflows reinforce the quality of institutions in boosting both leverage and the government's incentive to repay, thereby enhancing private investment and reducing public default risk. This aspect of complementarity resonates well with the empirical evidence on financial liberalization.

It is well known that the financial liberalizations of the 1990s were not uniformly beneficial for all countries (Eichengreen 2004). Formal econometric analyses (Kose et al. 2006) further suggest the presence of threshold effects, whereby financial liberalization has benefited only countries with sufficiently good institutions. Complementarity can help rationalize these threshold effects in the context of public default risk.[6] It suggests in particular that the large vulnerability of countries such as Russia, Ecuador, or Indonesia (but also of subsequent defaulters like Argentina, Ukraine, or Pakistan) to public defaults was due, at least in part, to financial liberalization that occurred in the absence of reforms aimed at strengthening domestic market institutions, the so-called second generation reforms.

CONCLUSION

We have illustrated how the notion of complementarity can shed light on the interaction between capital flows to the public and private sectors. We conclude this chapter by discussing some policy implications that are derived from this view.

Our analysis has important implications for the optimal sequencing of liberalization and reforms. At the most basic level, it suggests that emerging economies are more likely to gain from financial integration if they first develop their domestic financial markets. This is because developed markets provide the government with incentives to avoid public default crises.[7] Without prior market reform, financial liberalization will tend to exacerbate the financial fragility of these economies through public default risk. These considerations underscore the importance of prioritizing the reform of financial institutions such as creditor rights and corporate governance.

More broadly, our analysis has related implications for the privatization of the banking sector and for the decentralization of foreign borrowing.[8] Key to these latter reforms is that they produce a separation between public and private sector borrowing. Such separation is important, for it is precisely because private external debt and public debt are separated that a public default can hurt the private sector's access to foreign finance. In contrast, if a country's external borrowing is fully consolidated in the government budget (for example, through public ownership of banks), a public default always improves the net financial position of the country and government vis-à-vis foreigners. As a result, default ceases to inflict domestic costs, boosting public default risk.

Both of these implications point to an important change in perspective that may emerge from complementarity: Namely, that to successfully sustain financial integration, the reform of domestic market infrastructures is perhaps more important than the reform of the international financial architecture.

NOTES

1. The government may try to default and bail out domestic banks, de facto restoring discrimination. In the model of Gennaioli et al. (2010), bailouts are not feasible because of the very foundation for nondiscrimination, namely, the presence of secondary markets (Broner, Martin, and Ventura 2010). In reality, these bailouts are indeed not effective, also for a number of other reasons, including, for example, asymmetric information on the quality of banks.

2. Country fixed effects absorb all time invariant variation in the effects and prevalence of sovereign default across countries, stemming, for example, from cross-country differences in policy that are unrelated to creditor rights; time fixed effects absorb shocks that are common across countries such as changes in world interest rates.

3. Standard & Poor's defines sovereign default as the failure of an obligor to meet a principal or interest payment on the due date (or within the specified grace period) contained in the original terms of the debt issue. A debt restructuring where the new debt contains less favorable terms than the original issue is also counted as default. According to this measure, a fall in the number of defaults may also be generated by a reduction in the time needed to resolve debt crises. We checked for this possibility in the data and found that the fall in the number of defaults over time is, however, robust to controlling the duration of default episodes.

4. Private debt is a good proxy for the private foreign capital obtained by emerging economies in our sample, because debt accounts for the bulk of total private flows. Following the East Asian crisis, there has been a reallocation of these capital flows toward FDIs, but the volume of flows to emerging economies has continued to increase throughout and the share of these flows accounted for by private debt remains sizable.

5. For our immediate purposes, it is of secondary interest whether this pattern is due to increasing financial liberalizations (Henry 2000) or to other factors.

6. Others before us have noted that financial liberalization may fail if it is not preceded by reforms aimed at strengthening domestic markets, the so-called second generation reforms. Among these, our approach is perhaps closest to Caballero and Krishnamurthy (2001), who show how domestic financial frictions can aggravate the negative effects of

binding external borrowing constraints. In our model, it is domestic financial frictions themselves that determine the country's external borrowing constraint, which arises endogenously as a result of the government's incentives to repay its debt.

7. Of course, these normative considerations abstract from political economy constraints. In the presence of those constraints it might actually be optimal to liberalize, because only by doing so could it be possible to build a political coalition favorable to a more extensive institutional reform. See Caselli and Gennaioli (2008) for an argument along those lines.

8. This is in stark contrast to existing models of sovereign risk, which suggest that the government should oversee capital flows to avoid harmful overborrowing externalities among private borrowers. For a basic exposition of the overborrowing argument, see Eaton and Fernandez (1995). For more recent settings in which overborrowing may arise, see Jeske (2006), Wright (2006), and Broner and Ventura (2010).

REFERENCES

Alfaro, Laura, Sebnem Kalemli-Ozcan, and Vadym Volosovych. 2008. "Why Doesn't Capital Flow from Rich to Poor Countries? An Empirical Investigation." *The Review of Economics and Statistics* 90: 347–368.

Arteta, Carlos, and Galina Hale. 2008. "Sovereign Debt Crises and Credit to the Private Sector." *Journal of International Economics* 74: 53–69.

Broner, Fernando A., and Jaume Ventura. 2010. "Rethinking the Effects of Financial Liberalization." *Working Paper*. Barcelona, Spain: Centre de Recerca en Economia.

Broner, Fernando, Alberto Martin, and Jaume Ventura. 2010. "Sovereign Risk and Secondary Markets." *American Economic Review* 100: 1523–1555.

Caballero, Ricardo J., and Arvind Krishnamurthy. 2001. "International and Domestic Collateral Constraints in a Model of Emerging Market Crises." *Journal of Monetary Economics* 48: 513–548.

Caselli, Francesco, and Nicola Gennaioli. 2008. "Economics and Politics of Alternative Institutional Reforms." *Quarterly Journal of Economics* 123: 1197–1250.

Cowan, Kevin, Eduardo Levy-Yeyati, Ugo Panizza, and Federico Sturzenegger. 2006. "Sovereign Debt in the Americas: New Data and Stylized Facts." *Working Paper*, No. 577. Washington, DC: Inter-American Development Bank.

Djankov, Simeon, Caralee McLiesh, and Andrei Shleifer. 2007. "Private Credit in 129 Countries." *Journal of Financial Economics* 84: 299–329.

Eaton, Jonathan and Raquel Fernandez. 1995. "Sovereign debt." In G. Grossman and K. Rogoff, eds. *Handbook of International Economics III*. Amsterdam: Elsevier/North-Holland.

Eichengreen, Barry. 2004. *Capital Flows and Crises*. Cambridge, MA: MIT Press.

Gennaioli, Nicola, Alberto Martin, and Stefano Rossi. 2010. *Sovereign Default, Domestic Banks and Financial Institutions*. Barcelona, Spain: Centre de Recerca en Economia and Imperial College.

Henry, Peter Blair. 2000. "Stock Market Liberalization, Economic Reform, and Emerging Market Equity Prices." *Journal of Finance* 55: 529–564.

Holmström, Bengt, and Jean Tirole. 1993. "Market Liquidity and Performance Monitoring." *Journal of Political Economy* 101: 678–709.

Inter-American Development Bank. 2006. *Living with Debt: How to Limit the Risks of Sovereign Finance*. Cambridge, MA: David Rockefeller Center for Latin American Studies.

International Monetary Fund. 1999. "Second Generation Reforms: Reflections and New Challenges." Opening Remarks to IMF Conference on Second Generation Reforms by Michel Camdessus, Managing director of the International Monetary Fund. www.imf.org/external/np/speeches/1999/110899.htm.

———. 2002. *Sovereign Debt Restructurings and the Domestic Economy Experience in Four Recent Cases*. Washington, DC: International Monetary Fund, Policy Development and Review Department.

Jeanne, Olivier, and Anastasia Guscina. 2006. "Government Debt in Emerging Market Countries: A New Data Set." *IMF Working Paper* 06/98.

Jeske, Karsten. 2006. "Private International Debt with Risk of Repudiation." *Journal of Political Economy* 114: 576–593.

Kose, M. Ayhan, Eswar Prasad, Kenneth Rogoff, and Shang-Jin Wei. 2006. "Financial Globalization: A Reappraisal." *Working Paper*, IMF.

Kraay, Aart, and Vikram Nehru. 2006. "When Is External Debt Sustainable?" *World Bank Economic Review* 20:3, 341–366.

Lane, Philip R., and Gian Maria Milesi-Ferretti. 2007. "The External Wealth of Nations, Mark II: Revised and Extended Estimates of Foreign Assets and Liabilities, 1970–2004." *Journal of International Economics* 73: 223–250.

La Porta, Rafael, Florencio Lopez-de-Silanes, Andrei Shleifer, and Robert W. Vishny. 1998. "Law and Finance." *Journal of Political Economy* 101: 678–709.

Reinhart, Carmen M., and Kenneth Rogoff. 2008. "This Time Is Different: A Panoramic View of Eight Centuries of Financial Crises." *NBER Working Paper*, No. 13882.

Reinhart, Carmen M., Kenneth Rogoff, and Miguel A. Savastano. 2003. "Debt Intolerance." *Brookings Papers on Economic Activity* 1: 1–74.

Tirole, Jean. 2002. *Financial Crisis, Liquidity and the International Monetary System*. Princeton, NJ: Princeton University Press.

Wright, Mark L. J. 2006. "Private Capital Flows, Capital Controls, and Default Risk." *Working Paper*. Federal Reserve Bank of San Francisco.

ABOUT THE AUTHORS

Nicola Gennaioli earned his PhD in economics at Harvard University in 2004. He is currently a researcher at the Centre de Recerca en Economia Internacional (CREI) and an adjunct professor in the economics department at the Universitat Pompeu Fabra. He has had a Ramon y Cajal Fellowship since 2008. In 2009, he was awarded a European Research Council Starting Grant. His research interests include law and economics, contract theory, political economy and economic development. He can be reached at ngennaioli@crei.cat.

Alberto Martin is a researcher at the Centre de Recerca en Economia Internacional (CREI), an adjunct professor at Universitat Pompeu Fabra, and a research fellow at the Center for Economic and Policy Research. His research interests include financial economics, international economics, and macroeconomics. Within these areas, Professor Martin has conducted research on the effects of asymmetric information in financial markets, on sovereign risk and enforcement problems, and on the nature and consequences of asset bubbles. He has also worked as an economist in Argentina's Ministry of Economics and as a consultant for the United Nations Development Program. He holds a PhD and an MA in economics from Columbia University, an MA in economics from the Instituto Torcuato Di Tella in Buenos Aires, and an undergraduate degree in economics from the Universidad Nacional de Cuyo in Mendoza, Argentina. He can be reached at amartin@crei.cat.

Stefano Rossi is an assistant professor of finance at Imperial College Business School and a visiting assistant professor of finance at the Johnson Graduate School of Management at Cornell University. He is a research affiliate of the Center for Economic and Policy Research (CEPR), a research associate of the European Corporate Governance Institute (ECGI), and an associate editor of *European Financial Management*. Before joining Imperial College, he was a faculty member at the Stockholm School of Economics. His research focuses on bankruptcy and financial distress, corporate governance, international finance, and asset pricing and trading with frictions. His recently published research on ownership and control (with J. Franks and C. Mayer) has won two international prizes. He holds a BA and an MSc in economics from Bocconi University, and a PhD in finance from London Business School. He can be reached at srossi@imperial.ac.uk.

CHAPTER 11

Loans versus Bonds

The Importance of Potential Liquidity Problems for Sovereign Borrowers

ISSAM HALLAK
Assistant Professor, the Department of Finance of Bocconi University

PAUL SCHURE
Associate Professor, the University of Victoria, Canada

D o sovereign borrowers care whether they attract funds through the sovereign loan market or the sovereign bond market? Research on corporate debt suggests that loans and bonds are fundamentally different. Loans are usually associated with a limited number of credit relationships, while bond holdings tend to be more dispersed. Differences in the number of credit relationships implies that the incentives to screen and monitor borrowers are generally different for lenders and bond holders. Furthermore, banks, as important institutions on the supply side of the loan market, are special. Diamond and Rajan (2001) explain that their dependence on deposit financing can make banks superior monitors and Coleman, Esho, and Sharpe (2006) provides supporting evidence.

In this chapter we discuss a second reason why loans and bonds are different: Lenders and bond holders may differ in their treatment of illiquid borrowers.[1] In case illiquidity strikes, lenders may allow for relatively efficient renegotiation, while dispersed bondholders may face severe coordination problems, which can lead to substantial delay or a failure of loan renegotiations. This story is consistent with the models of Bolton and Scharfstein (1996) and Morris and Shin (2004) and the evidence of Sturzenegger and Zettelmeyer (2007) and Brunner and Krahnen (2008). Banks may also prove to be special lenders when it comes to addressing borrower illiquidity. For example, Elsas and Krahnen (1998), Boot (2000), and others show that relationship banks act as liquidity insurers in situations of liquidity problems of borrowers.

Until very recently, however, empirical evidence in the sovereign loans market failed to show that borrower illiquidity affects the interest spreads on sovereign bank loans, whereas indicators of borrower illiquidity do affect sovereign bond spreads (Edwards 1986; Eichengreen and Mody 2000). This evidence seems to suggest that the management of liquidity shortages is either unimportant to borrowers in the sovereign loan market or provided for free by lenders. We review in this chapter recent evidence that suggests both of these conclusions are wrong, thus underscoring that in the eyes of sovereign borrowers, loans and bonds are fundamentally different when it comes to illiquidity, and that sovereign loan contracts are structured such that borrowers pay lenders for their implicit promise to provide services in case of potential loan renegotiations. These services include coordinating the workout and liquidity insurance.

Specifically, we review our own recent contribution (Hallak and Schure 2010). This study is itself inspired by Hallak (2009) who shows, for the first time, that the pricing of sovereign loans does in fact capture the risk of liquidity shortages. (At the same time Hallak confirms the result of the above-mentioned studies that interest spreads are *not* affected by anticipated liquidity shortages.) When granting a loan, lenders typically charge a substantial up-front fee besides an interest spread. Hallak shows that upfront fees are positively affected by proxies for the likelihood of borrower illiquidity.

Hallak and Schure (2010) focus on what is by far the most important segment of the sovereign loans market, namely the market for sovereign *syndicated loans.* These are loans granted by multiple lenders. The next section deals with a widespread misconception that lenders all receive the same compensation in syndicated loan agreements. The section makes clear that lenders that commit a larger share of the syndicated loan generally obtain a higher percentage compensation. Hallak and Schure denote the excess return promised on the largest commitments over the smallest possible commitment as the *return premium.* While risk-aversion of lenders can perhaps explain why large lenders would demand a return premium, Hallak and Schure address the puzzle of why borrowers are prepared to pay larger lenders more, and thus seem to pay more than would be needed if the syndicate were composed of only small lenders.

The analysis then explains that the return premium tends to increase with standard proxies for the likelihood of borrower illiquidity. The return premium is also positively affected by factors that are known to aggravate coordination problems of lenders in case of loan renegotiations triggered by illiquidity. These findings suggest that large lenders obtain the return premium because they carry a disproportionately large share of the cost associated with potential workouts, which involve coordinating lenders, renegotiating the loan, and providing liquidity insurance. Such services of lenders are by implication valuable to sovereign borrowers.

In the final section, we address the hypothesis that banks are special lenders in the sovereign loan market. The evidence of Hallak and Schure supports this hypothesis. Banks seem to be equipped better than nonbank lenders to handle cases of idiosyncratic borrower illiquidity shocks in the sovereign debt market.

LARGER LENDERS EARN MORE

Our main data source is *Thomson One Banker.* We selected all foreign currency denominated syndicated loans issued or guaranteed by sovereign borrowers from developing countries between November 1982 and December 2006. In this context, sovereign borrowers are central governments, ministries, or central banks. Borrowers *guaranteed* by sovereigns are usually local authorities or state-owned firms, such as utility firms, grain boards, and import-export banks. Almost all loans are in U.S. dollars.

In the sample period, sovereign entities from developing countries successfully issued or guaranteed 1,228 variable interest rate publicly syndicated loans (the benchmark interest rate is almost always the 6-month U.S. dollar Libor). We removed loans for which information on either the interest spread, the loan amount, the lifetime of the loan, upfront fees, or the identity of the lenders is missing. This leads to the loss of quite a few observations despite the augmentation of our data with several additional sources, including the *International Financing Review,* the leading professional magazine on syndicated lending for practitioners.

Our data set eventually includes 288 loans issued by sovereign borrowers from 32 developing countries. (The bulk of the loans are so-called term loans.) Volumes in the sovereign syndicated loan market were relatively high in the first half of the 1980s, more or less at a stable level between 1986 and 2003, and somewhat lower from 2004 to 2006. The average loan amount is $181.3 million in 1995 U.S. dollars. The lifetime of the loan and the *average lifetime* (essentially the duration of the principal when the loan is granted) are 5.7 and 4.3 years, respectively, with quite a bit of variation across loans. The average number of lenders on the syndicate is 23.5, while on average, 19.6 lenders join during what is called the general syndication stage (see Rhodes 2004 for details on syndicated lending). Finally, the minimum and maximum up-front fees (received by the smallest and largest lenders that join the syndicate during the general syndication stage) are on average 32 and 52 basis points, respectively.

It can now be shown by looking at the all-in margins that syndicate members that commit the most funds earn the highest return. Amortizing (spreading out) the up-front fees over the average lifetime of a loan, and adding the amortized up-front fee and the interest spread, we obtain what is called the *all-in margin* on the loan. The all-in margin is essentially the lender's return net of funding costs, hence the lender's gross profits on the loan. Next, define the *return premium* as the difference between the maximum and minimum all-in margins expressed as a fraction of the minimum all-in margin; that is, for each loan i we have:

$$\text{Return premium}_i = \left(\frac{\text{all-in margin}_{high} - \text{all-in margin}_{low}}{\text{all-in margin}_{low}} \right)$$

The average return premium turns out to be 8.52 percent, meaning that the largest lenders in the syndicate earn an 8.52 percent higher return than the smallest lenders. The return premium varies substantially across observations. The lowest return premium is 0.86 percent, while the highest is 45.84 percent.

IDIOSYNCRATIC LIQUIDITY SHOCKS AND THE RETURN PREMIUM

Why are sovereign borrowers prepared to pay a return premium to larger lenders? As explained in the introduction, our main hypothesis revolves around idiosyncratic liquidity shocks.

Borrower liquidity hypothesis (BLH): The return premium compensates lenders that commit large amounts for a set of services they are expected to perform in case of borrower liquidity problems (illiquidity), for example, monitoring the borrower, renegotiating the loan, coordinating the lenders, and providing liquidity insurance in case of a workout.

A straightforward empirical implication of BLH is that the return premium increases in the likelihood of liquidity shortages as perceived at the time the loan contract is written. A second prediction is that the (anticipated) number of lenders that join the syndicate positively affects the return premium. This second prediction is based on Ongena and Smith (2000) and other studies that show that the number of lenders positively affects coordination costs during loan renegotiations. Finally, Brunner and Krahnen (2008) show that information asymmetries and other information problems between the borrower and the lenders also increase the coordination costs between lenders.

Hallak and Schure (2010) estimate the following system of equations.

$\text{Log(Return premium}_i) =$

$\quad \text{Constant1} + \psi_1 \text{ Number of joining lenders}_i + \psi_2 \text{ Reserves/Short-term debt}_{j,t}$

$\quad + \psi_3 \text{ St. dev. income growth}_{j,t} + \psi_4 \text{ Fraction of banks as large lenders}_i$

$\quad + \psi_5 \text{ Insolvency proxies}_{j,t} + \psi_6 \text{ Other controls}_{j,t} + \psi_7 \text{ Dummies1}_i + \text{Error1}_{i,j,t}$

$$(11.1)$$

$\text{Log(Number of joining lenders}_i) =$

$\quad \text{Constant2} + \varphi_1 \text{ Return premium}_i + \varphi_2 \text{ Credit market illiquidity}_i$

$\quad + \varphi_3 \text{ Log(Loan size}_i) + \Phi_4 \text{ Dummies2}_i + \text{Error2}_{i,j,t}$ (11.2)

In Equations 11.1 and 11.2 subscripts i are used for observations at the loan level, subscripts j to indicate the country of the sovereign borrower, and t the year. Lower-case Greek letters indicate scalars, and upper-case Greek letters vectors of coefficients. The two endogenous variables in Equations 11.1 and 11.2 are the *Return premium* and the *Number of joining lenders* (representing the number of lenders that joined the syndicate during the general syndication phase). While BLH makes clear that Equation 11.1 is the more interesting one, both equations need to be considered for estimation purposes. This is because the causality between *Return premium* and the *Number of joining lenders* may well be bidirectional. For example, the *Return premium* may be chosen in light of the anticipated number of lenders in the syndicate (BLH predicts $\psi_1 > 0$), while it may also affect the committed amounts by lenders and hence influence the *Number of joining lenders*. Hallak and Schure (2010) estimate Equations 11.1 and 11.2 are both using two-stage least squares (2SLS), which allows for bidirectional causality between the two endogenous variables, as well as using two separate ordinary least squares (OLS) regressions.

As for the other variables of Equation 11.1, *Reserves/Short-term debt* is the amount of foreign currency reserves available to the government and central bank of the sovereign borrower divided by the outstanding amount of short-term public debt denominated in foreign currencies. An increase in *Reserves/Short-term debt* improves the ability of the sovereign borrower to weather temporary financial troubles, and hence reduces the likelihood that the borrower needs to renegotiate its outstanding debt. Thus, BLH predicts that $\psi_2 < 0$. *St. dev. GDP growth* is the standard deviation of the GDP growth rate in the five years before the year t the loan is issued. Generally, greater values of *St. dev. GDP growth* mean a greater likelihood of borrower illiquidity. An increase in this variable has also been associated with greater information problems between the borrower and the lenders in the sovereign debt literature. Following either interpretation, BLH predicts $\psi_3 > 0$. The *Fraction of banks as large lenders* represents the fraction of banks among the lenders in the highest ranks of the syndicate. See Hallak and Schure (2010) for details on this, as well as on the *Insolvency proxies*, *Other controls*, and the *Dummies* in Equation 11.1.

Turning to Equation 11.2, *Credit market illiquidity* is the yield spread in basis points between representative portfolios of U.S. 30-year Corporate BAA bonds and 30-year U.S. Treasury bonds. A larger value of the yield spread indicates that, on the whole, lenders are more cautious about increasing their credit risk exposure. Such unwillingness to lend may mean smaller individual commitments, so that we anticipate that $\varphi_2 > 0$. *Loan size* is the size of the loan facility expressed in 1995 U.S. dollars. Ongena and Smith (2000) show that the loan size positively affects the number of lending relationships, suggesting $\varphi_3 > 0$.

The estimation results are found in Exhibit 11.1. Note that the 2SLS and OLS outcomes are close. The findings in the table strongly support the Borrower Liquidity Hypothesis. All three coefficients φ_1, φ_2, and φ_3 are statistically significant and have signs in line with the predictions clarified earlier. Thus, lenders appear to anticipate potential liquidity problems of borrowers, and they recognize that large lenders will step up in case of renegotiations and carry a disproportionally large share of the costs associated with renegotiation. Although syndicated lending arrangements do not explicitly bind larger lenders to monitor borrowers, coordinate lenders, and provide liquidity in workouts, their larger exposure may give them the incentives to take the lead. It may furthermore be that large lenders are in a better position to pressure the borrower and other lenders into signing a new agreement. Lending is a repeated game and larger lenders that do not act in a way that is consistent with their perceived role may lose reputational capital (see, for example, Sharpe 1990; Panyagometh and Roberts, 2010).

ARE BANKS SPECIAL LENDERS?

Godlewski (2010) shows in a cross-country study including 24 countries that the banking environment of a country affects the structure of lending syndicates. Hallak and Schure (2010) discuss several arguments for and against conjecturing that banks are special lenders when it comes to managing idiosyncratic liquidity risk and conclude that "the question . . . is an empirical one." However, they also show that *if* banks were indeed special, BLH suggests that the effect would surface among the large, active syndicate members. If so, greater values of the *Fraction of banks as large lenders* would be associated with higher return premiums.

Exhibit 11.1   Regression Results

Specification:	Equation 1-2		Equation 1	Equation 2
Dependent variable:	Log(Return Premium)	Log(Number of joining lenders)	Log(Return Premium)	Log(Number of joining lenders)
	(1)	(2)	(3)	(4)
Log(Return Premium)		0.123 [0.136]		0.166 *** [0.000]
Log(Number of joining lenders)	0.208 * [0.073]		0.260 *** [0.000]	
Reserves/Short-Term Debts	−0.055 ** [0.040]		−0.055 ** [0.040]	
St. Dev. GDP Growth	6.882 ** [0.028]		6.970 ** [0.024]	
Fraction of Banks as Large Lenders	0.747 ** [0.028]		0.751 ** [0.028]	
Long-Term Debts/GNP	0.030 [0.941]		0.052 [0.896]	
GDP Growth	−1.213 [0.680]		−1.182 [0.683]	
Investment	0.013 [0.231]		0.011 [0.247]	
Political Stability	−0.004 [0.374]		−0.005 [0.310]	
Log(GDP)	−0.093 ** [0.022]		−0.092 ** [0.022]	
Government Size	0.012 ** [0.037]		0.013 ** [0.029]	
Credit Market Illiquidity		0.133 [0.140]		0.137 [0.125]
Log(Loan Size)		0.435 *** [0.000]		0.436 *** [0.000]
dRefinance	−0.150 [0.341]	−0.246 ** [0.021]	−0.141 [0.379]	−0.236 ** [0.030]
dFirm	0.195 [0.126]		0.210 * [0.074]	
dRevolving Credit	−0.209 * [0.088]		−0.212 * [0.083]	
d1990_2006	−0.428 *** [0.007]	−0.255 *** [0.005]	−0.401 *** [0.006]	−0.243 *** [0.008]
Constant	−1.818 [0.139]	0.853 ** [0.012]	−2.010 * [0.084]	0.956 *** [0.001]
R-squared	36.1	44.9	36.3	45.1
Number of Observations	288	288	288	288

Note: The specifications of the models are found in Equation 11.1 and 11.2 in the main text. The first two columns report the two-stage least squares (2SLS) estimates of Equations 1 and 2, and the last two columns the ordinary least squares (OLS) estimates. Regression results for the dummies dTax Spare, dWorld Bank Co-Financing, dTrade, dGrace, and d1982−1983 are not reported. *p*-values are given in brackets and are based on robust variance estimators clustered on borrower; *, **, and *** indicate significance at the 10 percent, 5 percent, and 1 percent level, respectively.
Source: Hallak and Schure (2010).

Hypothesis 3 (banks-are-special hypothesis): A greater fraction of banks among the lenders in the higher ranks of the syndicate is associated with a higher return premium.

Equation 11.1 reveals that the coefficient of the *Fraction of banks as large lenders* is indeed positive and significant, suggesting that depository institutions are special in dealing with borrower liquidity problems, and that they charge borrowers more in light of this. This result was strengthened in an additional regression in which we replaced the *Fraction of banks as large lenders* by the *Fraction of banks as small lenders*. The estimated coefficient of the *Fraction of banks as small lenders* was insignificant and close to zero, which points to a generally passive role for small lenders.

Despite the appeal of finding supporting evidence for the banks-are-special hypothesis, we would like to interpret these results with caution. The main reason is that the average fraction of banks in the lending syndicates in our data set is quite high, namely 0.932 (more details in Hallak and Schure 2010).

CONCLUSION

This chapter discussed recent research that draws a link between borrower liquidity problems to the pricing of sovereign loan contracts. The results suggest that large lenders obtain higher returns than small lenders because they carry a disproportionately large share of the cost associated with loan renegotiations. This finding adds up with theoretical works, as well as with the syndicated loans literature that has shown that the large lenders on the syndicate are the most active in regard to managing the relationship with the borrower (for example, Lee and Mullineaux 2004 and Sufi 2007). It is also consistent with stylized evidence from sovereign debt workouts. For example, Cline (1995) reports that William R. Rhodes, then vice chairman of Citibank, the financial institution most involved in the sovereign debt markets during the 1980s, chaired most of the bank's advisory committees (London clubs) for the financially distressed Latin American countries.

Our results also suggest that banks are special syndicate members, which are better equipped at managing idiosyncratic liquidity shocks than nonbank lenders. This result does not enable us to distinguish whether banks are special because they are superior monitors as in Coleman et al. (2006); or because they are better at providing liquidity insurance than nonbanks (Gatev and Strahan 2006). Yet, the banks-are-special result is consistent with Huang and Ramírez (2010), who show that banks gravitate toward segments of the credit market where monitoring, renegotiation, and liquidation are important.

The results discussed in this chapter are important to understanding the choice of sovereign borrowers between loans and bonds. They are also important to assess the importance for borrowers of getting bankers on board. An avenue for future research is to study to what extent the findings of Hallak and Schure (2010) carry over to the corporate credit market.

NOTE

1. In a sovereign debt context, borrowers are said to be *illiquid* if they attempt to renegotiate the terms of the loan rather than to repudiate the contract outright (which is termed *insolvency*).

REFERENCES

Bolton, P., and D. S. Scharfstein. 1996. "Optimal Debt Structure and the Number of Creditors." *Journal of Political Economy* 104:1, 1–25.

Boot, A. 2000. "Relationship Banking: What Do We Know?" *Journal of Financial Intermediation* 9: 7–25.

Brunner, A., and J. P. Krahnen. 2008. "Multiple Lenders and Corporate Distress: Evidence on Debt Restructuring." *Review of Economic Studies* 75: 415–442.

Cline, W. R. 1995. *International Debt Reexamined*. Washington, DC: Institute for International Economics.

Coleman, A. D. F., N. Esho, and I. G. Sharpe. 2006. "Does Bank Monitoring Influence Loan Contract Terms?" *Journal of Financial Services Research* 30: 177–198.

Diamond, D. W., and R. G. Rajan. 2001. "Liquidity Risk, Liquidity Creation, and Financial Fragility: A Theory of Banking." *Journal of Political Economy* 109:2, 287–327.

Eichengreen, B., and A. Mody. 2000. "Lending Booms, Reserves and the Sustainability of Short-Term Debt: Inferences from the Pricing of Syndicated Bank Loans." *Journal of Development Economics* 63: 5–44.

Edwards, S. 1986. "The Pricing of Bonds and Bank Loans in International Markets." *European Economic Review* 30: 565–589.

Elsas, R., and J. P. Krahnen. 1998. "Is Relationship Lending Special? Evidence from Credit File Data in Germany." *Journal of Banking and Finance* 22: 1283–1316.

Gatev, Evan, and Philip Strahan. 2006. "Banks' Advantage in Hedging Liquidity Risk: Theory and Evidence from the Commercial Paper Market." *Journal of Finance* 61:2, 867–892.

Godlewski, C. J. 2010. "Banking Environment and Loan Syndicate Structure: A Cross-Country Analysis." *Applied Financial Economics* 20:8, 637–648.

Hallak, I. 2009. "Renegotiation and the Pricing Structure of Sovereign Bank Loans: Empirical Evidence." *Journal of Financial Stability* 5: 89–103.

Hallak, I., and P. Schure. 2010. "Why Larger Lenders Obtain Higher Returns: Evidence from Sovereign Syndicated Loans." Forthcoming in *Financial Management*.

Huang, R., and G. G. Ramírez. 2010. "Speed of Issuance, Lender Specialization, and the Rise of the 144A Debt Market." *Financial Management* 39:2, 643–673.

Lee, S. W., and D. J. Mullineaux. 2004. "Monitoring, Financial Distress, and the Structure of Commercial Lending Syndicates." *Financial Management* 33:3, 107–130.

Morris, S., and H. S. Shin. 2004. "Coordination Risk and the Price of Debt." *European Economic Review* 48: 133–153.

Ongena, S., and D. C. Smith. 2000. "What Determines the Number of Bank Relationships? Cross-Country Evidence." *Journal of Financial Intermediation* 9: 26–56.

Panyagometh, K., and G. S. Roberts. 2010. "Do Lead Banks Exploit Syndicate Participants? Evidence from Ex Post Risk." *Financial Management* 39:1, 273–299.

Rhodes, T., ed. 2004. *Syndicated Lending: Practice and Documentation* 4th ed. London: Euromoney Institutional Investor.

Sharpe, S. A. 1990. "Asymmetric Information, Bank Lending and Implicit Contracts: A Stylized Model of Customer Relationship." *Journal of Finance* 45: 1069–1087.

Sturzenegger, F., and J. Zettelmeyer. 2007. *Debt Defaults and Lessons from a Decade of Crises*. Cambridge, MA: MIT Press.

Sufi, A. 2007. "Information Asymmetry and Financing Arrangements: Evidence from Syndicated Loans." *Journal of Finance* 62: 629–668.

ABOUT THE AUTHORS

Issam Hallak is an assistant professor at the Department of Finance of Bocconi University. He received a PhD in Financial Economics at the European University Institute, Florence. He has done extensive work in sovereign debt and international finance, as well as on syndicated loans and corporate finance.

Paul Schure is associate professor at the University of Victoria, Canada. He received his PhD from the European University Institute in 2000. Before joining UVic, Paul spent one year as a postdoc researcher at the Hebrew University of Jerusalem and four months as a consultant at the European Investment Bank. Paul has held visiting positions at the Robert Schuman Centre of the European University Institute (2002 and 2005), the University of Bonn (2003), Utrecht University (2008), and the University of Amsterdam (2009). Paul's research interests include financial intermediation, entrepreneurial finance, industrial organization, and European economics. His work has appeared in various economics and finance journals, and a recent article appeared in European Union Politics. Paul was elected Secretary/Treasurer of the European Community Studies Association-Canada (ECSA-C) between 2004 and 2012 and co-organized the ECSA-C biennial conferences of 2008 and 2010.

CHAPTER 12

First-Time Sovereign Bond Issuers

Considerations in Accessing International Capital Markets

UDAIBIR S. DAS
IMF*

MICHAEL G. PAPAIOANNOU
IMF

MAGDALENA POLAN
Goldman Sachs International

B ased on recent experience of first-time sovereign issuers, this chapter presents some of the main advantages and disadvantages of international issuance and outlines some considerations that countries should take into account when contemplating or planning bond issuance in international capital markets for the first time. In this context, the chapter also discusses some typical pitfalls in accessing international capital markets by first-time issuers.

RECENT EXPERIENCE

While the objectives of first-time sovereign issuers may differ, past experience has shown that issuers had tried to access international capital markets under favorable domestic and external conditions. In general, these countries had prepared themselves by building a record of good economic performance over the preceding few years, and by maintaining a positive medium-term outlook.

---

*The views expressed herein are those of the authors and should not be attributed to the IMF, its executive board, or its management. Work for this article was completed when all authors worked at the IMF. The views expressed in this article are those of the authors and should not be attributed to the IMF, its executive board, management, or to Goldman Sachs International.

In most of these countries, growth was robust, inflation was under control, and the external current account deficit was being financed easily. These countries had prudent fiscal stances and were easily servicing existing public debt. Most had also made progress in data dissemination, transparency in the conduct of macroeconomic policy, and in carrying out structural reform. And typically, the political situation was supportive of the pursuit of appropriate economic policies.

Although the size of the initial bonds varied widely across first-time issuers, other characteristics of these bonds tended to be similar. Almost all recent first-time sovereign issuers placed fixed coupon, bullet bonds with maturities in the five-to-seven-year range. Almost all the initial issues were U.S. dollar denominated. Most initial bond issues were attractively priced to attract greater investor interest. All recent initial issues have included collective action clauses (CACs) and were issued as private placements or eurobonds rather than as global bonds.

BENEFITS AND RISKS OF INTERNATIONAL ISSUANCE

There are a number of potentially important benefits for a developing country issuing bonds in international markets. The main ones include:

- Supplementing domestic savings to finance public sector investment. This can lead to less crowding out of private investment by the public sector with benefits for growth and domestic capital market development.
- Diversifying external financing sources to reduce the government's reliance on bank financing from abroad and official financing.
- Obtaining longer maturities and typically lower interest rates than that available in local markets.
- Helping maintain steady momentum in carrying out critical macroeconomic and structural reforms due to closer international market monitoring.
- Establishing a pricing benchmark for external borrowing by the domestic banks and corporates.

However, issuing bonds in international markets also comes with risks, which can prove costly in adverse situations. These include:

- Increased exchange rate can lead to high ex post debt servicing costs in adverse circumstances.
- Refinancing risk can be significant because of abrupt changes in international financial conditions.
- These risks will be greater in situations in which a country is subject to wide swings in its terms of trade or when repayment of a bullet bond represents a significant fraction of export earnings. These considerations apply most frequently to smaller-sized economies.

MAIN ISSUES TO CONSIDER WHEN PLANNING AN INITIAL INTERNATIONAL BOND ISSUE

When planning for an initial international bond issue, the country will need to make a number of decisions at various points in the process. Some are more strategic in nature, and are best addressed in the context of a medium-term debt management plan, while others are primarily tactical, although no less important (Das, Papaioannou, and Polan 2008). Among the most important decisions to consider are the following:

- *Assessing the first issue in the context of an overall plan:* Before going to the international markets, it is essential that the authorities have developed a reasonable idea of how much they would like to raise from international markets over the next, say, three to five years. It is also important to have a clear idea of how the proceeds from bond issuance would be used (for example, for investment projects, for general government purposes, for changing the composition of public debt, and so on). This will provide a clearer picture of when funds will be needed, as it is costly to leave borrowed funds in international reserves for extended periods, which will help determine the size of the initial bond issue.
- *Size of the issue:* The size of the first-time issue is a critical consideration. In determining the appropriate size, principal consideration must be given to how much funds will need to be raised from markets in, say, the next one to two years, with the main question being whether to divide this total into more than one bond issue. The full desired funding can be obtained either by new issues or by reopening the first issue. In making this decision, the following are the key trade-offs:
  - Larger size bond issues are more liquid and if large enough can enter into the bond indexes, both of which are generally attractive to investors and can result in better pricing for the issuer. For liquidity purposes and to serve as a benchmark, the minimum size of an initial issue should be at least $100 million to $150 million.
  - Everything else being equal, a larger-size issue tends to increase the rollover or repayment risk, as the issuer has to raise larger funds before the maturity date under uncertain future market conditions.
  - Larger issues, in excess of immediate financing needs, can add to the government's costs, while excess funds are held in international reserves that yield less than the interest rate on the new bonds.
  - If the size of the initial issue is seen as too large relative to the size of the issuer's economy, raising questions about future debt sustainability, markets could charge a penalty rate outweighing liquidity benefits.
  - Market conditions at the time the bonds are placed can also have an effect on the size of the initial bond issue.
- *Maturity and repayment structure:* Another key choice is the repayment profile of the bonds. This involves deciding both the date of final payment (final

maturity) and the amounts of any intermediate principal repayments before that date.

- Markets generally prefer a rather short final maturity for an initial bond issue, five to seven years, because the country is less well known and has an unproven repayment history. Issuers also frequently prefer to issue at relatively short maturities, expecting that their credit spreads (country risk premiums) will come down before refinancing is needed, as economic performance improves and a record in servicing external debt is established. Depending on the use of proceeds and market conditions, however, it may be feasible and advantageous for the issuer to consider a longer maturity, even if the coupon rate is slightly higher.

- Small countries and issuers who anticipate going to the markets relatively infrequently should weigh very carefully the advantages of an amortizing structure rather than the heretofore more common bullet bond. Bullet bonds tend to increase the rollover risk for the issuer, as they create a hump in the debt repayment profile. Similarly, reopening such a bond at a later date would only increase the size of the payment due on the maturity date, while debt management operations to smooth out debt service humps (for example, prefunding or debt buybacks and debt exchanges) are often costly and not always easy to conduct.

- In contrast, amortizing bonds smooth the repayment profile, reducing the refinancing and rollover risk. This type of repayment structure can make reopening the issue more appropriate (in contrast with a bullet bond). Information asymmetry between the issuer and investors can be reduced, as regular payments help investors monitor the issuer, and reassure them that the issuer is able to honor the payments. This can lead to a more rapid reduction in risk spreads.[1]

- *Currency:* The currency denomination of the issue is an additional consideration. Generally, initial bond issues have been denominated in U.S. dollars since demand for such instruments is highest. However, the choice can be affected by factors such as the use of proceeds, currency composition of the countries' foreign trade, the investor base to be targeted, and the borrowing costs.[2]

- *Choice of investor base:* The issuer will need to decide the proper balance in targeting potential classes of investors. In particular, should there be extra focus on investors in one region (who may already be familiar with the country) or on retail investors (including emigrants willing to invest in their home country)? Should there be any initial sales to local financial institutions often anxious to have high-yielding, low-risk-weighted foreign currency assets? These decisions are typically best made in consultation with financial advisers.

- *Building demand:* Regardless of the chosen investor base, it is best to take time to build potential demand before issuing by properly introducing the country to international investors. One important way is to obtain a rating well before issuance from one or more credit rating agencies. Demand can also be effectively built through road shows that can be conducted before the bond issue or during the issue (pre-deal or deal road shows). In these, senior officials from the country would attempt to educate potential investors about the country's economic performance, stability, and creditworthiness. Financial advisers, including potential lead managers, can help in preparing materials for the credit rating agencies and in organizing pre-deal road shows.

- *Legal issues and documentation:* The issuer needs to decide various legal issues and nonfinancial terms that enter into the formal bond documentation. These issues include:
  - Which underlying law the bonds should be subject to and, relatedly, which market to issue into. If the broadest investor base is targeted, including retail investors in the United States, global bonds under New York law would be preferred. However, global bonds require more data transparency, which is not always feasible. On the other hand, issuing in the eurobond market, in U.S. dollars or euros, would typically be done under nonglobal English law. Sovereign bonds are frequently issued under New York law with restrictions limiting their sale to retail investors.
  - The issuer will have to decide other legal terms, including what form of CACs to include, and whether to use a trust agreement or fiscal agency agreement to intermediate between the issuer and investors during the life of the bonds.
  - These decisions should be made after discussion with legal and financial advisers.
- *Selecting lead managers:* The country will need to hire a lead manager (investment bank) or multiple lead managers (smaller countries may work with only one lead manager). This can be done once the country has decided on its basic issuance strategy. First-time issuers might find it advantageous to hire at an earlier stage pure financial advisers to help develop the issuance strategy, obtain ratings, and select the lead manager, but who would not be part of the syndicate earning fees from the sale of the new bonds. In deciding about hiring a lead manager, countries should seek competitive offers from potential lead managers. Issues to consider in selecting a lead manager should go beyond fees and would include:
  - The attractiveness of the lead manager's specific plans to market and distribute the new bonds.
  - The commitment of the lead manager to provide market support after issuance. Although post-issue support may increase the direct cost (fees), it may decrease the cost of servicing and managing the debt in the longer term and prove extremely valuable if the markets experience a downturn.[3] The extra implicit fee for these services may be very well worth it, as experience shows that a bond issued in a very cheap way may be underpriced (that is, priced away from the yield curve), resulting in higher debt service cost for the issuer.
  - The issuer will need to decide whether to pay additional fees for the bonds to be fully or partially underwritten (market risk assumed by the lead manager). In favorable market conditions such as in recent years, paying full underwriting generally will not be necessary or cost effective.

COMMON MISTAKES OF FIRST-TIME ISSUERS

While first-time issuers have been quite successful in recent years in placing bonds, most issues could have been designed or executed somewhat better. Among the most common, and most serious, pitfalls to be avoided are:

- *Too large an issue size:* A number of issues have been larger than the minimum size needed for liquidity and larger than could be put to near-term use by the issuer. This results in high carrying costs. Several issues have also been very large in comparison with GDP, sometimes in excess of 20 percent, resulting in high levels of risk for the country.
- *Not using amortizing structures:* Use of bullet bonds by small countries results in significantly high refinancing or roller risks, which can easily be avoided by amortizing the new issue gradually.
- *Rushing to market:* A number of first-time issuers have come to market without pre-deal road shows (in some cases without any road show) and shortly after obtaining a credit rating. This results in higher interest rates than could have been achieved through more patient building of investor demand.
- *Not choosing the lead manager competitively:* In several cases, there was no competitive process to select the lead manager. This has resulted in higher fees than necessary, precluding the government from getting the benefit of a wider set of opinions, and perhaps higher debt service costs.
- *Choosing the lead manager only on the basis of fees:* Selecting a lead manager only on the basis of fees has led in some cases to poor initial pricing and additional volatility in secondary trading.
- *Imprecise use of proceeds:* A number of new issues have specified only general governmental use when in fact proceeds were used to pay down expensive debt or to fund investment projects. This can lead to the underpricing of a first-time bond.
- *Not issuing global bonds:* Too frequently, issuers who had sufficient data to satisfy listing requirements for global bonds decided not to issue them solely on the basis of a modest additional cost and additional time to come to market. Particularly in cases in which there is a potential retail market, this can result in underpricing.
- *Not getting independent second opinions:* While advice from lead managers is invaluable, first-time issuers who have also sought the opinion of independent financial advisers or international financial institutions have found it beneficial, resulting in most cases in better structured bonds and better deal execution.

NOTES

1. An amortizing structure can take the form of a sinking fund, into which the issuer systematically commits funds that, depending on the market conditions, will be used to repay part of the outstanding debt. These funds can be used to service debt (when prices are above par) or to buy back outstanding bonds (if prices are below par).
2. It may make sense, however, to issue in U.S. dollars and use parallel instruments such as swaps to convert proceeds into the needed currency.

3. For example, if the lead manager maintains post-issue support by providing market-making services or enhancing liquidity, it could be easier for the issuer to engage in debt buybacks or swaps at a later date.

REFERENCE

Das, Udaibir S., Michael G. Papaioannou, and Magdalena Polan. 2008. "Strategic Considerations for First-Time Sovereign Bond Issuers." *IMF Working Paper,* WP/08/261.

ABOUT THE AUTHORS

Udaibir S. Das is an assistant director in the Monetary and Capital Markets Department of the IMF, where he heads the Sovereign Asset and Liability Management Division. Mr. Das leads a team that covers policy and operational issues relating to sovereign balance sheet risk management; debt, reserves, and sovereign asset management; and local and regional sovereign bond markets. He is also associated with country-specific vulnerability assessments and financial stability surveillance.

Mr. Das joined the IMF in 1996. Before joining the IMF, Mr. Das was with the Reserve Bank of India for 18 years. He has participated in various financial sector assessment programs, technical assistance missions, and has been closely associated with several international and regional initiatives in financial sector and capital market areas. He was the resident adviser in Guyana (South America) from 1996 to 1998. In his career with the Fund, he has represented Fund staff on various OECD Working Parties, the Basel-based Joint Forum and the International Association of Insurance Supervisors, and the International Working Group of Sovereign Wealth Funds.

Mr. Das is a Fulbright-Humphrey scholar with graduate degrees in economics (U.S.) and management (U.S.). He was a lecturer in economics and finance at Boston University from 1989 to 1991. He has published in several international and professional journals and holds a research interest in central banking, sovereign asset liability management, nonbank financial institutions, and different aspects of debt and fixed income markets.

Michael G. Papaioannou is a deputy division chief at the Sovereign Asset and Liability Management Division, Monetary and Capital Markets Department of the International Monetary Fund. While at the IMF, he served as a special adviser to the governing board of the Bank of Greece. Before joining the IMF, he was a senior vice president for international financial services and director of the foreign exchange service at the WEFA (Wharton Econometrics Forecasting Associates) Group and served as chief economist of the Council of Economic Advisors of Greece. He has also taught at Temple University's, School of Business and Management, Department of Finance, as an adjunct associate professor of finance, and was a principal research fellow at the University of Pennsylvania, Department of Economics, LINK Central. He holds a PhD in economics from the University of Pennsylvania and an MA in economics from Georgetown University.

Magdalena Polan is a senior European economist and executive director within the new markets economics team in the Global Investment Research division of

Goldman Sachs. Before joining Goldman Sachs, she spent six years with the International Monetary Fund in Washington, DC, working in the Monetary and Capital Markets, European, and Strategy and Policy Review departments, focusing on various issues related to economic policy in emerging market countries, including public financial management, crisis prevention and resolution, and sovereign debt restructurings. She also provided training and assistance in these areas to governments and central banks. Before joining the Fund, she was a research and teaching assistant at the University of Leuven, where her research agenda covered monetary policy, European monetary integration, and globalization. Her written work has been published in a number of economic journals, IMF Working Papers, and edited books. She holds degrees in economics from the University of Leuven and Warsaw University, and also studied political science.

CHAPTER 13

A Note on Sovereign Debt Auctions

Uniform or Discriminatory?

MENACHEM BRENNER
Stern School of Business Administration, New York University[*]

DAN GALAI
Jerusalem School of Business Administration, Hebrew University of Jerusalem

ORLY SADE
Jerusalem School of Business Administration, Hebrew University of Jerusalem

There is a long-standing debate regarding the auction system that a sovereign should use when it issues debt instruments. The most common pricing rules are the *uniform* and the *discriminatory*. In the *uniform price auction* (UPA) (also known as *single price auction*), the objects are awarded to bidders that bid above the market-clearing price. All bidders pay the same market-clearing price. In the *discriminatory auction* (DA) (also known as *multiple prices auction*), the objects are also awarded to bidders that bid above the clearing price but each bidder pays the price that he bid. The main objective of our research is to analyze the choices made by countries around the globe and what may explain these choices.

As early as 1960, Milton Friedman has argued that a discriminatory auction will drive out uninformed participants because of the "winner's curse" and attract better-informed, typically large players. Thus, the discriminatory mechanism will be more susceptible to collusion than the uniform one. Friedman predicted that the discriminatory auction would lead to lower revenues. Alternatively, a uniform price mechanism would lead to wider participation, which should result in lesser collusion and higher revenues. It is puzzling, therefore, to find that most countries in our study use the discriminatory price mechanism.

While sovereign bonds compose one of the largest primary markets, they are not the only financial asset that is initially sold through auctions. In a more general

---

[*]This chapter is based on our paper: "Sovereign Debt Auctions: Uniform or Discriminatory?" published in the *Journal of Monetary Economics* 56:2, 267–274.

setting, most of the current public and academic debate with respect to financial auctions revolves around two main issues. The first is whether to use an auction or another selling mechanism.[1] Given an auction offering, the second issue is the auction's specific design. The focus of this paper is on the very important feature of the design, specifically, the pricing rule: what may explain and determine the choice between a uniform auction and a discriminatory one.

It is important to note that this is a challenging academic question that has not been resolved. The academic literature since Friedman (1960) is not conclusive regarding the optimal offering system and pricing mechanism for repetitive bond auctions. In addition to the ongoing academic debate, this is also a very important practical issue that countries are coping with. Many countries in our sample have moved from one pricing rule to another after debating the issue, and in the case of the United States devoting time and resources for experimentation. The so-called Salomon Squeeze in May 1991 has triggered an examination of the auctioning system, in particular the pricing mechanism. The U.S. Treasury decided to carry out an experiment using the two pricing rules in parallel, for different bond issues. The results of this experiment are documented in Malvey, Archibald, and Flynn (1995), Nyborg and Sundaresan (1996), Malvey and Archibald (1998), and Goldreich (2007). While the experiment results did not provide a significant revenue improvement in the uniform mechanism versus the discriminatory, additional considerations have contributed to the decision to switch to the uniform price mechanism.

In the analysis of the markets for sovereign bonds, one must take into account the three major interested parties, or stakeholders: The first is the issuer, be it the national treasury or the central bank. The issuer's objective is to maximize revenues over time, taking into account long-term considerations. Hence, in addition to a short-term consideration like the revenues from a forthcoming specific auction, the issuer cares about the structure and quality of the secondary market, including the symmetry of allocation and the likelihood of collusion in the auction or the secondary market since it will affect the cost of future issues. Also, the sovereign may have additional objectives that can be related to macroeconomic considerations or foreign policy considerations such as the level of foreign holding of its debt. The second stakeholders are the intermediaries, who serve as the underwriters, designated dealers, dealers, and brokers. The designated dealers profit from purchasing the issue and selling it to the public, which can be either institutional investors or private investors. Their goal is to maximize the profit from this activity. They can potentially gain from market inefficiencies. The third stakeholder is the public, including financial institutions that invest in these debt instruments. They, of course, would like to pay the lowest possible price and at the same time they gain from market liquidity and efficiency.

Our research consists of two parts. First, we document the recent auction mechanisms employed by treasuries and central banks around the world (their revealed preferences). In the second part, we analyze, in a cross-sectional setting, the factors that are potentially related to the choice of a mechanism by country. We use several variables that were used in the academic literature to study the relationship between financial development and economic growth. Given our results, we provide an explanation, consistent with our empirical findings, that takes into account the bargaining power of the three stakeholders: the issuer, the intermediaries, and the investors.

Though the primary market for government debt is one of the largest financial markets in the world, there is no source of public data that provides information about treasury auctions. Since this information is not available in public databases, we had to use our own survey, which was sent by e-mails, mail, and faxes to central banks and treasuries around the world.[2] We received answers from 48 countries, listed in Exhibit 13.1. Our sample consists of countries from different continents and economic size, including almost all (83 percent) OECD countries.

We have screened these unique data and documented which country is using what mechanism (discriminatory, uniform, both, or other pricing rule). Our results indicate that most countries in our sample, 50 percent, use a discriminatory price auction, about 19 percent use a uniform price auction and about 19 percent use both methods, depending on the type of debt instruments being issued. The others, about 12 percent, use a method that is different from the two conventional ones (for example, Austria). Interestingly, even among countries with the same currency and relatively similar monetary policy (for example, the EU countries that use the euro) different types of auction mechanisms are used. Finland, for example, which used a uniform price mechanism, does not use auctions anymore,[3] while France

Exhibit 13.1 Survey Answers Regarding the Type of Auctions Used to Sell Sovereign Debt in Different Countries around the World as of April to October 2005

Discriminatory	Uniform	Both	Other
Bangladesh	Argentina	Brazil	Austria
Belgium	Australia	Canada	Finland[4]
Cambodia	Colombia	Ghana	Luxemburg
Cyprus	South Korea	Italy	Fiji
Ecuador	Norway	Mexico	Ireland
France	Singapore	New Zealand	Japan
Germany	Switzerland	Sierra Leone	
Greece	Trinidad and Tobago	Slovenia	
Hungary	United States	United Kingdom	
Israel			
Jamaica			
Latvia			
Lithuania			
Macedonia			
Malta			
Mauritius			
Mongolia			
Panama			
Poland			
Portugal			
Solomon Islands			
Sweden			
Turkey			
Venezuela			

and Germany use a discriminatory auction. We also find that in some countries the mechanism that is being used has changed over time (for example, the United States switched, in the 1990s, from a discriminatory mechanism to a uniform one while Mongolia switched from uniform auction to a discriminatory one). In about 50 percent of our sample, the country employed in the past a different selling mechanism from the one it currently uses. Some countries in our sample use more than one type of pricing rule to sell their debt instruments (for example, Canada and Brazil). Some use a different auction mechanism to issue debt than to buy back debt (for example, the United States).[5]

Given the different practices and the changes introduced by some countries,[6] it is clear that research—theoretical, experimental and/or empirical—about auction designs would be of great interest to a variety of issuers, be it governments or corporations. Thus, we examine the features that make up the profile of a country to see if there are common factors associated with one auction design or another. We collected several potential explanatory variables such as: Moody's sovereign debt ratings, indebtedness classification, civil (Roman) law versus common law, stock market capitalization as percentage of GDP, GDP, the Ease of Doing Business 2006 index, the CPI Corruption Index 2005, and the Index of Economic Freedom 2006, all of which describe the asset being sold and the issuer. They were obtained from different sources: the World Bank, Moody's, the International Finance Corporation (IFC), the *Wall Street Journal*, and Transparency International.

Exhibit 13.2 provides descriptive statistics of the countries according to the auction mechanism employed by them.

Civil (Roman) law versus common law. This variable was proposed by La Porta et al. (1998). We try to see whether the auction mechanism is associated with the legal system in a country.

Stock market capitalization as percentage of GDP (World Bank 2003). Market capitalization is the share price times the number of shares outstanding and is calculated as percentage of the GDP.

GDP (World Bank 2003). GDP is measured in current U.S. dollars.

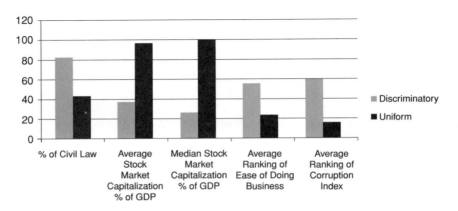

Exhibit 13.2   Factors that Are Associated with Auction Design

Ease of Doing Business 2006 (IFC 2005). The ease of doing business index ranks
economies from 1 (the best ranking) to 155.

The CPI Corruption Index 2005 (Transparency International) aims to measure
the overall extent of corruption (frequency and/or size of bribes) in the
public and political sectors. The index ranks countries from 1 to 158.

We conducted univariate and multivariate tests and found that countries that
have more market-oriented economies (as measured by capitalization or GDP) and
practice common law tend to use a uniform price auction (Exhibit 13.2). In other
countries in which the financial environment is less developed and barriers to
the public's participation in the auctions (direct or indirect) may exist, the central
planner needs to be more attuned to the preferences of the intermediaries, and
if they prefer a discriminatory price auction, the central planner will adopt this
mechanism.

So why do we find so many countries using the discriminatory pricing method?
Our conjecture is that the financial markets in many of these countries are dominated by a few large financial intermediaries and it is in their interest, paying
lower prices, to have a discriminatory price mechanism rather than a uniform
price mechanism. These few institutions are better informed than the rest of the
public simply because they hold a large portion of the potential bids either as
proprietary bidders or as agents for other bidders. This conjecture is supported by
our tests, which show that the discriminatory method is used more in countries
that have less-developed financial markets.[7]

To summarize, our paper belongs to the growing literature on divisible unit
auctions. The theory does not tell us whether the uniform auctions will generate
higher revenue than the discriminatory ones.[8] This remains an empirical issue
that our research is trying to contribute to. The relevant empirical work uses either an event study approach (for example, the U.S. experiment)[9] or employs
structural econometric models.[10] The novelty of our approach is that we use a
cross-sectional approach and look for explanatory variables that may help understand the sovereign's decision.[11] It makes a contribution to the literature on the
relationship between country characteristics and financial development.

NOTES

1. The recent Google and Morningstar auctions may have started a new approach to initial
   public offerings of stocks in the United States and elsewhere.

2. The survey was sent to all the central banks whose e-mail addresses were listed at
   the Bank for International Settlements international directory and to the treasuries and
   central banks whose e-mail addresses were listed at the IMF home page. In cases in which
   we did not get a response, we used personal contacts to get answers to the survey.

3. Though it now considers reinstating them in the future.

4. At the time of the survey, Finland indicated that it does not use auctions to sell its debt.
   Yet after the survey was conducted, we received information that Finland is considering
   using uniform auctions again in the future.

5. See Han, Longstaff, and Merrill (2007) for the description of the U.S. Treasury buyback
   auctions.

6. We also found that most countries using both mechanisms have the right to change the quantity after viewing the bidding results (67 percent for the discriminatory and 56 percent for the uniform), yet some of them do not use this right.

7. An additional explanation for the origin of using a given rule or method has to do with the evolution of financial markets around the world. Since the development of global financial markets has, by and large, lagged behind that of the United States, many countries have just followed the U.S example without questioning its rationale or whether it is appropriate and fits the market structure of that country.

8. See, for example, Wilson (1979), Back and Zender (1993), and Ausubel and Cramton (2002) for theoretical evidence on strategic bidding in multi-unit auctions.

9. The main issue with this approach (see also Tenorio 1993 and Umlauf 1993) is that one cannot claim *ceteris paribus,* that the economic conditions have not changed.

10. These papers (for example, Hortaçsu 2002) use a bidder's optimality condition to recover the distribution of the marginal valuations of the bidders. At its current stage, this literature does not provide a clear answer with respect to the mechanism choice.

11. A previous cross-country description of auction design issues is given in Bartolini and Cottarelli (1997). While their paper describes various aspects of the auction mechanism, our paper investigates recent practices and focuses on the determinants of the choice of the auction-pricing rule.

REFERENCES

Ausubel, L., and P. Cramton. 2002. "Demand Reduction and Inefficiency in Multi-Unit Auctions." *Working Paper*. University of Maryland.

Back, K., and J. F. Zender. 1993. "Auctions of Divisible Goods: On the Rationale for the Treasury Experiment." *Review of Financial Studies* 6: 733–764.

Bartolini, L., and C. Cottarelli. 1997. "Treasury bill auctions: Issues and uses." In M. Blejer and T. Ter-Minassian, eds. *Macroeconomic Dimensions of Public Finance: Essays in Honor of Vito Tanzi,* 267–336. New York: Routledge.

Friedman, M. 1960. *A Program for Monetary Stability*. New York: Fordham University Press.

Goldreich, D. 2007. "Underpricing in Discriminatory and Uniform Price Treasury Auctions." *Journal of Financial and Quantitative Analysis* 42:2, 443–466.

Han, B., F. Longstaff, and C. Merrill. 2007. "The 'Cherry-Picking' Option in the U.S. Treasury Buyback Auctions." *Journal of Finance* 62: 2673–2693.

Hortaçsu, A. 2002. "Mechanism Choice and Strategic Bidding in Divisible Good Auctions: An Empirical Analysis of the Turkish Treasury Auction Market." *Working Paper*. Chicago: University of Chicago Press.

La Porta, R., F. Lopez-de-Silanes, A. Shleifer, and R. Vishny. 1998. "Law and Finance." *Journal of Political Economy* 106: 1113–1155.

Malvey, P., C. Archibald, and S. T. Flynn. 1995. *Uniform Price Auctions: Evaluation of the Treasury Experience*. Washington, DC: U.S. Treasury, Office of Market Finance.

Malvey, P., and C. Archibald. 1998. *Uniform Price Auctions: Update of the Treasury Experience*. Washington, DC: U.S. Treasury, Office of Market Finance.

Nyborg, K., and S. Sundaresan. 1996. "Discriminatory versus Uniform Treasury Auctions: Evidence from When-Issued Transactions." *Journal of Financial Economics* 42.

Tenorio, R. 1993. "Revenue-Equivalence and Bidding Behavior in a Multi-Unit Auction Market: An Empirical Analysis." *Review of Economics and Statistics* 75: 302–314.

Umlauf, S. 1993. "An Empirical Study of the Mexican Treasury Bill Auction." *Journal of Financial Economics* 33: 313–340.

Wilson, R. 1979. "Auctions of Shares." *Quarterly Journal of Economics* 93: 675–698.

ABOUT THE AUTHORS

Menachem Brenner is a research professor of finance at the Stern School of Business, New York University. Brenner has served as an associate editor and referee to several finance journals. He co-founded the *Review of Derivatives Research.* He has published numerous articles in leading finance journals. His most recent work deals with volatility derivatives, executive stock options, and liquidity in the FX options markets. He co-invented (with Professor Dan Galai) the volatility index based on the prices of traded index options. Brenner has served as a consultant to leading stock exchanges, banks, and other financial institutions such as the New York Stock Exchange (NYSE), the American Stock Exchange, SOFFEX, the Tel Aviv Stock Exchange, the Bank of Israel, the Israel Securities Authority, and others. He was also a floor trader on the New York Futures Exchange and the NYSE. Professor Brenner was a member of the board of directors of the Tel Aviv Stock Exchange and the chairman of the new products committee. He was a member of the advisory panel on emerging markets at the International Finance Corporation.

Dan Galai is the Abe Gray Professor of Finance and Business Administration, and serves as the dean of the Jerusalem School of Business Administration of the Hebrew University in Jerusalem. He was a visiting professor of finance at INSEAD and at the University of California, Los Angeles. In 2006, he served as a visiting professor at the Stern School of Business at New York University and in the summer of 2008 was a visiting scholar at the IMF in Washington D.C. He has also taught at the University of Chicago and at the University of California, Berkeley. Dr. Galai holds a PhD from the University of Chicago and undergraduate and graduate degrees from the Hebrew University.

He has served as a consultant for the Chicago Board Options Exchange (CBOE) and the American Stock Exchange as well as for major banks. He co-invented (with Professor Menachem Brenner) the volatility index based on the prices of traded index options.

He has published numerous articles in leading business and finance journals, on options, financial assets, and corporate finance, and serves on the boards of academic journals. He is a co-author of *Risk Management,* McGraw-Hill (2000) and of *The Essentials of Risk Management,* McGraw-Hill (2005). He was a winner of the first annual Pomeranze Prize for excellence in options research presented by the CBOE.

He is a member of the blue ribbon panel and is the regional co-director for Israel of PRMIA (Professional Risk Managers International Association).

Dr. Galai is a principal in Sigma P.C.M. Ltd., which is engaged in portfolio management and corporate finance. In the company, he is responsible for risk management consulting to financial institutions as well as nonbank corporations. He is a co-founder of MutualArt Inc., a financial services company that provides pension-like benefits to selected artists worldwide. He also serves as a board member of several start-up companies.

Orly Sade, PhD, is a tenured senior faculty member and the head of the BA program at the Jerusalem School of Business Administration of the Hebrew University in Jerusalem. She joined the Hebrew University in 2002. Since 2006, Dr. Sade has also been a visiting associate professor of finance at New York University Stern School of Business. Dr. Sade also teaches at IE (Madrid) and at the NES (Moscow). She received her BA (economics and business) and MBA from Tel Aviv University and her PhD from the University of Utah.

Dr. Sade's primary research areas include the design of financial markets, financial auctions, and behavioral and experimental finance. She has published articles in these areas in leading scholarly journals. Dr. Sade was granted the Abe Gray research award by the president of the Hebrew University and received several other research grants and teaching recognition awards.

Dr. Sade has served as a member of investment committees of pension, providence, and mutual funds in Israel. She currently serves as a consultant to the Israeli Ministry of Finance and leading corporations.

CHAPTER 14

Pension Reform and Sovereign Credit Standing

ALFREDO CUEVAS
IMF's Representative, South Africa*

MARÍA GONZÁLEZ
Deputy Division Chief, International Monetary Fund

DAVIDE LOMBARDO
Senior Economist, International Monetary Fund

ARNOLDO LÓPEZ-MARMOLEJO
Senior Economist, BBVA Research

C an a reform designed to secure the long-term solvency of public finances by curbing the accumulation of unfunded liabilities end up reducing a country's creditworthiness? As most everything else in economics, social security reforms usually involve trade-offs and can have surprising side effects. Radical pension system reform, often described as *pension privatization*, provides an illustration of this principle. As we will explain, this reform raises challenges that demand a hard look at the well-known transition problem. Indeed, we argue that a successful pension reform along privatization lines will often require a program of adjustment in the nonpension fiscal deficit to limit the potential implications of pension reform for the evolution of government borrowing and, in consequence, for a government's creditworthiness.

Reform of public defined-benefit (DB) retirement programs has been an active element of the policy program in many countries since the last part of the twentieth century, as governments sought to address problems inherent to the financial sustainability of those programs. Many DB programs, typically introduced in the

---

*Cuevas, Gonzalez, and Lombardo are with the IMF; López-Marmolejo is with BBVA-Bancomer. This chapter presents the main findings from the authors' "Pension Privatization and Country Risk," prepared for Banca d'Italia's 2009 Conference on Pension Reform, Fiscal Policy, and Economic Performance and published in the volume of proceedings from that conference (see references for details). The views presented herein are the authors', and do not represent those of the IMF or BBVA-Bancomer.

middle of the last century, had for decades accumulated financial disequilibria that eventually came to threaten the long-term health of the public finances—in fact, they continue to do so in many countries. The reason was that the contributions paid by active workers over their lifetimes were insufficient to finance the benefits promised them upon retirement. The imbalance was in some cases evident only after the analysis of the long-run solvency of such programs that still yielded cash surpluses; in some other countries, social security programs were already chronically dependent on cash transfers from the government. In either case, the pension systems were net debtors to their current and future beneficiaries.

The present value of those net (current and future) *unfunded* liabilities is often described as *implicit pension debt* (IPD). IPD can be estimated as the amount of money that government would have to set aside today to allow the DB program to operate without recourse to any more subsidies (for a given projection of the future development of the economy and the workforce). It can be regarded as a *closed system* IPD (that is, what would be needed to face existing obligations only) or an *open system* IPD—what would be needed to finance existing and foreseeable additional obligations that would arise if the DB program were to operate on an unchanged basis into the indefinite future.

One of the reform options available to policy makers seeking to address these imbalances was the wholesale replacement of the DB retirement system with a defined-contribution (DC) program. Under this type of reform, pioneered by Chile in the early 1980s, the contributions made by each worker (or by others on her behalf) are deposited in an individual capitalization account. Pension administrators (often, but not necessarily, private firms) manage the funds in those accounts, investing them in approved assets, which typically include government bonds and selected stocks. Upon reaching retirement age, the worker's retirement benefit would be, in the general case, whatever the resources accumulated in her personal account could buy.

The appeal of introducing a DC system has been strong, as it makes no promises to its members beyond the promise to return to them their own accumulated contributions, plus any returns earned. In such a pure form, a DC system would be sustainable by definition, and would not represent a burden on the public purse; introduced *ab origine,* such a system would never create any IPD. That is, DC systems are by construction *fully funded.* In practice, reforms of this type have included some element of subsidy for the lowest-paid workers, but this is often designed with an eye to minimizing the resulting fiscal burden. In sum, the fiscal virtues of the DC program have made it an option worth considering for policy makers faced with unsustainable public DB systems. The list of countries that have implemented this type of reform following Chile's experience is by now long; and indeed it was seen as an integral component of the reform strategy recommended by the World Bank (1994).[1]

The replacement of a DB program with a DC program, however, is subject to a well-known cash flow problem. After the reform, workers' contributions are sent to their new capitalization accounts instead of going to the old social security agency, which, however, must continue to pay pension benefits to current retirees. This problem ends when the last beneficiaries of the old DB program die, so the transition period can be quite long. And while it lasts, a crucial decision must be made: Will the cash flow needs arising from the transition be financed with new public borrowing in financial markets, or with savings generated elsewhere in the fiscal accounts through measures such as new taxes and expenditure cuts?

Policy makers in reforming countries were well aware of the cash flow problem during the transition. Some of the countries that successfully implemented this type of pension reform, such as Chile and Mexico, accompanied their reforms with the increases of their underlying, nonpension fiscal balances. However, this has not been the case everywhere. Reform was often seen as a fail-safe option, good even when financed mostly with new borrowing. After all, the argument usually went, one would essentially just be making implicit pension debt explicit, and by arresting the accumulation of new unfunded liabilities, the balance of the reform would necessarily be positive. This line of thought, however, reflected an incomplete appreciation of the importance of the decision on how to finance the transition cash flow deficit. It roughly got right the idea that the cash flow deficits did not necessarily represent a loosening of fiscal policy, but just the expression of hitherto hidden (underlying or implicit) deficits (Mackenzie et al. 2003). It failed, however, to recognize the major differences that exist between implicit and explicit debt.

The mechanics of the transformation of IPD into explicit debt are easy to see once we look at a pay-as-you-go DB system as an intergenerational transfer mechanism that rolls over IPD. A worker acquires future pension rights with his contributions, which are a form of lending to the social security system, and this finances old pension liabilities falling due in the form of the obligation to pay benefits to current retirees. Public DB programs are continually borrowing from current workers so they can redeem their debt to current retirees. But after the introduction of a DC program, the social security agency is no longer able to borrow from current workers. If no fiscal adjustment takes place in the nonpension public sector, the general government must borrow from market participants to service its obligations to retirees. Thus, IPD is not replaced instantaneously by explicit financial debt. Rather, IPD falling due is gradually rolled into explicit financial debt.

Nevertheless, other things are not equal: Explicit or financial debt is a very different creature from IPD. IPD is a very long-term liability. If you consider a young worker accruing pension rights, it is easy to see that she may collect them for possibly 30, 40, or even 50 years. In contrast, for many sovereigns (mostly in the developing world) it has been traditionally difficult to borrow at maturities longer than 5 or 10 years. IPD is by definition payable in a country's own currency, whereas contractual or explicit financing may be available in only foreign currencies, especially at relatively longer maturities—the so-called original sin problem discussed by Eichengreen, Hausman, and Panizza (2003). Supported by the mandatory nature of social security, IPD's rollover risk was minimal, whereas financial debt is held voluntarily and thus subject to significantly higher rollover risk. Explicit financial debt is predetermined upon issuance, whereas the size of IPD is likely positively correlated with the tax base, which may make it easier to bear. In this sense, IPD is much like the new type of GDP-indexed liabilities being proposed by some observers as a means to enhance the sustainability of public finances. Lastly, financial debt is a contractually fixed commitment, or a firm liability. In contrast, IPD is a contingent liability; that is, its realization depends on a large number of factors, including invariance in the legal framework governing retirement and a variety of demographic and economic outcomes. While the latter may be beyond the control of the state, the legal framework is not. A slightly different way to say this is that IPD can be unilaterally restructured by the country's normal legislative process, whereas financial debt cannot.

Looking at the differences just listed, especially the last one, it is easy to see that IPD is much like equity, and thus stands in contrast with traditional debt. Under a DB system, workers hold a residual claim on government. Bondholders, on the other hand, hold a claim with specific contractual rights and which, in practice, is treated as if it were of higher seniority. In fact, countries in fiscal distress often modify the parameters of their DB systems (for example, by allowing inflation to erode the real value of pension benefits, or more quickly, by moving to tax pension benefits or increased payroll contributions) rather than default on their financial debt.

This last insight helps one understand more fully the replacement of a DB program with a DC one: It is, in a way, a debt equity swap in reverse. In effect, the reform elevates pension program contributors, formerly akin to equity holders, to the rank of creditors of government on a par with bondholders and other lenders. Before the reform, tightening the terms of a DB plan was a policy option that could be pursued unilaterally by the state in a bid to protect its ability to service financial debt. But after a DC plan has been introduced, workers are bondholders, enjoying the benefit of cross-default principles.

As it is natural, the reverse debt equity swap represented by pension reform increases the vulnerability of public finances, other things being constant. This rise in risk is the economic cost of pension reform, and it must be fully taken into account when evaluating pension reform options. Another way to look at this problem is to realize that, other things being equal, pension privatization will dilute over time the value of debt held by pre-existing creditors, who are now no longer ahead of workers and pensioners in the line for receiving payments from the state. The relative seniority of their claims has been weakened; this must be reflected in the value of such claims and, therefore, on the government's borrowing cost. The only way to prevent this from happening is to preserve the original trajectory of borrowing and debt by implementing real adjustment measures to finance transition costs.

In Cuevas et al. (2010), we present a statistical analysis designed to empirically test the reflections presented earlier.[2] The main hypothesis under assessment was that the financial markets do not regard standard financial debt and IPD as equivalent. As reported there, we followed two different strategies. In the first one, we looked directly at the separate impact of IPD and financial debt on a country's international investor rating, which is a standard credit rating. We looked at 33 countries at a point in time (1999 to 2000)—the largest set for which methodologically homogeneous measures of IPD could be obtained.[3] Our results showed conclusively that, in line with the literature, countries with higher financial debt get worse credit ratings, with the attendant repercussions on their borrowing cost. The other main determinant of a sovereign's credit rating was the level of its international reserves, indicating that these ratings focus largely on stock measures, and less so on flow indicators (the noninterest fiscal balance, in particular, turned out to be statistically unrelated to the credit rating, for example). However, despite trying various modeling specifications, we could not find evidence of any effect of IPD on credit ratings.

To further verify these results, we carried out a second exercise. In this case, we gathered a data set comprising 63 countries over the period from 1979 to 2003. The test consisted of trying to find whether, controlling for the level of financial debt and other variables, the credit rating of a sovereign improved with the implementation of pension privatization. Whereas the first exercise could be subject to the criticism that we were simply not using an accurate measure of IPD, the second was free of that problem, as the approval and implementation of pension reform can be dated accurately. Again, we tried several specifications, but were unable to uncover any independent positive effect on credit ratings from the introduction of a DC program in replacement of a DB program.

The implication of these results is clear: Creditworthiness can be adversely affected by radical pension reform implemented by replacing a DB program with a DC program, even if the reform does manage to reduce total (implicit plus explicit) public sector liabilities. Some might argue that this reflects a misunderstanding by market participants of the risks from imbalanced DB programs; but this would be yet another dimension in which IPD and financial debt differ. As noted earlier, however, beyond any possible misperceptions in the market, IPD and financial debt are different, and this is bound to affect the market's assessment of sovereign creditworthiness.

The corollary of this research is not to argue against pension reform, but to encourage a cautious implementation strategy that gives due weight to the question of how to finance transitional cash flow deficits. It may be necessary for the overall preservation of fiscal stability and the attainment of the goals of pension reform itself, that the nonpension fiscal balance be strengthened to finance at least some fraction of those cash-flow deficits. Also, pension privatization can be accompanied by measures to reduce unfunded liabilities in any residual components of the old DB program. The objective of these actions is to make sure that the implementation of pension reform does not excessively affect the level of public debt. The higher the level of public debt going into the reform, the larger the effort that should be made to finance transition costs with increased savings. To do otherwise could leave the country in a more vulnerable position, contrary to the very objectives of the reform.

NOTES

1. The appeal of pension reforms featuring the introduction of DC programs was made only stronger by the expectation that the capital deposited in individual accounts would boost national savings and thus finance investment for growth. As explained in Mackenzie, Gerson, and Cuevas (1997), this was often an unfounded expectation. Other features of the system have also been highlighted by its proponents. For example, the G. W. Bush administration played up the idea that enrolled workers would have part of their contributions invested in common stocks, which would allow them to partake of the growth in the market value of corporate America.

2. Our results are consistent with prior discussions in the literature, but are drawn from wider samples and involve a more systematic statistical work. See, for example, Truglia (2002), Fiess (2003), and Pinheiro (2004).

3. These estimates were compiled by Holzman, Palacios, and Zviniene (2004) in what represents a significant methodological effort.

REFERENCES

Cuevas, A., M. Gonzalez, D. Lombardo, and A. Lopez-Marmolejo. 2010. "Pension privatization and country risk." In Daniele Franco, ed. *Pension Reform, Fiscal Policy and Economic Performance*, 345–365. Rome: Banca d'Italia. www.bancaditalia.it/pubblicazioni/seminari_convegni.

Eichengreen, B., R. Hausman, and U. Panizza. 2003. "Currency Mismatches, Debt Intolerance and Original Sin." *NBER Working Paper*, No. 10036. Cambridge, MA: National Bureau of Economic Research.

Fiess, N. 2003. *Pension Reform or Pension Default? A Note on Pension Reform and Country Risk.* Washington, DC: World Bank.

Holzman, R., R. Palacios, and A. Zviniene. 2004. "Implicit Pension Debt: Issues, Measurement, and Scope in International Perspective." *Social Protection Discussion Paper.* Washington, DC: World Bank.

Mackenzie, G., P. Gerson, and A. Cuevas. 1997. "Pension Regimes and Saving." *Occasional Paper 153.* Washington DC: International Monetary Fund.

Mackenzie, G., P. Gerson, A. Cuevas, and P. Heller. 2003. "Pension Reform and the Fiscal Policy Stance." *Public Budgeting and Finance* 23:1, 115–127.

Pinheiro, V. 2004. "The politics of Social Security reform in Brazil." In K. Weyland, ed. *Learning from Foreign Models in Latin American Policy Reform*, 110–138. Washington, DC: Woodrow Wilson Center Press and Johns Hopkins University Press.

Truglia, V. 2002. "Sovereign Ratings and Aging Societies." Paper presented at the Rosenberg Institute of Global Finance's Conference on Financial Global Aging. www.brandeis.edu/global/rosenberg_papers/truglia_paper.pdf.

World Bank. 1994. *Averting the Old Age Crisis.* Washington, DC: World Bank, 432.

ABOUT THE AUTHORS

Alfredo Cuevas is the IMF's representative in South Africa. He was affiliated for many years with the fiscal affairs department of the International Monetary Fund. During that time, he led or participated in several technical assistance projects in the area of social security reform, mostly in Latin America. He has also written a number of research pieces on the relationship between pension reform and macroeconomic policy.

Maria González is a deputy division chief with the International Monetary Fund, where she has worked on several emerging market and low-income programs and surveillance countries. Her research interests and publications have mainly focused on political economy, fiscal, and monetary policy. She holds a PhD in economics from Princeton University.

Davide Lombardo is a senior economist with the International Monetary Fund, where he has worked on several emerging market programs. His research interests and publications have mainly focused on international and corporate finance. He holds a PhD in economics from Stanford University.

Arnoldo López-Marmolejo is a senior economist at BBVA Research. He received a PhD from the Autonomous University of Barcelona and has been a visiting scholar at the University of Minnesota and at the University of Pennsylvania. Before joining the BBVA group, Dr. López-Marmolejo was a financial specialist in the Central Bank of Mexico.

PART III

Sovereign Defaults, Restructurings, and the Resumption of Borrowing

A s we have already noted, the history of sovereign debt includes many episodes of default. Some nations have proven to be serial defaulters. Some observers have expressed amazement that a defaulting nation can secure repeated loans. This section examines the problem of defaults in detail. It begins by considering the reasons that nations default and also considers the means that their creditors use to command repayment. Furthermore, it asks the question of whether sovereign defaulters really are punished.

Few defaults are simple defaults with a total refusal ever to repay anything. Instead, a much more customary procedure is for the lender and borrower to agree to a rescheduling of the original obligation with reduced payment amounts stretched over a longer repayment horizon. In many instances, international financial institutions, such as the International Monetary Fund, intervene and assist in the restructuring process. While defaulting nations may be excluded from borrowing for some period after a default, this section also considers the conditions under which defaulting nations can reenter the market and secure new financing.

CHAPTER 15

Understanding Sovereign Default

JUAN CARLOS HATCHONDO
Economist, the Federal Reserve Bank[*]

LEONARDO MARTINEZ
Economist, the IMF Institute

HORACIO SAPRIZA
Research Economist, Division of International Finance

T his chapter discusses the economics of sovereign defaults, summarizing lessons from existing work on this issue.[1] First, we define sovereign defaults. Second, we describe costs of defaulting. Third, we identify circumstances that are likely to lead to a default. Finally, we discuss how default risk may help to account for distinctive features of emerging economies.

SOVEREIGN DEFAULTS

Sovereign debt refers to debt incurred by governments. Sovereign borrowing can be a key policy tool to finance investment or to respond to a cyclical downturn. There are different definitions of a sovereign default. From a legal point of view, a default event is an episode in which a scheduled debt service is not paid beyond a grace period specified in the debt contract. Credit-rating agencies consider a technical default an episode in which the sovereign makes a restructuring offer that contains terms less favorable than the original debt.[2]

Sovereign defaults do not necessarily imply a total repudiation of outstanding debt. Most default episodes are followed by a settlement between creditors and the debtor government. The settlement may take the form of a debt exchange or debt restructuring. The new stream of payments promised by the government typically involves a combination of lower principal, lower interest payments, and

---

[*]The views expressed herein are those of the authors and should not be attributed to the IMF, its Executive Board, or its management, the Federal Reserve Bank of Richmond, or the Board of Governors of the Federal Reserve System.

longer maturities. Credit rating agencies define the duration of a default episode as the amount of time that passes between the default event and when the debt is restructured (even though there may be holdout creditors).

COSTS OF SOVEREIGN DEFAULTS

Identifying the costs of sovereign defaults is essential in understanding why we observe sovereign debt in the first place. If there were no costs for defaulting, the sovereign would default under all circumstances. Anticipating this behavior, investors would never lend to sovereigns and there would be no sovereign debt. That is, for sovereign debt to exist, it is necessary that at least in some circumstances it would be more costly for a sovereign to default than to pay back its debt. Similarly, for sovereign defaults to exist, it is necessary that at least in some circumstances it would be more costly for a sovereign to pay back its debt than to default. This section describes two costs of sovereign default that are often mentioned in the literature: sanctions imposed by creditors, and signaling costs.

Sanctions

In this subsection, we first discuss the ability of creditors to increase the borrowing cost of defaulting sovereigns, and we then focus on other sanctions.

Borrowing Cost

Increasing a defaulting sovereign's borrowing costs would require coordination among holders of defaulted debt and all other potential lenders. It would require that potential creditors who find it beneficial to lend to a sovereign that has defaulted in the past would choose not to give credit to this sovereign, because these creditors want to punish the defaulter for its past behavior. In models of sovereign default, coordination among lenders can be sustained in infinitely repeated games in which a creditor wants to maintain his good reputation by not deviating from his agreement with other creditors so he can better keep his share of the profits obtained through coordination (see Wright 2002). Such a degree of coordination seems unlikely to occur in competitive credit markets with a large number of potential lenders. With more creditors, the share of the benefits from coordination for each creditor is smaller, and therefore deviations from a coordination agreement become relatively more attractive. Wright (2005) discusses how in the past three decades, the sovereign debt market has become more competitive.

Lenders can also try to impose financial sanctions that do not require such coordination. In their analysis of the legal consequences of sovereign default episodes, Sturzenegger and Zettelmeyer (2006b) discuss how holders of defaulted bonds succeeded in interfering with cross-border payments to other creditors who had previously agreed to a debt restructuring. If all cross-border payments could be blocked, a defaulting sovereign would not be able to borrow abroad—no creditor would lend if it were unable to collect the payments. From this, Sturzenegger and Zettelmeyer (2006b) infer that holders of defaulted bonds may have been able to exclude defaulting economies from international capital markets. Yet, at the same time they conclude that "legal tactics are updated all the time, and new ways are discovered both to extract payment from a defaulting sovereign as well as to avoid attachments." In particular, they expect that "the threat of exclusion may be less relevant for some countries or to all countries in the future." In any case, there are alternatives available to defaulting economies. They could issue bonds in local markets, obtain aid, or ask for official credit (from other governments or multilateral financial institutions). It is not obvious whether a sovereign forced to use these alternatives would face a significantly higher borrowing cost. A common finding is that a default leads to a drain in capital flows. However, the observed difficulties in market access after a default may be the result of the same factors that triggered the default decision itself. For example, both default and the difficulties in market access after default may be triggered by political turnover (see Hatchondo, Martinez, and Sapriza 2009). The empirical literature finds no clear evidence of defaulters being punished by creditors through exclusion or higher interest rates on new loans when sufficient control variables are used (see Eichengreen and Portes 2000 and Gelos, Sahay, and Sandleris 2004).[3]

Other Sanctions

Governments have on occasions intervened actively in support of their constituents who are holders of defaulted debt issued by other sovereigns (see Sturzenegger and Zettelmeyer 2006a). These interventions have taken the form of diplomatic dissuasion, withholding of official credit, threat of trade sanctions, and in exceptional cases, armed interventions (Mitchener and Weidenmier 2005 provide a case study of gunboat diplomacy).

Signaling Costs

A default may be costly because of the information it signals. For example, a default decision may signal that the policy makers in office are less prone to respect property rights. Furthermore, a default may disclose some of the government's private information about fundamentals of the economy to market participants, which in turn could increase borrowing costs. Furthermore, the signal transmitted by a default decision may have other consequences besides increasing the cost of future borrowing. Cole and Kehoe (1998) argue that a sovereign default may imply that the government is considered untrustworthy in other areas besides the credit relationship with lenders. Sandleris (2008) explains how by revealing negative information about itself or the economy, the government may affect firms' net worth and their ability to borrow, which may lower the desired level of investment. Arteta and Hale (2006) find that sovereign debt crises are systematically accompanied by a large decline in foreign credit to domestic private firms. IMF (2002), Kumhof (2004), and Kumhof and Tanner (2005) explain that domestic financial crises are observed after sovereign defaults. In contrast with the costs discussed in the beginning of this section, signaling costs reflect the increased perceived probability of a future default and not a punishment imposed by creditors.

The signals implied by a government's default decision may also have political consequences. The default may reveal important characteristics of the incumbent policy makers, such as their competence. Moreover, because the holdings of sovereign debt are not uniformly distributed across the population, a government's default may signal its redistribution goals.

Although the existence of signaling costs of defaulting seems plausible, it is not clear how important these costs are. More specifically, it is not clear how important the government's private information is, the extent to which this information is transmitted through the default decision, and the importance of the effects of communicating this information.

DETERMINANTS OF SOVEREIGN DEFAULTS

This section discusses which circumstances are likely to lead to a sovereign default. Identifying the set of states that are likely to trigger a sovereign default is closely related with identifying how the costs of defaulting discussed in the previous section depend on these states.

Resources

When the level of current resources is low, paying debt obligation may require large adjustments to expenditures or revenues. Such adjustments can be costly. Empirical evidence indicates that a sovereign tends to default in periods of low available resources. Using a historical data set with 169 sovereign defaults, Tomz and Wright (2007) report that 62 percent of these default episodes occurred in years when the output level in the defaulting country was below its trend. Cantor and Packer (1996) find that sovereign credit ratings strongly respond to macroeconomic factors such as the GDP growth rate and per capita income. The countercyclicality of the interest rate paid by governments in developing countries (see further on) is consistent with sovereigns being more likely to default when economic conditions are worse. Higher interest rates may reflect a higher compensation to lenders who estimate a higher default probability.

Fluctuations of terms of trade (the ratio of the price of exports to the price of imports) are an important driving force behind the business cycles in some emerging economies (see, for example, Mendoza 1995).[4] At the same time, several emerging economies strongly rely on commodity taxation as a source of public revenue and depend largely on imported intermediate goods that have no close substitutes. Studies find that terms of trade fluctuations are a significant predictor of sovereign default and interest rate spreads in emerging economies.[5] A recent example of the relevance of commodity prices is found in Ecuador, where falling commodity prices led to a deterioration of the macroeconomic conditions and a sovereign default in 1999.[6] The sharp declines in oil prices during the second half of the 1990s have also been linked to the worsening of the macroeconomic and fiscal situation that led to the Russian default of 1998 (see Sturzenegger and Zettelmeyer 2006a).

Furthermore, episodes of sovereign default may be triggered by wars or civil conflicts that adversely affect a country's productivity. Defaults may also be triggered by a devaluation of the local currency when a relatively large fraction of the sovereign's debt is denominated in foreign currency and its revenues rely heavily on the taxation of nontradable goods. The magnitude of crises triggered by a devaluation of the local currency is likely to be amplified by currency mismatches in the banking sector, the corporate sector, and households.

BORROWING COSTS

External factors that increase the cost of borrowing may also trigger a default episode. For example, both international interest rates and the total net lending to emerging economies may influence lending to a particular developing country. Borrowing costs are particularly important in periods in which a country is trying to roll over its debt. The importance of external factors for the borrowing cost of developing countries is suggested by empirical studies that find that the interest rates paid by these countries have tended to move in the same direction as U.S. interest rates (see Lambertini 2001, Arora and Cerisola 2001, and Uribe and Yue 2006).

Political Factors

In addition to pure economic variables, political factors may also play a nontrivial role as determinants of defaults.[7] Sturzenegger and Zettelmeyer (2006a) conclude that "a solvency crisis could be triggered by a shift in the parameters that govern the country's willingness to make sacrifices in order to repay, due to changes in the domestic political economy (a revolution, a coup, an election, etc.)." Similarly, Van Rijckeghem and Weder (2004) explain that it is reasonable to infer that a country's willingness to pay is influenced by politics, that is, by the distribution of interests and by the institutions and power structures. Santiso (2003) writes, "One basic rule of the confidence game [in international financial markets] is then to be very careful when nominating the official government voicer. For investors, it is mainly the ministry of economics or finance or the governor of the central bank."

The behavior of the sovereign spread in Brazil before and after the run-up to the presidential elections in October 2002 illustrates the importance of political factors as determinants of default decisions. The concerns raised by the left-wing presidential candidate Luiz Inacio "Lula" da Silva because of his past declarations in favor of debt repudiations is the most accepted explanation for the sharp increase in the country spread preceding the Brazilian election (see Goretti 2005). Spreads may have increased because of a decrease in the expected willingness to pay by the future government. Similarly, before winning the presidential elections in Ecuador, Rafael Correa declared his intentions to restructure the country's debt. On January 17, 2007, two days after taking office, Ecuador's minister of economics told a group of investors that the government may repay only 40 percent of its foreign debt as part of an effort to free up funds for health care and education. The day after, Ecuador's benchmark government foreign securities tumbled, driving the yield up 1.1 percentage points to 14.32 percent.

Empirical studies suggest that political factors are important in understanding sovereign defaults. Citron and Nickelsburg (1987) find that political instability is statistically significant as a determinant of a country's default probability. Balkan (1992) considers two dimensions of the borrower's political environment, a democracy index and a political instability index, and finds them statistically significant in explaining default probabilities. Rivoli and Brewer (1997) find that long- and short-term armed conflict in a country and changes in the long-term political legitimacy of the government are the most significant political predictors of debt rescheduling during the 1980s. Kohlscheen (2010) finds that parliamentary democracies experience a lower probability of default than presidential systems. He argues that this is explained by the higher number of veto players (that is, political players with power to prevent a default) in parliamentary systems. Moser (2006) finds a significant effect of changes of the finance minister or the minister of the economy on a country's interest rate spreads. He argues that such events may reveal important signals about the government's future policy course. These signals may contain information that affects expectations on both about how the government will influence future growth and the policy makers' willingness to service debt.

Alfaro and Kanczuk (2005), Cole, Dow, and English (1995), and Hatchondo, Martinez, and Sapriza (2009) present models in which both default and difficulties in market access after a default may be triggered by political turnover. In their models, policy makers with a different willingness to pay alternate in power. When policy makers with a weaker willingness to pay take power, they may default on the debt issued by pre-default governments with a stronger willingness to pay. Following such a default, as long as policy makers with a weaker willingness to pay stay in power, governments experience difficulties in market access. Furthermore, since it is more costly for post-default governments to borrow (because lenders understand that, other things being equal, these governments are more willing to default), they borrow less. Market access improves after the defaulting policy makers lose power. A clear example of this is discussed in Cole, Dow, and English (1995). They explain that "the ability of Reconstruction governments in Florida and Mississippi to borrow after the Civil War suggests that the old creditors could not block new loans once the states' reputations had been restored by an observable change in regime."

Hatchondo, Martinez, and Sapriza (2009) argue that the stability of creditor-friendly regimes is key for defaults triggered by political turnover to occur. Since the price received by the government for the bonds it issues incorporates a discount that mirrors the default probability, if a creditor-friendly government chooses borrowing levels that would lead a less-friendly government to default, it has to compensate lenders for this contingency, that is, for the contingency that less-friendly policy makers become the decision makers in the future. If the probability of this contingency is high enough (creditor-friendly regimes are not stable), it is too expensive for a creditor-friendly government to choose borrowing levels that would lead less-friendly governments to default. In this scenario, creditor-friendly governments choose borrowing levels that even less-friendly governments will most likely choose to pay, and therefore it is unlikely that political turnover triggers a default.

BUSINESS CYCLES IN EMERGING ECONOMIES AND SOVEREIGN DEFAULT

Default risk may help us account for distinctive features of business cycles in emerging economies. Neumeyer and Perri (2005) argue that the dynamics of interest rates are important for understanding business cycle fluctuations in emerging economies. To the extent that the interest rate paid by sovereigns is influenced by the probability of default, understanding default risk may help one to understand business cycles in emerging economies.

Several studies have documented that business cycles in small emerging economies differ from those in small, developed economies.[8] Compared with developed economies, emerging economies feature:

- More volatility—the volatilities of output, real interest rates, and net exports are higher.
- Higher volatility of consumption relative to income—the ratio of these volatilities is typically higher than one in emerging economies, while it is lower than one in developed economies.
- Countercyclical real interest rates in contrast with the procyclical real interest rates in developed economies.
- More countercyclical net exports.

Other distinctive features of emerging economies are that most of these economies exhibit a procyclical government expenditure (government expenditure is acyclical or slightly countercyclical in developed countries) and a countercyclical inflation tax (the inflation tax is procyclical in developed countries). These features are documented by Gavin and Perotti (1997), Talvi and Vegh (2005), and Kaminsky, Reinhart, and Vegh (2004).

Several authors have used the sovereign default framework proposed by Eaton and Gersovitz (1981) to account for the business cycle regularities of emerging economies.[9] In this framework, the high interest rates paid by developing countries reflect a compensation for the default probability. Furthermore, the countercyclicality of spreads paid by developing countries is consistent with the belief that sovereigns are more likely to default when economic conditions are relatively bad (see the earlier section on borrowing costs). The tendency of sovereigns to default in bad times implies that in such times, borrowing is more expensive, and thus borrowing levels may be lower. This is consistent with the more countercyclical net exports and higher volatility of consumption relative to income in developing countries. Furthermore, if borrowing is more expensive in bad times, then it may be optimal to tax more and decrease government expenditures in such times, which would help to explain the procyclicality of public expenditures and the countercyclicality of tax rates in emerging countries (see, for example, Cuadra, Sanchez, and Sapriza 2010). A complete understanding of the differences between developed and developing countries would require a theory of why default risk is higher in developing countries.

CONCLUSION

Sovereign default episodes are widespread throughout history and are likely to continue to occur in the future. More research is necessary on the topic, for example, to assess the magnitude of the different costs of defaulting and to understand the precise role played by the determinants of a sovereign default. Moreover, it is not clear what explains differences in recovery rates on defaulted debt or differences in the duration of a default episode. Answering these questions, and thus advancing our understanding of the economics of sovereign default, seems a necessary step to better comprehend the distinctive economic features of most economies.

NOTES

1. See Hatchondo, Martinez, and Sapriza (2007a) and Hatchondo, Martinez, and Sapriza (2007b) for a more detailed analysis of the different aspects of the economics of sovereign default.
2. See Peter (2002) for further discussion on rating agencies' definitions of default.
3. Hatchondo, Martinez, and Sapriza (2007b) discuss the role of assuming exclusion from capital markets of defaulting governments in quantitative models of sovereign default.
4. For many countries, the terms of trade for a few goods can significantly affect their income. For example, according to the United Nations Conference on Trade and Development, 57 developing countries depended on just three commodities for more than half of their exports in 1995 (see World Bank 1999).
5. See, for example, Catao, Kapur, and Sutton (2002), Catao and Kapur (2004), Min (1998), Caballero (2003), Caballero and Panageas (2003), Hilscher and Nosbusch (2004), Calvo, Izquierdo, and Mejia (2004), and Cuadra and Sapriza (2006).
6. Oil and bananas together accounted for 59 percent of Ecuadorian exports in 2001. Ecuador was the first country to default on Brady bonds (Brady bonds arose from an effort in the late 1980s to reduce the debt held by less-developed countries that were frequently defaulting on loans).
7. For a more detailed survey of the links between political factors and sovereign defaults, see Hatchondo and Martinez (2010).
8. See Aguiar and Gopinath (2007), Neumeyer and Perri (2005), and Uribe and Yue (2006), among others.
9. See Aguiar and Gopinath (2006), Arellano (2008), Cuadra and Sapriza (2008), Hatchondo and Martinez (2009), Hatchondo, Martinez, and Sapriza (2010), Lizarazo (2010) and Yue (2010), among others.

REFERENCES

Aguiar, M., and G. Gopinath. 2006. "Defaultable Debt, Interest Rates and the Current Account." *Journal of International Economics* 69:1, 64–83.

———. 2007. "Emerging Market Business Cycles: The Cycle Is the Trend." *Journal of Political Economy* 115:1, 69–102.

Alfaro, L., and F. Kanczuk. 2005. "Sovereign Debt as a Contingent Claim: A Quantitative Approach." *Journal of International Economics* 65:2, 297–314.

Arellano, C. 2008. "Default Risk and Income Fluctuations in Emerging Economies." *American Economic Review* 98: 690–712.

Arora, V., and M. Cerisola. 2001. "How Does U.S. Monetary Policy Influence Sovereign Spreads in Emerging Markets?" *IMF Staff Papers* 48:3, 474–498.

Arteta, C., and G. Hale. 2006. "Sovereign Debt Crises and Credit to the Private Sector." *Journal of International Economics* 74:1, 53–69.

Balkan, E. 1992. "Political Instability, Country Risk and Probability of Default." *Applied Economics* 24:9, 999–1008.

Caballero, R. J. 2003. "The Future of the IMF." *The American Economic Review, Papers and Proceedings* 93:2, 31–8.

Caballero, R. J., and S. Panageas. 2003. "Hedging Sudden Stops and Precautionary Recessions: A Quantitative Framework." *NBER Working Paper,* No. 9778.

Calvo, G. A., A. Izquierdo, and L. Mejia. 2004. "On the Empirics of Sudden Stops: The Relevance of Balance-Sheet Effects." *NBER Working Paper,* No. 10520.

Cantor, R., and F. Packer. 1996. "Determinants and Impact of Sovereign Credit Ratings." *Economic Policy Review* 2:2, 37–53.

Catao, L., and S. Kapur. 2004. "Missing Link: Volatility and the Debt Intolerance Paradox." *IMF Working Paper* 04/51.

Catao, L., S. Kapur, and B. Sutton. 2002. "Sovereign Defaults: The Role of Volatility." *IMF Working Paper* 02/149.

Citron, J., and G. Nickelsburg. 1987. "Country Risk and Political Instability." *Journal of Development Economics* 25:2, 385–392.

Cole, H., J. Dow, and W. English. 1995. "Default, Settlement, and Signaling: Lending Resumption in a Reputational Model of Sovereign Debt." *International Economic Review* 36:2, 365–385.

Cole, H., and P. Kehoe. 1998. "Models of Sovereign Debt: Partial versus General Reputations." *International Economic Review* 39:1, 55–70.

Cuadra, G., J. Sanchez, and H. Sapriza. 2010. "Fiscal Policy and Default Risk in Emerging Economies." *Review of Economic Dynamics* 13:2, 452–469.

Cuadra, G., and H. Sapriza. 2006. "Sovereign Default, Terms of Trade, and Interest Rates in Emerging Markets." *Working Paper* 2006-01. Banco de Mexico.

———. 2008. "Sovereign Default, Interest Rates and Political Uncertainty in Emerging Markets." *Journal of International Economics* 76: 78–88.

Eaton, J., and M. Gersovitz. 1981. "Debt with Potential Repudiation: Theoretical and Empirical Analysis." *Review of Economic Studies* 48:2, 289–309.

Eichengreen, B., and R. Portes. 2000. "Debt Restructuring with and without the IMF." Unpublished Manuscript. Berkeley, CA: University of California.

Gavin, M., and R. Perotti. 1997. "Fiscal Policy in Latin America." In B. S. Bernanke and J. J. Rotemberg, eds. *NBER Macroeconomics Annual* 1997, 12: 11–71. Cambridge, MA: MIT Press.

Gelos, G., R. Sahay, and G. Sandleris. 2004. "Sovereign Borrowing by Developing Countries: What Determines Market Access?" *IMF Working Paper* 04/221.

Goretti, M. 2005. "The Brazilian Currency Turmoil of 2002: A Nonlinear Analysis." *International Journal of Finance and Economics* 10: 289–306.

Hatchondo, J. C., and L. Martinez. 2009. "Long-Duration Bonds and Sovereign Defaults." *Journal of International Economics* 79: 117–125.

———. 2010. "The Politics of Sovereign Defaults." *Economic Quarterly* 96:3, 291–917.

Hatchondo, J. C., L. Martinez, and H. Sapriza. 2007a. "The Economics of Sovereign Defaults." *Economic Quarterly* 93:2, 163–187.

———. 2007b. "Quantitative Models of Sovereign Default and the Threat of Financial Exclusion." *Economic Quarterly* 93:3, 251–286.

———. 2009. "Heterogeneous Borrowers in Quantitative Models of Sovereign Default." *International Economic Review* 50:4, 1129–1151.

———. 2010. "Quantitative Properties of Sovereign Default Models: Solution Methods Matter." *Review of Economic Dynamics* 13: 919–933.

Hilscher, J., and Y. Nosbusch. 2004. "Determinants of Sovereign Risk." *Working Paper.* Cambridge, MA: Harvard University.

International Monetary Fund. 2002. "Sovereign Debt Restructurings and the Domestic Economy Experience in Four Recent Cases." Washington, DC: International Monetary Fund, Policy Development and Review Department.

Kaminsky, G., C. Reinhart, and C. Vegh. 2004. "When It Rains, It Pours: Procyclical Capital Flows and Macroeconomic Policies." In M. Gertler and K. Rogoff, eds. *NBER Macroeconomics Annual 2004* 19: 11–53. Cambridge, MA: MIT Press.

Kohlscheen, E. 2010. "Sovereign Risk: Constitutions Rule." *Oxford Economic Papers* 62:1, 62–85.

Kumhof, M. 2004. "Fiscal Crisis Resolution: Taxation versus Inflation." Unpublished Manuscript. Stanford, CA: Stanford University.

Kumhof, M., and E. Tanner. 2005. "Government Debt: A Key Role in Financial Intermediation." *IMF Working Paper* 05/57.

Lambertini, L. 2001. "Volatility and Sovereign Default." Unpublished Manuscript. Los Angeles: University of California.

Lizarazo, S. 2010. "Sovereign Risk and Risk Averse International Investors." *Working Paper.* Instituto Tecnológico Autonomo de Mexico.

Mendoza, E. 1995. "The Terms of Trade, the Real Exchange Rate, and Economic Fluctuations." *International Economic Review* 36:1, 101–37.

Min, H. G. 1998. "Determinants of Emerging Market Bond Spread: Do Economic Fundamentals Matter?" *Policy Research Paper*, No. 1899. Washington, DC: World Bank.

Mitchener, K., and M. Weidenmier. 2005. "Empire, Public Goods, and the Roosevelt Corollary." *The Journal of Economic History* 65:3, 658–692.

Moser, C. 2006. "The Impact of Political Risk on Sovereign Bond Spreads—Evidence from Latin America." Mainz, Germany: University of Mainz.

Neumeyer, P., and F. Perri. 2005. "Business Cycles in Emerging Economies: The Role of Interest Rates." *Journal of Monetary Economics* 52:2, 345–380.

Peter, M. 2002. "Estimating Default Probabilities of Emerging Market Sovereigns: A New Look at a Not-So-New Literature." *HEI Working Paper* 06-2002. Graduate Institute of International Studies, Economics Section.

Rivoli, P., and T. Brewer. 1997. "Political Instability and Country Risk." *Global Finance Journal* 8:2, 313–325.

Sandleris, G. 2008. "Sovereign Defaults: Information, Investment and Credit." *Journal of International Economics* 76: 267–275.

Santiso, J. 2003. *The Political Economy of Emerging Markets: Actors, Institutions and Crisis in Latin America*. New York: Palgrave Macmillan.

Sturzenegger, F., and J. Zettelmeyer. 2006a. "Defaults in the '90s." Unpublished Manuscript. Universidad Torcuato Di Tella.

———. 2006b. "Has the Legal Threat to Sovereign Debt Restructuring Become Real?" Unpublished Manuscript. Universidad Torcuato Di Tella.

Talvi, E., and C. Vegh. 2005. "Tax Base Variability and Procyclicality of Fiscal Policy." *Journal of Development Economics* 78:1, 156–190.

Tomz, M., and M. L. J. Wright. 2007. "Do Countries Default in 'Bad Times'?" *Journal of the European Economic Association* 5: 2–3, 352–360.

Uribe, M., and V. Yue. 2006. "Country Spreads and Emerging Countries: Who Drives Whom?" *Journal of International Economics* 69:1, 6–36.

Van Rijckeghem, C., and B. Weder. 2004. "The Politics of Debt Crises." Unpublished Manuscript. Mainz, Germany: University of Mainz.

World Bank. 1999. "Poverty Reduction and Economic Management." Note No. 13.

Wright, M. L. J. 2002. *Reputations and Sovereign Debt*. Unpublished Manuscript. Stanford, CA: Stanford University.

———. 2005. "Coordinating Creditors." *The American Economic Review, Papers and Proceedings* 95:2, 388–392.

Yue, V. 2010. "Sovereign Default and Debt Renegotiation." *Journal of International Economics* 80:2, 176–187.

ABOUT THE AUTHORS

Juan Carlos Hatchondo is an economist at the Federal Reserve Bank of Richmond. He received a PhD from the University of Rochester, and a degree in economics from the Universidad de la Republica, in Uruguay. Dr. Hatchondo has done extensive work in the area of international finance and his work has been published in the *International Economic Review, Journal of International Economics,* and *Review of Economic Dynamics.*

Leonardo Martinez is an economist at the IMF Institute and is on leave from his position at the research department of the Federal Reserve Bank of Richmond. He received a PhD in economics from the University of Rochester. Dr. Martinez's recent research has focused on models of equilibrium default. This includes his articles "Heterogeneous Borrowers in Quantitative Models of Sovereign Default" (co-authored with Juan Carlos Hatchondo and Horacio Sapriza), published in the *International Economic Review;* "Long-Duration Bonds and Sovereign Defaults" (co-authored with Juan Carlos Hatchondo), published in the *Journal of International Economics;* and "Quantitative Properties of Sovereign Default Models: Solution Methods Matter" (co-authored with Juan Carlos Hatchondo and Horacio Sapriza) forthcoming in the *Review of Economic Dynamics.*

Horacio Sapriza is a research economist at the Division of International Finance at the Federal Reserve Board, and an assistant professor of finance and economics at Rutgers Business School. He received an MA and a PhD from the University of Rochester, and his research interests are in international finance, macroeconomics, and finance. His studies on the effect of credit market imperfections and institutional factors on sovereign default risk and the business cycle dynamics of emerging market economies, and on the effect of financial constraints on firms' risk and stock returns have been published in leading academic journals.

CHAPTER 16

Are Sovereign Defaulters Punished?

Evidence from Foreign Direct Investment Flows

MICHAEL FUENTES
Central Bank of Chile

DIEGO SARAVIA
Central Bank of Chile

W hy do countries repay their debts? This question has originated a considerable amount of research in the economic literature. Unlike debt obligations among agents in the private sector, in which well-known bankruptcy laws and procedures apply in the case of default, when the debtor is a sovereign, there is no explicit legislation on the consequences of not complying with the contractual obligations to international lenders. Thus, to have international lending to sovereign agents in the first place, there should be some costs associated with not fulfilling those debt obligations. If this were not the case, countries would not pay their debts and lenders would not be willing to lend. Sovereign defaults must be costly in some dimensions to permit borrower-lender relationships to exist.

Several plausible costs associated with sovereign defaults have been identified in the theoretical and empirical literature. Some argue that exclusion from international capital markets, or the threat of this exclusion, would make countries repay their debts with international creditors and, in this way, invest in reputation. Other works focus on the reduction in trade flows as the punishment of defaults while other groups of work focus on supersanctions as, for example, military aggressions from disgruntled creditors or confiscation of foreign currency–generating assets.

The evidence presented in the empirical literature is not conclusive. Papers studying how defaults affect capital markets include, for example, Eichengreen (1989) and Lindert and Morton (1989), who found no evidence that defaulters were punished by creditors through higher interest rates on new loans. Ozler (1993) finds that past defaulters did have to pay a premium on the interest rate for sovereign debt issued in the 1970s. However, the premium is quantitatively small and does not constitute a punishment that appears likely to deter future defaults.

Obstfeld and Taylor (2004) also find a surprisingly small effect of past default on the interest rate spread of sovereign debt.

The evidence on trade flows as a punishment mechanism is not conclusive, either. For example, Rose (2005) finds that bilateral flows are reduced by 8 percent per year when a country defaults. This finding has been challenged by Martinez and Sandleris (2006), who argue that, even though countries' international trade declines after declaring sovereign default, the decay is not concentrated in the bilateral trade with creditor countries. Although supersanctions are not likely to be relevant nowadays, Mitchener and Weidenmier (2005) find, using early twentieth century data, that supersanctions appear to be an effective mechanism to deter new defaulters.

In Fuentes and Saravia (2010) we analyze how defaults affect the most important source of capital flows to emerging markets in the last decades, foreign direct investment (FDI), to defaulter countries. Thus, our paper is related to the literature that focuses on exclusion, maybe partial and temporal, from capital markets as the punishment of default.

Differently from previous research on the effects of default on capital flows, we use data in our work that allow us to disentangle if capital flows to defaulter countries originate in countries that were creditors at the time of default or from countries that were not affected by the default episode.

This is very important because it allows us to be more confident than in previous studies that, if a reduction on FDI inflows is observed after a default, it is a consequence of the default itself and not of other phenomena. Default episodes occur in difficult times when there are other things going on, like, for example, output drops. Also, arguably, defaults occur in countries with relatively weak institutions. In turn, in periods when there is a drop in output or in countries with weak institutions, capital flows tend to be lower than in normal times or than in countries with stronger institutions. For example, in countries with weak institutions there is a higher expropriation risk, which clearly disincentives capital flows. If we were not able to separate the countries that are the sources of FDI, we could attribute to defaults an effect that could actually be coming, for example, from the fall in output or a fear of expropriation. However, in our case, we can see if the reduction, if any, is coming specifically from disgruntled creditors or from everywhere. If the reduction is coming only from creditor countries, then we would attribute this effect to a punishment of default. On the other hand, if we observe a reduction from other countries that were not directly affected by the default, then we would not be able to be confident about the cause of this reduction. If the fall in output or the risk of expropriation were the causes of the reduction in capital inflows, then we would observe a reduction from a wide array of countries and not only from disgruntled creditors.

To give a real-world example of the dynamics of FDI after defaults and to illustrate the motivation of the exercises presented in Fuentes and Saravia (2010), it is interesting to recall the experience of Russia after its default in 1998. According to the information in OECD (2004), Germany and Japan were both among the biggest sources of FDI in the first part of the 1990s and creditors of Russia at the moment of the default. After the default, German FDI stocks in Russia declined by 10 percent, despite the fact that Germany's FDI stock in the world increased by 20 percent. Similarly, Japan's FDI stock in Russia was $940 million in 1997 but fell to 18 million of dollars in 1999. On the other hand, South Korea was not a creditor of Russia and its FDI in that country increased after the default. We try to uncover in our research if this pattern of foreign investment in Russia after its default is systematically observed in practice.

DATA AND RESULTS

One of the challenges to determine if defaulters are punished by its creditors is to obtain data on the identity of the parties involved in a sovereign debt contract. This hurdle is overcome using information from the Paris Club. In the Paris Club, representatives of lender countries meet several times a year to discuss possible restructuring deals for countries that are undergoing difficulties paying their debts. The debts renegotiated are only between governments, and the rules of the Paris Club ensure that all the creditors share the burden of restructuring on equitable terms. The Paris Club's web site publishes the information for each deal identifying all the lender countries that concur to each agreement, the total amount restructured, and, of course, the name of the defaulting country.

The other key piece of information we use to study if there is a cost for sovereign default is the data on FDI among countries. For this, we use data from the OECD that report the amount of FDI citizens of a country undertake each year in other countries. Our hypothesis is that a defaulting country will see its FDI inflows reduced after it defaults on its external debt but more so from the creditor countries, which, in turn, are identified with the data of the Paris Club. We used regression analysis to gauge the empirical relevance of this hypothesis. With this tool, we can isolate the effect of default on FDI flows after taking into account all of the other factors that the work of many other researchers has suggested should be considered. Among the many factors we considered might affect FDI are the measures of institutional quality and soundness of economic policy in the country that defaults. In statistical terms, it is important to control for these variables because, as discussed earlier, when a country defaults, it is usually undergoing a period of significant economic turmoil. Given this, the effect of FDI on default might be difficult to separate from the other developments in the country that almost surely also make foreign investors less willing to invest in that country. The use of these control variables in the context of regression analysis complements our identification strategy discussed earlier and allows us to assert with greater confidence that what we identify as the effect of default on FDI is indeed one of the possible punishments that countries might suffer.

An important caveat of our study is that we analyze the eventual punishment for *sovereign* (that is, government) default studying its eventual effect on an economic transaction between *private* parties (FDI). We discovered two channels in our research that can explain this apparent contradiction. First, governments of creditor nations can pressure firms to avoid conducting business in countries whose governments have declared a moratorium on payments of foreign debt. Apart from this, governments might refuse to provide insurance for the foreign investments of their countries' firms when that investment is destined to a defaulter country. These elements were mentioned in narrative sources such as newspaper stories and works written by authors directly involved in the restructuring negotiations and they can explain why FDI might decrease after a sovereign default.

Our results, reported at length in Fuentes and Saravia (2010), indicate that after a country defaults on its sovereign debt payments, the FDI inflows from each of its creditors decrease by 0.05 percent of GDP. This number might not seem significant but it turns out to be a relevant magnitude. The reason is that FDI appears to have a very significant effect on economic growth, according to other researchers (see Alfaro et al. 2004). In fact, combining our results with the estimated effect of FDI on economic growth, we estimate that economic growth in the defaulting country falls by 0.4 percentage points in the year of default, which is an economically significant magnitude. An interesting feature of our results is that the fall in FDI to the defaulter country occurs only from countries that we are able to identify as its creditors. In other words, default appears to have no effect on the FDI flows originating in countries that had not lent funds to the defaulter. This piece of evidence supports the view that countries that cease to comply with their foreign debt obligations are punished by their creditors through a reduction of FDI flows.

The next issue we analyzed is the duration of this punishment to defaulters. Our hypothesis here is that creditor countries do not exclude defaulters permanently from the investment portfolio. The empirical evidence we produce is indeed supportive of this view, although the punishment is fairly extended since it lasts approximately 17 years. Yet, other authors such as Rose (2005) also report punishments to defaulter countries of the order of 15 years. Both pieces of evidence lead one to think then that default to sovereign debt is indeed costly for countries that declare it. Another interesting feature of our research is that we do not find that the amount defaulted by the country has any influence on the size of the punishment. This element can be interpreted that the stigma of default is more important than the amount of debt renegotiated. Putting together all of these pieces of evidence, it seems that sovereign default is not a free lunch for countries that declare it. Perhaps this explains why default of sovereign debts remains a relatively infrequent phenomenon and one that countries seem to try to avoid.

A final possible punishment for defaulter countries that we try to measure is the curtailment of its investment opportunities abroad. One might think that apart from receiving less FDI *inflows*, creditors might shut the door to FDI outflows from the defaulter countries. This proved to be a much more difficult issue to settle with the available data, since FDI flows originating in developing countries (where all the defaulters are) is not very significant. With this caveat in mind, our results indicate that this punishment mechanism has not been used in practice.

In summary, the evidence we have discussed here suggests that countries that cease to comply with their sovereign debt obligations are punished by its creditors through diminished FDI inflows. This reduction in FDI inflows causes a noticeable decrease of the defaulters' economic growth and seems to be quite durable. Maybe these elements help us understand why countries try to avoid default on the significant sovereign debt issued in international capital markets.

REFERENCES

Alfaro, L., A. Chanda, S. Kalemli-Ozcan, and S. Sayek. 2004. "FDI and Economic Growth: The Role of Local Financial Markets." *Journal of International Economics* 64:1, 89–112.

Eichengreen, B. 1989. "The U.S. capital market and foreign lending, 1920–1955." In J. Sachs, ed. *Developing Country Debt and Economic Performance*, 107–155. Chicago: University of Chicago Press.

Fuentes, M., and D. Saravia. 2010. "Sovereign Defaulters: Do International Capital Markets Punish Them?" *Journal of Development Economics* 91:2, 336–347.

Lindert, P., and P. Morton. 1989. "How sovereign debt worked." In J. Sachs, ed. *Developing Country Debt and Economic Performance*, 39–106. Chicago: University of Chicago Press.

Martinez, J., and G. Sandleris. 2006. *Is it Punishment? Sovereign Defaults and the Decline in Trade.* Unpublished manuscript.

Mitchener, K., and M. Weidenmier. 2005. "Supersanctions and Sovereign Debt." *NBER Working Paper*, No. 11472.

Obstfeld, M., and A. Taylor. 2004. *Global Capital Markets: Integration, Crisis and Growth.* Cambridge, UK: Cambridge University Press.

Organisation for Economic Co-operation and Development. 2004. *International Direct Investment Statistics Yearbook.* OECD.

Ozler, S. 1993. "Have Commercial Banks Ignored History?" *American Economic Review* 83:3, 608–620.

Rose, A. 2005. "One Reason Countries Pay Their Debts: Renegotiation and International Trade." *Journal of Development Economics* 77:1, 189–206.

ABOUT THE AUTHORS

Miguel Fuentes is a senior economist in the research department of the Central Bank of Chile. He was previously an assistant professor of economics at the Pontifical Catholic University of Chile and a visiting scholar in the research department of the International Monetary Fund. He received his PhD in economics from the University of California at Berkeley and an MA in applied macroeconomics and a BA from the Pontifical Catholic University of Chile. Dr. Fuentes's main research interests are international finance and macroeconomics. His work has been published in peer-reviewed journals such as the *Journal of International Trade and Economic Development* and the *Journal of Development Economics.* He also serves as co-editor of the *Journal Economía Chilena* since 2009.

Diego Saravia is a senior economist in the research department of the Central Bank of Chile since 2008. He was an assistant professor of economics at the Catholic University of Chile (2004–2008) and an economic adviser at the Central Bank of Argentina (1997–1998). He holds a PhD in economics from the University of Maryland (2004), an MA in economics from the University of CEMA (Buenos Aires, Argentina) and a BA from the National University of Cordoba (Cordoba, Argentina). His main research areas are international finance and macroeconomics. His work has been published in such journals as the *Economic Journal, Journal of Development Economics,* and the *Journal of International Money and Finance.*

CHAPTER 17

Supersanctions and Sovereign Debt Repayment

KRIS JAMES MITCHENER
Robert and Susan Finocchio Professor of Economics, Santa Clara University and
National Bureau of Economic Research[*]

MARC D. WEIDENMIER
William F. Podlich Associate Professor of Economics, Claremont McKenna College
and National Bureau of Economic Research

W hy do sovereign debt defaulters ever repay? Unlike debt issued by public corporations, sovereign debt contracts offer little legal recourse for creditors when a nation defaults. Nevertheless, the continued operation of sovereign debt markets and the fact that outright repudiation is rare suggest that incentives exist to induce repayment by sovereign borrowers. Argentina's 2001–2002 default and large write-down on $88 billion of privately held debt is just one recent instance of sovereign debt default and subsequent renegotiation that has taken place regularly over the past two centuries (Reinhart and Rogoff 2004). Economists have suggested that the benefits of a good reputation or fear of economic sanctions might be sufficient to explain why borrowers repay (Eaton and Gersovitz 1981; Bulow and Rogoff 1989a, 1989b; Cole and Kehoe 1997; Obstfeld and Taylor 2004). The widespread historical incidence of default raises important questions about the need for coordinated and coercive mechanisms to regulate sovereign debt default.[1]

In contrast to recent history, the historical record (Borchard 1951; Kaletsky 1985; Suter and Stamm 1992) suggests that extreme and heavy-handed sanctions may have been employed from 1870 to 1913 to punish debt defaulters. We call instances when creditors imposed severe costs on sovereign debt defaulters *supersanctions*. In these episodes default was met with gunboat diplomacy or the loss of fiscal sovereignty. To our knowledge, extreme sanctions of a military, economic, or political nature have never been empirically tested for this period, in part because

---

[*]We thank Annalisa Yenne and Justin Jones for valuable research assistance, and the National Science Foundation (NSF Grant 0518661), the Leavey Fund, and the Dean Witter Foundation for financial support. This survey is based on Mitchener and Weidenmier (2010).

they were believed by economists and historians to be rare and isolated episodes (Lindert and Morton 1989; Lipson 1989; Suter and Stamm 1992).[2]

We find evidence that supersanctions were a particularly effective and commonly used enforcement mechanism over the period from 1870 to 1913. Although they were sometimes applied selectively during the gold standard era, all nations that defaulted on sovereign debt ran the risk of gunboats blockading their ports or creditor nations seizing fiscal control of their country if they defaulted. We find that, conditional on default, the probability that a country would be *supersanctioned* was almost 30 percent during the period from 1870 to 1913. Extreme debt sanctions were applied to more than 40 percent of defaulted debt during the first era of globalization. Supersanctions may have had a much broader effect on emerging market borrowing given that they influenced how policy makers perceived their choice set, as evidenced in the debt settlements of Argentina and Brazil in the 1890s. The historical record suggests that these two South American countries reduced the size of their *haircut*, in part because of the threat of debt sanctions. Consistent with what Caballero and Dornbusch (2002) have argued for restoring Argentina's reputation after its recent default, our results suggest that third-party enforcement mechanisms may be beneficial for resuscitating the capital market reputation of sovereign defaulters.

ENFORCEMENT MECHANISMS

The classical gold standard period is often described as the era of high bond finance, since firms primarily financed their investment projects through debt. The issuance of sovereign debt by European countries in other parts of the world, in particular the newly independent Central and South American countries, was another prominent feature of this period. Creditor nations were primarily located in Western Europe and were led by Britain. French, German, and Dutch capital played a secondary role. The majority of sovereign debt was issued on the London Exchange, both in terms of issues and size of issues (Clemens and Williamson 2004). As shown in Exhibit 17.1, 25 countries defaulted on their sovereign debt obligations by an amount equivalent to more than 200 billion U.S. dollars today.

Economists and historians have suggested a variety of coercive and coordinating mechanisms that may have been used to regulate sovereign debt default during the classical gold standard era. Most prominent was the Corporation of Foreign Bondholders (CFB), formed by British creditors in 1868. The Corporation published valuable economic data on sovereign debt burdens and tax revenues to discourage investment in countries that did not repay their debts. The CFB also established creditor committees of British bondholders to facilitate debt settlements between lenders and defaulters and even worked with creditor associations in Paris and Berlin to prevent debt defaulters from borrowing in international capital markets. Hence, the CFB may have played a role in denying countries with poor reputations access to capital markets. However, the fact that the CFB sometimes petitioned the British government to intervene and pressure a sovereign to repay or settle its debts also suggests that private creditor associations were not entirely effective at regulating debt defaults.

Exhibit 17.1 Sovereign Debt Default during the Gold Standard Era

Country	Default	Resumption	Default	Resumption	Default	Resumption	Default	Resumption
Argentina	1890	1894						
Bolivia	1872	1880						
Brazil	1898	1902						
Colombia*	1873	1877	1879	1896	1900	1905		
Costa Rica	1874	1886	1895	1898	1901	1912		
Santo Domingo	1872	1889	1892	1894	1897	1898	1899	1907
Ecuador	1868	1890	1894	1903	1906	1907	1909	1911
Egypt	1876	1881						
Greece	1826	1880	1894	1898				
Guatemala	1875	1889	1894	1896	1898	1913		
Honduras	1873	1927						
Liberia*	1874	1900	1912	1912				
Mexico	1867	1887						
Morocco*	1903	1904						
Nicaragua	1827	1875	1894	1896	1912	1912		
Paraguay	1874	1886	1892	1897				
Peru	1876	1890						
Portugal	1892	1903						
Salvador	1898	1900						
Serbia*	1895	1895						
Spain	1873	1876						
Tunis	1867	1871						
Turkey	1876	1882						
Uruguay	1876	1879						
Venezuela	1865	1882	1898	1906				

Sources: Corporation of Foreign Bondholders, *Annual Report* (various issues), Borchard (1951), and Correa (1926).
Note: Colombia (1873), Serbia (1895), Morocco (1903–1904), and Liberia (1912) all had multilateral reschedulings prior to the onset of open default (Suter and Stamm 1992, p. 651).
Turkey refers to the Ottoman Empire.

Although the CFB likely played a role in debt settlement and enforcement by punishing countries with poor reputations, other research suggests that reputation alone was insufficient to explain debt repayment during the classical gold standard. For example, Flandreau and Zumer (2004) find that interest rates increased by 500 basis points following a default. One year after a debt settlement was reached, markets assessed a penalty of 90 basis points, which fell to 45 basis points 10 years after a default. Flandreau and Zumer (2004, p. 49) conclude, "While there is indeed a penalty for defaulting, this penalty turns out to be, over the medium run, of a smaller order of magnitude than the savings associated with the amount of debt that has been repudiated."

Creditors therefore may have also relied on sanctions to encourage debt repayment and discourage future default during the gold standard period. In addition to the empirical evidence, which casts some doubt on the sufficiency of reputation as an enforcement mechanism during the gold standard era, theoretical work by Bulow and Rogoff (1989a, 1989b) suggests that reputation is an insufficient mechanism for ensuring debt repayment. They posit that creditors might instead punish defaulters by seizing assets of sovereigns, imposing restrictions on trade through tariffs or quotas, denying countries access to international trade, or carrying out gunboat diplomacy.

In addition to using trade-related sanctions to punish defaulters, private creditors and their countries appear to have been more willing to carry out even more extreme sanctions to regulate sovereign debt during the first era of globalization.[3] Exhibit 17.2 describes the supersanctions that were imposed during the classical gold standard period. They include episodes that put debtor nations under "house arrest" by imposing foreign administrators with fiscal authority and episodes in which gunboats were used.[4]

Historical Evidence on Supersanctions

Extreme sanctions used to enforce sovereign debt during the classical gold standard period can be characterized as having the following properties: (1) creditor governments' primary reason for intervention was in response to a debt default; (2) the defaulting country lost fiscal sovereignty or faced gunboats or the threatened use of them as punishment; (3) supersanctions improved a country's willingness to pay and led to a debt settlement with foreign creditors. To illustrate *fiscal house arrest*, we briefly discuss how this type of debt sanction was employed in three of the largest debt defaults of the gold standard period: Egypt, Turkey, and Greece. For an example of gunboat diplomacy, we discuss military actions by European powers and the United States in Central America and the Caribbean. We use primary source materials from the late nineteenth century and early twentieth century such as the annual reports of the Corporation of Foreign Bondholders, Fenn on the Funds (1883), and Fitch (1918), in addition to the secondary literature, to analyze how contemporaries viewed these episodes.

FISCAL HOUSE ARREST

A few studies have suggested that the British government was concerned that interventions violated sovereign immunity and undermined the confidence in

Exhibit 17.2   Sanctions during the Classical Gold Standard Period, 1870 to 1913

Panel A. Supersanctions

Country	Description of Sanction	Year(s)
Costa Rica	Roosevelt Corollary; United States threatens to take over customs houses	1911
Egypt	U.K. administers finances for the Khedive	1881–1913
Greece	International financial body administers finances of the defaulting republic	1898–1913
Guatemala	U.K. threatens Guatemala with gunboats; Guatemala agrees to settle long-outstanding defaulted debts with its creditors	1913
Liberia	United States administers customs houses and imposes debt restrictions	1912–1913
Morocco	International body appointed to oversee customs houses	1905–1911 (followed by the establishment of a French protectorate in April 1912)
Nicaragua	Roosevelt Corollary; threat of U.S. gunboat diplomacy helps lead to debt settlement; New York bank administers converted loan	1912
Santo Domingo	Roosevelt Corollary; United States administers customs houses	1905–1913
Serbia	International financial body helps to oversee country's finances following debt default; foreign bondholders have less control over Serbian finances than in other instances of financial control	1895–1913
Tunis	International financial body administers customs houses following debt default	1870–1881 (followed by the establishment of a French protectorate)
Turkey (Ottoman Empire)	International financial body administers customs houses following debt default	1882–1913
Venezuela	International blockade in response to debt default	1902–1903

Sources: Angell (1933), Borchard (1951), and Suter and Stamm (1992).

newly formed democratic nations. Some political historians have emphasized that the British Foreign Office maintained a noninterventionist position at least since the defaults of the early 1820s. But as Platt (1968) and Lipson (1985) argue, exceptions to this policy were often made for strategic interests even though the political and economic costs of a government-sponsored intervention could be large. For example, the Egyptian Khedive Ismail asked the British Foreign Office to send a delegation to examine the state of his country's finances in 1876. England and France both sent representatives to the North African country to assess its economic and financial health. After a series of additional inquiries, England and France recommended that Egypt turn over fiscal control to an international committee in the 1870s. Khedive Ismail opposed the surrender of financial control to an international creditors' committee and took several measures to prevent this from happening. The Egyptian leader ultimately lost his battle with the foreign powers and was forced to abdicate in favor of his son, who granted some external financial control to foreign creditors.

The British-led administration in Egypt established an efficient tax collection system and restored fiscal discipline. The power of the Egyptian assembly to authorize spending was limited, and Britain was able to negotiate a debt settlement for Egypt by 1883. Fiscal reform attracted additional foreign capital, and Egypt regained access to capital markets—borrowing at approximately half the rate of interest it had paid before Britain took control of the country's finances. Approximately 40 million dollars in new capital flowed into the country. Roads, railroads, and canals, including the Aswan Dam, were constructed using funds from tax revenues and new debt issues placed on international capital markets.

Greece was another large emerging market borrower that was supersanctioned during the gold standard period. The Mediterranean country defaulted on its external debt in May 1893 after announcing that it would repay only 30 percent of the interest on its debt. Over the next four years, the Greek government was unable to come to terms with its foreign bondholders. Prospects for a debt settlement changed in 1898 with the outbreak of war between Greece and Turkey. Not only did Greece lose the short war, but its financial position deteriorated as the country printed money to finance the conflict. Bondholders demanded that foreign powers protect their investments in Greek securities (Andreades 1925). The German government included a clause in the preliminary peace provisions of a treaty to end the Greco-Turkish War that called for the establishment of an international financial commission appointed by the major powers. The commission was given the power to ensure that the country repaid its defaulted debts incurred before the outbreak of war with Russia as well as the debt accumulated to finance the conflict. The Greek law of 1898 granted the council control over tax collection to service the country's debt and newly imposed war indemnity (Feis 1930, p. 260). The country serviced its external debt for the remainder of the gold standard period. An international financial committee remained in Greece until the Great Depression, when the country defaulted on its external debts.

Turkey was another important episode of a country placed under "financial house arrest" and forced to implement economic reforms and undergo sovereign debt restructuring by European powers in response to a default. Turkey sold its first debt issue on the London and French capital markets in 1854. Over the next two decades, the country borrowed more than 240 million pounds from European markets. The country paid increasingly higher interest rates as the size of its external debt rose. By 1875, over half of Turkey's expenditures were used for servicing its debts. High debt-service costs, in conjunction with a costly war and defeat to Russia in 1878, forced the country to default on its external debt (Nation's Encyclopedia).

In 1878, the major European powers met in Berlin to discuss Turkey's economic and political problems. At the Congress of Berlin, they recommended the establishment of a Financial Commission in Constantinople to examine the claims of the holders of Turkish debt and to propose the most effective means to give them satisfaction compatible with the financial situation of the country (Feis 1930, p. 332). Three years later, Turkey arrived at a debt settlement with its foreign bondholders and finally agreed to foreign financial control as suggested by the major powers. By the Decree of Mouharrem, a public debt administration was established to collect tax revenues and repay the country's external debts. The public debt administration was composed of representatives from the major powers, with Turkey given token representation. The Council of Administration remained in Turkey for the rest of the gold standard period. Turkey repaid its debts for the remainder of the gold standard. Interest rates on the country's sovereign bonds plummeted as the Council implemented fiscal reforms.

The view that house arrest was a credible and feared sanction used to enforce debt repayment—as opposed to civil order or some other reason—is perhaps best seen in the bond defaults of Argentina and Brazil. After Argentina defaulted in 1890, the largest default in the nineteenth century, the *Financial News* noted that Argentina might even benefit from foreign control of its purse strings, as had happened in Egypt and Turkey (*Financial News*, May 31, 1891, quoted in Fishlow, 1989, p. 100). Fishlow (1989) notes that the threat of foreign intervention in Argentina figured into the country's debt settlement plan with foreign bondholders in the early 1890s. As a result, Argentina's haircut was probably much smaller than it would have been in the absence of the threat of foreign financial control.

Like Argentina, Brazil also felt threatened by the possibility of external financial control in the late nineteenth century. In a move designed to prevent foreign intervention, Brazil opted to reschedule the country's interest payments rather than default on the principal of its debts in the late 1890s. Official correspondence of the Brazilian government indicates that the South American country considered three options before restructuring interest payments on its foreign debts: "(1) suspension of debt service, (2) reduction of interest, and (3) arrangement of a large loan. The first two hypotheses put at risk the very national sovereignty, with the country subject to foreign intervention against which it would be impossible to defeat" (Debes 1978, quoted in Fishlow, 1989, p. 100). The Brazilian government obviously believed that there was some probability that they would have to surrender their fiscal sovereignty to foreign creditors if they defaulted on the principal of their foreign debts.

GUNBOAT DIPLOMACY

Gunboat diplomacy was the second type of extreme sanction employed by creditor governments to enforce sovereign debt during the classical gold standard period. In these debt sanctions, creditor governments could employ the navy to bombard and punish a recalcitrant debtor or threaten it with the use of force. Sometimes the marines or other military forces were used to seize customs houses. The mechanism was primarily a tactic employed by foreign creditors in the Western Hemisphere.

In 1904, President Theodore Roosevelt announced the Roosevelt Corollary to the Monroe Doctrine, which stated that the United States had the right to intervene in the affairs of Central American and Caribbean countries that were unstable and did not repay their debts. This policy was designed to prevent European powers from intervening in the economic and political affairs of Central American and South American countries that did not repay their debts:

> If a nation shows to act with decency with regard to industrial and political matters, if it keeps order and pays its obligations, then it need fear no interference from the United States. Brutal wrong-doing, or an impotence which results in a general loosening of the ties of civilized society, may finally require intervention by some civilized nation, and in the Western hemisphere the United States cannot ignore the duty. (New York Times, "The President's Annual Message," December 7, 1904, p. 4)

The United States followed up this pronouncement by dispatching a battle-ship and taking control of customs houses in Santo Domingo after the Caribbean country defaulted on its external debts and European powers threatened to take action. American gunboat diplomacy produced a large bond market rally in Central American and Caribbean securities trading on the London market, with the average bond price rising more than 74 percent in the year after the change in U.S. foreign policy. The Roosevelt Corollary and the threat of American intervention led many Central American and Caribbean countries, including Costa Rica, Nicaragua, and Santo Domingo, to come to debt agreements with its foreign bondholders over the next several years.

EFFECTS OF SUPERSANCTIONS

There were 12 episodes of supersanctions from 1870 to 1913. As Exhibit 17.3 suggests, conditional on default, the probability of facing sanctions was quantitatively significant regardless of whether default is measured by the number of episodes, the number of countries, the number of years in default, or the size of defaults. Of the countries that defaulted during the gold standard era, 12 out of 25 (or 48 percent) were supersanctioned, and 7 out of 10 countries (or 70 percent) that defaulted *multiple* times during the gold standard period were supersanctioned. Sovereign debt defaulters were sanctioned a combined 131 years during the classical gold

Exhibit 17.3   Statistics for Sovereign Debt Defaults and Sanctions, 1870 to 1913

Panel A. Summary Statistics for Debt Default and Sanctions

Total number of default episodes	**43**
Total number of countries that defaulted	25
Number of default episodes with a supersanction	12
Percent of defaulted debt with a supersanction	40
Prob(Supersanction | Debt default episode)	$12/43 = 0.28$
Prob(Any type of sanction | Country defaulted more than once)	$7/10 = 0.70$

standard period. In terms of the size of defaults, we estimate that more than 40 percent of all defaulted debt during the classical gold standard was supersanctioned.[5] The average length of outside fiscal control by foreign powers was approximately 11.25 years.[6] For every year a country was in default, there was more than a one-in-four chance that it would be subjected to a supersanction.

We also examined yield spreads of long-term bonds to provide an ex post measure of the effects of supersanctions on country risk before and after the implementation of supersanctions. We compute country or political risk for a sample of defaulters during the classical gold standard period, measured as the yield on a representative sovereign bond minus the yield on the risk-free British consol (consolidated annuities) in the pre-supersanction and supersanction periods. After sovereign debt defaulters were subject to gunboat diplomacy or lost fiscal sovereignty, yield spreads fell by approximately 1,200 basis points, or nearly 90 percent.[7]

Before the implementation of supersanctions, countries in our sample spent nearly 47 percent of the classical gold standard era in default. In contrast, countries spent virtually no time in default after they were supersanctioned.[8] Also, countries that surrendered their fiscal sovereignty to external bondholder committees or foreign governments did not default for the remainder of the gold standard period. The fact that most of the countries in our sample were serial defaulters suggests that sovereign defaulters were unlikely to have enacted the necessary fiscal reforms to repay their debts without supersanctions.

We also computed yield spreads for supersanctioned countries for two different periods: (1) the period after a country had negotiated a debt settlement with bondholders (in all cases prior to heavy-handed sanctions) and (2) the period after the country was supersanctioned. Since Exhibit 17.4 focuses only on the set of countries that experienced both negotiated settlements and heavy-handed sanctions, it provides an additional method for comparison, while avoiding the potential problem that comparisons are based on countries that are somehow fundamentally

Exhibit 17.4 Comparing Average Yield Spreads Following a Debt Workout and Supersanctions

Country	Average Yield Spread after Bondholder Workout	Average Yield Spread after Supersanctions	Difference
Colombia	1286.75	355.95	−930.80
Greece	404.01	752.30	348.29
Liberia	456.99	183.09	−273.90
Nicaragua	616.44	313.76	−302.68
Turkey	461.80	163.27	−298.53
Venezuela	478.69	264.24	−214.45
Average	**617.45**	**338.77**	**−278.68**

Note: Column 1 shows the average yield spread after a country has negotiated a debt settlement with bondholders up until it defaults again. Column 2 shows the yield spread after supersanctions have been imposed and until the end of our sample period.

different (that is, that some countries might never be supersanctioned). Column 3 shows the average yield spread for a sovereign borrower following the negotiated debt settlement with bondholders up until the point when the country again defaulted on its debt. Column 3 shows the average yield spread for the supersanction period (none of the supersanctioned countries defaulted again before 1914). The fourth column shows the difference between Columns 2 and 3. Country risk was nearly 280 basis points lower during the supersanction period in comparison to the period after a negotiated debt settlement. The large decline in yield spreads after these countries were supersanctioned was accompanied by a more-than-50-percent increase in the average level of public debt. With the exception of Greece, country risk was substantially lower for every supersanctioned country after the imposition of fiscal control or gunboat diplomacy in comparison to the period after negotiated debt settlement.

NOTES

1. For a literature survey on sovereign debt, see Eaton and Fernandez (1993) and Obstfeld and Rogoff (1996).

2. For a discussion of the economic effects of sanctions since World War I, see Davis and Engerman (2003). Hogan (1906) surveys the use of minor interventions, called *Pacific Blockades*, during the nineteenth century. Fratianni (2004) examines how San Giorgio, a creditors' association formed by lenders to reduce the risk of debt repudiation, used various enforcement mechanisms to reduce the probability of default by the Republic of Genoa from 1407 to 1805.

3. This might not be that surprising, given the differences in international law and diplomacy that exist between today and the nineteenth century. For more on these differences, see Correa (1926) and Finnemore (2003).

4. For a discussion of the role of trade and private creditor sanctions in regulating sovereign debt during the gold standard era, see Mitchener and Weidenmier (2005).

5. To compute this figure, we gathered annual data from the *Investors' Monthly Manual* and secondary sources, and calculated the total outstanding defaulted debt (unredeemed debt at par value) over the entire sample period. For Tunis, Morocco, and Serbia, we used estimates from Correa (1926), Ling (1967), Stone (1999), and *The Times* (London).

6. We calculated this figure by averaging all episodes of gunboat diplomacy and financial control shown in Exhibit 17.2.

7. For the yield spread analysis, we do not employ debt issues that were explicitly guaranteed by the British government. Including issues with the label *guaranteed* by Her Majesty's government would only lead to a further decline in yield spreads and strengthen the empirical results. The results of the yield spread analysis are also robust to changing the representative interest rate for countries with multiple issues trading on the London exchange. We experimented with a variety of issues, including ones used by Obstfeld and Taylor (2004), Ferguson and Schularick (2006), and Flandreau and Zumer (2004) for the supersanctioned countries in our analysis. The results remained unchanged and are available from the authors by request.

8. Nicaragua briefly defaulted in 1912 on debt nominally guaranteed by U.S. authorities under the Roosevelt Corollary. But subsequent intervention by the United States in 1912

prodded Nicaragua to come to terms with its creditors. Nicaragua repaid its debts for the remainder of the gold standard period. Costa Rica remained in default even after the announcement of the Roosevelt Corollary and actions by the U.S. government in Santo Domingo that enforced the new U.S. foreign policy in 1904 and 1905. Costa Rica arrived at a debt workout with bondholders in 1912, however, following U.S. threats to take over control of the country's customs houses.

REFERENCES

Andreades, A. 1925. Lectures on Public Finances: National Loans and Greek Public Economics. Part I and II, Athens (in Greek).

Angell, J.W. 1933. *Financial Foreign Policy of the United States*. New York: Russell and Russell.

Borchard, Edwin. 1951. *State Insolvency and Foreign Bondholders: General Principles*. New Haven: Yale University Press.

Bulow, Jeremy, and Kenneth Rogoff. 1989a. "Sovereign Debt: Is to Forgive to Forget?" *American Economic Review* 79:1, 43–50.

———. 1989b. "A Constant Recontracting Model of Sovereign Debt." *Journal of Political Economy* 97:1, 155–178.

Caballero, Ricardo, and Rudiger Dornbusch. 2002. "Argentina: A Rescue Plan that Works." *Financial Times* Op-Ed.

Clemens, Michael A., and Jeffrey G. Williamson. 2004. "Wealth Bias in the First Global Capital Market Boom, 1870–1913." *Economic Journal* 114: 304–337.

Cole, Harold L.,and Patrick J. Kehoe. 1997. "Reviving Reputation Models of International Debt. *Federal Reserve Bank of Minneapolis Quarterly Review* 21: 21–30.

Corporation of Foreign Bondholders. Various Years Annual Report. London: CFB.

Correa, H. M. Alvares. 1926. *The International Controls of Public Finances: A Treatise of International Law*. Amsterdam: Drukkerij M. J. Portielje.

Davis, Lance, and Stanley Engerman. 2003. "Sanctions: Neither War nor Peace." *Journal of Economic Perspectives* 17:2, 187–197.

Debes, Celio. 1978. *Campos Salles: Perfil de Um Estadista. Volume 2: Na Republica*. Rio de Janeiro: Livraria F. Alves Editora.

Eaton, Jonathan, and Raquel Fernandez. 1995. "Sovereign debt." In G. Grossman and K. Rogoff, eds. *Handbook of International Economics*. Amsterdam: North-Holland.

Eaton, Jonathan, and Mark Gersovitz. 1981. "Debt with Potential Repudiation: Theoretical and Empirical Analysis." *Review of Economic Studies* 48: 239–309.

Feis, Herbert. 1930. *Europe: The World's Banker*. New Haven: Yale University Press.

Fenn on the Funds. 1883. *Fenn's Compendium of the English and Foreign Funds, Debts and Revenues of All Nations*, 13th ed. London: Effingham Wilson, Royal Exchange.

Ferguson, Niall, and Moritz Schularick. 2006. "The Empire Effect: The Determinants of Country Risk in the First Age of Globalization, 1880–1913." *Journal of Economic History* 66:2, 283–312.

Finnemore, Martha. 2003. *The Purpose of Intervention: Changing Beliefs About the Use of Force*. Ithaca, NY: Cornell University Press.

Fishlow, Albert. 1989. "Conditionality and willingness to pay: Parallels from 1890s." In Barry Eichengreen and Peter Lindert, eds. *The International Debt Crisis in Historical Perspective*. Cambridge, MA: MIT Press.

Fitch Record of Government Finances. 1918, 3rd ed. New York: Fitch Publishing Company.

Flandreau, Marc, and Frederic Zumer. 2004. *The Making of Global Finance*. Paris: Organisation for European Co-operation and Development.

Fratianni, Michele. 2004. "Government Debt, Reputation, and Creditors' Protection: The Tale of San Giorgio." *Indiana University Business School Working Paper.*

Hogan, Albert E. 1906. *Pacific Blockades.* Oxford, UK: Clarendon Press.

Kaletsky, Anatole. 1985. *The Costs of Default.* New York: Priority Press Publications and Twentieth Century Fund.

Lindert, Peter H., and Peter J. Morton. 1989. "How sovereign debt worked." In Jeffery Sachs, ed. *Developing Country Debt and Economic Performance* 1: 39–106. Chicago: University of Chicago Press.

Ling, Dwight L. 1967. *Tunisia: From Protectorate to Republic.* Bloomington: Indiana University Press.

Lipson, Charles. 1985. *Standing Guard: Protecting Foreign Capital in the Nineteenth and Twentieth Centuries.* Berkeley: University of California Press.

Mitchener, Kris James, and Marc Weidenmier. 2010. "Supersanctions and Sovereign Debt Repayment." *Journal of International Money and Finance* February: 19–36.

Mitchener, Kris James, and Marc Weidenmier. 2005. "Supersanctions and Sovereign Debt Repayment. *NBER Working Paper*, No. 11472.

Nation's Encyclopedia. Online. Washington, DC: Library of Congress. www.nations encyclopedia.com/.

Obstfeld, Maurice, and Kenneth S. Rogoff. 1996. *Foundations of International Macroeconomics.* Cambridge, MA: MIT Press.

Obstfeld, Maurice, and Alan M. Taylor. 2004. *Capital Markets: Integration, Crisis, and Growth.* Cambridge, UK: Cambridge University Press.

Platt, D. C. M. 1968. *Finance, Trade, and Politics in British Foreign Policy, 1815–1914.* Oxford, UK: Oxford University Press.

Reinhart, Carmen M., and Kenneth S. Rogoff. 2004. "Serial Default and the 'Paradox' of Rich to Poor Capital Flows." *American Economic Review, Papers and Proceedings* 94:2, 53–58.

Stone, Irving. 1999. *The Global Export of Capital from Great Britain, 1865–1913: A Statistical Survey.* New York: St. Martin's Press.

Suter, Christian, and Hanspeter Stamm. 1992. "Coping with Global Debt Crises: Debt Settlements, 1820 to 1896." *Comparative Studies in Society and History* 34: 645–678.

The Times. Various issues. London.

ABOUT THE AUTHORS

Kris James Mitchener is the Robert and Susan Finocchio Professor of Economics, Department of Economics, Leavey School of Business at Santa Clara University, and research associate at the National Bureau of Economic Research. His research focuses on international economics, macroeconomics, and economic history, and has been published in the *Journal of Political Economy, Economic Journal,* the *Journal of Law and Economics,* the *Journal of Economic Growth,* the *Journal of International Money and Finance,* the *Journal of Money, Credit, and Banking,* the *Journal of Economic History, Monetary and Economic Studies,* and *Research in Economic History.* He has held visiting positions at the Bank of Japan, the St. Louis Federal Reserve Bank, UCLA, and CRE at Universitat Pompeu Fabra, and serves on the editorial boards of the *Journal of Economic History, Cliometrica,* and *Economics.* He received his BA and PhD from the University of California, Berkeley.

Marc D. Weidenmier is the William F. Podlich Associate Professor of Economics and the director of the Lowe Institute of Political Economy at Claremont McKenna

College. Professor Weidenmier is a research associate at the National Bureau of Economic Research and a member of the editorial board of the *Journal of Economic History*. His research interests are in the area of monetary and financial economics. He has published in several leading economics and finance journals, including the *American Economic Review, Quarterly Journal of Economics, Journal of Financial Economics, Journal of International Economics,* and the *Journal of Economic History.*

CHAPTER 18

Debt Restructuring Delays

Measurement and Stylized Facts

CHRISTOPH TREBESCH
Free University Berlin and Hertie School of Governance

I n recent decades, sovereign debt restructurings have become a standard ve-
hicle to solve debt distress situations. There is surprisingly little systematic
data on debt restructurings and related debt renegotiations, however. This
chapter summarizes the data and results of Trebesch (2008), in particular a set of
new stylized facts from more than 90 sovereign restructurings in the period from
1980 to 2007. The focus lays on the duration of debt renegotiations with private
external creditors (banks and bondholders) and on the reasons of restructuring
delays.

The next section presents a new approach to measure restructuring episodes
and provides illustrative examples. The section after that sketches the three subphases of debt renegotiation processes and provides an overview on the duration
data. There is then a discussion on the role of creditor litigation and holdout events,
which are often seen as dominant reasons for debt restructuring delays. The final
section summarizes the key stylized facts in a concise manner.

MEASURING DEFAULT AND
NEGOTIATION EPISODES

There is no generally accepted definition on how to measure default and restructuring episodes. The most common data source used by researchers has been the
yearly list of default episodes by Standard & Poor's (Beers and Chambers 2006),
which has the advantage that it is easily accessible and goes back to the nineteenth
century. S&P has a clear definition of default: In any given year, a sovereign default
is coded in case one of the following two criteria applies: (1) missed payments, that
is, the government's failure to meet a principal or interest payment on the due
date or within the grace period, or (2) a distressed debt restructuring, defined as
an exchange of outstanding loans or bonds at terms less favorable than the original contracts. S&P does not measure the duration of negotiations or the start and
ending of restructuring processes. Given their definition, it is not possible to disentangle whether a default event in their data set is due to a debt exchange in that

year or due to missed payments. As a result, S&P data lump together defaults and restructuring processes into yearly distress episodes.

In Trebesch (2008), I propose a new monthly measure for the duration of debt restructuring and renegotiation events. The start of a restructuring process for sovereign loans or bonds is coded whenever the government misses first payments beyond the grace period (default month) *or* there is a public announcement to restructure the respective debt instruments. The episode is concluded with the final restructuring agreement and the implementation of the debt exchange. The main difference from S&P is that I code individual restructuring processes related to a specific bundle of loans or bonds being renegotiated, not aggregate default episodes. Negotiations over different types of debt (bonds, loans, trade credits) are thus coded as separate restructuring processes, even if the negotiations on different debt bundles are conducted in parallel.

The following examples, which are partly based on data by Cruces and Trebesch (2010), illustrate the differences between my definition of restructuring duration and the measurement of default episodes from Standard & Poor's data:

Example 1: Algeria's debt crisis in the early 1990s: Standard & Poor's codes this as one debt crisis event spanning the time from 1991 to 1996. I code this as two different events, involving two very distinct restructurings. The first restructuring event runs from October 1990 until March 1992 and relates to the restructuring of $1.457 million medium-term debt and letters of credit falling due until 1993. The restructuring was announced in October 1990, negotiations began in September 1991, and the agreement was signed and implemented in March 1992. The second episode concerns the restructuring of $3.2 million of principal and arrears, which was announced in December 1993 and concluded stepwise between September 1995 and July 1996.

Example 2: Brazil's debt crisis in the 1980s and 1990s: S&P codes this as one debt crisis event spanning the time from 1983 to 1994. I have coded five different restructurings and negotiation processes during that period. These include three shorter-term restructurings in 1983, 1984, and 1986 (each involving less than $10 billion), a large multiyear restructuring deal of 1988 (restructuring $62 billion), an intermediate deal to restructure $7.2 billion of arrears in November 1992, and finally the large Brady deal of April 1994 with a volume of $42 billion. Each of these restructurings affected different types of debt and had different negotiation processes and outcomes (for example, in recovery values).

Example 3: Russia's debt crisis in the late 1990s: S&P codes this as one event spanning the time from 1998 to 2000. I code three distinct restructuring processes. First, the renegotiation of domestic currency government short-term commitments (GKOs) held by nonresidents from July 1998 until March 1999 (exchanging the equivalent of $49 billion). Second, the restructuring of so-called MinFin3 bonds from May 1999 until February 2000 (restructuring $1.3 billion) and, third, the London Club negotiations on previously restructured bonds (principal bonds or PRINs and interest-arrears notes IANs) spanning the time from September 1998 until August 2000 (restructuring $32 billion).

These details show that aggregated *default episodes* as per S&P are not to be confused with *restructuring episodes*. Coding the negotiation process for individual restructurings provides a much more detailed overview on the time line of negotiations and the resulting debt exchange than using aggregate, yearly S&P data. In particular, it becomes apparent that the S&P data set does not capture the duration of negotiations of sovereign restructurings.

THE DEBT RESTRUCTURING PROCESS: THREE PHASES

This section proposes a new time line to categorize the process of sovereign debt restructurings. I suggest that debt renegotiations can be broken down into three subphases: First, the starting phase from the start of debt distress (default or restructuring announcement) until the beginning of formal negotiations or market sounding, that is, informal talks with creditor representatives. Second, the negotiation phase, which ends with a final exchange offer to creditors. And, third, the implementation phase, which ends with the final agreement and implementation of the debt exchange. The main advantage of this classification of restructuring phases is that it is general enough to be applied in different eras of debt restructurings and for different types of debt. The definitions provide comparable figures for bank debt restructurings deals of the 1980s and for the set of more recent restructurings, which mostly affected sovereign bonds.

To measure the three subphases of restructuring processes, I rely on four key dates:

1. *Starting Month of Debt Distress:* The start of a distress period is coded whenever the government misses first payments to private creditors beyond the grace period (default month) or whenever a key member of government[1] announces a restructuring of government debt to private creditors in public. Both events indicate that the government is in severe financial distress.
2. *Starting Month of Negotiations:* For commercial bank restructurings (particularly in the 1980s and early 1990s), the start of negotiations was coded as the first formal meeting of government officials with the London Club advisory committees. For the set of more recent bond restructurings, I coded the start of negotiations based on detailed press reports and available case study evidence. Thanks to the detailed case coverage, it was possible to identify the start of market sounding and formal or informal negotiations in each of the restructurings.
3. *Month of the Exchange Offer to Private Creditors:* For bond restructurings, this is the month in which the exchange is publicly opened. For commercial bank restructurings (particularly in the 1980s and early 1990s), I code the month in which an agreement in principle was reached with the bank advisory committee. After the principle agreement, the terms and respective contracts were routinely sent to all banks for them to sign and participate in the exchange deal.
4. *Month of Finalization of the Debt Restructuring:* The finalization of a deal is coded in the month in which either an official signing ceremony took place (such as with banks during the 1980s or 1990s), or for that month in which bonds were ultimately exchanged on the market.

Bringing these definitions to the data provides a series of new insights: First, I find a stunning variability in the length of sovereign debt restructurings. The average total duration from the start of debt distress to the finalization of the restructuring is about 28 months, with a very large standard variation of 32 months. In some cases, like Uruguay 2003, Pakistan 1999, Chile 1990, or Romania 1986, restructurings occurred at record speed, that is, in only three or four months. Other restructurings, such as Argentina 2001–2005, Jordan 1989–1993, or Peru 1983–1997, took many years to resolve.

Second, I find notable differences across time. Restructurings during the 1980s and 1990s took on average significantly longer (31 months) than restructurings in the "Post–Brady Era" since 1998 (17 months). Exhibit 18.1 provides an overview.

A third insight from the data is that the negotiation phase appears to be the most cumbersome of the three subphases of debt restructuring, with an average duration of more than 12 months. Interestingly, I find the last subperiod of debt restructurings (the implementation phase) to be the shortest, with an average duration of only seven months. During this period, creditor coordination problems and the risk of holdouts are likely to be most acute, as banks or bondholders are asked to accept or reject the exchange offer launched by the debtor. However, restructuring deals appear to be implemented relatively quickly once debtors issue a final exchange offer. This indicates that the problem of creditor-induced delay due to holdouts or litigation is only one of the many reasons for protracted restructuring processes.

A detailed overview on the sequencing of restructurings since 1998 is provided in Exhibit 18.2. As can be seen, most recent debt exchanges have been relatively quick, especially restructurings of sovereign bonds, which took an average of only

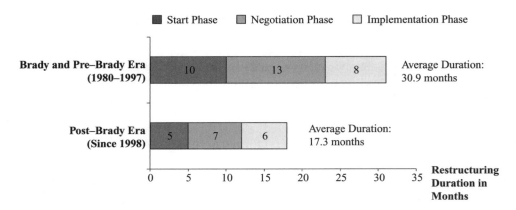

Exhibit 18.1   The Duration of Sovereign Debt Restructurings
Note: The figure summarizes the duration of individual debt restructuring processes between debtor governments and private external creditors since 1980. The post–Brady era begins after the last Brady deal was concluded by Vietnam in December of 1997. The sample includes 83 bank debt restructuring deals and 12 sovereign bond restructurings. The start of debt distress is defined as either default (missed payments beyond grace period) or the announcement or start of debt restructuring negotiations. The process ends with a final agreement or debt exchange. The data are mainly from Trebesch (2008) but complemented with data from Cruces and Trebesch (2010).

Exhibit 18.2 Dates and Duration of Selected Restructurings since 1998

	Announcement of Restructuring	Default Date	Start of Negotiations	Final Exchange Offer	Date of Exchange	Total Duration (Months)	Bond Exchange?
Pakistan (Bank debt)	Aug-98	Aug-98	Mar-99	May-99	Jul-99	11	No
Pakistan (Ext. bonds)	Aug-99	No (preemptive)	Sep-99	Nov-99	Dec-99	4	Yes
Ukraine (Ext. bonds)	Dec-99	No (preemptive)	Jan-00	Feb-00	Apr-00	4	Yes
Ecuador (Ext. bonds)	Jul-98	Aug-99	Sep-99	Jul-00	Aug-00	25	Yes
Russia (London Club)	Sep-98	Dec-98	May-99	Feb-00	Aug-00	23	No
Moldova (Ext. bonds)	Jun-02	No (preemptive)	Jun-02	Aug-02	Oct-02	4	Yes
Uruguay (Ext. bonds)	Mar-03	No (preemptive)	Mar-03	Apr-03	May-03	2	Yes
Moldova (Gazprom)	Sep-02	Mid 2001	Oct-02	Apr-04	Apr-04	34	No
Serbia and Montenegro	Dec-00	Since 1990s	Sep-01	Jun-04	Jul-04	43	No
Dominica (Bonds/loans)	Jun-03	Jul-03	Dec-03	Apr-04	Sep-04	15	Yes
Argentina (Ext. bonds)	Oct-01	Jan-02	Oct-01	Nov-01	Apr-05	42	Yes
Dominican Republic (Ext. bonds)	Apr-04	No (preemptive)	Jan-05	Apr-05	May-05	13	Yes
Dominican Republic (Bank debt)	Apr-04	Feb-05	Aug-04	Jun-05	Oct-05	18	No
Grenada (Bonds/loans)	Oct-04	Dec-04	Dec-04	Sep-0	Nov-05	13	Yes
Iraq (Bank/commercial)	in 2004	N/A	Jul-05	Jul-05	Jan-06	19	No
Belize (Bonds/loans)	Aug-06	Sep-06	Aug-06	Dec-06	Feb-07	6	Yes

Source: Trebesch (2008) and Cruces and Trebesch (2010).

13 months. This is less than half the average duration of bank debt restructurings, which took more than 30 months when considering the whole sample. It is also notable that, in recent years, only Argentina's 2005 bond exchange and Serbia's 2004 exchange of Yugoslav-era bank debt took more than three years to negotiate. Overall, one can conclude that debt restructuring duration has been decreasing significantly in the last decade, especially when it comes to bond debt.

EVIDENCE ON CREDITOR LITIGATION AND HOLDOUTS

In the public and academic debate, creditor coordination problems and related creditor actions such as holdouts or litigation are often seen as increasingly important stumbling blocks for quick and efficient debt restructurings (see Bi, Chamon, and Zettelmeyer 2009; Pitchford and Wright 2007, 2008, as well as IMF 2003 and Krueger 2002).

To gain a more systematic understanding, this section summarizes new data by Trebesch (2008) on the occurrence of creditor holdouts and litigation in 90 restructuring episodes. Inter-creditor disputes and holdouts are coded whenever such events reportedly led to a delay of more than three months in the restructuring process. Similarly, I code litigation events whenever creditors had filed suit against a foreign sovereign and when this was reported of being an obstacle in the related debt negotiations (see the Appendix for details on sources and coding). Note that I only consider pre-restructuring litigation, that is, cases filed before the completion of a debt restructuring. This is because I am mainly interested in whether legal conflicts were a relevant obstacle for debt exchanges with a majority of creditors.

Exhibit 18.3 provides a quick overview on the number of litigation and holdout events in the sample of 90 restructurings. I find surprisingly few instances of pre-restructuring litigation, which appears to have affected only 9 of the 90 restructuring cases surveyed. Of course, pre-restructuring litigation is only one side of the coin. Creditors often file suit against a sovereign only after the restructuring has been successfully completed. However, post-restructuring litigation typically

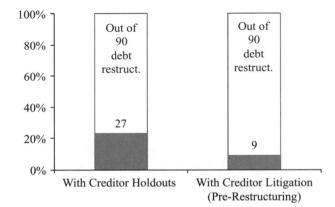

Exhibit 18.3 Holdouts and Litigation Cases

affects only minor parts of the total debt exchanged (the "race to the courthouse" in Argentina after 2002 being a notable exception).

Inter-creditor disputes and problems with holdout creditors were a more important stumbling block, affecting 27 restructurings. However, this is still less than 25 percent of all negotiation episodes surveyed. In most cases, holdout problems were caused by groups of smaller banks or minor bondholder groups. In some cases, however, major creditors also refused to participate in agreements arranged by a representative group (for example, Bankers Trust in Algeria 1992, Lloyds Bank in Argentina 1982, or Citibank in Chile 1987 and in the Philippines 1986). Overall, this coding exercise reveals that creditor actions such as litigation and holdouts could be observed only in a minority of debt restructurings. The data also show no increasing trend in the number of holdout attempts.

SUMMARY

The new insights summarized in this chapter can be structured along four stylized facts:

First fact: Many debt crisis episodes feature more than one restructuring and more than one round of debt renegotiations. The duration of a debt crisis of default episode, as measured, for example, by S&P data, is therefore not to be confused with the duration of individual debt renegotiation processes.

Second fact: The data show a very large variation in the duration of sovereign debt restructurings. The average duration in the time from 1980 to 2007 amounts to about 30 months, but has been decreasing over time. Since 1998, only Argentina's 2005 bond exchange and Serbia's 2004 exchange of Yugoslav-era bank debt took more than three years to negotiate.

Third fact: In the last decades, sovereign bond restructurings were implemented much quicker than bank debt restructurings. Bond restructurings took an average of only 13 months, less than half the duration of a typical bank debt restructuring (more than 30 months, on average).

Fourth fact: Creditor holdouts and pre-restructuring litigation against sovereigns could be observed only in a minority of debt restructurings. These creditor actions were an obstacle in less than 30 percent of the restructurings surveyed.

APPENDIX: THE DATABASE ON RESTRUCTURING DELAYS

Why construct a new data set if there are several standardized sources on sovereign debt restructurings? Some papers have, for example, relied on the list of private debt restructuring events in the World Bank's GDF (2003, 2004, 2006, 2007) publications. Unfortunately, however, these and other similar archives such as that by the Institute of International Finance (IIF) (2001) contained errors or inaccuracies regarding restructuring dates. Often, a date listed as a completion date was, in effect, the month of an agreement in principle, but not the final agreement. Drawing on a much broader information base, I therefore verify and correct the available data.

Moreover, the existing lists do not provide details on the beginning and length of negotiations, on creditor characteristics, or on possible reasons for delays such as litigation, inter-creditor disputes, or holdouts. This made my own coding effort necessary.

Case Selection and Coding

The database in Trebesch (2008) covers 90 debt restructuring cases from 35 developing and emerging economies in the period from 1980 to 2007. As such, the database covers all main emerging market economies covered in J.P. Morgan's Emerging Market Bond Index and large sovereign debtors rated by either Moody's or Standard & Poor's. I code only sovereign debt restructurings with private creditors, that is, commercial banks or bondholders. Note also that the data set includes only cases that were officially concluded, thus disregarding preliminary agreements that were never implemented. Hence, each case is coded from the beginning of negotiations or default until the first successful and final agreement. The cases were identified from existing lists on debt restructuring and default events, in particular by the World Bank (2003, 2004, 2006, 2007), the IIF (2001), and Stamm (1987).

The coding process extends the information basis collected by Enderlein, Trebesch, and von Daniels (2010), who construct an index of government behavior during sovereign debt crises. The coding was mainly based on the evaluation of 20,000 pages of articles from the financial press. The print media generally turned out to be the most rewarding information source. Given that debt crises are highly publicized events, the financial press provides extensive and detailed day-to-day coverage on the negotiation and restructuring process, including much behind-the-scenes information. I mainly relied on articles from six flagship media sources: the *Financial Times*, *Reuters*, the *Wall Street Journal*, *Dow Jones News Service*, the *New York Times*, and the Associated Press. The articles were extracted from the online news database Factiva, using a standardized search algorithm. Further important sources were case studies by academic researchers, policy reports by the IMF, and other international bodies. Each coding decision is backed by respective quotes and sources. For more details see Trebesch (2008).

NOTE

1. This refers to the president, the prime minister, the chief debt negotiator, or ministers of finance, economy, or planning (or their respective speakers).

REFERENCES

Beers, D., and J. Chambers. 2006. *Default Study: Sovereign Defaults at 26-Year Low, to Show Little Change in 2007*. New York: Standard & Poor's.

Bi, R., M. Chamon, and J. Zettelmeyer. 2009. *The Problem that Wasn't: Coordination Failures in Sovereign Debt Restructurings*. Washington, DC: International Monetary Fund.

Cruces, J., and C. Trebesch. 2010. *Pricing Haircuts: Do Markets Punish Lower Recovery Values in Sovereign Restructurings?* Berlin: Free University of Berlin.

Enderlein, H., C. Trebesch, and L. von Daniels. 2010. *Sovereign Debt Disputes*. Berlin: Hertie School of Governance.

Institute of International Finance. 2001. *Survey of Debt Restructuring by Private Creditors.* Washington, DC: Institute of International Finance.

International Monetary Fund. 2003. *Fact Sheet: Proposals for a Sovereign Debt Restructuring Mechanism.* Washington, DC: International Monetary Fund.

Krueger, A. 2002. *A New Approach to Sovereign Debt Restructuring.* Washington, DC: International Monetary Fund.

Pitchford, R., and Wright, M. L. J. 2007. *Restructuring the Sovereign Debt Restructuring Mechanism.* Los Angeles: UCLA.

———. 2008. *Holdouts in Sovereign Debt Restructuring: A Theory of Negotiation in a Weak Contractual Environment.* Los Angeles: UCLA.

Stamm, H. 1987. *Kooperation und Konflikt im Weltfinanzsystem. Eine Analyse multilateraler Umschuldungsaktionen seit 1956.* Zurich: Soziologisches Institut der Universität Zürich.

Trebesch, C. 2008. *Delays in Sovereign Debt Restructurings.* Berlin: Free University of Berlin.

World Bank. Various Issues. "Global Development Finance." Washington, DC: International Bank for Reconstruction and Development and World Bank.

ABOUT THE AUTHOR

Christoph Trebesch is a PhD candidate in economics at Free University of Berlin. He spent the 2009–2010 academic year at Yale University as a Fox Fellow, and holds a postgraduate degree from the Kiel Institute for the World Economy. He has worked for the International Monetary Fund and the World Bank, and is a research associate at the Hertie School of Governance in Berlin. As part of his doctoral thesis, he is currently finalizing a comprehensive new database on sovereign default cases and debt restructurings between 1970 and 2010, including detailed information on debt renegotiation processes and the scope of debt relief (*haircuts*).

CHAPTER 19

IMF Interventions in Sovereign Debt Restructurings

JAVIER DÍAZ-CASSOU
Teaching Fellow at the Development Studies Institute (DESTIN) of the London
School of Economics and Political Science*

AITOR ERCE
Research Economist, General Directorate of International Affairs of Banco De España

Since the 1980s debt crisis, the international monetary system has witnessed several sovereign debt restructurings, with the International Monetary Fund (IMF) being involved in many of them.[1] However, in spite of various attempts to create an international insolvency regime such as the Sovereign Debt Restructuring Mechanism (SDRM) proposed in the early 2000s, the IMF still lacks an instrument specifically designed to cope with these situations. In most cases, its interventions have been articulated around one of its facilities, which provide financial resources conditioned on the fulfillment of a program of macroeconomic and structural measures. But in what precise ways has the IMF made a contribution to the orderly completion of past sovereign debt restructurings? This chapter addresses this question using evidence from 10 recent episodes: Russia, Pakistan, Ukraine, Ecuador, Argentina, Uruguay, Dominica, Dominican Republic, Grenada, and Belize. It departs from Díaz-Cassou, Erce, and Vázquez Zamora (2008a), who provide an in-depth analysis of these experiences. We conclude that, in the context of the fiscal difficulties created by the ongoing financial crisis, a systematic approach to sovereign debt restructurings might be needed.

We argue that the Fund's interventions can potentially exert a constructive influence on sovereign debt restructurings by: (1) affecting countries' decision to restructure when their debt burden becomes unsustainable; (2) providing official finance to substitute for a loss of access to international financial markets; (3) setting a medium-term domestic adjustment path through conditionality; (4) providing independent information at a time of heightened uncertainty; and (5) providing incentives both to creditors and debtors. However, we also find that a lack of consistency has tended to characterize the Fund's involvement in past debt crises.

---

*The views displayed in this paper are those of the authors and do not necessarily coincide with those of the Banco de España or the Eurosystem.

To some extent, this reflects the flexibility with which the IMF has adapted its interventions to country-specific factors. Yet, we argue that this lack of consistency might have exacerbated the uncertainty that often surrounds these episodes and failed to provide the actors involved with adequate incentives.

OFFICIAL POLICY

The issue of sovereign debt restructurings has long figured in the international policy agenda. Until the late 1980s, however, the IMF did not lend to countries in arrears with private external creditors. This policy stance, while aimed at providing debtors and creditors with incentives to seek a prompt restructuring agreement so they could regain access to the Fund's resources and increase the sovereign's ability to repay, substantially constrained the role that the institution could play in these situations. The protraction of the debt crisis gradually undermined this rationale, as the recomposition of banks' balance sheets and the development of a secondary market for troubled debt weakened creditors' interest in the negotiations. Eventually, commercial banks' reluctance to settle came to be perceived as an unacceptable pseudo-veto power on the official sector's lending decisions. To override this problem, in 1989 countries in arrears were first allowed to draw from the IMF. This new policy of lending into arrears (LIA) paved the way for a more active IMF involvement in the resolution of the debt crisis and sovereign defaults.[2] However, besides legalizing lending in a very particular scenario, it did not specify the functions of the IMF during a debt restructuring.[3]

The succession of emerging market crises that followed the Mexican crash of 1995 provided another impetus to formalize the role of the IMF during debt crises. Indeed, after the Asian crisis, the international community embarked on a broad-based attempt to reform the international financial architecture, a crucial element of which was the reinforcement of the IMF's capacity to prevent and resolve emerging market crises. An aspect emphasized was the need to involve private creditors, ensuring that they would absorb part of the costs associated with these crises. This was not only a recognition of the fact that the volume of multilateral resources available for countries in distress had become dwarfed by the size of international financial transactions, but also a move to address the moral hazard problem that massive IMF bailouts were believed to have generated. As a result, private sector involvement (PSI) became a more or less explicit requirement in many of the IMF programs approved since the late 1990s.[4]

And yet, the traumatic experience of the 2001 Argentine default evidenced that if PSI was to play such a prominent role, further reforms would be needed to operationalize this concept and facilitate the orderly resolution of insolvency crises. In this context, adherents to the SDRM argued it would bring about prompt collective action to deal with unsustainable debt burdens. Had the SDRM been approved, it would have consolidated the IMF as the cornerstone of an international insolvency regime, with powers similar to those of domestic bankruptcy courts.[5] Nevertheless, no consensus could be reached, and the international community opted instead for a less ambitious market-based contractual approach: promoting the inclusion of collective action clauses (CACs) in sovereign bonds. Regardless of whether CACs will be up to the task (they have not been tested in a major restructuring yet), the international community succeeded in turning these clauses into a common feature of sovereign bond issuances.

Apart from entrusting the IMF with the task of promoting CACs, the adoption of the contractual approach left the institution's role essentially untouched. The discussions of the early 2000s, therefore, also failed to clarify an IMF policy on sovereign debt restructurings. Partly because of the fatigue generated by the SDRM debate, and partly because buoyant conditions in international financial markets in the mid-2000s rendered future sovereign insolvencies into a seemingly distant risk, international policy makers gradually lost interest in this issue. As a result, and in the face of mounting fiscal problems in various regions of the world, the lack of a well-specified policy on debt restructurings remains a significant gap in the IMF's toolkit.[6]

EXPERIENCE WITH PAST RESTRUCTURINGS: STYLIZED FACTS AND IMF'S INVOLVEMENT

The economics literature on sovereign debt events has tended to treat restructurings in relatively uniform terms. Yet, as summarized in Exhibit 19.1, our case studies exhibit substantial variation in various crucial aspects such as the duration of the restructuring, the period of exclusion from capital markets that followed the restructuring, the losses absorbed by private creditors, or the authorities' coerciveness in the negotiations. In Diaz-Cassou et al. (2008b) we argue that along with the degree of involvement of the IMF, and probably intertwined with it, there are a number of features of sovereign debt restructurings that are important to understand about the heterogeneous evolution and impact of these processes. Therein we defend that this heterogeneity can be in part attributed to strategic considerations on the part of the sovereign, such as whether to default on their obligations or to restructure them preemptively, the share and types of debt involved in the restructuring, or the degree of inter-creditor equity.

Our analysis shows that, when compared with post-default restructurings, those cases in which debt was restructured preemptively featured quicker re-access to capital markets and lower haircuts (see Exhibit 19.1). Although we believe that the IMF had a pivotal influence in this decision, the factors behind this decision are still an open issue. In most cases under scrutiny, country authorities tried to shield some debt or debtor categories from the restructuring. However, we find evidence that the more comprehensive cases, in the sense that the sovereign engaged most types of instruments and creditors, provided a faster and more durable solution to the debt problem. Ukraine, for example, went through various partial restructuring operations, but it was not until the comprehensive restructuring of 2001 that its debt problems were finally overcome. Similarly, we find a nonhomogeneous involvement of domestic creditors across crises. This varying role of domestic creditors is analyzed in further detail in Erce and Diaz-Cassou (2010a). There we show that the tendency to discriminate between resident and external creditors during a debt restructuring is influenced by factors such as the relative reliance of the domestic corporate sector on international financial markets and the ex ante health of the domestic banking system.

Exhibit 19.1 Restructuring Key Features

	1998 Russia	1999 Pakistan	1998 Ukraine	1999 Ecuador	2001 Argentina	2003 Uruguay	2004* Dominica	2004 Dom. Rep.	2004 Grenada	2006 Belize
Debt to GDP (%)[1]	51	84	42	100	62.2 (2001); 132 (2004)	104	130	56	129	98
Restructured debt (% GDP)	32	27	14.80	46	30 (2001); 53.4 (2005)	44	83	6	61	46
Restructured debt (USD billion)	71.6 (at pre-crisis exchange rates for 1998–1998 debt exchange)	19	4.7	7.81	162.3[10]	5.35	0.21	1.91	0.29	0.56
Rest. debt owed to the private sector (% GDP)	28.3	2.5	12.9	40.8	30 (2001); 53.4 (2005)	44.0	83	4.6	58.6	46.1
Paris Club reschedulings (% GDP)	4.14	24.9	1.85	5.52[11]	no resch.	no resch.	no resch.	1.28	2.83	no resch.
Announcement of the restructuring	Aug-98	Jan-99	Aug-98	Oct-99	June-01	March-03	Dec-03[4]	Apr-04	Oct-04[7]	Aug-06
Completion of the restructuring	Aug-00	Dec-01	July-01	End-00	June-05	May-03	June-04[5]	Oct-05	Nov-05	Feb-07
Duration (months)	24	35	35	14	46	2	6	12		6
Default on external private debt	N	N	N[8]	Y	Y	N	N[6]	N	Y	N
Default on domestic private debt	Y	N	N	Y	Y	N	N[6]	N	Y	N
Default on official debt	Y	Y	N[8]	Y	Y	N	N	N	Y	N
External debt restructuring	Y	Y	Y	Y	Y	Y	Y	Y	Y	Y
Domestic debt restructuring	Y	N[3]	Y	Y	Y	Y	Y	N	Y	N
Official debt restructuring	Y	Y	Y	Y	Y	N	N	Y	Y	N
NPV loss (%)	(40–75)	(29–33)	(5–59.2)	(9–47)	(25–82)	(5–20)[9]	50	(1–2)	(40–45)	(1–28)
Participation in the exchange (%)	92	99	99	98	76	93	79	97	91	98

Coerciveness index[2]	(3,6)	(2,4)	(0,1)	5	(0,7)	0	1	(1,3)	1	1
Capital controls	Y	Y	Y	N	Y	N	N	N	N	N
Deposit freezes	Y	Y	N	Y	Y	Y	N	N	N	N
Access to international capital markets[12]										
1st international bond issuance (3-month periods)	5	19	3	23	14	0	–	4	not yet	not yet
EMBI Global level below 1000 p.b.	11	9	7	16	16	1	–	2	–	0
Liquidity:										
Total debt service (% of exports of goods services and income—$t-1$)	7	22	7	30	69	40	11	8	15	35
TDS (% total reserves including gold, $t-1$)	40	126	57	87	107	162	28	290	33	306

Note: We consider 2004 as the year of the restructuring t even if the debt exchange offer was launched in December of the previous year.
[1] Closest available data to the launch of the exchange.
[2] Index of Government Coerciveness (Enderlein, Müller, and Trebesch 2007), ranging from 0 (cooperative restructuring without missed payments) to 9 (highest level of coerciveness).
[3] No domestically issued debt instrument was restructured but one third of the bonds exchanged in late 1999 were held by residents.
[4] The formal debt exchange offer was made in April 2004.
[5] The exchange offer formally closed in June 2004, but the deal was not completed until 2007 because of discussions with holdout creditors.
[6] Although this was a preemptive restructuring, two bonds were in legal dispute.
[7] The offer was launched in September 2005.
[8] Ukraine was in default for a short period.
[9] Some minor bonds carried a higher haircut (Sturzenegger and Zettelmeyer, 2005).
[10] Additionally, 58 billion USD of 2002 pesification were redollarized in 2003.
[11] 2003 Paris Club agreement not included.
[12] Quarters after the announcement of the restructuring (except Argentina's international bond issuance: quarters after December 2001 default).

Sources: Erce and Díaz-Cassou (2010b), Díaz-Cassou and Erce (2008b), World Bank World Development Indicators, Debt Indicator, International Monetary Fund, Moody's, European Central Bank, Paris Club, Datastream, Dealogic, United Nations Conference on Trade and Development, and authors' calculations.

183

As just argued, another important source of heterogeneity relates to the various channels though which the IMF's interventions affect debt restructurings. First, the IMF may influence sovereigns' decision to launch a restructuring. Such an influence might be desirable to the extent that, as described earlier, some countries have a tendency to gamble for redemption, avoiding comprehensive restructurings even when their debt stocks are unsustainable and, in so doing, potentially exacerbating the long-term cost of the crisis. As part of the Policy Support Instrument (PSI) policy adopted in the late 1990s, the IMF often requested governments under a program to induce private creditors to bear part of the adjustment cost. This contributes to an explanation of the proliferation of partial debt operations during those years, like the Argentine mega-swap of June 2001, the Russian pre-default debt exchange of July 1998, or the Ukrainian selective restructurings of 1998 and 1999. Ultimately, however, as mentioned earlier, many of these selective debt operations were costly in the long run.[7] On other occasions, such as Ecuador (1999), Ukraine (2000), or Uruguay (2003), the IMF adopted a more wide-ranging approach, encouraging sovereigns to engage in a more comprehensive restructuring, sometimes against their initial will.[8] Another scenario was that in which countries were forced to default as the suspension of the IMF's disbursements made it impossible for them to continue honoring their obligations. This occurred in Russia in August 1998 and in Argentina in December 2001 where, as a result of both governments' inability to implement the adjustment and reforms demanded, their respective programs went off track.

A second dimension of the Fund's interventions is the provision of financial assistance. IMF's support may be instrumental to avoid the collapse of trade finance or to smooth the haircut imposed on private creditors and increase the likelihood of a restructuring agreement. As shown in Exhibit 19.1, there is a great deal of variation in the size of the Fund's programs approved to support the restructurings under analysis. A particularly important distinction is the one between inherited programs that were in place before the launching of the restructuring and new programs approved just to deal with the crisis and support the restructuring. This distinction is relevant because countries with inherited programs could be facing demanding repayment schedules to the IMF on top of their obligations to private creditors. In this context, unless the Fund's financial exposure is increased after the launching of the restructuring through some sort of program augmentation, the country will not receive additional resources to deal with the debt restructuring. This was the case of Argentina after the 2001 default, with which all agreements with the IMF essentially rolled over preexisting obligations (see Exhibit 19.1). The problem associated with this scenario is not only that the concerned country does not receive fresh multilateral assistance to cope with the crisis, but also that the Fund's inherited financial exposure may undermine the institution's position as honest broker in the restructuring. Indeed, a conflict of interests came to be perceived by the various actors involved in the Argentine debt restructuring, as the IMF became increasingly concerned with the possibility of an Argentine default on its multilateral obligations. As a result, the credibility of the IMF as an adjustment agent and a provider of information and incentives became severely undermined.

A third dimension of the Fund's involvement is the setting of a macroeconomic adjustment path through the conditionality embedded in its programs. The Fund's role as an adjustment agent is undisputed in traditional IMF programs. During a restructuring, however, the level of domestic adjustment associated with the

Fund's conditionality, together with the program's macroeconomic projections, may leave the relief or haircut to be obtained from private creditors for the purpose of restoring debt sustainability as a quasi-residual. As this can strongly influence the negotiation, it is likely to be opposed either by the sovereign debtor or by private creditors. In most of our case studies, the IMF did play the role of an adjustment agent through its programs. This was particularly clear in the Dominican Republic and Pakistan, where the restructuring began with an agreement with the Paris Club.[9] The cases of Belize, Russia, and Argentina, however, constitute exceptions. Whereas in Belize no IMF program was in place at the time of the restructuring and the program was off-track in Russia, the case of Argentina is particularly interesting because the government did not compromise and the program's conditionality was short-term-oriented so as not to interfere with the negotiations.[10] As a result, domestic adjustment was left entirely to be determined by the bargaining process between the government and its creditors.

A fourth dimension of the Fund's involvement that may be relevant in the uncertain context of a sovereign restructuring is the provision of impartial information. Again, we find a substantial variation in the amount of information disclosed by the Fund in the various cases under consideration. This is probably due to member states having the right to preclude the Fund from disclosing certain market-sensitive pieces of information. The informational role of the Fund has been more intense in market-friendly restructurings than in the more contentious cases. For example, the Fund published most program-related documents in the cases of the Dominican Republic or Uruguay. Instead, few documents were published in Argentina and Ecuador. Although it could have been particularly useful in the context of these debt restructurings, in very few cases did the IMF disclose full-fledged debt sustainability analyses.

Finally, IMF programs may provide incentives to the parts involved in the process. We have already mentioned the Fund's potential role in the decision-making process, which may mitigate the cost of irrational decisions adopted in desperate situations and of an undue postponement of the debt restructuring. Also, IMF disbursements under a LIA program are explicitly conditioned on the authorities' good faith, which is aimed at inducing a collaborative stance in the negotiations. This good-faith criterion, however, is not included in preemptive debt restructurings and has proved to be highly judgmental, sometimes arbitrary, and a potential source of conflict between the IMF, its member states, and private creditors.[11] On the side of financiers, the managing director of the IMF has usually issued a letter to the members of the financial community in support of the authorities' economic program and the terms of the restructuring. In some cases, such as Uruguay, the IMF went as far as making it clear that an insufficient participation in the debt exchange could lead to a suspension of the Fund's financial support and, thereby, to a much higher likelihood of a default.

CONCLUSION

The failure to adopt an SDRM in the early 2000s left the IMF with no instrument specifically designed to cope with the challenges posed by insolvency crises. And yet, our case study analysis reveals that there is scope for the IMF to exert a significant influence on various important dimensions of sovereign debt restructuring without embarking on another unrealistic attempt to introduce an international bankruptcy court. Indeed, traditional financial programs have proved to be a rather flexible tool to customize the Fund's interventions to country- and crisis-specific factors. This flexibility, however, has sometimes come at the expense of consistency, meaning that the role played by the IMF in different crises has exhibited an excessive degree of heterogeneity. As a result, the Fund's interventions have sometimes added uncertainty to situations that were already plagued with informational asymmetries, feeding the perception that sovereign debtors and their private creditors have been treated unequally in different crises and potentially generating perverse incentives. Given the fiscal difficulties that are currently facing various countries as a result of the ongoing financial crisis, it may be worth reflecting on whether more predictability is required to guide future IMF interventions in sovereign debt restructurings. This would imply agreeing ex ante on the specific functions that the IMF should fulfill in these situations, which would reduce the ambiguities of the current system while contributing to anchor the expectations of the various actors involved.

A possible point of departure would be a reform of the policy of lending into arrears (Díaz-Cassou et al. 2008b). This would require not only broadening its scope to include all those situations in which a sovereign is renegotiating its contractual debt obligations, but also going beyond its current procedural nature so as to endow it with the economic substance that it currently lacks. The key for such a reform to have a desirable effect would be to reinforce the Fund's capacity to provide the right incentives both to sovereign debtors and their creditors. A priority should be to constrain countries' tendency to gamble for redemption in difficult situations. Indeed, when debt burdens become unsustainable, the IMF should be particularly vigilant to counter the sort of desperate measures that have generated an even greater economic dislocation in some past episodes. In some circumstances, this may require conditioning multilateral financial support on the launching of a comprehensive debt restructuring (but not on the sort of partial debt operations that have been encouraged in the past). In addition, we believe that the IMF has an important role to play as an adjustment agent and provider of information. In other words, we consider the IMF to be uniquely positioned to help determine the resource envelope of sovereign debt restructurings through its independent assessment of both the feasible level of domestic adjustment to be expected from sovereign debtors and of the haircut that would be required from creditors in order to restore debt sustainability.

NOTES

1. This chapter focuses on the restructuring of sovereign debt in the hands of private creditors, and only tangentially in the restructuring of bilateral debt.

2. The LIA policy is activated only when the sovereign falls into arrears with external private creditors. This means that it does not apply in purely preemptive restructurings such as Uruguay's, or when arrears arise only with official or domestic creditors, as was the case in Pakistan.

3. The difference between traditional and LIA programs is essentially of a procedural nature. LIA programs include only a few additional requirements, the most prominent being the so-called good faith criterion.

4. On the mildest end of the spectrum in terms of coerciveness, PSI referred to agreements with specific categories of creditors to roll over their loans, to maintain their exposure to a given country, or to take part in a preemptive voluntary debt exchange aimed at reestablishing the sovereign's creditworthiness and avoiding future losses. On the more coercive end of the spectrum, PSI referred to outright defaults and comprehensive debt restructurings.

5. Essentially, the SDRM was an international bankruptcy court, incorporating features that would entitle the IMF or another international body to sanction a standstill on debt payments, deter creditors from litigating during a legitimate restructuring, and bind all creditors to the restructuring terms agreed to by a qualified majority of them.

6. It should be recognized, however, that since the crisis erupted in 2008, several reforms have taken place to substantially reinforce the financial muscle of the IMF. This may have important consequences on the effectiveness of these interventions.

7. Some of these partial restructurings have been criticized as financial engineering operations providing a limited short-term relief at a very high long-term cost. The Argentine mega-swap, for instance, produced short-term savings of about US$12 billion, but increased long-term debt servicing obligations by a staggering US$66 billion.

8. This is the case of Uruguay, where the authorities were initially reluctant to restructure. Yet, as part of the program, IMF officials insisted that the Uruguayan government should default and restructure. The involvement of the U.S. government was instrumental in reaching a compromise: preemptively restructuring without interrupting debt servicing (Taylor 2007).

9. An IMF program setting a medium-term macroeconomic adjustment path constitutes a prerequisite for obtaining a Paris Club treatment. When a restructuring is opened by a Paris Club treatment, private creditors are involved later in fulfillment of the comparability of treatment clause. This clause, which constitutes a cornerstone of the Paris Club debt treatments, forces countries benefiting from the restructuring of their bilateral obligations to negotiate with their other nonmultilateral creditors in order to obtain a comparable debt relief from them.

10. The September 2003 SBA established a floor on the primary surplus of 3 percent of GDP, while fiscal targets for 2005 and 2006 were not even specified. Furthermore, the program was suspended in August 2004.

11. This is well illustrated by the Argentine case. Although many observers believed that, rather than engaging in a constructive dialogue, the authorities simply presented a series of take-it-or-leave-it offers clearly detrimental to creditors' interests, the IMF's program was not suspended on the basis of a breach of the good-faith clause. Yet the constant threat posed by the good-faith clause did also alienate the Argentine authorities who considered that, with the GDP-indexed bonds tendered in the debt exchange, it was offering an association agreement with its creditors. In their view, this was a proof of good faith that could eventually offset part of the haircut imposed in the restructuring if the Argentine economy performed better than expected.

REFERENCES

Díaz-Cassou, J., A. Erce, and J. Vázquez Zamora. 2008a. "Recent Episodes of Sovereign Debt Restructurings: A Case-Study Approach." *Banco de España Occasional Paper* 0804.

———. 2008b. "The Role of the IMF in Recent Sovereign Debt Restructurings: Implications for the Policy of Lending Into Arrears." *Banco de España Occasional Paper* 0804.

Enderlein, H., L. Müller, and C. Trebesch. 2007. "Sovereign Debt Disputes: Measuring Government Coerciveness in Sovereign Debt Crises." *Mimeo, Hertie School of Governance.*

Erce, A., and J. Díaz-Cassou. 2010a. "Creditor Discrimination during Sovereign Debt Restructurings." *Banco de España Working Paper* 1027.

Erce, A., and J. Díaz-Cassou. 2010b. "Sovereign Defaults and Creditor Discrimination." Documento de Trabajo de Banco de España (forthcoming).

Sturzenegger, F. and J. Zettelmeyer, 2007. "Haircuts: Estimating Investor Losses in Sovereign Debt Restructurings, 1998–2005." *Journal of International Money and Finance*, 27:5.

Taylor, J. B. 2007. "The 2002 Uruguayan Financial Crisis: Five Years On." Written version of remarks given at the Conference on the 2002 Uruguayan Financial Crisis and Its Aftermath, May 29, 2007, Montevideo, Uruguay.

ABOUT THE AUTHORS

Javier Díaz-Cassou is a teaching fellow at the Development Studies Institute (DESTIN) of the London School of Economics and Political Science, where he is finalizing his doctoral research. He has worked as an economist for the Bank of Spain, the European Central Bank, and the Inter-American Development Bank, and holds degrees from the School of Advanced International Studies (SAIS) of Johns Hopkins University and from Universidad Autónoma de Madrid.

Aitor Erce is a research economist at the General Directorate of International Affairs of Banco de España. He received an MBA from the Centro de Estudios Monetarios y Financieros (CEMFI) and a PhD from the European University Institute. He has worked as a researcher for the Bank of Spain and the European Investment Bank. Dr. Erce has done extensive work in the area of financial crises, capital flows, and international safety nets.

CHAPTER 20

Resuming Lending to Countries Following a Sovereign Debt Crisis

LUISA ZANFORLIN
International Monetary Fund*

It has been argued that international creditors are reluctant to resume lending to countries that default on their debt after having suffered catastrophic macroeconomic and financial crises, as this indicates either their unwillingness to repay or that claims are not enforceable. Interestingly, while the process toward resuming lending can be long and tortuous, several studies show that, ultimately, sovereign countries are able to regain their ability to borrow from international markets (International Monetary Fund 2003, 2005; Zanforlin 2007; others). In fact, with a couple of exceptions, most existing studies have overlooked demand and supply forces that may influence subsequent international lending conditions that may allow subsequent access of sovereign countries to international markets.

Whereas the literature on sovereign debt has shown that governments have an incentive to meet their obligations and to preserve their reputation as creditworthy borrowers both to ensure uninterrupted financing flows and to avoid enforcement of credible sanctions from creditors, they are also willing to lend to the extent that repayment will occur (Bulow and Rogoff 1989; Eaton and Gersovitz 1981).

BEYOND THE ISSUE OF REPUTATION

It has been argued that, despite an event of default, a sovereign will be able to borrow again, depending on the nature of such default. The nature of the crisis that led a sovereign to default can be crucial to explain the reasons why lending resumes. For example, if the default occurred as a result of external shocks exogenous to the policies of a country, creditors may be willing to resume lending, as the reputation of the country as a trustworthy borrower would remain untouched (Grossman and Van Huyck 1988). According to this view, a sovereign will be able to

---

*The views expressed herein are those of the author and should not be attributed to the IMF, its executive board, or its management.

regain its ability to borrow from the international capital markets provided it shows strong commitment to service its obligations and that it has the cash flow means to support it. The standard measures to reassure lenders that a country is committed to rebuilding its reputation are typically given in the form of consistent and sound economic policies. Thus, when testing for evidence on reputation issues, the explanatory variables of typical empirical equations will include macroeconomic variables that fluctuate within a reasonable range and are consistent among one another. They will signal a commitment to repay debt and, if investors are satisfied, resume borrowing.

Reputational issues may be reflected by focusing on the behavior of domestic policy indicators such as the fiscal deficit, the rate of inflation, the total stock of outstanding debt, and the stability of the political conditions and related institutions. For example, low inflation, debt ratios, and the fiscal deficit can provide an accurate reflection of sound domestic macroeconomic performance. Similarly, the inclusion of political stability and institutional variables can provide adequate reflections of good governance practices in the country. These variables best capture reputation building.

DEMAND AND SUPPLY FACTORS

Some researchers have questioned the narrow view that rebuilding credibility is the only thing that matters for countries to regain access to international financial markets. It appears that reputation is not all that is needed, but also other additional factors may be relevant for lending to resume. In this respect, one important factor is the sovereign's ability to repay foreign currency debt, another is the government commitment to repay debt, and, furthermore, the international liquidity conditions in the world economy.

The ability to repay is related to the capacity of the country to meet its commitments moving forward. This concept may be captured by external variables such as the total amount of reserves as a share of short-term debt, the total debt service as a share of reserves, the level of reserves in terms of months of imports, and the external current account balance. High levels of reserves and low current account deficits indicate a country's strong external position. Similarly, the presence of an International Monetary Fund program may be considered a signal for a country's ability to repay as it provides liquidity support (Zanforlin 2007). The expected returns to investors from resuming lending may be proxied by an indicator of economic activity, in particular, growth rates, which are typically reflected by the real return from investment in the country.

With respect to the issue of commitment to pay, it is important to note that the growth rates of gross domestic product and fiscal deficits may signal both the desired expected returns of investors and the sovereign's own demand. In fact, a sovereign that is emerging from a financial crisis signals its intention to become a creditworthy borrower by making a commitment to repay through the adoption of sound domestic macroeconomic policies and signals its ability to repay foreign debt through indicators of external soundness.

Finally, the higher the international liquidity conditions, as proxied by low yields on U.S. Treasury debt instruments, the more likely investors are to lend. In fact, recent evidence confirms the view that creditors evaluate the case to resume lending on the basis of their expected returns in the context of the global liquidity cycle. Foreign investors evaluate whether to resume lending on the basis of the expected rate of return of their investment subject to the international liquidity conditions. Here, following the lead of Zanforlin (2007), the aim is to explain which set of macroeconomic indicators increases the likelihood that a sovereign emerging from a crisis will regain its ability to borrow from international capital markets.

WHAT DOES THE EVIDENCE SAY?

A default is typically an episode in which an obligor fails to meet a principal or interest payment on the due date, or within the specified grace period, contained in the original terms of the debt issue. In particular, in the case of local and foreign currency bonds, notes, and bills, each issuer's debt is considered in default when either scheduled debt service is not made on the due date or when an exchange offer of new debt contains less favorable terms than the original issue; and in the case of bank loans, when either scheduled debt service is not made on the due date or a rescheduling of principal or interest is agreed to by creditors at less favorable terms than the original loan. Such rescheduling agreements covering short- and long-term bank debt are considered a default even when, for legal or regulatory reasons, creditors deem forced rollover or principal to be voluntary (Chambers and Alexeeva 2002).

While in the set of episodes compiled a financial crisis was eventually resolved by a debt reduction through a restructuring of its obligations, in other circumstances, exceptional liquidity support from multilateral financial institutions may have helped the sovereign to remain current on its bilateral obligations while facing a financial crisis. It is important to note that in the episodes in which the financial crisis was resolved through exceptional liquidity support, private creditors did not suffer any loss from lending, an outcome that is different from the episodes typically compiled in the literature. In both cases, however, the financial crisis entailed a loss of market access for the sovereign. As an additional observation, countries had to commit up front to sound macroeconomic policies to qualify for a disbursement under the exceptional financing facility, thus providing ipso facto a signal for a strong commitment to repay their external debt.

When using both definitions of crisis explained here, Zanforlin (2007) identifies a sample of 53 episodes of financial crisis that took place across 27 different countries for the time from 1980 to 2003. In 45 cases, the crisis entailed restructuring a bond or a loan to the sovereign, while in 8 cases the sovereign was granted exceptional liquidity support through access to financing from the International Monetary Fund without having to restructure any of its obligations. Episodes of restructuring both loans and bonds to the sovereigns were included in the sample because the greater part of sovereign lending in the period from 1980 to 1990 took the form of syndicated loans. The event of the resuming of international lending can be defined as the placement of a new sovereign bond in international markets for the first time after a financial crisis. For the sample of 53 financial crises over the period covered by the database, Zanforlin (2007) was able to identify 37 episodes of first successful international bond issues of market reentering by 26 different sovereigns. The data on financial crises were compiled by Standard & Poor's regular publications and comprised a set of episodes in which sovereigns either defaulted or restructured their external obligations, which resulted in a loss to the creditors.

While, in theory, the determinants of lending by international financial markets may appear easy to identify, it is important to note that sometimes the precise causal link between a specific determinant and the resumption of lending may remain unclear. For example, indicators such as the growth rate and fiscal deficits may signal to creditors not only the expected returns or the sovereign's commitment to repay but also reflect the sovereign's own demand for foreign financing. In effect, the fiscal deficit may also represent a financing need, while the rate of growth may very well reflect trends in the domestic demand. Including such variables in empirical work also provides a control for the sovereigns' demand for new financing. Ultimately, this implies that the expected sign for the estimated coefficient for fiscal deficits will be uncertain depending on which of the two effects, namely, commitment to repay or demand for financing, prevails. In fact, the estimated sign will provide an indication of which of them is more predominant in determining the event of regaining access to the international markets. In the case of GDP growth rates, both effects from the signaling of increasing returns and the domestic demand for new financing would increase the probability of regaining access to the markets.

As Zanforlin (2007) explains, another important problem that complicates an adequate understanding of the process of resuming lending by international financial markets is related to the so-called endogeneity issues. Variables that are not originally included in the empirical specification may be driving the results or, equally detrimental, the actual link between variables of interest may be contrary to what was originally conceptualized. For example, it may be the case that regaining access to the international markets may increase the ability of a sovereign to pay, and not the opposite. One way that allows a minimization of such issues of cross-correlation and joint endogeneity across explanatory variables is to take a parsimonious approach, by using only one indicator for each variable for each of the determinant groups discussed earlier. This makes it possible to better evaluate whether commitment to pay, ability to pay, or international conditions tend to be more significant in affecting the likelihood a country reentering international markets and to analyze the sensitivity of the estimates for coefficients.

The empirical evidence provided by Zanforlin (2007), among others, shows that the probability that a country may regain access to the international markets will be affected by the global liquidity cycle, total debt to GDP (to indicate the domestic policy stance), the level of the current account (to signal the external position), and the lagged GDP growth rate (to indicate the return from investment in the country). The elements that appear to affect most significantly the probability that international markets would resume lending to a sovereign are the perceived ability of the sovereign to repay, as signaled by the current account deficit, and the global liquidity cycle, as proxied by the yields on U.S. Treasury debt instruments. In fact, a one-percentage-point increase in the yields of U.S. Treasury notes reduces the probability of regaining access to the markets by, on average, 13 percent for any one year. In the case of indicators of ability to repay, a 1 percent improvement in the current account deficit was found to increase the probability of subsequent access by, on average, 20 percent. A sovereign's commitment to repay, as signaled indicators of sound domestic policies—debt levels, inflation levels, and domestic political conditions—also seemed to be a significant determinant of regaining access to international markets (the size of their impact appeared to be limited, however). Finally, investors' expected returns from the new lending, as proxied by lagged GDP growth rates, also appeared to affect the probability that lending would resume, but the estimates were not very robust.

Interestingly, indicators of commitment to repay, such as the total debt level to gross domestic product, appear to have a significant impact on the probability that lending by international financial markets would resume in those cases in which debt was restructured and creditors suffered losses. However, debt sustainability indicators tended not to be significant in those cases in which access to liquidity support was granted. In such cases, indicators of the ability to pay, such as the current account deficit and the level of debt service to reserves, which are more short-term in nature, appear to have a stronger impact on the probability of regaining access to the international financial markets than for the rest of the sample.

CONCLUSION

I provide evidence in this chapter that both commitment and ability to repay external obligations are statistically significant linked to the process whereby lending by international financial markets to a sovereign resumes after a financial crisis. In particular, it appears that external soundness indicators have a relatively larger impact on the probability that lending will resume, in particular, for those countries that, despite suffering a crisis, were able to avoid restructuring their debt (Zanforlin 2007). International investor demand is also a fundamental factor in regaining market access. Other important variables influencing international financial markets lending to resume were found to be the presence of an IMF program and sound macroeconomic policies. Overall, sound domestic policies coupled with a strong external position, in the context of a favorable global liquidity environment, were found to be the key factors in determining whether international financial markets lending would resume to sovereigns that suffered a financial crisis.

REFERENCES

Bulow, Jeremy, and Kenneth Rogoff. 1989. "A Constant Recontracting Model of Sovereign Debt." *Journal of Political Economy* 97:1, 155–78.

Chambers, John, and Dora Alekseeva. 2002. *Rating Performance 2002: Default, Transition, Recovery, and Spreads*. New York: Standard & Poor's.

Eaton, Jonathan, and Mark Gersovitz. 1981. "Debt with Potential Repudiation: Theoretical and Empirical Analysis." *Review of Economic Studies* 48:2, 289–309.

Grossman, Herschel, I., and John B. Van Huyck. 1988. "Sovereign Debt as a Contingent Claim: Excusable Default, Repudiation and Reputation." *American Economic Review* 78:5, 1088–1097.

International Monetary Fund. 2003. "Access to International Capital Markets for First-Time Sovereign Issuers—Country Cases." SM/03/218.

International Monetary Fund. 2005. "Assessing the Determinants and Prospects for the Pace of Market Access by Countries Emerging from Crises—Further Considerations." SM/05/76.

Zanforlin, Luisa. 2007. "Re-Accessing International Capital Markets after Financial Crises: Some Empirical Evidence." *IMF Working Paper* 07/136.

ABOUT THE AUTHOR

Luisa Zanforlin is a senior economist in the Monetary and Capital Markets Department in the International Monetary Fund. She holds a PhD from the European University Institute in Florence. Dr. Zanforlin has done extensive work in the area of international economics and finance and has done related work in several countries such as Portugal, Mexico, Iceland, Romania, and, more recently, Greece. She has written a number of articles in peer-reviewed journals such as *Public Choice*, the *Journal of International Development*, and the *IMF Staff Papers*, among others.

PART IV

Legal and Contractual Dimensions of Restructurings and Defaults

As with any loan agreement, sovereign debt contracts are encumbered with a variety of special conditions and restrictions, and these are most important when things go wrong—when debtors default or seek a restructuring. This section explores some of the most important of these features. For example, sovereign debt contracts typically provide for sovereign immunity. One effect of this immunity is that other nations cooperate with the sovereign debtor to prevent the seizure of its assets abroad. When Russia failed to include this condition in a debt agreement and then defaulted, the creditor made heroic attempts to seize assets of the Russian government outside of Russia, leading to effective restrictions on Russia's participation in air shows in Europe; the creditor's ardent pursuit of assets even kept Russian art treasures from being exhibited abroad.*

In many cases, sovereign default leaves numerous creditors scrambling for payment, so the matter of creditor priority becomes critical. Often a single creditor holds out and refuses to accept a general agreement that gives all creditors partial payment. Such *vultures* hope that the debtor will repay them in full in order to remove their objection to the general settlement. This kind of problem has led to collective action clauses, a stipulation in the loan agreement that allow a super-majority of creditors to enforce a general settlement on all creditors, stripping away the right of the vulture creditor to demand full payment.

A very serious legal and ethical question in sovereign debt arises in cases of so-called odious debt. Consider a military officer who seizes power in his country, rules as a dictator, borrows prodigiously in the name of the state, transfers the money away to his private Swiss bank account, and then falls from power, leaving a mass of sovereign debt obligations behind. In such circumstances, what are the obligations of the citizens of the beleaguered country to pay the debt? This matter can become even worse when there is a tacit agreement between the corrupt ruler and lender to encumber the natural resource revenues of the state.

---

*See Robert W. Kolb, "Sovereign Debt: Theory, Default, and Sanctions," the first article in this volume.

CHAPTER 21

A Code of Conduct for Sovereign Debt Restructuring

An Important Component of the International Financial Architecture?

KATHRIN BERENSMANN
German Development Institute

THE ROLE OF A CODE OF CONDUCT IN THE INTERNATIONAL FINANCIAL SYSTEM

The recent global financial crises point to the need for instruments that strengthen the functioning of the international financial system. In particular, appropriate mechanisms for preventing and resolving sovereign debt crises are needed because the debt crises in a number of emerging markets were accompanied by debt restructuring processes that were protracted and costly principally because of the ad hoc measures taken. The main reasons for these protracted debt restructuring processes were problems with coordination and collective action ultimately stemming from the growth in bond financing in emerging markets and an increasingly broad and diversified investor base (Ritter 2009, p. 9).[1]

The three main problems with collective action are, first, the *rush to the exit problem:* if creditors fear that a debtor may be heading for a debt crisis, they will seek to sell their claims; second, the *rush to the courthouse problem:* in the event of a default, creditors may take legal action to recover their claims, resulting in a fall in the value of the assets concerned, which could be detrimental to all the creditors involved; and third, the *holdout problem:* a minority of creditors may block a debt restructuring process that could be advantageous to the majority of creditors (Roubini 2002).

To solve these problems, three major instruments have been proposed and partly established. In the short term, a voluntary code of conduct and collective action clauses (CACs) constitute the most important market-based instruments for restructuring sovereign bond issues.

A code of conduct would lay down rules to be observed voluntarily by market participants in the period before and during a debt crisis. The first proposal for a code of conduct relating to sovereign debt restructuring was made in 2001 by Jean-Claude Trichet, who was at that time governor of the Banque de France (Banque de France 2003; Couillault and Weber 2003). The public and private sectors, and in particular the Institute of International Finance, in cooperation with other financial industry associations, put forward several proposals for "Principles for Stable Capital Flows and Fair Debt Restructuring in Emerging Markets" (hereinafter the Principles), on which sovereign debtors and private creditors agreed in autumn 2004 and which were implemented in late 2005. These Principles represent one kind of a voluntary and nonbinding code of conduct. In this respect, the code of conduct suggested by the Banque de France is the predecessor of the Principles (IIF 2009; Ritter 2009).

One interesting feature of the Principles is that they are a product of a transnational public-private partnership. The incentive for such a partnership can be explained by the history of sovereign debt restructuring. Mutual interests of the parties originated from the perceived risk of more government regulation in the area of sovereign debt restructuring in early 2000, when a number of proposals were presented for an insolvency procedure for sovereign states, such as the Sovereign Debt Restructuring Mechanisms suggested by the International Monetary Fund (Ritter 2009).

CACs represent a market-based approach and are included in bonds with the aim of simplifying procedures for the restructuring of sovereign bonds and of providing both creditors and debtors with an incentive to take part in debt restructuring. The collective majority clause authorizing a qualified majority of bondholders to involve minorities in their decisions is the most widely used type of collective action clause (Dixon and Wall 2000; Häseler 2009). In the medium term, an insolvency procedure (statutory approach) may play an important role in the restructuring of sovereign bond debt because it is a comprehensive instrument for coordinating different creditor groups before and during a debt crisis (Berensmann and Herzberg 2009; Bolton and Skeel 2004).

These three instruments complement each other. A code of conduct, for example, is complementary to an insolvency procedure because, before the outbreak of a crisis, it may serve as a complementary crisis prevention instrument by helping to provide timely information and to enhance transparency. In the time between a decision in favor of an insolvency procedure and its implementation, a code of conduct may help to improve the predictability of a restructuring process. During an insolvency procedure a code defines principles of conduct to which the participants commit themselves. A code of conduct is also an instrument that can be used to complement collective action clauses.

While CACs have been included in many sovereign bond contracts, codes of conduct have been adopted to only a limited extent and on a voluntary basis, and an insolvency procedure for sovereign debtors has yet to be implemented (Ritter 2009).

OBJECTIVES OF A CODE OF CONDUCT

One of the aims of a code of conduct is to contribute both to the prevention and to the resolution of sovereign debt crises. In the case of crisis prevention, a code of conduct will seek to avert restructuring procedures and to prevent a crisis from spreading to other countries by fostering transparency and a timely flow of information. A close debtor-creditor dialogue should also contribute to crisis prevention. As regards crisis resolution, a code of conduct serves to simplify restructuring procedures by enhancing the predictability and transparency of the negotiation processes involved in debt restructuring and by promoting cooperation between creditors and debtors. In addition, it represents a market-oriented approach designed to sustain and support existing contractual relations as long as possible.

For the debtor, compliance with a code could be important in enabling him to regain early access to international financial markets. For the creditor, it may help to reduce uncertainty over debtor moral hazard. Another purpose of a code of conduct is to balance the interests of creditors and debtors and of creditors among themselves with a view to achieving equitable burden-sharing among debtors and creditors (Berensmann 2003; IIF 2009, p. 27).

FEATURES OF A CODE OF CONDUCT

A code of conduct without a legal foundation lays down rules governing the behavior of all market participants both before and during a sovereign debt crisis. As a rule, it is voluntary and nonbinding in nature. In this regard, it represents a soft mode of governance. However, a code of conduct can, to some extent, become a hard mode of governance if compliance with it is monitored. While noncompliance with a code will have an adverse effect on reputation, compliance will send out positive signals to the market (Ritter 2009).

We concentrate on the design of the Principles in this chapter, because so far they represent the only code of conduct for sovereign debt restructuring that has been put into practice. The Principles set out in a code of conduct should apply equally to all market participants and are based on four pillars (Exhibit 21.1):

1. Transparency and timely flow of information
2. Debtor-creditor dialogue and cooperation aimed at avoiding restructuring
3. Good faith actions
4. Fair treatment (IIF 2009)

THE ADVANTAGES AND DISADVANTAGES OF A CODE OF CONDUCT

A well-formulated code of conduct can be one element of a road map that shows debtors and creditors how they should act before and during a restructuring process. While a code of conduct may help to mitigate the collective action problems mentioned earlier, it cannot eliminate them entirely. A code of conduct can neither prevent a *rush to the exit* nor offer any formal protection against a *rush to the courthouse* by creditors, nor can it provide any safeguards against *holdout behaviors*. It can help, however, solve the following coordination problems involved in restructuring debt through the application of, in particular, the third Principle, good-faith actions, which includes the coordination of various debt instruments in

Exhibit 21.1   Principles for Stable Capital Flows and Debt Restructuring in Emerging Markets

1. Transparency and timely flow of information
   - **General disclosure practice:** Debtors should ensure by disclosing relevant information that creditors are able to conduct thorough assessments of their economic and financial situation.
   - **Specific disclosure practice:** The debtor should disclose all information on the structure and amount of his debts to all creditors.
2. Debtor-creditor dialogue and cooperation aimed at avoiding restructuring
   - **Regular dialogue:** Debtors and creditors should take part in a regular dialogue.
   - **Best practices for investor relations:** An investor relations office should be set up to improve communication techniques.
   - **Policy action and feedback:** Debtor countries should conduct economic and financial policies designed to guarantee macroeconomic stability and promote sustainable economic growth.
   - **Consultations:** Debtors and creditors should look at alternative market-based instruments for restructuring debt.
   - **Creditor support of debtor reform efforts:** Creditors should take into account the voluntary, temporary continuation of trade and inter-bank advances. Moreover, creditors should consider a rollover of short-term maturities on public- and private-sector debt.
3. Good faith actions
   - **Voluntary, good faith process:** Debtors and creditors should warrant timely good-faith negotiations.
   - **Sanctity of contracts:** Contracts should be maintained and altered only if both parties are agreed.
   - **Vehicles for restructuring:** Creditor committees should be set up flexibly and on a case-by-case basis.
   - **Creditor committee policies and practices:** If a creditor committee is installed, it should stick to rules and practices relating, for example, to the coordination of various debt instruments and the protection of nonpublic information.
   - **Debtor and creditor actions during restructuring:** As far as possible, debtors should return to partial debt service payments and full payment of principal and interest. During a restructuring process, debtors and creditors should guarantee that trade lines are fully serviced and maintained.
4. Fair treatment
   - **Avoiding unfair discrimination among affected creditors:** Debtors should assure equal treatment of all creditors. However, some credits, including short-term trade-related facilities and inter-bank advances, should be dealt with separately.
   - **Fairness of voting:** The result of a vote among creditors on a restructuring effort should not be affected by bonds, loans, or other financial instruments owned or controlled by the sovereign debtor.

Source: For a more detailed description of this proposal, see IIF 2009, pp. 28–29.

creditor committees, and the fourth Principle, fair treatment, which incorporates a guarantee of fair treatment for all creditors:

- *Coordination in the restructuring of a single bond issue:* A code of conduct can help to prevent a minority of creditors from opting out of a restructuring procedure agreed upon by a majority.
- *Coordination in the restructuring of a number of bond issues:* A code of conduct can help to coordinate a number of bonds, particularly through the adoption of the principle of equal treatment.
- *Creditor coordination:* A code of conduct can help to coordinate creditors as they try to come to a decision on the approach to be adopted, particularly by ensuring timely good faith negotiations and the fair treatment of all creditors (Berensmann 2003; Roubini and Setser 2003).

Another advantage of a code of conduct is that, while the procedural principles it sets out establish a generally acceptable framework, it leaves sufficient room for proper and flexible account to be taken of a country's specific debt situation and repayment capacities.

The main objection to codes of conduct is that they are voluntary and nonbinding, which results in their not being especially effective. However, there are, first, a number of advantages associated with a soft mode of governance; second, the implementation of the Principles has shown that, to some extent, a transition from a soft to hard mode of governance has taken place; and third, the adoption of the Principles in several countries has contributed to a more orderly debt restructuring process.

The advantages of a soft mode of governance include, first, lower negotiating and contracting costs, which simplifies cooperative agreements between different stakeholders. Second, soft modes of governance lower such costs to the sovereign debtor as the institutional costs of establishing and enforcing soft laws. Third, soft laws may act as a tool of compromise with which actors have diverging preferences. Agreement on the Principles was reached in spite of incongruent preferences of debtors and creditors with respect to certain aspects of crisis prevention and resolution. Fourth, a nonmandatory law is better able to cope with uncertainties because it is more flexible if circumstances change. For these reasons, a soft law may be preferable to a hard law, since it is better able to reflect mutual interests of debtors and creditors and so facilitate agreement among them.

A binary distinction between mandatory and nonmandatory law is not sufficient, because a soft law can shift between the two extremes of soft and hard modes of governance. In the case of the Principles, a shift toward hard law has occurred over time because of the enhanced precision with which the Principles have been implemented. One example is the role of the creditor committees. In 2007, best-practice principles for the way creditor committees are formed and how they should operate were developed. Among other things, they offer guidance on the speed of establishing a committee or the significance of confidentiality.

Also, the application of the Principles to the debt restructuring procedures of a number of countries, including Belize, Congo, the Dominican Republic, and Grenada, and to Nicaragua's debt buyback contributed to the orderly resolution of those countries' debt crises. A good example of the successful application of the Principles is the restructuring of Belize's debt in 2006 and 2007, with the authorities and creditors engaging in an open and intensive dialogue. Moreover, the authorities guaranteed transparency in the dissemination of data. The Principles thus helped to ensure an orderly and successful debt restructuring process in which the creditor participation level reached more than 98 percent (Ritter 2009).

Nevertheless, the voluntary nature of a code of conduct makes it necessary to create incentives to actors in the international financial markets to adhere to it. The main incentive to sovereign debtors is that commitment to and compliance with a code of conduct signal their intentions and enhance their reputations. If the implementation of a code of conduct is perceived by market participants as an instrument for improving reputations and thus access to international financial markets, it is in a sovereign debtor's own interests to comply. Similarly, adopting a code of conduct will be beneficial to the debtor if failure to do so is likely to have a negative effect on its reputation. In this regard, peer and market pressure take on an important role (Couillault and Weber 2003; Ritter 2009).

CONCLUSION

A code of conduct is an important element of an improved international financial architecture. However, one instrument alone is not enough to prevent or resolve sovereign debt crises: A code of conduct, CACs, and the insolvency procedure for sovereign states must be deployed as complements, not as substitutes for one another. For this reason, a number of instruments designed to facilitate the orderly restructuring of sovereign debt are necessary.

Before and during a restructuring process, a code of conduct can help show debtors and creditors how best to communicate and coordinate debt restructuring in such a way as to ensure that a country's debt is sustainable. One factor crucial to the effectiveness of a code of conduct is that appropriate incentives are provided. In particular, reputation effects need to be associated with a code of conduct. If its effectiveness is to be enhanced, it is also important for a code of conduct to be accepted by market participants and for all involved to develop a sense of ownership. The Principles have been a good example of a public-private partnership in which debtors and creditors have participated in the formulation, approval, and implementation of a code.

The ultimate goal of implementing a code of conduct should be to ensure that it becomes a market standard to which the majority of (all) market participants subscribe, thus increasing the stability of the international financial markets. To strengthen the implementation process further and to increase awareness of and support for a code of conduct, it should be better included in the international policy dialogue, since this will strengthen the links between those who implement and monitor a code of conduct and the international policy forums and multilateral financial institutions.

NOTE

1. For an overview of recent sovereign debt restructurings, see Sturzenegger and Zettelmeyer 2006.

REFERENCES

Banque de France. 2003. *Towards a Code of Good Conduct on Sovereign Debt Re-Negotiation.* Paris: Banque de France. www.ifri.org/files/PropBdF.pdf.

Berensmann, K. 2003. "Involving Private Creditors in the Prevention and Resolution of International Debt Crises." *German Development Institute Studies* 8/2003. www.die-gdi.de/CMS-Homepage/openwebcms3.nsf/(ynDK_contentByKey)/ENTR-7BUKAZ/$FILE/BuG%209%202003%20EN.pdf.

Berensmann, K., and A. Herzberg. 2009. "International Sovereign Insolvency Procedure: A Comparative Look at Selected Proposals." *Journal of Economic Surveys* 23:5, 856–881.

Bolton, P., and D. A. Skeel Jr. 2004. "Inside the Black Box: How Should a Sovereign Bankruptcy Framework Be Structured?" *Emory Law Journal* 53: 763–822.

Couillault, B., and P.-F. Weber. 2003. "Towards a Voluntary Code of Good Conduct for Sovereign Debt Restructuring." *Financial Stability Review* (June 2003), 154–162. Paris: Banque de France.

Dixon, L., and D. Wall. 2000. "Collective Action Problems and Collective Action Clauses." Bank of England Financial Stability Review 8: 142–153. www.bankofengland.co.uk/publications/fsr/2000/fsr08art8.pdf.

Häseler, S. 2009. "Collective Action Clauses in International Sovereign Bonds—Whence the Opposition?" *Journal of Economic Surveys* 23:5, 882–923.

Institute of International Finance. 2009. "Principles for Stable Capital Flows and Fair Debt Restructuring in Emerging Markets." Washington, DC: Principles Consultative Group, Report on Implementation.

Ritter, R. 2009. "Transnational Governance in Global Finance: Principles for Stable Capital Flows and Fair Debt Restructuring in Emerging Markets." *Occasional Paper Series* No. 103. Frankfurt am Main, Germany: European Central Bank. www.ecb.de/pub/pdf/scpops/ecbocp103.pdf.

Roubini, N. 2002. "Do We Need a New Bankruptcy Regime?" *Brookings Papers on Economic Activity* 1: 321–333.

Roubini, N., and B. Setser. 2003. "Improving the Sovereign Debt Restructuring Process: Problems in Restructuring, Proposed Solutions, and a Roadmap for Reform." Paper prepared for the conference on improving the sovereign debt restructuring process, co-hosted by the Institute for International Economics and Institut Francais des Relations Internationales, March 9, Paris. www.iie.com/publications/papers/roubini-setser0303.pdf.

Sturzenegger, F., and J. Zettelmeyer 2006. *Debt Defaults and Lessons from a Decade of Crises,* 385. Cambridge MA: MIT Press.

ABOUT THE AUTHOR

Kathrin Berensmann has worked as a senior economist at the German Development Institute (DIE) in Bonn since 2000. Before joining the DIE, she was employed as an economist at the Institute of German Economy in Cologne. She received her PhD and "Diplom" (equivalent to a master's degree) in economics from the University of Würzburg (Germany). Her main areas of specialization are international financial architecture, international financial markets, debt policy, monetary and exchange rate policy, and financial sector development.

CHAPTER 22

Governing Law of Sovereign Bonds and Legal Enforcement

ISSAM HALLAK
Assistant Professor of Finance, Bocconi University

After each of the spectacular financial distresses of major sovereign states, serious concerns were raised about the economic inefficiency of the current international legal frames of sovereign debts. The sources of concern are the absence of an institutionalized renegotiation set-up that promotes orderly workouts and the limited ability of creditors to seize assets of the sovereign borrower in default (absence of collateral). In practice, each loan contract includes a governing law that provides the legal framework for any dispute. The governing law of the contract is a state law, for example, English law and New York law. The limitation in creditors' ability to seize foreign states' assets, the so-called foreign state immunity, is determined by the governing law of the loan contract. Unlike corporate debts, the governing laws of sovereign debts have major implications on the restructuring and the enforcement of the terms of the contract. In fact, the governing law constitutes the unique legal environment that governs any dispute that may arise. Instead, the jurisdiction where corporations are registered has major importance (for example, Ayotte and Skeele 2002; Wood 2008).

By looking at the characteristics and the impact of governing laws on international bond amounts, this chapter investigates the second source of concern, that is, the credibility of the legal threat of asset seizure (collateral) of sovereign defaulters. International bonds are nonlocal currency bonds, for example, a dollar-denominated bond issued by Argentina and listed in New York or Luxembourg.[1] I first analyze the foreign state immunity in English law and New York law, the governing laws of eurobonds that used most frequently. I then examine whether governing laws are selected according to the features of the governing law in general as well as in connection to the bond characteristics (listing market and currency). I also examine the impact of the governing law on international bond amounts.

Results are as follows. First, the governing law is determined by lenders' ability to take legal action against the sovereign defaulter under this law. Second, the credibility and the enforcement costs associated with each law have an impact on the size of the bond (yearly amounts and bond size relative to GNP). Therefore, the chapter provides evidence of the existence of a threat of legal enforcement.

NATIONAL LAWS: AD HOC INTERNATIONAL LEGAL FRAMES

Although the immunity of foreign states remains the general rule, major governing laws are inclined to breach the doctrine of sovereignty and adopt the restrictive doctrine of foreign state immunity. Provisions mainly apply to commercial activities that states carry out abroad. This is known as the restrictive view of sovereign immunity. There are three major issues associated with the determination of the deimmunization of foreign states contracting loans:

1. Define foreign state entities.
2. Define whether a loan is a commercial activity.
3. Determine whether the jurisdiction is relevant in taking a decision (forum conveniens).

I summarize the details regarding the English and Welsh and the New York laws that are the most common governing laws of sovereign eurobonds (see Exhibit 22.1).[2]

Foreign state. The definition in the U.K. act is narrower and is set to include only state and government entities. The U.S. act instead covers firms in which the foreign state holds a majority of shares or of votes.

Commercial activity. Both acts constrain sovereign immunities and deny the latter in commercial transactions entered into by the foreign state. However, if the U.K. code explicitly states loans as being a commercial activity, the U.S. act remains ambiguous. The U.S. act specifies that the commercial transaction should have a direct impact on the United States. Although the New York jurisprudence has assimilated some loans as being a commercial activity having an impact on the United States, the interpretation of the impact varies from the currency determination (U.S. dollars) to the country in which arbitrage takes place.

Jurisdiction. The U.S. act provides clearer insights on these regards since the statement that a federal law governs the transaction is sufficient to create jurisdiction in the respective federal state. Although the U.K. act is less specific, there are good reasons to believe that the Act applies after the courts create jurisdiction.

The U.K. act is therefore more specific and gives rise to almost no ambiguities. Moreover, the inaccurate U.S. Foreign Sovereign Immunities Act of 1976 exposes the creditor who attempts to sue the sovereign defaulter to higher risks of failure. Delaume (1994) also showed that judicial cases were time-consuming in the United States. English law incurs substantially lower enforcement costs and less uncertainty regarding the judicial outcome.

GOVERNING LAW AND CREDIT CONSTRAINTS

Governing Laws and International Bonds Characteristics

Exhibit 22.1 presents a group analysis of the governing laws and the related listing markets and currencies of denomination. In particular, the tables report the number of sovereign bonds denominated in the currency of the governing law and/or listed in the jurisdiction of the governing law. As detailed in the previous section, it matters for the forum conveniens and the eligibility for sovereignty restrictions. I also look at the measure of rule of law provided by La Porta et al. (1997), which indicates the strength of national law enforcement in general. Rule of law varies between 0 and 10, where 10 indicates the most stringent application of the law in the country.

Interestingly, all reported governing laws have a very high rule of law. England is the lowest with 8.57. Most other laws display a 10.0 rating. However, the main result of the combined analysis of governing laws, currencies, and listing markets is that issuers set governing laws of their tradable liabilities in accordance with their enforcement power given the listing markets and the currency. Among nonprivate placement bonds, New York law governs 67 nonprivate placement international bonds, of which 59 are either denominated in U.S. dollars or listed in New York. Only eight are neither of them. This is consistent with the previous analysis.

Besides, all international bonds governed by Japanese law are listed in Tokyo, and vice versa. All loans are denominated in Japanese yen. Similarly, all of the 65 German law–governed bonds are denominated in deutschmarks and traded in Germany. Last, English law governs all types of bonds whether they are listed in England or not (87 observations of 98 are not listed in London), and whether the currency is the U.K. pound or not (92 observations are not denominated in English pounds). A vast majority of the English law bonds are listed abroad and denominated in a foreign currency (84 out of 98, that is, 86 percent).

All other governing laws (that is, Austria, Luxembourg, Spain, and Switzerland) are associated with either the currency or the country of the listing market. Interestingly, Luxembourg is the place of listing of a majority of tradable debts but the Luxembourg law governs seven contracts only. This is consistent with practitioners' analysis (for example, Yianni 1999 and Rhodes 2009). Therefore, I find evidence that the governing law is not randomly designed. The governing law is determined so as to maximize the ability to obtain a favorable judicial decision to bondholders.

Jurisdiction Shopping and Credits Availability

Exhibit 22.2 and Exhibit 22.3 report the results of the statistical analysis. Main results are as follows. Individual amounts relative to GNP are lower in German and Japanese laws (0.24 percent of GNP), while New York law allows raising larger amounts on average at every issue (0.85 percent). England is in between at 0.57 percent. The debt creditworthiness indicator is hardly a factor of choice of governing law. Namely, more indebted countries would not issue under any

Exhibit 22.1 Currency Denomination, Listing Markets, and the Governing Law of Sovereign International Bonds

Governing Law	Rule of Law	Number of Contracts	One Listed Market = Governing Law	Private Placement	Currency = Governing Law	One Listing Market or Currency-Governing Law	Unknown Listing	Volumes in Million Constant USD
Austria	10.00	2	2	0	2	2	0	165
England	8.57	117	11	19	6	14	0	30,646
Germany	9.23	66	65	0	66	66	1	22,187
Japan	8.98	49	29	19	49	49	1	13,089
Luxembourg	N/A	1	1	0	0	1	0	472
New York	10.00	85	8	15	72	72	3	47,877
Spain	7.80	2	2	0	2	2	0	159
Switzerland	10.00	5	4	1	5	5	0	513
Unknown	–	2		1			1	314
Total		329	122	55	202	211	6	115,422

Note: The table lists national laws that govern one or more emerging markets' sovereign international bonds in the period January 1987 to December 1997 and their associated currency and listing markets. The first column reports the governing law. The second column reports the rule of law, namely the assessment by investors of law enforcement (average over the period from 1982 to 1995); scale from zero to 10. The third column reports the number of contracts governed by the respective laws. The fourth column reports the number of loans that are listed in the same country as the governing law. Column five reports the number of private placements. Column six reports the number of loans designed with the same country of currency as the governing law. The seventh column reports the number of contracts that are either listed in the same country or have the same currency as the governing law. The eighth column reports the number of contracts that report no listing markets. The last column reports the total amounts of debts governed by each law in millions of constant 1995 U.S. dollars. Note that the securities may be traded in several markets. Also, private placements are never listed, so listing and private placements are two exclusive features.

Source: La Porta et al. (1997).

Exhibit 22.2   The Selection of the Governing Law as a Function of the
Issuer Characteristics

	England	Germany	Japan	New York	All Sample
Individual bond amount to GNP (%)	0.57	0.24	0.24	0.85	0.52
Total debt to GNP (%)	39.00	40.90	38.00	43.80	40.10
Yearly amount to GNP (%)	1.20	0.43	0.49	1.48	0.91

Note: The table reports the selection of the governing law of sovereign international bonds in the period from January 1987 to December 1997. Lines include the individual loan amount normalized to the issuer's GNP, the country total debt to GNP, and the yearly amounts raised from capital markets relative to GNP. Only main governing laws are reported in columns, namely England, Germany, New York, and Japan.

specific law. For any governing law, the average ratio of outstanding debts to GNP of issuing countries is close to 40 percent. Therefore, laws do not catch specific types of debtors according to creditworthiness.

Exhibit 22.3 reports evidence that German and Japanese laws allow for lower amounts relative to English law at the levels of 0.01 percent and 0.03 percent. The New York law provides mixed results. There seems to be no differences between English and New York laws. This contrasts with the survey of laws presented in this section. This could be interpreted in different ways. On the one hand, the two laws provide the same enforcement power under certain conditions despite probable longer periods of court procedures. On the other hand, involving New York courts gives the creditors a higher chance of success for the seizure of the defaulter's assets. In additional untabulated results, I also find that the trade volumes toward the United States and the United Kingdom and Europe is a factor that determines the selection of the governing law. Traded goods constitute assets that can potentially be seized by creditors. For example, if a country trades more with the United States, the governing law is more likely to be New York law.

Exhibit 22.3   Regression Estimates

	Germany	Japan	New York	Debt to GNP	Constant
Yearly amount to GNP (%)	−0.86	−0.71	0.02	2.16	0.41
	0.00	0.03	0.92	0.00	0.16
$R^2 = 0.144$	Number of obs. = 181		Prob $> F = 0.0$		$F(4, 176) = 7.38$

Note: The table reports the impact of the governing law on the funds available yearly relative to GNP in the period from January 1987 to December 1997. The dependent variable is the sum of primary issues of bonds for a given country relative to GNP (in percentage). The country dummies, Germany, Japan, and New York, are dummy variables that take 1 if the group of bonds is governed, respectively, by Germany, Japan, and New York laws, and zero otherwise. English law is the omitted dummy variable and is therefore the benchmark. Debt to GNP is the indicator of creditworthiness of the issuing country.

CONCLUSION

This chapter explored whether the enforcement of governing laws of sovereign bonds are credible threats and whether they vary among major laws. Indeed, an essential difference among governing laws is their respective repayment enforcement power and costs. The analysis is based on the selection process of the governing law and amounts that can be accessed under the different laws. I find that the jurisdiction is determined by a set of factors that will imply effectiveness of the enforcement of the sovereign defaulter. The second result is that sovereign bond amounts are larger when governed by U.K. and U.S. law. The main implication of these findings is that there actually exists a legal threat that looks credible. In line with Rose (2002), this provides additional evidence to Bulow and Rogoff (1989) that predicts the existence of a stick to explain the presence of sovereign debts contracted from private creditors.

NOTES

1. International bonds are nondomestic currency-denominated bonds. Eurobonds are bonds whose currency of denomination is not the currency of the borrower or the currency of the country where the bond is listed. A dollar-denominated bond issued by Argentina is typically listed in Luxembourg.
2. See Hallak (2003) and Wood (2008) for further details.

REFERENCES

Ayotte, K. M., and D. A. Skeel. 2002. *Why Do Distressed Companies Choose Delaware? Venue Choice and Court Experience in Bankruptcy*. New York: Columbia Business School.

Bulow, J., and K. Rogoff, 1989. "Sovereign Debt: Is to Forgive to Forget?" *American Economic Review* 79: 43–50.

Delaume, G. R. 1994. "The Foreign Sovereign Immunities Act and Public Debt Litigation: Some 15 Years Later." *American Journal of International Law* 88: 257–279.

Hallak, I. 2003. "Courts and Sovereign Eurobonds: Credibility of the Judicial Enforcement of Repayment." *CFS Working Paper* 2003/34. http://ssrn.com/abstract=473187.

La Porta, R., F. Lopez-de-Silanes, A. Shleifer, and R. W. Vishny. 1997. "Legal Determinants of External Finance." *Journal of Finance* 52: 1131–1150.

Rhodes, T. 2009. *Syndicated Lending, Practice and Documentation*, 5th ed. London: Euromoney.

Rose, A. 2002. "One Reason Countries Pay Their Debts: Renegotiation and International Trade." *Centre for Economic Policy Research Discussion Paper* No. 3157.

Wood, P. R. 2008. *Law and Practice of International Finance*. London: Sweet and Maxwell.

Yianni, A. 1999. "Resolution of Sovereign Financial Crises—Evolution of the Private Sector Restructuring Process." *London School of Economics Financial Stability Review*, 78–84.

ABOUT THE AUTHOR

Issam Hallak is an assistant professor in the department of finance of Bocconi University. He received a PhD in financial economics at the European University Institute, Florence. He has done extensive work in sovereign debts and international finance as well as syndicated loans and corporate finance.

CHAPTER 23

Sovereign Debt Restructuring

The Judge, the Vultures, and Creditor Rights

MARCUS H. MILLER
University of Warwick, CEPR and CSGR[*]

DANIA THOMAS
Keele University, CSGR

The progressive switch from bank loans to sovereign bonds in lending to emerging markets—and the Brady Plan[1] in particular—triggered a lively debate on bond restructuring and the potential obstacles posed by holdout creditors.[2] The IMF proposal for a new sovereign debt restructuring mechanism (Krueger 2002) to tackle the issue found little favor with creditors or debtors, however. But the market-driven initiative for putting collective action clauses (CACs) into sovereign bond contracts backed by the U.S. Treasury was soon widely adopted.[3]

Nonetheless, Argentina successfully restructured the majority of its defaulted foreign debt in 2005 without mediation by the IMF and without clauses to promote creditor coordination. It was effected by a take-it-or-leave-it offer from the debtor, accepted by a supermajority of bondholders despite the substantial haircut involved.[4] Most of the international bonds issued by Argentina are in fact governed by U.S. law, and the Southern District Court of New York (SDNY), the lowest-level federal court in New York, has jurisdiction to deal with all legal matters that arise between Argentina and its creditors.[5] It is our contention that in the period leading

[*]This is a nontechnical version of a paper previously published in the *World Economy* 30:10, 1491–1509, October 2007. We thank Guillermo Calvo, Eduardo Cavallo, Christian Engelen, Rui Esteves, Jill Fisch, Javier García-Fronti, Anna Gelpern, Mitu Gulati, Sayantan Ghosal, Eric Helleiner, and seminar audiences at the Center for the Study of Globalization and Regionalization (CSGR), the Global Applied Research Network (GARNET) annual conference in Amsterdam, and the Inter-American Development Bank (IDB) in Washington for valuable feedback. The authors gratefully acknowledge comments and helpful criticisms from anonymous referees, research assistance from Parul Gupta, and financial support from the Economic and Social Research Council (ESRC) under project number RES-051-27-0125, "Debt and Development," and from CSGR, respectively. The usual disclaimer applies.

up to the swap, the U.S courts played a key role in promoting the swap by engaging the debtor and aggregating the claims of diverse creditors. In this chapter, we give an account of how the process of judge-mediated debt restructuring has operated in this case, and we speculate on future developments.

The size of the write-down involved in the Argentine case suggests to some observers that "rogue debtors, rather than rogue creditors, are the ones that pose the greatest threat to the integrity and efficiency of the international financial architecture." Despite the waiving of sovereign immunity, "the fact remains that it is exceedingly difficult to collect from a sovereign deadbeat [and] the sad truth is that only other governments . . . can hope to rein in a wayward sovereign debtor and persuade it not to walk away from its lawful obligations" (Porzecanski 2005, p. 331).

Others take a more optimistic view: For Sturzenegger and Zettelmeyer (2005c, p. 10) the Argentine swap was "in most dimensions, a textbook example of how to do an exchange." In reviewing recent litigation in international debt markets, however, they found no evidence that sanctions on trade and payments have been imposed in an effective way. Recent developments, they argue, provide support for the assumption made in the seminal paper by Eaton and Gersovitz (1981) that while "creditors cannot impose any sanction on defaulting countries, they can hinder sovereign access to international capital markets."

Sturzenegger and Zettelmeyer's (2005b, pp. 7, 51) careful examination of the Argentine debt swap of 2005 leads us to challenge both views. While Porzecanski concludes that the courts are irrelevant, we note that New York courts appear to have exploited creditor heterogeneity—between holdouts seeking capital gains and institutional investors wanting a settlement, in particular—first to achieve a swap and then to protect creditor rights. Likewise, the simple dichotomy between sanctions and reputation proposed by Sturzenegger and Zettelmeyer (as the only mechanisms to ensure a successful swap) misses a key factor, namely, judicial intervention.[6]

In regard to their effectiveness, our analysis of the opinions and orders of Judge Griesa's court draws a clear distinction between pre- and post-swap phases of judge-mediated debt restructuring. First, in the pre-swap phase, comes the engagement of the debtor: The judge finds in favor of holdouts and this encourages the debtor to make an offer. Second is promoting the swap: He alternatively refuses enforcement and threatens attachment. Then, once the swap has been accepted by a supermajority, it is time for the courts to maintain the threat of attachment (effectively denying the debtor access to primary capital markets).

In their discussion of sovereign debt restructuring, Fisch and Gentile (2004) emphasize the role of holdout litigation in the enforcement of sovereign obligations. We also see creditor litigation continuing to be important, but only in the period of transition to CACs do we consider that vultures play a pivotal role. In the future, when CACs are widespread, it may well be litigation by ex ante creditor committees that triggers the debtor to come up with an offer, with CACs cramming down potential holdouts.

The paper is organized as follows: The next section briefly reviews the literature on why sovereigns pay and indicates where our analysis fits in. In the section after that, we outline the salient features of the Argentine case. The fourth section analyzes the opinions and decisions of the New York courts: encouraging the debtor to make the first offer (in Dubai, September 2003); promoting the ensuing debt restructuring process (from Dubai to the final offer in March 2005); and acting to help resolve the holdout problem. The fifth section indicates how the widespread adoption of CACs will reduce the role of vultures in the future and sketches the role that the courts and creditor committees might play. The last section concludes.

WHY DO SOVEREIGNS PAY?

How does the analysis in this chapter relate to the existing literature on incentives for sovereigns to repay debt? What role have these incentives played in the Argentine case? The academic literature has stressed the role of direct sanctions, policy conditionality, and reputational sanctions imposed by creditors, as indicated in Exhibit 23.1, lines 1 to 3a. But such mechanisms played a minor role in the Argentine case: They were "the dogs that did not bark." Before outlining the role of the courts in helping to achieve the swap (see line 3(b) of Exhibit 23.1), we discuss in more detail the failure of the other mechanisms.

Sanctions—Private and Public

The use of direct military threats to enforce debt contracts may have been relevant in the nineteenth century when gunboat diplomacy was common, but not now. Moreover, WTO rules prohibit trade intervention for purposes of debt collection, and seizures not authorized by a court, are, by definition, illegal. As capital markets have become increasingly globalized, however, the waiving of sovereign immunity—often required as a precondition for issuing debt in London or New York—has allowed for the attachment of collateral assets under court procedures, and specialist vulture funds have developed litigation strategies to exploit these possibilities. Nonetheless, in the case of Argentina, efforts by holdout creditors to attach assets have been a failure, as indicated in the last column of the Exhibit 23.1.

A striking feature of modern capital markets is the ease with which creditors can exit; sovereign debtors are consequently exposed to capital flight with associated financial and exchange rate crises (Ghosal and Miller 2002). Reducing or avoiding the output losses that can be triggered by capital flight is now regarded as a strong incentive for sovereigns to honor their debts, as the references in note (2) to the table make clear.[7] The IDB Report (2006) stresses the political cost of sovereign default, which triggers a banking crisis.[8] In the Argentine case, severe output losses occurred but—since default was widely anticipated—they ensued well before default: While the debt was being restructured, recovery got well under way.

Another sanction that may have played a role in this case is the denial of trade credit, a device commonly used to put pressure on defaulting sovereigns (Kohlscheen and O'Connell 2003).

Policy Conditionality

Since the IMF policy of lending into arrears was initiated during the Latin American debt crises of the 1980s, the Fund has had to insist on explicit policy conditionality to avoid undermining debtors' incentives to repay; and signing

Exhibit 23.1 Why Do Sovereigns Honor Their Debts?

	Loss of	Agent/ Institution	Mechanism	The Case of Argentina
1. Sanctions	Exports Output	Gunboat (1) Gunboat (2) Crisis (3)	 Capital flight	Illegal under WTO Illegal under international law Yes (including anticipatory crisis) (4)
2. Policy Conditionality	Trade credit Collateral assets Sovereignty over policy	Banks (5) Court as enforcer (6) IMF as enforcer (7)	Deny rollovers to business Attachment Program conditions	Yes, short-term Unsuccessful Yes, but IMF repaid in December 2005
3. Market access denied by banks or denied by courts	International goodwill Reputation with leading banks Access to primary capital markets	Hegemon, G7 (8) "Anarchy" (9) Court as gatekeeper	"Cheat the cheater" Threat of attachment pending	Not evident from sovereign spreads A cautionary tale for holdouts in the future

1. Esteves (2005)
2. Bulow and Rogoff (1989)
3. Dooley (2000); Gai, Hayes, and Shin (2004); Irwin et al. (2005); Jeanne and Ranciere (2005)
4. Levy-Yeyati and Panizza (2005)
5. Kohlscheen and O'Connell (2003)
6. *E.M. Ltd. v. The Republic of Argentina* (Sept. 12, 2003)
7. Roubini and Sgard (2004b)
8. Kaletsky (1985); Aggarwal (1998a, b)
9. Eaton and Gersovitz (1981); Kletzer and Wright (2000)

a letter of intent that embodies such conditions is a precondition for obtaining IMF program assistance. In the cases of Korea in 1997 and Brazil in 2002, indeed, prospective presidents were persuaded to endorse targets for fiscal prudence before elections took place—an illustration of the loss of sovereignty mentioned in Exhibit 23.1. Conditions for rolling over IMF lending to Argentina after default did include the requirement that steps be taken to settle with holdout creditors, but, for the IMF, Argentina was effectively "too big to fail," and in any case, it freed itself from any such policy conditionality by early repayment of all its borrowing in 2006. Kaletsky (1985) stresses the role of international pressure from the G-7, but this does not seem to have played an important part in the Argentine case.

Market Access

An alternative incentive to repay debts would be the fear of damaging the sovereign's reputation, with a consequent widening of the bonds spread from junk bond levels[9] to what might be described as rogue-debt levels. Despite Porzecanski's characterization, this does not appear to be the case for Argentina—for which the spreads are close to those of Brazil. Kletzer and Wright (2000) analyze a self-enforcing mechanism—"cheat the cheater"—that could sustain equilibrium in debt markets with a limited number of creditors (see Exhibit 23.1, line 3a.)[10] Their analysis is, however, explicitly related to bank lending, as in the original Eaton and Gersovitz (1981) paper. How, if at all, it might be extended to a world of anonymous bondholders is unclear.

The argument of this paper is that in contrast with earlier judicial interventions, the courts have played a key role in the Argentine case: initially by threatening the debtor with attachments to prompt a credible offer, and reining in the holdouts to promote the swap. After the successful swap, the threat of attachment has effectively denied the debtor access to primary capital markets, namely London and New York. Could judicial intervention of this kind influence the courts in the future? This is discussed in the section on judge-mediated debt restructuring.

KEY ASPECTS OF THE ARGENTINE DEBT RESTRUCTURING

The Argentine case is notable for being the largest-ever sovereign debt default and for being conducted without decisive intervention by international institutions. Before providing our account of the role of the U.S. courts in this case, four salient features of the Argentine swap may be considered with the aid of Exhibit 23.2: These are the heterogeneity of creditor groups, the absence of creditor coordination, the size of the write-down and the long delay before it was accepted.

Pronounced Creditor Heterogeneity

Argentine debt in default contained a significantly higher number of bond issues than all the other cases listed in the exhibit: It involved many thousands of creditors in eight different legal jurisdictions. The sheer numbers posed a major obstacle to effecting a swap. Perhaps more significant, however, were the conflicting incentives affecting different groups.

Exhibit 23.2 Comparison of Recent Sovereign Debt Restructurings

	Argentina 2005	Ecuador 2000	Pakistan 1999	Russia 1998–2000	Ukraine 1998–2000	Uruguay 2003
Per Capita Income ($)*	11,586	3,363	1,826	6,592	3,841	8,280
Scope ($billions)	81.8	6.8	0.6	31.8	3.3	5.4
Number of Bonds	152	5	3	3	5	65
Jurisdictions Involved	8	2	1	1	3	6
Months in Default	38+	10	2	18	3	9
Principal Forgiveness	Yes	Yes	No	Yes	No	No
Haircut in Discount Bond (percent)	66.3	40	0	37.5	0	0
Participation Rate (percent of Eligible)	76	97	95	98	95	93

Sources: IIF, IMF, World Bank.
*Adjusted for purchasing power, latest (2003) data for Argentina, otherwise data correspond to year(s) of debt restructuring as noted.

As Fisch and Gentile (2004, p. 26) note "[o]nly certain large institutional investors, particularly commercial banks and investment banks, have ongoing relationships with the sovereign debtors... [and this] may drive these institutional investors to support restructuring plans that are unlikely to be acceptable to smaller investors, notably retail investors, who do not expect to gain from future transactions. . . ." Also, there is a specialized class of holdout litigants, popularly known as *vulture funds*, which purchase distressed debt at substantial discounts and seek capital gains through either the restructuring process or by holding out and seeking additional payments from the debtors. (The 24 percent of creditors still holding defaulted Argentine bonds include both vultures and retail investors.)

Absence of Creditor Coordination

Due in part to the aggressive negotiating stance taken by the sovereign, Argentina's creditors participated in the swap in the absence of either formal or informal creditor organizations. One exception was the short-lived Global Committee of Argentine Bondholders (GCAB). The GCAB was set up in 2003 to pool negotiating leverage and demand a better deal, claiming to represent U.S., European, and Japanese creditors holding about $40 million. But at the time of the swap, the GCAB had lost most of its institutional constituents and a majority tendered in the exchange. This attempt at creditor organization failed as each seemed to act in their own self-interest and took the opportunity to cut their losses and make short-term gains (Gelpern 2005).

Significant Debt Write-Down

On a total outstanding principal of $81.8 billion, the Argentine swap involved a 66.3 percent haircut, or write-down of face value (column 1). This is considerably larger than the other haircuts shown, namely 40 percent for Ecuador and

37.5 percent for Russia. The 76 percent participation rate in the swap is by far the lowest shown and implies that Argentina is still in default with 24 percent of its creditors by value.

Long Delay

It took more than three years for Argentina to restructure its debt—more than twice as long as it took Russia, for example. In part, the reasons were political, as the interim administration of President Duhalde had no mandate to negotiate a swap. Economic reasons for delay are also analyzed in the appendix.

JUDGE-MEDIATED DEBT RESTRUCTURING: FROM DEFAULT TO SWAP

In 1976, the United States (and, soon after, the United Kingdom) imposed statutory constraints on absolute sovereign immunity from suit in foreign courts (Buchheit 1995).[11] In the two decades that followed, creditors developed innovative litigation strategies to maximize the benefits of restricted sovereign immunity. In the absence of statutory regulation of sovereign debt, however, the litigation strategies have played a role—with common-law decisions influenced by the political and economic conditions in which the litigations were pursued.

Even in the absence of enforcement, restricted sovereign immunity has significantly improved the leverage of creditors in the restructuring process. In the case of *Elliot and Associates v. Banco de La Nación*, Perú decided in 1999, for example, the claimants were vulture funds that threatened the debtor with enforcement and consequent delay of the imminent swap. The debtor settled its claims out of court to avoid this outcome. Similarly, in the case of *Elliot and Associates v. Panamá*, decided in 1997, the threat of enforcement would have interfered with a new bond issue and consequently impaired Panama's ability to access capital markets. Again, the case was settled out of court, in favor of the vultures.

Moreover, in the case of *Pravin Banker v. Banco Popular del Perú*, decided in 1997, the court went as far as to lay down the guidelines that they would follow in sovereign litigation. The first guideline was to encourage orderly debt restructuring initiatives that involved the use of Brady bonds. The second guideline was to ensure the enforcement of contracts executed between U.S. investors and sovereign debtors. In line with U.S. foreign policy at the time, in most cases the second guideline dominates the first. Thus, in a situation in which ongoing debt restructuring negotiations were at the cost of the claims of U.S. creditors, the courts were bound to concede to the latter.

The Court's Role in the Argentine Swap of 2005

The Argentine swap was successfully concluded against the backdrop of more than 200 lawsuits (including 15 class action suits) filed in New York, Italy, and Germany. How was this achieved? We believe that in large part it was due to mediation by the judge, and we summarize the actions taken by Judge Griesa to promote restructuring.

In the first instance, the creditors who rushed to court on the election of President Kirchner and successfully obtained summary judgments, Judge Griesa had no option but to allow such claims (for example, *E.M. Ltd. v. The Republic of Argentina* [September 12, 2003]). This is only part of the story, however, as successful claimants have to enforce their judgments against the debtor by attaching its assets. This is when Judge Griesa exercised his discretion, dismissing pleas to attach specific assets of the debtor.

Also in 2003, relatively early on in the debt restructuring process, the creditors sought to certify class action suits. Judge Griesa accepted certain claims encouraging creditor coordination [*H.W. Urban GMBh v. The Republic of Argentina* (December 30, 2003)]. However, in his orders rejecting some class action suits, [for example, *Alan Applestein TTEE v. The Republic of Argentina* (May 12, 2003)], the judge encouraged a tighter definition of class: He also kept a decision on the interpretation of *pari passu* pending.

In the context of the class action suits, Judge Griesa's observations (*obiter dicta*) are instructive. At one point, he observes that "an important channel for attempting to resolve the Argentine debt problem will undoubtedly be the effort to negotiate a debt restructuring plan." He continues:

> *Judging from past national debt crises, these negotiations will be carried on largely, if not entirely, by debt holders who do not choose to engage in litigation. To the extent that the other debt holders, whether few or many, wish to pursue litigation, the litigation should be well defined and its participants should be reasonably identifiable. One reason for this is that those involved in the debt restructuring process should have a clear idea of who has chosen litigation and thus may not be candidates for participation in a voluntary restructuring plan.*

In early 2005, just before completion, the vultures attempted to stymie the swap. In the first instance, they succeeded in their bid to obtain an order to attach the contractual right of the debtor to receive old bonds (*NML Capital Ltd. v. The Republic of Argentina* [March 13, 2005]). But, in response to Argentina's submission that this would make it abort the swap, Judge Griesa overturned his own judgment. In his exercise of judicial discretion, the judge was motivated by a concern to promote restructuring and not only to enforce the claims of holdout litigants. Moreover, his decision was affirmed on appeal by the 2nd Circuit on the ground "[t]hat restructuring is obviously of critical importance to the economic health of the nation." The findings (in the decision to vacate the attachment orders) assure the creditors who may wish to participate in the swap that the court will effect its successful conclusion.

The process of judge-mediated debt restructuring is described as follows. Following default by the debtor, the court grants summary judgments in favor of holdout creditors as a means to prompt the debtor to make an offer. Then, in marked contrast to precedent, Judge Griesa reins in the holdout creditors so as to promote a settlement. The judge is concerned with the reasonableness of the swap and the percentage of creditors who consent to the amendment. Finally, the offer is accepted by a super majority vote (SMV), but this leaves a fraction of creditors outside the swap—and there are no CACs to ensure their compliance. Two particular aspects of this process are worth highlighting. First, Judge Griesa effectively aggregates across creditors in the swap by treating the debt as a consolidated whole; second, he keeps the claims of the holdouts distinct from those of creditors involved in the ongoing swap.

We turn now to the post-swap phase and the problem of holdouts. In a future with CACs, the swap can be crammed down on all creditors, as we argue further on. This option has not been available in the Argentine case. There has instead been a succession of unsuccessful attempts by professional holdouts to attach the assets of the sovereign—met with forthright denials of any compensation for them by Argentina. For Porzecanski (2005), the latter constitutes the actions of a *rogue debtor*—defined as a sovereign that can pick and choose the claims it wishes to satisfy and ignore the rest.

Such a rogue debtor would normally face high sovereign spreads,[12] but the market does not appear to share Porzecanski's view, as shown in Exhibit 23.1. Argentine sovereign spreads, which rose to extraordinary levels of more than 6,000 basis points during the restructuring, have moved sharply down to market levels as measured by the EMBI index, where Argentine spreads are marginally higher than the average. Despite the favorable spread, however, no new borrowing is being placed by Argentina in New York, as the court has effectively denied market access there.[13] While there is no legal restriction on the sovereign issuing new debt, there is little incentive to do so as proceeds will promptly be seized by vultures! In the meantime, Argentina is borrowing funds at low sovereign spreads[14] under Argentine jurisdiction in Buenos Aires.[15]

In a possible post-swap development, other than the rogue debtor scenario, for example, the debtor makes a late offer of a swap (consistent with the "most-favored-creditor" commitment made to those who accepted the swap) which, if accepted, leads to a final resolution with Argentina regaining full market access. While such a late offer is likely to be accepted by retail investors (especially as the bonds involved in the swap have increased substantially in value), vultures may well reject any substantial haircut, and they have the patience and skill to hold out for years. The latest offer[16] made by Argentina may still not be enough for it to regain access to primary capital markets as long as same creditors hold out for repayment of the face value of the debt.[17] This leads to the situation similar to what prevailed before the swap, when the debtor is denied access to primary capital markets.

As discussed earlier, with attachment orders outstanding, any new funds raised by the debtor in New York will go, first and foremost, to paying the hold-outs. Seizure of funds in this way may be how things end. Alternatively, the debtor may pay off the vultures in an out-of-court settlement. These uncertainties are, we believe, features of transition, illustrating the very problems CACs are designed to resolve.

CACS, COURTS, AND CREDITOR COMMITTEES

We have emphasized the role that courts (prompted by holdout litigation) have played, and are still playing, in the orderly resolution of a major sovereign debt crisis. Study of the opinions and orders of Judge Griesa's court suggests two distinct judicial roles—encouraging the debtor to make an offer and promoting a successful debt swap, which together protect creditor rights. It is now common with new issues of sovereign debt to include CACs. How will this affect the role of holdouts and of the courts?

Promoting the Swap and Handling Holdouts

Given that CACs are designed to reduce the profit opportunities available to holdouts, it should be easier for creditors to organize a swap, with an SMV requirement of 75 percent as the industry standard. As the IMF has warned, however, aggregation will remain a problem: The clauses operate only within a single bond issue (Krueger 2002). The judge in the Argentine case viewed the debt as a consolidated whole, thereby effectively aggregating a majority of the creditors (76 percent) that participated in the swap. Despite the requirement for unanimity in the bond contracts, the courts promoted a swap influenced by the economic, political, and financial factors in play at the time. Similar action may be called for in the future. With CACs, however, the issue of recalcitrant holdouts should disappear: If the swap achieves the necessary SMV, all holdouts will be compelled to accept the same terms. They cannot hold out for better.

While CACs and courts may well solve aggregation and resolve the holdout problem, this will not necessarily prompt the debtor into making an offer. Vultures may not have the incentive to initiate debtor engagement but existing creditors will, as we explain in the next section.

Debtor Engagement: Class Action Suits and Bondholder Organization

The historical record provides evidence of the effectiveness of formal and permanent bondholder committees like the British Corporation of Foreign Bondholders in the early part of the twentieth century (Eichengreen and Portes 1995; Esteves 2005). Mauro and Yafeh (2003, p. 26) point out that "... one of the roles of the Corporation of Foreign Bondholders (CFB) [was] to protect small bondholders from large bondholders who might otherwise arrange for a separate, advantageous deal for themselves in exchange for the promise to provide the country with new lending."

This is relevant to the Argentine case, in which many small creditors sold out to institutional investors at prices of less than 30 cents on the dollar. Esteves (2005) suggests that enhanced creditor organizations will substantially increase creditor payoffs, but because institutional investors acted to coordinate creditors and to negotiate with the debtor, the payoff to creditors as a whole would probably not have risen much.

Even without bondholder committees, there is one other opportunity for creditor coordination that can be considered. Buchheit and Gulati (2002) argue that class action suits could be used to involve courts in sovereign debt restructuring. According to them, creditors have a basic class interest,[18] distinguishable from that of an individual creditor. With CACs including SMV, this class interest is better defined.[19] Class action procedures would engender the formation of ex post, ad hoc creditor committees that would prompt the debtor into making an offer. In the latest judgment in the existing (and only) certified class action, Judge Griesa granted the motion of the class for summary judgment (*H.W. URBAN GMBH,*

Individually and on behalf of all others similarly situated v. The Republic of Argentina [March 9, 2006]).

To conclude, we see the vulture-initiated strategies for debt resolution as important principally in the period of transition to CACs. Unlike Fisch and Gentile (2004), who emphasize the continuing role of the vultures, we assume that SMV under CACs will reduce the threat of holdout litigation as we know it, but will nonetheless leave an important role for judicial intervention in debt restructuring.[20]

Instead of the threat of attachment by specialist creditors, it will hopefully be the formation of ex ante creditor committees, class action suits, and the possibility of judge-mediated debt restructuring that will prompt the debtor into successfully making an offer to restructure its debt.

CONCLUSION

Our interpretation of the Argentine litigation is that Judge Griesa used creditor heterogeneity to promote the swap—encouraging holdouts to bring the debtor to the negotiating table but restraining them when they threatened the swap itself. The outstanding attachment orders currently block Argentina's access to primary credit markets unless and until it deals satisfactorily with creditors outside the swap.

A possible argument against this view is that it is specific to the Argentine crisis and cannot be relied upon in the future restructurings. The New York court is still the preferred jurisdiction of sovereign bond contracts, however, and the Second Circuit decisions will surely form persuasive precedents for district courts in the future.

Our conclusions differ from those of Sturzenegger and Zettelmeyer (2005a), who are inclined to dismiss the role of holdout litigation in favor of reputational models. Our interpretation can also be contrasted with the view that holdout litigation represents a lasting solution to sovereign debt crises (Fisch and Gentile 2004). We agree with them that holdout litigation is "part of the solution and not the problem," but believe that to be true only in the period of transition to CACs, which is now over. Our description of judge-mediated debt restructuring emphasizes the role of the common law judges in the orderly resolution of sovereign debt crises, currently and in the future. From a recent survey by Gelpern and Gulati (2006),[21] it appears that market participants expect that CACs will be helpful only at the margins, and similar interventions, judicial or otherwise, will continue to influence sovereign debt settlements.

John Taylor (2002), then undersecretary of the treasury for international affairs, identified three main possibilities for debt restructuring: a decentralized, market-led approach; a centralized statutory approach; and a combination of the two, in which clauses are inserted into new debt instruments and a panel or court is created to deal with aggregation and other issues not captured in the clauses.[22]

While the second (centralized) approach has since been sidelined for the indefinite future, the first market-driven alternative favored by Taylor has become the norm. Our analysis of the Argentine debt restructuring, however, leads us to favor the third possibility, that of combining CACs with the judicial process. It may be that, in theory, bonds with CACs can be restructured to ensure engagement and to secure aggregation. In practice, it seems that the courts can do a great deal to help.

This is why we look to a future with CACs and courts, aided by creditor commit-tees and other creditor initiatives such as the Institute of International Finance (IIF) code of conduct.[23]

Stiglitz (2006) makes a similar point when he argues:

> *The fact that every advanced country has found it necessary to have a bankruptcy law reinforces the conclusions of economic theory that collective action clauses will not suffice; some judicial process is required.*

NOTES

1. Details available at www.emta.org/emarkets/brady.html.
2. These include so-called vulture funds, which buy distressed debt in default and sue for payment in full. See Fisch and Gentile (2004).
3. By 2004, close to 90 percent of new international bond issues had CACs, and the figure approached close to 100 percent in the first half of 2005. Note, however, that CACs and bankruptcy law are actually complementary, as can be seen from their coexistence in the United Kingdom.
4. Creditors who entered the swap suffered a loss of about two-thirds of the face value of their bonds. Those who did not received nothing from Argentina for more than a year after the swap.
5. The 2nd Circuit Court of New York hears appeals from the District Court.
6. Another missing factor, emphasized in the recent IDB report (2006), *Living with Debt*, is the domestic political fallout from sovereign default.
7. As with bank runs, there is a risk of self-fulfilling crises occurring: Schemes to reduce this risk include Cohen and Portes (2004) and Cordella and Levy-Yeyati (2005). IDB (2006) also stresses the political cost of default, which triggers a banking crisis.
8. See also Sussman and Guembel (2006), who argue that the interest of the median voter is a key factor in debt restructuring in the absence of default penalties.
9. As it is prone to restructuring, corporate debt in the United States is often referred to as *junk bonds.*
10. It should be noted, however, that not only Venezuela but also New York banks are happily lending into serious arrears by Argentina: Is this consistent with the Kletzer and Wright self-enforcing equilibrium?
11. More generally, see Buchheit (1998a, 1998b, 1999, 2000).
12. See Rochet (2005) for an analysis in which the government cannot control spending, defaults regularly, and faces high spreads.
13. A bid to seize official Argentine funds on deposit in New York by a holdout creditor was rejected by the appeals court on the grounds that the funds are owned by the Argentine central bank. This defense would not, of course, apply to funds accruing from the issue of new Argentine government debt.
14. In March 2006, for example, bonds were issued at a yield of 8.36 percent, a spread of 3.7 percent over U.S. Treasuries.
15. The fact that the purchasers include New York banks must throw some doubt on the mechanism proposed by Kletzer and Wright (2000). A possible explanation of continued

lending at low spreads is that foreign lenders know that many of these bonds are also held by domestic Argentine residents, and default will therefore be politically unpopular. See Chapter 12 of *Living with Debt* (IDB 2006).

16. "Argentina achieves 66.8 percent participation rate in debt swap." www.reuters.com/article/idUSN2722689420100628 (last accessed July 28, 2010).

17. "Argentina eyes legal strategy to force swap holdouts." www.reuters.com/article/idUSN0421531420100504 (last accessed July 28, 2010).

18. A class interest is one in which creditors as a class can achieve a settlement more effectively than individual creditors. This is the route currently adopted by creditors to force Argentina to make a better offer, so far with limited prospects for immediate gains. "Argentina wins appeals on inflated $2.24 bln award." www.reuters.com/article/idUSN2727215120100527 (last accessed July 28, 2010).

19. While Sturzenegger and Zettelmeyer (2005c) may dismiss class action procedures as ineffective for solving holdout problem, with CACs this is no longer an issue.

20. The incentives for vultures to litigate will arise from issues in which they have an SMV. They will use the courts to enforce hundred percent claims against the debtor. In the absence of unanimity, however, these claims will be isolated at the margin and will not affect the entire debt.

21. Gelpern and Gulati (2006).

22. Taylor (2002).

23. IIF (2005); and the report of implementation, IIF (2006).

REFERENCES

Aggarwal, V. K. 1998a. "Exorcising Asian Debt: Lessons from Latin American Rollovers, Workouts, and Write-downs." Paper presented at a conference on the aftermath of the Asian crisis, May 13–14, in Washington, DC.

———. 1998b. "Debt Rescheduling in Comparative Perspective." Paper prepared for presentation at a world conference on capital flows in crisis, October 27–28, in Washington, DC.

Buchheit, L. C. 1995. "The Sovereign Client." *Journal of International Affairs* 48: 527.

———. 1998a. "Changing Bond Documentation: The Sharing Clause." *International Financial Law Review* 17:7, 17.

———. 1998b. "The Collective Representation Clause." *International Financial Law Review* 17:9, 9.

———. 1999. "A Lawyer's Perspective on the New International Financial Architecture." *Journal of International Banking Law and Regulation* 14:7, 225.

———. 2002. "Sovereign Bonds and the Collective Will." *Emory Law Journal* 51: 1317.

Bulow J., and K. Rogoff. 1989. "Sovereign Debt: Is to Forgive to Forget?" *The American Economic Review* 79:1, 43–50.

Cohen, D., and R. Portes. 2005. "How to Avoid Self-Fulfilling Debt Crises." Paper presented at the Latin American and Caribbean Economic Association conference, October 27, in Paris, France.

Cordella, T., and E. Levy-Yeyati. 2005. "A (New) Country Insurance Facility." *IMF Working Paper*, No. 23.

Dooley, M. 2000. "Can Output Losses Following International Financial Crises Be Avoided?" *NBER Working Paper*, No. 7531.

Eaton, J., and M. Gersovitz. 1981. "Debt with Potential Repudiation: Theoretical and Empirical Analysis." *The Review of Economic Studies* 48:2, 289–309.

Eichengreen, B., and R. Portes. 1995. *Crisis, What Crisis? Orderly Workouts for Sovereign Debtors*. London: Center for Economic Policy Research.

Esteves, R. P. 2005. "Quis custodiet quem? Sovereign Debt and Bondholders' Protection before 1914." University of California, Berkeley.

Fisch, J. E., and C. Gentile. 2004. "Vultures or Vanguards? The Role of Litigation in Sovereign Debt Restructuring." *Emory Law Journal* 53: 1043.

Gai, P., S. Hayes, and H. S. Shin. 2004. "Crisis Costs and Debtor Discipline: The Efficacy of Public Policy in Sovereign Debt Crises." *Journal of International Economics* 62: 245–262.

Gelpern, A. 2005. "After Argentina: Policy Briefs in International Economics." www.piie.com/publications/interstitial.cfm?ResearchID=550.

Gelpern A., and M. Gulati. 2006. "Public Symbol in Private Contract: A Case Study." *Wash. U. L. Rev.* 84, 1627

Ghosal, S., and M. Miller. 2002. "Co-ordination Failure, Moral Hazard, and Sovereign Bankruptcy Procedures." *Economic Journal* 113: 276–304.

Inter-American Development Bank. 2006. *Living with Debt*. Washington, DC: Inter-American Development Bank.

Institute for International Finance. 2005. *Principles for Stable Capital Flows and Fair Debt Restructuring in Emerging Markets*. Washington DC: Institute for International Finance.

———. 2006. *Principles for Stable Capital Flows and Fair Debt Restructuring in Emerging Markets: Report on Implementation by the Principles Consultative Group*. Washington DC: Institute for International Finance (September).

Irwin, G., A. Penalver, C. Salmon, and A. Taylor. 2005. "Dealing with Country Diversity: Challenges for the IMF Coinsurance Model." Paper presented at the Latin American and Caribbean Economic Association conference, October 27, in Paris, France.

Jeanne, O., and R. Ranciere. 2005. *The Optimal Level of International Reserves for Emerging Market Countries: Formulas and Applications*. Washington, DC: International Monetary Fund.

Kaletsky, A. 1985. *The Costs of Default*. New York: Priority Press.

Kletzer, K. M., and B. Wright. 2000. "Sovereign Debt as Intertemporal Barter." *American Economic Review* 90:3, 621–639.

Kohlscheen, E., and S. A. O'Connell. 2003. *A Recontracting Sovereign Debt Model with Trade Credit*. Stockholm: Institute for International Economic Studies.

Krueger, A. 2002. *A New Approach to Sovereign Debt Restructuring*. Washington, DC: International Monetary Fund.

Levy-Yeyati, E., and U. Panniza. 2005. *The Elusive Costs of Default*. Washington, DC: Inter-American Development Bank.

Mauro, P., and Y. Yafeh. 2003. "The Corporation of Foreign Bondholders." *IMF Working Paper*, No. 107.

Porzecanski, A. C. 2005. "From Rogue Creditors to Rogue Debtors: Implications of Argentina's Default." *Chicago Journal of International Law* 6:1, 311–326.

Rochet, J. 2005. "Optimal Sovereign Debt: An Analytical Approach." University of Toulouse.

Roubini, N., and J. Sgard. 2004a. "Are There Such Things as International Property Rights?" *The World Economy* 27: 3.

———. 2004b. "IMF in Theory: Sovereign Debts, Judicialisation and Multilateralism." *Document de Travail du CEPII*.

Stiglitz, J. 2006. *Making Globalisation Work*. London: Penguin Books.

Sturzenegger, F., and J. Zettelmeyer. 2005a. "Has the Legal Threat to Sovereign Debt Restructuring Become Real?" www.utdt.edu/~fsturzen/legal.pdf.

———. 2005b. "Haircuts: Estimating Investor Losses in Sovereign Debt Restructurings, 1998–2005." *IMF Working Paper*, No. 137.

———. 2005c. "Argentina's Restructuring: Some Facts and Some Questions." Paper presented at the Latin American and Caribbean Economic Association conference, October 27, in Paris, France.

Sussman, O., and A. Guembel. 2006. "Sovereign Debt without Default Penalties." Mimeo. University of Oxford Said Business School.

Taylor, J. 2002. "Using Clauses to Reform the Process for Sovereign Debt Workouts: Progress and Next Steps." Prepared remarks at the Emerging Markets Traders Association annual meeting, December 5, New York City." www.treas.gov/press/releases/po3672.htm.

ABOUT THE AUTHORS

Marcus Miller is a professor of economics at Warwick University, teaching graduate macroeconomics and international macroeconomics courses. He is also a research fellow at the Center for Economic and Policy Research (CEPR) in London, a visiting fellow at the Peterson Institute for International Economics in Washington, and visiting lecturer at the International College of Economics and Finance in Moscow. Educated at Oxford University (Philosophy, Politics, and Economics) and Yale University (PhD), his previous academic career includes posts at the London School of Economics and Manchester University, with visiting teaching positions at University of Chicago Booth School of Business and Princeton University.

He has worked as an economist and as a Houblon-Norman fellow at the Bank of England; acted as adviser to the Treasury Committee of the House of Commons; was member and chair of an academic panel of the Treasury and joint director of the International Macroeconomics Program at CEPR in London. He has also, over the years, been a visiting fellow and economic consultant at the Organisation for Economic Co-operation and Development, TACIS (Technical Assistance to the Commonwealth of Independent States, on macroeconomic policy in Ukraine), the International Monetary Fund, the World Bank, the European Central Bank; and recently at the Inter-American Development Bank. He can be reached at marcus.miller@warwick.ac.uk.

Dania Thomas is a lecturer in business law in the School of Law at Keele University at Keele, United Kingdom. She received an LLB degree from Government Law College, University of Mumbai, and practiced as a counsel in the Supreme Court of India in New Delhi before completing her PhD in contract law from Keele University. Dania specializes in sovereign debt litigation, with a focus on U.S. law, on which she has published widely. She is currently examining the nature and creation of property rights in the sovereign debt market since securitization in the 1980s.

CHAPTER 24

Sovereign Debt Documentation and the *Pari Passu* Clause

UMAKANTH VAROTTIL
Assistant Professor, Faculty of Law, National University of Singapore

W hen a debtor defaults on its payment obligations to creditors, a collective action problem generally results. The problem is accentuated when the debtor has a large group of creditors with differing interests. The participating group of creditors tries to work with the debtor to reorganize its debts so they can be confident about recovering at least a portion of the debts owed to them. However, other creditors, known as holdouts, or *vultures*, generally believe they have a better chance of receiving the entire payment due to them if they press for it instead of negotiating with the debtor.[1] While participating creditors work with the debtor to optimize their returns in the given circumstances, holdout creditors stay outside any restructuring process, hoping to press their claims in court and force the debtor to pay the amounts due to them. Holdout creditors' efforts occasionally succeed.

This dynamic holds true even when the debtor is a sovereign.[2] Restructuring sovereign debts is fraught with delicate imbalances that threaten successful workouts and turnarounds. Holdout creditors have resorted to clutching at any straw to tip the scales in their favor. One such straw is the ubiquitous *pari passu* clause, a standard term in most debtor-creditor agreements. *Pari passu*, a Latin phrase, means *in equal step,* or *equally* (Buchheit and Pam 2004). The relevance of the *pari passu* clause to holdout creditors is best examined in the context of a holdout episode that occurred in relation to debts owed by the Republic of Peru.

THE ELLIOTT CASE

Banco de la Nacion, a Peruvian public sector bank, issued bonds in the international markets, guaranteed by Peru's government. Because of a default on the bonds, Peru was forced to negotiate a restructuring of the bonds with its creditors. Around the same time, Elliott Associates L.P., a vulture fund, purchased bonds issued by Nacion from certain bondholders. Elliott refused to participate in the restructuring, sued Nacion and Peru for full payment and obtained a judgment for more than $35 million in a New York court (*Elliott*, NY 2000). Despite the favorable outcome, Elliott faced a problem common to sovereign creditors—the inability to enforce judgments in an effective manner.[3] The *pari passu* clause redeemed Elliott from this weak position.[4]

Elliott knew Peru was prepared to pay participating creditors (to the exclusion of the holdouts) under its restructuring, which involved transferring funds through the Euroclear system in Belgium. Elliott initiated legal action in Belgium to prevent the Euroclear system from processing any payments received from Peru. Elliott stated that the payments by Peru violated the equal treatment principle laid down in the *pari passu* clause contained in Peru's agreements. It argued that under the *pari passu* clause, a sovereign debtor must pay all creditors ratably when it makes a payment to any of the creditors. On this interpretation, the *pari passu* clause requires debtors to make payments to creditors on a proportionate basis; debtors cannot make payments to some creditors to the exclusion of others. The Belgian Court of Appeals in 2000 accepted Elliott's interpretation of the *pari passu* clause and granted its request to block Peru's payment on bonds to other creditors (Bratton 2004; Buchheit and Pam 2004). Prevented from paying its creditors to make the restructuring successful, Peru settled with Elliott.

Elliot's success also led other holdout creditors to invoke the *pari passu* clause to prevent payments by sovereign debtors to participating creditors (Gelpern 2004). Thus, the *pari passu* clause constituted a powerful tool for holdout creditors to force sovereign debtors to make substantial payments to holdout creditors.

INTERPRETATION OF THE *PARI PASSU* CLAUSE

Although the *pari passu* clause is ubiquitous in debtor-creditor agreements, little interpretive authority from prior case law defines its scope or meaning.[5] It is under these circumstances that *Elliott* defined the *pari passu* clause.[6] *Elliott* caused a furor among creditors, lawyers, and academics in the sovereign lending community, who argued that the Belgian court's interpretation was incorrect and the *pari passu* clause does not allow an interpretation preventing a debtor from paying off one of its creditors without making a ratable payment to all of its creditors (Gulati and Klee 2001; Buchheit and Pam 2004; Financial Markets Law Committee 2005).

Several arguments against the ratable payment interpretation of the *pari passu* clause exist. First, the *pari passu* clause is about *ranking* and not about *payment*. It only prevents the debtor from incurring obligations that rank legally superior to the debt held by existing creditors. It does not prevent the debtor from making payments to certain creditors without making ratable payments to all creditors.

Second, the *pari passu* clause ought not to be confused with the timing of payment to unsecured creditors, as that would depend upon the contractual maturity of the debt. If the ratable payment interpretation is accepted, all creditors would need to be paid simultaneously even if some are not yet due to be paid according to the terms of their contract.

Third, in the corporate debt context, the practical consequence of the clause is most relevant during a bankruptcy or liquidation. However, unlike a corporate debtor, a sovereign cannot become bankrupt or be liquidated, and hence the *pari passu* clause in a sovereign debt obligation must have a different purpose.

Fourth, Buchheit and Pam (2004) allude to the previous existence of specific laws in Spain and the Philippines that enabled sovereigns to involuntarily subordinate creditors by utilizing certain prescribed procedures. This system posed a significant risk to the ranking of sovereign creditors, making the *pari passu* clause crucial for the protection of such creditors.

Fifth, several creditors, particularly multilateral financial institutions, have been conferred priority of payment by convention. These institutions have always received repayments in priority over other creditors of sovereigns and such priority has traditionally never been questioned. The ratable payments interpretation of the *pari passu* clause runs counter to the established priority held by such institutions.

On the basis of these arguments, the Belgian court considering *Elliott* should not have construed the *pari passu* clause as a ratable payments provision. The overwhelming number of arguments against the judgment in *Elliott* confirms that the court's interpretation cannot stand. The market should therefore be expected to react by clarifying the language in sovereign debt documentation to avoid similar results in the future.

However, this anticipated drafting change never occurred. Empirical evidence reveals sovereign borrowers continue to operate with the identical *pari passu* clause used before *Elliott* (Choi and Gulati 2006). There are several reasons why the clause may not have been altered despite interpretive shocks that reduce its value to sovereign debtors and participating creditors. The reasons may be either endogenous[7] or exogenous.[8] Existing studies on boilerplate terms like the *pari passu* clause focus primarily on endogenous reasons and empirical evidence for maintaining the status quo in boilerplate terms. The present analysis attempts to look beyond empirical evidence and examines exogenous reasons for the continued use of the unchanged *pari passu* clause despite its unconventional interpretation.

EXOGENOUS REASONING

This approach from a contract negotiation and bargaining standpoint helps determine the reasons for inaction with reference to certain boilerplate contractual terms like the *pari passu* clause. As a starting point during a contract negotiation, parties prefer deferring to boilerplate terms generally used in the marketplace (Ahdieh 2006). This induces an element of inertia between contracting parties that prevents them from changing boilerplate language. Deviation from standard terms usually occurs only if a term is costly to market participants. If status quo is costlier than change, then market participants gravitate toward change. An interpretive shock delivered by a court is a classic driver of change. But, as we have seen, interpretive changes do not always impel a drafting change in a contract.

Here, we need to look beyond the boilerplate term and its direct implications. Sometimes, exogenous factors operate to help maintain the status quo.[9] To illustrate this point, consider a scenario in which a boilerplate term is affected by an interpretive shock and logically requires a change. Exogenous factors operating simultaneously, however, may dilute the need for change, making the change less crucial than it would have been in the absence of the exogenous factors. Contracting parties, inherently inert as they are, prefer status quo over change if the benefits arising from the change are not substantial. (See Exhibit 24.1.) The logical reasoning behind interpretive shocks is set out here.

Applying this to the *pari passu* clause, the interpretive shock delivered in *Elliott* should have induced change. However, change did not occur. To determine the

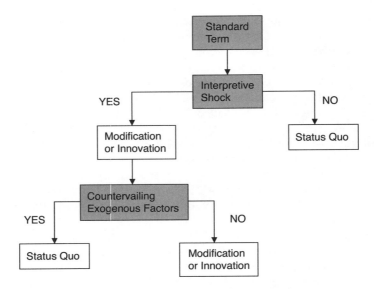

Exhibit 24.1   Effects of Interpretive Shocks on Boilerplate Contract Terms

reason for this, it is necessary to consider two other changes occurring in the sovereign debt market during the same time frame[10] and to determine if these changes affected the *pari passu* clause directly or indirectly, thereby explaining the status quo.

THE SHIFT FROM UNANIMOUS ACTION CLAUSES TO COLLECTIVE ACTION CLAUSES

A significant shift occurred between 2000 and 2003 in collective action mechanisms contained in sovereign bond documentation (Choi and Gulati 2004). This had an impact on the feasibility of sovereign debt restructuring exercises in light of the opposition by holdout creditors. Until 2003, sovereign bonds issued under New York law required unanimous bondholder approval to amend payment terms (mainly the principal and interest) (Buchheit and Gulati 2000). Such clauses were also known as *unanimous action clauses* (UACs). All other terms, being nonpayment terms, could be amended by a simple majority vote of all bondholders. Because of the high threshold requirement for amending payment terms, maverick creditors had an incentive to hold out because the restructuring could not be put into effect if there was even a single holdout creditor.

In due course, the market adopted a novel method of overcoming this difficulty. In 2000, Ecuador used exit consents to restructure its debt through an exchange offer (Choi and Gulati 2004).[11] The exit consent mechanism bound holdout creditors to the restructuring. There was initially no change to the UACs resulting from this interpretive shock. However, change came three years later when Mexico drafted collective action clauses (CACs) in its sovereign debt documentation instead of using the prevalent UACs. Following Mexico, other sovereign debt documents replaced their UAC clauses with CAC clauses. This ensured participating creditors with a 75 percent majority could restructure debt and bind holdout creditors to the restructuring without any remedy whatsoever to them. When this change was introduced in New York law–governed sovereign bond documentation, it tilted the balance in favor of the participating creditors, as the holdout creditors tended to follow the participating creditors that commanded the requisite majority and generally restructured the debts.

THE SHIFT FROM FISCAL AGENT TO TRUSTEE WITH SOLE ENFORCEMENT POWERS

Most sovereign bonds governed by New York law are issued pursuant to a fiscal agency agreement, whereby the fiscal agent is the agent of the sovereign issuer rather than of the bondholders (Fisch and Gentile 2004). In other cases, bonds are issued pursuant to a trust indenture, whereby the trustee is an agent or fiduciary of the bondholders and not the sovereign issuer. Until recently, either under the fiscal agency agreement or a conventional trust indenture, the right of an individual bondholder to bring an action against the sovereign debtor in recovery of its share of principal or interest that remained unpaid was inviolable. However, a Grenada bond offering document issued in 2005 introduced a novel provision, which did not provide individual enforcement rights to bondholders (Buchheit and Karpinski 2006). This set of provisions had two consequences.

All enforcement rights vested only with the trustee and were exercisable solely for the ratable benefit of all bondholders. This precluded individual bondholders from pressing for claims and recovering them to the detriment of other bondholders, reducing incentives for bondholders to hold out.

Individual bondholders were also precluded from initiating actions for repayment or acceleration unless a demand was made by holders of at least 25 percent of the outstanding amount of the bonds. Unless holdouts constituted at least 25 percent of the amount of the bonds, they were powerless to initiate actions against the sovereign debtor. Therefore, these provisions limited the powers of holdout creditors to initiate recovery actions.

REFLECTING ON THE EXOGENOUS FACTORS

The net impact of the preceding changes to sovereign bond documentation is that the powers of holdout creditors are substantially curtailed. How does this relate to the *pari passu* clause?

As explained, the interpretive shock delivered in *Elliott* arose from holdout litigation. Despite the interpretive shocks, the clause did not change. However, when exogenous reasons are examined, it becomes apparent the interpretive shock in the *pari passu* clause occurred simultaneously with two other changes that altered equations between the parties. This cushioned the interpretive shock delivered in *Elliott*; it was no longer relevant. After the changes, holdouts no longer possessed the same power as when *Elliott* was decided. The exogenous shifts (exit consents, the CAC clause, and indenture trustees) have largely shifted the incentives and negotiating positions of holdout creditors relative to the sovereign debtors and participating creditors. Holdout creditors cannot rely on their ability to bring about legal actions to frustrate debt restructuring processes unless they muster enough support to surpass the threshold percentage required to bring a legal action for recovery. The time, effort, and costs to holdout creditors likely exceed the benefits from such litigation. Accordingly, the risk of continued interpretive shocks like *Elliott* are substantially mitigated, inducing inertia in the drafters of *pari passu* clauses to keep the clauses within the confines of market practice.

CONCLUSION

The *Elliott* case and subsequent events suggest boilerplate contract terms may not necessarily change following interpretive shocks even if such terms are value-reducing in nature. The constancy of a clause following interpretive shocks may be explained by exogenous reasons that may affect the bargaining power and dynamics between contracting parties. These effects may cause boilerplate terms to continue unabated, although the terms may be ambiguous in nature because of the interpretation handed down by courts.

From a normative perspective, parties ought to continuously monitor exogenous factors because any changes in those factors modify a boilerplate contract term or (through any other appropriate mechanism) maintain the status quo. It is crucial to determine who will monitor the factors affecting boilerplate language. Contracting parties themselves do not have the incentives to monitor and induce change where necessary. Contracting parties are usually bogged down with inertia and collective action problems. Furthermore, the cost of monitoring activities is a disincentive to parties. Thus, this role is best carried out by market participants whose interests are represented in the aggregate. An association of market players usually possesses the necessary specialized knowledge and skills to monitor changes and determine the need for altering boilerplate terms. This association may be assisted by advisers such as law firms, which can assess the circumstances from a legal standpoint and provide expert input on whether to change boilerplate terms. Other advisers, such as investment bankers, can comment on the acceptability of such changes in the marketplace. These efforts will likely maximize the value of contract terms in sovereign debt documents, thereby enabling the unimpeded flow of transactions in the sovereign debt market.

NOTES

1. These creditors usually buy debts of issuers who are in financial distress, which they obtain from other debt investors in the secondary market. Because of the deteriorating financial position of the issuers, holdout creditors are able to purchase the debts at a substantial discount to the issue price. However, upon purchase of these debts, they acquire the right and entitlement to the full value of the debts (in the form of principal amounts and unpaid interest) against the issuer. Holdouts therefore have necessary incentives to stay out of any debt restructuring to press for full payment or at least to demand a substantially better deal than what is being offered to the participating creditors in the hope of making a handsome profit in a relatively short time.

2. Matters get somewhat complicated in the case of a sovereign debtor because of the diverse nature of its creditors, which may include banks, international financial

institutions, official bilateral creditors, trade creditors, and bondholders; add to that the absence of a bankruptcy or insolvency regime that governs delinquency of sovereigns.

3. Sovereigns rarely have assets situated outside their jurisdiction, making it cumbersome for creditors to recover meaningful judgments (Gulati and Klee 2001).

4. The Republic of Peru (being the guarantor) agreed to a *pari passu* clause in its bond documentation that provided: "[t]he obligations of the Guarantor hereunder do rank and will rank at least *pari passu* in priority of payment with all other External Indebtedness of the Guarantor, and interest thereon" (Bratton 2004).

5. Interestingly, the *pari passu* clause is often inserted by drafters of sovereign debt documentation who are uncertain of its meaning (Buchheit 1991).

6. The court determined that when a borrower without sufficient funds to pay its creditors wishes to pay some of its creditors, that borrower must pay all creditors on a ratable basis without paying some creditors more than others. This is the "ratable payment interpretation" of the *pari passu* clause.

7. For the present purposes, endogenous reasons or endogenous factors are those connected directly with the clause in question.

8. Exogenous reasons or exogenous factors are those that are not connected with the clause in question. These may include other clauses or groups of clauses in the same contract of which the clause in question is a part, or may include factors such as bargaining power or negotiating leverage between parties, market conditions, or other factors that may have an impact on the manner in which parties are likely to act in relation to the contract.

9. The exogenous factors may be either a single factor or a group of individual factors, or more likely, a mix of factors operating contemporaneously so as to alter the negotiating leverage and balance between the parties to a contract.

10. For the purposes of this study, the time from 2000 to 2005, namely a five-year period following *Elliott*, has been considered.

11. This requires an explanation of two terms, to wit, *exchange offers* and *exit consents*. Exchange offers are offers made by the sovereign debtor to restructure its bonds by issuing new bonds (which represent the restructured debt) in exchange for the old (pre-restructuring) debt held by the creditors. As part of the exchange offer, the sovereign debtor seeks the consent (exit consent) of the approving bondholders to amend provisions in the bonds that they are tendering in exchange (the original bonds) in order to render those bonds less attractive to any bondholder who may want to hold out. The nonpayment terms are usually amended because they require only a simple majority vote. However, mere amendment to the nonpayment terms (such as by delisting the bonds, deleting the *pari passu,* and other protective clauses) could still make the bonds highly unattractive so as to compel the holdout creditors to participate in the restructuring and exchange offer rather than hold on to bonds that are worth much less. This turned out to be a unique way of silencing holdouts.

REFERENCES

Ahdieh, R. 2006. "'Boilerplate': Foundations of Market Contracts Symposium." *Michigan Law Review* 104:5, 1033–1073.

Bratton, W. 2004. "Pari Passu and a Distressed Sovereign's Rational Choices." *Emory Law Journal* 53: 823–867.

Buchheit, L. 1991. "The Pari Passu Sub Specie Aeternitatis." *International Financial Law Review* 10:12, 11–12.

Buchheit, L., and M. Gulati. 2000. "Exit Consents in Sovereign Bond Exchanges." *UCLA Law Review* 48:1, 59–84.

Buchheit, L., and E. Karpinski. 2006. "Grenada's Innovations." *Journal of Banking Law and Regulation* 20: 227.

Buchheit, L., and J. Pam. 2004. "The Pari Passu Clause in Sovereign Debt Instruments." *Emory Law Journal* 53: 869–922.

Choi, S., and M. Gulati. 2004. "Innovation in Boilerplate Contracts: An Empirical Examination of Sovereign Bonds." *Emory Law Journal* 53: 929–996.

———. 2006. "Contract as Statute." *Michigan Law Review* 104:5, 1129–1173.

Elliott Assocs., L.P. v. Banco De La Nacion No. 96 Civ. 7916 RWS, 2000 WL 1449862. SDNY. September 29, 2000.

Financial Markets Law Committee. 2005. "*Pari Passu* Clauses: Analysis of the Role, Use and Meaning of *Pari Passu* Clauses in Sovereign Debt Obligations as a Matter of English Law." Issue 79. www.fmlc.org/papers/fmlc79mar_2005.pdf.

Fisch, J., and C. Gentile. 2004. "Vultures or Vanguards? The Role of Litigation in Sovereign Debt Restructuring." *Emory Law Journal* 53: 1043–1113.

Gelpern, A. 2004. "Building a Better Seating Chart." *Emory Law Journal* 53: 1115–1157.

Gulati, M., and K. Klee. 2001. "Sovereign Piracy." *Business Lawyer* 56:2: 635–651.

ABOUT THE AUTHOR

Umakanth Varottil is an assistant professor on the faculty of law, National University of Singapore (NUS). He specializes in corporate law and governance, cross-border investments, and financial sector regulation. He has co-authored a book on Singapore corporate governance, published articles in international journals, and founded the Indian Corporate Law Blog. He has also taught on a visiting basis at the Fordham Law School, New York, and the National Law School of India University, Bangalore. He is the recipient of several academic awards: the Lee Kong Chian Scholarship (at NUS), the Hauser Global Scholarship (at New York University School of Law), and eight gold medals (at the National Law School of India University). Before his foray into academia, Umakanth was a corporate attorney in India with the leading corporate law firm of Amarchand Mangaldas, where he was also a partner.

CHAPTER 25

Collective Action Clauses in Sovereign Bonds

SÖNKE HÄSELER

Research Associate, Institute of Law and Economics, University of Hamburg

The universal adoption of collective action clauses (CACs) was the most promising reform proposal in recent debates on sovereign debt crisis management. Academics and the public sector had been promoting CACs since 1995, yet market practice did not begin to change until 2003. This delay is often attributed to the opposition of investors and sovereign borrowers to CACs.

This paper evaluates the publicly stated as well as the suspected private motives of the two sides to block the spread of CACs. It draws on a wide range of existing evidence and adds some new theoretical considerations to show that there is no reason to be skeptical of CACs unless bailouts exist as an alternative crisis resolution mechanism. This conclusion may be of interest purely for the sake of historical accuracy. But more importantly, it may help to better understand and to assess any potential future resistance from market participants, for example, in the process of introducing CACs in bonds governed by German law.

BACKGROUND

When a sovereign government finds itself unable to service its bonds, it will ideally engage the bondholders in negotiations for debt relief according to a predefined, orderly procedure. Alas, until recently the majority of bonds would not provide for any such procedure. To change the payment terms of the bond—such as coupon rate, principal, or maturity—would usually require the consent of each and every bondholder, which is practically impossible to achieve. A debtor country would therefore typically resort to an exchange offer. Bondholders would be asked, under the implicit or explicit threat of default, to tender the existing bonds in exchange for ones with less stringent payment terms.

Bondholders may, of course, elect not to participate in the exchange. Free-riding on the debt relief provided by their peers, they may gamble for full repayment according to the old terms later on. Such holdout creditors can be a great nuisance to debtors because they retain their full legal rights under the old bond, which they may use in court, for example to interfere with the borrower's trade and finance flows. The debtor therefore has the unpalatable choice between facing potential legal action and paying the holdouts in full. The latter option is expensive, unfair to mainstream bondholders, and an outcome whose existence the debtor should deny for the purpose of discouraging holdouts in the first place. Given the holdout problem, the borrowing country will strive for as high a participation rate as possible. The exchange offer will thus have to be very attractive for bondholders, which implies it cannot bring much relief. Alternatively, the debtor may try to artificially boost participation by means of so-called exit consents (Buchheit and Gulati 2000), which are, however, regarded as coercive by investors and accordingly liable to make the debtor unpopular with the market.

Anticipating these troubles and potentially messy outcomes, debtor countries have tended to admit default only at the last possible moment, thereby aggravating the crisis up to the point at which requiring outside help becomes inevitable. Other countries and international financial institutions such as the International Monetary Fund (IMF) have regularly felt compelled to provide assistance to avert even larger damage to the debtor country and contagion to other regions—or so the official justification usually goes.

Such bailouts are perhaps the worst of all crisis resolution mechanisms in terms of equity and efficiency. Accordingly, there ensued a search for alternatives, which yielded, besides the stillborn sovereign debt restructuring mechanism (SDRM) (Krueger 2002), the rediscovery of CACs. These provisions had long been a regular feature of sovereign bonds governed by the laws of England, Japan, and Luxembourg (Liu 2002), which together accounted for less than 40 percent of the bonds outstanding in 2003 (IMF 2003). The clauses were generally not used in the two other popular jurisdictions, the state of New York and Germany. This omission was rooted in tradition and, arguably, market preferences, rather than in any legal impediments to collective action (Liu 2002). The universal adoption of CACs thus presented itself as a logical step.

Used wisely, CACs can facilitate an orderly, efficient restructuring process: A troubled debtor will approach bondholder representatives at an early stage to negotiate a proposed amendment of the bond terms. The proposal will then be put to the vote at a bondholder meeting. Approval by anywhere between two-thirds and 85 percent of the eligible principal, depending on the specifics of the clauses, will effectuate the amendment for the entire bond issue, including any dissenting creditors. The outcome of this process can be considered fair because all bondholders are treated equally; it is consultative in nature and thus more creditor-friendly than an exchange offer; and most importantly, it eliminates the holdout problem. Moreover, CACs are a natural complement to the appointment of a trustee, an institution that can suppress harmful individual bondholder action before a CACs-induced restructuring becomes effective (Häseler 2010).

Despite the evident advantages of collective over individual action, the universal adoption of CACs began to appear on the policy agendas only in the mid-1990s. Eichengreen and Portes (1995) can be credited with rediscovering CACs but were soon followed by a series of public sector (G10, G22, IMF) reports that called for the inclusion of CACs in New York law bonds. These calls remained unheard for several years until March 2003 when Mexico made what was widely perceived to be the first major issue with CACs in the U.S. market. The effects of this precedent were dramatic: Within a year, market practice was reversed; issuing

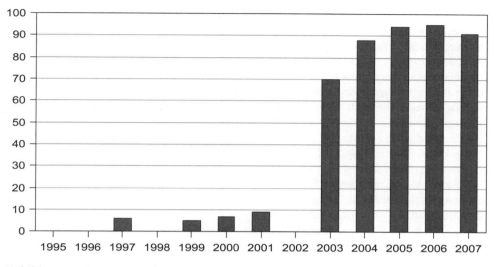

Exhibit 25.1 Percentage of New Issues that Contain CACs
Source: Bradley et al. (2008).

CACs under New York law went from being the exception to being the norm. Exhibit 25.1 illustrates the shift.

Gelpern and Gulati (2007) investigate, primarily through interviews with market participants, the factors that eventually led to these events. The authors emphasize the importance of politics and public symbolism. This paper, by contrast, asks why the change did not materialize sooner. Several sources report skepticism on the part of borrowers and outright opposition to the spread of CACs on the part of investors (Häseler 2009). We ask whether this discomfort with collective action was ever justified.

This question is relevant in at least two respects. First, we hope to shed some more light on a somewhat obscure episode of financial market history. But what is more important is that it is imperative to understand the incentives of investors and sovereign borrowers for the sake of pending reforms. Bonds are still being issued without CACs. And little progress has been made toward the proliferation of trust structures, which also hinges on the individual versus collective action divide (Häseler 2008). With this dual purpose in mind, we proceed to scrutinize in turn the position of investors and that of sovereign borrowers.

INVESTORS' PERSPECTIVE

Moral Hazard

"Sovereign bondholders are genuinely concerned that making sovereign bonds easier to restructure will make restructurings (even) more likely," said Michael Chamberlin (2002, p. 8), executive director of the Emerging Markets Trade Association. The possibility that CACs might exacerbate the moral hazard problem already inherent in sovereign lending was indeed the most common apprehension about the spread of the clauses. We comment on this concern from two perspectives.

First, it is not at all clear that there is a connection between the organizational ease and the incidence of restructurings. Fears about moral hazard appear to be premised on the assumption that the unpleasant prospect of a disorderly restructuring is a major factor in deterring borrowers from default. Häseler (2008) categorizes various views of sovereign default to argue that such a deterrence effect cannot be very large. A sovereign debtor who defaults opportunistically has much to lose besides the costs of restructuring, namely, first and foremost, its reputation with the financial markets.

Second, even if more CACs were to result in more restructurings, it is not quite clear why that should necessarily hurt investors. Existing bonds would be unaffected. New issues would conceivably trade at higher yields, which means investors are compensated for any additional risk. Those who are not prepared to bear that risk have an almost infinite number of alternative investments to choose from.

Esho et al. (2004) empirically test for a moral hazard effect. Sadly, their study is based on corporate bonds only and the methodology is not entirely convincing (Häseler 2009).

Fear of Abuse

Bondholder representatives have expressed concerns that majority action provisions could be abused by debtors who buy back a sufficient share of a particular issue to vote for a restructuring that runs squarely against the interest of the remaining bondholders (IMF 2002). This concern ignores the fact that CACs typically specify that bonds held by the issuer or by entities under its control are excluded from voting. And once again, the borrower's behavior is constrained by what the market deems fair, much more than by how the courts will read the provisions of the bond. Abuse of CACs is not an option for any issuers who value their reputation.

Ideology

Sovereign bonds issued under New York law traditionally followed the provisions of the Trust Indenture Act (TIA) of 1939, which postulates that no bondholder may be forced to cede any claims she has under the bond contract. The fact that the TIA applies only to corporate bonds but was nevertheless adhered to also in the sovereign bond market may be indicative of a dislike, particularly by U.S. investors, for being part of a minority upon whom a restructuring with CACs is imposed (Buchheit and Gulati 2002). Accordingly, Michael Chamberlin (2002, p. 5) speaks of the "legitimate right of creditors not to be bound to changes in debt payments made against their will." In that sense, opposition to collective action may be seen as a mere expression of individual freedom. Like the right to carry a gun, individual rights of action against a sovereign debtor have little practical value but the potential to do much social harm.

If ideology really played a role in the market's hesitation to embrace CACs, this reveals a certain degree of hypocrisy. Even before 2003, investors would have had to choose their bonds very carefully if they wanted to avoid being subject to CACs. Given their prevalence under English law, any larger sovereign debt portfolio likely contained the clauses. Furthermore, New York was never the sanctuary from collective action that some said it was. Gugiatti and Richards (2004), Gelpern and Gulati (2008), and Häseler (2010) all document large volumes of pre-2003 New York law bonds that nevertheless contained CACs. In all likelihood, the vast majority of investors are ignorant of the contractual details of the instrument they hold, which is inconsistent with their having any strong sentiments on the clauses.

Investor Surplus

In 2002, creditor representative organizations published a set of model collective action clauses. This move has been variously interpreted as a waning of investor opposition, or as bid to take the wind out of the public sector's pressure for the market to adopt measures that would encroach even more upon creditor rights than CACs, such as the SDRM.

These model clauses envisaged a voting threshold of 95 percent, which the drafters regarded as necessary to curb moral hazard. We impute an alternative motivation for the high voting threshold: It can be seen as a desperate attempt to achieve second best at a time when the political debate heralded the end of the first best—unanimous consent. Loosely speaking, the higher the voting threshold, the greater the creditors' bargaining power in a restructuring. This point can be illustrated graphically, as in Exhibit 25.2.

Imagine a troubled sovereign debtor who decides to make use of the CACs in its bonds by proposing an amendment to the financial terms. In our graphical model, the horizontal axis measures the proportion of bondholders who will support the restructuring. The vertical axis measures the inducement required to persuade bondholders to vote for the restructuring. This setup gives rise to a supply schedule for votes such as S_1: At the bottom of S_1 we find those bondholders who are most enthusiastic about the restructuring. They expect a large surplus or, in other words, require a negative inducement. Toward the top we find those who are most skeptical; they would require a side payment to tender their votes. Of course, no inducements can be paid in a restructuring; that is, we are at the

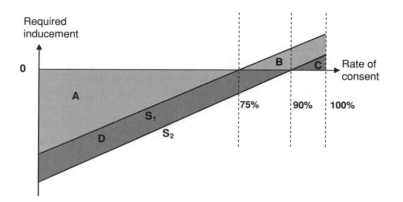

Exhibit 25.2 Voting Thresholds and Investor Surplus

point at which the supply schedule intersects the horizontal axis. The debtor must design the restructuring offer such that S shifts to the point at which the required threshold is achieved. To illustrate, we have picked supply schedules that achieve 75 percent and 90 percent consent rates, respectively. Under S_1, the net gain that investors would receive from a restructuring, let us call it *investor surplus*, is equal to the areas A minus (B + C). Under S_2, that area increases to (A + D) minus C. Increasing the voting threshold thus increases investor surplus by B + D. This is why it was no surprise to see investor representatives lobbying for high voting thresholds.

BORROWERS' PERSPECTIVE

Borrowing Costs

The fear that New York law covering bonds with collective action clauses could be less attractive to investors and thus imply higher borrowing costs is by far the most widely cited explanation for the sovereign borrowers' hesitation to incorporate the clauses in new bond issues, and was thus identified as the biggest obstacle to reform early on in the debate. As Jack Boorman (2003) of the IMF dramatically put it: "[T]he private sector seems to be going around to emerging market countries and trying to scare the hell out of them about the fact that [CACs] will lead to an increase in spreads. . . ."

Accordingly, much research has been devoted to empirically investigating the existence of any spread premiums on sovereign bonds with CACs. Häseler (2009) summarizes the five major studies in the period from 1999 to 2004 and concludes that higher borrowing costs are a myth. Although the empirical methodology improved over time in terms of sample sizes, accuracy of coding, and econometric sophistication, no study achieved stable results that stood the test of the next paper down the line. The same lack of spread premiums for CACs emerges from two more recent studies, Bradley et al. (2008) and Häseler (2010).

Signaling

The IMF (2002) discussed the possibility that borrowers might be afraid that the financial markets will view the use of CACs as a signal of deteriorating credit quality. After all, CACs have value only in a restructuring situation. A borrower who will never default has no reason to use the clauses. The concern here is that the issuer may unwittingly reveal information about its *type*, in addition to the apprehensions that investors may have about its *behavior* (moral hazard).

In practice, however, it is most questionable whether the act of issuing with CACs can possibly contain information that sophisticated investors and rating agencies do not already possess. Moreover, the contractual details of a new debt issue are rarely the result of the debtor's conscious choice but are instead typically left for legal advisers to negotiate. Investors would thus be interpreting a signal that was likely never sent in the first place. An interesting empirical test by Gugiatti and Richards (2003) accordingly yields no measurable signaling effect.

First Mover Problem

It was commonly thought at the time that the first country to issue bonds with CACs under New York law would incur substantial costs. Subsequent movers would benefit by being able to copy the contract terms from the first mover. Presumably the risk of investor hostility would also have declined. The tragedy of this constellation is, of course, that no one wants to be the first mover since the benefits provided to others cannot be internalized. The completeness of the shift in 2003 may be regarded as evidence of the first mover problem at work.

From an ex post perspective, however, it is not easy to make sense of the concerns about large up-front costs for the first mover. The lack of evidence on higher borrowing costs was already common knowledge, and indeed, Mexico suffered no noticeable spread premium on its celebrated bond issue. Furthermore, insiders must have known that market practice was much more varied at the time than was commonly thought, so that the introduction of CACs to the U.S. market was not really that daunting a task. Finally, the costs of drafting the new type of bonds can hardly have required a major effort, given that it had often happened before by accident (Gugiatti and Richards 2004).

Myopia

This is the intracountry, intergenerational version of the first mover problem. While the assumed costs of introducing CACs accrue at the time of borrowing, the benefits materialize only in the event of default, which is unlikely to happen during the borrowing finance minister's term in office. The decision makers would thus be providing a service to their successors, which is something politicians do not typically rush to do.

The catch with the myopia theory is the same as before: It is not clear why there should have been any substantial up-front costs. In fact, the opposite could be argued. The markets might even view the first mover as proactive, innovative, and thus worth investing in.

CONCLUSION

In search of an explanation for the delayed adoption of collective action clauses in sovereign bonds under New York law, we have scrutinized every major potential reason for opposition by investors or borrowers that has been suggested in the literature. None are convincing.

By way of conclusion, we offer two additional explanations. First: Much of the benefits of CACs accrue neither to borrowers nor to bondholders. By enabling smoother restructurings and reducing the risk of financial contagion, CACs may yield large positive externalities to the international financial institutions, to other countries, and to other markets. The universal adoption of CACs is in all likelihood a welfare-improving reform, but only a small fraction of the welfare gains falls on the parties that must implement the reform.

Second: CACs imply costs that accrue to both borrowers and bondholders but are invisible to the naïve observer. So far we have characterized the clauses as an option for collective action that as such precludes none of the crisis resolution strategies that were previously available. Market participants may have disagreed with this view. After all, the primary motivation for the stronger use of CACs was to obviate bailouts—which are by far the most convenient way out of a debt crisis for both borrowers and lenders. By potentially reducing the chances of a bailout, CACs thus impose a large indirect cost on the primary actors.

Where does this leave us? A credible commitment to no more bailouts would have sped up the adoption of collective action clauses and may yet be needed to complete the reform in the sphere of CACs and elsewhere. The recent case of Greece has demonstrated once more how third-party assistance relieves the market of any pressure to adopt more efficient structures. Furthermore, regulation is an option that should have been and perhaps should still be considered more seriously. When a welfare-improving reform fails to be implemented because of an unfortunate allocation of costs and benefits, an outside impetus may be needed. CACs could be made a listing requirement on the major stock exchanges, as has long been the practice in London with respect to the appointment of a trustee.

REFERENCES

Boorman, J. 2003. Remarks in a Panel Discussion at the IMF Conference on Sovereign Debt Restructuring Mechanisms (SDRM). www.imf.org/external/np/tr/2003/tr030122.htm.

Bradley, M., J. Fox, and M. Gulati. 2008. "The Market Reaction to Legal Shocks and Their Antidotes: Lessons from the Sovereign Debt Market." *Duke Law School Legal Studies Research Paper* No. 211.

Buchheit, L., and M. Gulati. 2000. "Exit Consents in Sovereign Bond Exchanges." *University of California Law Review* 48: 59–84.

———. 2002. "Sovereign Bonds and the Collective Will." *Emory Law Journal* 51: 1317–1364.

Chamberlin, M. 2002. *A Casual Observer's Commentary on the Taylor Proposal and the EMCA's Model Covenants for New Sovereign Debt Issues.* New York: Emerging Markets Trade Association.

Eichengreen, B., and R. Portes. 1995. *Crisis? What Crisis? Orderly Workouts for Sovereign Debtors.* London: Centre for Economic Policy Research.

Esho, N., I. Sharpe, and N. Tchou. 2004. "Moral Hazard and Collective Action Clauses in the Eurobond Market." Working paper, University of New South Wales.

Gelpern, A., and M. Gulati. 2007. "Public Symbol in Private Contract: A Case Study." *Washington University Law Quarterly* 84: 1627–1715.

———. 2008. "Innovation after the Revolution: Foreign Sovereign Bond Contracts Since 2003." *Capital Markets Law Journal* 4:1, 85–103.

Gugiatti, M., and A. Richards. 2003. "Do Collective Action Clauses Influence Bond Yields? New Evidence from Emerging Markets." www.rba.gov.au/rdp/rdp2003-02.pdf.

———. 2004. "The Use of Collective Action Clauses in New York Law Bonds of Sovereign Borrowers." *Georgetown Journal of International Law* 35:4, 815–836.

Häseler, S. 2008. "Individual Enforcement Rights in International Sovereign Bonds." *German Working Papers in Law and Economics.* www.bepress.com/gwp/default/vol2010/iss1/art1.

———. 2009. "Collective Action Clauses in International Sovereign Bonds—Whence the Opposition?" *Journal of Economic Surveys* 23:5, 882–923.

———. 2010. "Trustees versus Fiscal Agents and Default Risk in International Sovereign Bonds." *German Working Papers in Law and Economics.* www.bepress.com/gwp/default/vol2010/iss1/art1.

International Monetary Fund. 2002. "Collective Action Clauses in Sovereign Bond Contracts—Encouraging Greater Use." www.imf.org/external/np/psi/2002/eng/060602a.pdf.

———. 2003. "Progress Report to the International Monetary and Financial Committee on Crisis Resolution." www.imf.org/external/np/pdr/cr/2003/eng/090503.pdf.

Krueger, A. 2002. "Sovereign Debt Restructuring and Dispute Resolution." Speech on June 6. www.imf.org/external/np/speeches/2002/060602.htm.

Liu, Y. 2002. "Collective Action Clauses in International Sovereign Bonds." *IMF Working Paper.* www.imf.org/external/np/leg/sem/2002/cdmfl/eng/liu.pdf.

ABOUT THE AUTHOR

Sönke Häseler holds a master's degree in financial economics from the University of St. Andrews, Scotland, and is currently a research associate with the Institute of Law and Economics at the University of Hamburg. His PhD thesis focuses on the trade-off between individual and collective creditor rights in international sovereign bonds.

CHAPTER 26

Sovereignty, Legitimacy, and Creditworthiness

ODETTE LIENAU
Assistant Professor of Law, Cornell University

Those who imagine themselves practically minded may dismiss the issue of sovereignty in sovereign debt and international economic relations out of hand. Indeed, questions of sovereignty—that is, of the legitimate foundations for a state's rule over a given population and territory[1]—have been largely ignored by mainstream international finance. In particular, conventional wisdom in international finance today suggests that all sovereign state debt should be repaid, regardless of the arguable illegitimacy of the regime that signed a debt contract or the ultimate use of the loan proceeds.

This dismissal of the relevance of sovereign legitimacy to sovereign debt seems to derive from two sources. The first is theoretical path dependence. Under the current norms of international finance, it can be difficult to conceive of how different ideas of sovereignty would structure alternative sovereign debt regimes—or indeed how our current lending regime rests upon and reinforces a particular vision of sovereignty. The second reason for this dismissal is that it can be considered impracticable to upend the current lending structure, which assumes the irrelevance of questions of sovereignty. Most scholars agree that today's lending framework depends to a large degree on the mechanism of sovereign reputation or creditworthiness. That is, states maintain access to international capital markets by protecting their reputation for repayment. This mechanism, at least as it is currently understood, partially rests on the idea that states remain legally the same entity despite any internal regime changes, such as from a less to a more internationally legitimate regime.

In this chapter, I briefly address both of these threshold issues. I first argue for greater conceptual clarity in thinking about sovereign lending, highlighting how *any* sovereign lending regime is necessarily political in that it inherently relates to an underlying concept of sovereign rule. Different schools of sovereignty specify alternative relations of rulership and thus imply different answers to the question of who is authorized to enter into and abrogate sovereign debt contracts. As such, these foundational philosophical questions have significant distributional consequences for international finance. I also address the issue of reputation, or creditworthiness, underscoring how this mechanism is more flexible than it first appears and how it similarly relies on an implicit theory of sovereign legitimacy.

In short, the questions of sovereignty in sovereign lending and creditworthiness remain open and demand greater historical and policy analysis. This brief article is drawn from portions of a book on sovereignty, debt, and reputation forthcoming from Harvard University Press, *Rethinking Sovereign Debt: Debt and Reputation in the 20th Century.*

THE HIDDEN FOUNDATIONS OF SOVEREIGN LENDING

Although it is not frequently acknowledged in international finance, sovereignty constitutes one of the key concepts undergirding international transactions. Indeed, any arena that touches upon the actions of states—the sovereign debt regime being chief among them—necessarily presupposes the international legal concept of sovereignty. Adherence to any given vision of sovereignty—whether grounded in territorial control, democratic ideals, or basic constitutionalism—results in different expectations of appropriate outcomes in international politics and economics. And relatedly, an insistence that states act in certain ways can reinforce and entrench the concept of sovereignty implicated by those actions.

Perhaps unwittingly, a very distinct theory of sovereignty supports the international lending system's dominant norm of sovereign debt continuity—that is, the general rule that states should repay predecessors' debts even after a major regime change and the related expectation that they will otherwise suffer reputational consequences. Sovereign continuity effectively derives from what I call a strictly *statist* concept of sovereignty—the idea that the content of and changes in a state's internal structure, interests, and popular legitimacy are irrelevant to its status as sovereign and thus to its external political relations and financial obligations. Under a statist vision of sovereignty, a popular democracy succeeding an oppressive dictator constitutes the same sovereign and thus would remain subject to the same contractual obligations. Although this approach is frequently mischaracterized as being apolitical, it is in fact drawn from a very clear political theory; this school of thought posits the existence of a potentially eternal state entity that exists separate from either a particular ruler or a particular population. In Europe, this statist vision roughly emerged in the late medieval era, prior to which the idea of a disembodied state whose obligations existed after the demise of a concrete ruling family would have seemed foreign.[2] This statist tradition also allows for the acceptance and legitimation of dictatorial forms of rule, in which the binding authority of a state is disconnected from the interests and aspirations of the underlying people.

As should be clear to anyone with a passing interest in international politics, a statist approach to sovereignty—with its acceptance of even absolutist forms of rule and its rejection of the legal import of political change—is far from broadly accepted. Particularly starting in the early twentieth century, there has been considerable international contention about whether a concept of sovereignty that ignores ideas of self-determination or concern for the underlying population is practical or normatively appropriate. The clearest alternative would be the idea of popular or democratic sovereignty, which insists that a state's people are the true sovereign actors and which has gained traction since the American and French Revolutions. There is also what I call a *rule of law* concept of sovereignty, which insists that governments act legitimately not according to their whim but through their own internal legal framework. Finally, there is an approach that pays less attention to the *process* of sovereign decision-making and is more concerned with whether the *outcome* of any government decision is positive for the state as a whole.

Each of these nonstatist approaches to sovereignty challenges the doctrine of sovereign continuity in international debt by undermining its statist theoretical underpinnings. If we are concerned with the existence of a legitimate link between a state and its people, then the idea of certain types of principled debt cancellation makes sense; it seems philosophically and legally problematic to expect a state's people to pay back debt to which they did not consent and from which they derived no benefit. In other words, an application of nonstatist visions of sovereignty to international economic relations suggests that debt should *not* be continuous in some cases. This is the basic premise of the doctrine of *odious debt*, first formalized by Alexander Sack in 1927, by which debt should not be transferable to successor regimes if the debt is not authorized by and does not benefit a nation's people.[3] Thus emerging ideas about legitimate sovereignty ground the unease surrounding certain questions in the international debt regime: Should a new, black African–led South Africa really be expected to repay apartheid era debt? And given that Saddam Hussein was a dictator who used funds for the oppression of a majority of Iraq's population, would it be appropriate to require future Iraqi generations to pay for his iniquity?[4] While the answer to both of these questions under a statist political theory is an easy yes, accepting nonstatist concepts of sovereignty casts doubt on the viability of a strict rule of debt continuity. In short, the adoption of one philosophy of sovereignty over another significantly shapes expectations of continued payment as opposed to debt cancellation and thus has significant distributional consequences in the international debt regime.

SOVEREIGNTY AND CREDITWORTHINESS

In the face of these uncertainties, the dominant norm of debt continuity may find support from the argument that a country's reputation will necessarily suffer should it fail to accede to the repayment obligations of a predecessor regime. Without the assurance that debts will be repaid even in cases of regime change, creditors would be unwilling to take the risk of sovereign lending in the face of potential political volatility. And borrowing states, attentive to their reputation in the credit market, should never repudiate debt in a serious challenge to the system's principles, even if they default or restructure debt for other reasons and with reluctant creditor cooperation. Claiming that the doctrine of sovereign continuity grounds the entire lending system effectively assumes that creditors and other international actors would be unable to make reputational assessments incorporating a nonstatist concept of sovereignty. By contrast, I argue that different creditors may interpret reputation differently, and also that more flexible conceptions of sovereignty can be sustained within a reputational framework.

The Flexibility of Reputation

While an extensive literature review is not necessary for my purposes, evidentiary support exists for a general reputational effect in sovereign lending. For example,

Michael Tomz (2007) has highlighted the centrality of reputational factors in ensuring continued cooperation between creditors and sovereign borrowers. Tomz argues that creditors consider both payment record and the situational context of repayment to develop beliefs about a borrower's type—that is, whether it is a *lemon* that will default without justification, a *fair-weather* that will repay when times are good, or a *stalwart* that repays in good times and bad. This belief on the part of international investors in turn constitutes the borrower's reputation, which guides their risk assessments and lending decisions (Tomz 2007, pp. 17, 23).

While I agree that reputational mechanisms are a central reason for the success of cooperative sovereign lending, more attention should be paid to how the content of reputation depends on broader contexts that may change across time, place, and creditor. The practice of assessing sovereign creditworthiness ultimately remains subjective and may be contingent upon the assessor's position. As Ashok Vir Bhatia (2002) points out, the limited predictability of sovereign economic and political behavior, as well as the absence of widespread robust statistical testing, "leave[s] the task of credit ratings assessments poorly suited to formulaic straightjackets" (Bhatia 2002, p. 12). Research into sovereign creditworthiness necessarily blends objective analysis with subjective debate. Even in theoretical studies from economics and finance, there have been questions as to the degree to which reputation formation and perceptions of credibility are fully uniform and rational in the traditional sense. Robert Frank (1988), for example, has highlighted the ways in which emotion plays a key role in the formation of reputation, apart from any objective or material determinants. James Forder (2004) points out that definitions and perceptions of credibility are not a given across different professional groups. Academic economists and central bankers, among others, have very different views on the importance and definitions of credibility, and Forder contends that this has ramifications for the ways in which credibility as a concept can be abstracted for the purposes of both academic studies and policy proposals.

These studies of the microfoundations of reputation question whether it is constant and objective in the sense assumed by much international finance. It is not generally agreed upon that reputation is a stable factor with contours that remain uniform across time, context, or creditor. Even accepting creditors' basic profit orientations, their relative economic positions and larger social contexts will likely affect how they interpret sovereign creditworthiness. While creditworthiness may be uniformly important, its particular *content* vis-à-vis a statist principle of sovereign continuity or nonstatist ideas of odious debt will likely be embedded in a historically variable political and business framework.

The Theory of Sovereignty Implicit in Creditworthiness

Just as any claim about the validity of sovereign debt depends on an underlying political and legal theory, any assessment of sovereign reputation implicitly rests on an idea of who constitutes the legitimate sovereign in sovereign borrowing. In particular, while a state could never develop a *positive* reputation after a repudiation or debt cancellation on the basis of an odious debt idea, it is an open question as to whether a *negative* reputation should necessarily result. One might reasonably expect that the willingness of a country to repay a loan depends on the degree to which its population benefited from or authorized the loan.[5] If a previous obligation was used to oppress the population or was entered into so it could facilitate corruption, then a subsequent regime's degree of willingness to repay this debt may not have much bearing on its willingness to pay legitimately contracted or publicly beneficial loans in the future.

A more open idea of sovereignty in reputational analyses would correspond to greater acceptance of an odious debt idea, due to a nonstatist acknowledgment of the centrality of popular authorization or public benefit for legitimate sovereign borrowing. Nonstatist concepts of sovereignty at work after a regime change would lead to an incoming regime requesting a fresh start in international credit, and to creditors treating such a regime not as a lemon but rather as a new or unseasoned borrower. Conversely, a statist conception of sovereignty would not distinguish between legitimate and illegitimate debt in assessing a country's repayment record as part of its creditworthiness analysis. In fact, a strictly statist approach would be *most* hostile to repudiation on the basis of something like odious debt, given that there is no acceptable economic reason for the default.[6]

In a sense, a reputational assessment's acceptance or rejection of an odious debt idea necessarily carries with it an underlying judgment about sovereignty. The reputational interpretation and financial treatment of a borrower as new or unseasoned rather than as a lemon indicates tolerance of a more open approach to sovereignty on the part of that creditor. Thus, while I agree that reputation matters, this claim is far less dispositive than is usually acknowledged. A primary focus on state creditworthiness does not in itself mandate a practice of debt continuity. What counts as a reputational harm may differ dramatically across alternative theories of sovereignty.

CONCLUSION

If, as I argue, a particular and contested theory of sovereignty grounds the repayment norms and the current reputational mechanism of the international debt regime, what is the added value of this insight? First, it opens the way for a range of empirical questions. If multiple approaches to sovereign debt are possible according to different concepts of sovereignty, have these alternatives actually emerged historically? What factors make one or another approach to sovereign debt more likely? Relatedly, given that the mechanism of creditworthiness is itself bound up with particular definitions of sovereignty, have different creditors made contrary reputational assessments that suggest distinct approaches in sovereign lending? How does one rather than another reputational framework become dominant over time or lose sway?[7]

Second, this new analytical approach creates important avenues for policy inquiry. If the centrality of reputation itself is not sufficient to explain the dominance of a statist principle of sovereign debt continuity, might the current system simply be more welfare enhancing because of moral hazard concerns? Although the brief discussion provided here precludes a full explanation, concerns about moral hazard cut in both directions and are far from determinative—an orderly practice of odious debt cancellation might arguably be more welfare enhancing.[8] From another angle, if particular sovereign debt practices depend upon and reinforce specific concepts of sovereign legitimacy, is there room for engaging with those concepts more directly? For example, if policy makers disagree with the philosophical foundations and the political ramifications of a statist vision, to what degree should they support statist outcomes in international debt? Or, alternatively, is it consistent for a regime seeking to cancel debt on the basis of odiousness to then reject inquiry into the treatment of its own population on the basis of statist claims to absolute sovereignty? At a more general level, there is room to consider whether coherence across different issue areas is even desirable, or whether it is acceptable that a policy goal pursued in one arena may be undermined by practices in another. In short, failing to acknowledge the competing definitions of sovereignty that undergird divergent practices in debt payment does little to deepen our knowledge of the sovereign debt regime. It merely covers over key questions for policy and empirical analysis and obscures the significant financial consequences of a central concept in political and legal thought.

NOTES

1. This dimension of sovereignty has been labeled *internal sovereignty*, which has also been defined as the "fundamental authority relation within states between rulers and ruled" (Jackson 1999, p. 11). It is related to what might be called *external sovereignty*, or the legal authority of a state to represent and bind its population in the international political and economic arena, as determined by international law and practice. See ibid.

2. Jens Bartelson discusses this emergence of what he calls *proto-sovereignty* in *A Genealogy of Sovereignty* (1995, pp. 141–142).

3. The legal doctrine of odious debt, first developed after the Spanish-American War of 1898 and formalized by Sack in 1927, states that sovereign state debt is odious and should not be transferable to successors if the debt was incurred (1) without the consent of the people, *and* (2) not for their benefit (Sack 1927, p. 157). Although Sack's formulation is the one cited by scholars as "the doctrine of odious debt," one could come up with endless permutations by drawing from different schools of sovereignty and varying commitments to outcome orientation. For contemporary legal analyses of the doctrine, including potential modifications, extensions, and ramifications, see the double issue on odious debt of Duke's *Journal of Law and Contemporary Problems* 70 (2007).

4. This unease is not limited to debt cancellation activists outside of finance. As a *Wall Street Journal* editorial pointed out with regard to the Iraqi debt, some creditors, "while dismissing the idea of a total Iraqi debt write-off, are at least conceding the point that not all debts are created equal" (Opinion, "Iraq's Odious Debts," *Wall Street Journal*, April 30, 2003).

5. The two standard components of risk or creditworthiness analysis are the ability and willingness of a country to meet its obligations.

6. In Tomz's assessment, such countries would be interpreted as the worst lemons and thus the most likely to be subject to strict credit rationing.

7. These questions are addressed in *Rethinking Sovereign Debt: Debt and Reputation in the 20th Century*, forthcoming from Harvard University Press.

8. One of the most frequently cited academic papers on odious debt is an essay by economists Michael Kremer and Seema Jayachandran, who advocate the creation of an institution to assess the odiousness of a regime in advance of any credit extensions. Jayachandran and Kremer (2006) contend that an orderly system based on odious debt ideas could be more welfare enhancing than the current system.

REFERENCES

Bartelson, J. 1995. *A Genealogy of Sovereignty* (Cambridge, UK: Cambridge University Press).

Bhatia, A. 2002. "Sovereign Credit Risk Ratings Methodology: An Evaluation." *IMF Working Paper* WP/03/170 (2002). www.imf.org/external/pubs/ft/wp/2002/wp02170.pdf.

Forder, J. 2004. "'Credibility' in Context: Do Central Bankers and Economists Interpret the Term Differently?" *Econ Journal Watch* 1:3, 413–426.

Frank, R. H. 1988. *Passions within Reason: The Strategic Role of the Emotions.* New York: W.W. Norton.

Jackson, R. H. 1999. "Sovereignty and world politics: A glance at the historical and conceptual landscape." In Robert H. Jackson, ed. *Sovereignty at the Millennium.* Oxford, UK: Blackwell. Also, *Journal of Law and Contemporary Problems* 70 (2007).

Jayachandran, S., and M. Kremer. 2006. "Odious Debt." *American Economic Review* 96:1, 82–92.

Lienau, O. Forthcoming. *Rethinking Sovereign Debt: Debt and Reputation in the 20th Century.* Cambridge, MA: Harvard University Press.

Sack, A. N. 1927. *Les Effets des Transformations des États sur leurs Dettes Publiques et Autres Obligations Financières.* Paris: Recueil Sirey.

Tomz, M. 2007. *Reputation and International Cooperation: Sovereign Debt across Three Centuries.* Princeton, NJ: Princeton University Press.

Wall Street Journal. 2003. "Iraq's Odious Debts; Don't Stick Saddam's Victims with the Bill for His Rule,"April 30.

ABOUT THE AUTHOR

Odette Lienau is an assistant professor of law at Cornell University. She received her PhD in government from Harvard University and her JD from New York University School of Law. She has practiced law in New York City and is a member of the New York Bar. Her book, *Rethinking Sovereign Debt: Debt and Reputation in the 20th Century,* is forthcoming from Harvard University Press.

CHAPTER 27

Odious Debts or Odious Regimes?

PATRICK BOLTON
Barbara and David Zalaznick Professor of Business, Columbia University*

DAVID A. SKEEL JR.
S. Samuel Arsht Professor of Corporate Law, University of Pennsylvania
Law School

C urrent odious debt doctrine—using the term *doctrine* loosely, since it has never been formally adopted by a court or international decision maker—dates back to a 1927 treatise by a wandering Russian academic named Alexander Sack.[1] After surveying the handful of occasions in which a successor regime had repudiated the obligations of its predecessor as unenforceable, Sack suggested that debt obligations are odious and therefore unenforceable if they were incurred without the consent of the populace, they did not benefit the populace, and the lender knew or should have known about the absence of consent and benefit.[2]

The Sack definition contemplates a debt-by-debt approach to questionable borrowing. If a loan is used to benefit the population—to build a highway or water-treatment plant, for example—the obligation would be fully enforceable, no matter how pernicious the borrower regime. Loans that a ruler used to oppress the people, on the other hand, or diverted for his own purposes would be unenforceable if the lender knew or should have known the loan proceeds would be misused. The Sack definition is designed to nullify odious obligations without discouraging lenders from funding projects that provide genuine benefits.

As attractive as it sounds, however, the debt-by-debt approach has a debilitating weakness: Money is fungible. A loan ostensibly incurred for beneficent purposes often may simply free up other money for misuse. The fungibility of money seriously limits the efficacy of debt-by-debt strategies for policing the borrowing of pernicious regimes.

In this paper, we propose and defend an alternative approach: focusing on the odiousness of the regime, rather than on the nature of a particular loan. We begin

---

*An earlier version of this paper appeared in a 2008 symposium in *Law and Contemporary Problems*.

with the basic question, elided by the few commentators who have advocated similar approaches, of how to define an odious regime.[3] A regime is odious, we argue, if it engages in either systematic suppression or systematic looting. Odious regimes sometimes suppress a subgroup of the population, as with blacks in apartheid South Africa and Jews in Nazi Germany, and they sometimes suppress the entire population, as with Idi Amin's Uganda. The suppression is often, but not always, accompanied by looting. Every odious regime is marked by one, the other, or both.

Once *odious regime* is defined, the question is how to make the definition operative. We propose that two existing institutions, the United Nations (U.N.) and the International Monetary Fund (IMF), share responsibility for identifying odious regimes. The U.N. is best positioned to determine whether a regime is engaging in systematic suppression, while the IMF would assess concerns about looting and other, similar, financial depredations.

PRACTICAL OBSTACLES AND ALTERNATIVE APPROACHES

Despite its pedigree, Sack's intuitively appealing, three-part definition of odious debts—no consent, no benefit, and awareness of these facts by the lender—has never been formally adopted. One obvious reason for the doctrine's precarious status is the difficulty of applying it in practice. A robust odious debt doctrine might also have damaging implications for the cost of borrowing by sovereigns as lenders stiffened the terms of their loans to protect themselves against the risk those loans would later be deemed odious.

Spurred by the campaigns to cancel the debt of African nations and by the renegotiation of Iraq's Saddam Hussein–era debt, scholars have devised a variety of new proposals addressing these concerns. With one prominent recent exception, both current commentators and their predecessors have advocated a debt-by-debt approach to resolving sovereign-debt issues.[4] In principle, the debt-by-debt approach has a great deal to recommend it. Even corrupt regimes sometimes undertake some projects that benefit their citizens—for example, developing the nation's infrastructure by building roads or bridges. In practice, however, debt-by-debt strategy would be devilishly difficult to apply. One problem is that loans to corrupt rulers are often both good and bad, rather than entirely one or the other. A second problem is even more intractable: Money is fungible. As a result, a loan that is made for ostensibly beneficial purposes may free up other money to be used corruptly, even if the loan is in fact used as promised.

The limitations of the debt-by-debt strategy suggest that an alternative approach focusing less on particular debts and more on the nature of the regime is worth a closer look.

ODIOUS REGIMES: A DEFINITION

Odious debt scholars have yet to develop a definition of what constitutes an odious regime. In part, the vacuum seems to reflect a conclusion that the odiousness of regimes is too contentious an issue to get into. The perceived difficulty of devising a workable definition may also be a factor.

To more fully convey both the importance and the potential stumbling blocks of the project, it may be useful to begin by highlighting two key impediments. The first is widely divergent intuitions as to the odiousness of particular regimes. The U.S. government would no doubt be quick to label the Chavez government in Venezuela and Castro's Cuba as odious. The governments of other countries, on the other hand, including some in Europe, might not be so sure. Another difficulty is that the most obvious starting point—whether the country is a dictatorship or a democracy—turns out to be much less useful than one might wish. Venezuela and Peru are both democracies, but some might be inclined to characterize each as odious. On the other hand, although Singapore is a dictatorship, most would be hesitant to question its borrowing as potentially odious.

Perhaps the best way to move beyond the initial impasse is to identify the qualities of regimes that are undeniably odious. Most commentators would agree that Nazi Germany, Cambodia's Khmer Rouge, South Africa's apartheid, Zaire's Mobutu, Chile's Pinochet, Rwanda's Hutu government and Interahamwe and Impuzamugambi militia groups, Serbia's nationalist government of Slobodan Milosevic, Uganda's Idi Amin, Zimbabwe's Robert Mugabe, Liberia's Charles Taylor, or North Korea's regimes of Kim Il-Sung and Kim Jong-Il were or are odious. What do these regimes have in common? One common theme is that nearly all, by the standards of their time, used extreme oppression and brutality to suppress a particular ethnic group or the population at large. Some of the regimes are or were also characterized by systematic looting of their country's wealth by its leaders. Thus, an odious regime is, first, one that has an overt policy of terror and oppression, and denies the basic well-being, freedoms, and human rights of its people. And, second, it is a regime that is engaged in a policy of systematic looting for the benefit of the ruling elite. A regime that has either or both of these attributes is, in our view, an odious regime.

Systematic suppression, the first of the two alternative indicators of odiousness, is the broader of the two and requires some elaboration. A key component of systematic suppression is the absence of voice. Given that dictatorship removes the most obvious channel for citizen voice—the right to choose their leaders—it is not surprising that many of the patently odious regimes—Cambodia, Uganda, Nazi Germany—have been dictatorial. But citizens do not always lose their voice in a dictatorship or other autocratic government; they sometimes have alternative mechanisms for influencing their leadership. Civil society organizations can serve as a check on a dictatorial government if they are allowed to speak freely, as can the media if it is not controlled or censored by the government. An undemocratic regime may also be widely tolerated—if not accepted—by the population if it broadly rules in the interests of its people; preserves basic human rights, if not the rights to self-expression; and is seen as keeping a lid on potential costly conflicts, as in Tito's Yugoslavia.

Democracy has precisely the opposite relationship to voice. Robust democracy is the classic example of effective voice. But the presence of a democratic form of government, and even regular elections, does not by itself assure that citizens have a meaningful voice.

The key question, then, is not so much whether the government is a dictatorship, a democracy, or something in between. It is whether ordinary citizens, those who are governed, are themselves in a position to influence their rulers or are able to protect their basic rights. If they are not (or a large, identifiable subset is not), the citizens do not have a voice.

In a regime that engages in systematic suppression, the absence of voice invariably is accompanied by the brutal denial of basic rights. Citizens or a disfavored class may be systematically persecuted, have their property seized, and have their most basic freedoms denied; they may be murdered or jailed at the whim of the government; they may be prevented from leaving the country. These deprivations stifle potential dissent, completing the pattern of suppression.

The other indication of an odious regime is systematic plundering of a country's riches for the benefit of the ruling elite. The plundering is often facilitated by an absence of transparency with respect to the government's operations, its revenues, and how they are allocated. Nigeria's Abacha regime plundered much of Nigeria's tax and oil revenues. Several of the regimes identified as clearly odious in this section engaged in similarly pervasive plundering. In our view, a regime that exhibits this behavior is an odious regime.

A regime that is characterized *either* by systematic suppression or by systematic plundering is odious. Although many odious regimes will meet both criteria, some will not. South Africa's apartheid regime did not systematically plunder, for example, but it systematically suppressed the black population and would decidedly qualify as odious. Short of an international peacekeeping intervention to topple such regimes, these regimes should, to the extent possible, be denied access to international financial markets, and their citizens should not have to bear the financial burden of repaying the debts incurred by the regimes.

Consider how the definition might apply to three current and historical regimes. First, a particularly difficult case: the United States before the end of slavery. Although blacks were denied both the vote and basic human rights, antebellum the United States did not particularly stand out as odious compared with the rest of the world. As ugly as the history is, there probably would not have been widespread consensus for identifying the United States as odious. Second, Americans view Hugo Chavez's Venezuela as an odious regime, given the demagogic quality of Chavez's rhetoric and his aggressive anti-Americanism. But Venezuela does not meet either criterion for an odious regime. Finally, one current regime that does qualify as odious, as reflected in its inclusion on the list of odious regimes at the outset of the discussion, is Zimbabwe under Robert Mugabe. There are no genuine elections or free media, and civic-society organizations have been almost entirely stifled. He also has denied basic rights by jailing potential dissenters and engaging in a campaign of expropriation of white landowners, among others. The overall pattern is one of systematic suppression that can only be described as odious.

REMEDIES AND THE ROLE OF THE U.N. AND IMF AS DECISION MAKERS

How would an odious regime policy be operationalized? Rather than isolate and anoint a single decision maker, we envision a role for both the U.N.'s Security Council and the IMF's executive board in enforcing an odious regime policy. The U.N. is best placed to make the political judgment and to elicit an international consensus on whether a regime systematically denies a voice to its people and is engaged in unrelenting suppression. The IMF, on the other hand, is better placed through its Article IV surveillance mission to determine whether a regime is engaged in systematic plundering.

The Timing Question: When Should the Decision Be Made?

Before exploring the roles we envision for the U.N. and IMF in more detail, it may be useful to briefly address the question of timing. Should the determination of odiousness be made ex ante, while the regime is in place and before debts are incurred, or after the regime has been removed?

The timing of the condemnation of a regime should be flexible, determined both by the time when sufficient evidence of malfeasance has emerged and by political feasibility. Even if an early declaration is not possible and the regime or its bad policies have disappeared before a declaration has been made, an ex post declaration would still provide important benefits.

The U.N. Security Council as Arbiter of Systematic Suppression

The U.N. Security Council is empowered to impose sanctions under Chapter VII of its charter as an alternative and supplement to armed peacekeeping interventions. Under this provision, the Security Council already has the authority to implement an odious regime policy. Indeed, the U.N. and some of its member countries have recently introduced targeted financial sanctions, ranging from freezing financial assets to barring and even criminalizing financial transactions of targeted organizations and individuals.[5] There is thus a small step from implementing these types of sanctions to implementing an odious regime policy. The only innovation would be the added reach of denying enforcement of debt repayments for *any* debts incurred by an odious regime. Even here, the policy could be implemented flexibly, by targeting only the debts that have been incurred at a time when clear evidence confirmed the regime's odious policies.

There are inevitable concerns with a U.N.-overseen odious regime policy. Four in particular stand out. The first issue is the U.N. itself. Even apart from concerns about internal management at the U.N., the U.N. Security Council might fail to condemn odious regimes that happen to be on friendly terms with a majority of countries or are allies of a permanent member on the Security Council. The U.N.'s reluctance to attach the label of genocide to widespread persecution in Sudan and elsewhere is an illustration of this problem. Although the risk of foot-dragging must be acknowledged, in those instances when the Security Council did act, its pronouncement would better reflect international mores than that of another international decision maker. Moreover, even if the Security Council almost never condemned existing regimes, it might be more willing to condemn regimes after they lost power.

A second set of concerns relate to the scope of the proposal: Which debts would be invalidated by the determination that a regime is odious? If all of a country's debt were canceled, regardless of when and by which regime it had been incurred, the government succeeding an odious regime might default too liberally on the country's outstanding debts. This risk suggests an obvious limitation on the scope of debt cancellation: Only the debts incurred while the regime qualified as odious should be annulled. A more difficult question is how to treat debts incurred by the odious regime in the process of rolling over past debts it has inherited from a predecessor that was not odious. Should the originally legitimate debts be annulled? Yes: All the debts incurred by the odious regime should in principle be voided, whether these debts are incurred to service older debts or not, as this would allow for the strongest financial sanction on the regime.

In addition to these questions of scope, a third concern is that the implementation of an odious regime policy could result in the permanent exclusion of a few pariah states from the international community. It is thus important to include a procedure and conditions under which a regime branded as odious can reverse this international condemnation.

The final concern with the implementation of an odious regime policy, or for that matter, with any sanctions against an odious regime, is the humanitarian concern that the main victims of the sanctions may be the populations oppressed by odious regimes. The odious regime policy must be adjusted to allow access to credit even for an odious regime if the policy is likely to have destructive effects. A humanitarian escape clause to the odious regime policy would do this: It would permit the enforcement of debts by an odious regime in extreme circumstances to avoid a humanitarian crisis.

Taking Aim at Plundering: The International Monetary Fund's Executive Board

Under its Article IV surveillance mission, the IMF already conducts regular, extensive financial reviews of each of its members.[6] Not only will the review often uncover evidence of plundering, but the report that accompanies it could lay the groundwork for IMF action. If a regime were found to be odious, the IMF could impose two separate sanctions. First, the Fund would deny access to IMF liquidity assistance in a crisis. Second, it would declare any debts incurred by the odious regime unenforceable. The IMF board would decide whether to condemn a regime as odious in the same way the board decides on whether to grant a program to a member country facing a temporary liquidity crisis.

Although our approach bears a family resemblance to the IMF's use of ex ante conditionality in other contexts, an approach that has been harshly criticized, IMF implementation of an odious regime policy is far less troubling because of its much narrower scope. Rather than applying to every member country, as ex ante conditionalities would, the odious regime policy would be limited to extreme cases. That is, the policy would be enforced only against odious regimes, hopefully a rare occurrence.

Also, unlike with benign but financially precarious regimes, precipitating a financial crisis for an odious regime would be—*modulo* the humanitarian concerns discussed earlier—only for the better. Odious regimes tend to arise when there are civil wars or other forms of conflict between polarized factions. From this perspective, an odious regime policy would have the countervailing effect of raising the financial costs of conflict, as any victorious odious regime would not be able to borrow in international financial markets. If a plundering government is either forced to stop its pillage or forced out of power because of a financial crisis triggered by the IMF's condemnation of the odious predatory regime, the crisis would actually improve that country's welfare.

CONCLUSION

This chapter has made two main contributions to the odious debt debate. First, it states a case for shifting from debt-by-debt approaches to a policy that seeks to identity odious regimes. Because the literature seems to lack a well-developed definition of odious regime, a new definition is offered here: A regime is odious if it engages in either systematic suppression or systematic plundering. Second, the chapter provided a road map for implementing this definition of odious debt. The proposal set forth here could be implemented by existing decision makers employing their existing expertise.

It may be that odious regimes will always be with us. But we believe an odious regime policy could curb some odious regimes, and perhaps prevent others, by giving the international community a new tool for taking a stand against unconscionable regimes.

NOTES

1. Alexander N. Sack, *Les Effets des Transformations des Etats sur leurs Dettes Publiques et Autres Obligations Financieres* (Paris: Recueil Sirey, 1927), available at www.odiousdebts.org/odiousdebts/publications/dettes_publiques.html (last visited January 19, 2007).
2. Id. at 157.
3. See, for example, Seema Jayachandran, Michael Kremer, and Jonathan Shafter, "Applying Odious Debts Doctrine While Preserving Legitimate Lending" (2005) (hereinafter Jayachandran et al., "Legitimate Lending"); unpublished manuscript, available at www.economics.harvard.edu/faculty/kremer/papers/Odious_Debt_Doctrine.pdf; Seema Jayachandran and Michael Kremer, "Odious Debt," *American Economic Review* 96 (2006): 82.
4. See note 3. In their initial article, Jayachandran and Kremer considered only the odiousness of the regime. In their more recent article, Jayachandran et al., "Legitimate Lending," they develop a due diligence model that would enforce obligations owed to an odious regime if the lender conducted an adequate investigation before lending.
5. The U.N. Security Council does not have the authority under Chapter VII to directly alter the domestic laws of the U.N.'s member nations. Rather, it instructs the members to adjust their laws.
6. For an overview of the IMF's Article IV surveillance obligations, see, for example, "Legal Department, IMF, Article IV of the Fund's Articles of Agreement: An Overview of the Legal Framework" (2006), available at www.internationalmonetaryfund.com/external/np/pp/eng/2006/062806.pdf.

ABOUT THE AUTHORS

Patrick Bolton is the Barbara and David Zalaznick professor of business and member of the Committee on Global Thought at Columbia University. He is also co-director of the Center for Contracts and Economic Organization at the Columbia Law School. His areas of interest are in corporate finance, political economy, and law and economics. A central focus of his research is on the allocation of control and decision rights to contracting parties when long-term contracts are incomplete and when contracting parties are boundedly rational. This issue is relevant in many different contexts, including the firm's choice of optimal debt structure, corporate governance, the boundaries of the firm, and constitution design. He recently published *Contract Theory* (MIT Press, 2005) with Mathias Dewatripont and co-edited *Credit Markets for the Poor* (Russell Sage Foundation, 2005) with Howard Rosenthal.

David A. Skeel Jr. is the S. Samuel Arsht professor of corporate law at the University of Pennsylvania Law School. He is the author of *The New Financial Deal* (John Wiley & Sons, 2010), *Icarus in the Boardroom: The Fundamental Flaws in Corporate America and Where They Came From* (Oxford, 2005), and *Debt's Dominion: A History of Bankruptcy Law in America* (Princeton, 2001), as well as "Redesigning the International Lender of Last Resort" (*Chicago Journal of International Law*, 2005, with Patrick Bolton) and other articles on sovereign debt, bankruptcy, and corporate law. He also has written commentaries for the *New York Times*, the *Wall Street Journal*, the *Weekly Standard*, and other publications.

CHAPTER 28

Insolvency Principles

The Missing Link in the Odious Debt Debate

A. MECHELE DICKERSON
Arthur L. Moller Chair in Bankruptcy Law and Practice, The University of Texas School of Law

B ecause of the public international law concept of state succession, sovereigns remain liable for the debts of predecessor governments whether prior leaders are democratically removed from office or are replaced as a result of a violent overthrow or war. Even if the former leader or regime was brutal or despotic and the debts provided few (if any) benefits to the sovereign's citizens, the sovereign's citizens nonetheless are obligated to repay those debts.

Whenever a brutal leader (like Iraq's Saddam Hussein) or repressive regime (like the South African apartheid government) is replaced, members of the international human rights community inevitably argue that it is unfair to force the country's oppressed citizens to repay their loans. It seems especially unjust to make citizens liable for a former leaders' debts if the borrowed funds were used for activities that harmed the citizens or were used to purchase items that only benefited the leaders, their regimes, or their associates. The notion that a sovereign's citizens should be relieved of odious debts is grounded, almost exclusively, on philosophical and humanitarian considerations. To date, the global financial community has adamantly and consistently refused to restructure sovereign debts based solely on the humanitarian grounds that form the basis of the odious debt doctrine. To bolster the argument that sovereigns should be able to restructure odious debts, advocates for this doctrine should stop focusing exclusively on human rights principles and should, instead, incorporate the fundamental principles that permeate U.S. insolvency laws.

While sovereigns lend money to each other, private lenders finance most sovereign debt. The International Monetary Fund (IMF) provides humanitarian aid to sovereigns in its capacity as an international development institution. Members of the private financial community however, often criticize IMF lending practices because the lending criteria are rarely based on the debtor's creditworthiness or borrowing capacity. Indeed, critics argue that because the IMF often serves as the lender of last resort, its lending practices create a moral hazard problem that encourages sovereigns to borrow recklessly (and then wait for an IMF bailout) and encourages creditors to lend recklessly (and then assume that the IMF bailout will ensure their imprudent loans will be repaid). Human rights activists criticize IMF and World Bank lending policies as well, accusing those institutions of knowingly lending to repressive regimes that then divert the loan proceeds to their personal use or use the proceeds to finance activities that affirmatively harm the countries' citizens.

For the last several years, most sovereign debt has been unsecured bond debt. Even when the loans are secured by collateral, though, lenders' collection options are more tenuous than the ones they can exercise when a private entity is the borrower. For example, to preserve the collateral to satisfy the debt either before or after judgment, the lender must first locate the sovereign's assets and find a way to seize or preserve those assets before the assets are moved beyond the reach of the collecting creditor. Even if a lender has a security interest in immovable assets, like the sovereign's oil revenue or exports, the lender cannot easily take control of the oil wells or otherwise seize collateral located within the sovereign.

Lenders also are constrained in their ability to use the judicial process to collect sovereign debts. Specifically, the sovereign's courts (not surprisingly) will favor the sovereign in disputes with a lender (especially one based outside the sovereign). Adjudicating the dispute in another nation also poses procedural and political challenges, as courts in other nations may be unable or unwilling to resolve a commercial dispute between the sovereign and the lender unless the sovereign has consented to suit or is not otherwise immune from suit.

The combination of IMF lending policies and debt collection difficulties should, theoretically, give sovereigns an incentive to opportunistically default on their debts. Yet, sovereigns generally avoid defaulting on their debts. One reason sovereigns appear to avoid defaults is because defaults often trigger economic recessions, which then may force the sovereigns' leaders to raise taxes or make severe cuts in public expenditures on social programs. Leaders who are democratically elected justifiably avoid actions that threaten their political careers or otherwise give citizens an incentive to oust them during the next election cycle, and even dictators and despots have an incentive to avoid actions that may result in political upheaval.

Sovereigns fear that not repaying their loans will signal to the international capital markets that they are not creditworthy. Similarly, sovereigns also avoid defaulting because any attempt to restructure their debts necessarily will trigger a politicized, multistep process that will force them to engage in often prolonged negotiations with their domestic and external lenders. Restructuring sovereign debt is complicated because no uniform international statute, convention, or treaty governs sovereign debt restructurings. Because of this, sovereigns who owe debts to other sovereigns restructure these debts through an informal arrangement known as the Paris Club. These negotiations—though generally viewed as closed, nontransparent, and cumbersome—are efficient, quick, and relatively inexpensive because public creditors typically make concessions based on nonfinancial, geopolitical considerations. Private negotiations between sovereigns and their private commercial lenders most often occur in an arrangement known as the London Club. Unlike Paris Club restructurings, London Club negotiations tend to be longer and less efficient largely because commercial creditors have less of an incentive to forgive sovereign debts because of any perceived future or geopolitical relationships with the defaulting sovereign.

Because most leaders choose not to default on the sovereign's debts, successor governments must find a way to repay those debts since the old debts represent obligations of the state, not the debts of the former political party or leader. As demonstrated when Saddam Hussein was forcibly removed from power, forcing the oppressed citizens of a country to repay debts incurred by a former brutal leader who may have funded the acts of oppression using the proceeds of the very loans that the citizens are being forced to repay is controversial. The *odious debt* doctrine posits that successor governments are *not* liable to repay (in full, or at all) a prior regime's odious debts if the lender knew that the former political leader incurred debts or used the proceeds of loans to strengthen his regime, to repress political opponents, or to serve manifestly personal interests unrelated to the sovereign's interests.

Despite its laudable goals, the odious debt doctrine has never been formally acknowledged or endorsed by private or public lending institutions or by any powerful creditor nation, including the United States. The international financial community has refused to recognize the odious debt doctrine based on concerns that applying the doctrine would destabilize and generally create chaos in the international financial markets. Critics of the doctrine further contend that allowing sovereigns to repudiate debts based on humanitarian grounds will have unintended consequences because the resulting uncertainty in sovereign lending will retard the economic growth of emerging-market borrowers by making lenders less likely to lend funds to *all* developing nations—even those that have democratically elected regimes.

Notwithstanding these criticisms, basic insolvency principles embodied in the U.S. bankruptcy code (the Code) can and should be used to justify allowing a sovereign to repudiate debts if doing so enhances the sovereign's ability to reorganize itself politically and financially. At their core, U.S. insolvency laws are designed to ensure that people and businesses can shed some of their debts to ensure their long-term survival. The Code's fresh-start policy recognizes that allowing people to discharge some of their present debts makes it possible for them to have a viable ongoing financial future. The fresh-start policy embodied in Chapter 11 of the Code is designed to help financially distressed businesses modify their debts and continue to operate if the business is worth more as an ongoing concern than its parts would be if the business were to be liquidated. To preserve the value of viable businesses, Chapter 11 lets companies restructure and often eliminate some of their debts if doing so allows them to remain in operation and continue to perform their core business functions.

The U.S. insolvency system has long operated on the basis of the premise that an agreed-upon entity, that is, the U.S. Congress, applying clear factors, that is, federal bankruptcy laws, can allow a debtor to restructure its contractual obligations *even if* the restructuring causes a breach. Like businesses reorganizing under Chapter 11 or people who discharge some of their debts in a bankruptcy case, a sovereign will continue to exist and operate whether it repays odious debts, refuses to pay them, or has the debts forgiven. While the odious debt doctrine admittedly violates the basic principle that contracts should be honored, insolvency laws—by design—help debtors legally breach contracts. That is, though the Code respects the sanctity of contracts and makes it hard for debtors to breach contracts, it nonetheless allows debtors to restructure, and in some circumstances erase, some of their contractual obligations. Given this, the odious debt doctrine (carefully constructed and applied) could allow sovereigns to restructure (or, if needed, erase) some of their debt obligations.

Members of the global financial community have long been aware that their lending arrangements with U.S. businesses might be partially or totally restructured and, as a result, they might receive less than the full amount they are owed. Despite this knowledge, lenders remain willing to finance the future business operations of Chapter 11 debtors. Likewise, a sovereign's decision to restructure its debt structure and reduce its debt overhang (by eliminating its odious debts) should not make it impossible for them to borrow in the future or otherwise attract new investments as long as the sovereign's future lenders are assured (as Chapter 11 lenders are)[1] that the new capital will have a higher priority in payment.

For reasons based on U.S. insolvency principles, sovereigns should be allowed to modify their debts to powerful commercial lenders or creditor nations since the Code allows debtors to modify debts owed to favored creditor groups. For example, while secured creditors are favored by both insolvency and general commercial laws, under certain circumstances debtors can invalidate creditor's liens that otherwise would be enforceable under applicable nonbankruptcy law.[2] Likewise, debtors are allowed to refuse to perform (that is, reject) certain commercially unfavorable contracts and leases and can then pay the other nonbreaching party's claims for less than the creditor would be entitled to receive under nonbankruptcy laws.[3] Debtors also can force unsecured creditors who receive money from the debtor (whether innocently or as the result of aggressive collection efforts) just before the bankruptcy filing to return those preferential payments even if the creditor's conduct was proper and the creditor would be allowed to keep the payments under applicable state law.[4] Finally, while unsecured student educational loans generally cannot be restructured, debtors who have tried but are unable to repay their loans can restructure this debt upon a showing that forcing them to repay the loans would cause them or their families an undue hardship and that it is not likely that they will be able to repay the loans in the near future.[5]

Other favored creditors may face even more draconian treatment in bankruptcy. In recent years, businesses have used Chapter 11 to restructure their pension and health care obligations to employees and former employees. Though nonbankruptcy law generally prevents businesses from breaching contracts or terminating their labor obligations with their employees, the Code lets businesses reject or modify their obligations to current and former employees if they can show that these changes are necessary for the business to reorganize.[6] Indeed, a number of steel and airline companies have been allowed to use Chapter 11 to restructure their pension and health obligations to their employees based on their contention that making them honor these obligations would force them to liquidate an otherwise financially stable company.

Whether or not human rights principles support the odious debt doctrine, letting a nation restructure debts that provided little (or no) benefits to its citizens is consistent with the general insolvency principles and specific provisions found in the Code. That is, while most debtors fail the student loan undue hardship test, that the Code lets debtors discharge these favored loans supports the view that sovereigns should be allowed to restructure odious debts if forcing debt repayment would cause the debtor (the sovereign) or the debtor's dependents (the citizens) an undue hardship and if repaying the debts would impede the sovereign's efforts to attract future investments. Similarly, just as the Code lets businesses and people invalidate liens, recover prebankruptcy payments or repudiate their labor obligations to current and former employees if these actions are needed to help the company survive and continue to perform their core business functions, a sovereign should be allowed to breach contracts to avoid a state of functional insolvency that would prevent it from exercising its core business function of ensuring the safety, and providing for the general welfare of, its citizens. Indeed, even if a successor regime theoretically could use the country's resources (for example, oil reserves or other natural resources) to repay odious debts over an extended period, insolvency principles would justify excusing the sovereign from debt repayment upon a showing that forcing repayment would destroy the sovereign's credibility with its own (oppressed) citizens, render it incapable of investing in the country's physical infrastructure, force it to neglect the health, safety, or educational needs of its citizens, or prevent it from reentering the international community and attracting new investments.

One final insolvency principle, equitable subordination, also could justify allowing a sovereign to restructure odious debts. The equitable subordination doctrine lets debtors reorder the payment priority of certain claims or invalidate certain lenders' security interests in collateral if the creditor is found to have engaged in inequitable or fraudulent conduct that harms other creditors or confers an unfair advantage on the individual creditor.[7] Applying this principle to the odious debt debate would make lenders understand that their debts could be subordinated and this knowledge would give lenders an ex ante incentive to engage in due diligence before making a loan to a despotic leader. Knowing that their debts could be subordinated also would give lenders a greater ex ante incentive to monitor whether the loan proceeds were being used to benefit the nation's citizens or, instead, were being diverted to the personal use of the leader or his friends, political supporters, or family.[8]

In conclusion, just as parties involved in a commercial out-of-court debt restructuring negotiate in the shadow of bankruptcy, sovereigns and their human rights allies will always raise the specter of the sovereign repudiating odious debts whenever a repressive leader or regime is removed from power. Rather than continuing to frame the debate solely in human rights terms that suggest that a commercial lender has a moral or philosophical duty to renegotiate its debts, sovereigns and their allies should incorporate basic principles that permeate insolvency systems when they attempt to restructure their odious debts.

NOTES

1. 11 U.S.C. § 364.
2. U.C.C. § 9-317; 11 U.S.C. § 544.
3. 11 U.S.C. § 365(a), 502(g)(1).
4. 11 U.S.C. § 547(b). Under most state fraudulent transfer laws, only insiders who have knowledge that the debtor is insolvent will be forced to return preferential payments. See Unif. Fraudulent Transfer Act 5(b).
5. 11 U.S.C. § 523(a)(8).

6. 11 U.S.C. § 1113; 11 U.S.C. § 1114; 29 U.S.C. § 1342(c)(2)(B)(ii)(I)–(IV).

7. 11 U.S.C. § 510.

8. While there is no universally recognized list of odious regimes, it is disingenuous to suggest that international lenders cannot assess whether a regime is engaging in harmful activities or is making inappropriate uses of loan proceeds. International organizations, including the United Nations Security Council, routinely condemn nations that have despotic, brutal leaders or that otherwise engage in brutal practices, and the World Bank routinely lists countries with corrupt governments to whom it has refused to lend.

ABOUT THE AUTHOR

A. Mechele Dickerson is the Arthur L. Moller chair in bankruptcy law and practice at the University of Texas School of Law. She received her BA and JD from Harvard University and taught at William and Mary School of Law before joining the Texas faculty. She is a nationally recognized bankruptcy scholar and has written extensively in the consumer, business, and international insolvency areas. Her current research focuses on the U.S. housing crisis and the relationship between housing costs and education.

PART V

Historical Perspectives

S overeign borrowing has been around for as long as there have been states or even quasi-states, so the saga of sovereign debt has many chapters. The chapters in this section highlight some of the more dramatic events in this history, with a view to providing instruction about the management of sovereign debt in the future. Many of us today are aware of the demise of Barings Bank, a venerable British merchant bank that was destroyed by its notorious rogue trader, Nick Leeson, in 1995. Less well known is the almost fatal experience of Barings Bank in the general wave of defaults on sovereign debt that swept Latin America in the 1890s.

More recently, scholars have explored the performance of the sovereign debt market during the stresses of World War II. For example, one chapter in this section examines how the sovereign debt market anticipated the onset of war, while a second examines the political costs of default. Even more recently, the final chapter in this section examines the performance of sovereign debt spreads in emerging markets at the dawn of the twenty-first century.

CHAPTER 29

The Baring Crisis and the Great Latin American Meltdown of the 1890s

KRIS JAMES MITCHENER
Robert and Susan Finocchio Professor of Economics, Santa Clara University
and National Bureau of Economic Research[*]

MARC D. WEIDENMIER
William F. Podlich Associate Professor of Economics, Claremont McKenna College
and National Bureau of Economic Research

T he widespread occurrence of emerging market financial crises in the past several decades has sparked interest among economists and investors in understanding their nature, causes, and consequences. These episodes are often characterized by volatile capital flows, unsustainable or noncredible commitments to fixed exchange rates, currency mismatches, liquidity mismatches, and weak regulation and supervision of banking systems. Other studies have emphasized the role of contagion, the process through which a shock in one country can lead to a price movement in another country in excess of the underlying fundamentals.[1] For example, some research has pointed to the role of asymmetric information, informed and uninformed investors, and political variables in the transmission of the Asian financial crisis.[2] Other studies have noted the importance of common creditors in propagating crises. To reduce overall portfolio risk, financial institutions in the common-creditor country (one with large holdings of emerging market debt) reduce or sell off their assets in the entire region, especially in countries that have characteristics similar to the crisis country.[3]

To provide some historical insight into the global and regional effects of financial crises, we examine the most famous sovereign debt default of the nineteenth century—the Baring Crisis of 1890. The crisis originated in Argentina, and was then transmitted back to London through the House of Baring (an investment bank in London that held large amounts of Argentine debt that could not be placed in the London market). Most previous studies have examined the effect of the crisis on

---

[*]This survey is based on Mitchener and Weidenmier (2008).

Argentina or the Bank of England's rescue operation of the House of Baring.[4] We break new ground by thoroughly examining the global effects of the Baring Crisis on a sample of 41 emerging market borrowers. Using a new database of more than 15,000 weekly sovereign debt prices collected from *The Economist*, the empirical analysis of sovereign yield spreads suggests that the Baring Crisis was primarily a regional crisis. Interest rates for Latin American countries increased by more than 600 basis points between 1890 and 1895. In contrast, yield spreads for non-Latin emerging markets and core countries (high income European countries and the United States) were generally flat or unchanged during this period. This finding is consistent with the literature on modern crises and contagion that emphasizes their regional nature.[5]

THE BARING CRISIS OF 1890

The world debt crisis of 1873 and the ensuing recession had large economic effects on Argentina and Latin America. The region did not recover from the downturn until the early 1880s—after the resolution to wars with indigenous peoples living in the pampas in the late 1870s. With the election of the war hero, Julio Roca, as president, Argentina witnessed a resurgence of foreign trade and capital flows from Europe. Argentina absorbed roughly 11 percent of all new issues in the new London market between 1884 and 1890 and 40 to 50 percent of all lending that occurred outside the United Kingdom in 1889. (In contrast, North America had a population 20 times Argentina's and floated only 30 percent of the new issues in London.) Taylor (2003) suggests that "the 1880s stand out as a period of totally unprecedented capital inflows into an emerging market at any time in history." The current account deficit, as a percent of GDP, averaged 20 percent from 1884 to 1889.

Although the economic policies of the 1880s stimulated short-run economic activity in Argentina, they posed potentially serious long-run financing challenges. The financing of railroads and land improvement projects were aimed at promoting internal development, exports, and economic growth. The expanding national debt could only be serviced if the country had sufficient tax revenues for debt service. Unfortunately, it would take years before the government would realize significant revenues from commercial activity stimulated by the infrastructure investments.

Beginning in the mid-1880s, loose monetary and fiscal policies substantially worsened macroeconomic conditions in Argentina. The monetary base grew at an annual average rate of 18 percent (driven by the issuance of paper currency emissions), inflation averaged 17 percent, and the paper peso depreciated at an average rate of 19 percent between 1884 and 1890 (Ford 1956). Argentina was also running a substantial budget deficit. The Argentine economy worsened toward the end of the decade, with as much as 40 percent of foreign borrowing going toward debt service and 60 percent of imports going toward the purchase of (noninvestment) consumption goods. Railway net profits were declining and gold pesos were trading at a large premium (94 percent) relative to paper pesos. The former finance minister Jose Terry suggested that, "until the end of 1887, it was possible to save the patient. In 1888, it already was no longer possible."[6]

By the end of the decade, it was becoming clear to the financial community that paper pesos were inadequate to cover the normal service on the internal and external debt. In 1889, the government broke its promise and paid off some of its gold-denominated liabilities with paper currency. In response, primary issues on the London market were met with a tepid response, and investors dumped paper pesos in anticipation of a further decline in its value. The government used the gold (that backed the note issues) to defend the exchange rate, but by December 1889, the stock of gold at the Banco Nacional had dwindled such that it could no longer carry out this intervention in the currency market. Strikes, demonstrations, and a failed coup by military leaders erupted in 1889–1890 as the real wage of Argentine workers declined with the rising price level. Domestic political strife further reduced the willingness of foreign investors to hold Argentine securities. The questionable fiscal and monetary policies drained the banking system of specie, provoked multiple banks to experience runs beginning in 1890, and thus ushered in a financial crisis. A series of last-minute tax and fiscal reforms in the summer of 1890 slowed down the economic decline, but did not prevent the ensuing financial crisis.

Even though the Baring Crisis had its origins in Argentina, its effects were quickly felt in other parts of the world, including London.[7] Baring Brothers, the firm that underwrote most of Argentina's foreign debt issues, was not sheltered from that country's problems. On the verge of bankruptcy and unable to meet its debt obligations, the House of Baring notified the Bank of England of its financial problems in early November 1890. The central bank pooled resources from the Bank of France, Russia's central bank, and British financial institutions to form a rescue fund to save the troubled financial institution that threatened to bring down British financial markets. The rescue operation succeeded and prevented a general financial collapse on European markets. Although actions by the Bank of England avoided a major financial collapse on European markets, the central bank did little to help debt-ridden Argentina. The South American country defaulted on nearly £48 million of debt in 1890, which ended up constituting nearly 60 percent of the world's defaulted debt in the 1890s. Argentina's real GDP fell by 11 percent during 1890 and 1891. Argentina suffered a deep recession for several years and did not fully recover from the crisis until the turn of the century, following a debt workout and more than a decade of monetary and fiscal reforms.

MOVEMENTS IN EMERGING MARKET YIELD SPREADS

To provide some insight into the regional and global aspects of the Baring Crisis, we collected weekly prices on long-term government bonds with maturities greater than 10 years from *The Economist*.[8] The database contains over 15,000 weekly observations of bond price data from the London Stock Exchange for 41 countries and British colonies, for the period from 1887 to 1895. There are several reasons our analysis focuses on the sovereign debt market to measure the economic effects of the Baring Crisis. First, annual GDP estimates and other macroeconomic data (such as investment spending) are available only for high income countries and a handful of emerging markets for the gold standard period. Second, many scholars have questioned the quality of nineteenth-century GDP estimates, especially for the emerging market sample, since the figures are often constructed by back-casting and interpolation between decadal benchmarks.

We divided our entire sample of countries and colonies into three groups to analyze yields of (1) Latin American countries, (2) non-Latin emerging markets, and (3) core, or high income European countries and the United States in the period surrounding the Baring Crisis. Our unweighted yield index for Latin America consists of 12 countries: Argentina, Brazil, Chile, Colombia, Costa Rica, Guatemala, Honduras, Mexico, Nicaragua, Paraguay, Uruguay, and Venezuela. We construct an unweighted yield index of non–Latin American emerging markets using 22 countries and British colonies: Austria, British Guiana, Canada, the Cape of Good Hope, Egypt, Greece, India, Italy, Jamaica, Japan, Natal, New South Wales, New Zealand, Norway, Queensland, Russia, South Australia, Sweden, Tasmania, the Ottoman Empire (Turkey), Victoria, and Western Australia. The core country index consists of five high income European countries (Belgium, France, Germany, Netherlands) and the United States. As shown in Exhibit 29.1, interest rates are generally quite flat over the sample period for the non-Latin emerging markets and the core countries. The small increase in interest rates for the non–Latin Emerging Market Index can be completely attributed to Greece and its debt default in 1893. Bond yields are flat for the non-Latin emerging markets over the sample period if Greece is excluded. Interest rates for Latin American emerging markets, however, display a very different pattern, rising from about 800 basis points in 1887 to more than 1,200 basis points by the end of 1895. One reason that rates continued to rise

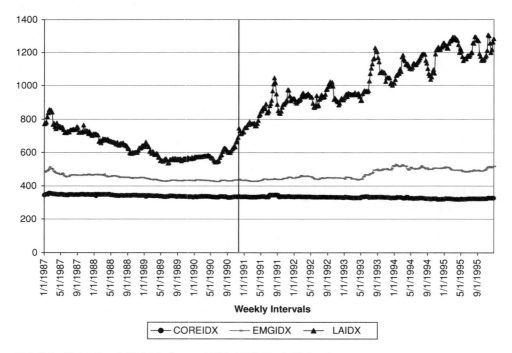

Exhibit 29.1   Bond Yield Indexes, 1887–1895 (Basis Points)

in other Latin American countries several years after the onset of the crisis may have been related to the ongoing failure of Argentina to fully renegotiate its debt and establish a stable monetary environment or the fact that European investors were unable to assess the severity of the crisis because of a lack of information or incomplete information.

Consistent with the graphical evidence, the weekly record of the sovereign bond market from the financial press suggests that, in addition to any country-specific events that moved sovereign spreads, the Baring Crisis may have been a common factor driving Latin American securities in the early 1890s. The newspaper clippings of the Corporation of Foreign Bondholders (a British entity representing the interests of sovereign debt holders) suggest that the Argentine crisis may have had real economic effects on other Latin American countries. For example, *The Bullionist* wrote:

> *Paraguay, like Argentina, Uruguay, and Brazil, is undergoing a financial crisis, and this crisis was recently described by the Finance Minister to Congress in the form of a report. . . . They were traceable, without a doubt, to the condition in the Argentine. There has been a general falling-off in trade, which has given rise to a feeling of uneasiness and want of confidence, and since the beginning of 1890 things have been getting worse.[9]*

It appears that financial markets may have also been reassessing the debt of the region en masse. The reassessment may be due to a wake-up call or a common-creditor channel, two explanations given for contagion during the Asian financial crisis.[10]

A wake-up call would suggest that Argentina's default signaled the potential for crises to occur in other countries; given this new information and the belief that other Latin American countries had characteristics that were broadly similar to Argentina, emerging market investors then sold their Latin American securities. This interpretation is similar to what some economists suggested occurred during the East Asian crisis. The fact that the bond spreads did not rise for the Latin American countries in the months preceding the crisis is consistent with a wake-up call interpretation of the Baring Crisis and similar to what has been observed during the East Asian Crisis.

Incomplete information about the financial health and growth prospects of particular Latin American countries may have made it difficult for investors to assess risk on a country-by-country basis before Argentina's default, and may have contributed to a sell-off of Latin American debt.[11] The fact that European investors lacked all the information they desired is well documented by the Corporation of Foreign Bondholders (CFB), which represented British lenders, and which was created, in part, to provide better information on sovereign borrowers (Mauro and Yafeh 2003). Finally, the presence of a common creditor may also help explain the large increase in Latin American interest rates following the onset of the Baring Crisis.[12] Investment banks that lent to Argentina were largely concentrated in London. Harmed by the Argentine default, they may have decided to cut back on their investments in the entire Latin American region to reduce their exposure to risk of a similar variety.

To help us further assess the regional nature of the crisis and control for country-specific factors, we analyzed the determinants of yield-spread movements over the time from 1886 to 1896. We constructed a panel data set consisting of annual data for our sample of 35 emerging market borrowers, which includes macroeconomic indicators, trade variables, institutional arrangements and political factors, and country-specific controls. We employed a series of country fixed-effects models to analyze the determinants of sovereign yield spreads. The country risk premium, ceteris paribus, is positively correlated with general movements in emerging-market interest rates, although the effect is only statistically significant at the 20 percent level. All else being equal, a country in debt default has yield spreads that are more than 387 basis points higher than a sovereign borrower that is servicing its debt. An improved budget deficit ratio reduces the country risk premium by nearly 30 basis points, but the effect is not statistically significant. The other macroeconomic and trade variables (the debt-to-revenue ratio, the trade-balance ratio, and exports and population) do not have statistically or economically significant effects on sovereign yield spreads.

Turning to the variables specifically concerned with the crisis, the Baring Crisis does not seem to have affected all sovereign borrowers: A crisis indicator variable is not statistically significant at conventional levels. However, consistent with the graphical evidence, the Latin-crisis variable (the interaction between a Latin America indicator variable and the Baring Crisis indicator) has a large positive effect on yield spreads that is statistically significant at the 5 percent level. The point estimate suggests that the crisis increased yield spreads in Central and South America by 214 basis points. It also appears that trade may have been a channel through which the crisis spread. The U.K. trade share variable interacted with the crisis dummy increases country risk by roughly 20 basis points (evaluating the point estimate of 1 at the mean U.K. trade share of 20), although the effect is not statistically significant at conventional levels (19 percent level of significance). The U.K. trade share variable interacted with the Latin American share raises country risk by approximately 80 basis points (evaluating the point estimate of 10 at the mean U.K. trade share in Latin America of 8). This additional effect on Latin American spreads is significant at the 20 percent level. To test the joint significance of the crisis variables, we took the partial derivative of yield spreads with respect to the crisis dummy variable. The three variables raise country risk by nearly 240 basis points for Latin American countries and are jointly significant at the 1 percent level.

The presence of a common creditor may also help explain the large increase in Latin American interest rates following the onset of the Baring Crisis. Investment banks that lent to Argentina were largely concentrated in London. Harmed by the Argentine default, they may have decided to cut back on their investments in the entire Latin American region to reduce their exposure to risk of a similar variety. Since other countries in their region had trade patterns, fiscal histories, and corporate governance similar to Argentina, this may have induced U.K. investors to reallocate their portfolios and shift funds to other parts of the world like the British Empire or other emerging markets. As a way to test the common creditor hypothesis, we re-estimated the empirical model adding two interaction terms to measure the effects of the Baring Crisis outside of Latin America. First, we interacted the Empire indicator variable with the crisis dummy to test the hypothesis that European investors may have sold off or reduced their holdings of Latin American securities and purchased British-guaranteed colonial bonds or debt in non-Latin emerging markets. Then, we interacted the non-Empire emerging market variable with the crisis dummy to capture the effect of the Baring Crisis on British colonies and developing countries outside of Latin America. Although the Empire interaction variable is not statistically significant, we find some evidence that yield spreads in non-Empire, non-Latin emerging markets actually declined about 42 basis points following the outbreak of the crisis. The falling yield spreads (and hence rising prices of non-Latin emerging market debt) provide some evidence that U.K. investors shifted some of their funds to non-Latin emerging markets during the early 1890s.

CONCLUSION

Our analysis suggests the existence of a large Latin American effect, even after controlling for both observed and unobserved differences across countries. Statistical and historical evidence suggests that European investors sold off or reduced their holdings of Latin American bonds. Investors reassessed sovereign risk in Latin America and reduced their holdings of government bonds issued by countries in the region, perhaps in part because of informational problems and in part to diversify away from region-specific risk.

NOTES

1. Forbes and Rigobon (2002), Forbes and Claessens (2001), and Kaminsky, Reinhart, and Vegh (2003).
2. Calvo (1999), Drazen (1998), Hahm and Mishkin (2000), Radelet and Sachs (1998).
3. Kaminsky and Reinhart (1998), Dornbusch, Park, and Claessens (2002).
4. For examples, see della Paolera and Taylor (2001), Eichengreen (1999), Ford (1956, 1962), and Williams (1920).
5. Glick and Rose (1999), Calvo and Reinhart (1996).
6. Quoted in Fishlow (1989).
7. Following (Eichengreen 1999 and della Paolera and Taylor 2001), we use the phrase "the Baring Crisis" to refer to both the distress in Argentina and the problems of the House of Baring in London. Some scholars, however, more narrowly refer to the Baring Crisis as applying only to the events in England and refer separately to the Argentine Crisis (Bordo and Murshid 2001). We view the two events as being importantly linked.
8. Par value for all bonds in our sample was 100 pounds sterling. Maturity length depended on availability.
9. *The Bullionist*, April 23, 1892.
10. See Radelet and Sachs (1998) and Eschweiler (1997) for evidence of a wake-up call in the 1997 East Asian Crisis.
11. There is some evidence that the wake-up call that may have occurred during the East Asian financial crisis was exacerbated by asymmetric information problems. According to Goldstein (1998, 19), "Creditors did not have accurate information on the creditworthiness of Asian borrowers (for example, external debt turned out to be much larger, and international reserves much smaller, than indicated by publicly available data)." Of course, for our period, the problems may have involved both inaccurate and incomplete information.
12. A common-creditor channel has been used to explain recent episodes of financial contagion in East Asia and Latin America (Dornbusch, Park, and Claessens 2002).

REFERENCES

Bordo, Michael D., and Antu P. Murshid. 1996. "Are financial crises becoming increasingly more contagious?" In Stijn Claessens and Kristin I. Forbes, eds. *International Financial Contagion,* 367–403. Boston: Kluwer Academic Publishers, 2001.

Calvo, Guillermo. 1999. "Contagion in Emerging Markets: When Wall Street Is a Carrier." College Park, MD: University of Maryland, Working Paper.

Calvo, Guillermo, and Carmen Reinhart. 1996. "Capital flows to Latin America: Is there evidence of contagion effects?" In Guillermo Calvo, Morris Goldstein, and E. Hochreiter, eds. *Private Capital Flows to Emerging Markets after the Mexican Crisis,* 151–171. Washington: Institute for International Economics.

della Paolera, Gerardo, and Alan M. Taylor. 2001. *Straining at the Anchor: The Argentine Currency Board and the Search for Macroeconomic Stability, 1880–1935.* Chicago: University of Chicago Press.

Dornbusch, Rudiger, Yung Chul Park, and Stijn Claessens. 2002. "Contagion: How it Spreads." *World Bank Research Observer* 15:2, 177–197.

Drazen, Allan. 1998. "Political Contagion in Currency Crises." *NBER Working Paper,* No. 7211.

Eichengreen, Barry. 1999. "The Baring Crisis in a Mexican Mirror." *International Political Science Review* 20:3, 249–270.

Eschweiler, B. 1997. "Emerging Asia: The Fallout after the FX Crisis." Singapore: J.P. Morgan, Asian Financial Markets.

Fishlow, Albert. 1989. "Conditionality and willingness to pay: Some parallels from the 1890s." In Barry Eichengreen and Peter H. Lindert, eds. *The International Debt Crisis in Historical Perspective,* 86–105. Cambridge, MA: MIT Press.

Forbes, Kristen, and Stijn Claessens. 2001. *International Financial Contagion.* New York: Kluwer Academic Publishers.

Forbes, Kristen, and Roberto Rigobon. 2002. "No Contagion, Only Interdependence: Measuring Stock Market Co-Movements." *Journal of Finance* 107:5, 2223–2261.

Ford, Alec G. 1956. "Argentina and the Baring Crisis of 1890." *Oxford Economic Papers* 8:2, 127–150.

———. 1962. *The Gold Standard, 1880–1914: Britain and Argentina.* Oxford: Clarendon Press.

Glick, Reuven, and Andrew K. Rose. 1999. "Contagion and Trade: Why Are Currency Crises Regional?" *Journal of International Money and Finance* 18:4, 603–617.

Goldstein, Morris. 1998. *The Asian Financial Crisis.* Washington, DC: Institute for International Economics.

Hahm, Joon-Ho, and Frederic S. Mishkin. 2000. "The Korean Financial Crisis: An Asymmetric Information Perspective." *Emerging Markets Review* 1: 21–52.

Kaminsky, Graciela, and Carmen Reinhart. 1998. "Financial Crises in Asia and Latin America: Then and Now." *American Economic Review* 88:2, 444–448.

Kaminsky, Graciela, Carmen Reinhart, and Carlos A. Vegh. 2003. "The Unholy Trinity of Financial Contagion." *Journal of Economic Perspectives* 17:4, 51–74.

Mauro, Paolo, and Yishay Yafeh. 2003. "The Corporation of Foreign Bondholders." *IMF Working Paper,* 03/107, Washington, DC.

Mitchener, Kris James, and Marc Weidenmier. 2008. "The Baring Crisis and the Great Latin American Meltdown of the 1890s." *Journal of Economic History* 68: 462–500.

Radelet, Steven, and Jeffrey Sachs. 1998. "The East Asian Financial Crisis: Diagnosis, Remedies, Prospects." *Brookings Papers on Economic Activity* 1: 1–74.

Taylor, Alan M. 2003. "Capital Accumulation." In Gerardo Della Paolera and Alan M. Taylor, eds. *A New Economic History of Argentina,* 170–196. Cambridge, UK: Cambridge University Press.

Williams, John H. 1920. *Argentine International Trade under Inconvertible Paper Currency, 1880–1900.* Cambridge: Harvard University Press.

ABOUT THE AUTHORS

Kris James Mitchener is the Robert and Susan Finocchio professor of economics in the Department of Economics at the Leavey School of Business at Santa Clara University, and a research associate at the National Bureau of Economic Research. His research focuses on international economics, macroeconomics, and economic history and is published in the *Journal of Political Economy, Economic Journal*, the *Journal of Law and Economics*, the *Journal of Economic Growth*, the *Journal of International Money and Finance*, the *Journal of Money, Credit, and Banking*, the *Journal of Economic History, Monetary and Economic Studies*, and *Research in Economic History*. He has held visiting positions at the Bank of Japan, the St. Louis Federal Reserve Bank, UCLA, and CREi at Universitat Pompeu Fabra and serves on the editorial boards of the *Journal of Economic History, Cliometrica*, and *Economics*. He received his B.A. and PhD from the University of California, Berkeley.

Marc D. Weidenmier is the William F. Podlich associate professor of economics and the director of the Lowe Institute of Political Economy at Claremont McKenna College. Professor Weidenmier is a research associate at the National Bureau of Economic Research and a member of the editorial board of the Journal of Economic History. His research interests are in the area of monetary and financial economics. He has published in several leading economics and finance journals, including the *American Economic Review, Quarterly Journal of Economics, Journal of Financial Economics, Journal of International Economics*, and the *Journal of Economic History*.

CHAPTER 30

How Government Bond Yields Reflect Wartime Events

The Case of the Nordic Market

DANIEL WALDENSTRÖM
Uppsala University and Research Institute of Industrial Economics (IFN)

BRUNO S. FREY
Institute for Empirical Research in Economics, University of Zurich

T his study examines how sovereign debt yields reflect wartime events and expectations about their future occurrence.[1] In particular, the analysis focuses on war threats during the years leading up to World War II, and to what extent historical government bond price data can be used to analyze these past views of the contemporaries in real time.

Historians of war generally ask many important questions to help them comprehend the main causes of war and its impact on societies and their citizens. One such question concerns whether the contemporaries anticipated the outbreak of a war. Of course, there are many possible answers, depending on what groups in society are targeted. For example, the perceived threat of war on the part of political and military leaders might (for informational or other reasons) differ from the threat of war perceived by the general public. Both groups are worth considering, particularly the latter, since it constitutes quite an important group in democratic societies when analyzing a country's actions.

The analysis centers on one of Europe's geopolitically most strategically important regions in the 1930s, the Nordic countries. The Swedish iron ore was pivotal to the German arms industry, Norway's coast offered an ideal starting point for a naval attack on Great Britain, and Finland's dominant position in the Gulf of Finland was a latent problem for the Soviet leaders. Hence, Europe's superpowers had strong vested interests in keeping their enemies out of the Nordic region, and they all had long-term plans of military interventions in line with these interests.

The main question asked is: *To what extent did contemporaries in the Nordic countries perceive this mounting threat of war?* Given the significance of public threat perceptions to the overall development of a country, it is not surprising that historians have gone to great lengths to analyze these questions. According to conventional Nordic World War II historiography, there were few, if any, people in the Nordic countries who truly believed a war in their own countries around the outbreak of World War II would include them. However, the traditional historical method used to generate these results is associated with various methodological problems. Historians primarily rely on in-depth analyses from various written sources, but widely held notions of pending threats of war are typically not systematically documented, and are therefore largely unobservable to historians. Another potential problem is that historians may be influenced by their own social and political context so that their selection and interpretation of historical facts depend on what they conjecture that their readers wish to read. Historians are, of course, well aware of these problems, and discussions on how to deal with them are found in Carr (1961) and Marwick (1970).

In the present paper, we contrast this historical writing with an alternative mode of analysis. This method, originally proposed by Willard, Guinnane, and Rosen (1996) in their study of currency price fluctuations around the time of the U.S. Civil War, is based on analyzing large sudden changes in sovereign debt yields and link these with major geopolitical prewar events. We argue that this will show if, and when, significant war risk increases occurred, as reflected by market prices. The underlying idea is that wars put extraordinary pressures on countries' fiscal balances and may even provoke governments to repudiate their sovereign debt. An increased risk of war will translate into an increased sovereign risk or, equivalently, higher yields on traded sovereign debt.

The empirical analysis is presented in two steps. First, we estimate war threat assessments from Nordic government bond yields recorded from prices quoted in the period from 1938 to 1940, that is, the years just before and around the outbreak of World War II. Second, these market-based estimates are contrasted with the conjectures of historians, retrieved from a close reading of the main writings of some of the most well-known Nordic historians, concerning public war threats during the exact same time. The final result is a comparative analysis, which not only conveys information about whether the Nordic political and military preparations for an enemy attack were in line with the general views about external threats of war, but also addresses the important question of whether conventional historiography is robust enough to consider alternative assessments of certain historical phenomena.

EMPIRICAL METHOD AND DATA

Our empirical analysis consists of collecting information on historical prewar threat assessments as characterized by, on one hand, historians and, on the other hand, quantitative estimates from historical sovereign yield data.

To characterize the conventional historical writing of World War II in the Nordic countries is, of course, a difficult and demanding task. We have read a large number of writings of some of the most established and reputable Nordic academic historians, searching for explicit discussions of war threat perceptions during the period under study. Of course, we do not claim to offer a complete coverage of this extensive and fragmented literature, but with a quite sizable coverage, we believe that we have captured the essence of what Nordic historians to date think about this issue. We have only examined the writings of Nordic scholars since we they have arguably a comparative advantage in describing past sentiments of the Nordic citizens.

We also use historical sovereign debt yields to describe the threat assessments before World War II. This is done using a time series econometrics technique (proposed by Bai and Perron 1998) that estimates statistically significant changes, called *structural breaks,* in the sovereign market yields.[2] These breaks are linked to simultaneously occurring political or military events, and from this we make an inference about the impact of the wartime events on contemporary society. The underlying idea is that wars put extraordinary pressure on a country's fiscal balances and may, in the worst case, provoke sovereign repudiations or defaults. This, in turn, increases the default risk of these government bonds, which implies that they should trade at lower prices on the secondary markets. By only basing the inference on the time series and not prior knowledge of what historical events historians consider important, the financial market approach is particularly useful for analyzing the true forward-looking assessments of the contemporaries, before the subsequent realization of the course of events that later became historical.

Our use of financial market data has particular advantages. First and foremost, financial asset prices contain a lot of informational value, as market actors always need to carefully evaluate the prevailing situation, as well as likely future developments, because errors directly affect them in monetary terms. This distinguishes capital market data from other types of data, in particular surveys and questionnaires, in which errors do not generally affect the persons committing them. Financial markets usually have a high predictive power, due to so-called marginal traders. This type of trader decides on a relatively unbiased basis, and carefully collects the relevant information. In the extreme case, even one such trader can drive the market price to the underlying equilibrium price.

Our data set consists of newly collected government bond prices, quoted between January 1938 and December 1940 on the secondary markets in all Nordic countries. The market prices recorded in Sweden are especially relevant for our purposes. Sweden was the only country in which all four Nordic countries floated their government bonds, and yield comparisons are improved by the fact that the loans were denominated in the same currency (the Swedish) and traded under the same institutional market conditions. Moreover, Sweden was never directly engaged in the war and did not implement many of the extremely restrictive trading and pricing regulations seen in most belligerent countries. This makes Swedish market data from this period particularly reliable and we therefore present only the results based on the Swedish data in the following discussion.

ESTIMATING STRUCTURAL BREAKS IN NORDIC SOVEREIGN YIELDS

This section first presents the results of the structural break estimations and then the findings from our main analysis, the comparison between the views of historians and financial markets regarding prewar threat assessments.

Exhibit 30.1 displays the sovereign yields of all four Nordic countries (solid lines) along with the fitted structural breaks (broken lines). The bond yields are

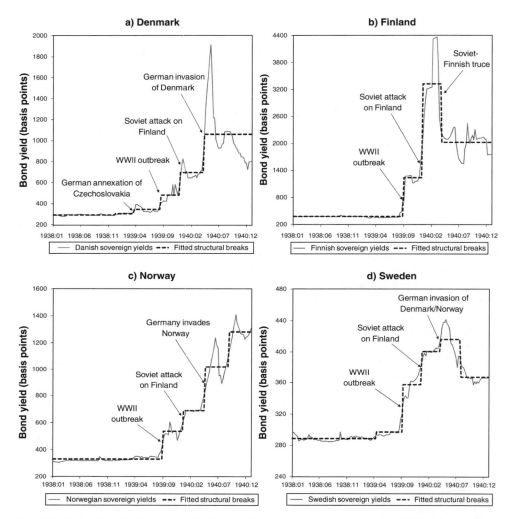

Exhibit 30.1   Nordic Sovereign Yields and Fitted Structural Breaks, 1938–1940

weekly and we use the ones recorded at the Stockholm market between 1938 and 1940. Consider first the Danish yields (panel a), where we record three notable structural breaks before the German invasion in April 1940. First, one in late March 1939, shortly after the German annexation of Czechoslovakia, a second one around the time of the war's outbreak in September 1939, and then a third one in early December 1939, directly after the Soviet attack on Finland. Finally, the German invasion of Denmark on April 9, 1940, produced a large and significant break of +361 basis points, but note that the initial spike the first week after the invasion amounted to +1,900 basis points! Altogether, these results show that the traders in Denmark and Sweden clearly perceived an increased war threat on Denmark well ahead of the German invasion. The invasion spike in the Stockholm yields, reflecting the yield under the realization of war, however, suggests that the Swedish investors still believed that a continued peace was more likely than the outbreak of war in Denmark.[3]

The Finnish yields in Stockholm (panel b) contain three statistically significant structural breakpoints, the first one in early September 1939 being +862 basis points. The second break in early December, that is, after the Soviet attack on Finland. This break measures to a massive yield shift, amounting to 2,083 basis points! The third break occurred in mid-March 1940, immediately after the Soviet-Finnish truce, and interestingly, it estimated a decrease in yields by 1,298 basis points. In other words, while both Finns and Swedes interpreted the German-Russo anti-aggression pact and the outbreak of war in Poland as strongly increased external threats to Finland, the actual outbreak of war in Finland further increased the sovereign risk (in Sweden).

Now consider the Norwegian yields in Stockholm (panel c). They exhibit breaks in early September and late December, clearly indicating that traders in Sweden perceived increased war threats to Norway at this time. A third break is recorded just after the German invasion, in April 1940, measuring +333 basis points. This break indicates that the eventuality of war was not entirely capitalized by the Swedish market actors. Later in 1940, there is a fourth break of –243 basis points, which most likely signals the resolved uncertainty about the effects of the German occupation on Norway's economy and, perhaps, even status as a sovereign nation.

Finally, consider the Swedish yields (panel d). Note first that the magnitude of the Swedish breaks is markedly smaller than those of its neighboring countries. Still, they are recorded at the time of several major war events: the outbreak of the war in early September 1939 (+66 basis points), the Finnish-Soviet war in December 1939 (+44 basis points), and the German invasion of Denmark and Norway in early April 1940 (+15 basis points). An interesting observation is that the yield increases get smaller the closer the war gets to Scandinavia. This could signal that Swedes regarded the risk of an attack on Sweden as being independent of the risk of attacks on the other Nordic countries. Given the vast importance of the Swedish iron ore exports to, in particular, the German war industry, such a conjecture may actually have been plausible at the time.

COMPARING THE VIEWS OF HISTORIANS AND MARKETS

We now turn to our comparative analysis in which we contrast the estimates of historians and bond markets. Neither approach is free from methodological and data-related problems and this exercise is consequently not about any version being right or wrong or better or worse. Rather, we wish to shed light on whether they differ at all and, if so, why and in what way.

There are several points of agreement between the historians and the bond markets. In particular, both views agree that Nordic citizens perceived little external threat before August 1939. Even if the Danish yields rose in March of that year, the substantial yield increases came first after the significant events around the war's outbreak in September. This suggests that the Nordic people did not relate to Austria and Czechoslovakia in regard to foreign policy relations with Germany, at least judging from the lack of major threat increases recorded after their annexations in 1938 and 1939, respectively. Another example of concurrence is the that the realization of war in Finland, Denmark, and Norway gave rise to yield spikes in the respective countries' bonds traded in Stockholm. If anything, this indicates that there was no one who fully anticipated the wars, which hence supports the claims of historians. Judging from the magnitudes of the estimated breaks relative to the short-term spikes, which reflect the prospected yield under the realization of war, the market actors viewed the probability of war in Denmark, Finland, and Norway as being somewhere around 50 percent.[4]

Having said this, our comparative analysis also points at several cases of stark disagreement between the two versions of history. Most importantly, the financial markets signal substantially higher war risk expectations than historians do. For example, historians report that the Danes and Norwegians felt largely secure up until the German invasions, but the markets display several dramatic yield increases following some of the most important war-related events: the German-Russo Pact, the outbreak of World War II, and the war between Finland and the Soviet Union as well as some minor events in early 1940.

CONCLUSION

Did the people in the Nordic countries expect that their own countries would be drawn into war activities during the turbulent years from 1938 to 1940? This paper examines and compares two different empirical methodologies and their answers to this question.

Several findings come out of the analysis. In particular, we find several instances of disagreement between the two interpretations of history. Historians claim that the Nordic peoples felt safe up until the autumn of 1939 (in the case of Finland), the winter of 1939 (Sweden) and early April 1940 (Denmark and Norway). The sovereign yield analysis, however, indicate increased threat perceptions considerably before these conjectured dates, often as direct responses to major geopolitical events such as the announcement of the Molotov-Ribbentrop Pact in late August 1939 or the Soviet attack on Finland in late November of that year. We also find, however, points of agreement between historians and markets. For example, Norwegian yields in Oslo dropped after the truce between Finland and the Soviet Union, thereby somewhat reinforcing the widely held sentiments of reassurance described by historians.

Note that even if we find notable discrepancies between the two versions of history, our comparative analysis says little about any of them being either right or wrong. Both approaches suffer from methodological and data-related problems. For example, historians predominantly use text-based sources while past public opinions may hardly be evident in such data material. Historians' selection and interpretation of the historical facts may also reflect views of their own political and social context, which might bias their conjectured war historiographies. On the other hand, the financial market-based analysis relies on the quality of the historical statistical data, which can often be questionable. Furthermore, the econometric method used relies on modeling choices and various assumptions that could be discussed. In other words, there are pros and cons with both approaches and we would therefore recommend a broad methodological approach when analyzing subtle issues concerning the mindsets of large populations in the past.

NOTES

1. This paper is a condensed version of Waldenström and Frey (2008). For further details about data, Nordic World War II historiography, and the econometric analysis, see the original contribution.

2. Technically, this method consists of first estimating a system of linear equations using least squares regressions. Then a number of statistical tests are conducted to assess whether any breaks exist and, if so, their number and exact timing. A structural break is here defined as a lasting significant mean-shift in the series analyzed and we estimate it only using the information contained in the actual time series and do not rely on any prior notions of when breaks should have occurred.

3. An "assessed war probability," calculated as the Stockholm yields right before the war divided by the tip of the yield spike right after the war's outbreak, for Denmark is roughly 40 percent (750 basis points/1,150 basis points = 0.395).

4. The "assessed war probabilities," calculated as the prewar yields (just before the outbreak of war) divided by the tip of the yield spike right after the outbreak of war, are for Denmark, 40 percent; for Finland, 35 percent (1,100 bp/3,200 bp = 0.344); and for Norway, 54 percent (700 bp/1,300 bp = 0.538).

REFERENCES

Bai, J., and P. Perron. 1998. "Estimating and Testing Linear Models with Multiple Structural Changes." *Econometrica* 66:1, 47–78.

Carr, E. H. 1961. *What Is History?* London: MacMillan.

Marwick, A. 1970. *The Nature of History*. London: MacMillan.

Waldenström, D., and B. S. Frey. 2008. "Did Nordic Countries Recognize the Gathering Storm of World War II? Evidence from the Bond Markets." *Explorations in Economic History* 45:2, 107–126.

Willard, K. L., T. W. Guinnane, and H. S. Rosen. 1996. "Turning Points in the Civil War: Views from the Greenback Market." *American Economic Review* 86:4, 1001–1018.

ABOUT THE AUTHORS

Daniel Waldenström is professor in economics at Uppsala University and fellow at the Research Institute of Industrial Economics (IFN), Stockholm, Sweden. He holds doctorate degrees in both economics and economic history. His research concerns income and wealth distribution and historical financial development.

Bruno S. Frey, a professor of economics at the University of Zurich, received an honorary doctorate in economics from the Universities of St. Gallen, Goeteborg, the Free University of Brussels, and the University of Aix-en-Provence, Marseille. He has been distinguished professor of behavioral science at the Warwick Business School at the University of Warwick (U.K.) since 2010. Current research interests include behavioral economics, public choice, and law and economics. He has numerous articles published in professional journals and 21 books, including *Not Just for the Money; Economics as a Science of Human Behaviour; Arts and Economics; Inspiring Economics; Successful Management by Motivation; Happiness and Economics; Dealing with Terrorism—Stick or Carrot; Economics and Psychology: A Promising New Cross-Disciplinary Field; Happiness: A Revolution in Economics,* and *Glück: Die Sicht der Ökonomie.*

CHAPTER 31

How Important Are the Political Costs of Domestic Default?

Evidence from World War II Bond Markets

DANIEL WALDENSTRÖM

Uppsala University and Research Institute of Industrial Economics (IFN)

I n traditional economics models of sovereign debt default, the main focus is put on countries' external debt, that is, their foreign currency denominated government bonds issued to foreign capital markets. When these models explain why governments refrain from defaulting, the reasons are based on the impact of the default on foreign creditors and how they will respond. For example, a default deteriorates a country's credit reputation on international capital markets which, in turn, makes future borrowing more expensive (Eaton and Gersovitz 1981). Alternatively, if the foreign creditors have political connections in their home countries an external default could trigger direct political sanctions (Bulow and Rogoff 1989) or curb trade flows (Rose 2005).

While this traditional literature captures several relevant aspects of sovereign default risk, it misses one dimension of reality. When examining the stylized facts of how sovereign debt is allocated geographically, it turns out that a majority of public debt is in fact issued domestically and not to foreign capital markets. In a new comprehensive analysis of the evolution of sovereign default around the world over the past 800 years, Carmen Reinhart and Kenneth Rogoff find that domestic government debt has been an important part of public finance for a long time and accounts for about two thirds of all public debt today (Reinhart and Rogoff 2010).

What determines whether governments default on their domestic or external debt? There is a small but growing literature on domestic defaults and their costs to governments. The focus in this literature lies in the political and economic aspects of a default. In an influential theoretical model by Drazen (1998), domestic creditors are described as agents belonging to a political constituency upon which the government relies for its political support. Unlike foreign creditors, domestic debt holders are able to credibly threaten to punish the government in case of a domestic default, for example, by refusing to reelect it. Domestic creditors can also be local elites, for example, commercial banks, which are typically large bondholders. They can be expected to exert all their influence to prevent the government from repudiating its domestic debt, possibly even pushing it to instead repudiate its foreign loans.[1] Taken together, these models complement the traditional sovereign default models cited earlier, their main message being that if the groups holding domestic and external debt and their means to punish a defaulting sovereign differ, the expected costs of domestic and external defaults will most likely also differ.

The previous empirical work on sovereign defaults has, just as the theoretical models, focused primarily on the external sovereign debt of countries.[2] There are in fact only a handful of studies of domestic debt default and the role of political-economic channels to government default decisions, as forwarded by Drazen (1998). In Tomz (2004), the expected distributional effect of a domestic debt default is linked to individual voter preferences through an extensive survey database, and the findings are in line with Drazen's political default cost channel. Van Rijckeghem and Weder (2009) examine the likelihood of defaulting on both domestic and external debt, finding that political institutional variables such as democratic standards or type of electoral systems matter, but primarily in conjunction with severe macroeconomic stability, for example, low levels of inflation.

In this study, the link between changes in the expected costs of domestic and external defaults and the differential in sovereign risk on domestic and foreign bond markets is analyzed. The study uses data from a unique historical episode, World War II, during which several exogenous geopolitical shocks shifted the relative cost of domestic and external defaults. Furthermore, the war also abruptly segmented international capital markets, which allows for an examination of what effect these shocks had on creditors and investors in domestic and foreign capital markets. Hence, while the exogeneity of the cost shocks is important for the interpretation of the measured effects, capital market segmentation is necessary for being able to contrast the different theories on external and domestic default costs, as it ensures a stable linkage between creditor nationality and debt type with no arbitrage trading or debt buybacks by borrowing governments.

An econometric analysis uses newly assembled market yields on Danish government bonds that were traded in Denmark and Sweden from 1938 to 1948. The yields in Denmark are the domestic yields and the yields in Sweden are the external yields. A yield differential is computed between these markets, and all nondefault risk-related influences such as differences in macroeconomic fluctuations and portfolio diversification opportunities are factored out. The resulting sovereign risk differential is then regressed on a set of exogenous wartime shocks that, arguably, influenced the Danish government's domestic and external default costs differently. This is how the role of the political-economic cost of domestic default is estimated.

INSTITUTIONAL SETTING AND DATA

When analyzing historical financial asset prices, one must pay close attention to the institutional framework of the markets where the prices were generated. Inefficient market microstructures as well as restrictive regulations often made these markets dysfunctional in ways that affected the price mechanism negatively. The Danish and Swedish secondary bond markets of the late 1930s and 1940s, however, seem to have functioned relatively smoothly. Both countries hosted frequent and regular secondary bond trading, transaction taxes and fees were modest, and financial information channels were relatively sophisticated. Especially important for the present study, which conducts an empirical analysis based on comparing asset prices in Denmark and Sweden, is that the institutions governing securities trading were quite similar in these countries throughout the study period. There were some extraordinary wartime regulations that primarily affected the Danish market, but there is little evidence that these rulings affected the pricing of bonds.[3]

The degree of market integration between Danish and Swedish capital markets also has some bearing on the analysis. Bilateral capital flow data for Sweden and Denmark, recorded on a quarterly frequency throughout this period, suggest that there were three phases of market integration. The first phase is the interwar era ending in September 1939. Here, markets appear to have been highly integrated and one should hence expect Danish sovereign yields to be effectively equal because of the law of one price. The second phase is World War II, between September 1939 and May 1945. Immediately after the outbreak of war, market integration abruptly broke down, as indicated by the registered capital flows as well as contemporary newspapers. Wartime markets were entirely segmented and the prices on the domestic Danish sovereign debt, traded in Denmark, were only influenced by domestic (Danish) investors and domestic market forces. Similarly, the Danish external sovereign debt floated in Sweden was during the war only set by the Swedish traders. There were also no signs of "third market integration," that is, a situation in which the Danish external debt was traded by domestic Danes in some third market, for example, London, as there were no recorded capital flows from any other countries during this period. The third phase is the postwar era, when markets were once again integrated. Altogether, the wartime market segmentation enables us to interpret Danish government debt policy with respect to the identity of the creditors holding and trading its debt in the respective countries.

The data set consists of yields to maturity on Danish long-term government debt, priced and traded in Denmark and Sweden from 1938 to 1948.[4] To have as similar loans as possible from each market, I use a domestic 4 percent 25-year loan of 1934 issued in Danish *kronor* and a foreign 4 percent 20-year loan of 1936 issued in Swedish *kronor*. Available official documentation and financial press in both countries suggest that all bondholders, both home and abroad, received coupon payments throughout the period. Exhibit 31.1 displays the nominal yields of these loans. One may take notice of the relatively low yield levels of the Danish domestic loan traded in Copenhagen, with a yield not exceeding 5 percent at any point in time and exhibiting a downward sloping trend during the war.

In the econometric analysis, a set of additional macroeconomic and financial variables from both markets, collected from official statistical sources, are also included. These include local inflation rates, interest rates, and stock market returns. See Waldenström (2009) for more details.

EMPIRICAL ANALYSIS

The main objective of this study is to analyze the importance of political costs of domestic sovereign default. As suggested by the model of Drazen (1998), when governments repudiate their domestic debt, they get punished by domestic creditors, either through lost votes in coming elections or through losses of other

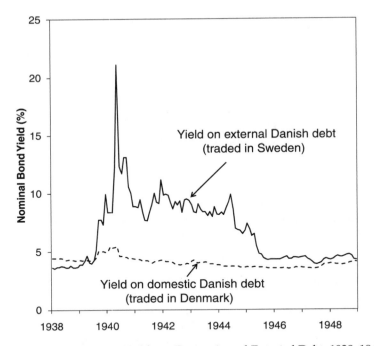

Exhibit 31.1   Danish Sovereign Yields on Domestic and External Debt, 1938–1948

kinds of political or financial support coming from local elites. One implication is that whenever the domestic creditors become relatively more important,
one should expect a lowered default risk on the domestic debt vis-à-vis the
external debt.

The empirical analysis is based on comparing the Danish domestic and external yields, recorded on the segmented domestic and foreign bond markets during
the wartime era. All influences on the yields that are not related to the default risk
are factored out in the estimation. Specifically, different inflation rates across countries are controlled for, as are returns to local opportunity investments for which
market interest rates and stock market returns are used as proxies. To estimate
the impact of political default costs on the sovereign yields, I employ exogenous
geopolitical wartime events that arguably affected the Danish government's costs
of defaulting on its domestic and external debt differently. The shocks are retrieved
from combining sovereign debt theory with the political and economic historiography of Denmark and Sweden (Johansen 1986; Lidegaard 2005). From these shocks,
changes in the relative cost of defaulting on the domestic over the external debt
are retrieved.

Exhibit 31.2 presents the econometric estimation results from linear regressions
of Danish nominal and real yield differentials on a set of dummy variables, representing the geopolitical shocks, and the other control variables. The outbreak of
World War II significantly increased the sovereign risk differential from its prewar
level by almost four percentage points (*War outbreak*), depending on the specification. Before the war, the Danish government faced a high default cost on all of

Exhibit 31.2   Sovereign Spreads and Relative Default Costs, 1938–1948

	Nominal Yield Differential	Real Yield Differential
War outbreak (1939:9–1940:3)	0.036***	0.039***
	(0.006)	(0.005)
German occupation (1940:4–1943:8)	0.058***	0.056***
	(0.005)	(0.005)
Martial laws (1943:9–1945:5)	0.035***	0.034***
	(0.004)	(0.003)
Postwar period (1945:6–1948:12)	0.008***	0.007***
	(0.002)	(0.002)
Market interest rate differential	0.416	1.004***
	(0.390)	(0.046)
Stock market return differential	0.013	0.028
	(0.026)	(0.020)
Constant	0.004	0.011***
	(0.005)	(0.001)
Observations (months)	129	129
F-statistic	85.7	459.2
R^2	0.87	0.96

Note: Dependent variables are nominal and real differentials between Danish long-term external and domestic government bonds based on market prices in Stockholm and Copenhagen. ***, **, and * denote statistical significance at the 1%, 5%, and 10% levels, respectively. Standard errors are heteroskedasticity and autocorrelation consistent.

its debt. External default costs were high since Denmark had a default-free credit history, which meant that a default would make future borrowing more expensive. Domestic costs were also high since bondholding was widespread among the Danish people and creditors were likely an important group in the government's constituency. The war outbreak brought down external default costs for two reasons. First, the reputational costs of a default are likely to be smaller if the default is driven by exogenous fiscal shocks, as during wars, and not purely by the will of sovereigns. Second, historians report that the Danish government disliked the fact that in early 1940, the Swedish government refused to promise to support Denmark in case of an attack (Lidegaard 2005, p. 150). The domestic default costs remained high, however, since the economic difficulties caused by the war made the Danish people more inclined to check that the government did not try to inflate away public debt, for example, by printing extra money.

The second severe political shock was the German invasion of Denmark in April 1940, which was followed by three years of German occupation. The domestic political situation was largely unchanged and domestic default costs hence remained high. Historians emphasize that the Germans were keen on keeping the Danish people reasonably satisfied during the war in order to prevent any disruptions in the important Danish-German trade and to keep occupation costs low (Johansen 1986, p. 72). By contrast, expected external default costs dropped further as a result of the new political and fiscal influence of the notorious defaulter Germany. Fully in line with this prediction, the estimated change in sovereign risk differential, that is, *German occupation–War outbreak*, shows an increase by roughly 2.4 percentage points.

A third political shock in Denmark occurred in August 29, 1943, when the Germans, after a long raid by the Danish resistance movement, finally dissolved the Danish government, proclaimed martial law and took control over most political and fiscal issues (Johansen 1986, p. 87). If anything, this must have reduced the ability of the Danish people to punish the domestic debtor, that is, now the German occupants, thereby reducing domestic costs of default. By contrast, the costs of an external default hardly changed after this event as they were already on a quite low level. The point estimates in Exhibit 31.2 show that the relative cost of a domestic default decreased by the decrease in the sovereign risk spread by about 2.7 percentage points. (*Martial law–German occupation*).

Finally, the peace in May 1945 was a major political event that restored the Danish debt servicing policy to its prewar situation. The estimates in Exhibit 31.2 fully reinforce this picture by reporting a decrease in the sovereign risk spread, *Postwar–Martial laws,* by 2.7 percentage points. This drop hence eliminated the remaining wartime spread between domestic and external debt, fully in line with the simultaneous equalization of the default costs of these two debt types.

CONCLUSION

There is a new literature on sovereign debt default and its determinants, focusing on the role of domestic government debt. As suggested by, for example, Drazen (1998) and Reinhart and Rogoff (2010), both domestic and foreign creditors matter to borrowing governments and they may choose strategically on which of these debts to default, depending the size of their political and economic costs.

This study is one of the first to provide an empirical backing to this new literature. It examines how the cost of domestic sovereign default influences financial market-assessed sovereign risk. The analysis draws on the unique situation during World War II, when market segmentation geographically separated the trading of Danish domestic and external debt. By linking some of the most important geopolitical wartime shocks to the effective cost of domestic and external defaults to the Danish government, an econometric analysis shows that these shocks explain a significant part of the variation in the sovereign risk differential between Danish domestic and external debt.

NOTES

1. Gelpern and Setser (2004) have pointed out the importance of local elites as domestic creditors to the government. Furthermore, Reinhart, Rogoff, and Savastano (2003) argue that another cost of a domestic default is the possible resulting turbulence on domestic banking markets, which could hurt government finances.

2. See Waldenström (2009) for an extended discussion of these studies.

3. In Waldenström (2009), a detailed examination of the role of price caps and trading halts show that they mattered quite little to the quoted bond prices.

4. Prices come from official statistical publications and contemporary financial press. See Waldenström (2009) for details.

REFERENCES

Bulow, J., and K. Rogoff. 1989. "A Constant Recontracting Model of Sovereign Debt." *Journal of Political Economy* 97:1, 155–178.

Drazen, A. 1998. "Towards a political-economic theory of domestic debt." In G. Calvo and M. King, eds. *The Debt Burden and Its Consequences for Monetary Policy: Proceedings of a Conference held by the International Economic Association at the Deutsche Bundesbank in Frankfurt, Germany.* New York: St. Martin's Press.

Eaton, J., and M. Gersovitz. 1981. "Debt with Potential Repudiation: Theoretical and Empirical Analysis." *Review of Economic Studies* 48:2, 289–309.

Gelpern, A., and B. Setser. 2004. "Domestic and External Debt: The Doomed Quest for Equal Treatment." *Georgetown Journal of International Law* 35:4, 795–814.

Johansen, H. C. 1986. *The Danish Economy in the Twentieth Century.* London: Croom Helm.

Lidegaard, Bo. 2005. *Kampen om Danmark 1933–1945.* Copenhagen: Gyldendal.

Reinhart, C., and K. S. Rogoff. 2010. *This Time Is Different: Eight Centuries of Financial Folly.* Princeton, NJ: Princeton University Press.

Reinhart, C., K. S. Rogoff, and M. A. Savastano. 2003. "Debt Intolerance." *Brookings Papers on Economic Activity* 1: 1–74.

Rose, A. K. 2005. "One Reason Countries Pay Their Debts: Renegotiation and International Trade." *Journal of Development Economics* 77:1, 189–206.

Tomz, M. 2004. "Voter Sophistication and Domestic Preferences Regarding Debt Default." Unpublished Working Paper. Palo Alto, CA: Stanford University.

Van Rijckeghem, C., and B. Weder. 2009. "Political Institutions and Debt Crises." *Public Choice* 138:3–4, 387–409.

Waldenström, D. 2009. "Why Does Sovereign Risk Differ for Domestic and External Debt? Evidence from Scandinavia, 1938–1948." *Journal of International Money and Finance* 29:3, 387–402.

ABOUT THE AUTHOR

Daniel Waldenström is professor in economics at Uppsala University and a fellow at the Research Institute of Industrial Economics (IFN), in Stockholm, Sweden. He holds doctoral degrees in both economics and economic history. His research concerns income and wealth distribution and historical financial development.

CHAPTER 32

Emerging Market Spreads at the Turn of the Twenty-First Century

A Roller Coaster

SERGIO GODOY
ING Investment Management

This paper focuses on a very turbulent period for emerging financial markets and draws on Godoy (2008). Between 1997 and 2001, these markets suffered several episodes of an extreme financial instability or crisis. The most important crises were (in chronological order) the Asian crisis, the Russian default, the Brazilian devaluation, the Ecuadorian default, the Turkish crisis, the Argentine default. These events were not only particularly painful for the specific countries involved but also some of them reverberated across global financial markets.

In particular, we examine here the variability of monthly secondary emerging market spreads from 18 economies located in three continents (Asia, Eastern Europe, and Latin America) from October 1997 to September 2002. At that time, international bond investors mainly used these bonds for taking positions in emerging markets. In consequence, these spreads were (and still are) widely watched by market participants as a proxy of the market perception of the specific country risk. We attempt in this paper to explain this spread variability using, as explanatory variables, several macroeconomic and financial factors and dummy variables that seek to capture those mentioned crises.

More specifically, we perform individual and panel data estimations for the first principal components of spreads for Latin America, Asia, and Eastern Europe.[1] Exhibit 32.1 shows the evolution of each regional first principal component in the sample period.

In a nutshell, the principal components analysis is a statistical method that allows us to obtain a set of uncorrelated linear combinations of the original variables, the so-called principal components, in which the first principal component retains most of the variability existing in the set of original variables, the second variable retains the second most variability existing in the original variables, and so on. In our case, the original variables correspond to three distinct regional sets

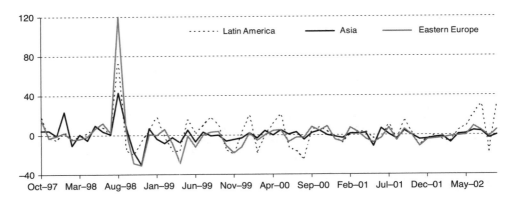

Exhibit 32.1 First Principal Components
Source: Author's calculation based on data from Goldman Sachs, reproduced with the permission of Revista Análisis Económico.

of emerging market spreads, and for each set, we secure the first principal component. We interpret these first components as regional spreads over the default-free international interest rate.[2] Thus, changes in these components reflect changes in the international perception on regional risk.

We chose macroeconomic and financial variables based on two branches of the literature, which are the literature on determinants of sovereign spreads and the theoretical and empirical literature on contagion. Notwithstanding this academic setting, we consider that these variables are really very intuitive for market practitioners and economists. These variables are the following:

1. *The six-month U.S. dollar Libor interest rate.* This is a proxy for the world interest rate and we deem this variable as a good benchmark of global liquidity conditions. A higher interest rate means tighter global liquidity conditions and, thus, higher emerging market spreads. Thus, we expect a positive sign for this variable.
2. *The changes in sovereign credit.* These changes correspond to +1 (−1) for one notch downgrade (upgrade) for the credit rating of any country in the region. The literature has shown that sovereign credit ratings are determined by the country's long-term economic fundamentals.[3] Therefore, the expected effect of this variable on sovereign spreads is positive.
3. *The ratio of international reserves to six-month average imports.* This captures the short-term country external liquidity and higher ratio, which means that the country can more safely face capital outflows. Thus, its expected effect on sovereign spreads is negative.
4. *Interest arrears as a percentage of GDP.* We include this variable as a proxy of the country's willingness to pay. Some important authors[4] convincingly explained that the main difference between corporate and sovereign default is that there is no established modern mechanism for recovering assets or collateral in the case of the sovereign. We proxy this willingness using the interest arrears. Hence, the expected sign of this variable is positive.

5. *The region's exports to developed countries as a percentage of its total exports.* The idea is that countries with larger trade links to developed markets would be less shocked by the contagious effects of an emerging market crisis. Thus, the expected sign of this variable is negative.

As we explained before, in our estimations, we used the fact that emerging markets suffered important crises in our sample period. Theoretically speaking, these severe events can be captured with timely placed dummies.[5] A dummy variable is a variable that takes the value +1 when the event occurs and is zero otherwise. In our case, we create six dummies for the following events: the Asian crisis (November 1997), the Russian default (August 1998), the Brazilian devaluation (January 1999), the Ecuadorian default (June 1996), the Turkish crisis (October 2000), and the Argentine default (December 2001). Though all these crises shared a common expected feature—that is, the region affected suffered a huge spread widening—they can also have potential disruptive effects on other emerging regions. The dummies included are the following:

1. The first dummy is associated with the Asian Crisis. Specifically, we chose November 1997 based on the fact that this month the Korean government stopped defending the won. Korea was by far the largest and richest Asian country involved in this crisis. In consequence, we deem that this event played a significant role in Asia.
2. The second dummy corresponds to the Russian default and the collapse of the Long-Term Capital Management hedge fund. We believe that this is the most extreme single event that occurred during our sample period. A casual visual inspection of Exhibit 32.1 permits us to conjecture on the importance of this event for emerging market yields.
3. The third dummy is related to the Brazilian devaluation, which occurred in mid-January 1999 when the Brazilian central bank stopped openly managing the currency. The Brazilian currency had been under pressure for several months because of market doubts on whether Brazil was capable of meeting its (external) debt payments.
4. The fourth dummy is explained by the default of Ecuador government, which, in turn, is explained by a banking crisis and political turmoil. At the time, this event was important because it was the first time a sovereign was defaulting on Brady bonds.[6]
5. The fifth dummy captures the 2000 Turkish banking and currency crisis. This country's banking system had clear weaknesses and the expected burden on the budget of a massive bailout precipitated a confidence crisis on the local currency.[7]
6. The sixth and last dummy is associated with the biggest default in the emerging markets' history. After two years of wrestling with the market doubts, in December 2001, the Argentine government announced its default on $155 billion of debt. An unavoidable casualty of this default was the fallout of the decade-old currency board system.

We explain our empirical results in the remainder of the paper and, in particular, we provide a taxonomy of the emerging market crises mentioned earlier.

Our first important result is that we find that the economic and financial variables have almost no explanatory power. This outcome is not similar to other authors' findings. A possible explanation for this difference is the particular sample period considered in this paper. Our paper focused on a particular turbulent period when the crises dominated the emerging market landscape. However, the period before our sample (between mid-1995 [after the Tequila Crisis] and mid-1997) and the era after our sample period (from the beginning of 2003 until today, with the important exception of the fourth quarter of 2008) were certainly much more tranquil.[8]

Second, and not surprisingly, based on the dummies that capture the effect of crisis events, we find evidence showing that emerging market crises have a regional character. In particular, the dummies showed that regional measure of spreads widened robustly in every region that faced a crisis, except for the Ecuadorian default and the Argentine default.

Third, and most crucially, some important differences among crises surfaced when we checked the impact of these regional crisis events on other regions. First, we can classify the Asian crisis as an event of emerging market portfolio rebalancing because spreads in other regions significantly narrowed in tandem over this period.[9] Second, the crisis in Russia—and its collateral effect on the fall of the huge hedge fund Long-Term Capital Management—caused a huge and significant widening of stripped spreads all across the emerging market spectrum. We attributed this robust widening to a big pull out of capital flows from all emerging markets.[10] Third, the devaluation in Brazil at the beginning of 1999 produced a spread widening in Latin America and Eastern Europe (with the exception of Russia) and there was no clear effect on the Asian economies. We see this episode as an important portfolio outflow from Latin America and Eastern Europe.

Fourth, the Ecuadorian default caused a strong spread widening in this country[11] and just mildly narrowed in almost all other developing economies. Thus, this evidence is consistent with a country-specific episode that produced some mild rebalancing of emerging market portfolios.

Fifth, the crisis in Turkey made the spreads soar across all emerging markets but in a mild way relative to the Russian default. In consequence, we consider that the Turkish crisis was an event of portfolio outflows from emerging bond markets but smaller when compared to the Russian default. Finally, notwithstanding being the biggest emerging market default ever, in the Argentine default, there was a huge increase in only this country spread and some decrease in almost all other emerging market spreads. Therefore, this crisis looked like a small rebalancing portfolio episode. However, there was some evidence that market participants anticipated this crisis, which, in turn, can explain the mild effect of this crisis on other emerging markets.

We believe that this empirical work offers an important insight to emerging countries' policy makers. They should recognize that their economies can be seriously affected by these crisis events, over which they do not have much control whatsoever.[12] Thus, as a long-term challenge for the country, it is necessary to design policies that provide some cushion against the most violent effects of these crises. For example, if the private sector develops important currency mismatches because the international interest rates are very low, then the sovereign should redesign this capital structure through compensating currency mismatches.

Market practitioners can also draw some important conclusions from this article. First, emerging market crises can be very dissimilar in nature. Thus, different portfolio strategies can be profitable, depending on the nature of the crisis. For example, being short in emerging market spreads (that is, shorting an emerging market bond index and going long in a U.S. Treasury bond of similar duration) would have worked beautifully in a crisis like the Russian default or the Turkish crisis (or even in the more recent crisis caused by the fall of Lehman Brothers). However, this strategy is not so profitable in the case of the Brazilian devaluation, for which a relative strategy of shorting Brazilian spread and going long in Asian spreads would have been much more profitable.

Second, economic and financial fundamentals might be useful for emerging market bond pricing in more tranquil periods. For example, the literature has found some evidence that international interest rates, country indebtedness, and credit ratings, among others, help explain emerging market variability. However, when a crisis strikes the emerging market spectrum, these economic and financial fundamentals are not really useful for pricing these bonds since all spreads start to comove or some unusual negative correlations among spreads develop, depending on the nature of the crisis.

NOTES

1. In the Latin American set, we include sovereign spreads from Argentina, Brazil, Colombia, Ecuador, Mexico, Peru, and Venezuela. The Asian set comprised sovereign spreads from China, Indonesia, Malaysia, the Philippines, Thailand, and South Korea. Finally, the Eastern European group includes sovereign spreads from Bulgaria, Poland, Turkey, Russia, and South Africa, as there is no natural group for it.

2. This interpretation is based on the highly negative correlation vis-à-vis the J.P. Morgan bond price indexes.

3. These include, among others, GDP growth rates, fiscal policy, inflation rate, external debt-to-GDP ratio, and export growth. Therefore, we chose not to include these macroeconomic performance variables in our estimation.

4. See Bulow and Rogoff (1989) and Eaton and Gersovitz (1981).

5. These dummies are based on the recollection of events explained in Fuentes and Godoy (2004).

6. These bonds were created to solve the Latin American debt crisis of the early 1980s, and at the time, they had a very active secondary market.

7. A quick IMF package in early 2001 helped stabilize the financial system.

8. An alternative explanation is that we were the first in this literature to estimate large sample statistic estimators for our regressors, which have the property of being consistent. For doing this, we performed bootstrapping resampling. Using this method, it is possible to estimate large sample statistic estimators by repetitive sampling with replacements from the same sample that these estimators come from. This method strengthens the significance of the crisis dummies and diminishes the significance of the economic variables.

9. Other authors have pointed out a similar result. See, for example, Pettis (2001) and Van Royen (2002).

10. Emerging market bond spreads saw more recently a very similar cataclysmic episode—the fall of Lehman Brothers in September 2008.

11. Ecuador is a very small country. In fact, its external debt was only 0.96 percent of the 1999 total external debt of the countries included in our sample.
12. González Rozada and Levy Yeyati (2008), in a much more recent work, obtained a very similar conclusion.

REFERENCES

Bulow, Jeremy, and Kenneth Rogoff. 1989. "Sovereign Debt: Is to Forgive to Forget?" *American Economic Review* 79:1, 43–50.
Eaton, Jonathan, and Mark Gersovitz. 1981. "Debt with Potential Repudiation: Theoretical and Empirical Analysis." *Review of Economic Studies* 48:2, 289–309.
Fuentes, Mónica, and Sergio Godoy. 2005. "Co-movements in Emerging Market Spreads: A Principal Component Analysis." *Central Bank of Chile Working Paper* 332.
Godoy, Sergio. 2008. "Emerging Market Spreads at the Turn of the Century: A Roller Coaster." *Economic Analysis Review* 23:2, 57–94.
Gonzalez-Rozada, Martin, and Eduardo Levy Yeyati. 2008. "Global Factors and Emerging Market Spreads." *Economic Journal* 118:533, 1917–1936.
Pettis, Michael. 2001. *The Volatility Machine: Emerging Economics and the Threat of Financial Collapse.* New York: Oxford University Press.
Van Royen, Anne-Sophie. 2002. "Financial Contagion and International Portfolio Flows." *Financial Analysts Journal* 58:1, 35–49.

ABOUT THE AUTHOR

Sergio Godoy received an MBA and a PhD in financial economics from Columbia University and a master's degree in applied macroeconomics from Pontificia Universidad Católica de Chile. He is currently vice president of fixed income strategy at ING Investment Management. He was previously the head of fixed income strategy at Larrain Vial AGF, a senior economist at the Central Bank of Chile, and the chief economist of the Chilean National Chamber of Commerce. He has been a part-time finance professor at the MBA and master's in finance of the Pontificia Universidad Católica de Chile, Universidad Adolfo Ibañez, and Universidad del Desarrollo. He has published several columns on macrofinancial issues in Chilean newspapers.

PART VI

Sovereign Debt in Emerging Markets

U ntil very recently, when the supposedly rich nations awoke to their own problems, sovereign debt has been associated most particularly with the debt of developing nations. This section focuses on sovereign debt in emerging markets—both as investment vehicles and in terms of fiscal management in the borrowing countries.

For example, a default on sovereign debt may have profound implications for a borrower nation's fiscal policies. Restricted government funding may in turn lead to social unrest and political upheaval. Some countries fall into a default trap that leads to an apparently endless cycle of borrowing and default, so a persistent problem is understanding and correcting the circumstances that lead to such a miserable result.

The rate of interest that a sovereign borrower must pay depends largely on the sovereign's credit rating. For example, in 2010, downgrades of the quality of Greek bonds played a significant role in heightening the crisis in Greek public finances. Several contributions in this section consider the determinants of sovereign credit ratings. As these discussions show, both economic and political factors play important roles. We have seen that Venezuela is reckoned as a terrible credit risk, but this is due very largely to its current political structure rather than a lack of economic resources adequate to repay as promised. Sovereign debt markets are not independent of other markets, so this section also explores how changes in sovereign debt ratings affect stock markets as well.

CHAPTER 33

Sovereign Default Risk and Implications for Fiscal Policy

GABRIEL CUADRA
Senior Economist, Banco De México[*]

HORACIO SAPRIZA
Research Economist, Division of International Finance, Federal Reserve Board

I n the recent global crisis, the implementation of expansionary fiscal policies mostly in developed economies, along with the relaxation of monetary conditions and policy actions aimed at supporting financial markets and institutions, contributed to break the negative feedback loop between financial conditions and economic activity. In this setting, fiscal stimulus packages supported aggregate demand and consequently contributed to promote economic recovery. However, they also led to a sharp worsening of fiscal positions, mainly in a number of advanced economies from the Eurozone. As for emerging economies, policy makers in these economies were, in general, significantly less able to provide fiscal stimulus than their counterparts in advanced economies.

In light of these events, this paper discusses the reasons behind the limited margin of maneuver that emerging economies' policy makers have to adopt fiscal stimulus packages during economic contractions. In particular, it mostly focuses on how the countercyclical pattern of default risk and the lesser access to external financing in recessions significantly constrain the policy options available to fiscal authorities during the downward phase of the business cycle. In this scenario, it discusses some policy recommendations that could help overcome this problem and consequently increase the degrees of freedom on this matter for policy makers.

To help explain the limited room to provide fiscal stimulus in emerging economies, a useful starting point is to describe a number of empirical regularities for these economies that have been documented in the economic literature. For example, fiscal policy usually follows a procyclical pattern in most middle- and low-income economies. In particular, a procyclical fiscal policy means that public expenditures are increased and tax rates reduced during economic expansions, while the opposite type of fiscal measures are adopted during recessions.

---

[*]The views expressed in this paper are those of the authors, and do not necessarily reflect those of Banco de México or the Federal Reserve System.

These stylized facts have been well documented by several authors. For example, Gavin and Perotti (1997) showed that fiscal policy is procyclical in economies from Latin America. Later, Talvi and Vegh (2005) found that not only do Latin American economies exhibit a procyclical fiscal policy but emerging economies from other regions also do. More recently, Ilzetzki and Vegh (2008) analyzed data from low- and middle-income countries, finding evidence of a procyclical fiscal policy in these economies.

A procyclical fiscal policy implies that instead of adopting a fiscal stimulus package to support economic activity in bad times, emerging economies' policy makers typically implement a tightening fiscal program during recessions, which may lead to an even further decline in the production of goods and services. Also, this stylized fact is at odds with both the standard neoclassical theory on fiscal policy based on the work of Barro (1979) and with Keynesian prescriptions regarding fiscal policy. In particular, neoclassical theory suggests that fiscal policy should be noncyclical, while Keynesian theory suggests that it should be countercyclical. In this scenario, it is crucial to analyze why fiscal authorities usually increase taxes and reduce public spending during the downward phase of the business cycle.

A common explanation for the procyclicality of fiscal policy in middle- and low-income economies is related to the lack of strong political and legal institutions in these economies. For example, according to Lane and Tornell (1999), weak institutions typically lead to a *voracity effect* during economic expansions. That is, in good times there is an increase in fiscal revenues associated with the expansion in the tax base. This windfall in public revenues tends to intensify the struggle for public resources among interest groups, which leads to a sharp increase in public spending. However, once the economic boom ends and public sector income falls, policy makers have to adjust fiscal expenditures.

Gavin and Perotti (1997) suggested another explanation for the procyclicality of fiscal policy in emerging economies, mainly associated with the loss of access to international financial markets during bad times, which typically makes the adoption of either countercyclical or noncyclical fiscal policies extremely difficult. These authors presented some evidence that emerging economies face increasing difficulties to get external financing in recessions. Although it is not possible to directly observe tight credit constraints, they infer them from the use of IMF emergency credit, which is typically granted when there are no alternative sources for financing. Gavin and Perotti (1997) documented that the use of these credits is more common in recessions, which implied that the access to external credit markets is more difficult and expensive during that phase of the business cycle. However, they only emphasized the importance of borrowing constraints in explaining the pattern of fiscal policy observed in emerging economies, without developing a formal model or providing any quantitative analysis.

Other authors have also found evidence of a diminished access to external borrowing for emerging economies during recessions. For example, Neumeyer and Perri (2005) and Uribe and Yue (2006) document that foreign credit is more expensive in bad times than in good times. Thus, emerging economies face countercyclical interest rates when borrowing from abroad. Usually, this pattern in the cost of external financing is associated with default risk being higher in recessions than in expansions. For example, empirical studies (Peter 2002) have shown that default episodes are more common during economic recessions. Therefore, in response to the higher default probability in that phase of the business cycle, foreign creditors usually require a high risk premium.

Based on these stylized facts, Cuadra, Sanchez, and Sapriza (2010) (from now on, CSS) formalized the idea that reduced access to foreign borrowing in recessions and countercyclical default risk are behind the procyclical character of fiscal policy in emerging economies. The setup of the model developed by these authors consists of a small open economy inhabited by domestic households and a benevolent government. Households value private and public consumption, as well as leisure. From their point of view, private consumption and public spending are substitute goods. That is, the government provides goods and services that are valued by the private sector. Households also prefer a smooth path of both private and public consumption over a volatile one. Also, the economy uses labor to produce and it is subject to productivity shocks that generate business cycles.

In the model economy, the government finances its public expenditures through taxes and foreign borrowing. Credit markets are incomplete, in the sense that the government can issue only noncontingent bonds. Furthermore, these international financial contracts are not enforceable, so it is possible for the government to default on previously acquired debts. Given the possibility of a default episode, foreign lenders are aware of this situation and are therefore willing to lend to the government only if they are compensated for the risk of default they face. This compensation takes the form of a default premium that generates a spread between the interest rate that the government pays and the international risk-free interest rate.

Since asset markets are incomplete, that is, at the maturity date, the bond will pay the same, independent of the state provided the government does not default, so sovereign debt repayment imposes a higher burden in recessions than in economic expansions. This higher debt burden together with households' desire for consumption makes the default option more attractive for the government during periods of recession. Under these circumstances, the risk of default is higher during the downturn of the cycle, which generates a higher risk premium in bad times and consequently, countercyclical interest rates.

The fact that the access to external financing is easier and less expensive in good times than in bad times induces the government to rely on foreign borrowing to finance its expenditures during economic booms. This situation leads to a widening in fiscal deficit and to an increase in public debt levels. Therefore, when the economic expansion ends and the economy moves toward an economic recession, the government finds itself with a weak fiscal position and a high level of public debt. In turn, the economic slowdown leads to a decline in fiscal revenues due to the contraction in the tax base, which generates an even further deterioration in fiscal accounts. This situation also contributes to further increase the risk premium during economic contractions.

This interaction between fiscal variables and default risk is also in line with the findings of several papers in the economic literature, which have documented that fiscal positions and public debt levels also have an impact on sovereign risk indicators. For example, Afonso, Gomes, and Rother (2007) found that fiscal deficit and public debt levels, along with economic growth rates, are among the main determinants of sovereign ratings, while Akitoby and Stratmann (2006) showed that higher public debt-to-GDP ratios typically lead to increases in sovereign spreads.

In this setting, more expensive external financing during recessions makes it harder for the government to finance public spending and forces it to rely more heavily on taxes for financing public spending in that phase of the business cycle. As a result, taxes are procyclical, that is, they are low during economic expansions when financing through debt is easy and not too costly, and high during economic contractions when access to credit markets is reduced and the cost of borrowing is high.

Within the framework developed by CSS, the heavier reliance on taxes and the higher cost of international credit during contractions imply that the level of public expenditures that the government is able to finance in recessions is smaller than in times of expansion, when the tax base is larger and the access to international financing is easier and less costly. Hence, public spending is also procyclical: low in bad times and high in good times. The joint cyclical behavior of public spending and tax rates generates a fiscal policy that follows a procyclical pattern.

Summing up, two factors help explain the procyclical pattern of fiscal policy in emerging economies and the limited margin of maneuver that policy makers enjoyed in many of these economies to provide fiscal stimulus during the recent global crisis: first, a voracity effect associated with weak political and legal institutions; and second, a countercyclical default risk related to higher incentives to default in bad times than in good times, mainly due to an incomplete asset market structure. Although these theories are usually presented in the economic literature as two alternative explanations for the procyclicality of fiscal policy in middle- and low-income economies, in practice they complement each other. The voracity effect argument in particular may play a more important role in explaining the increase in public spending typically observed during the upward phase of the business cycle, while the lesser access to international financial markets during economic recessions mainly explains the need to adopt a tightening fiscal policy in that phase of the business cycle.

In light of the previous discussion, a number of policy actions may contribute to reduce the procyclical pattern of fiscal policy in emerging economies and increase the scope to provide fiscal stimulus in these economies during future economic contractions. First, further efforts are needed to improve fiscal policy frameworks in emerging economies. In particular, increasing the degree of transparency in fiscal management is crucial. This would make those authorities in charge of designing and implementing fiscal policies more accountable. Furthermore, fiscal transparency can help significantly reduce the influence of particular interest groups on the allocation of public sector resources, which would contribute to attenuate and eventually eliminate the voracity effect analyzed, among others, by Lane and Tornell (1999). This would allow fiscal authorities to save the extraordinary revenues associated with economic expansions and use them during economic contractions, facilitating the adoption of expansionary fiscal policies in recessions. Second, it is necessary to adopt policy actions aimed at inducing a further development of financial markets in emerging economies, which would increase economic agents' ability to pool and distribute risks more efficiently, as well as to smooth both private and public consumption. For example, it may be convenient to analyze the possibility of developing a market for GDP indexed bonds, whose payments would be contingent to the economic growth rate (Borensztein and Mauro 2002, 2004, and Sandleris et al. 2010). These financial instruments may lead to an asset market structure closer to the complete market framework, and consequently would help to reduce the incentives to default in recessions, contributing to overcome the problems associated with a countercyclical default risk. In particular, this would avoid the large increase in sovereign spreads typically observed during economic contractions. Under these circumstances, in that phase of the cycle, policy makers would be more able to borrow from abroad, and they would consequently enjoy more degrees of freedom to provide fiscal stimulus during recessions.

REFERENCES

Afonso, A., P. Gomes, and P. Rother. 2007. "What 'Hides' Behind Sovereign Debt Ratings?" *European Central Bank Working Paper* 711.

Akitoby, B., and T. Stratmann. 2006. "Fiscal Policy and Financial Markets." *IMF Working Paper* 06/16.

Barro, R. 1979. "On the Determination of Public Debt." *Journal of Political Economy* 87: 940–971.

Borensztein, E., and P. Mauro. 2002. "Reviving the Case for GDP-Indexed Bonds." *International Monetary Fund Policy Discussion Paper* 02/10.

———. 2004. "The Case for GDP-Indexed Bonds." *Economic Policy* April, 165–216.

Cuadra, G., J. Sanchez, and H. Sapriza. 2010. "Fiscal Policy and Default Risk in Emerging Economies." *Review of Economic Dynamics* 13:2, 452–469.

Gavin, M., and R. Perotti. 1997. "Fiscal Policy in Latin America." *NBER Macroeconomics Annual*, 11–61.

Ilzetzki, E., and C. Vegh. 2008. "Procyclical Fiscal Policy in Developing Countries: Truth or Fiction?" *National Bureau of Economic Research Working Paper* 14191.

Lane, P., and A. Tornell. 1999. "The Voracity Effect." *American Economic Review* 89: 22–46.

Neumeyer, A., and F. Perri. 2005. "Business Cycles in Emerging Economies: The Role of Interest Rates." *Journal of Monetary Economics* 52:2, 345–380.

Peter, M. 2002. *Estimating Default Probabilities of Emerging Market Sovereigns: A New Look at a Not-So-New Literature.* Geneva: The Graduate Institute of International Studies.

Sandleris, G., H. Sapriza, and F. Taddei. 2010. "GDP Indexed Bonds: An Applied Framework." *Collegio Carlo Alberto Working Paper* 104.

Talvi, E., and C. Vegh. 2005. "Tax Base Variability and Pro-Cyclical Fiscal Policy." *Journal of Development Economics* 78: 156–190.

Uribe, M., and V. Yue. 2006. "Country Spreads and Emerging Countries: Who Drives Whom?" *Journal of International Economics* 69: 6–36.

ABOUT THE AUTHORS

Gabriel Cuadra holds a PhD in economics from the University of Rochester and is a senior economist at Banco de México. His fields are macroeconomics and international finance. He is the author of papers about sovereign default published in academic journals such as the *Review of Economic Dynamics* and the *Journal of International Economics.* He can be reached at gcuadra@banxico.org.mx.

Horacio Sapriza is a research economist at the Division of International Finance at the Federal Reserve Board, and an assistant professor of finance and economics at Rutgers Business School. He received an MA and a PhD from the University of

Rochester and his research interests are in international finance, macroeconomics, and finance. His studies on the effect of credit market imperfections and institutional factors on sovereign default risk and the business cycle dynamics of emerging market economies, and on the effect of financial constraints on firms' risk and stock returns have been published in leading academic journals. He can be reached at hsapriza@andromeda.rutgers.edu.

CHAPTER 34

Default Traps

LUIS A.V. CATÃO
Inter-American Development Bank and International Monetary Fund, USA

ANA FOSTEL
George Washington University and International Monetary Fund, USA

SANDEEP KAPUR
Birkbeck, University of London, U.K.

INTRODUCTION

The history of sovereign borrowing is replete with evidence of serial default: Countries that default once are often the ones that default again. An early study by Lindert and Morton (1989) found that countries that defaulted at least once in the period between 1820 and 1929 were, on average, 69 percent more likely to default in the 1930s; countries that incurred arrears in repayment or were forced into rescheduling between 1940 and 1979 were 70 percent more likely to default in the 1980s.[1]

The experience of serial defaulters typically involves a vicious circle of default, penal interest rates, and greater borrowing to service the higher interest rates. In contrast, other countries enjoy virtuous circles of borrowing and repayment with declining sovereign spreads. While history suggests that individual countries can graduate from the former group to the latter, the process is typically very slow and not immune to setbacks. At the time this chapter was written, for example, countries in southern Europe that had reputedly graduated from serial default seem to be at risk of falling back into that state. Understanding the causes of serial default is a matter of considerable policy interest. It has potentially profound implications for explaining observed growth divergences across groups of countries as well as for the design of a sound international financial architecture.

Strikingly, however, theoretical models of serial default remain in short supply in the otherwise voluminous literature on sovereign debt.[2] We describe in this chapter a model in which a sovereign borrower's output volatility and persistence of its income shocks interact with informational asymmetry about the nature of such shocks to create an environment in which serial default occurs spontaneously.[3] We also present empirical evidence in support of our theoretical model.

EXPLAINING SERIAL DEFAULT

At its simplest, serial default might be a consequence of persistence in factors that make a country vulnerable to adverse macroeconomic shocks. If poor economic management or weak institutions make a country prone to default, repeated default may reflect only the slow evolution of these structural factors. Similarly, if default is triggered by negative shocks to a country's output, any persistence in shocks will generate serial default. While persistence is indeed a crucial ingredient of the model we describe, we argue that even mild forms of informational asymmetry can exacerbate the impact of the underlying persistence.

Formal economic modeling of sovereign default usually treats default as the outcome of a calculated choice between the long-term consequences of default versus repayment. In particular, default avoids the short-term pain of repayment, but imposes long-term costs: The loss of reputation as a creditworthy borrower might hinder future access to international capital markets, thereby compromising defaulters' ability to smooth consumption in the face of future income shocks. Default may also be punished through economic sanctions and disruption of trading arrangements, which lower future output. Many of these models focus on how severe these penalties need to be in order to incentivize borrowers to repay their debts.

We build a theory of serial default—what we call *default traps*—by combining the template of previous economic models with two stylized facts. First, many countries vulnerable to serial default display considerable volatility and persistence in their national output: shocks to output not only tend to be large but, quite notably, are also very persistent. Second, such countries are characterized by poor institutional transparency: information on economic fundamentals, which is of considerable relevance to lenders' assessment of the borrower's future repayment capacity, is hard to come by. This may be due to poor data-collection capabilities in these countries, or obfuscation of relevant statistical information, especially in times of economic upheaval. Recent ambiguities about Greek national statistics provide an example. With limited information about fundamentals, any act of default (or, conversely, the act of repayment) provides a valuable signal about future economic prospects. Characteristically, when market expectations are shaped by observations on a binary choice—default versus repayment—beliefs become quite fragile. An act of default can lead investors to assume the worst, generating excessive pessimism about the country's future economic trajectory. Conversely, repayment, even when only narrowly achieved, can spawn confidence beyond that which is merited by the fundamentals.

Such fragility of expectations exacerbates the risk of serial default. Consider a sovereign borrower that finances its investment needs through issuing short-term debt (bonds) in international markets. Suppose that its ability to meet repayment obligations depends on its realized output, so that negative shocks to output can trigger default. If output shocks are persistent—so that a negative shock to output is likely to result a prolonged period of below-average performance—any direct observation of negative shocks will lead investors to reassess the likelihood of future default. When sovereign spreads are determined competitively and reflect the market assessment of sovereign default risk, we would expect the spread to rise. However—and this is the crucial point—if investors are unable to observe the economic fundamentals directly, they can only make inferences from observing default events. In such situations, an act of default triggers a dramatic revision of market expectations, and the greater pessimism result in a surge in sovereign spreads. We label this discrete jump in a country's sovereign spread following a default event as the *default premium*.

The discrete adjustment of market expectations to default events is reinforced by a feedback mechanism. The surge in sovereign spreads following default increases the cost of future borrowing, and this higher cost in turn makes it harder for the country to repay in the future. Investors, who set interest rates in competitive markets, must internalize this risk, so the interest rates for countries that default tend to rise sharply. On the other hand, countries that repay get the benefit of any market-held doubts, with lower interest rates; the lower borrowing costs reduce the risk of default, and market-determined interest rates are even lower for this reason. Given this feedback mechanism, the default premium—outcome of the gap between the pessimistic and optimistic assessments—can be quite large. Importantly, small chance events can tip a country from one trajectory to the other. For example, if default triggered by purely transitory shocks is misread by markets as a sign of future repayment difficulty, the resulting rise in sovereign spreads can have self-confirming consequences.

It is intuitive to see in this setting that this default trap becomes more acute when the output shocks display greater persistence. The underlying argument is intrinsically technical, but the intuition is plain to see. If income shocks are purely transitory rather than persistent, default in one period provides no information on the risk of future default. If so, the belief revision mechanism and the feedback process that support our model of serial default are of little relevance.

EMPIRICAL EVIDENCE

Our model of default traps gives rise to some testable hypotheses:

Hypothesis 1: Controlling for economic fundamentals, countries with a history of sovereign default face higher sovereign spreads; that is, there is a positive default premium.

Hypothesis 2: Countries with greater persistence of output shocks face higher sovereign spreads. The default premium rises with the persistence of output shocks.

Hypothesis 3: Countries with higher conditional volatility of output (that is, subject to sizable bad shocks) face higher spreads.

To test these hypotheses, we compiled a data set that spans a long period, starting from the early globalization years of the 1870s through to 2004 (see Catão, Fostel, and Kapur 2009 for details and data sources). We start by examining how a country's default risk depends empirically on various explanatory variables. The dependent variable in our regressions is the sovereign spread, measured as the (average) interest rate on a country's sovereign bonds relative to the benchmark foreign interest rate of similar maturity: that benchmark is the United Kingdom for the initial period, and the United States for the later periods in our long sample.

Exhibit 34.1 Determinants of Sovereign Spreads, 1870–1913

	1	2	3	4
U.K. real interest rate	0.013	0.011	0.012	0.012
	(2.430)*	(2.620)**	(2.380)*	(2.380)*
Debt/GDP	0.010	0.015	0.012	0.012
	(13.060)**	(22.170)**	(12.140)**	(13.260)**
Export/GDP	−0.005	−0.011	−0.011	−0.010
	(−2.050)*	(−8.090)**	(−3.370)**	(−2.990)**
Volatility	0.151		0.109	0.122
	(9.520)**		(6.520)**	(6.470)**
Persistence	0.004		0.003	0.002
	(5.630)**		(3.140)**	(2.470)*
Volatility instrument		0.180		
		(5.570)**		
Persistence instrument		0.004		
		(4.120)**		
Default history			0.059	0.065
			(9.910)**	(6.440)**
Default history * volatility				−0.895
				(−3.80)**
Default history * persistence				0.032
				(3.670)**
Observations	619	598	570	570
Number of countries	23	22	21	21
R-squared	0.24	0.23	0.27	0.28

Note: Robust z-statistics in parentheses; * denotes significance at 5%; ** significance at 1%.

The explanatory variables we consider are the international risk-free interest rate, the country's indebtedness (the ratio of external debt to GDP), its openness (ratio of exports to GDP), measures of volatility and persistence of output shocks,[4] and a default history indicator to capture the time-varying shifts in default premiums. Further, because the default history interacts with persistence and with volatility, interactive terms are included in the regressions.

Exhibit 34.1 spans the pre–World War I era, reporting the pooled ordinary least squares regressions of the country sovereign spread as the dependent variable. Column (1) reports our baseline specification without a default premium term. The estimated coefficients have signs that are consistent with our theoretical model and are statistically significant at 5 percent. The point estimates show that a one percentage point increase in the conditional volatility implies a 14 basis point increase in sovereign spreads, while a 10 percentage point increase in persistence raises spreads by 5 basis points, everything else being constant. These effects may appear small by the standards of the 1980s or 1990s, but not by those of the pre–World War I era. Column (2) shows that these results are robust to endogeneity problems, since similar estimates are obtained once volatility and persistent indicators are instrumented out.

Column (3) introduces default history as an explanatory variable. This country-specific credit history indicator gauges how much of the default premium following the borrower's action (default versus repayment) helps explain the evolution of spreads over and above the information contained in other fundamentals. Our indicator of default history is defined as the share of years in default since the beginning of the sample. As such, a positive default indicator decays over time with successive repayments and bounces back up every time a new default occurs. In terms of our model, we expect this variable to be positively correlated with current spreads and statistically significant. Its point estimate indicates that a country with a default history at the sample mean (0.08) has its spread boosted by over 40 basis points relative to a country that has never defaulted. Once again, since spreads for the period from 1870 to 1913 averaged some 200 basis points, the effect was substantial. In particular, for those countries in the sample that spent up to 30 percent of the time incurring arrears on foreign debt, the default premium could exceed 150 basis points. Column (4) measures how persistence and volatility of output interact with the default premium. Consistent with our model, conditional upon default, countries with higher persistence tend to have a higher default premium. In contrast, the negative sign on the interactive volatility variable (default history * volatility) indicates that higher conditional output volatility tends to dampen the default premium.

Exhibit 34.2 turns to the interwar period. For this period, neither the international risk-free rate nor the debt-to-GDP ratio is statistically significant at conventional levels though both retain their expected theoretical signs. The volatility and

Exhibit 34.2   Determinants of Sovereign Spreads, 1925–1939

	1	2	3	4
U.K. real interest rate	0.005	0.005	0.006	0.005
	(0.530)	(0.660)	(0.690)	(0.580)
Debt/GDP	0.004	0.001	0.008	0.009
	(1.540)	(0.230)	(5.440)**	(7.000)**
Export/GDP	−0.057	−0.051	−0.039	−0.04
	(−4.610)**	(−3.970)**	(−4.990)**	(−5.020)**
Volatility	0.333		0.187	0.305
	(3.930)**		(4.190)**	(4.020)**
Persistence	0.014		0.009	0.01
	(2.200)*		(2.610)**	(3.280)**
Volatility instrument		0.168		
		(2.950)**		
Persistence instrument		0.007		
		(1.810)		
Default history			0.099	0.192
			(18.700)**	(3.160)**
Default history * volatility				−3.447
				(−3.490)**
Default history * persistence				0.183
				(3.250)**
Observations	305	305	305	305
Number of countries	25	25	25	25
R-squared	0.12	0.11	0.62	0.64

Note: Robust z-statistics in parentheses; * denotes significance at 5%; ** significance at 1%.

persistence indicators remain significant at 5 percent and effect of persistence on spreads is now larger than in the pre–World War I sample: A 10 percentage point increase in persistence leads to 14 basis point increase in spreads. Instrumenting both variables out as in column (2) halves the respective coefficients, but both variables remain significant at close to 5 percent.

Column (3) in Exhibit 34.2 shows that introducing the default history as an explanatory variable has a major impact on the regression fit and also on the statistical significance of the debt-to-GDP ratio. This may not appear surprising since there were many defaults during this short period. However, the results signal the presence of a positive and large default premium, the existence of which has previously been disputed in the literature on the interwar period (Eichengreen and Portes 1986; Jorgenson and Sachs 1992). Introducing the interactive term between the default history and persistence also brings out results that clearly support our model.

Exhibit 34.3 reports the results for our last subsample, 1994–2004. Once again, the persistence and volatility variables are found to be statistically significant and so are the other two relevant model-dictated variables—the risk-free U.S. interest rate and the debt-to-GDP ratio. Once again, there is clear evidence of a positive and significant default premium, as shown in column (2). This is so even though the 1994–2004 sample is severely biased toward countries that have defaulted serially in the past (mostly issuers of Brady bonds), excluding all advanced countries that were previously present in the two pre–World War II samples. Regression results in column (3) reflect these two sample limitations—the very limited time-series

Exhibit 34.3 Determinants of Sovereign Spreads, 1994–2004

	1	2	3	4
U.S. real interest rate	0.161	0.161	0.177	0.173
	(2.140)**	(2.260)**	(2.330)**	(2.300)**
Debt/GDP	0.024	0.023	0.04	0.051
	(3.280)***	(2.940)***	(4.070)***	(4.540)***
Export/GDP	−0.044	−0.039	(0.050)	−0.057
	(−5.490)***	(−4.210)***	(5.720)***	(−6.120)***
Volatility	0.522	0.621	0.265	0.321
	(3.870)***	(3.850)***	(1.000)	(2.120)**
Persistence	0.020	0.019	0.028	0.022
	(3.320)***	(2.390)**	(5.290)***	(3.840)***
Default history		0.044	0.090	
		(1.970)**	(1.160)	
Default history * volatility			−0.138	
			(−1.510)	
Default history * persistence			0.415	1.544
			(0.320)	(2.510)**
Observations	189	189	189	189
Number of countries	28	28	28	28
R-squared	0.51	0.52	0.57	0.55

Notes: Robust z-statistics in parentheses; * denotes significance at 5%; ** significance at 1%.

dimension and the bias toward countries that with higher output volatility and persistence that have defaulted serially in the past. The resulting multicolinearity between the stand-alone default history variables and its interactive terms with conditional output volatility and persistence renders them statistically insignificant individually at 5 percent, when included together in the regression, although yielding the expected sign. Looking at the underlying data, the reason is clear: the correlation coefficients between default history and the two interactive terms are 0.89 and 0.92, respectively. In other words, not much new information can be drawn from such interactive terms once default history, persistence, and volatility are already present in the regression. Indeed, column (4) shows that once the two key variables of our model—namely, default history and shock persistence—are interacted, their joint significance is clear.

CONCLUSION

Theoretical models of sovereign debt typically assume that default is punished by denial of access to international capital markets. Our model builds instead on a punishment that takes the form of a long-lasting rise in the cost of issuing fresh debt, something widely observed in practice. In contrast with previous models, ours also highlights how imperfect information between lenders and borrowers exacerbates this cost: When lenders are poorly informed, a sovereign borrower's repayment choice can trigger a sharp shift in lenders' expectations about the risk of future default. Default causes the lenders to assuming the worst about the repayment prospects on future loans, while repayment creates a more favorable outlook. The difference between interest rates commensurate with these differing scenarios generates a default premium in sovereign spreads. The default premium raises the cost of future repayments beyond what is justified by the fundamentals, creating the possibility of default traps. That is, a country that has defaulted once will face a long-lasting higher cost of repaying which, in turn, makes it more prone to default again once hit by a sufficiently bad shock in the future. We argue that this is a key causal mechanism of serial default.

Our empirical estimations are fully consistent with such a mechanism: Previous default history and higher underlying persistence of output shocks are highly significant in explaining the evolution of sovereign spreads and risk of further defaults, over and above other determinants of country risk. To the extent that higher output persistence reflects deep structural features of some economies (such as poor institutions and widespread market failures) and that greater asymmetry of information between borrowers and lenders exacerbates market punishment of defaulters through higher spreads, mitigating these structural and informational weaknesses are key to avoiding default traps. Yet, history also indicates that tackling these deep-rooted weaknesses is bound to be a hard and long process, and one potentially subject to great reversals. As a result, graduation from serial default is hardly a trivial path, and will possibly remain a nonmonotonic one in practice.

NOTES

1. A list of sovereign default and debt rescheduling episodes can be compiled from various sources, including Lindert and Morton (1989), Borensztein and Panizza (2009),

Sturzenegger and Zettelmeyer (2007), Reinhart and Rogoff (2009), and Moody's (2009). While there are discrepancies among these sources when it comes to classifying events as default or rescheduling, the identification of serial defaulters, broadly defined, is unequivocal.

2. See, for example, the well-known surveys of the sovereign debt literature, such as Eaton and Fernandez (1995), Obstfeld and Rogoff (1996), Sturzenegger and Zettelmeyer (2007), and Reinhart and Rogoff (2009).

3. This analysis is based on Catão, Fostel, and Kapur (2009).

4. One issue in constructing volatility and persistence measures to input as regressors is whether the shocks in the model should be interpreted as shocks to trends or shocks to cycle. It turns out that our findings are robust to this choice. Hence, we report results based on a standard measure of stochastic persistence the slope coefficient of a regression of detrended real GDP (obtained by the standard HP-filter method, which makes the series stationary) on its first-order lag. Using the same regression, we compute stochastic volatility as the standard deviation of the residuals. To allow for gradually evolving changes in volatility and persistence, we compute both measures recursively over a 20-year rolling window, except for earlier in the sample, where we use 10-year windows to economize on degrees of freedom.

REFERENCES

Borensztein, E., and U. Panizza. 2009. "The Costs of Sovereign Default." *IMF Staff Papers* 56: 4, 683–741.

Catão, L.A.V., A. Fostel, and S. Kapur. 2009. "Persistent Gaps and Default Traps." *Journal of Development Economics* 89:2, 271–284.

Eaton, J., and R. Fernandez. 1995. "Sovereign Debt." In G. Grossman and K. Rogoff, eds. *Handbook of International Economics*, vol. 3, 2031–2077. Amsterdam: Elsevier.

Eichengreen, B., and R. Portes. 1986. "Debt and Default in the 1930s: Causes and Consequences." *European Economic Review* 30, 599–640.

Jorgensen, E., and J. Sachs. 1992. "Default and Renegotiation of Latin American Foreign Bonds in the Interwar Period." In B. Eichengreen and P. Lindert, eds. *The International Debt Crisis in Historical Perspective*. Cambridge, MA: MIT Press.

Lindert, P., and P. Morton. 1989. "How Sovereign Debt Has Worked." In Jeffrey Sachs, ed. *Developing Country Debt and Economic Performance: The International Financial System*. Chicago: National Bureau of Economic Research.

Moody's. 2009. "Sovereign Defaults and Recovery Rates, 1983–2008," New York and London: Moody's.

Obstfeld, M., and K. Rogoff. 1996. *Foundations of International Macroeconomics*. Cambridge, MA: MIT Press.

Reinhart, C., and K. Rogoff. 2009. *This Time Is Different: Eight Centuries of Financial Folly*. Princeton, NJ: Princeton University Press.

Sturzenegger, F., and J. Zettelmeyer. 2007. *Debt Defaults and Lessons from a Decade of Crises*. Cambridge, MA: MIT Press.

ABOUT THE AUTHORS

Luis A.V. Catão is a senior economist at the research department of the International Monetary Fund. His research spans international finance and open economy macroeconomics, including sovereign debt and emerging market risk, exchange rate modeling and empirics, monetary policy and inflation, international business cycles, and long-term economic growth, with particular reference to Latin America.

Dr. Catão was graduated in electrical engineering and also in economics (with honors) at the Federal University of Rio de Janeiro, and holds a master's and PhD degrees from the University of Cambridge. He has been an associate professor at the University of London, a research fellow at the Institute of Latin American Studies of the same university, and a visiting scholar at UCLA. More recently, he also held a senior position in the office of chief economist at the Inter-American Development Bank. He has published in academic and policy-oriented journals, including the *American Economic Review*, the *Journal of Monetary Economics*, the *Journal of Development Economics*, and the *IMF Staff Papers*. His research has received press coverage in *The Economist*, *Dow Jones International News*, *The Herald Tribune*, the *Washington Post*, and *Valor Economico*, among other newspapers and magazines.

Ana Fostel is an assistant professor at George Washington University. She earned a PhD in economics from Yale University in 2005 under the direction of John Geanakoplos, Andres Velasco, and Herb Scarf. Her research interests are in economic theory and finance. Her research has focused on two areas. The first is leverage. The main objective is to explain what determines leverage in general equilibrium models with incomplete markets, if market leverage levels are optimal, and asset price implications of leverage as well as its impact on investment and output. The second is sovereign debt and default risk. The main objective is to explain what are the main determinants of sovereign risk and their impact on international capital flows. She teaches undergraduate and graduate courses in international financial markets. She is currently visiting the IMF as a research visitor scholar.

Sandeep Kapur is a professor of economics at Birkbeck, University of London. He has a PhD in economics from the University of Cambridge, and has previously held teaching positions at Cambridge, University of Pennsylvania, and George Washington University. His research output spans the areas of financial intermediation, the design of pension systems, economic and financial regulation, and the economics of new technologies. More recently, his interests include the growing internationalization of firms from China and India, and the design of policy responses to this emerging trend. Dr. Kapur has served as an advisor to many government departments in the United Kingdom.

CHAPTER 35

Self-Fulfilling and Self-Enforcing Debt Crises

DANIEL COHEN
Paris School of Economics

SEBASTIEN VILLEMOT
Paris School of Economics

International debt crises are (very) costly. Why do we observe that so many countries fall into that trap? Should we not expect more prudent behavior from such countries? The theoretical answer in fact is: It depends. Take the simplest form of financial crisis driven by an exogenous shock. Spreads on sovereign bonds are high because the country is expected to be vulnerable to a financial earthquake or to a long-lasting commodity shock that is beyond its control. The country should then indeed behave with increased prudence: The greater the debt the country might have to repay, the heavier the cost of the earthquake relative to a favorable state of nature. Yet, on the other hand, if the expected earthquake is so large that the country knows that it will actually default on its debt, then a *Panglossian attitude* (as Krugman has coined it) may become rational: The debt will lose all value after the earthquake, and it would then be absurd not to have borrowed more beforehand. The country then behaves as if the risk of unfavorable shocks can be ignored. Following Dr. Pangloss, the character of Voltaire's book *Candide,* the country acts as if only "the best of all possible worlds" will occur. In this case, debt endogenously leads to more debt; we call this the self-enforcing case.

Let us now consider the case when crises are driven by the lack of confidence of financial markets toward a given country, making the country financially fragile through self-fulfilling behavior. Self-fulfilling debt crises have been analyzed in different forms. In the model of Cole and Kehoe (1996 and 2000) self-fulfilling crises are a variant of a liquidity crisis, by which a lack of coordination among creditors leads a solvent country to default. As argued by Chamon (2007), however, such crises can readily be avoided when lenders manage to offer contingent loans of the kind organized by venture capitalists. If any individual creditor offers a line of credit conditionally on other creditors following suit, then liquidity crises can be easily avoided.

Self-fulfilling crises have also been analyzed as the perverse outcome of a snowball effect through which the build-up of debt becomes unmanageable out of the endogenous fear that it can indeed become unmanageable (Calvo 1988). Relying on an intuition developed in a simpler model in Cohen and Portes (2004), Cohen and Villemot (2010) show that snowball spirals can occur only in cases in which a debt crisis has the potential of damaging the fundamentals of the indebted country. If a crisis reduces the GDP of a country by, say 10 percent, then it is clear that the lack of confidence toward a country can degenerate into a self-fulfilling crisis. If instead the fundamentals are not altered by the crisis, we show that self-fulfilling crises of the Calvo type are (theoretically) impossible.

At the end of this argument, a simple characterization of a self-fulfilling debt crisis is possible, as one that is the outcome of an endogenous weakening of the country's fundamentals. In the self-fulfilling case so defined, it is the crisis that reduces GDP, originating from the various disruptions that a weakening of the confidence in a country may bring about (capital flight, exchange rate crisis, and so on). In the earthquake case, the sequence of causation is inversed: the fundamentals are first destroyed, then the crisis occurs.

A simple typology of cases is then obtained. Below a critical level of debt, a country tends to act prudently, aiming, for example, to reduce its debt in response to a permanent adverse shock. Past a critical level of the debt-to-GDP ratio, which can be the outcome of a sequence of repeated unfavorable exogenous shocks, a country will begin to behave in the Panglossian mode, rationally ignoring the bad news, increasing the level of debt to its upper limit in a self-enforcing process. A crisis may then occur either because of the occurrence of another adverse exogenous shock, or because of a self-fulfilling shock, one that endogenously weakens the ability of a country to service its debt.

We approach the data with this type of typology. We use a slightly modified version of the database that has been compiled by Kraay and Nehru (2004), which we updated to cover all debt crises that have occurred until 2004. Following and adapting the work of these authors, we show that the likelihood of a debt crisis is well explained by three factors: the debt-to-GDP ratio, the level of real income per capita, and a measure of overvaluation of the domestic currency.

To best estimate the risk of a self-fulfilling debt crisis, we then distinguish the law of motion of debt in tranquil times from the motion triggered by the onset of the crisis. We define a self-fulfilling crisis as one that would not have happened, had debt simply been driven along the pre-crisis path. We also calibrate the strength of the Panglossian effect. We show that countries do appear to have behaved as if the distribution of the risk was truncated, leading the country to ignore risk. The influence of both mechanisms is tested through Monte Carlo simulation. They add up to about 20 percent of all debt crises.

DATA SET

Our empirical strategy relies on a data set of *debt distress* and *normal times* episodes, following the methodology of Kraay and Nehru (2004).

More precisely, for a given year, a country is considered to be in debt crisis if at least one of the following three conditions holds:

1. The country receives debt relief from the Paris Club in the form of a rescheduling or a debt reduction.

2. The sum of its principal and interest in arrears is large relative to the outstanding debt stock.
3. The country receives substantial balance of payments support from the IMF through a nonconcessional standby arrangement (SBA) or an extended fund facility (EFF).

For the last two conditions, we choose the same thresholds as do Kraay and Nehru (2004), that is, a country is considered to be in crisis if its arrears are above 5 percent of the total stock of its outstanding debt, or if the total amount agreed to under SBA/EFF arrangements is above 50 percent of the country's IMF quota. Moreover, a country receiving Paris Club relief for a given year is also considered to be in crisis for the following two years, since the relief decision is typically based on three-year balance of payments projections by the IMF.

Having defined when a country is considered to be in crisis or not, we then define debt distress episodes as periods of at least three consecutive years of crisis. Moreover, we impose the restriction that a distress episode should be preceded by at least three years without crisis, so that we are able to consider macroeconomic variables before a crisis episode as being exogenous to the crisis.

We also define normal times episodes as five consecutive years without any crisis (imposing no other restriction).

For identifying debt distress and normal times episodes, we use the following data sources:

The World Bank's Global Development Finance 2006 for data on debt levels and payment arrears
The Paris Club web site (www.clubdeparis.org)

For information on debt relief:

The IMF's International Financial Statistics 2006 for data on SBA/EFF commitments.

In our subsequent econometric estimations, we also use two other sources:

The World Bank's World Development Indicators 2006 for general macroeconomic variables
The Penn Word Tables (version 6.2) for data on Purchasing Power Parity (PPP) variables.

The set of countries for which the computations are made consists of the 135 developing countries as defined by the World Bank, from which we removed the 38 countries that have absolutely no access to private financial markets. We define market access as in Gelos, Sahay, and Sandleris (2004). The countries we removed are those that never accessed international credit markets between 1980 and 2000, in accordance with the authors' definition.

We choose to remove them since their situation of indebtedness is somewhat different from that of the rest of the developing world (in particular, they have a much higher proportion of concessional lending). From the standpoint of the model, they probably fall into the category of countries that have no access to risky markets, and their debt dynamics must consequently be different.

We are therefore left with a sample of 97 countries. From the time angle, our data cover the period from 1970 to 2004. Before the elimination of certain observations in our econometric estimations (due to missing data), our largest sample of episodes consists of 70 distress episodes, and 223 normal times episodes.

To summarize, the differences between our data set and that of Kraay and Nehru are twofold: First, we update their data to 2004, which is relatively minor but allows us to include the Ecuadorian debt crisis of 2000, for example. Second, we restrict our analysis to the emerging countries that have access to private credit markets.

The Econometric Model

Our empirical framework is given by a system of three simultaneous equations explaining, respectively, debt dynamics, growth, and crises. Each law of motion is affected by independent shocks.

The first equation reflects a debt dynamics equation, from past debt to new one, incorporating the potential of a Panglossian effect. We interpret the shock as pure noise, in the spirit of Campos et al. (2006), who show that the dynamics of debt are barely explained by deficit and much more by unforeseeable shocks (such as valuation effect, hidden contingent liabilities, and so on).

In the growth equation, the shock is the driver of the country's growth exogenous uncertainty. Depending on the occurrence of a debt crisis, growth can be endogenously reduced.

Finally, in the debt crisis equation, the shock corresponds to the variability of the threshold level of debt default, such as driven by the variability of the financial markets.

There is a circular dependency between the three endogenous variables. This feature is precisely the possibility of multiple equilibria that we are trying to modelize. When multiple equilibria are possible, we introduce a stochastic variable (with only two possible values) that determines which equilibrium to choose: It is a sunspot variable, as it is sometimes called in the literature, that is, a variable with no relation to economic fundamentals but which makes agents coordinate on one equilibrium when several are possible.

Simulating the Model

Our strategy is that we simulate the dynamic model described by equations over several periods, for a given trajectory of random draws.

We start from an initial debt-to-GDP ratio of 60 percent. We simulate 2,500 series of five periods (that is, of 10 years, since lagged variables are taken 2 years earlier).

The dynamics of the model are affected by four shocks that may be switched off for comparison purposes: shocks to the law of motion of debt, to growth, to the crisis equation, plus the self-fulfilling shock. We also consider simulations in which the Panglossian effect is switched off (just by removing the corresponding

Exhibit 35.1 Causes of Debt Crises

Effect	Contribution
Crisis shock	55.80%
Debt shock	15.20%
Panglossian effect	12.00%
Growth shock	11.00%
Self-fulfilling	6.10%
Total	*100%*

term in the debt equation). Thus, there is a total of $2^5 = 32$ possible combinations according to whether or not we activate these five effects.

When the five effects are activated, 89.4 percent of the simulations exhibit a crisis episode in at least one of the five simulation periods. This high occurrence rate of crisis is the consequence of the relatively high level of the debt-to-GDP ratio that we have chosen as the starting point for simulations.

To most accurately compute the contribution of each of these five effects to these crises, we shut off each of them one by one, and observe by how much the number of crises diminishes, which gives the contribution of each one. An issue is that the results depend on the order in which the effects are shut down: We solve this problem by making these computations for the 120 possible orders, and by computing the average contributions.

We present the results in Exhibit 35.1, which reports the contribution of each effect: It shows the percentage of crisis episodes that can be considered a direct consequence of each effect.

One can see that the largest contributor is by far the crisis shock, which explains more than 55 percent of crises: This means that most crises are triggered by events not related to the level of the debt-to-GDP ratio, but related to the uncertainties due to the financial market themselves. For the remaining crises, the Panglossian effect comes third, explaining about 12 percent of the crises, while the self-fulfilling effect accounts for about 6 percent.

CONCLUSION

We have tried to distinguish two attitudes toward debt: the attitude of prudent borrowers, who attempt to stabilize their debt at low levels, even in the event of an adverse shock, and Panglossian borrowers, who only take into account the best scenarios possible, rationally anticipating to default on their debt if hit by an unfavorable shock (or by a sequence of them). We have shown empirically that this distinction is consistent with the data. We have also distinguished two types of debt crises: those that are the effect of an exogenous shock, and those that are created in a self-fulfilling manner by the financial markets themselves.

We have shown that the majority of crises are due to the uncertainties regarding the financial market themselves. Self-fulfilling and Panglossian crises explain together about 18 percent of the crises. This is more important than growth or debt uncertainties taken in isolation, although both of them (the traditional channels in the theory) account for about a quarter of the cases.

REFERENCES

Calvo, G. A. 1988. "Servicing the Public Debt: The Role of Expectations." *The American Economic Review* 78: 647–661.

Campos, C. F., D. Jaimovich, and U. Panizza. 2006. "The Unexplained Part of Public Debt." *Emerging Markets Review* 7: 228–243.

Chamon, M. 2007. "Can Debt Crises Be Self-Fulfilling?" *Journal of Development Economics* 82: 234–244.

Cohen, D., and R. Portes. 2004. "Towards a Lender of First Resort." *Centre for Economic Policy Research,* Discussion Paper 4615.

Cohen, D., and S. Villemot. 2010. "Endogenous Debt Crises." Forthcoming, Paris School of Economics.

Cole, H. L., and T. J. Kehoe. 1996. "A Self-Fulfilling Model of Mexico's 1994–1995 Debt Crisis." *Journal of International Economics* 41: 309–330.

———. 2000. "Self-Fulfilling Debt Crises." *The Review of Economic Studies* 67: 91–116.

Gelos, R. G., R. Sahay, and G. Sandleris. 2004. "Sovereign Borrowing by Developing Countries: What Determines Market Access?" *Working Paper* 04/221. International Monetary Fund.

Kraay, A., and V. Nehru. 2004. "When Is External Debt Sustainable?" *Policy Research Working Paper* 3200. The World Bank.

ABOUT THE AUTHORS

Daniel Cohen is a professor of economics at the Paris School of Economics and the director of Centre pour la Recherche Economique et ses Applications (CEPREMAP). He is also a research fellow at the Centre for Economic Policy Research (CEPR).

Sebastien Villemot is a research fellow at CEPREMAP.

CHAPTER 36

The Impact of Economic and Political Factors on Sovereign Credit Ratings

CONSTANTIN MELLIOS
Professor of Finance, the University of Paris 1 Panthéon-Sorbonne

ERIC PAGET-BLANC
Professor of Finance, the University of Evry

T he important role played by rating agencies raises the question of the main determinants of the ratings they assign to sovereign bonds. The purpose of this study is to examine the factors affecting sovereign credit ratings provided by the three major rating agencies: Fitch Ratings, Moody's, and Standard and Poor's. Instead of choosing these factors a priori, we follow a rigorous methodology by using a principal component analysis and a logistic model to detect the most (statistically) significant of them. Our results, in accordance with other studies, show that sovereign ratings are mostly influenced by government income, real exchange rate changes, inflation rate, and domestic savings. In contrast, default history and corruption turn out to be crucial factors, which appear as proxies for both economic development and the quality of the governance of a country.

INTRODUCTION

Rating agencies[1] play a crucial role in the assessment of the risk of default of sovereign bonds. It turns out to be of great importance to identify which factors affect the agencies' decisions. The current debt crisis in the many developed countries, in particular in the European Union, illustrates the importance of the debt issued by states—or sovereign debt—on capital markets. The U.S. Treasury is the largest debtor in the world, and developed countries as a whole are the largest issuers of debt on the international bond markets. Emerging countries, which long relied upon bank financing, have also increasingly resorted to the bond markets since the 1990s, which has outpaced the growth in bank lending in the 2000s. Governments can issue debt in local or in foreign currency. The former is generally easier to repay, as governments can ask their central bank to purchase their bonds, a process known as monetization because it involves creation of money and, eventually, inflation. By contrast, countries have to generate foreign exchange revenues to repay their debt denominated in foreign currencies.

In the late 1980s and in the 1990s, a number of emerging countries[2] were confronted with debt crises, and some of them defaulted on their debt in foreign currency. According to Standard and Poor's, the average default on sovereign debt in foreign currency reached its peak in 1992 at 34.8 percent, from 1.2 percent in 1975. In the late 1990s and early 2000s, a number of Eastern Europe (Russia and Ukraine) and Latin American (Argentina) countries defaulted on their foreign currency bonds. As there is no bankruptcy code for sovereign debt, it is difficult for a foreign investor to seize the assets of a government, which is in arrears on the service of its debt—though some so-called vulture funds have managed to do so. The alternative for creditors is to renegotiate the terms of their debt. This is done through an association of creditors, including official lenders—Paris Club—or private financial institutions—London Club—that ensure that all the creditors are equally treated, and hence reinforces the creditors' bargaining power. In the 1980s, 1990s, and 2000s, a number of emerging countries had to restructure their debt in foreign currency. As a consequence, the demand for sovereign credit ratings has significantly increased since the 1990s, as foreign bondholders purchasing government debt need information on the risk of default of sovereign issuers (see Exhibit 36.1).

A sovereign credit rating is an assessment of the risk of default of government bonds assigned by an independent entity called a rating agency. They allow estimating the probability of default of a government on its public debt, but they do not address the default risk of other issuers in the same country.[3] Rating agencies distinguish local and foreign currency sovereign ratings. Typically, ratings of foreign currency denominated debt are lower than those of domestic currency debt,

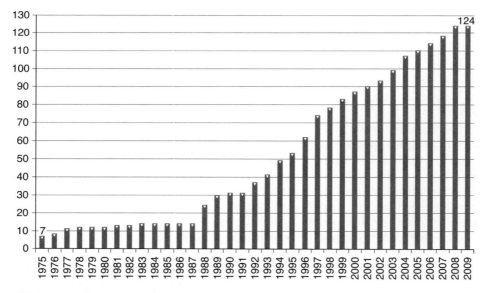

Exhibit 36.1   Sovereign Debt Ratings by S&P (1975–2009)

as the latter can be repaid more easily through monetization (see Trevino and Thomas 2001).

Rating agencies assign a grade to a borrower according to its degree of relative creditworthiness. The grades range from AAA, the highest rate, (Fitch and S&P) or Aaa (Moody's) to, respectively, D and Caa, the lowest rate. A credit rating between AAA and BBB– is used to denote an investment grade debt, while a debt rated BB+ to D is considered as speculative, or high yield. Although the three agencies use different symbols for their ratings, there is a correspondence between the different rating systems. Sovereign credit ratings greatly influence the terms and the extent to which government can access international bond markets. The downgrade of the ratings of Greece by the three international rating agencies in 2010 considerably increased the interest rate paid by this country on its public debt, as investors willing to buy these bonds required a higher risk premium.

The remainder of this paper is organized as follows. The next section provides a brief discussion on sovereign debt and default that can explain the choice of the explanatory variables. In the section after that, we present and discuss our main results. Finally, the last section concludes our discussion.

Potential Explanatory Variables of Sovereign Credit Ratings

Rating agencies use a combination of several quantitative and qualitative variables (economic, social, and political) to assign a credit rating to a debtor or to a debt instrument. These criteria are listed in methodological documents published and regularly updated by the three main rating agencies. The quantitative variables include a number of economic and financial measures, while the political and policy aspects constitute mostly a qualitative appraisal of default. An important question is thus to determine the number and the nature of the factors, which are statistically significant in explaining sovereign credit ratings. Exhibit 36.2 summarizes the most important variables affecting the probability of sovereign default and thus the sovereign ratings.

Explanations of sovereign default can be divided in two main approaches. In the first one, since, when a default occurs, the lender to a country may not have recourse to a bankruptcy code and thus to a procedure to force payment, the main question is to know why do sovereign debtors repay their debts. Eaton and Gersovitz (1981) and Grossman and Van Huyck (1988) suggest that a country may be motivated to pay its debt so it can better keep its good reputation and to maintain future access to credit markets. If a country decides not to honor its debt to keep up their good reputation for repayment, lending to small countries is then possible, if additional, economic, political, and legal sanctions are imposed (Bulow and Rogoff 1989b). A country rarely makes an outright default but, rather, it renegotiates its original debt. The rescheduling of (or default on) a country's debt results from a bargaining game between creditors and the borrower (Bulow and Rogoff 1989a). The choice made by the latter is based on an assessment of the costs and benefits of rescheduling or defaulting.

The second approach to sovereign default risk is described by Haque et al. (1996) as the debt-servicing capacity approach. In this approach, it is the unintended deterioration of the country's capacity to service its debt that could cause its default. The capacity of a country to pay its debts depends on its solvency or liquidity.

Exhibit 36.2   Description of the Potential Explanatory Variables

Variable	Economic Rationale	Theoretical Predictions
Per capita income	An increasing of the per capita income implies a larger potential tax base and a greater ability of a country to repay debt.	−
GDP growth	An increasing rate of the economic growth tends to decrease the relative debt burden. Moreover, it may contribute to avoid insolvency problems.	−
Inflation rate	A low inflation rate reveals sustainable monetary and exchange rate policies. It can be also seen as a proxy of the quality of economic management.	+
Economic development	Developed countries are integrated with the world economy and are less incited to default on their foreign debts so as to avoid sanctions from the lenders.	−
Current account	A large current account deficit implies the dependence of a country on foreign creditors. A persistent deficit affects its sustainability.	+
Foreign debt/GDP	This ratio is negatively related to default risk.	+
Real exchange rate	The real exchange rate assesses the trade competitiveness of the economy.	+
Default history	A country's default history affects its reputation.	+
Ratio debt/GDP	The higher this ratio is, the greater the occurrence of a liquidity crisis.	+
Ratio reserves/ imports	The higher this ratio is, the more reserves are available to service foreign debt.	+
Corruption Index	This index is a measure of political risk and can reduce a country's willingness to pay.	+
Aggregate Governance Indicators	This composite index allows evaluating the governance of a country and affects a country's willingness to pay.	−

Note: For theoretical predictions, a sign + (−) means that the theory predicts a positive (negative) relation between the explanatory variable and the risk of default.

For example, macroeconomic variables, economic policy, currency crisis, short-term budget mismanagement, and internal or external shocks may affect short-term liquidity or long-term solvency. In recent years, the case of some countries may illustrate debt-servicing difficulties ranging from liquidity crises to outright defaults (South Korea, Brazil, Turkey, Russia, Ecuador, Argentina, and Greece). In some cases, outright default has been avoided by the intervention of international financial institutions.

Many of the economic variables are common in the two approaches since they affect the opportunity cost of a country to make debt payments as well as its capacity to service its debt. However, the impact of the political risk on the probability of default is different in the two approaches. In the first one, political risk has an impact not only on the ability but also on the willingness of a country to pay its debt. In the second one, political risk relies on the quality of economic management and influences the debt-servicing ability of a country.

Many empirical studies have examined the impact of economic factors on sovereign ratings and on the difficulties of a country to service its external debt (Cantor and Packer 1996; Haque et al. 1996; Larrain et al. 1997; Jüttner and McCarthy 2000; Monfort and Mulder 2000; Mulder and Perrelli 2001; Afonso, 2003). Based on the preceding arguments, these authors choose a priori a parsimonious subjective set of economic explanatory variables. Although the reasoning of the choice of the variables is rigorous, some important factors may have been omitted. Moreover, since the payment of a country's debt depends on its willingness, political factors should play a crucial role in determining sovereign ratings. Unfortunately, the limited existing empirical evidence on political risk (see, for example, Brewer and Rivoli 1990; Cosset and Roy 1991; Lee 1993; Haque et al. 1998; Mckenzie 2002) is an obstacle to a better understanding of the rating agencies' decisions. The political situation of many emerging countries and some developed countries is an informative example. Some countries may have sound economic indicators, but a low rating due to corruption or a deteriorating economic situation may be explained by a corrupt political regime. Political variables can also have a strong influence on the estimation of the parameters of economic variables.

Instead of postulating the variables affecting sovereign credit ratings, we suggest a rigorous methodology to determine the factors explaining these ratings, including political risk.

MAIN RESULTS

The main results are extracted from Mellios and Paget-Blanc (2006). The data used in this paper include the foreign currency ratings assigned by three rating agencies—Fitch, Moody's, and Standard & Poor's—based on the ratings of 86 countries, published in December 2003, and a series of 46 variables available at the end of 2002. All countries were rated by Fitch, 75 by Moody's, and 74 by S&P. The ratings do not differ significantly across the three agencies. The average rating score difference between Fitch and Moody's is 0.34 notch; between Fitch and S&P, 0.04 notch; and between S&P and Moody's, 0.36 notch.

To identify the possible factors that explain sovereign ratings, a two-step procedure is followed. First, the principal components analysis (PCA) method has been employed to reduce the initial set of the explanatory variables and to identify a small group of factors that best describe these ratings. Second, the impact of the factors on the ratings has been assessed using an ordered logistic model of the rating levels.[4]

The PCA allows us to reduce the original data from 49 variables to 13 factors with a low loss of information. Exhibit 36.3 reports the list of extracted factors and their meaning. Although 12 of them are economic factors, one of them can be clearly assimilated to a political factor. It is worth pointing out that the importance of the factors is similar to that used by rating agencies in their methodology. In contrast, the heavy weight of the development level is not explicitly taken into account in their methodology. Moreover, the corruption level—measured by a Transparency International Index—which could be a priori considered as a

Exhibit 36.3   Identification of Extracted Factors

Factor Significance

1. Development level	8. Inflationary pressure
2. Public indebtedness	9. Net investment inflows
3. Quality of governance/ political stability	10. Size of the economy
4. Economic growth	11. Competitiveness
5. Money supply	12. Debt servicing
6. External liquidity	13. Balance of payments
7. External indebtedness and openness	

political factor, appears highly correlated with variables associated with the level of development. It follows that this index can also be considered as a proxy for the level of development. The PCA method, however, does not provide information regarding the effect of each factor on the ratings assigned by agencies.

The second step of our methodology allows us to precisely measure which variables have the most significant impact on agencies' rating. The logistic model further reduces the number of variables to nine. As shown in Exhibit 36.4, six of them seem to be the most prominent. As would be expected from economic or financial arguments, the changes of the real exchange rate, the gross domestic savings, and the government's income have a positive effect on the ratings, while the inflation rate has a negative one. Moreover, the default history of a country turns out to be a crucial determinant of sovereign ratings. This indicates that countries that have defaulted once on their official debt are rated, on average, 1.4 notches below countries with a good track record. This result has to be analyzed with caution, as the default history is related to a country's GDP and government debt, which have been captured in other variables. However, it constitutes an important indicator of a country's willingness to repay its debt: several countries

Exhibit 36.4   Logistic Regression: Model Specification

Independent Selected Variables	Estimated Coefficient
Real effective exchange rate (% change)	0.115
Gross domestic savings	0.079
Gross public external debt (in % of current external receipts)	−0.013
Gross national income PPP per capita (in USD)	0.000
Consumer prices (% change)	−0.133
Trade dependency	−0.034
Government revenue (% of GDP)	0.070
Corruption perception index	0.736
Default history (dummy)	1.394

Note: Significance at the 1% level.

Exhibit 36.5 Comparison between Observed and Predicted Rating Values

	Total	Cumulative	% Cumulative
4 notches and more	1	1	1.16%
3 to 4 notches	2	3	3.49%
2 to 3 notches	11	14	16.28%
1 to 2 notches	25	39	45.35%
Less than one notch	47	86	100.00%

rescheduled their official debt in recent years while their economic fundamentals did not deteriorate to the point at which they could not assume the service of external debt. This was the case, for example, of Gabon and Nigeria. It is interesting to mention that the corruption index has the second most important impact on ratings. The developed and more competitive countries have high ratings.

Another important aspect of the logistic model is its predictive power. Indeed, for our sample of 86 countries, the difference between predicted and observed rating values is less than two notches for 72 countries, and three notches for 83 countries.

As shown in Exhibit 36.5, only one estimated rating, Luxembourg, deviates by more than four notches from the observed ratings and two by three rating notches, Ecuador and Ukraine. For Luxemburg, the model predicts a rating four notches higher than AAA, which is the maximum of the scale, and hence cannot be considered as a prediction error. Ecuador and Ukraine, which defaulted on official debt in 2000 and 2001, respectively, provide a good illustration of the negative impact that recent defaults produce on creditworthiness perception. They are both rated on average three notches below the predicted rating score. Although their economic fundamentals have been somewhat improved since then, rating agencies prefer to wait before upgrading the rating to a level corresponding to economic fundamentals. The same argument can be brought forward to explain the low ratings assigned by agencies to Cape Verde and Indonesia, which restructured their debt in 2002, and Uruguay, which defaulted in 2003. The Dominican Republic, with an observed rating 2.3 notches below its predicted score, saw its financial situation deteriorate considerably in the course of the year 2003, which was reflected in December 2003 rating, but does not appear in the economic data of 2002. These facts highlight the difficulty in using a prediction model based on lagged independent variables.

CONCLUSION

The main objective of this paper was to study the determinants of sovereign credit ratings of the three major rating agencies. Our methodology allows us to show that among the 49 variables used by these agencies to assign a rating to a sovereign debt, six of them turn out to be significant. Although some of them are economic factors (real exchange rate, government revenue, inflation rate, and domestic savings), two of them may be viewed as political factors.

NOTES

1. The three major rating agencies are Fitch Ratings, Moody's, and Standard & Poor's (S&P).
2. See Dailami, Kalsi, and Shaw (2003), Chapter 3. An annex provides a list of commercial debt restructuring activities of developing countries since 1980.
3. Notice that sovereign ratings affect corporate ratings and debt markets. When investors have little information about a country and its firms, they tend to associate sovereign ratings to country risk.
4. The logistic model is well adapted to model sovereign ratings. Its objective is to express the probability of a rating score assigned to a country as a function of the economic and political determinants of this country.

REFERENCES

Afonso, A. 2003. "Understanding the Determinants of Sovereign Debt Ratings: Evidence of the Two Leading Agencies." *Journal of Economics and Finance* 27: 56–74.

Brewer, T., and P. Rivoli. 1990. "Politics and Perceived Country Creditworthiness in International Banking." *Journal of Money, Credit and Banking* 22: 357–369.

Bulow, J., and K. Rogoff. 1989a. "A Constant Recontracting Model of Sovereign Debt." *Journal of Political Economy* 97: 155–178.

———. 1989b. "Sovereign Debt: Is Forgive to Forget." *American Economic Review* 79: 43–50.

Cantor, R., and F. Packer. 1996. "Determinants and Impact of Sovereign Credit Ratings." *Reserve Bank of New York Economic Policy Review* 2: 37–53.

Cosset, J.-C., and J. Roy. 1991. "The Determinants of Country Risk Ratings." *Journal of International Business Studies* 22: 135–142.

Dailami, M., H. Kalsi, and W. Shaw. 2003. "Coping with Weak Private Debt Flows." In *Global Development Finance*, Chapter 3. Washington, DC: World Bank.

Eaton, J., and M. Gersovitz. 1981. "Debt with Potential Repudiation: Theoretical and Empirical Analysis." *Review of Economic Studies* 48: 288–309.

Grossman H., and J. Van Huyck. 1988. "Sovereign Debt as a Contingent Claim: Excusable Default, Repudiation and Reputation." *American Economic Review* 78: 1088–1097.

Haque, N., M. Kumar, N. Mark, and D. Mathieson. 1996. "The Economic Content of Indicators of Developing Country Creditworthiness." *IMF Staff Papers* 43: 688–724.

Haque, N., N. Mark, and D. Mathieson. 1998. "The Relative Importance of Political and Economic Variables in Creditworthiness Ratings." *IMF Working Paper* 98/46.

Jüttner J., and J. McCarthy. 2000. "Modeling a Rating Crisis." Working Paper. Macquarie University.

Larrain G., H. Reisen, and J. Maltzan. 1997. "Emerging Market Risk and Sovereign Credit Ratings." OECD Development Center. *Technical Paper* 124.

Lee, S. 1993. "Relative Importance of Political Instability and Economic Variables on Perceived Country Creditworthiness." *Journal of International Business Studies* 24: 801–812.

McKenzie, D. 2002. "An Econometric Analysis of IBRD Creditworthiness." *Policy Research Working Paper* 2822. Washington, DC: World Bank.

Mellios, C., and E. Paget-Blanc. 2006. "Which Factors Determine Sovereign Credit ratings?" *The European Journal of Finance* 12: 361–377.

Monfort, B., and C. Mulder. 2000. "Using Credit Ratings for Capital Requirements on Lending to Emerging Market Economies: Possible Impact of a New Basel Accord." *IMF Working Paper* 00/69.

Mulder, C., and R. Perrelli. 2001. "Foreign Currency Credit Ratings for Emerging Market Economies." *IMF Working Paper* 01/191.

Trevino, L., and S. Thomas S. 2001. "Local versus Foreign Currency Ratings: What Determines Sovereign Transfer Risk?" *The Journal of Fixed Income* 11:1, 65–75.

ABOUT THE AUTHORS

Constantin Mellios is a professor of finance at the University of Paris 1, Panthéon-Sorbonne, where he is in charge of the master in Financial Markets and head of the research center in business studies, PRISM-Sorbonne. He earned his PhD in finance from the University of Paris 1, a master's in finance from the University of Aix-Marseille, and a master's in econometrics from the University of Bourgogne. He won awards for his PhD thesis and his papers. He has written several academic papers on sovereign credit ratings, asset allocation, and derivatives. He can be reached by e-mail at constantin.mellios@univ-paris1.fr.

Eric Paget-Blanc is a professor of finance at the University of Evry, France, where he is in charge of the master of finance program. He also teaches development finance at the University of Perpignan, and in the professional training program of Agence Française de Développement, the French development agency. His researches focuses on credit risk and development finance. He has published a book on credit rating in 2007, as well as several papers in academic reviews. He is also performs sovereign credit research for a major rating agency.

Eric Paget-Blanc has a PhD in finance from the University of Paris-Nord, a master's in business administration from the University of Denver, and a bachelor's degree from the Toulouse Business School. He can be reached by e-mail at epagetblanc@yahoo.fr.

CHAPTER 37

Sovereign Bond Spreads in the New European Union Countries

IOANA ALEXOPOULOU
European Central Bank

IRINA BUNDA
IMF–Singapore Regional Training Institute

ANNALISA FERRANDO
European Central Bank

The new European Union countries (Bulgaria, Czech Republic, Latvia, Lithuania, Hungary, Poland, Romania, and Slovakia)[1] were strongly affected by the global financial crisis. For many years these countries had been considered as a group in their path toward economic and financial integration with the euro area, although growing macroeconomic imbalances and short-run discrepancies started to play an important role in investors' perceptions of the countries' creditworthiness in the aftermath of the crisis. The impact of the crisis, the policy response to it and the various interventions by international policy authorities varied significantly across countries and crucially depended on the varying degrees to which countries had built up their external and internal imbalances and vulnerabilities before the crisis.

We investigate in this paper the developments of sovereign bond spreads in some of the new EU countries[2] taking into account the long-run determinants of their spreads together with their short-run dynamic behavior.[3] Exhibit 37.1 displays the spreads on long-term government bonds since 2001. As can be seen, they experienced a downward trend from mid-2001 to mid-2007 in the context of ample and favorable global liquidity conditions, low investors' risk aversion due to formal prospects to join the Economic and Monetary Union (EMU). Spreads started rising thereafter and accelerated significantly once the financial turmoil intensified in September 2008, reaching the highest levels in the first quarter of 2009.

Even though there is some comovement discernible in Exhibit 37.1, new EU country spreads show a considerable amount of heterogeneity that reflect differences in domestic macroeconomic policies eventually priced in by the market. Countries like Poland and the Czech Republic experienced significant declines in

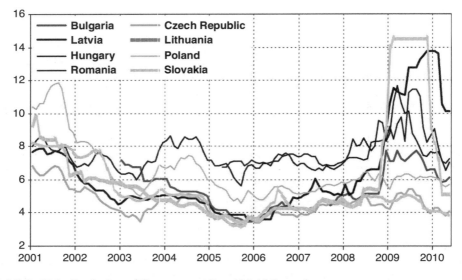

Exhibit 37.1 Evolution of Government Bond Yield Spreads
Source: European Central Bank.

their cost of sovereign borrowing since 2001, only partially reversed during the financial crisis. For the other countries, however, the peaks recorded during the crisis stand out as historical highs.

WHAT EXPLAINS GOVERNMENT BOND SPREADS? A MODEL AND EMPIRICAL RESULTS

In what follows, we employ the Pesaran, Shin, and Smith (1999) pooled mean group technique (PMG) that allows disentangling the respective roles of fundamentals, euro area factors, and market behavior in determining the government bond yields against a euro area average. This technique allows separating the short-run and the long-run dynamics and models the long-run convergence process, under the form of unique coefficients for the variables in the long run and heterogeneous ones in the short run.

The model to be tested can be written as

$$\Delta Spreads_{it} = \phi_i \left(Spreads_{it-1} - \alpha_i - \beta_i^{(1)} F_{it}^{(1)} - \ldots - \beta_i^{(n)} C_t \right) - \gamma_{2i0}^{(1)} \Delta F_{it}^{(1)} - \ldots$$
$$- \gamma_{2i0}^{(n)} \Delta C_t + \varepsilon_{it}$$

in which *Spreads* is the monthly average spreads computed from yields on long-term government bonds for the eight new EU countries[4] relative to the euro area average, F and C denote the fundamentals and the common factors, respectively. The term in brackets is the long-run relationship, with α_i, the country-specific intercept and $\beta_i^{(1)}, \ldots, \beta_i^{(n)}$ the long-run coefficients on the explanatory variables. These are restricted in the long run to satisfy the slope homogeneity condition.

Moreover, for a long-run relationship to exist, the error correction coefficients φ have to be different from zero.

As for the choice of the explanatory variables, we start from the idea that spreads reflect the premium required by investors to hold government securities issued by the new EU countries compared to equivalent bonds issued by the euro area member states. This compensation reflects the credit (or default) risk, liquidity and exchange rate risk, as well as other factors like transaction costs and market behavior. Regarding the default risk, when investors put into question the government's ability to repay its outstanding debt on time, the yield on government bonds will rise for the purpose of compensating debt holders for the increased risk. The liquidity and exchange rate risks refer to the barriers in the secondary market to trading domestic currency denominated assets, whereas the transaction costs capture inefficiencies related to cross-border payments and securities settlement, differences in taxation, standards and legislation, and so on.

Based on the existent literature on the determinants of government bond spreads,[5] the convergence criteria set by the Maastricht Treaty (public debt, fiscal deficit, and inflation) and data availability, sovereign spreads are explained in terms of domestic fundamentals and a common (euro area) factor. We group the domestic fundamentals according to their possibility to explain country differences in fiscal, external, and money market conditions as well as country differences in the nominal convergence and in their international openness.

The long-run results of the pooled mean group estimation are given in Exhibit 37.2. As main long-run determinants of government bond spreads, the model has picked up the sustainability of external finances (as reflected by the significant positive coefficient on external debt-to-GDP ratio), short-term interest rate spreads, as reflected by the significant positive coefficient, the exchange rate (negative coefficient), inflation rate (positive coefficient), the fiscal balance, and the euro area equity volatility, though both are entering with nonsignificant negative coefficients. Trade openness is a key variable to external solvency of a country in the sense that a high degree of openness may indicate that the required expected trade surpluses to meet future foreign debt repayments may materialize and this therefore tends to reduce bond spreads. For the long-run relationship to be valid, the error correction coefficients have to be different from zero for each country.

Exhibit 37.2 Long-Run Determinants of Government Bond Spreads, from January 2001 to December 2008

External debt	5.01***
Fiscal Balance	−5.94
Trade Openness	−2.26**
Inflation	17.36***
Exchange rate	−2.70**
Short interest rate spread	0.39***
Euro area equity volatility	−0.98

*indicates significance at 10%.
**indicates significance at 5%.
***indicates significance at 1%.

Exhibit 37.3 Error Correction Coefficients of Government
Bond Spreads, from January 2001 to December 2008

	Error Correction Coefficient
Bulgaria	−0.08***
Czech Republic	−0.10***
Latvia	−0.05**
Lithuania	−0.09***
Hungary	−0.10***
Poland	−0.16***
Romania	−0.21***
Slovakia	−0.17***

*indicates significance at 10%.
**indicates significance at 5%.
***indicates significance at 1%.

As is the case in Exhibit 37.3, Latvia, Bulgaria, Lithuania, and the Czech Republic exhibit the lowest error correction values (below −0.1), suggesting that their government bond spreads would be relatively less affected in the long run by changes in the underlying fundamental determinants. Conversely, Poland, Slovakia, Hungary, and Romania display higher coefficients. Therefore market perceptions on the quality of their fundamentals or the impact of the external environment are going to have a bigger long-lasting impact on their government bond spreads.

THE ROLE OF MACROECONOMIC AND FISCAL FUNDAMENTALS

The evolution of spreads illustrated in Exhibit 37.4 may suggest that countries for which spreads are constantly higher throughout the sample period (for example, Hungary and Romania) may be characterized by higher equilibrium level spreads than countries such as the Czech Republic or Slovakia, where long-run spreads are small and closer to zero. Thus, different groups are proposed to be formed in order to reflect the heterogeneity in the determinants.

The formation of the groups is done according to their relative position to the median of cross-country fundamentals (mainly the external debt-to-GDP, inflation, and current account-to-GDP). With the exception of Lithuania and Hungary, the three criteria send similar signals in regard to financial vulnerability. Based on fundamental values, we assign Czech Republic, Lithuania, Poland, and Slovakia to one group, formed by countries broadly characterized by a sustainable current account balance and/or external debt-to-GDP ratios and relatively lower inflation. The group showing high negative current account balance (below 8 percent) or high external debt-to-GDP (above 50 percent) and relatively higher inflation rates (above 5 percent) comprise Bulgaria, Latvia, Hungary, and Romania, as Exhibit 37.5 shows.

For the first group, the main drivers of the rise in spreads are inflation rates and short-term interest rates. Compared to the long-run results for the whole sample, the current account balance has now a role to play in driving spreads in

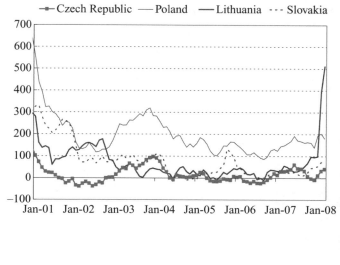

Long-run determinants and error correction terms	
External Debt	1.56
CA	−3.01**
Fiscal Balance	−5.38
Trade Openness	−0.94
Inflation	23.54***
Short I.R. Spread	0.36***
EA Equity Vol.	−1.69***

	Error correction
Czech Rep.	−0.23***
Lithuania	−0.07***
Poland	−0.19***
Slovakia	−0.12***

Exhibit 37.4 Evolution of Government Bond Spreads for Country Group 1 (in Basis Points)

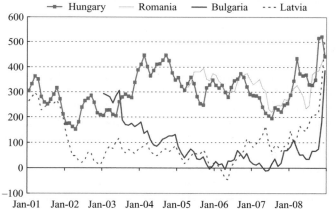

Long-run determinants and error correction terms	
External Debt	5.56***
Interest Payment	170.30***
Trade Openness	−2.85***
Exch. Rate	−3.63**
Short I.R. Spread	0.22***
EA Equity Vol.	2.03**

	Error correction
Bulgaria	−0.43***
Latvia	−0.11***
Hungary	−0.11**
Romania	−0.36***

Exhibit 37.5 Evolution of Government Bond Yield Spreads for Country Group 2 (in basis points)

these countries. Short-term interest rate differentials continue to drive spreads in the long run and the common factor—the euro area equity market volatility—now enters with a negative and statistically significant sign in the long-run specification. This suggests that investors treat bonds issued by countries in this group similarly to the average euro area ones.

By contrast, spreads in the most vulnerable group seem to be mainly driven by fiscal fundamentals. While external debt-to-GDP ratio enters with a similar and statistically significant sign for the whole group of countries, interest payments on government debt-to-GDP ratio plays now a much bigger role. Differently from the other group, the common factor enters with a positive and statistically significant coefficient. This suggests that investors treat sovereign bonds issued by countries in the second group as relatively riskier.

During the last two years, the financial crisis had particularly adverse effects for the second group of countries, reflecting their vulnerabilities to external shocks because of the deterioration of their fundamentals. Regarding the period of market turmoil that started in the summer of 2007, the results suggest that the rise in spreads in countries like Hungary and Romania was driven by a mix of deteriorating fundamentals and increased dependence on external conditions. In Bulgaria, Latvia, and Lithuania, fundamentals became prevalent in 2008 and their abrupt deterioration had immediately translated into higher risk premiums required by investors to hold government bonds. For other countries in the sample—like the Czech Republic—we observe that fundamental-driven spreads were, at times, slightly higher than actual ones. This feature suggests increased investors' differentiation in a context of heightened uncertainty and risk aversion.

POLICY MEASURES

During 2009, the IMF and the EU agreed to joint programs for Hungary, Latvia, and Romania. The aim of the programs was not only to ensure balance of payments sustainability but to avoid second round speculative attacks, and thereby ensure policy credibility. The responses reflected the need to balance increasing concerns regarding the sustainability of public finances and other macroeconomic imbalances and at the same time to implement fiscal stimuli to mitigate the adverse impact of the crisis on economic activity.

The requirements of the programs across the three countries included strict fiscal consolidation through wide-ranging revenue and expenditure measures for the next few years. Some of the policy actions included minimizing government expenditures, reducing pension benefits and other entitlements, lowering public sector wages, and increasing the revenue base through a wide range of tax increases.

The Latvian authorities requested a 27-month standby arrangement under the exceptional access policy of the IMF, of special drawing rights (SDR) 1.521626 billion (approximately €1.7 billion). An initial purchase of SDR 0.54 billion became available. The aim of the funding was to remedy the immediate banking liquidity crisis and to ensure long-term external stability, while maintaining the exchange rate peg of the Latvian lat. The program aimed to stabilize the financial sector and restore depositor confidence. It also included substantial fiscal policy tightening, especially for the public and government sectors. As a result, the economy

Exhibit 37.6   Financial Support by International Institutions or Countries During the Financial Crisis (Outstanding Amount as a Percentage of GDP) by billions per Euro

	2008	2009	Ceiling[1]
Latvia			
Total loan	2.5	16.9	39.6
provided by			
European Union[2]	0.0	11.7	16.5
IMF	2.5	4.1	8.8
World Bank	0.0	1.1	2.1
EBRD, Czech Republic, and Poland	0.0	0.0	2.1
Nordic countries[3]	0.0	0.0	10.1
Hungary			
Total loan	6.6	14.4	20.8
provided by			
European Union[2]	2.0	5.8	6.7
IMF	4.6	8.6	13.0
World Bank	0.0	0.0	1.0
Romania			
Total loan	0.0	7.3	16.8
provided by			
European Union[2]	0.0	1.3	4.3
IMF	0.0	5.7	10.7
World Bank	0.0	0.3	0.9
EBRD, EIB and IFC	0.0	0.0	0.9
Poland			
Total loan	0.0	0.0	4.6
provided by			
IMF	0.0	0.0	4.6

Source: ESCB, European Central Bank "Convergence Report 2010."
[1]Including provisions of future financial support.
[2]European Commission responsible for implementing the disbursement and the conditionality.
[3]Finland, Sweden, Estonia, Denmark, and Norway.

contracted sharply by almost 19 percent as an effect of a sharp slowdown in domestic demand. However, competitiveness has improved recently and the fiscal deficit is on a downward trend. Expenditure has been lowered through structural reforms, and cuts in administration, social spending, and the public sector wage bill. The recession has contributed to a large current account surplus and capital outflows have been less than expected more recently.

Hungary was affected significantly by global deleveraging because of its high levels of government and external debt (see Exhibit 37.6). Gross financing needs became more difficult to meet, necessitating both a stronger policy response and significant external assistance from the IMF (12.5 billion euro), the EU (6.5 billion euro), and the World Bank (1 billion euro). The Hungarian authorities requested a 17-month SDR 10.5 billion (€12.5 billion) standby arrangement under the exceptional access policy. An initial purchase of SDR 4.2 billion became available. The two key objectives of the funding program were substantial fiscal adjustment to ensure that the government's financing needs will decline and to maintain adequate liquidity and strong levels of capital in the banking system. The authorities planned to incorporate reductions in government expenditures, to introduce a rules-based fiscal framework, to create new facilities to inject public funds into banks, and to guarantee interbank borrowing.

The Romanian authorities requested a 24-month SDR 11.443 billion (€12.95 billion) standby arrangement under the exceptional access policy. An initial purchase of SDR 4.37 billion became available. The policy steps that were outlined by the government were to:

- Strengthen fiscal policy further to reduce the government's financing needs and improve long-term fiscal sustainability.
- Maintain adequate capitalization of banks and liquidity in domestic financial markets.
- Reduce inflation.
- Secure adequate external financing and improve market confidence.

The authorities' plan incorporated reductions in government expenditures, the introduction of fiscal reforms to improve the budgeting process and reduce key expenditure pressures, and financial sector reforms to better protect against banking difficulties.

Acute macroeconomic imbalances have been avoided in Poland because of a booming economy in previous years. Notwithstanding Poland's favorable fundamentals and the authorities' strong policy response, the economy was being severely affected by the global financial crisis through both the real and financial sector channels. Exports and credit growth were slowing sharply, with a deceleration in output growth. Risks to the banking sector also increased. The Polish authorities believed that access under a flexible credit line (FCL) arrangement in the amount of SDR 13.69 billion, which it treated as precautionary, would help maintain market access and safeguard against downside risks during a time of high volatility and retrenchment in international capital markets. This credit line has not been exercised yet.

CONCLUSION

We presented an empirical investigation of the main determinants of government bond spreads in new EU countries, taking into account some specific features that distinguish these countries from other emerging economies. These are a persistence of short-run heterogeneities and an adjustment trend to equilibrium values over the medium to long run as part of the convergence process to the euro area. The investigation was based on the convergence criteria set by the Maastricht Treaty (public debt, fiscal deficit, and inflation), highlighting potential fundamentals that may influence market perception of those countries' creditworthiness. We also put into light that there may be two clusters among new EU countries that evolve in different long-run paths with respect to fundamentals and common factors characterizing the euro area. A joint criterion based on their external position and inflation rates offered the best split determining one group with relatively better fundamentals (Czech Republic, Lithuania, Poland, and Slovakia) and a second group with higher external vulnerability (Bulgaria, Latvia, Hungary, and Romania).

Following the intensification of the financial crisis, it became clear that the funding needs of some countries grew abruptly with the result of asking for help from international authorities on specific funding programs. This entailed for Latvia, Hungary, and Romania to impose strict fiscal tightening, especially in the government and public sectors.

NOTES

1. In May 2004, the European Union (EU) grew from 15 to 25 countries in what was the biggest enlargement since its foundation. The Czech Republic, Estonia, Cyprus, Latvia, Lithuania, Hungary, Malta, Poland, Slovenia, and Slovakia joined the EU on May 1, 2004, followed by Bulgaria and Romania on January 1, 2007. Upon their accession to the EU, these 12 countries participated in the Economic and Monetary Union with the status of a "Member State with a derogation," which implies that they are committed to preparing for euro area participation, under the conditions set out by the Treaty. Since their accession to the EU, four countries—namely Cyprus, Malta, Slovenia, and Slovakia—have met the convergence criteria specified in the Treaty and adopted the euro at different points in time. Estonia joined the euro area at the beginning of 2011.

2. No comparable long-term government bond interest rate is available for Estonia.

3. See Alexopoulou, Bunda, and Ferrando (2009) for an extended analysis.

4. Slovakia is included because the estimations are done for the period 2001 to 2008.

5. See Ferrucci 2003 and Ciarlone, Piselli, and Trebeschi 2009.

REFERENCES

Alexopoulou, I., I. Bunda, and A. Ferrando. 2009. "Determinants of Government Bond Spreads in New EU Countries." *European Central Bank Working Paper* 1093.

Ciarlone, A., P. Piselli, and G. Trebeschi. 2009. "Emerging Markets Spreads and Global Financial Conditions." *Journal of International Financial Markets, Institutions and Money* 19: 2, 222–239.

European Central Bank. 2010. *Convergence Report 2010*. Frankfurt: European Central Bank.

Ferrucci, G. 2003. "Empirical Determinants of Emerging Market Economies' Sovereign Bond Spreads." *Bank of England Working Paper* 205.

Pesaran, M. H., Y. Shin, and R. P. Smith. 1999. "Pooled Mean Group Estimation of Dynamic Heterogeneous Panels." *Journal of the American Statistical Association* 94: 621–634.

ABOUT THE AUTHORS

Ioana Alexopoulou is a senior portfolio management expert at the European Central Bank. She is a graduate of Birkbeck College, University of London. Her publications include "The New Basel Capital Accord and Its impact on Japanese Banking: A Qualitative Analysis" in *The New Basel Capital Accord*, edited by Benton E. Gup; "Globalization of the Bond and Stock Markets: The Japanese Case—An International Perspective," in *Capital markets, Globalization and Economic Development*, edited by Benton E. Gup; "What Accounts for the Low Level of Interest Rates?" in *Institutional Investors, Global Savings and Asset Allocations,* Committee on the Global Financial System Working Group and European Central Bank working papers.

Irina Bunda is an international consultant economist at the IMF–Singapore Regional Training Institute, which provides training in the formulation and implementation of macroeconomic and financial policies to government officials from the Asia-Pacific region. Before joining the IMF's regional training center in Singapore, she worked for two years at the European Central Bank in Frankfurt, Germany, in the Economics, Monetary Policy, and International Relations directorates. She has also visited the Bank of England's International Finance and the IMF's Policy Development and Review and Research departments. Her areas of expertise are in the fields of international macroeconomics, banking, and finance. She conducts applied research on international financial crises, monetary policy and exchange rates, financial contagion, and asset price dynamics, and has published in a number of journals. She received a master of science and technology in market finance, an MSci in economics and finance, and a PhD in economics from University of Orléans, France.

Annalisa Ferrando is a principal economist at the Capital Markets/Financial Structure Division of the European Central Bank. She received an MPhil from Oxford University, a postgraduate diploma in energy economics and management at Scuola Superiore E. Mattei in Milan, and a degree in economics at the Universita' Ca' Foscari Venezia. She has worked in the research department of the Bank of Italy and the Directorate General for Enterprise and Industry of the European Commission. She has done extensive work in the area of European financial integration, corporate finance in the euro area and on the convergence assessment of Central and Eastern European countries.

CHAPTER 38

Can Sovereign Credit Ratings Promote Financial Sector Development and Capital Inflows to Emerging Markets?

SUK-JOONG KIM
Associate Professor of Finance, the University of Sydney, Sydney, Australia

ELIZA WU
Senior Lecturer in Banking and Finance, the University of New South Wales, Sydney, Australia,

C redit rating agencies have on occasion been criticized for doing a poor job in rating debt instruments. In particular, their reactive rather than proactive stance on revising credit ratings has been blamed for exacerbating financial crises. For example, their belated and split decisions to downgrade the sovereign ratings of some of the peripheral Eurozone countries in 2010 caused investors to panic, which led to episodes of sovereign debt crises in the affected countries. The calls for reforming the credit rating process have already become louder with the recent subprime debt crisis. Rightly or wrongly, credit ratings provided by agencies like Standard and Poor's, Moody's Investor Services, and Fitch Ratings, are observed worldwide by financial market participants and they help reduce the information asymmetries that exist in international financial markets. Sovereign credit ratings in particular are deemed to be a reference assessment on country risk.

In emerging capital markets, the information asymmetries faced by participants in all financial sectors are arguably even greater than in the developed economies of the West. To the extent that the major rating agencies would have access to various types of data for individual sovereign obligors that other interested parties (for example, international banks and investors) might not have, their ratings decisions would convey information on the investment climates within those rated countries that otherwise would not have been available. As such, information pertaining to sovereign credit rating revisions reduces the extent of variations in information availability, and this could potentially be beneficial for emerging economies as the resulting international capital inflows could significantly contribute to financial and economic development.

We explore this issue in this chapter and formally investigate whether sovereign credit ratings provided for entire countries may be beneficial for the development of financial sectors in emerging economies. One of the key functions of financial sectors is the matching of savers and borrowers within a financial system. Hence, the development of financial sectors is important for the process of financial intermediation and for channeling scarce capital to efficient and productive uses within societies. This brief chapter draws on a more extensive academic article by the authors (Kim and Wu 2008).

We consider the sovereign credit ratings information provided by Standard and Poor's on a sample of 51 emerging economies from across Asia, Latin America, Central and Eastern Europe, and Africa and the Middle East over the years from 1995 to 2003. We identify a significant amount of rerating activity over this period for the cohort of emerging markets reflecting the economic and political developments that have taken place. For example, there were a total of 15 ratings revisions made by Standard and Poor's for Argentina over this period but 8 of these were made in 2001 alone during the Argentine debt crisis.

Sovereign credit ratings are typically assessments provided by independent rating agencies such as Standard and Poor's at the cost of a rating fee paid by sovereign obligors wanting to be rated. Sovereign credit ratings are solicited by sovereign issuers to help generate investor interest and get potentially better terms and lower costs of borrowing so they can fund fiscal expenditures. Once initiated, the rating agencies will continue to monitor the latest developments affecting the ability of these governments to repay and service their debt on an ongoing basis. As such, the rating decisions of the rating agencies will be revised as underlying fundamental conditions warrant changes in the credit quality of the sovereign borrowers. The credit assessments given by rating agencies are not only for the long-term perceived default risks (conveyed in the form of sovereign credit ratings) but also for the perceived developments within a country that may ultimately affect its sovereign credit rating in the short or intermediate term (conveyed in the form of watch lists or outlooks). The shorter-term assessments, in essence, provide potential warnings on relevant developments over the next six months to two years. Sovereign debts are rated on an ordinal scale that ranges from AAA (being the highest credit quality) to D/SD (default or selective default being the worst rating possible).[1] Moreover, the outlooks range from credit watch—positive to credit watch—negative indicating that closer attention is either being given for potentially upgrading or downgrading the country, respectively, in the next few months. For the purpose of our analyses, we combine the two aspects of credit assessments into a composite credit rating measure to reflect the full value of credit ratings information provided by Standard and Poor's. From an earlier study performed by former Federal Reserve Bank economists Cantor and Packer (1996), sovereign credit ratings are known to be determined to a large extent by country-specific economic conditions, past debt history, institutional quality, and degrees of political and financial stability. As such, they are regarded and widely used within financial systems as reference measures on the potential risks associated with investing in specific countries.

In examining the role of sovereign credit ratings information for future levels of financial development, we consider the three main financial sectors of stock, banking, and bond markets. A typical feature of emerging market economies is that there usually isn't a balanced development across these three key market segments, with the banking sector being particularly more dominant in the earlier stages of financial development when banks have a clear advantage and can better serve as delegated monitors for savers. As such, sovereign ratings information may have different roles to play in the development of each of these segments. Furthermore, in trying to better understand how the different rating assessments work for financial development, we also relate them to international capital flows. Considering the importance of foreign capital for economic development, an understanding of the informational content of sovereign ratings for international capital inflows is imperative. For completeness, we consider multiple measures for international bank flows, longer-term foreign direct investments and shorter-term portfolio investment flows (often called *hot money* because of the speed at which it can move out of financially stricken economies). In general, we expect ratings improvements either in terms of ratings upgrades or moves to positive outlooks (under the same rating grade) to provide a positive influence on both financial market development and foreign capital inflows to emerging economies.

The investigation results of the impacts of sovereign ratings on domestic financial market development are summarized in Exhibit 38.1. Four different types of sovereign credit ratings are considered. These are long- and short-term ratings of debt issued by sovereign obligors denominated in both foreign and domestic currencies. A positive sign suggests a statistically significant and positive influence of a prior ratings grade on an underlying financial market development measure, and vice versa for a negative sign. Where there is no significant relationship, no sign is allocated.

It can be observed that foreign currency long-term ratings induce bond market development, which is as expected. However, it has a negative influence on the development of stock markets in the 51 emerging economies we considered. Local currency long-term ratings show somewhat different impacts. Both stock market and banking sector developments are encouraged by ratings improvements but bond market developments are hampered. The overall results of long-term ratings suggest that there are some trade-offs between different market segments, and this perpetuates unbalanced financial sector development.

Exhibit 38.1   Summary of Impact of Sovereign Ratings on Financial Market Development

	Financial Market Development		
	Stock Market	**Banking Sector**	**Bond Market**
Foreign Currency Long-Term	−		+
Local Currency Long-Term	+	+	−
Foreign Currency Short-Term	−		−
Local Currency Short-Term	−	−	−

Short-term ratings in both foreign and local currencies have negative impacts on financial development in all cases. This suggests a switch from long-term to short-term financing occurring as short-term ratings improve, given long-term ratings. Overall, we report that improvements in long-term ratings selectively contribute to financial market development, but improvements in short-term ratings are detrimental.

Our analyses clearly point to an important influence of sovereign credit ratings on investors' financial decisions (inferred from the subsequent changes observed in aggregate financial activity) and ultimately on financial development. Boot et al. (2006) provide a theoretical basis for how credit ratings in general can serve as a focal point in financial markets, as they provide a commonly understood assessment for all financial market participants. Our evidence suggests that with these focal points, emerging economies are better able to flourish as both local and international market participants can make use of these credit assessments to distinguish between the risks and returns associated with investments in emerging economies where informational asymmetries are more problematic. Improvements in sovereign credit assessments can boost financial development, as they serve as comprehensive signals of improved institutional quality and better protection for creditor rights to all financial market participants. They effectively help reduce monitoring costs for investors in emerging markets and facilitate the special process of financial intermediation.

The investigation results of the impacts of sovereign ratings on international capital flows to emerging economies are summarized in Exhibit 38.2.

The credit ratings on long-term sovereign debt denominated in foreign currencies are most powerful in stimulating all forms of foreign capital flows, and it is through this avenue that they are able to support financial sector development in emerging economies. Upgrades in sovereign credit assessments can help emerging markets open up their economies to international investments. This is because improvements in a sovereign obligor's perceived ability to honor its financial obligations in hard (foreign) currencies sends a very strong signal to existing and potential foreign investors that the country's currency is strong and is unlikely to plummet in value and consequently wipe out their foreign investment returns. Sovereign ratings for debt denominated in local currencies, however, discourage capital inflows. We conjecture that improvements in the local currency ratings provide market participants with a clearer guide on domestic conditions and are helpful in inciting confidence and providing the grounds for domestic

Exhibit 38.2 Summary of Impact of Sovereign Ratings on International Capital Inflows

	Capital Inflows to Emerging Economies		
	FDI Inflows	**Bank Inflows**	**Portfolio Inflows**
Foreign Currency Long-Term	+	+	+
Local Currency Long-Term		−	−
Foreign Currency Short-Term	−		
Local Currency Short-Term	−	−	+

financial development. This then reduces the need for externally sourced capital in all forms.

Credit ratings on debt with short-term maturities unequivocally deter international capital inflows and hamper domestic financial market development, as the reliance on short-term debt (encouraged by more favorable borrowing terms with improvements in short-term ratings) is perceived by market participants to be risky and enhances financial fragility. Investors are likely to infer from the changes in sovereign credit ratings on short-term debt the potential reliance on short-term borrowings and are therefore discouraged from partaking in any financial activity in the country's financial sectors.

While we do not explicitly address whether sovereign credit ratings exacerbate financial crises or not in this chapter, our results suggest that while rating downgrades (which are rampant in times of financial crises) do subsequently reduce the hot money flows into emerging markets (along with international banking flows and foreign direct investments), the longer-term benefits that sovereign credit rating improvements have on financial development appear to outweigh the potential propagation of financial crises through sovereign rating news releases into international financial markets.

As this chapter has briefly discussed, sovereign credit ratings information is not all the same and different kinds of sovereign credit ratings provided by rating agencies like Standard and Poor's work to encourage financial sector development in emerging markets through the different signals that they send to market participants. Sovereign credit ratings on long-term sovereign debt are more beneficial for financial development and international finance than those on short-term debt. While sovereign credit ratings on debt denominated in foreign currencies work to promote financial sector development by stimulating additional international capital flows into emerging markets, ratings on debt denominated in local currencies can still facilitate domestic growth and development without assistance from foreign capital sources. Moreover, we find that short-term sovereign rating improvements have a detrimental impact on both domestic financial market development and in attracting all forms of capital from abroad. This reflects the potential pitfall of financing longer-term projects with cheaper shorter-term borrowings, thereby increasing duration mismatch and potentially retarding the development of longer-term domestic credit markets. These findings on the differential effects of the various types of sovereign credit assessments provided by rating agencies hold up even against other governance conditions (like the effectiveness of the government and low levels of corruption) that are also necessary ingredients for stimulating financial development.

In conclusion, the policy emphasis on sovereign credit ratings under Basel II and other financial regulatory regimes restricting financial institutions like pension funds and insurers to hold only investment grade assets have, without a doubt, made sovereign credit ratings closely watched by financial observers. A beneficial side effect from this increased attention is that sovereign credit ratings provided by the rating agencies actually aid in the development of necessary financial sectors in emerging economies, generating real economic growth and development in the long run. There is an undeniable relationship between sovereign credit ratings and future levels of financial development and capital flows in emerging markets. In this way, we argue that there are important anchoring and monitoring roles played by sovereign credit ratings in emerging markets finance, and policy makers should not, in a sense, throw the baby out with the bathwater in their making of future reforms to international financial regulations.

NOTE

1. To examine their impact on measures of financial development, we transform these sovereign credit ratings into a linear numerical scale following earlier studies like Gande and Parsley (2005). The rating scale for sovereign ratings on short-term debt are made on a more condensed scale (from A-1+ to D/SD).

REFERENCES

Boot, A. W., T. T. Milbourne, and A. Schmeits. 2006. "Credit Ratings as Coordination Mechanisms." *Review of Financial Studies* 19: 81–118.

Cantor, R., and F. Packer. 1996. "Determinants and Impact of Sovereign Credit Ratings." *Federal Reserve Bank of New York Economic Policy Review* 2: 37–53.

Gande, A., and D. Parsley. 2005. "News Spillovers in the Sovereign Debt Market." *Journal of Financial Economics* 75: 691–734.

Kim, S.-J., and E. Wu. 2008. "Sovereign Credit Ratings, Capital Flows, and Financial Sector Development in Emerging Markets." *Emerging Markets Review* 9: 17–39.

ABOUT THE AUTHORS

Suk-Joong Kim is an associate professor of finance in the Discipline of Finance, at the University of Sydney, in Australia. He received a PhD in financial economics from the University of Sydney. He previously held a teaching position at the University of New South Wales. Dr. Kim has conducted extensive work in the area of international finance, foreign exchange markets, and international capital movements. His research output has been widely cited by fellow researchers in the fields. His publications have appeared in the journals *Journal of International Money and Finance, Journal of Financial Research, Journal of Banking and Finance*, and *Pacific Basin Finance Journal*, among others. He has recently edited two research books with an international focus: *Asia-Pacific Financial Markets: Integration, Innovation and Challenges*, and *International Banking in the New Era: Post-Crisis Challenges and Opportunities*. These are volumes 8 and 11, respectively, of the International Finance Review research book series.

Eliza Wu is a senior lecturer in the School of Banking and Finance at the University of New South Wales (UNSW). She received a PhD in finance and an honors degree in economics from the University of New South Wales in Sydney, Australia. Dr. Wu has broad experience in teaching and researching within international finance and specializes in sovereign credit risk, financial market integration, cross-border finance, and emerging financial market issues. Her research has been published in the *Journal of Banking and Finance, Journal of Financial Research, Journal of International Financial Markets, Institutions and Money, Journal of Fixed Income, Emerging Markets Review,* and the *International Journal of Finance and Economics.* Outside of academia, Eliza has worked at the Reserve Bank of Australia and at the Bank for International Settlements in the representative office for Asia and the Pacific in Hong Kong.

CHAPTER 39

Country Debt Default Probabilities in Emerging Markets

Were Credit Rating Agencies Wrong?

ANGELINA GEORGIEVSKA
BNP Paribas, London, U.K.

LJUBICA GEORGIEVSKA
Goldman Sachs, London, U.K.

DR. ALEKSANDAR STOJANOVIC
Head of Department of Accounting and Finance, Director of Centre for Governance,
Risk and Accountability, University of Greenwich Business School, London, U.K.

DR. NATASA TODOROVIC
Senior Lecturer in Investment Management, Cass Business School, London, U.K.

S overeign credit ratings and their associated default probabilities have historically been used by leading international banks for determining their capital
allocation in a particular country, pricing of sovereign bonds and loans and,
most importantly, as an input to their credit risk management models. Such credit
ratings and default probabilities are traditionally provided by the leading credit
rating agencies (CRAs). According to the Basel Capital Accord–Basel II, banks were
allowed to use their internal sovereign ratings or CRAs' ratings and their associated
default rates in determining their required regulatory capital against credit risk.
When this is applied to emerging markets, because of the lack of data on sovereigns,
the sovereign credit ratings are mainly based on corporate defaults, assuming the
latter is a good proxy for the former. However, corporations and governments are
fundamentally different borrowers both in terms of their legal status and solvency,
making this assumption doubtful. Therefore, in this chapter, which draws upon a
recently published paper, "Sovereign Rescheduling Probabilities in Emerging Markets: A Comparison with Credit Rating Agencies' Ratings,"[1] we assess whether
country default probabilities derived from the empirical models we specifically

designed for sovereigns are more appropriate measures of sovereign default than CRAs' corporate default rates. Specifically, in search of the most accurate approach to predicting sovereign debt rescheduling, we compare the real-world probabilities estimated using historical data in our models with the assigned probabilities of three major international rating agencies, namely, Moody's, Standard & Poor's (S&P), and Fitch. Basing our probabilities of sovereign default on models using 124 emerging countries over the period from 1981 to 2002, we show that CRAs underestimate sovereign debt default probabilities, which brings into question banks' and investors' reliance on the CRAs' credit ratings.

DEBT RESCHEDULING PROBABILITY MODEL

When deriving a model that would be specific for the estimation of sovereign default probabilities in emerging markets, one needs to be aware that a potentially large number of economic, political, and market factors determine the extent of a country's debt repayment difficulties. Sovereign default may be caused by a country's politically motivated unwillingness to repay its external debt or simply by an inability stemming from insolvency or illiquidity. Solvency is often measured by the GDP, government revenues, or exports, and it also depends on the exchange rate regime (an overvaluation of currency can lead to external imbalances and hence to accumulation of debt). Macroeconomic factors such as inflation and money growth affect foreign investors' risk attitude; for example, an increase in inflation would inversely affect the amount of foreign capital invested in a country. Illiquidity, as another variable contributing to a country's inability to repay its debt, is usually measured by the short-term debt to reserves or M2 to reserves. Moreover, political and institutional factors are very important determinants of probability of default because they affect a country's stability and debt repayment policies. Furthermore, financial ratios that have most commonly been identified in literature as significant determinants of probability of sovereign default are: reserves to imports (for example, Aylward and Thorne 1998); total external debt to GDP (for example, Balkan 1992; Detragiache and Spilmbergo 2000; and so on); and total debt service payment to exports (for example, Solberg 1988 and Rivoli and Brewer 1997). Finally, it has been documented that a country's past debt repayment record can be used as an excellent indicator of their current likelihood to default. The list of variables that could potentially affect sovereign default presented here is not exhaustive, so for a more detailed review of these and other variables, see Georgievska et al. (2008). To select the most appropriate variables out of a large pool, which could be used in building an empirical model for estimating probability of sovereign default, we deploy the principal component analysis technique. Our selection method[2] leads us to adopt variables that can be grouped into four main categories and are expected to have either a positive or negative impact on the probability of rescheduling, as described in Exhibit 39.1.

The event of debt default or rescheduling is defined as a binary variable:

$Rescheduling_{it}$ if country i reschedules its external debt in year t, that is, if its total amount of debt rescheduled is above zero in year t

if country i does not reschedule its external debt in year t

Exhibit 39.1   The Impact of Selected Variables on the Probability of Default or Rescheduling

Variables	Impact of the increase in value of the variable on the probability of default or rescheduling	
	Positive	Negative
Past rescheduling record:		
Lagged Rescheduling	x	
Political Variable:		
ICRG Rating[a] (50% political, 25% financial and 25% economic risk)		x
Solvency Variables		
Total Debt/GNP	x	
Arrears/Exports	x	
Exports/GDP		x
Liquidity Variables:		
International Reserves/GDP		x
Macroeconomic Variables		
Current Account Balance/GDP		x
Imports/GDP[b]	ambiguous	ambiguous

[a] A higher number, obtained as a weighted average of points assigned for political, economic, and financial risk of a country, indicates the lower potential risk and vice versa.
[b] When the imports in relation to the GDP are higher, the country is more vulnerable to foreign shocks, and more likely to external debt rescheduling (Frenkel 1983). However, Odedokun (1995) argues that the higher this ratio, the more open the economy is, which in effect reduces the probability of default.

There were 519 debt defaults or reschedulings[3] in our sample in total. Although 22 countries had no defaults in this period, some, for example, Gabon, Zambia, Tanzania, and Nicaragua, faced a dozen or more default or rescheduling events.

Applying the panel logic models, traditionally used in this setting, we estimated the probabilities of sovereign default in emerging market countries in our sample. In search for the most accurate model, we considered those that (1) maximize the percentage of correct predictions (that the default had occurred) and (2) minimize the false negatives, that is, minimize the error that the actual defaults are classified by the model as nondefaults (known as a Type I error). Using the variables described earlier, we have derived two models that satisfy criteria (1) and (2), respectively, and give us empirical estimates of debt rescheduling probabilities in emerging markets. Specifically, Model 1, which included prior rescheduling events (over the past one year), total debt/GNP, exports/GDP, current account balance/GDP and international reserves/GDP, gave us 82.68 percent of correct predictions of actual defaults and 9.13 percent Type I error. Model 2, which, in addition to past rescheduling and total debt/GDP, included the political variable (International Country Risk Guide index), arrears/exports and imports/GDP had 82.54 percent correct predictions and 8.33 percent Type I error. Overall, our determinants of debt rescheduling suggest that to reduce their probability of default or rescheduling and get better access to international capital markets, emerging countries should maintain a good past debt repayment record; reduce their current account deficit; improve their political stability; increase their exports relative to imports; keep close control of international reserves relative to GDP (which is of particular relevance for countries with an underdeveloped banking system); and limit the size of the external debt compared to their resource base (GNP).

EMPIRICAL VERSUS CRAs' PROBABILITIES OF EMERGING MARKETS SOVEREIGN DEBT RESCHEDULING

A direct comparison between empirical one-year default probabilities from our Models 1 and 2 and the one-year sovereign credit ratings from Moody's, Standard and Poor's, and Fitch cannot be done, because the CRAs use letter ratings that range from AAA (for S&P and Fitch, Aaa for Moody's) to C, while our models provide quantitative probability of default. To enable this comparison, we use transformation of letter ratings into their associated one-year cumulative default probabilities (or ranges of default probabilities).[4] More specifically, to derive one-year cumulative default probabilities, all three CRAs use periods of up to 20 years. For example, a credit rating of B1 corresponds to the average one-year cumulative default rate of 2 percent, which represents the percentage of historical number of debtors that have defaulted within one year of being assigned rating B1, within a total number of countries and companies with the B1 rating over the same one-year period. The year selected for comparison is the final year in our sample, 2002, when, at the beginning of the year, 42 countries have been rated by the three CRAs.

Striking findings emerged from the comparison of empirical versus CRAs' probabilities of default: 95.59 percent of the countries rated by Moody's, 85.71 percent of those rated by S&P, and 96.3 percent of Fitch-rated countries had lower one-year cumulative default probabilities than equivalents generated by our Model 1 (corresponding numbers of comparison with Model 2 are 97.3 percent, 88.57 percent, and 92.59 percent). Exhibit 39.2 sets out the default and rescheduling probabilities derived from our models, along with the CRAs' one-year cumulative default probabilities, focusing on the sample of nine countries that have actually rescheduled or defaulted in 2002.

One of the reasons why CRAs' default rates are underestimating emerging country sovereign defaults over a one-year horizon lies in the fact that CRAs' sovereign ratings are mainly based on historical corporate default rates (the exception are Fitch's ratings, which specifically follow sovereign defaults). Given that characteristics of borrowers in each case are very different (government versus corporation), corporate bond credit ratings and their associated default probabilities generally do not appear to be good proxies for sovereign default probabilities.

IMPLICATIONS

It is well known that leading banks and international investors rely on sovereign default probabilities to estimate credit risk exposure in one country, price sovereign bonds and loans, and decide upon country capital allocation. However, using CRAs' default probabilities for this purpose may have serious implications for

Exhibit 39.2 Model 1 and Model 2 One-Year Default and Rescheduling Probabilities versus CRAs' One-Year Default Rate in 2002: Sample of Countries That Have Actually Defaulted or Rescheduled

Country That Has Defaulted in 2002	Model 1 Default Probabilities	Model 2 Default Probabilities	Moody's Associated Default Probability	S&P's Associated Default Probability	Fitch's Associated Default Probability	Moody's Rating	S&P Rating	Fitch Rating
Bolivia	12.90%	14.09%	2.00%	2.63–3.33%	—	B1	B+	—
Honduras	46.33%	58.62%	6.81%	—	—	B2	—	—
Indonesia	66.63%	76.43%	6.86%	100.00%	1.68–21.97%	B3	CCC	B-
Jordan	36.29%	48.18%	1.58%	2.63–3.33%	—	Ba3	BB-	—
Mexico	7.83%	6.89%	1.78%	0.00–2.63%	0.27–1.55%	Baa3	BB+	BB+
Moldova	8.65%	9.12%	13.95%	—	21.97%	Caa1	—	CC
Nicaragua	76.25%	85.31%	6.81%	—	—	B2	—	—
Pakistan	65.88%	70.98%	13.95%	3.33–100%	—	Caa1	B-	—
Russian Federation	61.73%	55.17%	1.58%	2.63–3.33%	1.00–1.68%	Ba3	B+	B+

Notes: — Indicates that the data are not available (countries are not rated). For a majority of the selected countries, the one-year cumulative default rates implied from their CRAs ratings at the beginning of 2002 are very low, mostly being well below 10 percent, giving no signal of potential default (the exception is Indonesia, for which the S&P correctly assigns 100 percent probability of default). Conversely, most of the default probabilities generated by our empirical models were above 50 percent (particularly when Model 2 is taken into consideration), indicating that rescheduling is likely to occur. For example, in the case of Nicaragua, Model 1 and Model 2 give very high default probabilities of 76.25 percent and 85.31 percent respectively, while Moody's assigns it a B2 rating and associated cumulative default probability of only 6.81 percent. This and further analysis in Georgievska et al. (2008), leads us to conclude that CRAs did not effectively predict 2002 defaults or reschedulings. That is not to say that empirical models are always correct. If some empirical models (and CRAs) use past rescheduling or default event as one of the determinants of probability of default, then, a country that has defaulted in the recent past (up to one year ago) may be classified by empirical models (and some CRAs) as "likely to default" in the next period. However, in reality, one default *does not have to* follow another. The example of Argentina (which defaulted in 2001, but not in 2002 despite the predictions of default from our empirical models and all CRAs but Fitch) bears this out.

both banks and countries in question, as their problems may outweigh the benefits. For example, CRAs' continuous underestimation of sovereign default risk for emerging countries will cause underestimation of credit risk for banks, underpricing of sovereign bonds and loans and increasing capital allocation to emerging countries with underestimated probabilities of default. Therefore, if an actual default of a sovereign occurs, it is likely that CRAs will downgrade the country rating very quickly. The banks may then experience difficulties in reducing the amount of capital allocation in these (now riskier) countries. Nevertheless, the capital outflows will be imminent under such circumstances. Once the considerable amount of foreign capital is withdrawn from a downgraded country, its fundamentals are likely to deteriorate further, leading subsequently to the new downgrades by CRAs and deepening the crisis.

Finally, although this article favors the use sovereign debt default probabilities from empirical models and historical data over those provided by the CRAs, it is important to draw the attention of the reader to the cost of applying each method, which varies with the size of investors. Large financial institutions already have the analytical setup needed for obtaining and processing the data required for the empirical models, so, in that case, the information cost of generating their own sovereign default probabilities is marginal. For individual investors, who by and large do not have adequate analytical frameworks in place, the cost advantage lies with the existing (readily available) CRAs' default probabilities, but—as this paper suggests—these should be used with caution.

NOTES

1. For more details, please refer to Georgievska et al. (2008).
2. The following were the selection criteria: the variables are individually and jointly significant in the econometric model; the coefficients on the variables included in the model show their expected sign; and the variables included optimize the fit of the model.
3. Data obtained from the World Bank *Global Development Finance*.
4. Data obtained from: Moody's Investors Service (2003); Standard & Poor's (2002); Fitch Ratings (2002).

REFERENCES

Aylward, L., and R. Thorne. 1998. "An Econometric Analysis of Countries' Repayment Performance to the International Monetary Fund." *IMF Working Paper* WP/98/32.

Balkan, M. E. 1992. "Political Instability, Country Risk and Probability of Default." *Applied Economics* 24: 999–1008.

Detragiache, E., and A. Spilmbergo. 2000. "Crises and Liquidity: Evidence and Interpretation." Unpublished Manuscript. Washington, DC: International Monetary Fund.

Fitch Ratings. 2002, "Fitch Corporate Finance 2002 Rating Migration and Default Study." *Corporate Finance*. New York: Fitch Ratings.

Frenkel, J. 1983. "International Liquidity and Monetary Control." *NBER Working Paper* 1118.

Georgievska, A., L. Georgievska, A. Stojanovic, and N. Todorovic. 2008. "Sovereign Rescheduling Probabilities in Emerging Markets: A Comparison with Credit Rating Agencies' Ratings." *Journal of Applied Statistics* 35:9, 1031–1051.

Moody's Investors Service. 2003. *Default and Recovery Rates of Corporate Bond Issuers: A Statistical Review of Moody's Ratings Performance, 1920–2002.* New York: Moody's Investor Service, Special Comment.

Odedokun, M.O. 1995. "Analysis of Probability of External Debt Rescheduling in Subsaharan Africa." *Scottish Journal of Political Economy*, 42: 82–98.

Rivoli, P., and L. T. Brewer. 1997. "Political Instability and Country Risk." *Global Finance Journal* 8: 309–321.

Solberg, R. L. 1988. *Sovereign Rescheduling: Risk and Portfolio Management.* London: Unwin Hyman.

Standard & Poor's. 2002. "Sovereign Ratings 2001: The Best of Times, The Worst of Times." *Sovereigns.* New York: Standard & Poor's.

ABOUT THE AUTHORS

Angelina Georgievska has an investment banking background where for the past seven years she has been running the emerging market Central and Eastern Europe fixed-income business at BNP Paribas. Angelina has been pivotal in developing, selling, and implementing risk management solutions as well as hedging and structured investments for the bank's corporate and institutional clients. She holds an MSc (honors) in investment management from the Cass Business School and has published scientific work in the area of EM sovereign credit risk modeling. Her specialty is debt and derivatives in EM and valuing and hedging financial risks so as to improve returns. She has worked on such issues with EM governments, government-owned utilities, telecoms, banks, and other large companies in the CEE region.

Ljubica Georgievska's international banking career started in the corporate and public sector derivatives division at J.P. Morgan Chase, London. She then moved to Merrill Lynch as part of a team to set up the EM derivatives business. She is currently at Goldman Sachs, on the global markets emerging markets team. Ljubica has extensive experience in commodity derivatives, structured financings, private equity investments, and structured products. She holds an MSc in investments management, with honors, from the Cass Business School, and finance specialization, Strategic Financial Analysis for Business Evaluation, at the Harvard Business School.

Aleksandar Stojanovic, PhD, is the head of the department of accounting and finance at the University of Greenwich Business School, London. He was formerly a founding member and director of research at Bradley Financial, a City of London–based equity research and financial consulting agency.

He gained a first-class degree in economics from Belgrade University, an MBA (finance) and a PhD (finance) from City University (Cass) Business School, London. In addition to his extensive undergraduate and postgraduate teaching experience, Alex has won praise as an executive education professional, most notably as a visiting lecturer in finance at the Cass Business School's executive MBA program. Alex worked on various international banking projects, including work on international payment systems in association with the Bank of England and work on the impact of the euro on the U.K. banking industry in association with the Corporation of London.

Stojanovic is director of the Centre for Governance, Risk, and Accountability (gra@gre.ac.uk), a research center and forum active in the areas of corporate governance, corporate social responsibility, risk management, behavioral finance, and banking regulation.

Natasa Todorovic obtained a PhD in finance from Cass Business School (City University, London), where she currently holds a post of senior lecturer in investment management. Her current research interests are in asset management, with an emphasis on profitability of trading strategies, and emerging markets debt, focusing on Eastern Europe. She has published articles in several peer-reviewed finance journals. Todorovic links to finance industry and professional bodies include the current post as a chief examiner for fund management diploma program at the Chartered Institute for Securities and Investment (London), and prior posts in executive training at the Aviva Group, as well as advisory board membership at MP Asset Management (Slovenia).

CHAPTER 40

The International Stock Market Impact of Sovereign Debt Ratings News

MIGUEL A. FERREIRA
Universidade Nova de Lisboa—Faculdade de Economia[*]

PAULO M. GAMA
Universidade de Coimbra—Faculdade de Economia

I s sovereign rating news of one country relevant for other countries' stock markets? Specifically, we focus on spillovers of Standard & Poor's (S&P) credit rating, or outlook, for one country (the event country) to stock market return spreads (the return differential vis-à-vis the United States) of all other countries (the nonevent countries). If rating changes are seen as country-specific issues, little information impact would be expected. On the contrary, either rational behavior due to liquidity constraints or irrational herding of investors and financial and real sector linkages across countries can act as transmission vehicles for country shocks (see, for example, Karolyi 2003).

A sovereign credit rating represents a rating agency assessment of the capacity and the willingness of a sovereign obligor to meet its debt service payments in a timely fashion. In most cases, the rating assigned to nonsovereign debt issues (or issuers) is the same as or lower than the rating assigned to the sovereign of the country of domicile (sovereign ceiling doctrine).

Several mechanisms reveal a link between sovereign ratings revisions and stock markets. The country's ability to borrow in international markets may be damaged by an unfavorable revision of the sovereign debt instruments rating, thus contributing to a credit crunch. Ratings revisions may increase the awareness of market players may have about the future economic health of the rated country. Governments can take policy actions that directly affect companies' future prospects (for example, raising corporate taxes to compensate for increased debt service following a downgrade).

---

[*]A more thorough analysis of this issue can be found in Ferreira and Gama (2007).

There is published research on this issue. Kaminsky and Schmukler (2002) show that emerging market sovereign rating news is contagious for bond and stock markets in emerging markets, particularly during periods of turmoil and particularly for neighboring countries. Brooks, Faff, Hillier, and Hillier (2004) find that sovereign rating downgrades have a negative impact on the rerated country's stock market (one-day abnormal returns of 197 basis points), but upgrades have an insignificant effect. Gande and Parsley (2005) find asymmetric international spillover effects on sovereign debt markets. Downgrades abroad are associated with a significant increase in sovereign bond spreads (12 basis points), but upgrades have an insignificant effect.

We find evidence of a robust asymmetric spillover effect. A one-notch rating downgrade abroad is associated with a statistically significant negative return spread of 51 basis points, on average, across nonevent countries. No significant impact is found for rating upgrades.

The spillover impact is attenuated by geographic distance and by the degree of financial development. Ratings news has a more pronounced effect in nearby countries and among emerging countries.

RESEARCH DESIGN

We define a rating event as a change in either the explicit credit rating or the credit outlook assigned to a specific sovereign foreign currency debt, that is, the variable of interest is the changes in a comprehensive credit rating (CCR) measure; see Ferreira and Gama (2007) for details on the CCR construction.

Since July 3, 1989 (the first complete month S&P debt rating and credit outlook information are available), through December 31, 2003, there are 106 upgrades and 109 downgrades. The vast majority of events are announced individually (for one country on a given day), although multiple event days occur for 14.1 percent of the upgrades, and 3.7 percent of the downgrades. Approximately 50 percent of the events (54 upgrades and 59 downgrades) occur within a window of two weeks (10 trading days). The strong temporal association of events suggests the use of a short event-window in evaluating the impact of rating revisions and to explicitly control for worldwide recent rating activity.

We examine the cross-country spillover effects of sovereign rating revisions using the S&P history of sovereign ratings for 29 countries that meet two criteria: they have publicly traded U.S. dollar denominated sovereign debt, and country-level portfolio total return index data are available in the T.F. Datastream database.[1]

We use data on several country-specific control variables that proxy for underlying similarities between countries that could heighten common spillover effects; see Gande and Parsley (2005). A country is classified as *emerging* if it is listed as emerging by Morgan Stanley Capital International, S&P, or ISI Emerging Markets. Bilateral dummy variables are used to identify the sharing of a common language, adjacency (or common land border), legal tradition, and membership in a formal trade bloc, like NAFTA, Mercosur, the EU, or ASEAN. The great circle distance between capital cities allows for an explicit control for physical distance between countries. We explicitly control for crisis periods by including dummy variables for the European Exchange Rate Mechanism crisis of 1992–1993, the Tequila crisis of 1994, the Asian Flu of 1997, and the recent crises in Russia, Brazil, Turkey, and

Argentina. Finally, we use the Bekaert and Harvey (2000) and Bekaert, Harvey, and Lundblad (2003) official liberalization dates to control for emerging market segmentation from the world market due to regulatory constraints on international capital flows.

To study the impact of rating changes in international stock markets, we measure the nonevent country $j(\neq i)$ stock market response to a rating event in country $i(\neq j)$ by the daily logarithmic change in the country j total return index relative to the equivalent change in the U.S. market total return index (the benchmark). Daily returns are cumulated in a two-day window [0,1] to account for time zone differences between stock markets. We add a country-matched random sample (with replacement) of 215 nonevent days (the total number of rating events) to our sample of event days.

We pool the data for all countries (j) excluding the event country (i), at each event or randomly selected nonevent time (t), and separately estimate a benchmark regression for upgrades and downgrades:

$$r_{j,t} = \acute{a} + \acute{a}_1 Event_{i,t} + \sum_k \acute{a}_k X_k + \acute{a}_{ij,t}, \forall j \neq i \tag{40.1}$$

in which $r_{j,t}$ represents the cumulative [0,1] return spread. $Event_{i,t}$ takes a value equal to the change in the CCR measure on event days and zero on nonevent days. For ease of interpretation, we use the absolute value of $Event_{i,t}$ in the downgrade regression. In the basic specification, matrix X includes full sets of year and country dummies and the levels of event and nonevent country CCR. In the extended specification, matrix X is expanded to include additional controls for the time-invariant country-specific characteristics mentioned previously.

EMPIRICAL RESULTS

Exhibit 40.1 reports estimates of the coefficients in Equation 40.1. Sovereign debt rating upgrades are associated with a positive effect on stock market prices relative to the United States, and downgrades with a statistically significant negative effect. In other words, on the days a sovereign credit rating for a particular country is downgraded (or a credit outlook worsens), our results suggest that the remaining countries do much worse than the U.S. market does.

Only for downgrades is the effect statistically significant at the 5 percent level. The downgrade effect is also economically more meaningful than the upgrade effect. A one-notch negative event in one country is associated with an average negative two-day stock market return spread abroad of about 51 basis points, while positive events are associated with positive return spreads of less than 4 basis points (see specifications 1a and 1b).

Ratings downgrades, but not upgrades, seem to have an impact on nonevent countries' stock markets. One possible explanation are information leakages (or pre-event information disclosure) of the imminent upgrade by the event country government. In the case of a downgrade, rating agencies probably try harder to avoid an information leakage. Another possible explanation is marketing reasons. Rating agencies are more reluctant to downgrade a sovereign rating than to upgrade; see, for example, Larrain, Reisen, and Maltzan (1997).

The level of event country CCR is significant only for upgrades. The higher the event country CCR, the lower the nonevent country stock market response for rating upgrades, suggesting that the effect of upgrades is most marked for low-quality sovereign rating. Moreover, the coefficient of the lag event variable (the control for clustering in events in other countries by measuring rating activity in the prior two weeks) is insignificant, which suggests that rating history does not matter. This reinforces the intuition that the stock market understands downgrades as surprises.

Controlling for time-invariant characteristics that proxy for underlying similarities between countries (specifications 2a and 2b) leaves the main results unchanged.

We interpret the opposite sign of the physical distance variable relative to the event variable as evidence that added distance between countries diminishes the average wealth impact of spillovers. Therefore, there is a greater stock market effect of rating news abroad when countries are closer, which is consistent with the information asymmetry hypothesis.

The coefficient of the emerging market dummy variable (which takes a value of one when both event and nonevent countries are classified as emerging) has the same signal as the event variable coefficient (and is significant in the upgrade regression), suggesting a more pronounced impact among emerging country stock markets (excluding the event country) of events in an emerging market country.

We next perform several robustness checks to our results. We address the issues of currency effects, return definition, crisis periods, capital market liberalization, and country size. Specifically we reestimate model (1), considering first local currency denominated returns to compute the differential return vis-à-vis the U.S. market. Second, we follow Goh and Ederington (1993) and we use a rolling window of 36 months (excluding the event months –1, 0, and +1) centered on each event month (or the month of randomly selected observations), to compute the market model parameters using monthly returns (taking the U.S. stock market as a benchmark). Third, we resume the original data and use a dummy variable to control for periods of capital market turmoil (the 49 events that occurred during the international financial crisis could be driving our results). Likewise, we find that the liberalization effect is not statistically significant. A strong message emerges. The basic asymmetric effect holds when we control for these country-specific characteristics.

Larger countries are more important in the international debt market and receive more attention from global investors, thus rendering information spillovers from them to be economically more significant. To investigate this hypothesis, we focus on the 15 countries with purchasing power-adjusted GDP of more than 300 billion USD in 2002. We find that downgrades of large countries have a more pronounced impact than downgrades of small countries.

Finally, we look with further detail into the international impact of downgrade events. Specifically, we test whether the estimated downgrade spillover effect affects the cross-country correlations and we look at the stock market reaction at the local industry level.

We use a simulation procedure to characterize cross-country correlations. We randomly select (with replacement) a matched (across countries) sample of nonevent (CCR downgrade) date return spreads for each event, imposing the

Exhibit 40.1 International Stock Market Impact of Sovereign Rating News

	Upgrades				Downgrades			
	(1a)		(2a)		(1b)		(2b)	
	Coeff	t-stat	Coeff	t-stat	Coeff	t-stat	Coeff	t-stat
Constant	1.324	3.55	0.425	0.74	0.802	2.10	0.750	1.18
Event	0.036	0.59	0.038	0.61	−0.514	−5.73	−0.509	−5.68
Lag Event	0.000	0.00	0.007	0.14	0.060	1.27	0.060	1.26
CCR (event country)	−0.130	−6.29	−0.128	−6.18	−0.025	−1.27	−0.024	−1.21
CCR (nonevent country)	0.023	0.92	0.029	1.14	−0.030	−1.01	−0.027	−0.93
Emerging			0.993	2.09			−0.252	−0.49
Developed			−0.474	−0.97			0.678	1.25
Adjacent			−0.055	−0.30			0.218	1.12
Distance			−0.010	−1.06			0.021	1.91
Language			0.057	0.55			0.107	0.94
Trade bloc			0.213	1.40			0.041	0.22
Common law			−0.085	−0.59			0.007	0.04
Year dummies	yes		yes		yes		yes	
Event country dummies	yes		yes		yes		yes	
Nonevent country dummies	yes		yes		yes		yes	
Adjusted R^2	0.03		0.03		0.04		0.04	
Number of observations	7745		7745		7760		7760	

Notes: This table presents the coefficient estimates of Equation 40.1 using a sample of event days and randomly selected (with replacement) nonevent days. Event is the change in the comprehensive credit rating (CCR) on event days and zero on nonevent days. Lag event is the cumulative change in the CCR of nonevent countries during the two weeks preceding the event. Matrix X includes the levels of event and nonevent country CCR, country status as emerging or developed, adjacency (sharing of land border), distance between countries, sharing a common official language, membership in a trade bloc, origin of legal systems, and full sets of year and country (event and nonevent) dummies. The dependent variable is the cumulative two-day [0,1] nonevent country stock market return spread relative to the U.S. stock market, denominated in U.S. dollars. All t-statistics (t-stat) are heteroskedasticity-robust using the White correction.

additional condition that the nonevent days are sampled within the window [−60,−21] days relative to the event day. The sampling exercise is performed 10,000 times, and a cross-country correlation matrix is computed using each randomly selected sample of nonevent day return spreads. The simulations yield a median Jennrich (1970) test statistic of 577.96; the 5 percent critical value is 453.98 (for a chi-square distribution with 406 degrees of freedom). We reject at the 5 percent level the null hypothesis that correlation matrices are equal across all 10,000 simulations. Thus, our results strongly suggest that the correlation structure itself changes on event days. Moreover, across all 10,000 matrix evaluations, we find higher proportions of net increases than of net declines 70.6 percent of the time. Thus cross-country correlations increase during downgrade event periods.

The local industry impact of sovereign downgrades abroad relies on T.F. Datastream Level 3 local industry portfolios cumulative two-day return spreads.[2] As with the country portfolios the local industry portfolios impact of downgrades abroad is negative (65 basis points) and statistically significant. Moreover, classification of industries into traded and nontraded goods industries (Griffin and Karolyi 1998) shows that though the impact is significant in both subsamples, it is economically more important for traded goods industries (81 basis points versus 49 basis points). Similarly, the impact is also more noticeable for small industries than for larger industries (86 basis points versus 45 basis points) and is statistically significant in both subsamples.

CONCLUSION

As with own-country stock market reaction to rating changes, the evidence reveals asymmetric spillovers as only downgrades convey (new) information to stock markets abroad. Downgrades are associated with an economically and statistically significant negative return spread. On the other side, ratings upgrades abroad have no discernible impact on stock market return spreads.

Our findings are robust to control variables that proxy for possible linkages across markets, crisis periods, the nature of affected markets, and the currency in which returns are measured. Furthermore, we find that geographic distance is inversely related to the spillover impact. This is consistent with the hypothesis that rating news has a more pronounced effect in countries nearer to each other, where there is less information asymmetry. We also find that a country's status as an emerging market is positively associated with the downgrade impact. Rating downgrades have a greater economic impact for large-country events, small industries, and industries with greater foreign exposure.

NOTES

1. The countries are: Argentina, Austria, Belgium, Brazil, Canada, Chile, China, Colombia, Denmark, Finland, Greece, Hungary, Indonesia, Ireland, Israel, Italy, Korea, Malaysia, Mexico, New Zealand, Philippines, Poland, South Africa, Spain, Sweden, Thailand, Turkey, the United Kingdom, and Venezuela.

2. The 10 industries are: basic industries, cyclical consumer goods, cyclical services, financials, general industries, information technology, noncyclical consumer goods, noncyclical services, resources, and utilities.

REFERENCES

Bekaert, G., and C. Harvey. 2000. "Foreign Speculators and Emerging Equity Markets." *Journal of Finance* 55: 565–613.

Bekaert, G., C. Harvey, and C. Lundblad. 2003. "Equity Market Liberalization in Emerging Markets." *Journal of Financial Research* 26: 275–299.

Brooks, R., R. Faff, D. Hillier, and J. Hillier. 2004. "The National Market Impact of Sovereign Rating Changes." *Journal of Banking and Finance* 28: 233–250.

Ferreira, M. A., and P. M. Gama. 2007. "Does Sovereign Debt Ratings News Spill Over to International Stock Markets." *Journal of Banking and Finance* 31: 3162–3182.

Gande, A., and D. Parsley. 2005. "News Spillovers in the Sovereign Debt Market." *Journal of Financial Economics* 75: 691–734.

Goh, J., and L. Ederington. 1993. "Is a Bond Rating Downgrade Bad News, Good News, or No News for Stockholders?" *Journal of Finance* 48: 2001–2008.

Griffin, J., and G. Karolyi. 1998. "Another Look at the Role of the Industrial Structure of Markets for International Diversification Strategies." *Journal of Financial Economics* 50: 351–373.

Jennrich, R. 1970. "An Asymptotic Chi-Square Test for the Equality of Two Correlation Matrices." *Journal of the American Statistical Association* 65: 904–912.

Kaminsky, G., and S. Schmukler. 2002. "Emerging Markets Instability: Do Sovereign Rating Affect Country Risk and Stock Returns?" *World Bank Economic Review* 16: 171–195.

Karolyi, G. 2003. "Does International Financial Contagion Really Exist?" *International Finance* 6: 179–199.

Larrain G., H. Reisen, and J. Maltzan. 1997. "Emerging Market Risk and Sovereign Credit Ratings." OECD Development Center. *Technical Paper* 124.

ABOUT THE AUTHORS

Miguel A. Ferreira is an associate professor of finance at the New University of Lisbon (NOVA). He has a PhD in finance from the University of Wisconsin-Madison, a master's in economics from the New University of Lisboa, and a B.A. in business from the Instituto Superior das Ciências do Trabalho e da Empresa (ISCTE). He teaches corporate finance and risk management in the undergraduate and graduate programs at NOVA. He is currently a member of the executive committee of the European Finance Association. His research interests include international investments and corporate finance. His research has been published in academic journals such as the *Journal of Finance, Journal of Financial Economics, Journal of Financial and Quantitative Analysis, Review of Financial Studies,* and the *Journal of Banking and Finance.* He has been a recipient of research grants from the FDIC, the Institute for Quantitative Investment Research, the Bank of Portugal, and the Portuguese Science Foundation. He is a chair of the department of finance at ISCTE Business School in Lisbon.

Paulo M. Gama is an assistant professor of finance at the University of Coimbra where he teaches corporate finance and financial investments in the management undergraduate course and in the M.B.A. and MSc. programs. He received a PhD in finance from ISCTE Business School in 2005. He has published several articles in refereed finance journals. His research interests cover international capital markets, investments, and corporate governance and performance.

PART VII

Sovereign Debt and Financial Crises

P roblems with sovereign debt are clearly related to broader financial crises. A sovereign default, or even a downgrade of sovereign debt, can play an instrumental role in fomenting a financial crisis. By the same token, we are seeing in current times that a widespread financial crisis can lead to serious recession, and this reduced economic activity can have an adverse impact on a nation's ability to service its sovereign debt.

The chapters in this section focus generally, but not exclusively, on the interaction between the financial crisis of 2007–2009 and the world of sovereign debt. For example, one chapter explains how a crisis that originated as a banking crisis became a sovereign debt crisis in Europe. Other articles in this section focus on the wider European experience with sovereign debt in the wake of the financial crisis.

Formerly an arcane term of bank regulation, the phrase *too big to fail* has become a common term in recent years. It has been applied to financial institutions that are so big that their failure would impair the wider financial system and through that the real economy. The final chapter of this book raises an even more daunting question: What happens when a sovereign debtor is too big to fail? Policy makers have addressed the banks that are too big to fail through massive bailouts financed by taxpayers. But what happens when a really large country has massive debts and faces its own sovereign debt crisis?

CHAPTER 41

Equity Market Contagion and Co-Movement

Industry Level Evidence

KATE PHYLAKTIS
Professor of International Finance and Director of the Emerging Markets Group,
Sir John Cass Business School in London

LICHUAN XIA
Chief Economist and Director of Cypress House Asset Management in Hong Kong

Financial crises seem never far away from us. A series of crises were witnessed in the last 20 years: the 1992 ERM attacks, the 1994 Mexican peso collapse, the 1997 Asian crisis, the 1998 Russian collapse, the 1998 Long-Term Capital Management crisis, the 1999 Brazilian devaluation, the 2000 technological crisis, and most recently, the 2007 U.S. subprime mortgage crisis. A striking feature of crises is that markets tend to move more closely together during volatile times than during tranquil times. Such strong comovement is usually beyond the explanation of real and financial linkages and is often referred to as a *contagion*. For example, during the Asian crisis, following the collapse of the Thai baht's peg in July 1997, the financial markets of East and Southeast Asia—in particular, Thailand, Malaysia, Indonesia, the Philippines, and Korea—headed in a similar, downward direction during late 1997 and early 1998. The closer linkage between markets during the crisis episode makes it possible that external shocks are transmitted across different markets. Shocks from one market are especially propagated to the markets that have no real or financial linkages with the market in crisis and to the markets that are in different geographic locations.

What is the driving force behind the transmission of shocks from one country to the others? Is it fundamentals driven, or is it just a case of pure contagion such as a herd mentality displayed by panic-stricken investors? Understanding contagion and its origin is important for policy markers and fund managers aiming to diversify risks. For policy markers, if the crisis is mainly due to contagion, that is, due to temporary, nonfundamental factors, then short-run isolation strategies, such as capital controls, could be highly effective in reducing the effect of the crisis. On the other hand, if the crisis is transmitted mainly through permanent fundamental factors, then these short-run isolation strategies will only delay a country's adjustment to a shock (Forbes and Rigobon 2001; Dungey et al. 2003). For fund managers, if contagion prevails in times of crisis, the benefit of international diversification will be hampered when it is needed most.

The contagion on financial markets has been extensively studied. The results are, however, mixed. The early studies make use of correlation analysis and find that contagion exists. The central idea is to assess whether the correlation coefficient between two equity markets changes across tranquil and volatile periods. If the correlation increases significantly, it suggests that the transmission between the two markets amplifies after the shock, and thus contagion occurs. For example, King and Wadhwani (1990), find that cross-market correlations between the United States, the United Kingdom, and Japan increased significantly after the 1987 U.S. stock crash. Calvo and Reinhart (1996) focus on emerging markets and find that the correlations in equity prices and Brady bonds between Asian and Latin American emerging markets increased significantly during the 1994 Mexican peso crisis. Baig and Goldfajn (1999) test for contagion in equity indexes, currency prices, interest rates, and sovereign spreads in emerging markets during the 1997–1998 Asian crisis. They document a surge of significant cross-market correlations during the crisis for many of the countries.

Later studies have recognized that focusing on correlations can be misleading. For example, Forbes and Rigobon (2002) show that looking at unadjusted correlation coefficients is not appropriate, as the calculated correlation coefficient is an increasing function of the variance of the underlying asset return, so that when coefficients between a tranquil period and a crisis period are compared, the coefficient in the crisis period is biased upward as volatility rises substantially. After correcting for this bias, they find no contagion during the 1997 Asian crisis, the 1994 Mexican peso collapse, and the 1987 U.S. equity market crash. Instead, a high level of market interdependence is found during these crisis periods, which reflects a continuation of strong cross-market linkages globally present. Bekaert, Harvey, and Ng (2003) avoid the preceding correlation analysis and develop a two-factor (global and regional) asset pricing model to examine the equity market contagion in the regions of Europe, Southeast Asia, and Latin America during both the Mexican and Asian crises in the 1990s. By defining contagion as correlation among the model residuals after controlling for the local and foreign shocks, the authors show that there is no evidence of additional contagion caused by the Mexican crisis. Economically meaningful increases in the residual correlation have been found, however, especially in Asia, during the Asian crisis, a result of contagion confirmed by Dungey et al. (2003) and others who have studied the contagion on Asian equity markets.

Studies on equity market contagion unanimously focus on the empirical evidence at the market level and examine whether contagion exists across markets. The question they try to answer is whether idiosyncratic shocks from one particular market or group of markets are transmitted to the other markets during financial crises. In this paper, however, we take a different perspective and explore the equity market contagion at the disaggregated industry level, an issue that has not yet been examined in the previous literature. The question we endeavor to answer is whether unexpected shocks from a particular market (group of markets) or a particular sector, are propagated to the sectors in other countries.

Studying the contagion effect at the sector level is important for several reasons. First, studying the contagion at the market level may mask the heterogeneous performances of various sectors. Sector contagion can be asymmetric, in the sense that some sectors are more severely affected by external shocks than the other sectors within a market. Forbes (2001) shows that trade linkage is an important determinant of a country's vulnerability to crises that originate from elsewhere in the world. If this is so, sectors with extensive international trade (for example, traded goods sectors) would tend to be more prone to external shocks than sectors with less international trade (for example, nontraded goods sectors). Some sectors (for example, banking) may even constitute a major channel in transmitting the shocks across markets during crises (see, for example, Tai 2004). From the point view of portfolio management, the sector heterogeneity of contagion implies that there are sectors that can still provide a channel for achieving the benefit of international diversification during crises despite the prevailing contagion at the market level. Second, there is evidence showing that in recent years the global industry factors are becoming more important than the country specific factors in driving the variation of international equity returns (for example, Phylaktis and Xia 2006a, 2006b). Industries have overcome the cross-border restrictions and become increasingly correlated worldwide, which increases the likelihood of industries' role in propagating the global shocks and providing a channel for transmitting the contagion effect. Third, the industrial composition varies across global markets. Large, mature markets (for example, the United States and the United Kingdom) are composed of more diversified industries, whereas small, less mature markets (for example, Switzerland) are usually concentrated on a few industries. It is thus interesting to know whether markets with similar industrial structures will comove more closely with each other and be more prone to contagion during crises compared to the markets with different industrial structures.

Although the exact definition of contagion is not agreed upon in the literature, we define *contagion* in this paper as excess correlation—that is, correlation over and above what one would expect from economic fundamentals. Our paper takes an asset pricing perspective based on the methodology of Bekaert, Harvey, and Ng (2003) and examines two sources of risk: one from the U.S. equity market (proxy for the world market) and the other from the regional market, nesting an international capital asset pricing model and a regional capital asset pricing model, after controlling for local fundamental factors. Our framework essentially decomposes the correlations of sector returns into two components: the part the asset pricing model explains and the part the model does not explain. The explained part provides potential insights about sector level integration, and the unexplained part allows us to examine the correlations of model residuals, which we define as the contagion effects at the sector level. Our sample covers 10 broad sectors in 29 smaller countries across the regions of Europe, Asia, and Latin America (see Exhibits 41.1 and 41.2) with a time span from January 1990 to June 2004.

In terms of sector level integration, we find that two sectors exhibited common features in the three regions: the information technology sector showing a global nature, and the utilities sector a local regional nature. This is not surprising, as the information technology sector is considered more international in nature while the utilities sector is subject to local country-specific factors. However, the rest of the sectors performed variably across regions. In Europe and Latin America, those

Exhibit 41.1 Financial Times and London Stock Exchange Actuaries (Sector and Industry Classification)

Sector	Industries Included
Basic Industries	Chemicals Construction and Building Materials Forestry and Paper Steel and other Metals Chemicals, Construction, and Building Materials, Forestry and Paper Steel and other Metals
Cyclical Consumer Goods	Automobiles and Parts Household Goods and Textiles
Cyclical Services	General Retailers Leisure Entertainment and Hotels Media and Photography Support Services Transport
General Industries	Aerospace and Defense Electronic and Electrical Equipment Engineering and Machinery
Information Technology	Information Technology Hardware Software and Computer Services
Noncyclical Consumer Goods	Beverages Food Producers and Processors Health Personal Care and Household Products Pharmaceuticals and Biotechnology Tobacco
Noncyclical Services	Food and Drug Retailers Telecommunication Services
Resources	Mining Oil and Gas
Financials	Banks Insurance Life Assurance Investment Companies Real Estate Specialty and other Finance
Utilities	Electricity Gas Distribution Water

Exhibit 41.2   Sample Countries Included in the Analysis

Region	Countries Included
Europe	Belgium, Denmark, Spain, Finland, Greece, Ireland, Luxemburg, Netherlands, Norway, Austria, Portugal, Sweden, Switzerland, Turkey
Asia	Hong Kong, Malaysia, Korea, Indonesia, Singapore, Thailand, Taiwan, the Philippines
Latin America	Argentine, Brazil, Colombia, Chile, Mexico, Peru, Venezuela

sectors are dominated by the regional factors and, as such, are more strongly integrated at the regional level. Financials, general industries, and cyclical services are the top three sectors with the greatest regional integration in magnitude. In contrast, in Asia, those sectors are more heavily influenced by the U.S. market and more integrated at the global level. The strongest globally integrated sectors are general industries, financials, and cyclical goods.

Our finding of regional dominance in Europe is consistent with the results of other studies (see, for example, Fratzscher 2002). This regional dominance can to a large part be attributed to the drive toward Economic and Monetary Union and in particular, the elimination of exchange rate volatility and uncertainty in the process of monetary unification after the introduction of the euro. The dominance by the regional market in Latin America is also reported in other papers as well (see, for example, Heaney et al. 2002). Similarly, the stronger connection to the U.S. market in Asia is also documented in Bekaert, Harvey, and Ng (2003).

In regard to contagion, we find an overall contagion exists over our entire sample period for most of the sectors, but the transmission channels and magnitude of contagion vary across regions. For possible transmission channels, contagion across the three regions is transmitted by global and regional shocks. But in Europe and Asia, an additional channel is identified, which is the shocks from equivalent sectors within the region. This confirms our prior expectation that contagion occurs at the sector level and sectors provide channels in propagating unexpected shocks. For the magnitude of contagion, in Europe and Latin America, the most severe contagion comes from the regional shocks, whereas in Asia, it is mainly driven by the shocks from equivalent sectors within the region.

In this paper, we also examined whether there is additional contagion during the periods of the Mexican crisis in 1994–1995 and the Asian crisis in 1997–1998. Our results reveal the following: first, contagion is transmitted in some sectors and not in others. This explains the mixed results found in studies of contagion at the market level. Second, the results also point out that even though contagion might be prevalent at the market level, there are still some sectors that are immune from the contagion effect during a crisis. Third, for the financials sector, in our analysis of the Mexican crisis, we found that it did exhibit additional correlation with respect to the United States in Europe and Asia during Mexican crisis, but it didn't in Latin America. Meanwhile, correlations with equivalent sectors in the region were not found. This demonstrates that financial links with the United States might have transmitted the Mexican crisis in the region. This result is supported by Frankel and Schmukler (1998), who examined the behavior of mutual funds in international equity markets. They found that the Mexican crisis spread to other equity markets in Latin America through New York rather than directly. In Europe and Asia, trade links might have been the transmission mechanism of the crisis.

In the case of the Asian crisis, the scenario is different. Our analysis indicates that contagion can be observed only in Asia. Also, the financials sector is among the sectors that displayed additional correlation with respect to the United States. This again confirms the financial links through the United States for the propagation of the crisis. This result is supported by Van Rijckeghem and Weder (2001, 2002), who examined shifts in portfolios of European, North American, and Japanese banks during the Asian crisis. They found that North American banks shifted their lending amid emerging markets from Asia to Latin America and Europe, explaining our findings as to why the last two regions were unaffected. In short, our analysis lends support to the importance of financial links through a financial center, such as the United States, in propagating a crisis, at least within the region of the initial disturbance.

To conclude, by applying a two-factor asset pricing model, we examined the equity market integration and contagion at the industry level. With regard to integration, we have found that the sector level integration displays a distinct pattern across regions: Sectors in Europe and Latin America have higher betas with respect to the regional market than with respect to the U.S. market, suggesting the stronger integration at the regional level. Conversely, sectors in Asia are more responsive to the U.S. market than to the regional market and thus more integrated at the global level. Our findings of regional differences are also confirmed in other papers studying the international equity market comovements. The heterogeneous performance of sectors across regions indicates that those sectors are less globally correlated than we have expected and are still subject to the regional effects.

With regard to contagion, an overall contagion over our entire sample period is found for the majority of sectors in Europe, Asia, and Latin America. The transmitting channels and the magnitude of contagion vary, however, across regions. Sector shocks do play a role in contagion propagation. Finally, in examining whether the Mexican and Asian crises provide additional contagion effects, we find that nearly half of the sectors in the three regions were affected by the global shocks during the Mexican crisis. During the Asian crisis, no additional contagion is found in Europe or Latin America, but a worsened contagion transmitted by the global and regional shocks is found for most sectors in Asia. In reviewing the affected sectors, we note that the financials sector exhibited additional correlation with respect to the United States in Latin America during the Mexican crisis and in Asia during the Asian crisis, supporting the importance of financial links through a financial center in propagating a crisis.

Thus, our results confirm the sector heterogeneity of contagion, and this has implications for portfolio managers aiming to diversify risks. On the one hand, industries and sectors are found to have crossed national boundaries and become integrated with the rest of the world. This means that domestic risk factors now matter less, and nondomestic factors matter more. Diversification across countries may be losing merit and diversification across industries is preferable. The divergence of integration across regions, however, points to the fact that industries and sectors are not as globally correlated as we expect and regional effects still play a role. Therefore, selecting portfolios across regions rather than within regions would be more efficient. International investors and portfolio managers are concerned with diversification in volatile times, however, especially during crisis periods when it is most needed. Our evidence indicates that some sectors are plagued with contagion during crises, so investors and portfolio managers should avoid choosing individual securities from those contagious sectors. Our evidence also demonstrates, however, that there are sectors that are immune from external shocks or contagion during financial crises. Those sectors can provide a tool to diversify risks during crisis periods and achieve the benefits of diversification.

REFERENCES

Baig, T., and I. Goldfajn. 1999. "Financial Market Contagion in the Asian Crisis." *IMF Staff Papers* 46:2, 167–195.

Bekaert, G., C. R. Harvey, and A. Ng. 2003. "Market Integration and Contagion." *NBER Working Paper* 9510.

Calvo, S., and C. Reinhart. 1996. "Capital Flows to Latin America: Is There Evidence of Contagion Effects?" In G. Calvo, M. Goldstein, and E. Hochreiter, eds. *Private Capital Flows to Emerging Markets.* Washington, DC: Institute for International Economics.

Dungey, M., R. Fry, and V. L. Martin. 2003. "Equity Transmission Mechanisms from Asia and Australia: Interdependence or Contagion?" *Australian Journal of Management* 28: 157–182.

Forbes, K. 2001. "Are Trade Linkages Important Determinants of Country Vulnerability to Crises?" *NBER Working Paper* 8194. www.nber.org/papers/w8194.

Forbes, K., and R. Rigobon. 2001. "Contagion in Latin America: Definitions, Measurement, and Policy Implications." Paper prepared for the World Bank Conference: "How It Spreads and How It Can be Stopped," Washington, DC, February 3–4, 2000. www.worldbank.com.

———. 2002. "No Contagion, Only Interdependence: Measuring Stock Market Co-Movements." *Journal of Finance* 57: 2223–2262.

Frankel, J., and S. Schmukler. 1998. "Crises, Contagion, and Country Funds: Effects on East Asia and Latin America." In R. Glick, ed. *Managing Capital Flows and Exchange Rates: Perspectives from the Pacific Basin,* 232–266. New York: Cambridge University Press.

Fratzscher, M. 2002. "Financial Market Integration in Europe: On the Effects of EMU on Stock Markets." *International Journal of Finance and Economics* 7:3, 165–194.

Heaney, R. A., V. Hooper, and M. Jagietis. 2002. "Regional Integration of Stock Markets in Latin America." *Journal of Economic Integration* 17: 745–760.

King, M., and S. Wadhwani. 1990. "Transmission of Volatility between Stock Markets." *The Review of Financial Studies* 3:1, 5–33.

Phylaktis, K., and L. Xia. 2006a. "The Changing Role of Industry and Country Effects in the Global Equity Markets." *European Journal of Finance* 12: 627–648.

———. 2006b. "Sources of Firms' Industry and Country Effects in Emerging Markets." *Journal of International Money and Finance* 25: 459–475.

Tai, C. 2004. "Can Bank Be a Source of Contagion During the 1997 Asian Crisis?" *Journal of Banking and Finance* 28: 399–421.

Van Rijckeghem, C., and B. Weder. 2001. "Sources of Contagion: Is it Finance or Trade?" *Journal of International Economics* 54: 293–308.

———. 2002. "Spillovers Through Banking Centres: A Panel Data Analysis." *Journal of International Money and Finance* 22: 483–509.

ABOUT THE AUTHORS

Kate Phylaktis is currently a professor of international finance and the director of the Emerging Markets Group at the Cass Business School in London. She received an MSc in economics from the London School of Economics and a PhD in banking and finance from City University. Dr. Phylaktis has held various positions at the school, including head of the department of banking and finance. Before joining the school, she worked at the London School of Economics. Visiting appointments include the research department of the International Monetary Fund, the University of Bordeaux, the Athens Laboratory of Business Administration, and the Warsaw University.

She has published in prestigious journals in the areas of foreign exchange markets, capital markets, and emerging markets finance. Current work focuses on microstructure issues, financial market integration, dual listing of securities, and international diversification. She has written three books and is an associate editor of five journals.

Lichuan Xia is the chief economist and director of Cypress House Asset Management in Hong Kong. He received an MBA and a PhD in finance from the Cass Business School, London, and an MA in economics from the graduate school of the People's Bank of China. Having worked with China's central bank and several financial and securities companies in Hong Kong and Singapore, Dr. Xia has more than 15 years of practical research experience in macroeconomics and financial markets. His numerous academic papers have been published in top journals such as the *Journal of International Money and Finance* and *Financial Management Journal*, among others.

CHAPTER 42

An Insolvency Procedure for Sovereign States

A Viable Instrument for Preventing and Resolving Debt Crises?

KATHRIN BERENSMANN
German Development Institute[*]

ANGÉLIQUE HERZBERG
Department of Economics, Heinrich Heine University

G lobal financial crises and the related sovereign debt crises since the mid-1990s have highlighted the need for a reform of the current ad hoc arrangements for sovereign debt restructurings, which have often been disorderly, delayed, and inefficient. They have given rise to undue costs for both debtors and creditors and led to losses in currency reserves and generally to a decline in economic output (IMF 2002a). One viable instrument for resolving the debt crises of sovereign states in good times would be an insolvency procedure that above all else required the countries concerned to restructure their debts in accordance with set rules. Also, restructuring would be based on majority creditor decisions that were binding on minorities.

REASONS FOR ESTABLISHING AN INSOLVENCY PROCEDURE FOR SOVEREIGN STATES

An orderly insolvency procedure for sovereign states could considerably shorten the restructuring period (particularly by increasing the speed with which creditors came to an agreement), thereby reducing the economic costs of an ad hoc restructuring process (IMF 2002b).

---

[*]This paper is mainly based on Berensmann, K., and A. Herzberg, 2009. "International Sovereign Insolvency Procedure: A Comparative Look at Selected Proposals." *Journal of Economic Surveys* 23:5, 856–881.

Sovereign debt restructuring under ad hoc arrangements can, however, be time-consuming for several reasons. First, owing to the lack of a specified restructuring procedure, or road map, the parties involved face uncertainties about the process itself. Second, highly indebted countries may tend to protract debt restructuring for fear of the high costs associated with it. Third, a lack of the information needed to decide how different creditor groups should be treated could also prolong a restructuring process (Berensmann 2003; IMF 2002a).

Finally, a delay can result from problems of creditor coordination because of the size and the heterogeneous structure of creditor groups and from collective action problems, including the holdout problem, the rush-to-the-exit problem, and the rush-to-the-courthouse problem. A holdout, or free rider, problem may occur when some creditors refuse to participate in a restructuring process in order to have their claims met in full after other creditors have agreed to restructuring. A rush to the exit may ensue if creditors fear a default and seek to sell off (or not to roll over) their claims on a sovereign debtor at the earliest opportunity. The rush-to-the-courthouse problem may arise when some creditors try to attach a sovereign debtor's assets through early litigation (Roubini 2002).

Currently, there is no one instrument capable of resolving all the problems associated with coordination and collective action. The most practicable short-term approaches include a code of conduct (a voluntary approach) and collective action clauses. A code of conduct sets out general principles to be observed by market participants in the period prior to and during a debt crisis, such as a timely dialogue between creditors and debtors, a fair exchange of information among all parties involved, speedy and cooperative negotiations, equal treatment of all creditors and continued adherence to the terms of existing contracts (Banque de France 2003; Cardona and Farnoux 2002; Ritter 2009). Being no more than a voluntary agreement, a code of conduct cannot offer any formal protection against creditor litigation or provide any safeguards against a holdout. One solution to this problem would be to include a code of conduct in contracts. Collective action clauses (a contractual approach) are provisions in sovereign bond contracts designed to simplify restructuring procedures for sovereign bonds and in particular to offer both creditors and debtors incentives to participate in restructuring negotiations. The most common type of collective action clause is the collective majority clause, which authorizes a qualified majority of bondholders to agree to a restructuring program that is binding on all bondholders (Berensmann 2003; Dixon and Wall 2000).

The economic consequences of debt restructuring and their transmission channels have been analyzed, for example, by the IMF (IMF 2002b) on the basis of four debt crises: Russia (1998), Ecuador (1999), Ukraine (2000/2001), and Pakistan (1999).[1] In all four cases, the wealth of domestic holders of restructured debt decreased owing to a reduction in the net present value of their assets, and the announcement of the sovereign debtor's inability to pay led to a significant depreciation. The cost of capital increased significantly even before the default (bond spreads rose considerably, in particularly in Russia and Ecuador). At least in three cases (Russia, Ecuador, and Ukraine) a reduction in money demand and a substitution of foreign currency for domestic currency denominated assets contributed to the devaluation of national currencies and boosted barter trade. In Russia and Ecuador in particular, capital inflows to the bank and nonbank sectors plummeted. Interbank lending also fell sharply in Ecuador and Russia (IMF 2002b).

An insolvency procedure causes concern in a number of respects. Debtor states fear losing access to international capital markets once an insolvency procedure has been opened. The experience of some countries (for example, Russia in 1998) shows, however, that access to private financing can be regained soon after a default. Creditors worry that an insolvency procedure may promote opportunistic defaults by facilitating debt restructuring. The risk of a rush to default (Roubini 2002) can be reduced by establishing clear rules that prevent restructuring from becoming too easy an option. Finally, the opponents of a statutory approach argue that an insolvency procedure could be installed only in the long run since it would require a legally binding international framework, which would then have to be transposed into national law (as, for example, envisaged by Schwarcz 2000). However, the establishment of an insolvency procedure under international law is not essential (see, for example, the proposal by Raffer 1990, 2005). Despite the aforementioned concerns, an insolvency procedure is a highly comprehensive instrument for preventing and dealing with sovereign debt.

A number of proposals have been put forward for an insolvency procedure for sovereign states. Most of them take the U.S. bankruptcy law (Chapter 9 and Chapter 11) as a model, since similar collective action problems also arise in the corporate context.[2]

- Raffer's proposal, first published in 1990, builds on the most important principles of Chapter 9, Title 11 of the U.S. Bankruptcy Code, which concerns debts of municipalities (Raffer 1990, 2005). Several nongovernmental organizations, such as the Jubilee Campaigns, recommend a similar approach, known as the "fair and transparent arbitration process for indebted southern countries" (Kaiser and Schroeder 2002).
- Based mainly on Chapter 11, Title 11 of the U.S. Code, Schwarcz's proposal (2000) develops a concrete design for an international convention on sovereign insolvency procedures. The main reasons for applying Chapter 11 are to provide for debtor rehabilitation and distributional equity among creditors.
- Perhaps the best-known proposal, the sovereign debt restructuring mechanism (SDRM), was presented in November 2001 by Anne O. Krueger, the then–first deputy managing director of the International Monetary Fund (Krueger 2001). At the spring meeting of the IMF and the World Bank in 2003, the SDRM (IMF 2003) was rejected as being impracticable. It similarly incorporates the main features of Chapter 11 (IMF 2003).
- The proposal tabled by Bolton and Skeel (2004) aims at improving selected aspects of the SDRM. The authors focus in particular on protecting priority creditor rights when claims are classified.
- The international debt framework (IDF) suggested by Berensmann and Schroeder (2006) is a nonstatutory approach linked to the G-20 countries. It comprises two institutions: an IDF secretariat, designed to improve the transparency of information on debtor countries and the ways in which it is made available by instituting a regular debtor-creditor dialogue, and an IDF commission, whose main task would be to help ensure orderly debt restructuring.

THE MAIN FEATURES OF AN INSOLVENCY PROCEDURE

This section outlines the key design features of an international sovereign insolvency procedure. They include, first, the framework conditions required for the efficient restructuring of sovereign debt, such as the right to open and to terminate an insolvency procedure, the arbitration body and ways of achieving creditor coordination. Second, the actual core features of any insolvency procedure are the rules on the restructuring of debt, including the definition of debt sustainability, the inclusion of claims, and the stay of enforcement and cessation of payments.

The Right to Open an Insolvency Procedure

With a view, first and foremost, to protecting sovereignty, most proposals suggest assigning the right to open an insolvency procedure to a sovereign debtor. To reduce the risk of a rush to default, the petition of a debtor state could be examined by an arbitration body or by creditors (Berensmann and Herzberg 2009). An examination of this kind would require, in particular, an assessment of the debt of the country in question. The difficult task of determining a government's insolvency or illiquidity could be facilitated by applying debt sustainability indicators, such as the level of debt or debt service as a fraction of export revenue, gross domestic product, or national income.

Arbitration Body

Most of the proposals for sovereign insolvency procedures argue that debt restructuring should not be left entirely to the parties affected and that a neutral third party should take on the role of arbiter (mediating between the parties and performing such administrative tasks as the verification of claims) and approve the restructuring solution, which would be binding on both sides.

The first issue to be clarified is whether there are any institutions that could act as arbiter. Using the expertise and reputation of an existing institution would have many advantages, and the time and expense of launching a new institution would be saved. However, finding an appropriate institution appears to be difficult. National courts (Bolton and Skeel 2004) bear a risk of being partial; such other institutions as the International Court of Justice and the Dispute Settlement Body of the World Trade Organization (Schwarcz 2000) do not have any expertise in bankruptcy procedures.

It would seem easier to meet the requirements of impartiality and acknowledged expertise by establishing a new institution (for example, Raffer 1990; Paulus 2002; IMF 2003; Berensmann and Schroeder 2006). A new arbitration panel might consist of a small number of impartial experts in bankruptcy issues. Each party could appoint the same number of arbiters (two or four), who would elect one of their members as chairman. Giving the chairman two votes would yield an uneven number of votes and ensure clear majority decisions. Such an ad hoc arbitration panel would not require major legal changes and could therefore be set up in the short to medium term. In the long run, however, the predictability of sovereign insolvency procedures could be enhanced by laying the legal foundations for a whole procedure and, among other things, for the arbitration panel (for example, an international convention as suggested by Schwarcz 2000).

Creditor Treatment and Coordination

To ensure that all creditors are treated equally, all categories of external debt (debt held by bilateral and multilateral public creditors and private creditors) should be included in a restructuring procedure. Domestic debt should be taken into account when overall debt sustainability is assessed, but should not be included in a restructuring procedure since, first, countries have national restructuring instruments and, second, it might increase opportunistic defaults by making restructuring too easy.

Claims of the same priority could be grouped in one class. Unsecured claims could be further classified by the first-in-time rule: the older a claim, the higher its priority. The first-in-time priority rule would help to prevent overborrowing, since new creditors run higher risks than older creditors (see Bolton and Skeel 2004 for details). During the restructuring process, the debtor typically needs interim financing. To provide creditors with incentives to lend to an insolvent debtor, their claims against the debtor could, for example, be exempted from the restructuring. A system of previously defined classification rules would protect creditors from any violation against the priority of their claims and also accelerate the restructuring process by eliminating the struggle among creditors for payment flows (Gelpern 2004).

The classification of claims could also facilitate the voting on the restructuring plan submitted by the debtor. In general, majority enforcement provisions or unanimity in combination with the cramdown rule should solve the holdout problem (Roubini 2002). Within the various classes, a simple or qualified majority—based on the amount or volume of claims—would ensure that a class could vote even if some creditors did not participate in the voting. Among the classes, either majority decisions or unanimity combined with a cramdown could be required. The cramdown rule would allow the arbitration body to agree to the restructuring plan even if some classes voted against it—provided that it was fair and equitable. Since the revision of the plan by the arbitration body would take time, creditors would have an incentive to reach an agreement and avoid the cramdown (Schwarcz 2000).

Stay of Enforcement

With the aim of protecting a debtor country from a rush to the courthouse and a rush to the exit, an insolvency procedure should incorporate stay provisions. A (temporary) stay of enforcement could protect the debtor against a rush to the courthouse and against disruptive litigation. A rush to the exit could be avoided by a (temporary) stay of debt payments (for example, as part of a moratorium). A stay of payments would also allow the debtor to use its scarce foreign-exchange earnings for investment instead of debt servicing. Both types of stays would give creditors an incentive to take part in restructuring negotiations. Also, these stays could help to ensure equal treatment of all creditors because no creditor would be able to enforce payments during a stay or receive any payments. However, both stays could raise credit costs for sovereign debtors since creditors might try to compensate for the lack of opportunity to attach sovereign debtors' assets by demanding a higher return (Schwarcz 2000). Another concern is that stays would trigger capital flight or have contagion effects on other countries (Berensmann and Schroeder 2006, Berensmann 2003).

Proposals for insolvency procedures range from no stay at all (Schwarcz 2000) to an automatic stay (Raffer 2005; Paulus 2002). A middle course is a conditional stay coming into force upon the approval of the supermajority of creditors (IMF 2003a) or G-20 countries (Berensmann and Schroeder 2006) or a stay that applies only to asset seizures with ordinary litigation taking its normal course because it does not hamper the debt restructuring (Bolton and Skeel 2004). To accelerate a procedure, a stay with a specified duration (say, 90 days) that takes effect automatically on the opening of the procedure would be most suitable.

CONCLUSION

The current international financial architecture does not include a comprehensive procedure, or road map, for the restructuring of a country's foreign debt. This lack of a comprehensive approach to debt restructuring is very costly, mainly because of the consequent delays in initiating restructuring processes. For this reason, an orderly debt restructuring mechanism that is both predictable and based on a general set of principles recognized by creditors and debtors alike could lead to the initiation of restructuring processes at an earlier stage.

NOTES

1. It must be remembered that it is difficult to distinguish between the primary effects of debt restructuring on an economy and the effects of such policy measures as the introduction of capital controls or a change in the exchange rate regime (IMF 2002b).

2. For an overview of the main proposals for international insolvency procedures, see Berensmann and Herzberg (2009). A history of ideas on international insolvency procedures can be found in Rogoff and Zettelmeyer (2002). Other overviews have been compiled by Bernhard and Kellermann (2008) and Hagan (2005).

REFERENCES

Banque de France. 2003. *Towards a Code of Good Conduct on Sovereign Debt Re-Negotiation*. Paris: Banque de France. www.ifri.org/files/PropBdF.pdf.

Berensmann, K. 2003. "Involving Private Creditors in the Prevention and Resolution of International Debt Crises." *DIE Studies* 8/2003. www.die-gdi.de/CMS-Homepage/ openwebcms3.nsf/%28ynDK_contentByKey%29/ENTR-7BUKAZ/$FILE/BuG%209% 202003%20EN.pdf.

Berensmann, K., and A. Herzberg. 2009. "International Sovereign Insolvency Procedure: A Comparative Look at Selected Proposals." *Journal of Economic Surveys* 23:5, 856–881.

Berensmann, K., and F. Schroeder. 2006. "A Proposal for a New International Debt Framework for the Prevention and Resolution of Debt Crises in Middle-Income Countries." *DIE Discussion Papers* 2/2006. www.die-gdi.de/CMS-Homepage/openwebcms3.nsf/ (ynDK_ contentByKey)/ADMR-7BRMCG/$FILE/2-2006.pdf.

Bernhard, R., and C. Kellermann. 2008. "Against All Debts? Solutions for Future Sovereign Defaults." *Journal for International Relations and Global Trends* 1: 116–130. http:// library.fes.de/pdf-files/ipg/ipg-2008-1/09_a_bernhard.pdf.

Bolton, P., and D. A. Skeel, Jr. 2004. "Inside the Black Box: How Should a Sovereign Bankruptcy Framework Be Structured?" *Emory Law Journal* 53: 763–822.

Cardona, M., and M. Farnoux. 2002. "International Codes and Standards: Challenges and Priorities for Financial Stability." *Banque de France Financial Stability Review* 1: 143–154. www.banque-france.fr/gb/publications/telechar/rsf/2002/et8_1102.pdf.

Dixon, L., and D. Wall. 2000. "Collective Action Problems and Collective Action Clauses." *Bank of England Financial Stability Review* 8: 142–153. www.bankofengland.co.uk/publications/fsr/2000/fsr08art8.pdf.

Gelpern, A. 2004. "Building a Better Seating Chart for Sovereign Restructurings." *Emory Law Journal* 53: 1119–1161.

Hagan, S. 2005. "Designing a Legal Framework to Restructure Sovereign Debt." *Georgetown Journal of International Law* 36:4, 299–402.

International Monetary Fund. 2002a. "Sovereign Debt Restructurings and the Domestic Economy Experience in Four Recent Cases." Paper Prepared by the Policy Development and Review Departments in Consultation with the Other Departments." *International Monetary Fund*, February 21, 2002. www.imf.org/external/np/pdr/sdrm/2002/022102.pdf.

———. 2002b. "The Design of the Sovereign Debt Restructuring Mechanism—Further Considerations." Paper prepared by the Legal and Policy Development and Review Departments in consultation with the International Capital Markets and Research Departments." *International Monetary Fund*, November 27, 2002. www.imf.org/external/np/pdr/sdrm/2002/112702.htm.

———. 2003. "Proposed Features of a Sovereign Debt Restructuring Mechanism." Paper prepared by the Legal and Policy Development and Review Departments in consultation with the International Capital Markets and Research Departments." *International Monetary Fund*, February 12, 2003. www.imf.org/external/np/pdr/sdrm/2003/021203.htm.

Kaiser, J., and F. Schroeder. 2002. "New Steps to Faster and Broader Debt Relief for Developing Countries." *Dialogue on Globalization Occasional Papers* 1. Friedrich Ebert Foundation. http://library.fes.de/pdf-files/iez/01451.pdf.

Krueger, A. 2001. "International Financial Architecture for 2002: A New Approach to Sovereign Debt Restructuring." Address by Anne Krueger, first deputy managing director, International Monetary Fund, given at the National Economists' Club Annual Members' Dinner, American Enterprise Institute, Washington DC, November 26, 2001. www.imf.org/external/np/speeches/2001/112601.htm.

Paulus, Christoph G. 2002. "Some Thoughts on an Insolvency Procedure for Countries." *The American Journal of Comparative Law* 50:3, 531–553.

Raffer, K. 1990. "Applying Chapter 9 Insolvency to International Debts: An Economically Efficient Solution with a Human Face." *World Development* 18:2, 301–311.

———. 2005. "Internationalizing US Municipal Insolvency: A Fair, Equitable, and Efficient Way to Overcome a Debt Overhang." *Chicago Journal of International Law* 6:1, 361–379. http://cjil.uchicago.edu/past-issues/sum05.html.

Ritter, R. 2009. "Transnational Governance in Global Finance: The Principles for Stable Capital Flows and Fair Debt Restructuring in Emerging Markets." *European Central Bank Occasional Paper* No. 103.

Rogoff, K., and J. Zettelmeyer. 2002. "Bankruptcy Procedures for Sovereigns: A History of Ideas, 1976–2001." *IMF Staff Papers* 49:3, 470–507.

Roubini, N. 2002. "Do We Need a New Bankruptcy Regime?" *Brookings Papers on Economic Activity* 1: 321–333.

Schwarcz, S. L. 2000. "Sovereign Debt Restructuring: A Bankruptcy Reorganization Approach." *Cornell Law Review* 85: 956–1033.

ABOUT THE AUTHORS

Kathrin Berensmann has worked as a senior economist at the German Development Institute (DIE) in Bonn since 2000. Before joining the DIE, she was employed as an economist at the Institute of German Economy in Cologne. She received her PhD and Diplom (equivalent to a master's degree) in economics from the University of Würzburg (Germany). Her main areas of specialization are international financial architecture, international financial markets, debt policy, monetary and exchange rate policy, and financial sector development.

Angélique Herzberg is a PhD candidate at Heinrich Heine University, Düsseldorf, Germany, where she also works as an instructor. Her PhD thesis, written under the supervision of Professor H. D. Smeets, focuses on current account imbalances. Other research interests include sovereign debt crises and sovereign insolvency procedures. She graduated from Heinrich Heine University in 2006 with a Diplom (equivalent to an MSc) in economics and business administration as a German National Academic Foundation scholar.

CHAPTER 43

From Banking to Sovereign Debt Crisis in Europe

BERTRAND CANDELON
Professor of International Monetary Economics, Maastricht University School
of Business and Economics, the Netherlands

FRANZ C. PALM
Professor of Econometrics, Maastricht University School of Business
and Economics, the Netherlands

O ne may get the feeling from reading the daily press that since 2007, developed economies are suffering from one long-lasting financial crisis. At a closer look, however, the term *financial crisis* appears to be too vague to be meaningful. The turmoil began with a real estate bubble in the United States that crashed in 2007, leaving financial institutions with serious liquidity problems or even insolvency. The real estate crisis mutated into a banking crisis. Partly as a result of measures taken to rescue financial institutions in distress, some euro area countries faced difficulties in balancing their budgets and financing their debt, signaling hence the upcoming mutation of the crisis into a sovereign debt one. These tensions are now affecting the currency market, signaling a new mutation into a currency crisis. At the same time, as private banks hold large portions of public debt, a sovereign debt crisis might put the banking sector in distress. Hence, it appears that the 2007 turmoil is not monolithic. Instead it evolves as a sequence of specific crises. Discerning this feature will be crucial for understanding the crises.

Economic literature on financial crises has paid attention to the links between currency and banking crises, denominated as twin crises (for example, Glick and Hutchinson 2000; Bordo et al. 2001). However, only a few studies have integrated sovereign debt crisis effects.[1] This paper intends to shed light on the potential linkages between the different types of financial crises. The paper first presents the theoretical linkages and empirical evidence and then turns to scrutinize the current European situation.

THEORETICAL LINKAGES AND EMPIRICAL EVIDENCE

The Balance Sheet Approach

Theoretical models, as presented in Flood and Garber (1984), apprehend the occurrence of a currency crisis, considering jointly well-known relationships (such as uncovered interest rate parity and money demand), and the balance sheet of the central bank, through an accounting relationship between foreign reserves and domestic credit. When foreign reserves are exhausted, currency market turmoil might be avoided by controlling money supply growth.

Adopting a balance sheet approach (BSA), we illustrate the mutation of a crisis using the linkages[2] between financial sector, nonfinancial sector (firms and households), external sector, and central bank and government sector balance sheets. This framework allows us to investigate some main causal links behind the recent crises.

The burst of the real estate bubble affected the nonfinancial sector balance sheet because households were unable to service their mortgages. The subsequent losses incurred by banks, in particular by those that held toxic assets bundling risky mortgage loans, affected assets on the financial sector balance sheet, the turmoil turning into a banking crisis. Stock markets crashed, destroying wealth, affecting final demand, and deteriorating further the asset side of financial and nonfinancial sectors' balance sheets. Authorities implemented safety plans or guarantees to rescue the financial sector. These interventions, coupled with the contraction of the domestic demand, shrank the asset part of the government balance sheet initiating a sovereign debt crisis. The turmoil could now initiate a new banking or currency crisis. The depreciation of some government bonds, which became labeled as risky, may induce liquidity problems for the financial institutions holding them. Similarly, the turmoil weakens the balance sheet of the external sector and the central bank, transmitting the trouble into the currency market. With a flexible exchange rate, the currency will strongly depreciate. In a monetary union, extreme internal tensions might lead to its termination. Besides, the nonfinancial sector balance sheet will be also weakened directly, by the costs of refinancing the public debt, the depreciation of government bonds and the austerity measures required to restore a balanced budget, and indirectly by the credit crunch and the depreciation of residents' wealth. Adjustments will continue until an equilibrium is reached, the overall effects depending on the mismatches between the different balance sheets.[3]

Empirical Evidence

Empirical evidence on the mutation of a currency into a banking crisis has been provided by numerous studies (for example, Kaminsky and Reinhart 1996, 1999; Bordo et al. 2001; Glick and Hutchison 2001; von Hagen and Ho 2008). They all found a strong relationship between these two types of crises and an important incidence on real economic variables as GDP. There is no consensus, however, on whether causation runs from banking crisis to currency crisis or the reverse, indicating that mutations can occur in both directions.

Only a few studies have investigated the link between banking and sovereign debt crises. Reinhart and Rogoff (2009) find that three years after a banking crisis, the stock of public debt is increased by a factor of 1.86. This effect pushes up default risk and may cause a sovereign debt crisis in countries with initially fragile public finances. Focusing on the subprime crisis period for European countries, Candelon and Palm (2010) corroborate this relationship. They provide evidence that the mutation of the banking crisis into a sovereign debt crisis is not due to the fiscal costs of governments' saving and guarantee plans to financial institutions, but rather to stock market losses leading to a fall in wealth, GDP, and fiscal income, and an increase of debt and of the debt-to-GDP ratio and thus a higher probability of debt default.

The Financial Crisis in Europe

The Facts

Since the collapse of the real estate market in the United States, European countries have been hurt by banking and sovereign debt crises. U.S. branches of European financial institutions were directly hit by the subprime crisis. After financial stabilization using rescuing plans, fiscal stability in Europe turned out to be shaken: In 2009, most European members did not meet the fiscal criteria imposed by the Maastricht Treaty.[4] In Greece and Italy, the level of debt now exceeds their GDP. The weakest European countries (labeled as the five PIIGS[5]) feel the pressure by financial markets and face increasing refinancing rates.[6] Investors, losing confidence in the ability of these countries to service their debt, request higher risk premiums. The subprime turmoil has hence muted into banking and sovereign debt crises.

The institutional frame of the Economic and Monetary Union is not well equipped to address a sovereign debt crisis at the European level, as fiscal policy is largely a matter of individual member states, and the European Central Bank (ECB) is prohibited to be a lender of last resort to the governments of member states. As long as the Stability and Growth Pact is not adhered to and effectively monitored, it cannot serve as a substitute for a European fiscal authority.

At this stage, two questions request an answer: Does the mutation come to an end with the sovereign debt crisis? And which policy measures would freeze or at least dampen this transformation?

The End of the Story?

Unfortunately, the mutation will most probably not be terminated with the sovereign debt crisis.

First, we observe increasing heterogeneity between countries experiencing a loss of reserves (the PIIGS, for example) and those (as Germany) benefiting from capital inflow, due to a flight to quality effect. Interest rate spreads are diverging within the euro area, endangering hence the monetary union. Weakened by these threats, the euro lost 25 percent of its value with respect to the U.S. dollar since November 2009 when it sold for US $1.50 and June 2010 when the exchange rate was US $1.20. A similar evolution can be observed with respect to the Japanese yen, the British pound, or the Russian ruble. Tensions, both within and outside euro area, may pave the way to a currency crisis.

Second, European private banks have massively invested in foreign debt issued by the PIIGS countries and are now holding large amounts of assets that could become troubled. For example, German banks hold \$703.9 billion[7] and French banks hold \$911.2 billion[8] of shaky foreign debt issued by these countries. Compared with the banks' total capital and reserves (\$565.2 billion in Germany and \$579.3 billion in France) these amounts are such that even a partial default of Spain and Italy could cause major distress in the banking sector in France and Germany.

Finally, these backfire effects could potentially create the conditions for speculators to generate a self-fulfilling currency or, although less likely, a banking crisis (see Obstfeld 1996 for a theoretical model of a self-fulfilling currency crisis). The mechanism at the origin of such an event is relatively simple to outline: As markets are uncertain about the future value of a currency, any rumor or news could provoke a massive sell-off of the euro, leading to its depreciation.

Policy Recommendations

To provide policy recommendations, it is worthwhile to consider similar historical events. The Russian 1998 crisis episode constitutes an interesting benchmark despite its specificities (post-communist era, huge reserves of energy and raw materials, and so on). In 1997 and 1998, Russia also faced a conjunction of banking, currency, and sovereign debt crises.

The first measures in response to the turmoil consisted in a fiscal cure. The Russian authorities severely cut expenditures like military procurement and rationalized fiscal income in particular through better tax collection at the regional level.[9] Similar measures have now been implemented by countries like Greece and Spain, both of which decided to reduce civil servants' salaries. Those moves should help regain credibility from investors, and to reward these countries by smaller risk premiums and refinancing rates. Nevertheless, an excessive contraction of the final demand may lead to a complete pass-through of such actions into further fiscal deficits. Indeed, to guarantee the positive effect of the austerity measures, it is essential to check that the elasticity between private demand and tax level is lower than unity. Finally, this policy should be concerted among the members of the euro area so as to avoid higher heterogeneity.

The second action concerns monetary policy. During the Russian crisis, the central bank was not authorized to finance public deficit,[10] forcing the government to issue government bonds (government short-term commitments [GKO] and federal loan obligations [OFZ]). This legal prohibition has been removed in order to finance the Russian public debt. A similar constraint applies to the European Central Bank, which is not allowed to directly finance the EU countries.[11] According to the EU treaty, a no bail-out clause is in effect for the purpose of avoiding moral hazard problems.[12] A structural institutional solution has to be found to solve the one-way issue. The solution requires the creation of an institutional European body that acts in the case of sovereign debt crises and a more effective and credible role of the European Commission in publicly monitoring the member states within areas defined in the Stability and Growth Pact.[13] The initial step has been taken by the EU when member states agreed on the support loan program by creating the European Financial Stability Facility for a member countries facing public debt problems.

The third action concerns exchange rate stabilization policies. In a monetary union, a member country cannot use exchange rate adjustments to the extent needed to address its problems induced by a sovereign debt crisis and regain external competitiveness and credibility, not even if a currency crisis followed the foreign debt crisis. The exchange rate of the monetary union currency will likely always reflect the economic conditions in the whole union and the credibility of its policies. Breaking the monetary union, by excluding the weakest currencies, would allow them to adopt floating exchange rates. This constitutes, of course, an extreme measure.

In last resort, if the fiscal situation in some countries became unsolvable, a restructured debt could also constitute the ultimate solution. After a three-month moratorium, the public debt in Russia was restructured in 1998. Debt restructuring might naturally induce a loss of credibility for foreign investors but would temporarily freeze the degradation of the situation. It does not constitute a long-run strategy, however, contrary to previous recommendations.

NOTES

1. With the exception of Reinhart and Rogoff (2008) and Candelon and Palm (2010).
2. See Rosenberg et al. (2005) for a version where central bank and government balance sheets are aggregated.
3. See Rosenberg et al. (2005) or Candelon and Palm (2010).
4. Debt-GDP ratio below 60% and a public deficit-GDP ratio below 3%.
5. PIIGS refers to Portugal, Ireland, Italy, Greece and Spain.
6. See Candelon and Palm (2010) for the recent evolution of the government bond spread in Euro area.
7. Data are issued by the Bank of International Settlements (http://www.bis.org/statistics/provbstats.pdf#page=90). They represent the foreign claims by nationality of reporting banks (Table 9B) and correspond to the following U.S. dollar amounts: $45.0 billion in Greece, $237.9 billion in Spain, $47.4 billion in Portugal $183.8 billion in Ireland, and $189.7 billion in Italy.
8. It corresponds to $75.2 billion in Greece, $219.6 billion in Spain, $44.7 billion in Portugal, $60.3 billion in Ireland and $511.4 billion in Italy.
9. See Sutela (2010).
10. This decision aims at curving down inflation.
11. Even if ECB violated this rule to help Greece.
12. Article 100 of the Maastricht Treaty could however be invoked to allow EU governments to freely bail out a country if needed.
13. According to the Stability and Growth Pact, the European Commission should monitor the member countries' public finance, such that they respect the fiscal criteria imposed by the Maastricht Treaty in 1992.

REFERENCES

Bordo, M. D., B. Eichengreen, D. Klingebiel, and M. S. Martinez-Peria. 2001. "Financial Crises: Lessons from the Last 120 Years." *Economic Policy* 16: 51–82.

Candelon, B. and F. Palm. 2010. "Banking and Debt Crises in Europe: The Dangerous Liaisons?" *De Economist* 158: 81–99.

Flood, R. P., and P. M. Garber. 1984. "Collapsing Exchange Rate Regimes: Some Linear Examples." *Journal of International Economics* 17: 1–13.

Glick, R., and M. Hutchison. 2000. "Banking and Currency Crises: How Common Are the Twins?" Hong Kong Institute for Monetary Research. *Working Paper* 01/2000.

Kaminsky, G., and M. Reinhart. 1996. "The Twin Crises: The Causes of Banking and Balance-of-Payments Problems." *International Finance Discussion Papers* No. 544. Washington, DC: Board of Governors of the Federal Reserve System.

———. 1999. "The Twin Crises: The Causes of Banking and Balance-of-Payments Problems." *American Economic Review* 89: 473–500.

Obstfeld, M. 1996. "Models of Currency Crises with Self-fulfilling Features." *European Economic Review* 40: 1037–1048.

Reinhart, C., and K. Rogoff. 2009. *This Time Is Different: Eight Centuries of Financial Folly.* Princeton, NJ: Princeton University Press, Preface.

Rosenberg, C., I. Halikias, B. House, C. Keller, J. A. Pitt, and B. Setser. 2005. "Debt-Related Vulnerabilities and Financial Crises: An Application of the Balance Sheet Approach to Emerging Market Countries." *IMF Occasional Paper* 240.

Sutela, P. 2010. "The Financial Crisis in Russia." In J. R. Bisignano, W. C. Hunter, and G. Kaufman, eds. *Global Financial Crises: Lessons from Recent Events.* Boston: Kluwer Academic Publishers; Basel, Switzerland: Bank of International Settlements; Chicago: Federal Reserve Bank of Chicago.

von Hagen, J., and T. K. Ho. 2008. "Twin Crises: An Examination of the Empirical Links." Bundesbank. *Working paper.*

ABOUT THE AUTHORS

Bertrand Candelon is a professor in international monetary economics. He received a PhD from the Universite Catholique de Louvain. After a postdoctoral fellowship at the Humboldt Universität zu Berlin, he joined University Maastricht School of Business and Economics in 2001. Bertrand Candelon has written an extensive number of papers in the field of international finance, in particular on contagion and on the analysis of financial market comovements. He is one of the founders of the methods in international finance network.

Franz C. Palm studied economics at the Universities of Louvain and Chicago. He has been a professor of econometrics at the Free University, Amsterdam, and since 1985 at Maastricht University. For almost eight years he has been dean of Maastricht University School of Business and Economics. He is a foreign member of the Royal Netherlands Academy of Arts and Sciences. He currently holds a (research) professorship at this academy. He is a founding co-editor of the *Journal of Empirical Finance*. In 2009, he received a doctorate honoris causa from Université de Fribourg, Switzerland.

CHAPTER 44

From Financial Crisis to Sovereign Risk

CARLOS CACERES
International Monetary Fund*

VINCENZO GUZZO
International Monetary Fund

MIGUEL SEGOVIANO
Comisión Nacional Bancaria y de Valores (Mexican Financial Authority)

O ver the past few years, euro area sovereign yields and spreads[1] have exhibited an unprecedented degree of volatility (see Exhibit 44.1). These
movements can have significant macroeconomic consequences. A rise in
sovereign yields tend to be accompanied by a widespread increase in long-term
interest rates in the rest of the economy, affecting both investment and consumption decisions. On the fiscal side, higher government bond yields imply higher
debt-servicing costs and can significantly raise funding costs. This could also lead
to an increase in rollover risk, as debt might have to be refinanced at unusually
high cost or, in extreme cases, cannot be rolled over at all. Large increases in government funding costs can thus cause real economic losses in addition to the purely
financial effects of higher interest rates.

As the crisis unfolded, several factors might have affected the valuations
of sovereign bonds. First, the global market price for risk went up, as investors
sought higher compensation for risk. Deleveraging and balance sheet–constrained
investors developed a systemically stronger preference for a few selected assets
vis-à-vis riskier instruments. This behavior not only benefited sovereign securities
as an asset class at the expense of corporate bonds and other riskier assets, but also
introduced a higher degree of differentiation within the sovereign spectrum itself.

Second, as policy authorities stepped in to support troubled financial institutions, the crisis spread to the public sector and probabilities of distress went up
across governments. In this context, two distinct channels may be identified: a
domestic channel, as fundamentals started deteriorating, and an external channel,

*This section is an excerpt from Caceres, C., V. Guzzo, M. Segoviano, 2010, "Sovereign
Spreads: Global Risk Aversion, Contagion or Fundamentals?" *IMF Working Paper* 10/120.

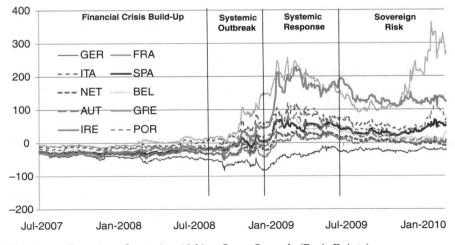

Exhibit 44.1   Euro Area Sovereign 10-Year Swap Spreads (Basis Points)
Source: IMF Staff calculations on DataStream and Bloomberg data.

as higher probabilities of distress spread among sovereigns. This section explores how much of the observed large movements in sovereign spreads reflect shifts in the market price of risk or country-specific risks, arising directly from worsening fundamentals or indirectly from spillovers originating in other sovereigns.

Explicitly modeling sovereign spreads on measures of global risk aversion and distress dependence is one of the key aspects of this study. Other research papers have attempted to include proxies for global risk aversion in the analysis of sovereign spreads. Some of these measures, however, tend to be overly simplistic and to be affected by a wide range of factors, thus not capturing the specific concept of global risk aversion. For example, the spreads of U.S. corporate bonds over Treasury bonds,[2] which are likely to be affected by a large number of institution-specific or country-specific factors, cannot be considered an exclusive measure of global risk aversion.

Other methods rely on extracting the (unobserved) risk aversion component from the actual (observed) sovereign spread series—in other words, filtering.[3] Although statistically viable, these measures depend on the adopted data sample, as global risk aversion is assumed to be proxied by the time-varying common factor of the analyzed series. Our measure of global risk aversion is independent of our data sample, and does not change according to which countries are being considered.

The inclusion of a measure of distress dependence—or a spillover coefficient—is another original twist in this study. In particular, by explicitly differentiating among distress dependence, global risk aversion, and country-specific fundamentals, this analysis can separately identify the effects of each of these factors on sovereign spreads. In fact, the common factor obtained through the use of filtering techniques mentioned earlier might be explained by global risk aversion as well as contagion.[4]

To explore the dynamics governing sovereign spreads, we introduce a dynamic model in which each of these spreads is regressed on the factors described earlier. Namely:

1. *Global Risk Aversion.* The price of an asset reflects both market expectations of the asset's returns and the price of risk, that is, the price that investors are willing to pay for receiving income in distressed states of nature. The index of global risk aversion (IGRA) typifies the market price of risk. It allows us to extract from asset prices the effects of the price of risk and thus to compute the market's expectation of the probability of distress. This result is achieved by using the methodology developed in Espinoza and Segoviano (2010). The authors propose an original method to estimate the market price of risk under stress, which can be seen as the expectation of the market price of risk exceeding a certain threshold. The latter is computed from its two moments: the variance of the market price of risk and its discount factor, which is simply the inverse of the expected market price of risk. The price of risk can be estimated through different methods. For example, it can be derived from the VIX or from the factors in a Fama-MacBeth regression.[5]

For this analysis, the IGRA was constructed using the formula:

$$IGRA_t = -(1 - PoR_t) \qquad (44.1)$$

in which PoR_t is the share of the market price of risk in the actual probability of the stress event (as estimated in Espinoza and Segoviano 2010). This index reflects the market perception of risk at every point in time, and—as highlighted in Exhibit 44.2—it captures the sharp increase in global risk aversion observed after September 2008, followed by a gradual reduction throughout most of 2009.

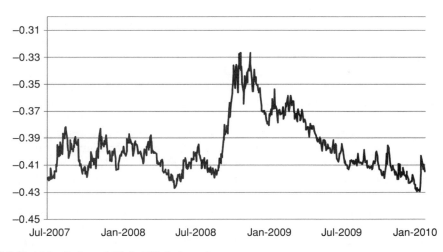

Exhibit 44.2 Index of Global Risk Aversion
Source: IMF Staff calculations.

2. *Contagion,* captured by a measure of distress dependence—the spillover co-efficient (SC)—which characterizes the probability of distress of a country conditional on other countries (in the sample) becoming distressed. This indicator embeds distress dependence across sovereign credit default swaps (CDS) and their changes throughout the economic cycle, reflecting the experience that dependence increases in periods of distress. The SC is based on the methodology developed by Segoviano and Goodhart (2009).

For each country A_i, the SC is computed using the formula:

$$SC(A_i) = \sum P(A_i / A_j) \cdot P(A_j) \qquad \text{for all} \quad j \neq i \qquad (44.2)$$

which is essentially the weighted sum of the probability of distress of country A_i, given a default in each of the other countries in the sample. This measure of distress dependence is appropriately weighed by the probability of each of these events to occur.

3. *Country specific fundamentals,* identified by each country's stock of public debt and budget deficit as a share of GDP.[6]

As mentioned earlier, the inclusion of measures of global risk aversion and contagion in the analysis of sovereign swap spreads represents a novel approach. The IGRA and the SC were developed to disentangle the effect of country-specific fundamentals from that of increased market risk aversion or contagion on these spreads. This is a critical step, as sovereign bond spreads might well exhibit significant movements without any noticeable change in their fiscal position.

In particular, the SC measure quantifies the distress dependence between the various countries in our sample. This dependence captures the macrofinancial linkages among these countries, including trade, capital flows, financial sector linkages, and contingent liabilities among sovereigns. This last element is important, as the countries included in the sample belong to a monetary union in which fiscal transfers are (implicitly) absent. Yet the market might attribute a high probability to the event that a country experiencing sovereign distress would be ultimately supported by other countries in the union. The country in distress is effectively considered as a contingent liability for the other countries.

These factors were found to have different effects across different periods and countries. During the first phase, which we call financial crisis build-up (Phase I), between July 2007 and September 2008, securities from Germany and, to some extent, other core euro area sovereigns, benefited from flight-to-quality flows, whereas bonds from peripheral countries saw their yields rising versus swap yields as global risk aversion was weighing adversely on these lower-rated issuers. In general, fundamentals were supportive of sovereign bonds, as both the deficit and the debt were still improving at this stage (see Exhibit 44.3).

During the systemic outbreak phase (Phase II), between October 2008 and March 2009, characterized by sovereign interventions in support of financial institutions, government bond yields rose relative to swap yields across the board, on contagion from countries more directly involved in the financial crisis and fundamentals, which had started deteriorating. Global risk aversion was not playing

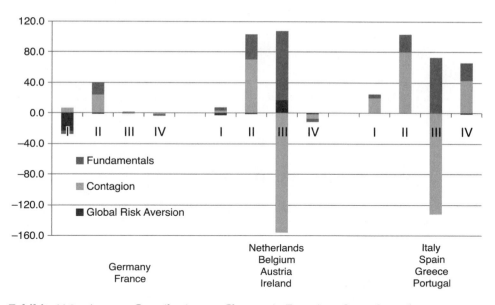

Exhibit 44.3 Average Contributions to Changes in Euro Area Swap Spreads
Source: IMF Staff calculations.

such a favorable role any longer as crisis-related interventions and fiscal stimulus packages had started diluting the perception of sovereigns as a riskless asset class.

During the systemic response (Phase III), between April 2009 and September 2009, all government bond yields fell back toward swaps, as the lower probability of distress in some countries was favorably affecting others. The correction was larger among those bonds such as Italy and Greece, which had underperformed during the systemic outbreak as weaker contagion was offsetting further deterioration in fundamentals.

Finally, in the sovereign risk phase (Phase IV), since October 2009, swap spreads have started to be driven by country-specific developments. They have been broadly unchanged for most countries, but tightening substantially for Greece and Portugal, where bond yields have surged well above swap yields on further weakening in fundamentals and the great risk of contagion.

Overall, it is worth noting that earlier in the crisis, the sources of contagion could be found among those countries hit hardest by the financial crisis, such as Austria, the Netherlands, and Ireland (see Exhibit 44.4). These countries are characterized by relatively large financial sectors compared to the size of their economy. However, in the most recent period, the countries putting pressure on euro area sovereign bonds were primarily Greece, Portugal, and Spain. In other words, the market shifted its attention from exposure to banking sector distress toward short-term refinancing and long-term fiscal sustainability risks.

The increased emphasis on country-specific risks, directly from worsening fundamentals, or indirectly from spillovers originating in other sovereigns, leads to a number of policy implications. With acute debt vulnerabilities, elevated funding needs, and looming sovereign risk, countries need to invest in their debt management framework and focus on macroeconomic linkages between debt

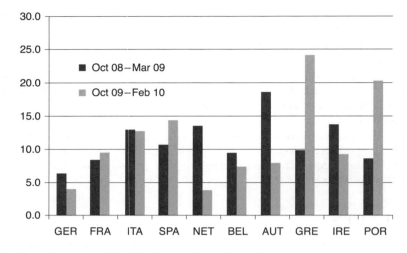

Exhibit 44.4 Percentage Contributions to Euro Area Contagion
Source: IMF Staff calculations.

management and financial stability. Debt sustainability and appropriate management of sovereign balance sheets are necessary conditions for preventing sovereign risk from feeding back into broader financial stability concerns. Rising sovereign risk requires credible medium-term fiscal consolidation plans as well as a solid public debt management framework. Emphasis should be given to the presence of significant contingent risk on sovereign balance sheets and the need for sovereigns to gradually disengage from a number of measures supporting the financial sector. More importantly, the crisis has made the link between debt management and financial stability more explicit suggesting the need for closer coordination with monetary and financial stability authorities.

While credible medium-term reforms are implemented and public debt management is improved, immediate steps should be taken to reduce the possibility of projecting longer-term sovereign credit risks into short-term financing concerns. Debt managers across the world have already turned to a broad range of strategies to alleviate this intense funding pressure, including adding new instruments to their debt portfolios and making more intensive use of syndication techniques as well as raising the size and the frequency of the auctions or revising their format. This effort should be pursued further.

NOTES

1. Sovereign spreads are measured as spreads of 10-year sovereign bond yields to the euro interest rate swap of the same maturity. The latter is the yield at which one party is willing to pay a fixed rate in order to receive a floating rate from a given counterparty.
2. Used in, for example, Codogno et al. (2003) and Schuknecht et al. (2010).
3. For example, Geyer et al. (2004) extract the common factor embedded in EMU spreads based on the use of a Kalman filter. Sgherri and Zoli (2009) apply a Bayesian filtering technique to extract the time-varying common factor from a nonlinear model of the sovereign spreads.

4. For example, one could think of developments in an individual country affecting all other countries in the sample, without any changes in global risk aversion. In that case, the common trend cannot be considered as a measure of global risk aversion, but rather of contagion.

5. VIX is the Chicago Board Options Exchange Volatility Index, a popular measure of implied volatility of S&P 500 index options. The Fama-MacBeth regression is a method used to estimate parameters for asset pricing models such as the capital asset pricing model (CAPM).

6. The daily series for the fiscal variables were obtained by using a linear interpolation on the underlying quarterly data. This is based on the assumption that these variables tend to explain the low frequency movements in the swap spreads, with almost no impact on high frequency (daily) variations.

REFERENCES

Caceres, C., V. Guzzo, and M. Segoviano. 2010. "Sovereign Spreads: Global Risk Aversion, Contagion or Fundamentals?" *IMF Working Paper* 10/120.

Codogno, L., C. Favero, and A. Missale. 2003. "Yield Spreads on EMU Governments Bonds." *Economic Policy* 18:37, 505–532.

Espinoza, R., and M. Segoviano. 2010. "Probabilities of Default and the Market Price of Risk in a Distressed Economy." *IMF Working Paper* 10/120.

Geyer, A., S. Kossmeier, and S. Pichler. 2004. "Measuring Systematic Risk in EMU Government Yield Spreads." *Review of Finance* 8: 171–197.

Schuknecht, L., J. von Hagen, and G. Wolswijk. 2010. "Government Bond Risk Premiums in the EU Revisited: The Impact of the Financial Crisis." *ECB Working Paper* 1152.

Segoviano, M., and C. Goodhart. 2009. "Banking Stability Measures." *IMF Working Paper* 09/4.

Sgherri, S., and E. Zoli. 2009. "Euro Area Sovereign Risk During the Crisis." *IMF Working Paper* 09/222.

ABOUT THE AUTHORS

Carlos Caceres is a national of both Italy and El Salvador, and works in the Fiscal Affairs Department at the International Monetary Fund (IMF). Before joining the Fund, Carlos worked as an economist at the European Investment Bank (EIB) in Luxembourg, in the development and economic advisory services division. Before that, he spent two years working in the European economics team at Morgan Stanley in London. Carlos holds an MEng degree in engineering with business and finance degrees from the University College of London and the London School of Economics, respectively, and MPhil and DPhil (PhD) degrees in economics from the University of Oxford (Nuffield College).

Vincenzo Guzzo is a senior economist in the Sovereign Asset and Liability Management Division of the Monetary and Capital Markets Department at the International Monetary Fund. He joined the IMF in April 2009, when he moved from Morgan Stanley in London, where he was executive director and senior European interest rate strategist. He had previously worked for the same firm as the economist responsible for Italy, Spain, Portugal, and Greece and was in charge of the analysis of the fiscal policies in the euro area. Vincenzo had started his career in investment banking as a sovereign analyst on Southeast Asia for Lehman Brothers in New York and then worked as an economist at Merrill Lynch, where he was also responsible for the Italian economy. Vincenzo holds a master of arts and a PhD in economics from New York University.

Miguel Segoviano is the director general of risk analysis and quantitative methodologies, at Comisión Nacional Bancaria y de Valores (CNBV), the Mexican financial authority. Before joining the CNBV, Miguel worked at the IMF for more than five years developing and implementing models for systemic macrofinancial stress testing and financial stability assessment, which have been widely used by the IMF in the Global Financial Stability Report, Financial Sector Assessment Programs, highly specialized technical cooperation and assistance missions, and risk assessment and surveillance projects, all of these allowing Miguel to work in a wide set of developed and developing countries, including major central banks around the world. Academically, he has collaborated with diverse institutions, including the Financial Markets Group at the London School of Economics, the U.K. Department for International Development, and the Bank for International Settlements. In the private sector, he worked for Deutsche Bank and Citibank. Miguel holds a PhD in finance from the London School of Economics and has won several research awards, including the 2004 first prize in financial research by Global Asset Management (GAM).

CHAPTER 45

Sovereign Spreads and Perceived Risk of Default Revisited

ABOLHASSAN JALILVAND
Dean of the School of Business Administration and Graduate School of Business,
Loyola University Chicago

JEANNETTE SWITZER
Financial Consultant, Chicago

S imilar to its predecessor crisis in the mid-1970s and early 1980s, the recent global financial crisis has also induced a significant degree of volatility on interest rates and spreads demanded by lenders on sovereign borrowers. Collectively, this increased global volatility has pushed long-term government bond yields higher, deteriorating government default prospects through higher debt servicing costs and elevated debt rollover risk. It has also deteriorated the level of global confidence in efficient movement and allocation of capital flows. This paper discusses the conceptual development and empirical implications of a simple credit pricing model to determine sovereign spreads. Our discussion deviates from the conventional debt sustainability framework in its treatment of sovereign default as an endogenous financial decision with some carefully specified costs and benefits mainly captured by the borrower's future growth prospects. Theoretical, empirical, and public policy implications associated with the two approaches are discussed and elaborated.

INTRODUCTION

The recent global financial crisis has induced a significant degree of volatility on interest rates and spreads demanded by lenders on sovereign borrowers. The volatility has been more pronounced among the higher-debt, lower-rated sovereign bonds. Examining the pattern of some selected euro spreads over a five-year overlapping period, Figure (1) from the article by Caceres, Guzzo and Segoviano in this volume, and reproduced here as Exhibit 45.1, shows relative stability in euro area 10-year swap spreads during the financial crisis build-up period, followed by a significant divergence around the systemic outbreak of the financial crises in

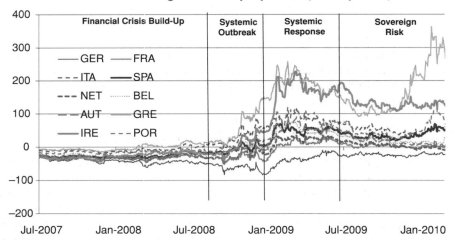

Exhibit 45.1 EUR Sovereign 10-Year Swap Spreads (basis points)
This figure originally appeared in C. Caceres, V. Guzzo, and Miguel Segoviano. 2010. "Sovereign Spreads: Global Risk Aversion, Contagion or Fundamentals." *IMF Working Paper*, IMF Monetary and Capital Market Department.

late 2008 and early 2009 and a return to some levels of stability in mid-2009 as the so-called contagion effect was contained and the overall level of risk subsided. The increased volatility has deteriorated the level of global confidence in efficient movement and allocation of capital flows. It has further pushed long-term government bond yields higher, deteriorating government default profile through higher debt servicing costs and elevated debt rollover risk.

A similar pattern to sovereign debt problems also occurred during the 1970s and early 1980s. *Euromoney* magazine reported a significant increase in the number of rescheduling incidents during this period. More than $20 billion of sovereign loans were renegotiated during the period from 1979 to 1981, involving 16 different countries. In 1982 alone, loans amounting to $60 billion were rescheduled. Although the size of the borrowing involved was dramatically lower than what is transacted today, recent studies continue to show that the underlying economic variables and influences determining the dynamics of sovereign spreads have principally remained the same, including country-specific risk factors and the spillover pressures or the contagion effects.

Conceptually, the prevailing approach in examining the risk of default in international capital flows and its impact on the magnitude and volatility of sovereign spreads is still motivated by the concept and principles of debt sustainability. This concept implies that default is an environment exogenously forced on the borrowing country by uncontrollable domestic and global economic and social events. There is, however, a competing and well-argued notion that builds on one of the most fundamental and differentiating characteristics of sovereign lending—unenforceability of sovereign, as opposed to domestic, lending. Following Merton (1974) and Galai and Masulis (1976), it is motivated by the application of the contingent claim model to examine default on corporate liabilities recognizing the economic role of leverage and its moral hazard consequences.

This paper discusses the conceptual development and empirical implications of a simple credit pricing model to determine sovereign spreads. Our discussion deviates from the debt sustainability framework in its treatment of sovereign default as an endogenous financial decision of the borrowing country, which may or may not be exercised given some carefully specified costs and benefits mainly captured by the magnitude of a borrowing country's future growth prospects.

CONCEPTUAL FRAMEWORK: A PROPOSAL

Researchers applying the debt sustainability framework have been preoccupied with explaining the size of the spread (risk premium) on sovereign loans ex post using a number of predetermined exogenous variables viewed as proxies for country risk. By and large, the prevailing empirical results have remained unstable over time. This situation is best indicated in a recent paper by Tao Sun (2010). The paper focuses on the role of bank-specific and global financial indicators in explaining the differences between intervened (perceived as higher default risk) and nonintervened financial institutions during the subprime crisis. Using a sample of global financial institutions, his results are mixed, questioning the relevance of some frequently supported variables such as capital adequacy ratios, traditional liquidity ratios, asset quality indicators, and standard measures of earnings and profits. The results on some contagion indicators are also mixed. On the other hand, he finds support for the influence of basic leverage, return on assets, provisions for loan losses, global financial stress, and global excess liquidity in identifying the differences between the intervened and nonintervened financial institutions.

Examining the pattern of some selected euro sovereign spreads, Caceres, Guzzo, and Segoviano (2010) find that the surge in global risk aversion was a significant factor influencing the sovereign spreads during the earlier part of the crisis. However, more, recently, country-specific factors have begun to play a more important role. Regarding the contagion effect, there has been a geographic shift from countries such as Australia, the Netherlands, and Ireland, in the earlier part of the crisis, toward Greece, Portugal, and Spain.

While informative, the instability and arbitrary nature of the explanatory variables used in the previous literature have hindered their use for ex ante prediction of country risk. There is a need for an underlying analytical formulation for pricing sovereign risk, which introduces a set of stable processes and factors to explain the dynamics of sovereign spreads. In case of default on sovereign loans, in general, the ability of a lender to garnish directly a portion of the sovereign borrower's current or future income streams or to seize the borrower's domicile assets is extremely limited. Put differently, the size and scope of the lender's direct collateral is very small. Sovereign loans are not directly enforceable. However, a lender may have an indirect collateral (or insurance) against default whose value depends on the magnitude of the future economic costs or penalties (credit embargos, higher cost of future credit, disruptions of trade, and so on) that may be imposed on the sovereign borrower if the default is declared. In other words, by defaulting, while a borrowing country may enjoy the windfall gains amounting to the principal and interests on the existing loan (or a portfolio of loans), it may face current and future costs associated with lower economic growth prospects. Hence, a borrowing country may be viewed as having to choose (or to possess an option) between the windfall gains of default and the loss of future growth opportunities.

Furthermore, the disciplining nature of leverage to avoid costly bankruptcy could also support the treatment of default as a rational financial decision by the borrower. The default costs for sovereign borrowers will be equal to the value of future growth opportunities lost in case of default. Finally, treating default as a rational decision is also consistent with the borrowers' awareness and expectation that the international community might forgive their debt obligation or there will be subsidies to cover losses when the prospect of collection deteriorates—a regular practice in previous and, especially, current debt crises. The moral hazard associated with the too-big-to-fail idea would strengthen this type of incentive.

Doukas and Jalilvand (1987) used this option framework within an equilibrium credit pricing model to determine a bank's rate of interest on a sovereign loan. According to this model, a given sovereign spread is then shown to be influenced by the distribution of the borrower's future costs of default and the bank's opportunity cost of capital. It is argued that the size of the direct collateral and (or) the conventional measures of outstanding debt may not adequately assess the borrower's creditworthiness without also considering the future growth potential reflected in the borrower's investment opportunities and therefore its cost of default. Hence, rational pricing of international loans should reflect a borrowing country's growth prospects as a major determinant of its propensity to default.

Empirically, using nonparametric statistical methodologies, Doukas and Jalilvand (1987) showed a stable and significantly positive association between sovereign rankings by their observed market spreads and expected future growth rates of GNP and exports. Sovereign borrowers with higher (or lower) future growth potentials consistently obtained lower (or higher) average spreads on their international loans. Furthermore, borrowers' growth prospects were also shown to have considerable ex ante predictive ability in identifying future rescheduling. Their predictive power was superior to that provided by the respected Institutional Investor Credit Rating Index published by *Euromoney* magazine.

FURTHER RESEARCH AND POLICY IMPLICATIONS

Treating default as a rational decision by borrowers has significant implications for modeling and testing the determinants of sovereign spreads. As mentioned before, it also lends itself to developing more accurate forecasts of future defaults and debt rescheduling by borrowing countries. Three primary areas are highlighted here.

1. Controversy on Country Specific Variables and Volatility Measures
   Treating default as a rational decision by the borrower provides us with a theoretical (as opposed to econometric) explanation on why the size of the direct collateral and (or) the conventional measures of outstanding debt may not adequately assess the borrower's creditworthiness. The mixed results on the impact of balance sheet–related country specific factors on sovereign spreads have always been a major limitation of the previous studies. Furthermore, the positive relationship between the extent of a country's future growth opportunities and volatility of future exports and (or) GDP

provides a systematic justification for a positive relationship between measures of volatility and the size of sovereign spreads. This is not the conventional wisdom and, once again, the empirical evidence on this issue is still inconclusive.

2. Econometric Insights in Detecting the Contagion Effect

One could also identify a number of modifications to the application of the conventional orthogonal least-square regression models to explain sovereign spreads. To the extent that borrowers view default as a rational financial decision, empirical measures of a sovereign's spreads and the extent of its future growth opportunities may be endogenously determined and thus need to be simultaneously estimated. Alternatively, a recursive estimation process, or system, may be called for whereby spreads are determined by future growth opportunities that themselves are instrumentally estimated through a separate relationship.

Also, direct empirical measures of contagion reflected in correlation matrices among various economic metrics are of limited applicability and scope. By definition, the contagion effect reflects the spillover consequences of economic problems experienced by countries whose capital markets and trades are fairly integrated. It is, therefore, an unobservable effect that cannot be directly measured and is best captured through the structure of the error terms resulting from estimating the principal regression equation. Exploring the impact of the variance-covariance matrix of the error terms within the estimation process should be very worthwhile in detecting the contagion effect. Generalized least square estimation approaches are more applicable in this regard.

3. Policy Issues

There are also implications for the nature and extent of monetary and fiscal interventions by international financial bodies such as the International Monetary Fund and the World Bank. Regular austerity policy prescriptions may actually increase the prospect of default by countries experiencing debt servicing problems. On the other hand, reforms targeting the advancement of future growth opportunities, and thus increasing the future cost of default, may have a better chance of encouraging the borrowing countries to take the necessary steps toward solvency and future prosperity. There is also a need for developing a fresh perspective on approaches needed to manage sovereign debt and achieve debt sustainability targets. Borrowing countries should be advised to manage their financing and investment decisions in a manner to achieve their maximum future growth opportunities. To this end, they may increase debt financing in periods when interest rates are favorable to ensure the availability of sufficient funds to take advantage of future investment opportunities. Hence, what may be perceived as an irrational build-up of debt may, in fact, clearly correspond with a planned investment and financing strategy designed to achieve maximum future growth for a given borrowing country. Managing the maturity, type, and schedule of such borrowings will be an important consideration in this context.

The economics of sovereign spreads and the crucial role they play in guiding the future growth opportunities of the borrowing countries will continue to be an important topic for policy makers and academic researchers.

As shown in this study, recent developments in the field of corporate debt management and the firm's incentive structure may provide direct applications for pricing international loans and assessing the riskiness of sovereign borrowers.

REFERENCES

Caceres, C., V. Guzzo, and M. Segoviano. 2010. "Sovereign Spreads: Global Risk Aversion, Contagion or Fundamentals." *IMF Working Paper,* IMF Monetary and Capital Market Department.

Doukas, J., and A. Jalilvand. 1987. "Perceived Risk of Default and Banks' International Lending Decision." *Journal of Economics and International Relations* 1:4, 323–332.

Galai, D., and R. Masulis. 1976. "The Option Pricing Model and the Risk Factor of Stocks." *The Journal of Financial Economics* 3: 53–81.

Merton, R. 1974. "On the Pricing of Corporate Debt: The Risk Structure of Interest Rates." *Journal of Finance* 29:2, 449–470.

Sun, T. 2010. "Identifying Vulnerabilities in Systemically Important Financial Institutions in a Macro-Financial Linkages Framework." *IMF Working Paper,* IMF Monetary and Capital Market Department.

ABOUT THE AUTHORS

Abol Jalilvand received his PhD in finance from the University of North Carolina at Chapel Hill, a master of business administration degree from Oklahoma State University and a bachelor of commerce degree in banking from the Iranian Institute of Banking. His scholarly work on corporate debt structure, risk management, cost of capital, and international capital flows has appeared in top refereed journals and been presented at major academic conferences. Professionally, he has been editor-in-chief of the *Canadian Journal of Administrative Sciences;* president, Mid-Continent East AACSB Conference; a consultant to major corporations and has testified before a number of regulatory bodies. He was formerly dean of faculty of management and Herbert S. Lamb chair in business education at Dalhousie University, Canada. He is presently dean of the School of Business Administration and Graduate School of Business at Loyola University Chicago.

Jeannette Switzer received her PhD from the University of Oklahoma and BA in music and foreign languages from Southern Methodist University. Her scholarly work on mergers and acquisitions, capital structure, and corporate governance has appeared in top refereed journals and been presented at major academic conferences. She is also the author of several textbooks in finance and is presently a private financial consultant in Chicago.

CHAPTER 46

What Explains the Surge in Euro Area Sovereign Spreads During the Financial Crisis of 2007–2009?

MARIA-GRAZIA ATTINASI
Economist, Fiscal Policies Division, European Central Bank[*]

CRISTINA CHECCHERITA
Economist, Fiscal Policies Division, European Central Bank

CHRISTIANE NICKEL
Head of the Fiscal Analysis Section, Fiscal Policies Division, European Central Bank

Between the intensification of the financial crisis in September 2008 and the early signs of stabilization in financial markets in March 2009, government bond yields in the euro area reacted strongly. Ten-year government bond yield spreads relative to the benchmark German bond increased dramatically for most euro area countries. As of March 2009, the spread between the Greek government bonds and the German bund had widened to almost 300 basis points (bps) from about 35 bps, the average spread after Greece's accession to the Economic and Monetary Union (EMU). Ireland also experienced the largest increase in its bond spreads, followed by Portugal, Italy, Belgium, Austria, and Spain, as Exhibit 46.1 indicates. This development is even more striking from a historical perspective: Before the financial crisis and since the start of the EMU in January 2000, euro area bond spreads relative to the German bund had generally been relatively compressed and averaged about 16 basis points,[1] indicating a very modest differentiation of countries by financial markets.

The surge and the widening of sovereign bond yield spreads reflected increasing concerns in financial markets about some governments' capacity to meet their

[*]This chapter is based on the paper by Attinasi, M.-G., C. Checcherita, and C. Nickel. 2009. "What Explains the Surge in Euro Area Sovereign Spreads During the Financial Crisis of 2007–09?" *ECB Working Paper* No. 1131.

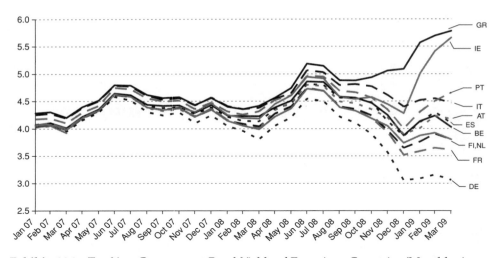

Exhibit 46.1 Ten-Year Government Bond Yields of Euro Area Countries (Monthly Averages; Percentages per Annum; January 2007 to March 2009)
Sources: Bloomberg and authors' calculations.

future debt obligations.[2] In addition to the higher cost of borrowing, the increase in sovereign bond yield spreads may signal that investors are less willing to provide funding to sovereign borrowers; thus in the extreme threatening the latter's ability to gain access to capital markets. In this respect, the economic literature on the determinants of long-term government bond yields has found evidence of the market-based fiscal discipline hypothesis, according to which financial markets ask a higher default premium to countries that borrow excessively (Goldstein and Woglom 1992; Bayoumi et al. 1995).

Furthermore, the announcement by many euro area countries of bank rescue packages directed at banks experiencing liquidity or solvency problems, may have fueled investors' concerns about those countries' creditworthiness.[3] Indeed, the governments' commitment to provide financial support to ailing banks may have been interpreted by investors as a transfer of credit risk from the private financial to the public sector. The packages were announced after the Lehman Brothers default, between the end of September and the end of October 2008, and the amount of resources committed varied across countries to a great extent. Ireland announced a guarantee scheme of €400 billion (above 200 percent of its GDP) including the retail bank deposit guarantee. Countries such as the Netherlands, Austria, and Germany committed resources above 20 percent of their GDP. Overall, about 23 percent of the euro area GDP was committed to bank rescue packages. Exhibit 46.2 shows the composition and size of bank rescue packages in euro area countries.

The widening of sovereign bond spreads vis-à-vis Germany was interpreted by many observers as a welcome reassessment and differentiation of country risks. This is also in the spirit of the European fiscal framework: The Stability and Growth Pact not only hinges upon the concept of peer pressure (that is, European countries among themselves urge countries with excessive deficits to correct them), but also on the idea that financial markets exert pressure, through higher bond risk

Exhibit 46.2 Bank Rescue Packages (as a Percentage of Country GDP)

Country	Date of (First) Announcement	Cumulative Recapitalization	Cumulative Guarantees
Austria	10/13/08	5.0	26.0
Belgium	09/26/08	5.1	74.0
Germany	10/06/08	3.5	19.0
Spain	10/07/08	2.8	9.1
Finland	10/20/08	2.1	26.4
France	09/30/08	2.0	16.4
Greece	10/15/08	5.2	6.0
Ireland	09/29/08	5.0	259.0
Italy	10/08/08	3.0	—
Netherlands	09/26/08	18.0	33.7
Portugal	10/13/08	2.3	11.9

Notes: The table reflects the cumulative amounts of bank rescue packages as released in some countries in subsequent announcements. Cumulative guarantees include retail deposit guarantees.
Source: Authors' calculations.

premiums, on countries with unsustainable fiscal positions. Before the current financial crisis, this differentiation of country risk across the euro area was virtually absent.

Against this unprecedented rise in sovereign bond yield spreads, the question arises as to whether it was driven by general factors such as liquidity risk or international risk aversion or whether differentiation between countries' fiscal positions or macroeconomic fundamentals also played a role.

Following the existing literature on the determinants of government bond yield spreads, this chapter looks at the main determinants of 10-year sovereign bond yield spreads, namely: a country's credit risk, as captured by the relative soundness of its expected fiscal position; international risk aversion (that is, investor sentiment toward this asset class for each country), which in times of heightened uncertainty could be higher for some euro area countries than for others; and market liquidity risk, which may be related to the relative size of sovereign bond markets. Finally, we also investigate whether the announcement of broad-based bank rescue packages played a role by way of a transfer of credit risk from the private financial sector to the public sector.

THE EMPIRICAL EVIDENCE

The analysis uses a dynamic panel specification to explain the determinants of 10-year sovereign bond yield spreads over Germany (spread) in 10 euro area countries during the time from July 31, 2007, to March 25, 2009. The empirical model is the following:

$$spread_{it} = \alpha + \rho spread_{it-1} + \beta_1(ANN)_{it} + \beta_2 E(FISC)_{it} + \beta_3 Intl.Risk_t$$
$$+\beta_4 LIQ_{it} + \varepsilon_{it}$$

in which: *ANN* is a country dummy variable on the announcements of bank rescue packages;[4] *E(FISC)* denotes governments' expected fiscal positions, as measured by the general government balance or gross government debt as a percentage of GDP, relative to Germany; *Intl.Risk* is our proxy for international risk aversion; *LIQ* is a proxy for liquidity of euro area governments' bond markets; ε_{it} is the error term.

In line with the existing empirical literature, we find that the widening of sovereign bond yield spreads in the euro area during the period under consideration reflected concerns about a country's credit risk and liquidity risk as well as higher international risk aversion.

Higher expected budget deficits or higher expected government debt relative to Germany have contributed to higher government bond yield spreads in the euro area over the period under consideration. The results are robust if the analysis is restricted to after the crisis intensified, that is, from the end of August 2008 to the end of March 2009. The announcements of bank rescue packages, used here as an additional measure of a country's credit risk, increased, on average, the perceived risk of government borrowing compared with Germany. The results remain robust if the analysis starts from September 2008 instead of the end of July 2007. Interestingly, the results remain unaffected if Ireland is excluded from the panel. This shows that investors' discrimination across sovereign borrowers was triggered by the governments' credible commitment to extend support to the banking sector. Investors may have anticipated that governments would provide as much support as needed to shore up ailing banks regardless of the amounts explicitly announced in the first place (that is, in case of systemic banking risk, significant implicit guarantees may add up to the explicit ones). This evidence is corroborated if we investigate the impact of the announced size of bank rescue operations on investors' perception of euro area governments' borrowing risk relative to Germany. When in Equation (1) the *ANN* variable is replaced by the size of the packages, the significance of the expected budget balance remains unaffected, whereas the impact of the new variables is less conclusive. The absence of, or at best weak, correlation between the size of bank rescue packages announced by the countries in our sample and the widening in sovereign bond yield spreads is not surprising. With the exception of Ireland, the countries that experienced the highest volatility and the largest increase in their bond spreads are not those that have committed the largest amount of resources to the bank rescue packages. It can be argued that the size of bank rescue packages depends, on average, on the country's fiscal room for maneuver: Countries with limited fiscal space committed relatively less resources for the purpose of broad based rescue packages. The evidence presented in this section is that a country's expected fiscal position matters for investors' perception of its credit risk. In particular, the crisis seems to have triggered a flight to quality effect, whereby investors started to discriminate among sovereign borrowers on the basis of their fiscal outlook.

To conclude, investors seem to have reacted on average more forcefully to the announcement of financial support whereas they have been less responsive to the size of the packages, except in the case of Ireland, whose package size was extremely large.

The liquidity of government bond markets also played a role in the widening of sovereign bond yield spreads. Countries with a more liquid bond market seem to enjoy relatively lower bond yield spreads during periods of financial turmoil.

Finally, and in line with the existing empirical literature, the international risk aversion is an important factor in explaining sovereign bond yield spreads.

RISK TRANSFER FROM THE PRIVATE TO THE PUBLIC SECTOR: THE ROLE OF BANK RESCUE PACKAGES

Our empirical analysis also directly tests the credit risk transfer hypothesis through the impact of the announcement of bank rescue packages on the difference between sovereign CDS premiums and CDS premiums for European financial corporations. Under this hypothesis, the announcement of bank rescue packages should lead to a widening of the difference between the sovereign and the corporate CDS premiums, as risk is perceived to be transferred from the private financial to the government sector.

Concurrent with the announcement of bank rescue packages in euro area countries, pressures on the financial sector eased while the opposite occurred at the general government level. This was felt through a sharp increase in sovereign credit default swap premiums for most euro area countries, whereas the credit default swap premiums for European financial corporations (that is, those covered by the iTraxx financial index),[5] reversed their upward trend and started to decline. Exhibit 46.3 illustrates these developments and depicts the cumulative changes

Exhibit 46.3 Cumulative Changes in Average Five-Year Sovereign Credit Default Swap Premiums for Euro Area Countries and iTraxx Financial Index (September 15, 2008, to March 25, 2009; bps)

Note: The vertical bars indicate the dates on which bank rescue packages were announced in euro area countries. Countries included in the analysis were: Austria, Belgium, Finland, France, Germany, Greece, Ireland, Italy, the Netherlands, Portugal, and Spain.

Sources: Datastream and authors' calculations.

since mid-September 2008 in the average five-year sovereign credit default swap premiums for 11 euro area countries and in the credit default swap premiums for European financial institutions covered by the iTraxx index.

The announcement of bank rescue packages proved to be a robust and statistically significant determinant of the differential between sovereign credit default swap premiums and the iTraxx financials over the period of analysis. This suggests that government commitments to support ailing financial institutions led to a reassessment of sovereign credit risk from the part of investors, through a transfer of risk from the banking sector to the government. Investors' perceptions may have been driven by expectations that governments would provide as much support as needed to shore up ailing banks regardless of the amounts explicitly announced in the first place.

ROBUSTNESS CHECKS AND RELATIVE CONTRIBUTION OF FACTORS

Our findings are robust to the use of different time frequencies (daily and monthly), various estimation techniques, and to the inclusion of additional control variables. In this respect, we also found that the reduction in the ECB main refinancing operations rate contributed significantly to narrowing sovereign bond spreads for the period under consideration. Similarly, private external imbalances relative to Germany have an influence on sovereign bond spreads, whereas the expected economic growth rate does not seem to matter for the period covered in our analysis. Controlling for other types of announcements, such as the release of macroeconomic data and lead indicators for the euro area, Germany, France, Italy, and the United States, does not change our conclusions regarding the impact of announcements of bank rescue packages on sovereign spreads.

Finally, we also calculate the relative contribution of each explanatory variable in the sample to the daily change in average sovereign bond spreads relative to Germany.[6] This allows gauging the relative importance of each factor in explaining movements in sovereign bond spreads. For the sample as a whole, we find that each explanatory variable contributes to the change in daily sovereign bond yield spreads in the following maximum proportions:

- International risk aversion (56 percent).
- Expected fiscal position (expected budget balance and debt) (21 percent).
- Liquidity proxy (14 percent).
- Announcement of bank rescue packages (9 percent).

POLICY LESSONS

The large relevance of international risk aversion for changes in sovereign bond yield spreads can be explained by the extraordinary severity of the financial crisis during the period of our analysis. Moreover, the fact that fiscally relevant variables account for about one-third of the movements in euro area sovereign spreads during the financial crisis points to the importance of preserving the public's trust in the soundness of public finances. This is essential to anchor market expectations about a government's ability to meet its future debt obligations. Therefore, an important lesson from the financial crisis is that countries should consolidate during good economic times to more easily build a fiscal cushion that provides sufficient room for maneuver during an economic downturn or a crisis. Many euro area countries failed to do so and entered the crisis with high fiscal deficits and debt ratios that limited the scope of their fiscal actions at a time when it was needed the most. Moreover, when announcing bank rescue operations and fiscal stimulus packages, a credible commitment to maintain longer-term fiscal sustainability could have limited the negative market reaction.

NOTES

1. This average is computed for the period January 2000 to July 2008, using daily 10-year sovereign bond yield spreads relative to Germany. Greece is included in the sample only since January 2001, the year of its EMU accession. The data source is Bloomberg.

2. On this point, also see Sgherri and Zoli 2009, De Grauwe 2009, and Schuknecht et al. 2009.

3. The fiscal stimulus packages announced by euro area governments to boost aggregate demand are not considered. Their effect on the fiscal variables would already be captured by the expected budget deficits and debt ratios, given their direct statistical recording, thus making the two sets of variables strongly correlated.

4. The variables included in Equation (46.1) are specified in terms of differentials to Germany. However, the *ANN* variable cannot be defined as a differential to Germany being based on calendar dates. Therefore, to ensure consistency in the model specification, we dropped the dates of the announcement of bank rescue packages by Germany in the dummy variable *ANN*.

5. A credit default swap (CDS) is a contract in which a protection buyer pays a periodic premium to a protection seller and, in exchange, receives a pay-off if the reference entity (a firm or a government issuer) experiences a credit event, for example, a failure to make scheduled interest or redemption payments on debt instruments (typically bonds or loans). The iTraxx financial index contains the CDS spreads of 25 European financial institutions, including institutions from the United Kingdom and Switzerland.

6. When computing the relative contributions, we transfer the first lag of the dependent variable to the left hand side of Equation (46.1), thus broadly explaining the contribution of our variables of interest (fiscal variables, liquidity risk, and international risk aversion) to the *change* in sovereign bond yield spread. In the analysis, we include only those explanatory variables that are statistically significant.

REFERENCES

Attinasi, M.-G., C. Checherita, and C. Nickel. 2009. "What Explains the Surge in Euro Area Sovereign Spreads during the Financial Crisis of 2007–09?" *ECB Working Paper* 1131.

Bayoumi, T., M. Goldstein, and G. Woglom. 1995. "Do Credit Markets Discipline Sovereign Borrowers?" *Journal of Money, Credit and Banking*. 27:4, 1046–1059.

De Grauwe, P. 2009. "Why Should We Believe the Market This Time?" *ECMI Commentary* No. 22/20. www.ceps.eu/files/book/1801.pdf.

Goldstein, M., and G. Woglom. 1992. "Market-Based Fiscal Discipline in Monetary Unions: Evidence from the U.S. Municipal Bond Market." In M. Canzoneri, V. Grilli, and P. Masson, eds. *Establishing a Central Bank*. Cambridge, UK: Cambridge University Press.

Schuknecht, L., J. von Hagen, and G. Wolswijk. 2009. "Government Bond Risk Premiums in the EU Revisited: The Impact of the Financial Crisis." *CEPR Paper* 7499.

Sgherri, S., and E. Zoli. 2009. "Euro Area Sovereign Risk During the Crisis." *IMF Working Paper* 09/222.

ABOUT THE AUTHORS

Maria-Grazia Attinasi is an economist in the fiscal policies division of the European Central Bank. She received an MSc from the University of Oxford and a PhD from Bocconi University. As an economist for the Asian Development Bank, she has done extensive work in the design and implementation of public financial management programs in developing countries.

Cristina D. Checherita is an economist in the fiscal policies division of the European Central Bank. She holds an MPA in economic policy management from Columbia University, New York, and a PhD in public policy from George Mason University, VA. She previously worked in the Ministry of Public Finance of Romania as head of section and adviser to the minister on macroeconomic issues. Her main research interests include the role of fiscal policy in the process of economic growth, economic convergence and spatial analysis, and the economics of public-private partnerships.

Christiane Nickel is the head of the fiscal analysis section of the fiscal policies division at the European Central Bank in Frankfurt, Germany. She previously worked as an economist at the International Monetary Fund in Washington D.C. and as a senior economist at the European Bank for Reconstruction and Development in London. She holds a PhD in economics from the WHU–Otto Beisheim School of Management in Vallendar, Germany, and a diploma in economics from the Johann Wolfgang Goethe University in Frankfurt, Germany. Dr. Nickel's research interests lie in fiscal policy and international macroeconomics. In both fields, she has published numerous journal articles and working papers.

CHAPTER 47

Euro Area Sovereign Risk During the Crisis

SILVIA SGHERRI
International Monetary Fund

EDDA ZOLI
International Monetary Fund

ollowing the onset of the global financial crisis, sovereign risk premium differentials in the euro area widened. Although the perceived risk of default for euro area countries has remained generally low until the unraveling of the Greek crisis, markets appear to have been increasingly discriminating among government issuers since the Lehman collapse, while requiring overall higher risk premiums (Exhibit 47.1). Specifically, the spreads on the yield on 10-year government bonds over Bunds spiked in January 2009 for various euro area members, accompanied by downgrades of sovereign debt ratings for Greece, Spain, and Portugal, and a warning for Ireland. The rebound of euro area sovereign spreads is particularly noticeable from a historical perspective, as it follows a prolonged period of remarkable compression of sovereign risk premium differentials, which had been raising doubts about financial markets' ability to provide fiscal discipline across euro area members.

In this context, the observed widening of sovereign spreads might reflect increased financial markets' concerns about the worsening fiscal accounts of most euro area countries on the heels of the financial crisis. Indeed, while the use of public resources has been critical to stem further job losses and to break the adverse loop between the financial system and the real economy, it has also implied a significant deterioration in the budget positions of most euro area members and ballooning government debts.

In addition to fiscal vulnerabilities and—hence—default risk concerns, discrimination among sovereign issuers may reflect considerations about the relative liquidity of different government bond markets. Indeed, the financial turmoil may have led to a flight to safety and liquidity, resulting in a decline in the yields of the most liquid sovereign bond markets—such as the benchmark Bunds. The literature tends to recognize the importance of liquidity risk in explaining interest rate differentials within the euro area, although the size of this effect remains somewhat controversial.[1]

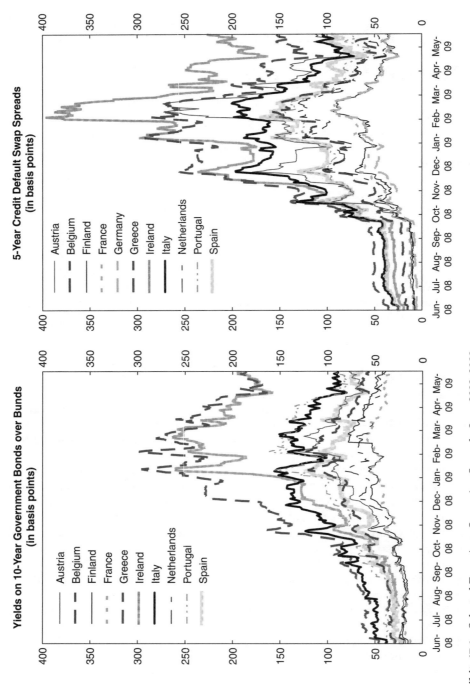

Exhibit 47.1 Selected Euro Area Sovereign Spreads, June 2008–2009

Government exposure to weaknesses in the financial sector may have also become a factor in explaining sovereign spreads in the euro area. In this respect, some countries have committed large resources to guarantee financial institutions, thereby establishing a potentially important link between financial sector distress and public sector bailouts. In Ireland, for example, sovereign spreads started to increase after the government extended a guarantee to the banking system.

Global risk repricing may have also contributed to the widening of sovereign risk premium differentials, in a sign of discrimination among different classes of default risk. Owing to the abrupt reversal in market sentiment and the severe liquidity squeeze, euro area sovereign bond markets have certainly come under strain. Previous empirical studies have indeed found that spreads tend to co-move over time and are mainly driven by a single time-varying common factor, typically identifying international risk appetite.[2]

Understanding what has prompted recent developments in sovereign risk is key for policy making. If the observed widening of sovereign spreads mainly mirrors an abrupt reversal in market sentiment due, for example, to a severe liquidity squeeze, liquidity provision measures will prompt knock-on beneficial effects on governments' marginal funding costs. Otherwise, if rising sovereign spreads reflect financial markets' concerns about the solvency of national banking systems and their consequences for fiscal sustainability, investors will keep requiring higher sovereign default risk premiums for most countries and discriminating among sovereign issuers until a credible financial system restructuring plan and a clear commitment to long-run fiscal discipline are envisaged.

DISSECTING COMMON RISK

There is unanimous consensus in the literature that euro area government bond spreads are mostly driven by a single time-varying common factor, associated with shifts in international risk appetite. In theory, risk appetite—the willingness of each investor to bear risk—depends on both risk aversion—a deep parameter representing the degree to which agents dislike uncertainty—and the level of macroeconomic uncertainty itself. Periodic shifts in risk appetite are generally more likely to respond to changes in uncertainty than to changes in investors' risk aversion. In practice, shifts in investors' risk appetite are not directly observable. What is observable is the (asset-specific) risk premium—the expected return required to compensate investors for holding one specific asset: this is jointly defined by a common component—the common price of risk, that is the inverse of investors' risk appetite—and the inherent riskiness of that asset.

To estimate the extent to which (unobservable) shifts in international risk appetite may have contributed to the (observed) increase in sovereign spreads for the individual countries, we rely on a very simple asset pricing model.[3] Specifically, by assuming that risk premiums embedded in country-specific sovereign yields are determined jointly in the market and influenced by both the riskiness of the specific asset and the common price of risk, the latter component can be identified and thereby be filtered out.

The estimated dynamic common factor in sovereign bond spreads is plotted in Exhibit 47.2. For the sake of comparison, the estimated common factor is pictured along with an index measuring the implied volatility in the German stock

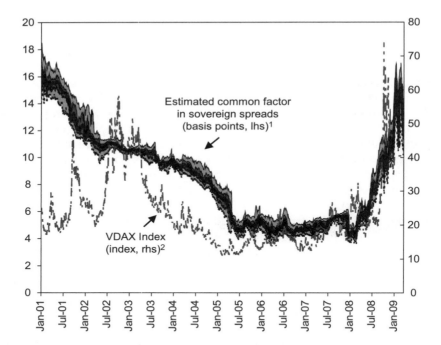

[1]The fan chart plots, at each point in time, the 5th, the 50th, and the 95th, percentile of the estimated probability distribution for the expected common component across euro area sovereign spreads. Hence, there is a 90 percent chance that the common spread will be inside the gray-shaded range. The central thick black line denotes the estimated median common spread.
[2]Implied volatility of German stock market.

Exhibit 47.2 Estimated Common Component in Sovereign Spreads (*in Basis Points*)
Sources: Datastream; Bloomberg L.P.; and IMF staff calculations.

market—a variable extraneous to the filtering procedure used to extract the component itself.

To a first approximation, the estimated common risk component seems able to capture four distinct developments in euro area sovereign bond spreads: the narrowing of risk premium differentials due to EMU convergence over 2001–2002; the decline in financial market volatility over 2003–2005; the abundant liquidity and muted risk aversion characterizing international financial markets over 2005–2007; and the jarring risk repricing commencing at the end of 2007 and receding at the very end of the sample.

Which economic forces are behind the movements in such a time-varying common factor? Over the long run, a common widening of euro area sovereign bond spreads is found to be driven by expected *de*flationary risks and *declining* interbank rates. On average, inflation and wholesale money market developments appear to account for more than half of the changes in the common component of euro area sovereign spreads. Also, common shifts in euro area risk premium differentials tend to be *positively* correlated with volatility—and, hence, uncertainty—in stock, currency, and emerging markets. Over the short run, only 12 percent of the *daily* variation in the common component of euro area risk premium differentials can be explained—most of which is induced by endogenous dynamic adjustments.

These findings seem to confirm previous evidence from the finance literature: Time-varying risk aversion is typically associated with expectations about the state of the economy and uncertainty in financial markets. Risk aversion increases as economic downturns loom on the horizon—that is, when inflation is expected to decline and monetary policy to be accommodative—while it decreases in periods of forthcoming expansion—when the opposite holds true. The intuition behind this is certainly not new.[4] As the economy enters into recession, investors will take less risky positions in financial markets, as their income is already at risk.

EXPLAINING DEVELOPMENTS IN EURO AREA SOVEREIGN RISK DURING THE CRISIS

To assess the determinants of spreads during the crisis, a simple panel model of the spread between the yield on 10-year sovereign bonds among 10 euro area countries and Germany is estimated over the period from January 2003 to March 2009, using monthly data.

A general-to-specific approach is adopted, commencing with a general equation encompassing a range of explanatory variables on the basis of existing empirical work and theory. The general degree of risk aversion is measured by our previously estimated common factor. Variables used to proxy for investor assessments of country-specific credit risk include expected changes in debt stock and future fiscal balances. Also, the possible effect on spreads arising from vulnerabilities in national financial systems is captured by the expected default frequency of the median financial institution of each country. The market value of a country's traded euro-denominated long-term government bonds is included among the regressors as a proxy for the liquidity of the country's bond market. Finally, projected growth and current account imbalances, also from the economist intelligence unit, are additional explanatory variables.

A preliminary look at the determinants of spreads and how they have changed before and after the crisis is provided in Exhibit 47.3. Strikingly, Greek and Irish sovereign bonds appear to have been severely punished by the markets. This is out of line with evidence before the crisis, and cannot be fully explained by either expected debt developments or the bond markets' liquidity measures. What accounts for such dramatic shifts in sovereign risk premium differentials?

Overall, the estimates show that changes in sovereign default risk premiums continue to reflect mainly global risk factors—such as shifts in risk aversion in financial markets. There is also evidence, however, that the sensitivity of sovereign spreads to projected debt changes significantly increased after September, suggesting that the markets may now be able to provide more fiscal discipline than in the early years of the common currency. In a few countries, markets also appear to be progressively more concerned about the solvency of national banking systems. Finally, the liquidity of sovereign bond markets appears to remain a relevant factor in explaining spread behavior.

Country-specific issues also matter (Exhibit 47.4). Decomposing the contributions to the actual change in country-specific sovereign spread between the end of

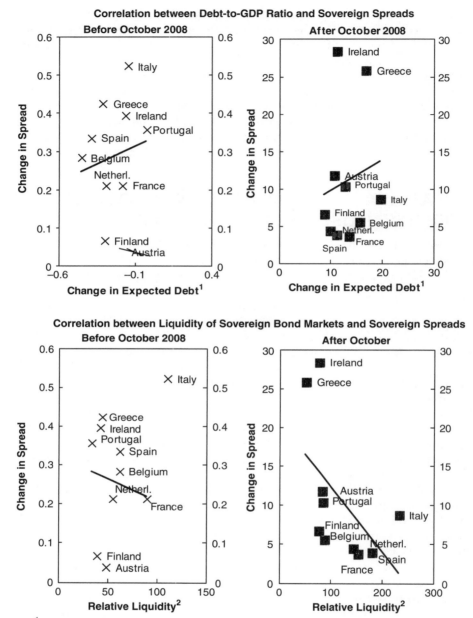

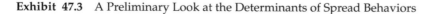

[1]Projected change in the debt-to-GDP ratio over the next year (percent).
[2]Traded volume of government debt relative to the German bond market (percent).

Exhibit 47.3 A Preliminary Look at the Determinants of Spread Behaviors

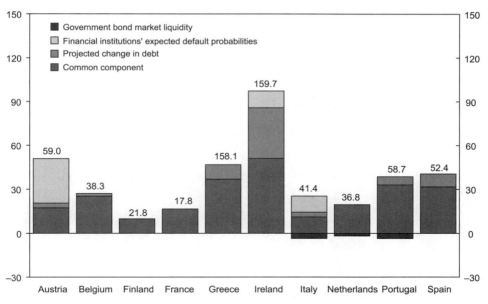

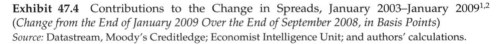

[1]For each country, the explanatory variables included in the model are the changes in: the common factor, the EDF of the median financial institution, the projected debt-to-GDP ratio over the next year, and the traded volume of government debt.
[2]For each country, the actual change in spread over the period is reported above the corresponding histogram.

Exhibit 47.4 Contributions to the Change in Spreads, January 2003–January 2009[1,2] (*Change from the End of January 2009 Over the End of September 2008, in Basis Points*)
Source: Datastream, Moody's Creditledge; Economist Intelligence Unit; and authors' calculations.

January 2009 and the end of September 2008 indicates that concerns about fiscal sustainability are significant for countries like Greece, Ireland, Spain, and—to a lesser extent—Austria, Italy, and Portugal. The extent to which rising default risks in the financial sector translate into increases in government spreads is found to be large and significant in Austria, Ireland, and Italy. Finally, *ceteris paribus*, the liquidity of the sovereign bond market appears to lessen the Italian government's financing costs. Nonetheless, a sizable part of the actual change in spreads since September 2008 remains unexplained, notably in the case of Greece.

The picture has changed substantially, though, from the end of January to the end of March 2009 (Exhibit 47.5). Investors' risk appetite appears to play a much smaller role by the end of March, while concerns about the solvency of the national financial sectors have risen, particularly in Austria, Finland, Greece, and Portugal. On the other hand, concerns about domestic fiscal sustainability have mounted in Belgium, Ireland, and Italy. This seems to indicate an improvement in the market's perception of the euro area cyclical outlook starting from 2009Q2 but, at the same time, it suggests that markets have become progressively more concerned about the potential fiscal implications of national financial sectors' frailty and future debt dynamics. The liquidity of sovereign bond markets still seems to play a significant (albeit fairly limited) role in explaining changes in euro area spreads in few countries.

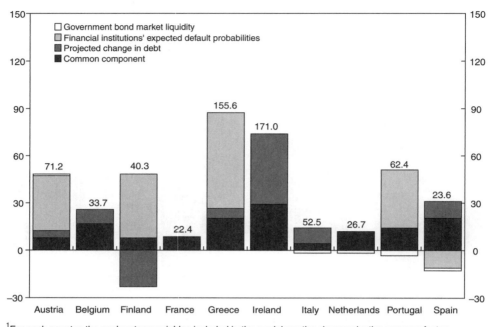

¹For each country, the explanatory variables included in the model are the changes in: the common factor, the EDF of the median financial institution, the projected debt-to-GDP ratio over the next year, and the traded volume of government debt.

²For each country, the actual change in spread over the period is reported above the corresponding histogram.

Exhibit 47.5 Contributions to the Change in Spreads, January 2003–March 2009 1, 2 (*Change from the End of March 2009 Over the End of September 2008, in Basis Points*)
Sources: Datastream; Moody's Creditedge; Economist Intelligence Unit; and authors' calculations.

CONCLUSION

In response to the deepening financial crisis, fiscal policy has been providing important backing through the use of public balance sheets to shore up the financial system and to support activity in the face of the current unprecedented slowdown. While the use of public resources has been critical to bolster aggregate demand and to break the adverse loop between the financial system and the real economy, it is key that the entailed fiscal cost not be seen by markets as undermining fiscal sustainability.

Financial markets seem to have responded to the significant deterioration in fiscal positions by requiring higher sovereign default risk premiums for most countries, and differentiating across sovereign issuers much more than before. While global risk factors continue to play a significant role in explaining movements in euro area sovereign interest rate differentials, country-specific developments—in particular, rapidly rising projected debt levels as well as concerns about the solvency of national banking systems and their budgetary consequences—are becoming increasingly more evident.

Evidence of the increased financial market's awareness is extremely compelling from a policy point of view. In particular, it seems to support the position that restoring trust in the financial system is key—not only to shape the recovery, but also to increase the effectiveness of fiscal stimulus measures while reducing future governments' financing costs. At the same time, it strengthens the argument for a credible commitment to long-run fiscal discipline and a clear exit strategy from a supportive policy stance as the crisis abates. Casting short-term fiscal expansion within a credible medium-term framework and envisaging fiscal adjustments as economic conditions improve could conceivably help euro area governments curb solvency concerns in financial markets. Structural reforms—enhancing potential growth and, thereby, medium-term revenue prospects—are also likely to work in the same direction. Together, these measures may be able to ensure that yesterday's global financial crisis does not sow the seed of tomorrow's vicious domestic debt dynamics.

NOTES

1. See, for example, Codogno et al. (2003), Beber et al. (2009), the European Central Bank (2009), and Manganelli and Wolswijk (2009).
2. See, for example, Codogno et al. (2003), Geyer et al. (2004), and Favero et al. (forthcoming).
3. The theoretical and empirical underpinnings of the model are explained in greater detail in Lombardi and Sgherri (forthcoming).
4. See also Manganelli and Wolswijk (2009).

REFERENCES

Beber, A., M. Brandt, and K. Kavajecz. 2009. "Flight-to-Quality or Flight-to-Liquidity? Evidence from the Euro-Area Bond Market." *Review of Financial Studies* 22:3, 925–957.

Codogno, L., C. Favero, and A. Missale. 2003. "Yield Spreads on EMU Government Bonds." *Economic Policy* 18:37, 503–532.

European Central Bank. 2009. "New Evidence on Credit and Liquidity Premia in Selected Euro Area Sovereign Yields." *September Monthly Bulletin*, 35–54.

Favero, C., M. Pagano, and E-L. von Thadden. Forthcoming. "How Does Liquidity Affect Bond Yields?" *Journal of Financial and Quantitative Analysis*.

Geyer, A., S. Kossmeier, and S. Pichler. 2004. "Measuring Systematic Risk in EMU Government Yield Spreads." *Review of Finance* 8:2, 171–197.

Lombardi, M., and S. Sgherri. (Forthcoming), "Risk Repricing and Spillovers across Assets." *IMF Working Paper*.

Manganelli, S., and G. Wolswijk. 2009. "What Drives Spreads in the Euro Area Government Bond Market?" *Economic Policy* 24:4, 191–240.

ABOUT THE AUTHORS

Silvia Sgherri is a senior economist at the International Monetary Fund. During her career, she has carried out research at the Research Directorate General of the European Central Bank, the Economics and Research Division of De Nederlandsche Bank, and the ESRC Macroeconomic Modeling Bureau. She received a degree and a doctorate in economics and management from the Sant'Anna School of Advanced Studies of Pisa (Italy), and an MSc and a PhD in economics from the University of Warwick (UK). She has done wide-ranging work in the area of applied econometrics, macromodeling, and international economic policy, and is the author of a number of articles and working papers in these fields.

Edda Zoli is a senior economist in the European Department of the International Monetary Fund. She has worked in the past for the World Bank and the Bank for International Settlements. Her research interests include international macroeconomics and finance. She has contributed to recent editions of the IMF *Regional Economic Outlook* on Europe. She holds an MPhil and PhD in economics from the University of Cambridge.

CHAPTER 48

Facing the Debt Challenge of Countries That Are "Too Big To Fail"

STEVEN L. SCHWARCZ
Stanley A. Star Professor of Law and Business, Duke University School of Law, and Leverhulme Visiting Professor, University of Oxford*

T he recent financial woes of Greece and other nations have reinvigorated the debate over whether to bail out defaulting countries or, instead, restructure their debt. Bailouts are expensive, in the case of Greece costing potentially hundreds of billions of euros. Although the European Union and the International Monetary Fund (IMF) are underwriting the Greek bailout, the IMF's payment is funded by all IMF member nations—the United States, for example, provides 17 percent of IMF funding—so we all share in the burden.[1]

In the case of Greece, a bailout was virtually inevitable because a default on Greek debt was believed to have the potential to bring down the world financial system, whereas an orderly debt restructuring was impractical. This is a growing problem. As global capital markets increasingly (and inevitably) embrace sovereign bonds, the potential for a country's debt default to trigger a larger systemic collapse becomes even more tightly linked.

TOO BIG TO FAIL

This reveals a phenomenon viewed until recently as limited to large banks—the problem of "too big to fail." A bank whose default could trigger an economic domino effect is, or at least may be perceived to be, too big to fail. It therefore must be bailed out by public funds. This can foster moral hazard: anticipating a bail-out, the bank may lack incentive to take a prudent economic course.[2]

Countries, even those as small as Greece, can likewise be seen as too big to fail if their default could trigger a wider economic collapse. That too can foster moral

---

hazard. The Greek government, for example, did little to impose fiscal austerity even as debts accumulated.

An Alternative to Bailouts

Bailouts are not, however, the only way to prevent defaults. Just as policymakers have been proposing orderly resolution procedures for troubled banks and other large financial institutions, an orderly resolution procedure for troubled countries can bypass the need for a bailout.

Countries are very different from banks, of course. Nonetheless, there are meaningful ways to create debt resolution procedures for troubled nations. Perhaps the most notable is the concept of a sovereign debt restructuring mechanism (SDRM), originally proposed by scholars (including the author) and later refined by the IMF into a template for an international convention. The template was never adopted as a treaty, however, because of political opposition in the United States by President George W. Bush's administration. Although the basis of the administration's opposition was not clearly articulated, it appeared to reflect the philosophical dogma that free-market solutions always ought to trump legislative ones.

The Holdout Problem and the Funding Problem

In the sovereign debt restructuring realm, however, free-market solutions are inadequate because of market failures—of which the two most important are the holdout problem and the funding problem. The holdout problem is that any given creditor has an incentive to strategically hold out from agreeing to a reasonable debt-restructuring plan, hoping that the imperative of others to settle will persuade them to allocate the holdout more than its fair share of the settlement or purchase the holdout's claim.[3] The funding problem is that a country is likely to need to borrow new money to pay critical expenses during the debt restructuring process but no lender is likely to be willing to lend such funds unless its right to repayment has priority over existing debt claims. Any effective SDRM would at least have to address these two problems.

Addressing the Holdout Problem

The holdout problem can be addressed by legislating, through international treaty, a form of "super-majority" voting on sovereign debt-restructuring plans, in which the vote by the overwhelming majority of similarly situated creditors can bind dissenting creditors. This is the tried-and-true method by which insolvency law, including Chapter 11 of the Bankruptcy Code in the United States, successfully and equitably addresses the holdout problem in a corporate context and achieves consensual debt restructuring. Because only similarly situated creditors can vote to bind dissenting creditors, and because any outcome of voting will bind all those creditors alike, the outcomes of votes should benefit the claims of holdouts and dissenters as much as the claims of the super-majority.[4]

Many have argued, nonetheless, that the holdout problem can be addressed contractually through what are referred to as collective-action clauses (CACs), allowing essential payment terms of a loan facility to be changed through super-majority, as opposed to unanimous, voting.[5] There are, however, two fundamental problems with CACs. First, CACs are not always included in sovereign loan and bond agreements. In the Greek debt crisis, for example, 90 percent of the total debt was *not* governed by CACs.[6] Although creditors could consider agreeing during a crisis to include those clauses in their agreements, the likelihood of achieving that is small.[7]

Second, even if every sovereign loan and bond agreement included CACs, such clauses would work on an agreement-by-agreement basis. Therefore, any one or more syndicate of banks or group of bondholders that fails to achieve a super-majority vote would itself be a holdout vis-à-vis other creditors. It therefore is unlikely that CACs can ever effectively resolve the holdout problem in sovereign-debt restructuring.[8]

It also is unlikely that the holdout problem will be addressed judicially. To the contrary, some courts have encouraged holdout behavior. In *Allied Bank Int'l v. Banco Credito Agricola de Cartago*,[9] for example, the court upheld a holdout-creditor's claim. A member of a bank syndicate that refused to join a restructuring agreement between Costa Rican sovereign debtors and other syndicate members sued in the United States for repayment of its defaulted loan.[10] The court granted summary judgment in favor of the holdout bank on the basis that the loan was clearly due and payable, notwithstanding Costa Rica's unilateral regulation suspending its external debt payments.[11] Similarly, in *Elliott Assocs. v. Banco de la Nacion*,[12] the holdout was a vulture fund (one that invests in distressed debt) that had bought debt of two government-guaranteed Peruvian banks at a deep discount. The fund then received, but refused to participate in, an offer to exchange that debt for new bonds, instead suing Peru for payment. The fund was granted judgment on appeal, but the parties ultimately settled.[13]

Addressing the Funding Problem

For these reasons, I believe that an international convention, in which super-majority voting can bind all of a nation's creditors, is needed to solve the holdout problem. Such a convention also could address the funding problem by granting a first priority right of repayment to loans of new money made to enable a country to pay critical expenses during the debt restructuring process. Existing creditors can be protected by giving them the right to object to a new-money loan if its amount is too high or its terms are inappropriate. Existing creditors will also be further protected because a country that abuses new-money lending privileges will be unlikely to receive super-majority creditor approval for a debt-restructuring plan.

Consensus and Disputes

Once these two market failures have been addressed, the remainder of the sovereign debt restructuring process can be consensual. A consensual process would not undermine the rule of law, as would an attempt by a nation to impose a "haircut" on its bonds such as by unilaterally reducing the principal amount of the bonds or the rate of interest payable thereunder. Nor should a consensual re-structuring increase borrowing costs for other nations. Indeed, a nation whose debt has been consensually restructured should itself be able to borrow new money at attractive rates. In the nonsovereign context, by analogy, lending rates to companies with consensually restructured debt are much lower than rates charged before the restructuring. Admittedly, the lower rates in part reflect that companies, after restructuring their debt, have a more conservative capital structure. After a *consensual* debt restructuring, however, new-money lenders are less likely to charge a risk premium reflecting uncertainty as to whether the debtor will again try to unilaterally reduce its debt.

Nor would a sovereign debt restructuring process need to depend on the creation of a "bankruptcy-like" court or other costly institutional arbiter. Indeed, the experience of corporate debt restructuring in the United States under Chapter 11 confirms that the parties themselves do most of the negotiating.[14] There may nonetheless be circumstances when parties have disputes. I have suggested that a relatively low-cost and straightforward procedure already exists under international law for this purpose.[15] The International Centre for Settlement of Investment Disputes (ICSID), an autonomous body created under the auspices of the World Bank, provides facilities for arbitration of investment disputes.[16] The ICSID arbitration procedure is well established, commonly used, and widely accepted, and it should be a useful model to the extent that a tribunal is needed to resolve sovereign debt restructuring disputes.[17] Others have similarly proposed the creation of an international arbitral panel for this purpose.[18]

CONCLUSION

As finance becomes more intertwined, sovereign debt defaults will become even more likely to trigger larger systemic collapses. That, in turn, will make most nations too big to fail. Without an effective sovereign debt restructuring mechanism, defaulting nations will expect to—and in most cases, by necessity, almost certainly will—be bailed out by the international community. We then will all end up subsidizing nations that lack the political will or ability to be fiscally responsible.

NOTES

1. Nor are IMF payments made to bail out sovereign countries necessarily profitable investments for the member nations. Member nations earn interest on their deposits in the IMF, but repayment by the IMF, although anticipated, is not assured. Furthermore, the IMF pays member nations less than a market rate of interest on their deposits. Steven L. Schwarcz, "'Idiot's Guide' to Sovereign Debt Restructuring," *Emory Law Journal* 53, 2004, 1189, 1195–96.

2. Moral hazard more generally refers to the tendency of people who are protected from the consequences of risky behavior to engage in such behavior.

3. "Idiot's Guide," supra note 2, at 1193.

4. Steven L. Schwarcz, "Sovereign Debt Restructuring: A Bankruptcy Reorganization Approach," (*Cornell Law Review* 85, 2000), 956: 1006.

5. See, for example, Barry Eichengreen, *Towards a New International Financial Architecture*, 65–70 (1999); Christopher Greenwood and Hugh Mercer, *Considerations of International Law*, in Barry Eichengreen and Richard Portes, *Crisis? What Crisis? Orderly Workouts for*

Sovereign Debtors (1995), 110; Lee Buchheit & Mitu Gulati, *Exit Consents and Sovereign Debt Workouts*, 48 UCLA L. REV. 59 (2000).

6. Lee Buchheit and Mitu Gulati, *Buchheit and Gulati on How to Restructure Greek Debt*, The Faculty Lounge (blog), May 9, 2010 (last visited May 13, 2010).

7. "Idiot's Guide," supra note 2, at 1203.

8. See Hal S. Scott, "A Bankruptcy Procedure for Sovereign Debt" (*Int'l Law.* 37, 2003) 103: 129 (concluding that "[t]he insertion of collective action clauses in sovereign bonds is an exercise in futility").

9. 757 F.2d 516 (2d Cir. 1985).

10. Ibid. at 519.

11. Ibid. at 522–23.

12. 194 F.3d 363 (2d Cir. 1999).

13. "Idiot's Guide," supra note 2, at 1193 n. 14.

14. James B. Hurlock, *The Way Ahead for Sovereign Debt*, Int'l Fin. L. Rev., July 1995, at 12 ("most U.S. bankruptcies are self-executing in that creditors, in concert with the debtor, collectively determine the economic terms upon which the enterprise will be restructured."); David G. Epstein et al., *Bankruptcy* § 10-2, (1993) at 734 ("It would be wrong to think of the Chapter 11 process as primarily a litigated, judged-ruled adversarial process. Plans proposed and adopted in Chapter 11 almost always have been produced by negotiation, not by litigation").

15. "Idiot's Guide," supra note 2, at 1210.

16. Convention on the Settlement of Investment Disputes Between States and Nationals of Other States, *opened for signature* Mar. 18, 1965, art. 1, 17 U.S.T. 1270, 575 U.N.T.S. 159. The ICSID Convention applies to disputes between contracting countries and nationals of other contracting countries, but I suggest it as a model for a parallel sovereign debt dispute adjudication procedure.

17. See "Idiot's Guide," supra note 2, at 1210–1211.

18. Christoph G. Paulus and Steven T. Kargman, *Reforming the Process of Sovereign Debt Restructuring: A Proposal for a Sovereign Debt Tribunal*, April 7, 2008, unpublished draft.

REFERENCES

Buchheit, Lee and Gulati, Mitu. 2000. "Exit Consents and Sovereign Debt Workouts." *UCLA Law Review* 48.

Buchheit, Lee and Gulati, Mitu. 2010. "Buchheit & Gulati on How To Restructure Greek Debt." The Faculty Lounge (blog), May 9.

Eichengreen, Barry. 1999. *Toward a New International Financial Architecture: A Practical Post-Asia Agenda*. Washington, D.C.: Institute for International Economics.

Epstein, David G. et al., 1993. *Bankruptcy*. St. Paul: West Publishing.

Greenwood, Christopher and Mercer, Hugh. 1995. "Considerations of International Law" *Crisis? What Crisis? Orderly Workouts for Sovereign Debtors* Ed. Barry Eichengreen and Richard Portes. London: Centre for Economic Policy Research.

Hurlock, James B. 1995. "The Way Ahead for Sovereign Debt." *International Financial Law Review*.

Paulus, Christoph G. and Kargman, Steven T. 2008. "Reforming the Process of Sovereign Debt Restructuring: A Proposal for a Sovereign Debt Tribunal." Unpublished draft.

Schwarcz, Steven L. 2000. "Sovereign Debt Restructuring: A Bankruptcy Reorganization Approach." *Cornell Law Review* 85: 956.

Schwarcz, Steven L. 2008. "Systemic Risk." *Georgetown Law Journal* 97: 193.

Schwarcz, Steven L. 2004. "Idiot's Guide' to Sovereign Debt Restructuring." *Emory Law Journal* 53: 1189.

Scott, Hal S. 2003. "A Bankruptcy Procedure for Sovereign Debt." *The International Lawyer* 37: 103.

1985. *Allied Bank Int'l v. Banco Credito Agricola de Cartago*. 757 F.2d 516 (2d Cir.).

1999. *Elliott Assocs. v. Banco de la Nacion*. 194 F.3d 363 (2d Cir.).

ABOUT THE AUTHOR

Steven L. Schwarcz is the Stanley A. Star professor of law and business at Duke University, founding director of Duke's Global Capital Markets Center, a fellow of the American College of Bankruptcy, and founding member of the International Insolvency Institute. He was a partner at two leading international law firms before joining Duke, and also taught at the Yale and Columbia law schools. In the fall of 2010, he was the Leverhulme visiting professor at the University of Oxford. Schwarcz's scholarly works include "Sovereign Debt Restructuring: A Bankruptcy Reorganization Approach," *Cornell Law Review* 85, 956 (2000), available at http://scholarship.law.duke.edu/faculty_scholarship/50; "'Idiot's Guide' to Sovereign Debt Restructuring," *Emory Law Journal* 53, 1189 (2004), available at http://scholarship.law.duke.edu/faculty_scholarship/1141; "Global Decentralization and the Subnational Debt Problem," *Duke Law Journal* 51, 1179 (2002), available at www.law.duke.edu/shell/cite.pl?51+Duke+L.+J.+1179; and "Systemic Risk," *Georgetown Law Journal* 97, 193 (2008), available at http://ssrn.com/abstract_id=1008326.

Index

A

Ability to repay, 190, 192
Afonso, A., 305
Aggregation of claims, 220
Akerlof, G., 55
Akitoby, B., 305
Alesina A., 56
Alfaro, L., 142
Algeria, 170, 175
Allied Bank Int'l v. Banco Credito Agricola de Cartago, 427
All-in-margin, 103
Amortizing structure, 114, 116
Anthony Gibbs and Sons, 10
Apartheid era debt, 247, 263
Archibald, C., 120
Argentina, 15, 45, 84, 90, 95, 156, 161, 172, 174, 175, 179, 184, 185, 205, 211, 212, 213, 215, 217, 218, 219, 220, 221, 269, 270, 271, 272, 273, 295, 297, 298, 326, 328, 346
Argentine debt reconstruction,
   absence of creditor coordination, 216
   creditor heterogeneity, 215–216
   long delay, 217
   significant debt write-down, 216–217
Arnone, M. B., 18
Arteta, C., 139
Asia, 93, 180, 295, 297, 362, 371, 375, 376
Asset seizure, 205
Associated Press, 176
Asymmetric international spillover,
   effects in sovereign debt markets, 362
Attachment of collateral assets, 213, 218, 219, 221

Auction design, 120
Auction mechanisms, 121
Australia, 272, 403
Austria, 121, 206, 272, 283, 397, 407, 408, 421
Autocratic regimes and poor institutions, 54
Average life time, 103

B

Backward induction, 5
Baig, T., 372
Bailouts,
   alternative to, 426
   vs. collective action clauses (CACs), 242
   costs of, 425
   de facto restoring discrimination from,
   equity and efficiency problems with, 236
   moral hazards from, 261
Balance sheet approach (BSA), 388
Balkan, E., 141
Banco de La Nación, 227
Bank accounts, freezing, 10
Bank rescue packages, 408, 409, 410, 411–412, 412
Bank runs, 25
Banking crises, 27
Banking crisis to sovereign debt crisis,
   about, 387
   balance sheet approach (BSA), 388
   empirical evidence, 388–389
   financial crisis in Europe, 389–391

Banks. *See also* Central banks,
    fraction of, as large lenders, 107
    fraction of, as small lenders, 107
    as large lenders, 105, 107
    rescue of commercial, 59
    in sovereign loan market, 102
Banks as special lenders, 105–107
Baring crisis of 1890, 269–275
Barro, R., 304
Bekaert, G., 363, 372, 373, 375
Belgium, 10, 228, 229, 272, 407, 421
Belize, 179, 185, 201, 202
Berensmann, K., 381
Berg, A., 18
Berk, Jonathan, 45
Bhatia, A., 248
Bilateral trade flows, 150
Boilerplate contractual terms, 229, 232
Bolton, P., 101, 381
Bond spreads, 85
Bonds,
    vs. loans, 101–107
Boom-based borrowing and lending, 54
Boom-based borrowing capacity, 53
Boorman, J., 240
Boot, A., 101
Borensztein, Eduardo, 44
Borrower illiquidity, 101, 102, 104, 105
Borrower liquidity hypothesis (BLH),
    104
Borrowers' perspective,
    borrowing costs, 240
    first mover problem, 241
    myopia, 241
    signaling, 240–241
Borrowing costs,
    collective action clauses (CACs)
        effect on, 240
    from coordination of lenders,
        138–139
    political factors, 141–142
    of sovereign default, 141–142
Bradley, M., 240
Brady bonds, 170, 211, 217, 314
Brazil, 66, 122, 141, 156, 161, 170, 215,
    272, 295, 297, 298, 299, 328, 362, 371
Brewer, T., 141
Britain, 63, 156

British Guiana, 272
Broader financial crisis costs, 25–28
Broner, Fernando, 91
Brooks, R., 362
Brunner, A., 101, 104
Bryan, William Jennings, 64
Buchheit, L., 220, 228
Building Demand, 114
Bulgaria, 335, 338, 340
Bullet bond, 114
Bulow, J., 6, 59, 158, 210
Bulte, E., 53
Busby, G., 53
Business cycles in emerging counties,
    and sovereign defaults, 142–143
Butler, Alexander W., 84

C

Caballero, Ricardo, 156
Caceres, C., 401, 403
CACs (collective action clauses). *See*
    Collective action clauses (CACs)
Calvo, G. A., 320
Calvo, S., 372
Calvo type crisis, 320
Cambodia, 255
Campos, C. F., 322
Canada, 122, 272
Candelon, B., 389
Cantor, R., 140, 346
Cape Verde, 331
Capital accumulation, with and
    without lending structure, 57
Capital flight, 213
Capital flow drain, 139
Capital flows,
    global volatility and, 401
    public defaults and
        complementarity, 92–95
    sovereign defaults effect on, 150
Capital inflows, 270, 348, 380
Capital outflows, 358
Caprio, Gerard, 46
Caribbean countries, 161
Carr, E. H., 280
Cash flow problem, 128
Central America, 156, 161, 162, 273

Central banks,
   double role of, 17
   independence of, 16, 17, 18
Central government weakness, 7
Chamberlin, M., 237, 238
Chamon, M., 319
Checks and balances, 16, 77
Chile, 84, 128, 129, 172, 175, 255, 272
Cicero, 1
Ciocchini, Francisco, 84, 85
Citron, J., 141
Civil (Roman) law vs. common law, 122
Class action suits, 218, 221
Class action suits and bondholder
      organizations, 220–221
Cline, W. R., 107
Closed system IPD, 128
Code of conduct,
   advantages and disadvantages of,
      199–202
   in contracts, 380
   features of, 199
   objectives of, 198–199
   role of, 197–198
   conclusions, 202
Cohen, D., 320
Cole, H., 139, 142, 319
Coleman, A. D. F., 101, 107
Collateral assets, attachment of, 213,
      218, 219, 221
Collective action clauses (CACs), 112,
      180, 211, 212, 213, 222, 237–238,
      242, 380, 426
Collective action clauses (CACs),
      courts, and creditor committees,
   about, 219–220
   class action suits and bondholder
      organizations, 220–221
   swaps and holdouts, 220
Collective action clauses (CACs) in
      sovereign bonds,
   about, 235–237
   investors' perspective, 237–240
   conclusions, 241–242
Collective majority clause, 380
Collier, P., 54
Colombia, 272
Commercial banks, rescue of, 59

Commitment to repay, 190, 193
Commodity prices,
   international lending and, 52
Common creditors, 273
Common law vs. civil (Roman) law, 122
Complementarity,
   financial integration, institutions
      and, 88–97
   between private and public sector
      borrowing, 90
Comprehensive credit rating (CCR),
      362
Conditionality, 179
Conditionality requirement, 185
Confrontational debtor policies, 38
Congo, 201
Consensual debt reconstructuring, 428
Consensus and disputes, 427–428
Contagion,
   described, 371
   distress dependence used as
      measure of, 396
   indicators of, 403
   sector stocks role in, 376
Contagion effect, 405
Contagion risk,
   sources of, 373
Contingent claim model, 403
Coordination agreement, 138–139
Corporate access to finance, 33, 34
Corporation of Foreign Bondholders
      (CFB), 156, 157, 220, 273
Correa, Raphael, 141
Corruption,
   aggregate effects of, 85
   effect on creditworthiness of, 84
Corruption and creditworthiness,
      79–86
Corruption index, 329, 331
Corruption Perception Index (CPI),
      80–81, 123
Costa Rica, 162, 272, 427
Costs of sovereign defaults,
   borrowing costs, 141–142
   sanctions, 138–139
   signaling costs, 139–140
Countercyclical fiscal policy, 304
Countercyclical inflation tax, 143

Countercyclical pattern of default risk, 303
Countercyclicality of interest rates, 140
Country default probabilities, 353
Country risk, 295, 403
Country shocks, 361
Country-specific factors, 403
Country-specific issues, 419
Country-specific variables and volatility measures, 404
Cramdowns, 219, 383
Credit default swaps (CDSs), 411
Credit market illiquidity, 105
Credit pricing model for sovereign spreads, 403
Credit rating agencies (CRAs), 137, 325, 329, 353, 354, 358. *See also* Fitch; Moody's; Standard & Poor's
Credit rating spillovers, 362
Credit reputation, 287
Credit risk transfer hypothesis, 411
Creditor coordination problems, 174, 380
Creditor heterogeneity, 212, 215, 221
Creditor holdouts. *See* Holdouts
Creditor litigation and holdouts, 174–175
Creditor sanctions, 12
Creditor sanctions as sovereign defaults,
  about, 7
  Peru and guano deposits, 9–10
  Russian Federation, 10–11
  Spanish Empire defaults, 8–9
  conclusions, 11–12
Creditworthiness, 73–77, 127, 209, 245, 248–249, 262, 331
Cross-country correlations, 364, 365
Crowe, C., 18
Cuadra, G., 305
Cuba, 255
Cuevas, A., 130
Cukierman A., 18
Currency crises, 27
Currency risk, 28
Current account balance, 338
Current account deficit, 192

Current expenditure-based, adjustments vs. revenue-based adjustments, 73
Custom house control, 162
Cyclical debt, 5
Czech Republic, 335, 338, 340
Czechoslovakia, 282, 283

D

Damania, R., 53
De Paoli, B. S., 24, 25, 27
Deacon, R., 53
Debasement, 64
Debt cancellation, 247, 250, 253, 258
Debt crises, self-fulfilling and self-enforcing,
  about, 319
  data, 320–323
  econometric model, 322
  model simulation, 322–323
  conclusions, 323
Debt crisis cost,
  broader financial crisis, 24–25
  measures of costs of, 25–28
  penalty costs, 24
Debt intolerance, 17
Debt intolerance, institutional determinants of,
  about, 15
  lessons for current crisis, 19
  monetary institutions role, 16–19
  political institutions role, 16
Debt renegotiations,
  collective action clauses (CACs) for, 235
  duration of, 169, 170
  good faith, 38
  odius debt and, 264
  phase of, 169
Debt rescheduling, 354–355
Debt rescheduling probability model, 354–356
Debt restructuring,
  creditor litigation and holdouts, 174–175
  delays, 169–176

loss of credibility for foreign investors through, 391
measuring default and negotiation episodes, 169–171
process and phases of, 171–174
Debt rollover risk, 401
Debt service, 270
Debt service payment-to-exports ratio, 354
Debt servicing costs, 401
Debt settlement, 160
Debt sustainability, 16, 19, 402, 405
Debt sustainability framework, 403
Debt-by-debt approach to debt cancellation, 253, 254
Debt-financed spending vs. tax-financed-based spending, 73
Debtor states, denomination currency of, 140
Debtor-creditor restructuring, 29
Debt-servicing capacity, 327
Debt-to-GDP ratio, 193, 314, 320, 322, 323, 389, 410. *See also* External debt-to-GDP ratio
Debt-to-GNI ratio, 75
Decree of Mouharrem, 161
Default episodes vs. restructuring episodes, 171
Default history, 315
Default premia, 311, 313, 314, 315
Default risk,
    countercyclical pattern of, 303, 305
    different classes of, 417
    domestic debt vs. external debt, 290
Default traps,
    about, 309
    empirical evidence, 311–315
    serial default, 310–311
    conclusions, 315
Default-prone countries, 15
Defined-benefit (DB) plan, 129, 131
Defined-contribution (DC) plan, 128, 131
Deininger, K., 18
Delaume, G. R., 206
Demand and supply factors, 190–191
DeMarzo, Peter, 45

Democracy, 76
Democratic sovereignty, 246
Denial of trade credit, 213
Denmark, 282, 283, 284, 288, 289, 290, 292
Denomination currency, 114
Depken, Craig, 84
Determinants of sovereign defaults, 140–141
Developed economies vs. emerging economies, 143
Diamond, D. W., 101
Dictator's choice, 55
Dictator's tradeoff, 56
Discriminatory auction (DA), 119, 122
Discriminatory price mechanism, 123
Distress dependence, 394, 396
Diversification across countries, 376
Domestic conflict, 52, 54
Domestic creditors,
    punishment by, 287, 289
    role of, 181
Domestic currencies, overvaluation of, 320
Domestic currency denominated debt vs. foreign currency denominated debt, 325
Domestic currency short-term committments (GKOs), 170
Domestic debt, 383
Domestic debt vs. external debt default risk, 290
Domestic default,
    empirical analysis, 289–292
    institutional setting and data, 288–289
    political costs of, 287–292
    political-economic cost of, 288
    conclusions, 292
Domestic policy indicators, 190
Dominica, 179
Dominican Republic, 179, 185, 201, 331
Dornbusch, Rudiger, 156
Doukas, J., 404
Dow, J., 142
Dow Jones News Service, 176
Downgrade spillover effect, 364
Downgrades, 363

Drazen, A., 287, 288, 289, 292
Drelichman, Mauricio, 8
Dubai, 213
Dungey, M., 372
Durbin, Erik, 84, 85
Dutch disease, 52, 54, 55, 56

E

Ease of doing business, 123
Eaton, J., 143, 212, 215, 327
The Economist, 81, 271
Ecuador, 90, 94, 95, 140, 141, 179, 184,
    185, 217, 230, 295, 297, 298, 328,
    331, 380
Ederington, L., 364
Edwards, S., 75
Egypt, 3, 158, 159, 160, 161, 272
Eichengreen, B., 129, 149, 236
Elections, 76
Elliot and Associates v. Banco de La
    Nación, 217, 231, 232, 427
Elliot and Associates v. Panamá, 217
Elliot Associates L.P., 227
Elsas, R., 101
EMBI (Emerging Markets Bond Index),
    74, 176
Emerging countries, functional,
    definition of, 362
Emerging economies,
    vs. developed economies, 143
    private capital flows to, 92
Emerging market economies (EMEs),
    23
Emerging market spreads, 295–300
Emerging markets,
    contagion and market integration,
    376
    yield spreads, 271–275
Emerging Markets Bond Index (EMBI
    Global), 74, 176
Emerging Markets Review, 346
Endogeneity issues, 192
Enforcement mechanisms and
    sovereign debt repayment,
    156–157
England, 159, 160, 206, 236
English, W., 142

English law, 205, 206, 208, 209, 234, 238
Equilibrium pricing model, 404
Equitable subordination principle, 265
Equity market contagion and
    co-movement, 371–377
Esho, N., 101, 107, 238
Espinoza, R., 395
Esteves, R. P., 220
Euro area sovereign risk during crisis,
    about, 415–416
    common risk, 417–419
    explanation of, 419–422
    conclusions, 422–423
Euro sovereign spreads, 403
Euro spreads, 401
Euromoney, 402, 404
Europe, 64, 209, 372, 373, 375, 376
European sovereign debt, 19
European Union,
    countries in, 335
    Greek bailout underwriting, 425
    membership impact on debt, 83
    membership of, 81
Ex-ante conditionality, 258
Ex-ante prediction of country risk,
    403
Exchange offers, 235
Exchange rate depreciation, 25
Exchange rate stabilization, 391
Exit consent mechanism, 230, 236
Exogenous shocks, 189, 290–291, 319
Expenditure-based adjustments vs.
    revenue-based adjustments, 74
Explicit debt vs. implicit debt, 129
Expropriation, 89, 150
Extended fund facility (EFF), 321
External creditors, 181
External debt as permissive cause of
    war, 67
External debt issuance, 35
External debt-to-GDP ratio, 28, 338,
    340, 354

F

Faff, R., 362
Fauver, Larry, 84
Fear of abuse, 238

Federal loan obligations [OFZ], 390
Fenn on the Funds, 157
Finance integration, complementarity institutions and, 88–97
Financial crisis, mutations of, 387
Financial crisis to sovereign risk, 393–399
Financial debt, impact of, 130
Financial institutions and public default, 90
Financial liberalization, 95
Financial market uncertainties, 322, 323
Financial News, 161
Financial reform, 89
Financial Times, 176
Finland, 84, 121, 279, 282, 283, 284, 421
First mover problem, 241
First-in-time priority rule, 383
First-time sovereign bond issuers, benefits and risks of international issuance, 112
   common mistakes made by, 115–116
   issues to consider, 113–115
   recent experience, 111–112
Fiscal adjustment, 73
Fiscal agents vs. trustees, 231
Fiscal balance, 81
Fiscal cure, 390
Fiscal deficits, 305, 413
Fiscal house arrest, 157, 158–161
Fiscal policy, government institutions, and sovereign creditworthiness, analytical framework, 73–74
   key findings, 74–76
Fiscal policy shocks, 73, 74
Fiscal sovereignty, loss of, 155
Fiscal transparency, 306
Fisch, J. E., 212, 216
Fishlow, Albert, 161
Fitch, 325, 329, 345, 354, 356
Fitch Record of Government Finances, 158
Flandreau, Marc, 158
Flexible credit line (FCL), 342
Flight-to-quality effect, 389, 410
Flight-to-quality flows, 396
Flynn, S. T., 120
Forbes, K., 372, 373

Forder, J., 248
Foreign currency denominated debt vs. domestic currency denominated debt, 325
Foreign direct flows, reduction as punishment, 149
Foreign direct investments (FDI), 150, 151, 152, 347
Foreign exchange reserves, 29
Foreign investment insurance, 151
Foreign state immunity, 205–206
Fox, J., 240
France, 23, 64, 66, 121, 156, 159, 160, 272, 390, 412
Frank, R. H., 248
Frankel, J., 44, 46, 375
Freedom House index, 76
Free-market solutions, 426
Fresh-start policy, 263
Friedman, Milton, 119, 120
Fry, R., 372
Fuentes, M., 150, 151
Fully funded plans, 128
Funding problem, 426, 427
Future borrowing costs, 24, 65
Future debt obligations, 413
Future finance access, 23
Future growth opportunities, 404, 405

G

Gabon, 331, 355
Galai, D., 402
Gambling for redemption theory, 43, 184
Gambling theory, 47
Gande, A., 362
Gaon, Nessim, 10
Gapen, M., 24
Gavin, M., 143, 304
Gelos, R. G., 24, 321
Gelpern, A., 221, 237, 239
Gennaioli, Nicola, 89, 90, 91, 92, 94
Genoese, 8
Gentile, C., 212
Georgievska, A., 353, 354
Georgievska, L., 353, 354
German law, 208, 235

Germany, 3, 122, 150, 156, 160, 206, 217,
    236, 254, 255, 272, 282, 283, 284,
    291, 292, 389, 390, 396, 407, 408,
    410, 412
Gersovitz, M., 143, 212, 215, 327
Gini coefficient, 18
Global bonds, 115, 116
Global Committee of Argentine
    Bondholders (GCAB), 216
Global financial indicators, 403
Global liquidity, 296
Global liquidity cycle, 192
Global risk aversion (GRA), 394, 395,
    396, 403
Global volatility, 401
Globalization and sovereign defaults,
    93
Godlewski, C. J., 105
Godoy, S., 295
Goh, J., 364
Gold standard period, 156, 158–164,
    271
Goldfajn, I., 372
Goldreich, D., 120
Gomes, P., 305
Gonzalez, M., 130
Governing law of sovereign bonds,
    about, 205
    and credit constraints, 208
    jurisdiction shopping, 208–209
    national laws, 206–207
    conclusions, 210
Government bond spreads, long-run
    determinants of, 337
Government bond yields, 393
Government bonds, 16
Government bonds during wartime,
    about, 279
    empirical method and data, 280–281
    historians vs. bond markets, 283–284
    structural breaks in sovereign yields,
        281–283
    conclusions, 284–285
Government coerciveness index, 37
Government institutions and sovereign
    creditworthiness, 73–77
Government short-term commitment
    [GKO], 390

Government spending changes and
    spreads, 75
Government strength, 6–7
Great Britain, 3, 9, 64
Greece, 158, 160, 164, 242, 272, 301, 310,
    327, 328, 389, 390, 397, 403, 407,
    415, 419, 421, 425, 427
Greisa, Thomas (judge), 217–219
Grenada, 179, 201, 231
Grilli, V., 18
Gross domestic product (GDP). *See also*
    Debt-to-GDP ratio; External
    debt-to-GDP ratio,
    auction mechanism, 122
    external balance, 81
    per capita, 81
    public, and sovereign spreads,
        305
    stock market capitalization as
        percentage of, 122
Grossman, H., 327
Guano deposits, 9
Guatemala, 272
Gugiatti, M., 239, 240
Guinnane, T. W., 280
Gulati, M., 220, 221, 237, 239, 240
Gunboat diplomacy, 155, 157, 161–162,
    164, 213
Guzzo, V., 401, 403

H

Haircuts, 156, 181, 184, 211, 427
Hale, G., 139
Hallak, I., 102, 104, 105, 107
Hapsburg default, 8
Haque, N., 327
Harvey, C. R., 363, 372, 373, 375
Häseler, S., 238, 239, 240
Hatchondo, J. C., 142
Hausman, R., 129
Hillier, D., 362
Hillier, J., 362
Historical perspectives, 267
Hoeffler, A., 54
Hoggarth, G., 24, 25, 27
Holdout litigation vs. reputational
    models, 221

Holdout problem, 213, 219, 236, 380, 383, 426–427
Holdouts, 174–175, 215, 227, 230, 231
Holdouts/holdout problem, 197, 199
Honduras, 272
Hot money, 347, 349
House of Baring, 269, 271
Huang, R., 107
Humbolt, Alexander von, 9
Hume, David, 63
Hungary, 335, 338, 340, 341

I

Idiosyncratic liquidity shocks and return premia, 103–105
Illiquid borrowers. *See* Borrower illiquidity
Illiquidity, 101, 102, 105, 354, 382. *See also* Borrower illiquidity
Ilzetzki, E., 304
IMF (International Monetary Fund),
  as adjustment agent, 184, 185, 186
  bailouts by, 180, 425
  on collective action clauses (CACs), 240
  conditionality requirement, 185
  early warning role of, 28
  economics of debt restructuring study, 380
  financial assistance role, 184
  as international development institution, 261
  role in sovereign default, 139
  sovereign debt restructuring activities, 179
Implicit debt vs. explicit debt, 129
Implicit pension debt (IPD), 128
Income inequality, 18
Increased indebtedness, 52
Indebtedness, 312
Index of coerciveness, 37, 38
Index of debtor coerciveness, 37
Index of global risk aversion (IGRA), 395
Index of political rights, 76
India, 83, 272

Indirect collateral, 403
Indonesia, 85, 94, 95, 331, 371
Inflation, 81, 338
Informal sector economy, 79
Information asymmetry, 366
Information leakage, 363
Information spillover effect, 364
Informational asymmetry, 310, 315, 345, 348, 364
Insolvency law, 426
Insolvency principles, 261–266
Insolvency procedure for sovereign states,
  about, 379
  arbitration body, 382–383
  creditor treatment and coordination, 383
  features of, 382–384
  reason for establishing, 379–381
  right to open, 382
  stay of enforcement, 383–384
  conclusions, 384
Insolvency procedure proposals, 381
Insolvency proxies, 105
Instability from liquidity, 56
Institutional Investor Credit Rating Index, 404
Institutional transparency, 310
Institutions, financial integration, and complementarity,
  about, 89–91
  capital flows. public defaults and complementarity, 92–95
  institutions and public default risk, 91–92
  threshold effects and finance integration benefits, 95
  conclusions, 95–96
Institutions and public default riisk, 91–92
Inter-American Development Bank (IDB), 45
  IDB report, 213
Intercreditor disputes, 175
International bank flows, 347
International bankruptcy court, 185–186
International capital flows, 402

International Country Risk Guide (ICRG),
 democratic accountability index of, 74, 76
 government accountability measured by, 76
 political risk index, 76
International debt framework (IDF), 381
International Financial Review, 103
International issuance, benefits and risks of, 112
International lending and commodity prices, 52
International liquidity, 190–191
International risk aversion, 409, 411
Interpretive shocks, 229, 231–232
Investor base, 114
Investor surplus, 239–240
Investors' perspective,
 borrowers' perspective and, 240–241
 fear of abuse, 238
 ideology, 238–239
 investor surplus, 239–240
 moral hazards, 237–238
IPD,
 credit rating impact of, 131
 impact of, 130
Iraqi debt write-off, 247, 254, 263
Ireland, 397, 403, 407, 410, 417, 419, 421
Isham, J., 53
Issue size, 113, 116
Italy, 3, 16, 217, 272, 389, 390, 397, 407, 412, 421

J

Jaimovich, D., 322
Jalilvand, A., 404
Jamaica, 272
Japan, 16, 64, 150, 206, 236, 272, 372
Japanese laws, 206
Jennrich, R., 365
Jensen's inequality, 44
Jordan, 172
Jorgensen, E., 24
Journal of Economic Literature, 44

Judge-mediated debt restructuring, 212, 217–219
Jurisdiction shopping, 208–209

K

Kaletsky, A., 215
Kaminsky, G., 143, 362
Kanczuk, F., 142
Kant, Immanuel, 63
Kehoe, P., 139
Kehoe, T. J., 319
Kim, S.-J., 346
King, M., 372
Kletzer, K. M., 215
Klingebiel, Daniela, 46
Klingen, C. A., 59
Kohlscheen, E., 142
Korean War, 64
Kraay, A., 320, 321, 322
Krahnen, J. P., 101, 104
Krueger, A., 381
Krugman, Paul, 45, 324
Kubota, Megumi, 46
Kumar, M., 327
Kumhof, M., 139

L

La Porta, R., 91, 208
LaFountain, Courtney, 84
Lagged default, 81
Lane, P., 304, 306
Large lenders' earnings, 102–103
Larrain G., 363
Latin America, 93, 267, 270, 273, 304, 372, 373, 375, 376
Latvia, 335, 338
Laurens, J., 18
Lead managers, 114, 115, 116
Left wing governments vs. right wing governments, 75
Legal and contractual issues, 195
Legal enforcement. *See* Governing law of sovereign bonds
Legalized breach of contracts, 263–264
Leite, C., 53
Lenders, upfront fees of, 102

Lending, marginal impact of, 58
Lending into arrears (LIA), 180, 185, 186
Liberia, 255
Lienau, O., 245
Lindert, P., 24, 149, 309
Lipson, Charles, 159
Liquidity,
  instability from, 56
  of sovereign bond markets, 421
Lithuania, 335, 338, 340
Loans,
  banks as special lenders, 105–107
  vs. bonds, 101–107
  idiosyncratic liquidity shocks and
    return premia, 103–105
  large lenders' earnings, 102–103
  conclusions, 107
Loans renegotiations, 101, 102
Local currency, 65–66
Lombardo, D., 130
London Club, 170, 171, 262, 326
Londregan, J. B., 56
Long-cycle theory, 64
Long-term foreign currency,
  denominated debt, 80
Long-term local currency denominated
  debt, 80
Looting,
  probability of, 58
  vs. staying, 55
Looting indicator, 56, 58
Lopez-de-Silanes, F., 91, 208
Lopez-Marmolejo, A., 130
Lula da Silva, Luiz Inácio, 66, 141
Lundblad, C., 363
Luxembourg, 205, 206, 236, 331

M

Maastricht Treaty, 337, 342, 389
Majoritarian electoral systems, 76
Majority-rule countries, 76
Malaysia, 371
Malone, Samuel, 43, 45, 46
Maltzan, J., 363
Malvey, P., 120
Manasse, Paolo, 46

Manzano, O., 53, 54
Marginal traders, 281
Mark, N., 327
Market access, 215
Market integration, 289
Market liquidity risk, 409
Market price of risk, 395
Market segmentation, 292
Market-based fiscal discipline, 408
Martin, Alberto, 89, 90, 91, 92, 94
Martin, V. L., 372
Martinez, J., 150
Martinez, L., 142
Marwick, A., 280
Masciandaro, D., 18
Masulis, R., 402
Mathieson, D., 327
Maturity and repayment structure,
  113–114
Mauro, P., 220
Meade, E. E., 18
Measuring default and negotiation
  episodes, 169–171
Medeiros, C., 24
Mellios, C., 329
Merton, R., 402
Mexico, 129, 180, 230, 236, 241, 272, 362,
  371, 372, 375, 376
Middle class, 16, 18
Mitchener, K., 150
Modelski, George, 64
Monetization, 325
Moody's, 122, 176, 325, 327, 329, 345,
  354, 356
Moral hazards, 52, 55, 58, 59, 180,
  237–238, 240, 249, 261, 390, 404
Morris, S., 101
Mortal, Sandra, 84
Morton, P., 24, 149, 309
Moser, C., 142
Multiple prices auction, 119
Mutations of crises, 387–388
Mutual interest in peace, 65

N

Natal, 272
National laws, 206–207

Nehru, V., 320, 321, 322
The Netherlands, 8, 156, 272, 397, 403, 408
Neumeyer, A., 304
Neumeyer, P., 142
New South Wales, 272
New York law, 230, 231
New York Times, 176
New Zealand, 272
Neyapti, B., 18
Ng, A., 372, 373, 375
Ng, David T. C., 84, 85
Nicaragua, 162, 201, 272, 355
Nickelsburg, G., 141
Nigeria, 256, 331
Noga, 10, 11
Noncyclical fiscal policy, 304
Nonstatist concept of sovereignty, 247, 249
Nordic countries, 279
North America, 270
North Korea, 255
Norway, 272, 279, 283, 284
Number of joining lenders (variable), 104
Nyborg, K., 120

O

Obstfeld, Maurice, 149
Odious debt, 247, 248, 249
Odious debts vs. odious regimes,
  about, 253
  definitions, 254–256
  IMF role, 256–259
  obstacles and alternatives, 254
  remedies, 256–259
  systemic suppression, 257–258
  timing issues, 257
  U. N. Security Council role, 256–259
  conclusions, 259
Odius debt, 58, 263
OECD, 150
Ongena, S., 104, 105
Openness, 312
Ottoman Empire (Turkey), 272
Output losses,
  cumulative, 27
  per year, 28
Oxford Economic Papers, 43, 45
Özler, S., 24, 56, 149

P

Packer, F., 140, 346
Paget-Blanc, E., 329
Pakistan, 90, 95, 172, 179, 185, 380
Palm, F., 389
Pam, J., 228
Panama, 217
Panglossian effect, 319, 323
Panizza, U., 44, 129, 322
Paper currency, 270, 271
Paraguay, 272
Pari passu clause, 218, 228
Paris Club, 151, 185, 262, 320, 321, 326
Parliamentary systems vs. presidential systems, 142
Parsley, D., 362
Partial debt operations, 184
Pasha, Ismail (Khedive), 3, 159–160
Peace, mutual interest in, 65
Peace dividend, 65
Penalty costs of debt crisis, 24
Pension privatization, 127
Pension reform,
  economic cost of, 130
  and sovereign credit standing, 127–132
Perceived threat of war, 279, 282, 283, 284
Permissive cause of war,
  external debt as, 67
  sovereign debt as, 63–64
Perotti, R., 143, 304
Perri, F., 142, 304
Personal wealth, 16
Pertamina crisis, 54
Peru, 10, 172, 217, 227, 228, 255, 427
Peru and guano deposits, 9–10
Pesaran, M. H., 336
Philip, King, 8, 9
Philippines, 175, 228, 371
Platt, D., 159
Plundering, 256, 258–259

Poland, 283, 335, 338, 340, 342
Policy conditionality, 213, 215
Policy gambles,
    sovereign debt problems and, 43–48
Policy gambling for redemption, 47
Policy support instrument (PSI), 184
Political default cost channel, 288
Political economy of sovereign debt, 1
Political factors, 141–142
Political instability, 54, 141
Political objectives, 15
Political risk, 76
Political turnover, 141
Political-economic cost of domestic
    default, 288
Polity index, 76
Poole, K. T., 56
Pooled mean group technique (PMG),
    336
Poor governance, 55, 58
Poor institutions, 52, 54
Popular sovereignty, 246
Pork barrel spending, 76
Portes, R., 149, 236, 320
Portfolio investment flow, 347
Portugal, 403, 407, 415
Porzecanski, A. C., 219
Pravin Banker v. Banco Popular del Perú,
    217
Principal components analysis (PCA)
    method, 329
"Principles for Stable Capital Flows
    and Fair Debt Restructuring in
    Emerging Markets," 198, 199, 200,
    201–202
Pritchett, L., 53
Private access to capital, sovereign, 34
Private and public sector borrowing,
    complimentarity between, 90
Private capital flows to emerging
    economies, 92
Private corporations, sovereign, 33
Private sector investment, 180
Private to public risk transfer, 409,
    411–412
Procyclical fiscal policy, 303, 304, 306
Procyclical government spending, 143
Proportional electoral systems, 76

Public debt, 16
Public default, financial institutions
    and, 90
Public-debt-to-GDP ratios and
    sovereign spreads, 305
Public-defined-benefit (DB) program
    retirement,
    cash flow problem, 128, 129
    reform of, 127
Punishment,
    by domestic creditors, 287, 289
    of serial defaulters, 310
Punishment to sovereign defaulters,
    duration of, 152
    foreign direct flows reduction as, 149

Q

Queensland, 272

R

Raffer, K., 381, 382, 384
Rajan, R. G., 101
Ramírez, G. G., 107
Ranking of sovereign creditors, 229
Ratable payment interpretation, 228,
    229
Rating agencies, 76. *See also* Credit
    rating agencies (CRAs)
Ratings of different classes of debt, 80
Real GDP per capita growth, 81
Real income per capita, 320
Reforms,
    financial liberalization in absence of,
    95
Regime changes, 245, 246
Reinhart, C. M., 15, 17, 23, 24, 93, 143,
    287, 292, 372, 389
Reisen, H., 363
Renegotiation of loans, 101, 102
Rent seeking, 52
Renter state effect, 54
Repression effect, 54
Reputation, 247–248
Reputational explanations, 4–5
Reputational factors, 248
Reputational issues, 189–190

Reputational spillovers, 6–7, 11, 156, 158
Reserve currency, U.S. dollars as, 64
Reserves/short-term debt, 104
Reserves-to-imports ratio, 354
Resource collateral, 55
Resource curse and sovereign debt, 51–59
Resource wealth, 52
Resource-based collateral, 53
Resource-rich countries with poor governance, 58
Restricted sovereign immunity, 217
Restructuring, options before, 161
Resumption of lending, 192
Rethinking Sovereign Debt: Debt and Reputation in the 20th Century (Lienau), 246
Return premia, 103–105
Reuters, 176
Revenue-based adjustments,
    vs. current expenditure-based adjustments, 73
    vs. expenditure-based adjustments, 74
Rhodes, William R., 107
Ricardo, David, 63
Richards, A., 239, 240
Right wing governments vs. left wing governments, 75
Rigobon, R., 53, 54, 372
Risk appetite, 417
Risk aversion, 419
Risk premia, 28
Risk spillovers,
    of sovereign and private sector, 34
    top-down, 33
Rivoli, P., 141
Rogoff, K., 6, 15, 17, 23, 93, 158, 210, 287, 292, 389
Rogue debtors, 219
Rollover risk, 393
Romania, 172, 335, 338, 340, 342
Romer, P., 55
Roosevelt, Theodore, 161
Roosevelt Corollary to Monroe Doctrine, 162
Rose, A., 150, 152, 210

Rosen, H. S., 280
Ross, M., 54
Rossi, Stefano, 89, 90, 91, 92, 94
Rother, P., 305
Roubini, N., 46, 56
Rule of law concept of sovereignty, 246
Rush-to-default risk, 382
Rush-to-the-courthouse problem, 197, 199, 380, 383
Rush-to-the-exit problem, 197, 199, 380, 383
Russia, 25, 64, 90, 94, 95, 140, 150, 160, 170, 179, 184, 185, 195, 217, 272, 295, 297, 298, 299, 326, 328, 362, 371, 380, 390, 391
Russian crisis, 28
Russian Federation default, 10–11
Russo-Japanese War, 64
Rwanda, 255

S

S&L crisis, 55
Sachs, J., 18, 24, 45, 52, 53
Sack, A., 247, 253
Sack of Antwerp, 8
Sahay, R., 24, 321
Sanchez, J., 305
Sanctions,
    borrowing costs, 138–139
    in government lending, 9
    other, 139
    role of direct, 213
Sandleris, G., 24, 139, 150, 321
Santiso, J., 141
Santo Domingo, 162
Saporta, V., 24, 25, 27
Sapriza, H., 142, 305
Saravia, D., 150, 151
Savastano, M. S., 17, 24
Scharfstein, D. S., 101
Schimmelpfennig, Axel, 46
Schmukler, S., 362, 375
Schroeder, F., 381
Schure, P., 102, 104, 105, 107
Schwarcz, S. L., 381
Sector contagion, 373

Sector stocks,
  contagion role of, 376
Segalotto, J. F., 18
Segoviano, M., 395, 401, 403
Seignorage, 64
Seizure, 10, 11
Self-fulfilling effect, 323
Serbia, 174, 175, 255
Serial default, 315
Serial defaulters, 24, 162, 163, 310, 314,
  355
Sharpe, I., 101, 107, 238
Shin, H. S., 101
Shin, Y., 336
Shleifer, A., 91, 208
Shock persistence, 315
Short-run isolation strategies, 371
Short-term debt, 80
Short-term foreign currency
  denominated debt, 80
Short-term local currency denominated
  debt, 80
Signaling, 240–241
Signaling costs, 139–140
Singapore, 255
Single price auction, 119
Sinyagina-Woodruff, Yulia, 11
Skeel, D. A., Jr., 381
Slovakia, 335, 338, 340
Smith, D. C., 104, 105
Smith, R. P., 336
Social security, mandatory nature of,
  129
Solvency, 354
Sommer, M., 18
South Africa, 247, 254, 255, 256
South America, 156, 162, 273
South Australia, 272
South Korea, 150, 215, 328, 371
Southeast Asia, 372, 373
Sovereign bond spreads in European
  Union countries,
  about, 335
  government bonds spreads, 336–338
  macroeconomic and fiscal
    fundamentals, 338–340
  policy measures, 340–342
  conclusions, 342–343

Sovereign bond yield spreads, 407
Sovereign bonds, CAC spread premia,
  240, 241
Sovereign ceiling doctrine, 361
Sovereign continuity, 247, 248
Sovereign credit ratings,
  about, 325–329
  country risk assessment through, 345
  credit rating agencies (CRAs) and,
    85, 353
  determinants of, 331
  economic and political factors,
    325–332
  emerging market development and
    capital flows, 345–350
  explanatory variables, 327–329
  and international banks' capital
    allocation, 353
  results, 329–331
  conclusions, 331
"Sovereign Credit Ratings, Capital
  Flows and Financial Sector
  Development in Emerging
  Markets" (Kim and Wu), 346
Sovereign credit risk, 409
Sovereign creditworthiness, 73–77
Sovereign debt,
  as constraint on belligerence, 65–67
  in emerging markets, 301
  and financial crises, 369
  inefficient contract effect, 56
  as permissive cause of war, 63–64
  and taxes, 63
Sovereign debt and military conflict,
  sovereign debt as constraint on
    belligerence, 65–67
  sovereign debt as permissive cause
    of war, 63–64
  conclusions, 67–68
Sovereign debt and the resource curse,
  51–59
Sovereign debt auctions, 119–124
Sovereign debt crises, 90
Sovereign debt crisis, lending
  resumption after,
  about, 189
  demand and supply factors, 190–191
  reputational issues, 189–190

Sovereign debt crisis, lending
     resumption after, (*Continued*)
  conclusions, 191–192
Sovereign debt documentation and *pari
     passu*,
  Elliott case, 227–228
  exogenous factors, 231–232
  exogenous reasoning, 229–230
  fiscal agents vs. trustees, 231
  pari passu interpretation, 227–228
  Peru's use of, 233
  unanimous action classes vs.
       collective action classes,
       230–231
  conclusions, 232
Sovereign debt, making it work, 71
Sovereign debt markets, 362
Sovereign debt problems and policy
     gambles,
  about, 43–44
  background, 44–46
  political gambling for redemption
       theory, 46–47
  conclusions, 47–48
Sovereign debt ratings, international
     stock market and,
  about, 361
  empirical results, 363–366
  research design, 362–363
  conclusions, 366
Sovereign debt restructuring,
  about, 211–213
  Argentine debt reconstruction,
       215–217
  CACs, courts, and creditor
       committees, 219–221
  IMF interventions of, 179–186
  judge-mediated debt restructuring,
       217–219
  why sovereigns pay question,
       213–215
  conclusions, 221–222
Sovereign Debt Restructuring
     Mechanism (SDRM), 179, 180, 185,
     198, 381, 426
Sovereign debt, theory, defaults, and
     sanctions,
  about, 3

beyond reputational explanations,
     5–7
creditor sanctions as sovereign
     defaults, 7–12
reputational explanations, 4–5
Sovereign debt yields changes and war
     risk, 280
Sovereign default,
  causes of, 354
  debt rescheduling probability model,
       354–356
  definition of, 169
  in emerging market countries,
       353–358
  empirical vs. CRA probabilities, 356
  as endogenous financial decision,
       401
  higher interest rates, 149
  implications, 356–358
  wars and civil conflicts, 140
Sovereign default database, 17
Sovereign default, output costs of,
     23–30
Sovereign default risk, 358
Sovereign default risk, fiscal policy
     implications, 303–307
Sovereign default risk, spillovers from,
  about, 33
  corporate access to finance, 34
  data and empirical strategy, 35
  sovereign risk and sovereign default,
       35–37
  summary, 37–38
  conclusions, 38
Sovereign defaulters, foreign direct
     flows reduction and, 149–152
Sovereign defaults,
  about, 137–138
  business cycles in emerging counties
       and, 142–143
  costs of, 138–140
  determinants of, 140–141
  and domestic financial crisis, 139
  duration of episode, 137
  economics of, 137
  globalization and, 93
  impact on banking system, 25
  impacts of, 17

output loses of, 25
restructuring and resumption of
    borrowing, 135
understanding, 137–144
conclusions, 143–144
"Sovereign Indebtedness, Default, and
    Gambling for Redemption"
    (Malone), 43
Sovereign legitimacy, 245
Sovereign loan spreads, 75
Sovereign looting, 58
Sovereign reputation, 245
"Sovereign Rescheduling Probabilities
    in Emerging Markets: A
    Comparison with Credit Rating
    Agencies' Ratings," 353
Sovereign risk. *See also* Sovereign
    default risk,
    and corporate access to finance, 33
    and sovereign default, 35–37
Sovereign risk differential, 290,
    291–292
Sovereign risk premiums, 422
Sovereign risk pricing, 73
Sovereign risk-created equity premia,
    34
Sovereign spreads,
    credit pricing model for, 403
    determinants of, 313, 314
    public-debt-to-GDP ratios and, 305
    from worsening fundamentals or
        indirectly from spillovers, 394
Sovereign spreads and perceived risk
    of default,
    about, 401–403
    conceptual framework, 403–404
    future research and policy
        implications, 404–406
Sovereign spreads surge during
    financial crisis,
    about, 407–408
    bank rescue packages, 411–412
    empirical evidence, 409–411
    factors contributing, 412
    policy lessons, 412–413
    private to public risk transfer,
        411–412
Sovereign yields, 393

Sovereignty, legitimacy and
    creditworthiness,
    about, 245
    sovereign lending foundation,
        246–247
    sovereignty and creditworthiness,
        247–249
    conclusions, 249–250
Soviet Union, 282, 284. *See also* Russia
Spain, 8, 9, 23, 206, 228, 390, 403, 407,
    415, 421
Spanish Empire defaults, 8–9
Special drawing rights (SDR), 340
Spillover coefficient (SC), 394, 396
Squire, L., 18
Stability and Growth Pact, 408
Standard & Poor's, 80, 92, 169, 170, 176,
    191, 325, 326, 329, 345, 346, 349,
    354, 356, 361
Standby arrangement (SBA), 321
State succession concept, 261
Statist concept of sovereignty, 246
Staying vs. looting, 55
Stiglitz, J., 222
Stock market capitalization as
    percentage of GDP, 122
Stojanovic, A., 353, 354
Stratmann, T., 305
Structural breaks, 281
Sturzenegger, F., 44, 45, 101, 138, 141,
    212, 221
Sun, T., 403
Sundaresan, S., 120
Super majority vote (SMV), 218,
    220–221, 426
Supersanctions,
    effects of, 162–164
    Egypt, 158–159
    Greece, 160
    gunboat diplomacy as, 3
    historical effectiveness of, 150
    historical evidence of, 155, 158
    probability of, 156
    as the punishment of defaults, 149
    sovereign borrowers avoidance of, 4
    and sovereign debt repayment,
        155–164
Swagel, P., 56

Swaps and holdouts, 220
Sweden, 272, 279, 281, 282, 283, 288,
    289, 290, 291
Switzerland, 206
Sy, Amadou N., 83
Systemic suppression, 255, 256,
    257–258

T

Tabellini, G., 18
Talvi, E., 143, 304
Tanner, E., 139
Tanzania, 355
Tasmania, 272
Taxes, sovereign debt and, 63
Tax-financed-based spending vs.
    debt-financed spending, 73, 75
Taylor, Alan M., 150, 270
Taylor, John, 221
Tchou, N., 238
Term loans, 103
Terry, J., 270
Thailand, 371
The Bullionist, 273
The International Centre for Settlement
    of Investment Disputes (ICSID),
    428
Threat of attachment, 212
Threshold effects and finance
    integration benefits, 95
Todorovic, N., 353, 354
Tomz, M., 140, 248, 288
Too-big-to-fail idea, 369, 404, 425–428
Tornell, A., 304, 306
Trade flows, 150
Trade openness, 82
Tranquil periods, 371, 372
Transparency International Index,
    329
Triple crises, 27, 28
Truman, H. S., 64
Trust Indenture Act (TIA), 238
Trust relationships, 6, 7
Tunisia, 84
Turkey, 160, 161, 295, 297, 298, 299, 328,
    362
Twin crises, 25

U

Uganda, 84, 85, 254, 255
Ukraine, 90, 95, 179, 183, 326, 331,
    380
Unanimous action classes vs. collective
    action classes, 230–231
Unanimous action clauses (UACs), 230
Unfunded liabilities, 128
Uniform price mechanism, 121, 123
Uniform pricing auction (UPA), 119
United Kingdom, 205, 209, 217, 270,
    372. *See also* Britain; England;
    Great Britain
United States, 66, 76, 83, 120, 205, 209,
    217, 255, 272, 363, 372, 375, 376,
    412, 426
Uribe, M., 304
Uruguay, 172, 179, 184, 185, 272
U.S. Bankruptcy Code, 263, 264, 381,
    426
U.S. courts, 211
U.S. dollars as reserve currency, 64
U.S. Foreign Sovereign Immunities Act
    of 1976, 206
U.S. government, 64
Usui, N., 53

V

Van Huyck, J., 327
Van Rijckeghem, C., 141, 288, 376
Vegh, C., 143, 304
Venezuela, 3, 255, 256, 272, 301
Ventura, Jame (Jaume), 91
Vietnam, 172
Villemot, S, 320
Vishny, R. W., 91, 208
Volatile periods, 372
Voracity effect, 304, 306
Voth, Hans-Joachim, 8
Vulture funds, 216, 325
Vultures, 195, 212, 218, 219

W

Wadhwani, S., 372
Wake-up call, 273

Wall Street Journal, 176
War, 140, 142. *See also* Domestic
    conflict; Gunboat diplomacy;
    Perceived threat of war;
    Permissive cause of war, and
    civil conflicts
War costs, 66
War risk,
    financial market signals of, 284
    sovereign debt yields and, 279
    sovereign debt yields changes and,
       280
Warner, A., 52, 53
Wartime inflation effects, 65
Wartime shocks, 288
Weak institutions, 150
Weder, B., 59, 141, 288, 376
Weidenmier, M., 150
Weidmann, J., 53
"Why sovereigns pay" paradox
    market access, 215
    policy conditionality, 213
    sanctions, 213
Willard, K. L., 280
Willingness to pay, 327, 330

Wilson, Woodrow, 64
Winners' curse, 119
Woolcock, M., 53
World Bank, 128
World interest rate, 296
Wright, B., 215
Wright, M. L. J., 138, 140
Wu, E., 346

Y

Yafeh, Y., 220
Yield spreads, 271–275, 273
Yue, V., 304
Yugoslavia, 255

Z

Zaire, 255
Zambia, 355
Zanforlin, L., 24, 191
Zettelmeyer, J., 44, 45, 59, 101, 138, 141,
    212, 221
Zimbabwe, 255, 256
Zumer, Frederic, 158